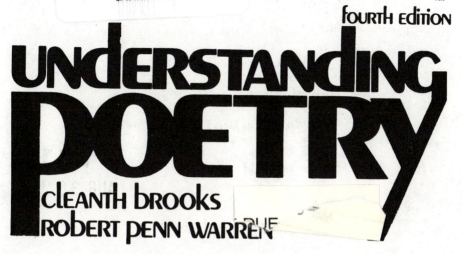

fourth edition

UNDERSTANDING POETRY

cleanth brooks
robert penn warren

Holt, Rinehart and Winston

New York   Chicago   San Francisco   Atlanta   Dallas
Montreal   Toronto

Library of Congress Cataloging in Publication Data

Brooks, Cleanth, ed.
  Understanding poetry.

  Includes index.
  1. English poetry. 2. American poetry. I. Warren,
Robert Penn, joint ed. II. Title.
PR1109.B676 1976   821'.008   75–25539
ISBN 0–03–076980–9

Editor Harriett Nolte
Developmental Editor Pamela Forcey
Designer Arthur Ritter

Acknowledgments

LÉONIE ADAMS. "Grapes-Making" from *Poems, A Selection* (Funk and Wagnalls, New York, 1954, copyright 1954 by Léonie Adams), is reprinted by permission of Léonie Adams.

CONRAD AIKEN. "Beloved, Let Us Once More Praise the Rain" from *Collected Poems* by Conrad Aiken (copyright © 1953, 1970 by Conrad Aiken) is reprinted by permission of Oxford University Press, Inc.

A. R. AMMONS. "Hardweed Path Going" from *Collected Poems, 1951–1971* by A. R. Ammons (copyright © 1972 by A. R. Ammons) is reprinted by permission of W. W. Norton & Company, Inc.

JOHN ASHBERY. "These Lacustrine Cities" from *Rivers and Mountains* by John Ashbery (copyright © 1962, 1963, 1964, 1966 by John Ashbery) is reprinted by permission of Holt, Rinehart and Winston.

W. H. AUDEN. The following poems are reprinted from *Collected Shorter Poems 1927–1957* by W. H. Auden by permission of Random House, Inc. and Faber & Faber Ltd.: "As I Walked Out One Evening," "In Memory of W. B. Yeats," "Lullaby," and "The Unknown Citizen" (all copyright 1940 and renewed 1968 by W. H. Auden); "The Fall of Rome" (copyright 1947 by W. H. Auden); "Paysage Moralisé (copyright 1937 and renewed 1965 by W. H. Auden); excerpts from "Missing," "The Secret Agent" ("It Was Easter As I Walked"), and "1929" (all copyright 1934, renewed 1962 by W. H. Auden); and excerpt from "Twelve Songs, IX" (copyright 1940, renewed 1968 by W. H. Auden).

CHARLES BALLARD. "Sand Creek" from *Voices of the Rainbow,* edited by Kenneth Rosen (copyright © 1975 by Kenneth Rosen) is reprinted by permission of The Viking Press, Inc.

IMAMU AMIRI BARAKA. See LeRoi Jones.

JOHN BERRYMAN. Excerpt from "Eleven Addresses to the Lord" from *Love & Fame* by John Berryman (copyright © 1970 by John Berryman) is reprinted by permission of Farrar, Straus & Giroux, Inc.

JOHN BETJEMAN. "The Cottage Hospital" from *Collected Poems* by John Betjeman is reprinted by permission of Houghton Mifflin Co. and John Murray (Publishers) Ltd.

ELIZABETH BISHOP. "Little Exercise" from *The Complete Poems* by Elizabeth Bishop (copyright 1946 by Elizabeth Bishop; copyright renewed 1974 by Elizabeth Bishop) is reprinted by permission of Farrar, Straus & Giroux, Inc.

LOUISE BOGAN. "Night" and "Song for the Last Act" from *The Blue Estuaries* by Louise Bogan (copyright © 1923, 1929, 1930, 1931, 1933, 1934, 1935, 1936, 1937, 1938, 1941, 1949, 1951, 1952, 1954, 1957, 1958, 1962, 1963, 1964, 1965, 1966, 1967, 1968 by Louise Bogan) are reprinted by permission of Farrar, Straus & Giroux, Inc.

J. KEIRN BRENNAN. "Let the Rest of the World Go By" (copyright © 1919 by M.

from *Lord Weary's Castle* by Robert Lowell (copyright 1946, 1974 by Robert Lowell) is reprinted by permission of Harcourt Brace Jovanovich, Inc.

ARCHIBALD MACLEISH. "Frescoes for Mr. Rockefeller's City" from *Poems, 1924–1933* by Archibald MacLeish (copyright 1924, 1926, 1928, 1932, 1933 by Archibald MacLeish) are reprinted by permission of Houghton Mifflin Company.

PHYLLIS MCGINLEY. "The Day After Sunday" from *Times Three* by Phyllis McGinley (copyright 1952 by Phillis McGinley) is reprinted by permission of The Viking Press, Inc. It appeared originally in *The New Yorker*.

CLAUDE MCKAY. "If We Must Die" from *Selected Poems of Claude McKay* (copyright 1953 by Twayne Publishers, Inc.) is reprinted by permission of Twayne Publishers, A Division of G. K. Hall & Co.

WILLIAM MEREDITH. "The Open Sea" from *The Open Sea and Other Poems* by William Meredith (copyright © 1953 by William Meredith) is reprinted by permission of Alfred A. Knopf, Inc.

JAMES MERRILL. "Thistledown" from *The Country of a Thousand Years of Peace* by James Merrill (copyright © 1970 by James Merrill) is reprinted by permission of Atheneum Publishers.

W. S. MERWIN. "The Widow" from *The Lice* by W. S. Merwin (copyright © 1967 by W. S. Merwin) is reprinted by permission of Atheneum Publishers. It appeared originally in *The New Yorker*.

EDNA ST. VINCENT MILLAY. "The Cameo" and "I Shall Go Back" (copyright 1923, 1928, 1951, 1955 by Edna St. Vincent Millay and Norma Millay Ellis) and "Wild Swans" (copyright 1921, 1948 by Edna St. Vincent Millay) from *Collected Poems* by Edna St. Vincent Millay, Harper & Row, are reprinted by permission of Norma Millay Ellis.

N. SCOTT MOMADAY. "Earth and I Gave You Turquoise" from *Angle of Geese and Other Poems* by N. Scott Momaday (copyright © 1974 by N. Scott Momaday) is reprinted by permission of David R. Godine, Publisher.

MARIANNE MOORE. "A Grave," "No Swan So Fine" and "Poetry" from *Collected Poems* by Marianne Moore (copyright 1935 by Marianne Moore; renewed 1963 by Marianne Moore and T. S. Eliot) are reprinted by permission of Macmillan Publishing Co., Inc. "A Grave" is also reprinted by permission of Faber and Faber Ltd.

FREDERICK MORGAN. "I Saw My Darling" from *A Book of Change* by Frederick Morgan (copyright © 1972 by Frederick Morgan) is reprinted by permission of Charles Scribner's Sons.

HOWARD MOSS. "Long Island Springs" from *Selected Poems* by Howard Moss (copyright © 1971 by Howard Moss) is reprinted by permission of Atheneum Publishers. It appeared originally in *The New York Quarterly*.

FRANK O'HARA. "Life on Earth" is reprinted by permission of Daisy Aldan.

WILFRED OWEN. "Dulce et Decorum Est" from *The Collected Poems of Wilfred Owen* edited by C. Day Lewis (copyright 1946, © 1963 by Chatto & Windus, Ltd.) is reprinted by permission of Chatto & Windus, the Executors of the Estate of Harold Owen, and New Directions Publishing Corporation.

MARGE PIERCY. "The Quiet Fog" is reprinted by permission of the poet.

SYLVIA PLATH. "Daddy" from *Ariel* by Sylvia Plath (copyright © 1962 by Ted Hughes) is reprinted by permission of Harper & Row, Publishers, Inc. and Olwyn Hughes.

COLE PORTER. "You're the Top" (copyright © 1934 Harms, Inc.; copyright renewed; all rights reserved) is used by permission of Warner Bros. Music.

EZRA POUND. "Envoi," excerpt from "Hugh Selwyn Mauberly," "In a Station of the Metro," "The River-Merchant's Wife: A Letter" and "Separation on the River Kiang" from *Personae* by Ezra Pound (copyright 1926 by Ezra Pound) are reprinted by permission of New Directions Publishing Corporation. "Hugh Selwyn Mauberly" is also reprinted by permission of Faber and Faber Ltd.

JOHN CROWE RANSOM. "Bells for John Whiteside's Daughter" and "Winter Remembered" (copyright 1924 by Alfred A. Knopf, Inc. and renewed 1952 by John Crowe Ransom) and "Lady Lost" (copyright 1927 by Alfred A. Knopf, Inc. and renewed 1955 by John Crowe Ransom) are reprinted from *Selected Poems, Third Edition, Revised and Enlarged* by John Crowe Ransom by permission of Alfred A. Knopf, Inc.

HENRY REED. "Chard Whitlow" and "Naming of Parts" from *A Map of Verona* by Henry Reed are reprinted by permission of Jonathan Cape Ltd.

ISHMAEL REED. "The Feral Pioneers" from *Conjure* by Ishmael Reed (copyright © 1972 by Ishmael Reed) is reprinted by permission of the poet.

ADRIENNE RICH. "Living in Sin" from *The Diamond Cutters*, published by Harper & Row, New York, 1955, is reprinted by permission of Adrienne Rich.

EDWIN ARLINGTON ROBINSON. "Mr. Flood's Party" from *Collected Poems* by Edwin Arlington Robinson (copyright 1921 by Edwin Arlington Robinson; renewed 1949 by Ruth Nivison) is reprinted by permission of Macmillan Publishing Co., Inc. "Luke

PREFACE

This fourth edition of *Understanding Poetry* has been much more thoroughly and radically changed than were the second and third editions. What we began as merely another revision became, during several years of conversation and argument, an attempt to re-inspect, to re-think, from tne start. This revision is thus the result of a new immersion in poetry for both of us.

We have tried always to keep in mind that this book should be both *teachable* and *flexible*. These two qualities interact in our minds—and, we believe, in the book—with what we feel is the most natural and fruitful way to approach any poem: To begin with as full and innocent an immersion in the poem as possible; to continue by raising inductive questions that lead students to examine the material, the method, and their relations in the poem—that is, to make an appeal to students' "understanding" of the poetic process; then to return students as far as possible to the innocent immersion—but now with a somewhat instructed innocence to make deeper appreciation possible. The purpose of such a process is to lead each student, not to a set of clichés that may be parroted about any poem, but to an *experience* of the poem—an experience that is at first immediate in its impact and then gradually acquires greater and greater resonance. Students, in other words, can be encouraged to understand poetry both as a continuity with, and a comment on, their own experience. They can be led to understand poetry as a means of imaginatively extending their own experience and, indeed, probing the possibilities of the self.

The most obvious result of seeking to achieve these goals is the changed organization and table of contents:

1. In the third edition, there were 215 poems; in this edition, there are 345. But these figures do not tell the whole story. There are actually 188 poems new to *Understanding Poetry*. Believing in the vital continuity of past and present, we have greatly increased the number of contemporary poems; in fact, there is now a whole new section entitled "Representative Poems of Our Time."

2. We have tried to emphasize more strongly the relation of traditional to twentieth-century work by placing the poems according to the two principles *contrast* and *continuity*. For example, in Section 3, "Tone," under the subheading "Against the Establishment" (pp. 149–161), we include three traditional poets from the late eighteenth and early nineteenth

centuries, a protest piece from the Depression, two ballads, Lowell's poem on modern Boston ("For the Union Dead"), two noteworthy pieces of black protest, and Ginsberg's lament for America ("A Supermarket in California").

Among other instances of such interweaving of periods under a single rubric is Section 4, "Analogical Language: Metaphor and Symbol" (p. 196). In one of the several subsections dealing with the various strategies in the use of metaphor and symbol, we include "She Dwelt Among the Untrodden Ways" (Wordsworth), as well as "You're the Top" (Cole Porter).

3. The mere juxtaposition of old and new inevitably involves cultural differences, but we have undertaken to dramatize the matter of poetry and cultural difference not only by chronological and geographical spread, but also by a variety of cultural sources. We should emphasize here that this is not a handbook of comparative literature and that it is confined to the English-American language. Even within the limitations of that language, however, there are a great variety of cultural sources, traditions, and techniques from which we have drawn. There are certain obvious sources of variety: here are 45 poems by women, 24 by black Americans and Indians (including examples of the rich poetic tradition of spirituals and blues), a number of examples of folk poetry of various orders, and an appendix of parodies.

4. Another new feature is the reorganization of material in the individual sections to provide a more effective pedagogical progression. This process of revision is most obvious in Sections 3, 4, and 5. Section 3, "Tone," for example, is divided into eleven subsections (A–K), each concerning a general topic that clearly invites differences in tonal treatment. We have already commented on the variety in Subsection F, "Against the Establishment," but we should also note the variety in Subsection D, "A Garland of Love Poems" (pp. 138–145), which juxtaposes a cry of yearning ("Western Wind"), almost naked passion (Tennyson's "Fatima"), sentimentality (Brown's "When Love Meets Love" and E. B. Browning's "If Thou Must Love Me"), intellectualized passion (Shakespeare's "Let Me Not to the Marriage of True Minds"), and a blend of intellectual paradox and tenderness (Auden's "Lullaby").

The point here is that the variety is not for the sake of variety as such. The fact of the variety dramatizes, in a pedagogical progression, the fundamental question: how do the elements in a poem relate to its overall meaning and "feel"? That is, how does the poem come to be what it is, even though its topical concern is the same as that of a number of other poems? As for a similar intention, but with a somewhat different method, we should point to Section 4, "Analogical Language: Metaphor and Symbol," which, in its six subsections, surveys various aspects of meaning and strategy in the use of imagery.

To sum up, then, the organization of this edition emphasizes progression by smaller units—or "clusters"—of concern arising from the general topic of a section.

5. An entirely new feature in this edition, Section 6 (p. 341), is organized about the relation of a number of poems to a common subject, a way of dramatizing the variety of the attitudes, meanings, and methods available when "the poet looks at a bird."

6. Perhaps our most marked departure from ordinary practice is in the method of treating metrics and other technical problems. All instructors know that when this type of material is offered in terms of abstract principles, the result, for many students at least, is boredom and alienation. Yet there is a systematic body of such material which is essential to an understanding of the nature of poetic practice—not merely in an intellectual sense, but, more importantly, as a way of sharpening the ear and the feelings of the reader. Our conviction is that only the instructor, who knows the specific class, can finally decide on the best way of handling this most difficult of problems. We have therefore sought a method flexible enough to give the instructor room for maneuver, but without sacrificing the possibility of a systematic treatment of the subject.

We offer Appendix B, "Metrics" (p. 493), which consists of a systematic treatment of both meter and other technical questions, including such topics as theoretical variation, unity and texture, musicality of verse, stress meter, and free verse. Except, perhaps, in certain advanced groups, this appendix should not, in the beginning at least, be studied as a whole. The ideal is for students to grasp the relevance of the technical material bit by bit as it applies to the poetry they have already made some basic connection with and, presumably, immersed themselves in, even as a rhythmic experience.

What we have done is to insert six "Rhythm and Meter" subsections in Sections 1–5 that discuss topics—and refer to pages—in Appendix B that are most fruitfully considered in connection with certain poems in the specific sections. Additional exercises related to the poems are often included in these subsections. Also, there are page references to Appendix B elsewhere, when appropriate. Note that the sections of Appendix B assigned in the "Rhythm and Meter" subsections and elsewhere are not consecutive. For example, early in the book, the student encounters poems in free verse and poems in stress (not accentual-syllabic) meter; therefore, we send the student to Appendix B for further information on those topics at those points, even though, for systematic reasons, stress meters and free verse are treated late in Appendix B itself. That is, our references meet the student's immediate need.

Our hope is that by the time students have reached the end of Section 5, they will have covered all of Appendix B, in constant association with poems they have come to know well, reinforced by poems in the appendix itself. Thus we have tried to devise a method by which the study of technical matter is geared to the student's needs and curiosities while progressing—a method that constantly emphasizes the expressive aspect of the technical details and constantly suggests our governing idea of the massive unity of the good poem.

.   .   .

The first edition of this book was published in 1938 and the following editions in 1950 and 1960. During all the years that these three earlier editions have been in use, we have benefited from comments, suggestions, and criticisms from a great number of instructors who have used the book. These constructive reactions have had much to do with the fact that each edition, including this one, has, we believe, been a decided improvement over the last. We wish to make formal acknowledgment here of our debt to these colleagues.

C.B.
R.P.W.

CONTENTS

Asterisks indicate poems that are analyzed

Supplemental Poems 164

7   POEMS FOR STUDY   369

8   REPRESENTATIVE POEMS OF OUR TIME   406

APPENDIX A
HOW POEMS COME ABOUT: INTENTION AND MEANING   464

APPENDIX B
METRICS   493

APPENDIX C
METAPHOR AND SYMBOL
COMPARED AND CONTRASTED   577

APPENDIX D
PARODIES   582

Poetry as a Way of Saying

Poetry is a kind of "saying." It is, however, a kind that many people, until they become well acquainted with it, feel is rather peculiar and even useless. They feel this way for two reasons: the "way of the saying" and the "nature of the said." As for the "way of the saying," the strongly marked rhythms, the frequent appearance of rhyme, and the figurative language may seem odd and distracting; and as for the "nature of the said," it generally contains neither a good, suspenseful story nor obviously useful information. Poetry, in short, may seem both unnatural and irrelevant.

Yet poetry has existed from the time of the emergence of the human race from shadowy prehistory and has survived, in one form or another, in every society since that time. When we realize this, we may be inclined to consider the possibility that poetry only *seems* unnatural and irrelevant. We may even decide, on reflection, that it does spring from deep human impulses and does fulfill human needs.

Let us look first at the way of the saying. Probably its most obvious feature is its strongly marked rhythm. Rhythm is, we know, the repetition in time of a perceptible pattern. The pattern may be visual, as in the flashing of a light or the advance and retreat of waves on the beach, or it may be a

1

pattern of repetition not in time but in space—we sometimes even speak of the rhythmic elements in a scene or a painting. In poetry, however, we are characteristically concerned with aural (heard) rhythm, that of sound. Aural rhythm is most obvious and assertive in the ticking of a clock or a metronome, but we are commonly aware of many more vital rhythms around us—in the sound of insects on a summer night, in a pulse beat, in a human voice. In fact, the world we live in pulses with rhythms of all kinds—visual, aural, tactile: the procession of the seasons, the wax and wane of the moon, the pattern of tides, the migration of birds. The human body itself is a locus of rhythms: the beat of the heart, the inhalation and exhalation of breath, waking and sleeping, effort and rest, hunger and satiety.

Rhythm is a principle of all life and all activity and is, of course, deeply involved in the experience of, and the expression of, emotion. We all know how the expressions, verbal or other, of love, hate, pain, joy, or grief tend to fall into rhythmic patterns; the very origin of language involves rhythm. This is not to say, of course, that poetry is merely a direct expression of emotion or that the only function of rhythm in poetry is to express emotion. But it is to say that emotional expression is an essential element of poetry, that rhythm is a natural and not an artificial aspect of poetry and is, therefore, an indication of the relation of poetry to the common experience of life.*

Rhyme, too, has a direct connection with our human constitution. It is related, as is rhythm, to the very origins of language, as we sense when we observe babies in their cribs playing delightedly with sounds. This "lalling," as it is termed, gives babies a certain satisfaction; they are acting on a pleasurable impulse. But at the same time, though they don't know it, they are working hard on the great, serious project of learning a language. When they are older, they will be fascinated by tongue-twisters and nonsense rhymes. They will repeat "Peter Piper picked a peck of pickled peppers" and will enjoy the tangled glitter of syllables. Or they will almost effortlessly memorize a nursery rhyme such as

> Hinx, minx, the old witch winks,
> The fat begins to fry.
> There's nobody home but Jumping Joan
> And Father, and Mother, and I.

Here we find only teasing hints of a story, and the hints don't make sense. True, they are provocative, they set the imagination working, but what we are left with is the chime of language in a verbal structure: that is, because the teasing possibilities of sense really come to nothing, the purely verbal effects are more sharply accentuated than if there were no hints of meaning at all.

We have just used the phrase "a verbal structure"—in this case, a struc-

---

* This whole question is more fully discussed in Section 3, "Tone."

ture of rhyme and rhythm; and this notion of a verbal structure, or verbal form, points to another aspect of the "naturalness" of poetry. When we resort to the jingle "Thirty days hath September" in order to remember the number of days in a month, we illustrate our need of a form to make remembering easy. In preliterate cultures, the myths and history of the tribe, the magical incantations, and the religious rituals went into verbal forms which facilitated transmission from generation to generation. In this aspect the form had a practical efficacy in preserving and transmitting information, but the form also, we must remember, combined the urgencies of the material being transmitted with the urgencies of rhythm and, sometimes, rhyme, alliteration, and so on. No doubt the aspect of utility is involved in the origin of all the arts, but even so, whatever the fusion of the practical and specifically poetic aspects of the form, the key fact is that man is a form-making animal, and that to the "natural" origins of rhythm, rhyme, and other verbal factors, we must add the "natural" impulse to create forms by means of them. Man creates forms in order to grasp the world. Even the act of perception is, in a complex way, a creation of forms.

As rhythm and rhyme are natural, so with metaphor, that is, using words in figurative, nonliteral ways.* But to the purely practical person, metaphor—when it appears in poetry, at least—often seems unnatural, strained, merely decorative, and superfluous. This attitude toward metaphor was seemingly justified by a theory of the origin of language that for a time was widely accepted: the theory that language developed by equating a word with a thing in a no-nonsense fashion, one kind of sound meaning "bear" and another kind meaning "fire," and that in such a language of practical equivalents metaphorical usage developed as a sort of degenerative disease.

That notion of the origin of language and the corollary notion of metaphor as a disease of language has long since been rejected. For instance, Owen Barfield wrote:

> The most conspicuous point of contact between meaning and poetry is *metaphor*. For one of the first things that a student of etymology—even quite an amateur student—discovers for himself is that every modern language, with its thousands of abstract terms and its nuances of meaning and association, is *apparently* nothing, from beginning to end, but an unconscionable tissue of dead, or petrified, metaphors. If we trace the meanings of a great many words—or those of the elements of which they are composed— about as far back as etymology can take us, we are at once made to realize that an overwhelming proportion, if not all, of them referred in earlier days to one of these two things—a solid sensible object, or some animal (probably human) activity. Examples abound on every page of the dictionary. Thus, an apparently objective scientific term like *elasticity*, on the one hand, and the metaphysical *abstract*, on the other, are both traceable to verbs meaning "draw" or "drag." *Centrifugal* and *centripetal* are composed of a noun

* See Appendix C for a comparison of metaphor and symbol.

meaning "a goad" and verbs signifying "to flee" and "to seek" respectively; *epithet, theme, thesis, anathema, hypothesis,* etc., go back to a Greek verb "to put," and even *right* and *wrong,* it seems, once had the meaning of "stretched" and so "straight" and "wringing" or "sour." *

In other words, language did not develop in a mechanically "pure" form, without the contamination of emotion, but in a form that embodied and expressed the density of experience—the interpenetration of stimulus and response, of object and perception, of idea and emotion, of action and feeling. The word for "bear" not only pointed in a disinterested fashion to a certain kind of creature, but also embodied "bearness"—the terror, awe, power, majesty, and other qualities associated with that creature. Furthermore, language developed in a more specifically metaphorical way by embodying the relation of thing to thing as expressions of human response and feeling. One thing might be like another in various ways. A man might be like a bear, or a bear like a man, not merely by, let us say, their common ability to stand erect. A certain tribe might be "of the bear," and a member of the tribe would carry a certain "bearness" in him. Or the massive power of the stroke of the bear's paw might equate "bear" with "storm" or "storm" with "bear." The naming process might, in fact, embody such relations. When we find in the Anglo-Saxon poem *Beowulf* the sea being called the "swan's way" or the "whale's bath," we stand at a kind of crossroads: one road leads back to the naming process in the development of language, and the other leads forward toward metaphor as we know it in the formal poetry of highly developed literatures. In common speech we find, too, traces of such a process of naming. There is the "leg" of a table, the "bed" of a river, the "eye" of a needle; and a plumber getting ready to connect two pieces of pipe refers to the "female" and the "male" joinings. The process of naming by metaphor is illustrated here, but the mere name, in such cases, has long since absorbed the metaphorical element.

Looking back on the history of mankind we see that metaphor has been a natural—even essential—way of expression, and looking around us now, we see the same thing. We think of slang as lurking on the outskirts of the accepted language; yet, slang expressions are stretchings and twistings of the ordinary meanings of words and thus are metaphoric, and so are related to the healthy growth of the language.

When slang is "bad," it is bad because its metaphors are ineffective rather than pungent and imaginative, or because constant, mechanical repetition dulls us to its original imaginative force. But, in fact, nothing proves more clearly than slang the persistent vitality and natural function of metaphor. Slang is simply the bastard brother of poetry. Through both slang and metaphor a language continually reinvigorates itself.

* Owen Barfield, *Poetic Diction: A Study in Meaning.* Faber and Faber, 1928, pp. 63–64.

In discussing rhythm, rhyme, and metaphor, we have been referring to the "way of saying" in poetry. But metaphor represents not only the "way of saying" but also the "said." Poetry is not always metaphorical. It does make plain statements that are, or pretend to be, facts. It may make clear demands and may make direct exhortations. But sometimes, very often in fact, the metaphor is, finally, the main body of content. To take one of the more famous of Shakespeare's sonnets (No. 73):

> That time of year thou may'st in me behold
> When yellow leaves, or none, or few, do hang
> Upon those boughs which shake against the cold,
> Bare ruin'd choirs where late the sweet birds sang.
> In me thou see'st the twilight of such day   5
> As after sunset fadeth in the west,
> Which, by and by, black night doth take away,
> Death's second self, that seals up all in rest.
> In me thou see'st the glowing of such fire
> That on the ashes of his youth doth lie,   10
> As the death-bed whereon it must expire,
> Consum'd with that which it was nourish'd by.
>   This thou perceiv'st, which makes thy love more strong,
>   To love that well which thou must leave ere long.

The main body of the poem consists of three comparisons, each of which is developed in some detail (with metaphors hung upon the primary metaphor): "I am autumn; I am twilight; I am a dying fire." That is all that the poem specifically offers in the first twelve lines; and that is merely a metaphorical way of saying, "I am getting old." Then comes the concluding couplet of the sonnet, which says: "The fact that I am getting old ought to make me dearer to you, for people especially value what they may soon lose."

In other words, in this poem, as in many others, metaphor constitutes a large part (here almost all) of the verbal content—constitutes not only the "way of saying," but also the "said."

But, we ask ourselves, if this is all that Shakespeare had to say, why didn't he simply say it straight out: "I am getting old"? Or if he wanted to use metaphors, why didn't he stick to the three basic ones (I am autumn; I am twilight; I am a dying fire) and omit all the wordy details? Certainly we could get the idea that autumn, twilight, and a dying fire stand for old age without all the elaboration about bare boughs being like ruined choirs, and so on. Something must be involved here beyond the mere statement of information.

What is that "something"?

Perhaps an indirect approach to our answer is best. As practical people going about our daily occupations, we live by information. We watch for road signs, study football scores and stock market quotations, read the menu in a restaurant, take inventory of the stock in our hardware store, follow the directions on the can of weed-killer. It is only to be expected, then, that we assume, offhand, that discourse is—or should be—primarily concerned with information. But after Mr. X has obeyed the road signs, after he has punched the time clock at the factory or given an order to his broker or ordered new stock for his store, after he has weeded his lawn and eaten his dinner, he may be surprised to reflect on the number of non-practical matters his discourse that day has been concerned with. He had told the office boy a joke, had commented on the fine fall weather to the traffic officer (who could observe the weather as well as he), had told an old friend he was glad to see him again, had reminded his wife of some little episode of their early life together, an event of no importance, something merely pleasant or amusing.

What common denominator, we may ask, would these pieces of non-practical conversation exhibit? They are all concerned, we immediately realize, with attitudes and feelings. They do not point outward to action in the world, to the control of experience, as communications involving practical information characteristically do; instead, they point inward to the self as it confronts the world—as it makes an assessment of experience. That is, we have feelings and attitudes *concerning* the world of action, just as we have them concerning ideas; and poetry, we may add, does not treat feelings and attitudes except as they come specifically into experience—that is, as they come into the realm of action and ideas.

Poetry, however, does characteristically *focus on the feelings and attitudes* in such a context, and not on the action or ideas as such; this distinction, as we shall see in looking at the particular poems to come, is crucial. As we shall later try to illustrate, poetry is concerned with the massiveness, the *multidimensional quality,* of experience. In a sense, this whole book will be concerned with this issue.

To return to the day of Mr. X, we observe that the realm of practical action and that of attitudes and feelings are not sharply separated from each other. In ordinary life the two realms constantly intersect and interpenetrate.

To sharpen our notion of the realm of attitudes and feelings, then, we may contrast the concern of poetry, not with that of practical action, but with the more specialized concern of science. Science aims to make statements of absolute precision. (Poetry may be said to have its precision too, but it is of a very different kind.) The scientist carefully cuts away from his technical terms all associations, emotional colorings, and implications of attitude and judgment. Science aspires to the condition of mathematics, and the really exact scientific statement can be expressed in mathematical formulae. The chemist describes water as H_2O. The molecule of water consists of two atoms of hydrogen joined to one atom of oxygen. This formula differs tremendously from the common word *water,* for that word, neutral as it seems in connotation, has a potential of all sorts of associations—with drinking, bathing, boating, the mystery of distance and the thrill of adventure on the high seas, the pull of the moon to create tides, the sea from which the goddess Aphrodite rose, or, as Keats puts it,

> The moving waters at their priestlike task
> Of pure ablution round earth's human shores.

As with the liquid, so with the word: the scientist needs a distilled product.

The language of science represents an extreme degree of specialization of language in the direction of a certain kind of precision. It is unnecessary, of course, to point out that in this specialization tremendous advantages inhere, and that the man of the twentieth century is rightly proud of his scientific achievements. But it is more often necessary to point out that scientific precision can be attained only in regard to certain materials. Here is an example of an eminent scientist trying to make a precise statement about a subject different from his professional concern:

> For sentimental pacifism is, after all, but a return to the method of the jungle. It is in the jungle that emotionalism alone determines conduct, and wherever that is true no other than the law of the jungle is possible. For the emotion of hate is sure sooner or later to follow on the emotion of love, and then there is a spring for the throat. It is altogether obvious that the only quality which really distinguishes man from the brutes is his reason.*

The author of this statement was Robert Andrews Millikan, an internationally famous physicist and winner of the Nobel Prize. He was making a plea for the scientific attitude in political and international affairs, but when one inspects this statement carefully one finds that it is not "scientific." Some of the propositions asserted could not be proved by Millikan, or by anyone else, in the same way that one can prove certain formulas of physics in the laboratory. The comparisons concerning the jungle and the leap of one infuriated beast at the throat of another represent the sort of comparison one finds in poetry, for the comparisons are not based on any scientific analogy; the resemblance is prompted by the emotional attitude of the speaker and is calculated to incite a corresponding attitude in the reader. But the coloring of the general statement—that is, the bringing in of an implied interpretation of the statement—extends beyond the mere use of a "poetic" comparison.

In the first sentence, for example, the word *pacifism* is qualified by the word *sentimental;* presumably, it is a particular sort of pacifism to which Millikan's objections applied. But does the adjective *sentimental* really set off a "bad" kind of pacifism from a "good" kind? Could the reader determine from Millikan's statement whether or not he would consider the pacifism of Jesus Christ, the Prince of Peace, a sentimental or a nonsentimental sort? Since the only kind of pacifism that Millikan admired was a scientific pacifism operating through an organization of sociologists and economists, one might conceivably assume that Jesus Christ would fall

* "Science and Modern Life," *The Atlantic Monthly,* April, 1928.

into the former classification. Or, to state the matter otherwise: is the basic argument for peace to be found in the fact that war is unprofitable or is horrible, or in the belief that it is wrong to kill one's fellow man? As a matter of fact, the adjective *sentimental* is, on logical grounds, a bogus qualification: its real function is to set up an attitude in the reader that will forbid the inspection of the basis of the statement.

Whether or not the general statement is logically sound, Millikan did not state it with scientific precision. In his defense it may be said that *the proposition is one that cannot be stated with scientific precision by anyone.* Millikan, a scientist trying to state the virtues of a scientific method in human relationships, was forced to resort to devices which we associate with poetry. He would never have colored a mathematical formula by referring to a "sentimental figure four" or described a well-known chemical reaction by saying that two ferocious atoms of hydrogen spring at the throat of one defenseless atom of oxygen.

For better or worse, certain kinds of material and certain kinds of concern are not amenable to scientific treatment, and when science does attempt to treat such things, it is so much the less science. The specialized language of science permits precision of statement in—but only in—its special field. Literature in general represents a specialized language that permits precision of statement in—but only in—its special field.

One of the concerns that is inaccessible to scientific treatment is the individual as individual. Walker Percy, in a recent book, puts the matter forcefully:

> There is a secret about the scientific method which every scientist knows and takes as a matter of course, but which the layman does not know. The layman's ignorance would not matter if it were not the case that the spirit of the age had been informed by the triumphant spirit of science. As it is, the layman's ignorance can be fatal, not for the scientist but for the layman.
>
> The secret is this: Science cannot utter a single word about an individual molecule, thing, or creature in so far as it is an individual but only in so far as it is like other individuals. The layman thinks that only science can utter the true word about anything, individuals included. But the layman is an individual. So science cannot say a single word to him or about him except as he resembles others. It comes to pass then that the denizen of a scientific-technological society finds himself in the strangest of predicaments: he lives in a cocoon of dead silence, in which no one can speak to him nor can he reply.*

This special field of literature, in contrast to that of practical and that of scientific concerns, involves, as we have said earlier, feelings and attitudes. At first glance, the field of feeling and attitudes may seem trivial when thought of in contrast to the great bustling practical business of the world or in contrast to the vast body of organized knowledge which science is and which allows man to master, to a certain degree, nature and his own fate.

* *The Message in the Bottle,* Farrar, Straus & Giroux, 1975, p. 22.

The field of feeling and attitude may seem to be "merely personal" and "merely subjective," and therefore of no general interest. But at second thought, we may realize that all the action and knowledge in the world can be valuable only as these things bring meaning to life—to our particular lives especially.

Poetry, then, is a response to, and an evaluation of, our experience of the objective, bustling world and of our ideas about it. Poetry is concerned with the world as responded to sensorially, emotionally, and intellectually. But—and this fact constitutes another significant characteristic of poetry that cannot be overemphasized—this response always involves all three of these elements: a massive, total response—what we have called earlier *the multidimensional quality of experience.* As Coleridge put it, poetry "in ideal perfection, brings the whole soul into activity." A major concern of this book will be to investigate, directly or indirectly, how this massive effect is achieved and what it means in human experience.

Poetry enables us to know what it "feels like" to be alive in the world. What does it "feel like," for instance, to be in love, to hate somebody, to be conscience-stricken, to watch a sunset or stand by a death-bed, to be willing to die for a cause or live in a passionate devotion to some chosen ideal? Only poetry—in the broadest sense of the word—can help us to answer such questions, and help us, thus, to an understanding of ourselves and of our own values. We may say, in fact, that literature is the most sophisticated example of the process by which we come to grasp our own environment, especially our human environment, with its complex and ambiguous values; you become aware through imaginative enactment and an imaginative logic that all the possibilities of fate are your own, for better or worse. Literature is the most complicated language that man has invented for talking not only to others but to himself; or rather, it is the language he has invented so that he may be *himself.* As J. Bronowski has put it, in literature, we "enter the contraries of the human predicament more fully" and what "distinguishes literature from other forms of knowledge is that it cannot be understood unless we understand what it is to be human."* In other words, we may have a child chess champion or musical prodigy, but not a child literary critic or dramatist.

Poetry, it is clear, is not cut off from life, but is basically concerned with life—that is, with the lived fullness of the world. It extends our own limited experience by means of imagination. By imagination, it sharpens our sense of the physical world on the one hand, and on the other, it deepens our sense of the emotional, intellectual, and moral implications of human situations and actions. It does not accomplish such things by general description, logical analysis, or abstract reasoning (though it may, as we shall see, involve such activities), but by *imaginative enactment,* by our sense of "living into" the world portrayed by a poem.

---

* *The Identity of Man,* Natural History Press, 1971, pp. 82ff.

To take a simple case, we may go back to the sonnet by Shakespeare. The poet does not merely say, "I am like autumn" (that is, "I am getting old"), but gives a picture that in itself is vivid—boughs bare or with a few last yellow leaves hanging. He goes, however, beyond this relatively superficial identification of the self and the boughs. The boughs do not, literally, feel the cold of the season. When they shake, it is because they are being moved by the wind. But as the poet puts it, they "shake against the cold"—and the human identification has subtly, by suggestion, been deepened. The poem goes on to deepen the imaginative involvement. The "autumn-ness" of the aging man is projected beyond the immediate metaphor of the stripped and quivering boughs; the bare boughs become "bare ruined choirs"—that is, the choir section that might be found in the ruins of a medieval church. And this image continues into the metaphorical fusion of birds and human beings who had once sung in joy and devotion. The comparison "I am like autumn" becomes "real" by the sharpness of the physical perception and the evocation of emotional responses; and this implies, of course, the reader's direct imaginative involvement.

In discussing such involvement, we must return to the function of rhythm, which acts to intensify this imaginative involvement. It does so in two ways: first, by its essential part in the "forming" process, which provides a frame and focus of attention, thereby making the material "graspable"; second, by the general emotional association of rhythm, which merges with the particular material here presented. Later we will give a great deal of detailed attention to these ideas, but for the moment, if students make a prose version of the sonnet, with all the details faithfully kept, they will immediately recognize what is lost.

There is one more important element involved in the effect of this sonnet. As we have seen, the poem ends in a general statement. Taking the statement by itself, we may very well say, "Yes, sure, that's true," and pass on. But the business of the poem is not to elicit such merely intellectual assent. It is to make us "feel" the statement—to make us feel what the statement signifies in experience. In other words, the metaphors and the rhythm of the sonnet have made it possible for the statement to come to us as a "lived truth"—and that is the only kind of truth poetry is immediately concerned with. We must here emphasize the word *immediately*, for whatever ideas are stated by a poem exist not only in the poem but in a context of ideas and "truths" outside the poem, including, of course, the deepest convictions of the reader. The relation between a poem's "truth" and what the reader holds to be true is enormously complex and, though we shall discuss it later, we can scarcely promise a ready solution.

The general concern of the last several paragraphs has been the fusion of metaphor, rhythm, and statement as the end a poem seeks to achieve. We are using each of these terms—metaphor, rhythm, and statement—in its broad sense. We take metaphor as whatever kind of aura exists around literal aspects of the world; rhythm as including phonetic qualities in general, with such things as rhyme, alliteration, and sound variation; and statement as literal content, including objects, facts, events, and ideas. What is crucial to poetry is that these elements—metaphor, rhythm, and statement—are absorbed into a vital unity. The poem, in its vital unity, is a "formed" thing, a thing existing in itself, and its vital unity, its form, embodies—*is*—its meaning. Yet paradoxically, by *the fact of its being "formed" and having its special identity, it somehow makes us more aware of life outside itself.* By its own significance it awakens us to the significance of our own experience and of the world.

We see, then, that a poem is not to be thought of as merely a bundle of things that are "poetic" in themselves. Nor is it to be thought of as a kind of box, decorated or not, in which a "truth" or a "fine sentiment" is hidden.

Certainly it is not to be thought of as a group of *mechanically* combined elements—meter, rhyme, figurative language, idea, and so on—put together to make a poem as bricks are put together to make a wall. The total relationship among all the elements in a poem is what is all important; it is not a mechanical relationship but one that is far more intimate and fundamental. If we must compare a poem to the makeup of some physical object, it ought to be not to a wall but to something organic like a plant.

We may investigate this general principle by looking at some particular examples. The following lines could scarcely be called melodious. Indeed, they may be thought to have a sibilant, hissing quality rather than that of melody.

> If it were done when 'tis done, then 'twere well
> It were done quickly: if the assassination
> Could trammel up the consequence, and catch,
> With his surcease, success, that but this blow
> Might be the be-all and the end-all here,
> But here, upon this bank and shoal of time,
> We'd jump the life to come.

This is the speech of Macbeth at the moment when he is debating the murder of Duncan; innumerable critics and readers have considered the passage to be great poetry. We are not to consider that the passage is great poetry *in spite* of its lack of ordinary melodious effects; but rather we are to see that the broken rhythms and the tendency to harshness of sound are essential to the dramatic effect that Shakespeare wished. The piling up of the *s* sounds in the second, third, and fourth lines helps to give an impression of desperate haste and breathless excitement; the effect is of a conspiratorial whisper. The rhythm and sound effects of the passage, then, are poetic in the only sense that we have seen to be legitimate: they are poetic because they contribute to the total significance of the passage.

Or we may approach the general problem in another way. Here are two lines by Robert Burns that were greatly admired by the poet William Butler Yeats:

> The white moon is setting behind the white wave,
>   And Time is setting with me, O!

Let us suppose that the lines had been written as follows:

> The white moon is setting behind the white wave,
>   And Time, O! is setting with me.

Literally considered, the two versions would seem to say exactly the same thing: they describe a scene and give an exclamation provoked by it. But if we read the two versions carefully with an ear for the rhythm, we shall discover that the transposition of the word *O* has made a great difference in the movement of the lines.

This difference is not finally important merely because the first version may be in itself more melodious than the second. The movement of the first version is superior primarily because it contributes to the total effect, or to what we might call the total interpretation, of the scene. The placing of the cry at the emphatic position of a line-end implies that the speaker had scarcely realized the full force of his own statement until he had made it. The lingering rhythm caused by the position of the exclamation at the end of the second line coincides with the fact that the poet sees in the natural scene a representation of the pathos of the passing of time and of his own life. If we place the exclamation anywhere else we impair this relationship between the rhythm and the other elements involved—the image of the moonset and the poet's statement about the passing of time. Yeats summarizes the general effect of the passage and the relationship of the parts as follows:

> Take from them [the lines] the whiteness of the moon and of the wave, whose relation to the setting of Time is too subtle for the intellect, and you take from them their beauty. But, when all are together, moon and wave and whiteness and setting Time and the last melancholy cry, they evoke an emotion which cannot be evoked by any other arrangement of colours and sounds and forms.*

The remarks by Yeats here apply, as we can see, to the elements of the scene itself as well as to the rhythm. He is not praising the lines merely because the scene of the white moon setting behind the white wave amounts to a pretty picture. As a matter of fact, a white moon may not appear as beautiful as a golden moon, but if we rewrite the lines with a golden moon, we have lost something:

> The gold moon is setting behind the gold wave,
>   And Time is setting with me, O!

* W. B. Yeats, "The Symbolism of Poetry," *Essays and Introductions*, Macmillan, 1961, pp. 155–156.

The "something" that has been lost obviously depends on the relationship of the color to the other elements in the general effect. The whiteness of the moon and the wave in connection with the idea of "setting," and then more specifically in connection with the idea of the irrevocable passage of time, suggests, even though unconsciously to most readers, a connection with the paleness of something waning or dying. The connection is not a logical connection, as Yeats intimates when he says the "relation . . . is too subtle for the intellect," but it is nonetheless a powerful one. All of this merely means that Yeats is saying that the beauty—by which he means the total poetic effect—of the lines depends on the relationship of the parts to each other. And here we may again quote Coleridge: the good poem must "contain in itself why it is so and not otherwise." Or as Shelley said, it must "contain the principle of its own integrity," by which Shelley meant that the parts of the good poem are unified, are "integrated" in an expressive whole in which all parts by their interrelation participate.

In the discussion of the "naturalness" and the "relevance" of poetry, which has occupied us up to this point, we have deliberately postponed discussing one fundamental element. We began by remarking that poetry is a kind of "saying" and then discussed the "way of the saying" and the "nature of the said." But if poetry is a "saying," there must be a "sayer," and what we have postponed is the question, "Who does the saying?" And that leads to another question: "What provokes the saying?"

Let us take the last question first. A situation underlies every poem, and the poem is what the situation provokes. The poem is a response to a particular situation. It is, then, a little—or sometimes a big—drama. In some poems the situation is quite explicit, as in "Sir Patrick Spence" (p. 23) or "Waking in the Blue" (p. 39). But in other poems it is only implied. For instance, in "Western Wind" (p. 138) and "Go, Lovely Rose" (p. 213) the situation is suggested in only the vaguest terms, while in "The Main-Deep" (p. 99), "In a Station of the Metro" (p. 71), and "If Poisonous Minerals" (p. 330) there is only the most general implication. It does not matter how explicit or implicit the situation may be in a particular poem; the only thing necessary is that it be adequate to spark the poem, and if "Sir Patrick Spence" requires a full-bodied narrative, "The Main-Deep" requires only the impression of a moving wave as viewed by an unidentified observer.

The situation, as we have pointed out, provokes a response which is the poem, and so, for the poem to make sense, we must have some idea of the identity of the "sayer" who responds to the situation. Ultimately, the sayer is, of course, the poet, but for present purposes let us look at the matter more narrowly—that is, scrutinize the poem itself. At one end of a scale we may place the impersonal poem with a totally unidentified speaker. Obviously, such a poem as "The Main-Deep" or "In a Station of the Metro" is of this sort; and the overall "voice," as we may call it, of "Sir

Patrick Spence," even though in the course of the poem clearly identified characters do speak in the first person, is equally not identifiable. Somewhere toward the middle of the scale, we might place a poem like Housman's "Farewell to Barn and Stack and Tree" (p. 36), in which the whole poem is spoken by one clearly identifiable speaker, but a speaker who is fictional: the speaker is presented as a farm boy who has killed his brother and is about to flee, and we know that Housman, the poet, was a highly respectable professor of Latin at Cambridge University and never killed anybody in his life. If we take "Go, Lovely Rose" or "Western Wind," we again find a first person, but there is no reason for us to assume that the "I" is any less fictional than that of Housman's poem. To proceed to the other end of the scale, we do find poems in which the identity (and sometimes the character) of the speaker in a poem tends to fuse with the literal identity of the poet—that is, a poem which the poet proclaims to be directly autobiographical. "Waking in the Blue" is such a poem, and the description there of morning in a mental hospital is drawn from the author's experience—even to the name of the hospital.

We have said that, since a poem is a little drama, we must have some sense of the identity of the speaker, that the voice of a poem is not heard in a vacuum. In fact, we shall come to consider in detail how what we call the tone of a poem, its style in general, and its basic feeling, may be regarded as springing from the identity of the speaker and the situation confronted. Therefore, we must always begin by thinking of the identity of the speaker as revealed in the particular poem, no matter whether the image is identifiable only in the vaguest, most general way (as in "The Main-Deep") or more specifically identifiable as the actual poet (as in "Waking in the Blue").

In an important sense, all poems are fictional, even poems that profess to be autobiographical, for the voice of the poem is inevitably a creation and not a natural and spontaneous outburst. The sly, wise, ironic yet sensitive, somewhat folksy Yankee farmer and cracker-barrel philosopher who is the speaker in many of Robert Frost's poems is very far from the actual man who voted and paid taxes. The actual Robert Frost had been born in San Francisco and been named for Robert E. Lee; and though he was of New England blood and had farmed in that section, his poetic career actually began in England. When he returned to America he deliberately set out, as he himself records in a letter, to "Yankee-fy" himself—that is, to develop the character that speaks in the poems. William Butler Yeats, to take another example, distinguished between himself as poet and himself as man; in fact, he thought of the poet's role as a dramatic role, or as a sort of mask—a persona—to conceal the literal man.* But not only to conceal the literal man; to enable him to speak with

---

* *Persona* is the Latin word for the mask worn by actors in classic tragedy. Our word *personality* is derived from it.

clarity. As Oscar Wilde, in an essay called "The Truth of Masks," puts it: "Man is least himself when he talks in his own person. Give him a mask and he will tell you the truth." And a writer as different from Wilde as Emerson (in his Journal of 1841) agrees: "Many men can write better in a mask than for themselves."*

The notion of the mask—of the voice special to the poem—does not imply that the poet specifically, in the literal person, is not the ultimate speaker and that we are not, in the end, concerned with that person. After all, the poet is the creator of the poem's world and of its persona, and that experience provides the material of the poetry. Later we shall go more fully into such questions, but for the present, and always when we are making acquaintance with a poem, we must answer these questions: (1) Who is speaking? (2) Why?

The title of this book is *Understanding Poetry.* It might, however, with equal reason have been called *Experiencing Poetry,* for what this book hopes to do is to enlarge the reader's capacity to experience poetry. What is at stake in the choice between the two titles is a matter of emphasis. The title *Experiencing Poetry* would emphasize the end to be hoped for— a richer appreciation of poetry, a fuller enjoyment. Our chosen title emphasizes the process by which such an end may be achieved.

We speak of an enlarged capacity for the experience of poetry as an end to be gained. But some people assume that no preparation, no effort, no study, no thought, is necessary for that experience, and that if a poem seems to make such demands it is so much the less poetry. This assumption is sadly erroneous, but the error represents the distortion of a fundamental truth. When we do truly make contact with a poem, when we are deeply affected by it, the experience *seems* to come with total immediacy, with total naturalness, without effort. It comes with the ease of a revelation.

Let us, however, inspect this situation. When is a reader ready for such an experience of immediacy, naturalness, effortlessness? To begin with, we know that a child of eight years is not ready for the poem that a child of twelve happily seizes on, and that the child of twelve is not ready for *Romeo and Juliet, Lycidas,* or *King Lear,* which may please his big brother (or sister) in college. To be "ready" means to have had more experience of life and the world, directly as well as by education and imagination. We assume, in other words, that the child grows into "readiness" for poetry. And once we assume that much, we must realize, too, that the experience that leads to a sensitive reading of *Romeo and Juliet, Lycidas,* or *King Lear* is not merely the experience of life but of poetry.

We scarcely think of the experience of life, literal or otherwise, as a

* The created "self"—the persona—is more coherent and more "knowable" than the literal man, even to himself; and is therefore more effective dramatically. But another factor may enter: in the mask, instinctive concealments and reticences can be relaxed.

preparation for the experience of poetry: it is simply the self-justifying process of living. And, too, the preparation for poetry by the reading of poetry may be largely unconscious. For instance, James Dickey, a prominent contemporary poet, while a fighter pilot in World War II, simply stumbled into reading poetry out of the boredom of life at a base in the Pacific; and as he immersed himself in poetry he was not looking beyond the momentary satisfaction, certainly not toward a career as a poet and a teacher of poetry.

Given intelligence and sensitivity in some degree, much of our learning of anything is accomplished unconsciously. But to speak specifically of poetry, mere immersion does little good unless the reader is making, however unconsciously, some discriminations, comparisons, and judgments; if he merely wallows in a vague, pleasurable reaction, the immersion can mean little or nothing. And here is where "understanding" may come in. The more or less unconscious process of making discriminations, comparisons, and judgments can be lifted into consciousness and, to a degree, systematized; and that is one of the things this book undertakes to do. By trying to understand the *nature* and *structure* of poetry, how that nature and structure are expressive, and how we respond to them, readers may accelerate and deepen the natural and more or less unconscious process by which they enlarge their experience of poetry.

By way of conclusion we must emphasize two related matters of the greatest importance:

First, criticism and analysis, as modestly practiced in this book and more grandly elsewhere and by other hands, is ultimately of value *only insofar as it can return readers to the poem itself*—return them, that is, better prepared to experience it more immediately, fully, and, shall we say, innocently. The poem is an experience, yes, but it is a deeply significant experience, and criticism aims only at making the reader more aware of the depth and range of the experience.

Second, there is no point at which a reader can say, "I am now ready to experience poetry." The reader may, indeed, be more or less ready for one poem or one poet, yet not for another. But the law of life is change and, ideally, the law of change should imply growth. We, as readers, may grow as we continue to explore the poetry of the past and the new poetry that will be written tomorrow.

Dramatic Situation

1

Foreword

We have said that the "stuff of poetry" is not something separate from the ordinary business of living, but itself inheres in that business. We hear someone say that a farm boy has suffered a fatal accident while cutting wood with a buzz-saw; or we read in the newspaper that a woman has shot her lover; or we remember that there was once an outlaw from Missouri named Jesse James, who was killed by treachery. This sort of thing, even though it may not strike us as beautiful, instructive, or elevating, appeals to the interest people have in other people and the shocks of life and turns of fate.

That interest, as we have indicated, is not scientific or practical but is simply the general curiosity we feel about people as human beings. Even though the account of a painful accident or a sordid murder seems almost as far removed as possible from poetry, it arouses the kind of interest which poetry attempts to satisfy, and comprises the "stuff of poetry." In the case of the three incidents mentioned—the death of a farm boy, the murder of the lover, and the betrayal of the outlaw—the "stuff of poetry" has actually been turned into poems. That is, the "human interest" has been put into a *form** that preserves it, even after the accidental and temporary curiosity has been satisfied.

The phrase "put into a form that preserves it" can be misleading, if we think of poetic form as a kind of container, a kind of box, in which the stuff of poetry has been packed. The form does more than "contain" the poetic stuff: it organizes it; it shapes it; it defines its meaning. Much of our subsequent discussion will have to do with what form is and what it does.

"Out, Out—"

Robert Frost [*1874–1963*]

The buzz-saw snarled and rattled in the yard
And made dust and dropped stove-length sticks of wood,
Sweet-scented stuff when the breeze drew across it.
And from there those that lifted eyes could count
Five mountain ranges one behind the other   5
Under the sunset far into Vermont.
And the saw snarled and rattled, snarled and rattled,
As it ran light, or had to bear a load.
And nothing happened: day was all but done.
Call it a day, I wish they might have said   10
To please the boy by giving him the half hour
That a boy counts so much when saved from work.
His sister stood beside them in her apron
To tell them "Supper." At the word, the saw,
As if to prove saws knew what supper meant,   15
Leaped out at the boy's hand, or seemed to leap—
He must have given the hand. However it was,
Neither refused the meeting. But the hand!
The boy's first outcry was a rueful laugh,
As he swung toward them holding up the hand   20
Half in appeal, but half as if to keep
The life from spilling. Then the boy saw all—
Since he was old enough to know, big boy
Doing a man's work, though a child at heart—
He saw all spoiled. "Don't let him cut my hand off—   25
The doctor, when he comes. Don't let him, sister!"
So. But the hand was gone already.
The doctor put him in the dark of ether.
He lay and puffed his lips out with his breath.
And then—the watcher at his pulse took fright.   30
No one believed. They listened at his heart.
Little—less—nothing!—and that ended it.
No more to build on there. And they, since they
Were not the one dead, turned to their affairs.

---

* In its most comprehensive sense, the term "form" means a shape, a pattern, a structure, an articulation. In poetry, of course, the form is an articulation of words, so selected and so arranged as to communicate a total experience.

Frankie and Johnny

Anonymous

Frankie and Johnny were lovers, O how that couple could love.
Swore to be true to each other, true as the stars above.
He was her man, but he done her wrong.

Frankie she was his woman, everybody knows.
She spent one hundred dollars for a suit of Johnny's clothes.   5
He was her man, but he done her wrong.

Frankie and Johnny went walking, Johnny in his bran' new suit,
"O good Lawd," says Frankie, "but don't my Johnny look cute?"
He was her man, but he done her wrong.

Frankie went down to Memphis; she went on the evening train.   10
She paid one hundred dollars for Johnny a watch and chain.
He was her man, but he done her wrong.

Frankie went down to the corner, to buy a glass of beer;
She says to the fat bartender, "Has my loving man been here?
He was my man, but he done me wrong."   15

"Ain't going to tell you no story, ain't going to tell you no lie,
I seen your man 'bout an hour ago with a girl named Alice Fry.
If he's your man, he's doing you wrong."

Frankie went back to the hotel, she didn't go there for fun,
Under her long red kimono she toted a forty-four gun.   20
He was her man, but he done her wrong.

Frankie threw back her kimono; took out the old forty-four;
There was her lovin' Johnny a-lovin' up Alice Fry;
He was her man, but he done her wrong.

Frankie threw back her kimono; took out the old forty-four;   25
Roota-toot-toot, three times she shot, right through that hotel door.
She shot her man, 'cause he done her wrong.

Johnny grabbed off his Stetson. "O good Lawd, Frankie, don't shoot."
But Frankie put her finger on the trigger, and the gun went roota-
    toot-toot.
He was her man, but she shot him down.   30

"Roll me over easy, roll me over slow,
Roll me over easy, boys, 'cause my wounds are hurting me so,
I was her man, but I done her wrong."

With the first shot Johnny staggered; with the second shot he fell;
When the third bullet hit him, there was a new man's face in hell.   35
He was my man, but he done me wrong."

Frankie heard a rumbling away down under the ground.
Maybe it was Johnny where she had shot him down.
He was her man, and she done him wrong.

"Oh, bring on your rubber-tired hearses, bring on your rubber-tired
    hacks,   40
They're takin' my Johnny to the buryin' groun' but they'll never
    bring him back.
He was my man, but he done me wrong."

The judge he said to the jury, "It's plain as plain can be.
This woman shot her man, so it's murder in the second degree.
He was her man, though he done her wrong."   45

Now it wasn't murder in the second degree, it wasn't murder in the
    third.
Frankie simply dropped her man, like a hunter drops a bird.
He was her man, but he done her wrong.

"Oh, put me in that dungeon. Oh, put me in that cell.
Put me where the northeast wind blows from the southeast corner of
    hell.   50
I shot my man 'cause he done me wrong."

Frankie walked up to the scaffold, as calm as a girl could be,
She turned her eyes to heaven and said, "Good Lord, I'm coming to
    thee.
He was my man, and I done him wrong."

Jesse James

Anonymous

It was on a Wednesday night, the moon was shining bright,
    They robbed the Danville train.
And the people they did say, for many miles away,
    'Twas the outlaws Frank and Jesse James.

Jesse had a wife to mourn him all her life,   5
    The children they are brave.
'Twas a dirty little coward shot Mister Howard,
    And laid Jesse James in his grave.

Jesse was a man was a friend to the poor,
    He never left a friend in pain.   10
And with his brother Frank he robbed the Chicago bank
    And then held up the Glendale train.

It was Robert Ford, the dirty little coward,
    I wonder how he does feel,
For he ate of Jesse's bread and he slept in Jesse's bed,   15
    Then he laid Jesse James in his grave.

It was his brother Frank that robbed the Gallatin bank,
    And carried the money from the town.
It was in this very place that they had a little race,
    For they shot Captain Sheets to the ground.   20

They went to the crossing not very far from there,
    And there they did the same;
And the agent on his knees he delivered up the keys
    To the outlaws Frank and Jesse James.

It was on a Saturday night, Jesse was at home   25
    Talking to his family brave,
When the thief and the coward, little Robert Ford,
    Laid Jesse James in his grave.

How people held their breath when they heard of Jesse's death,
    And wondered how he ever came to die.   30
'Twas one of the gang, dirty Robert Ford,
    That shot Jesse James on the sly.

Jesse went to rest with his hand on his breast;
    He died with a smile on his face.
He was born one day in the county of Clay,   35
    And came from a solitary race.

The first of these poems was written by Robert Frost, a professional poet, who felt in the fatal accident to an obscure farm boy the pathos and horror of the unreasonable and unpredictable end that at any moment may come to life. (The title is taken from Shakespeare's *Macbeth,* Act V, sc. 5, ll. 73–78.) We do not know who composed the second poem, but certainly not a professional poet. Apparently some ordinary person felt so strongly the force of the murder of Johnny that this reaction was conveyed in the song. And the song did succeed in conveying something of the re-actions of the unknown composer, for it has been passed down from mouth to mouth, probably being constantly altered in the process.* Poems like "Frankie and Johnny," narratives to be sung, that ordinarily spring from unknown sources and are transmitted by word of mouth, and that may experience alteration in this process, are usually called *ballads.*

The most ordinary way by which we express the interest we as human beings have in other human beings is by telling or attending to stories. Since poetry derives from this basic human interest we expect to find, and do find, many poems in which the element of story is large. As a matter of fact, the three poems we have just read, and all the poems in the first section of this book, give enough of the explicit action of a story to appeal

---

* In fact, the early version of the ballad now generally known as "Frankie and Johnny" was called "Frankie and Albert," Albert being the name of the lover of the original Frankie, a prostitute in the sporting section of St. Louis. The early version is much simpler than that presented here.

to the usual curiosity we feel about how any situation will turn out. But this is not the only appeal the poems make to us, just as it is not the only appeal any good piece of fiction makes. We are interested not merely in getting the information about the conclusion, but in following the process by which the conclusion is reached. As a matter of fact, we do not even want all the details of the process, but just enough to make us experience the central feeling and grasp the central meaning of the events. But this is not all: we like a poem, not because it satisfies our curiosity or because it gives us an idea we can "carry away with us," as people sometimes put it, but because *the poem itself is an experience.*

We can illustrate by a comparison with a football game. If a man reads the Sunday sports section account of a game he missed on Saturday, he may really have more accurate information about it than if he had been present. But if he had had his choice he would probably have gone to the actual game or watched it on television. He wants the *experience* of the game itself—the suspense, the excitement, the empathy with the action. Without the experience, the statistics of score, yardage, and so on, may be rather a bore.

This general principle is clear if we remember that the mere fact, as a fact, that a woman in the slums shot her lover Johnny is of little interest to us. If we enjoy hearing "Frankie and Johnny" sung, we do so because of something more than the statistical importance of the subject. Further-more, we do not enjoy it merely because it satisfies our curiosity about the outcome; for we enjoy the song for an indefinite length of time after we know the conclusion. It is obvious, then, that if we like it at all, we like it because of its particular nature as an experience—just as we like the foot-ball game.

The story element in a poem, then, whether it is prominent as in "Frankie and Johnny" or relatively unimportant as in "Out, Out," is only one of many elements that work together to give the total experience of the poem. We already know what some of these other elements are: rhythm, figurative language, and so on. But in these poems, where the story ele-ment is prominent, we may proceed best by studying the way in which this one element is treated in specific cases to give the effect we call poetry.

Let us give a little attention now to "Jesse James." Its hero was born in 1847 and was shot to death in 1882 by a member of his own band of outlaws, a man named Robert Ford, who betrayed him in order to win the reward of $10,000 that had been placed on James's head. Jesse and his brother Frank, citizens of the border state of Missouri, had sided with the Confederacy in the Civil War and served with a guerrilla band until the war ended. In 1866 Jesse was declared an outlaw and thenceforward lived as a desperado, committing daring crimes, holding up banks and trains. Poorer folk came to think of him as an American Robin Hood, the outlaw who fleeced the rich in order to be generous to the poor.

Out of this admiration for Jesse's skill and courage, gratitude for his generosity to the poor man, and pity and outrage at his death, the ballad grew. Like the traditional folk ballads—of which we have some examples, for instance, in "Sir Patrick Spence" (below) and "The Three Ravens" (p. 54)—"Jesse James" is anonymous, and the fact of anonymity implies that there was a background of attitudes and feelings held in common that made the ballad become popular. It also implies that the story was generally known, so that mere factual suspense, as we may observe, was not the main concern of the nameless narrator. We are given, quite objectively, certain key facts, but there is no attempt to explain what the outlaw's motives and feelings were.

As early as line 8 we are told how Jesse died, and the narrator apparently takes for granted that in general the facts leading up to that event are well known. The concern here is to celebrate the bravery and generosity of his hero and to vent scorn on the base betrayer Robert Ford. (James for a time went under the name of Howard, and the poet prefers to use that alias in the refrain—presumably because it furnishes such an apt rhyme for *coward*.)

This folk ballad stumbles and blunders a bit. For example, the last two lines will seem—at least at first reading—inept and anticlimactic. Yet we must not jump to conclusions: on reconsideration we may decide that they possess a kind of left-handed effectiveness after all. To sum up, the ballad of Jesse James is objective and circumstantial in its telling. We are told what Jesse did and how he died. Yet the poem, in spite of its apparently "objective" treatment, was evidently generated by strong emotion. Its author keeps emphasizing Jesse's bravery and generosity and voicing contempt for the "dirty" Robert Ford who shot Jesse James "on the sly."

Questions

1. Write an account of the poets' attitudes toward Frankie and Robert Ford. Both are killers, but with a difference. How is the attitude conveyed in each case? How is the difference in attitude justified by details in the two poems?

2. Compare the line of the narrative in the two poems. Where and how are events consecutive and where out of their natural sequence? What narrative purposes do these differences serve? What elements that might ordinarily be expected in the narratives are omitted?

Sir Patrick Spence

Anonymous

> The king sits in Dumferling toune,
>   Drinking the blude-reid wine:
> "O whar will I get guid sailor,
>   To sail this schip of mine?"

Up and spak an eldern knicht,   5
  Sat at the kings richt kne:
"Sir Patrick Spence is the best sailor,
  That sails upon the se."

The king has written a braid[1] letter,
  And signd it wi his hand,   10
And sent it to Sir Patrick Spence,
  Was walking on the sand.

The first line that Sir Patrick red,
  A loud lauch lauchèd[2] he;
The next line that Sir Patrick red,   15
  The teir blinded his ee.[3]

"O wha is this has don this deid,
  This ill deid don to me,
To send me out this time o' the yeir,
  To sail upon the se!   20

"Mak hast, mak haste, my mirry men all
  Our guid schip sails the morne:"
"O say na sae, my master deir,
  For I feir a deadlie storme.

"Late, late yestreen I saw the new moone,   25
  Wi the auld[4] moone in hir arme,
And I feir, I feir, my deir master,
  That we will cum to harme."

O our Scots nobles wer richt laith[5]
  To weet their cork-heild schoone;[6]   30
Bot lang owre a'[7] the play wer playd,
  Thair hats they swam aboone.

O lang, lang may their ladies sit,
  Wi thair fans into their hand,
Or eir they se Sir Patrick Spence   35
  Cum sailing to the land.

O lang, lang may the ladies stand,
  Wi thair gold kems[8] in their hair
Waiting for thar ain deir lords,
  For they'll se thame na mair.   40

Haf owre,[9] haf owre to Aberdour,
  It's fiftie fadom deip,
And thair lies guid Sir Patrick Spence,
  Wi the Scots lords at his feit.

---

[1] broad   [2] laughed   [3] eye   [4] old   [5] loath   [6] cork-heeled shoes   [7] ere all   [8] combs
[9] Half over

This poem is a folk ballad, probably dating from about the fifteenth century. The anonymous Scots author gives us a narrative poem having to do with an expedition, sent out by the Scottish king, in which Sir Patrick Spence, the captain of the ship, perishes at sea with all hands aboard.

Notice that the poet has preferred to present the story through a series of individual scenes. The first (lines 1–10) describes the king sitting at ease in his palace, drinking the blood-red wine, and almost casually signing the order that will send this fine seaman to his death.

The second scene (lines 11–28) takes us abruptly to the seaside, where we see Sir Patrick, who is walking along the seaside near his ship, receive the king's letter. At first he laughs in astonishment at the notion that he is to make an expedition at this dangerous time of the year, but the next moment "the teir blind[s] his ee" when he realizes that this is no joke but a serious command. He can only conjecture (lines 16–20) that some enemy has recommended him to the king's attention. But at once (lines 21–22) he orders the ship to be made ready for the voyage, though the news that they are to sail elicits cries of consternation from the seamen who, like Sir Patrick, are well aware of the dangers in which they will be placed. One of them speaks of the weather sign (lines 25–26) which he interprets as foreboding a terrible storm.

We expect that the next scene will present the onset of the storm and the sinking of the ship, but not so. The last stanzas of the poem (lines 29–44) have to do with a time *after* the ship has gone down. We are forced to create the storm scene in our own imaginations, and that very fact perhaps makes the storm more vivid. We are given, to be sure, one scenic detail, a glimpse of the hats of the drowned lords floating on the sea. The poet's calling attention to that clutter of eloquent flotsam suggests the entire event to us more powerfully than any narration.

Beginning with line 29 we no longer have a relatively objective reporting of what people did and said. Instead, we begin to sense an ironic voice pointing to the contrast between the Scots nobles who were Sir Patrick's passengers and the brave captain himself. The scenic method is not abandoned, of course. Our attention is next called to other objects of vanity, to the fans and gold combs of the ladies who wait at home.

In the last stanza, the ballad comes to a final focus on the scene of Sir Patrick on the sea floor, with a climactic force deriving from what has gone just before. Here, as with the hats floating on the sea, suggestion does the work of narration and explanation. The nobles, the captain, and crew, all now lie at the bottom of the sea.

In referring to their ladies, the anonymous author is hardly bitter; but it is made clear that the ladies, like their husbands or lovers, were not prepared for the grim happenings that occurred; like their husbands, they too belonged to an elegant world that was out of touch with the harsher aspects of reality. Their costly fans and golden combs point out the contrast between their life and that of the weather-beaten and tough-minded Sir

Patrick, who well knew what the voyage entailed and that his own life was at stake.

In the last stanza, the ironic voice comes close to making a direct evaluation of the situation; yet even here the comment is somewhat oblique. The poet does not say in so many words that Sir Patrick was superior to the Scots lords since he consciously accepted his fate and moved toward his death with open eyes, whereas drowning for them was simply an unforeseen accident. What the voice does suggest is that the fastidious Scots lords lie at Sir Patrick's feet, not he at theirs. In life they may have outranked him, but not now in death. The manner of his dying proved him the nobler man.

Questions

We have noted that the ballad provides no specific account of the storm. Sir Walter Scott, in his *Minstrelsy of the Scottish Border,* printed a longer version of this ballad in which the storm is described. Here are five of those stanzas:

14

They hadna sailed a league, a league,
    A league but barely three,
When the lift[1] grew dark, and the wind blew loud,
    And gurly grew the sea.

15

The ankers brak, and the topmasts lap,[2]
    It was sic[3] a deadly storm;
And the waves cam o'er the broken ship,
    Till a' her sides were torn.

    • • •

19

"Gae, fetch a web o' the silken claith,[4]
    Another o' the twine,
And wap them into our ship's side,
    And let na the sea come in."

20

They fetched a web o' the silken claith,
    Another of the twine,
And they wrapped them round that gude ship's side,
    But still the sea came in.

    • • •

[1] sky [2] were sprung [3] such [4] cloth

22

And mony was the feather-bed,
   That flattered on the faem;
And mony was the gude lord's son,
   That never mair cam hame.

1. Do these stanzas from Scott's longer version add to the dramatic power of the poem? Or are they irrelevant to the main theme and actually a distraction? Compare this description of the storm with the storm that we create in our own imagination. Is there something to be said for not trying to tell everything?

2. At least one editor of this ballad disapproves of some of the descriptive detail. He writes that "certain expressions . . . such as 'eldern knicht,' 'cork-heild shoon,' and 'gold kems in their hair'—seem to betray the art of the fripperer"; that is, he is saying that the poet is dressing up the poem in worn finery taken second-hand from other ballads. Do you agree? If you don't, how would you defend the poet's use of these concrete details?

The Demon Lover

Anonymous

"O where have you been, my long, long love,
   This long seven years and mair?"
"O I'm come to seek my former vows
   Ye granted me before."

"O hold your tongue of your former vows,   5
   For they will breed sad strife;
O hold your tongue of your former vows,
   For I am become a wife."

He turned him right and round about,
   And the tear blinded his ee: 10
"I wad never hae trodden on Irish ground,
   If it had not been for thee.

"I might hae had a king's daughter,
   Far, far beyond the sea;
I might have had a king's daughter,   15
   Had it not been for love o thee."

"If ye might have had a king's daughter,
   Yer sel ye had to blame;
Ye might have had taken the king's daughter,
   For ye kend[1] that I was nane.[2]   20

"If I was to leave my husband dear,
   And my two babes also,

[1] knew   [2] none

O what have you to take me to,
   If with you I should go?"

"I hae seven ships upon the sea—   25
   The eighth brought me to land—
With four-and-twenty bold mariners,
   And music on every hand."

She has taken up her two little babes,
   Kissd them baith³ cheek and chin: 30
"O fair ye weel, my ain⁴ two babes,
   For I'll never see you again.

She set her foot upon the ship,
   No mariners could she behold;
But the sails were o the taffetie,   35
   And the masts o the beaten gold.

She had not sailed a league, a league,
   A league but barely three,
When dismal grew his countenance,
   And drumlie⁵ grew his ee.   40

They had not sailed a league, a league,
   A league but barely three,
Until she espied his cloven foot,
   And she wept right bitterlie.

"O hold your tongue of your weeping," says he,   45
   "Of your weeping now let me be;
I will shew you how the lilies grow
   On the banks of Italy."

"O what hills are yon, yon pleasant hills,
   That the sun shines sweetly on?"   50
"O yon are the hills of heaven," he said,
   "Where you will never win."

"O whaten a mountain is yon," she said,
   "All so dreary wi frost and snow?"
"O yon is the mountain of hell," he cried,   55
   "Where you and I will go."

He strack the tap-mast wi his hand,
   The fore-mast wi his knee,
And he brake that gallant ship in twain,
   And sank her in the sea.   60

Questions

   1. What finally motivates the woman to yield to the lover's entreaties?
   2. What is the implication of the fact that the ship's sails are taffeta
and the masts, gold? Is the ship too good to be true?

---

³ both   ⁴ own   ⁵ dark

3. When the woman spies the "cloven foot"—the devils, for all tneir power to disguise themselves, are not permitted to conceal one mark of their deviltry—she knows that her supposed lover is a demon. How justify, then, the keeping up of the pretense until line 55? Is the portrayal of the woman and the demon from 43 to 55 acceptable? Is the psychology sound?

4. What actually happens in the last stanza? Read carefully, noting the details of the action, and describe the picture that emerges. What, physically, has happened to the lover?

In the version of this ballad printed by Sir Walter Scott in his *Minstrelsy of the Scottish Border,* two stanzas (made up by Scott's friend William Laidlaw) precede the last stanza. The first of these reads as follows:

> And aye when she turn'd her round about,
>   Aye taller he seem'd to be;
> Until that the tops o' that gallant ship
>   Nae taller were than he.

This stanza "explains" what happens in the last stanza; but is the explanation needed? Does its inclusion strengthen or enfeeble the effect of the last stanza?

Mama and Daughter

Langston Hughes   [*1902–1967*]

> Mama, please brush off my coat.
> I'm going down the street.
>
> Where're you going, daughter?
>
> To see my sugar-sweet.
>
> Who is your sugar, honey?   5
> Turn around—I'll brush behind.
>
> He is that young man, mama,
> I can't get off my mind.
>
> Daughter, once upon a time—
> Let me brush the hem—   10
> Your father, yes he was the one!
> I felt like that about him.
>
> But it was a long time ago
> He up and went his way.
> I hope that wild young son-of-a-gun   15
> Rots in hell today!
>
> Mama, dad couldn't still be young.
>
> He *was* young yesterday.
> He *was* young when he—
> Turn around!   20
> So I can brush your back, I say!

Questions

Write a prose narrative of 250 words or so, fleshing out the episode with a setting, description of the characters, and any relevant information. That is, try to convert the poem into a little short story. What have you gained? What have you lost?

The Echoing Green

William Blake [*1757–1827*]

> The Sun does arise
> And make happy the skies;
> The merry bells ring
> To welcome the Spring
> The skylark and thrush,   5
> The birds of the bush,
> Sing louder around
> To the bells' cheerful sound,
> While our sport shall be seen
> On the Echoing Green.   10
>
> Old John, with white hair,
> Does laugh away care,
> Sitting under the oak,
> Among the old folk.
> They laugh at our play,   15
> And soon they shall say:
> "Such, such were the joys
> When we all, girls and boys,
> In our youth time were seen
> On the Echoing Green."   20
>
> Till the little ones, weary,
> No more can be merry;
> The sun does descend,
> And our sports have an end.
> Round the laps of their mothers   25
> Many sisters and brothers,
> Like birds in their nest,
> Are ready for rest,
> And sport no more seen
> On the darkening Green.   30

It would be hard to imagine a simpler poem than this. The first stanza presents a bright spring morning as a setting for the sports of the young on the Echoing Green. The second presents the healthy and contented old people benevolently watching the girls and boys and remembering how, when young, they too played on the same spot. In the third, evening comes, "sports have an end," and sleepy and contented the children gather around their mothers "Like birds in their nest." The little narrative, so unpretending and simple, and written in language equally simple and unpretentious making no attempt at sophisticated poetic effects, suggests how man can be happy in the acceptance of his lot in nature and time, of life and a self-fulfilling natural process with a sense of community and warmth in it.

Questions

What do you make of the phrase "Echoing Green," which appears in the title and provides a refrain for the first two stanzas a refrain which is altered in the last line? What is "echoing" (what, that is, repeats what) in the poem? Why is this idea central to the poem? Why is the word *echoing* changed in the last line? How do the title and earlier refrain prepare for this change? Is the basic notion of the poem altered by this, or merely reiterated in another way?

Battle of the Bonhomme Richard and the Serapis

Walt Whitman [*1819–1892*]

I

Would you hear of an old-time sea-fight?
Would you learn who won by the light of the moon and stars?
List to the yarn, as my grandmother's father the sailor told it to me.

Our foe was no skulk in his ship I tell you, (said he,)
His was the surly English pluck, and there is no tougher or truer,
    and never was, and never will be;   5
Along the lower'd eve he came horribly raking us.

We closed with him, the yards entangled, the cannon touch'd,
My captain lash'd fast with his own hands.

We had receiv'd some eighteen pound shots under the water,
On our lower-gun-deck two large pieces had burst at the first fire,
    killing all around and blowing up overhead.   10

Fighting at sun-down, fighting at dark,
Ten o'clock at night, the full moon well up, our leaks on the gain,
    and five feet of water reported,
The master-at-arms loosing the prisoners confined in the afterhold to
    give them a chance for themselves.

The transit to and from the magazine is now stopt by the sentinels,
They see so many strange faces they do not know whom to trust.   15

Our frigate takes fire,
The other asks if we demand quarter?
If our colors are struck and the fighting done?

Now I laugh content for I hear the voice of my little captain,
We have not struck, he composedly cries, *we have just begun our
    part of the fighting.*   20

Only three guns are in use,
One is directed by the captain himself against the enemy's main-mast,
Two well serv'd with grape and canister silence his musketry and clear
    his decks.

The tops alone second the fire of this little battery, especially the main-top,
They hold out bravely during the whole of the action.   25

Not a moment's cease,
The leaks gain fast on the pumps, the fire eats toward the powder-
    magazine.

One of the pumps has been shot away, it is generally thought we are
    sinking.

Serene stands the little captain,
He is not hurried, his voice is neither high nor low,   30
His eyes give more light to us than our battle-lanterns.

Toward twelve there in the beams of the moon they surrender to us.

II
Stretch'd and still lies the midnight,
Two great hulls motionless on the breast of the darkness,
Our vessel riddled and slowly sinking, preparations to pass to the one
    we have conquer'd,   35
The captain on the quarter-deck coldly giving his orders through a
    countenance white as a sheet,
Near by the corpse of the child that serv'd in the cabin,
The dead face of an old salt with long white hair and carefully curl'd
    whiskers,
The flames spite of all that can be done flickering aloft and below,
The husky voices of the two or three officers yet fit for duty,   40
Formless stacks of bodies and bodies by themselves, dabs of flesh upon
    the masts and spars,
Cut of cordage, dangle of rigging, slight shock of the soothe of waves,
Black and impassive guns, litter of powder-parcels, strong scent,
A few large stars overhead, silent and mournful shining,
Delicate sniffs of sea-breeze, smells of sedgy grass and fields by the
    shore, death-messages given in charge to survivors,   45
The hiss of the surgeon's knife, the gnawing teeth of his saw,
Wheeze, cluck, swash of falling blood, short wild scream, and long,
    dull tapering groan,
These so, these irretrievable.

"Song of Myself," 35–36

Questions

1. Here is a very vivid account of John Paul Jones's most famous victory. The poem does celebrate the "little captain," but is that the main intention of the poem? To answer this we may think of the context in which the action is set. To begin, let us ask what Whitman intends by his second line:

> Would you learn who won by the light of the moon and stars?

Certainly the fact that the battle lasted for hours, into the night, is implied by the line. But is that all? If so, why do we return to the night scene in line 32, at the end of Part I, and again in line 42, where among other effective details is the "shock of the soothe of waves," and, 45, the "smells of sedgy grass and fields by the shore"? If a mere celebration of Jones's courage were all that were intended, what would, in fact, be the use of most of Part II?

But is this to imply that Whitman means to underrate the courage of captain and crew, and to deplore the event? Is it not, rather, that he intends to put the courage into a special context? What are the elements of this context? What added dimension do you feel from the context? What we are now trying to do is to work toward the main idea—the theme—of the poem. How would you state it?

2. If we have some notion of the theme of the poem—and as a corollary, the main effect the poet is trying to give—we can begin to think of what principle governs his selection of detail. The action, historically speaking, was very complicated. Whitman has ignored most of it. Why?*

It may be said that Part I deals with the main outlines of the battle, the stages in the action. What keeps this from being a mere summary? Rhythm? Flashes of dramatic action? Shrewdly observed detail and image? Sharp *simile* or *metaphor*?† A progression toward a climax? (What, by the way, is the climax of Part I?)

The action is narrated in fits and starts; we are made to leap from one thing to another more athletically, we may say, than in ordinary prose narrative. Does it make for greater imaginative involvement? Let us look at one striking example of such a leap, the break in continuity between line 5 and line 6. Lines 4 and 5 describe "the surly English pluck" of the enemy. Then, suddenly, comes the line

> Along the lower'd eve he came horribly raking us.

What is the effect of this leap? Can you find similar effects elsewhere in Part I, especially toward the end? See also Question 4 of "The Demon Lover." Poetry does often work by presenting vivid and unexpected details that stimulate the imagination, but once this imagination has been aroused, poetry may, with equal force, work by withholding detail in order

---

* For a fascinating historical account of the engagement, see Samuel Eliot Morison, *John Paul Jones,* Atlantic-Little, Brown, 1959. If that account is read in connection with Whitman's poem, we have a clear example of the difference in obligation and intention between an historical and a poetic treatment.

† A comparison using "like" or "as" (*simile*) or implied (*metaphor*). See pp. 68–71 and 196 and Appendix C.

to force the reader's imagination to supply them. That is, compression, economy, ellipsis, and suggestion are as useful as direct stimulation of the imagination. But both principles are to be used in relation to each other.

3. We have said that Part I deals with the main outline of the action. What is the concern of Part II? In the massing of the images—the details of the scene—do you find any startling transitions that correspond in effect to the leaps in action in Part I?

4. Go back over the whole poem and point out the words, phrases, and images that seem especially effective—things like the word *cluck* in line 47, or the old salt's curled whiskers in line 38. (What associations, for example, are imported into the poem by the word *cluck?* Does the shock here make for vividness?)

5. Let us investigate some details:

(a) Why, in line 19, does the narrator say "my little captain" instead of "our" or "the"? What is the effect of the word *little* here? Jones was very small, but is the word merely factual?

(b) What is the significance of the word *Stretch'd* in line 33? Of the word *breast* in line 34?

(c) Why does Whitman use the word *conquer'd* and not "captur'd" in line 35?

(d) Why is the phrase "through a countenance white as a sheet," better than "with a countenance white as a sheet" (line 36)?

(e) In line 42, in the phrase "slight shock of the soothe of waves," what do you make of the apparent contradiction between *shock* and *soothe?* In fact, if it is a calm sea, why use the word *shock* at all? Or do the waves now give a shock that ordinarily would pass unobserved? Let us notice that the word *soothe* is used here as a noun. What does this distortion do for us? And does the word *soothe* here carry more meaning than the factual description? If so, to what other elements—details and interpretations—would you link it?

(f) Do you find any principle of progression in feeling and/or idea in the passage from line 45 to the end? If so, try to define it.

(g) Let us return to the contrast, pointed out at the very beginning of our discussion, between the celebration of "my little captain" and the heroic victory, and the human pain and waste that is so vividly presented after the victory. Certainly, the poem is not a simple celebration. But, by the same token, is it a "protest" against war? Is it "pacifistic"? Do not the two lines of thought and feeling—the celebration of heroism and the awareness of pain and waste—coexist as the poles of the poem? That is, can it be said that the poem is concerned ultimately with the tragic—and ironic—fact that both the glory of heroism and the pain and death are inevitable aspects of life and history? Can the same thing be said about "Sir Patrick Spence"?

Danny Deever

Rudyard Kipling   [*1865–1936*]

"What are the bugles blowin' for," said Files-on-Parade.
"To turn you out, to turn you out," the Color-Sergeant said.
"What makes you look so white, so white?" said Files-on-Parade.
"I'm dreadin' what I've got to watch," the Color-Sergeant said.
  For they're hangin' Danny Deever, you can hear the Dead March play,
  The Regiment's in 'ollow square—they're hangin' him today;   6
  They've taken of his buttons off an' cut his stripes away,
  An' they're hangin' Danny Deever in the mornin'.

"What makes the rear-rank breathe so 'ard?" said Files-on-Parade.
"It's bitter cold, it's bitter cold," the Color-Sergeant said.   0
"What makes that front-rank man fall down?" said Files-on-Parade.
"A touch o' sun, a touch o' sun," the Color-Sergeant said.
  They are hangin' Danny Deever, they are marchin' of 'im round,
  They 'ave 'alted Danny Deever by 'is coffin on the ground;
  An' 'e'll swing in 'arf a minute for a sneakin' shootin' hound—   15
  O they're hangin' Danny Deever in the mornin'!

" 'Is cot was right-'and cot to mine," said Files-on-Parade.
" 'E's sleepin' out an' far to-night," the Color-Sergeant said.
"I've drunk 'is beer a score o' times," said Files-on-Parade.
" 'E's drinkin' bitter beer alone," the Color-Sergeant said.   20
  They are hangin' Danny Deever, you must mark 'im to 'is place,
  For 'e shot a comrade sleepin'—you must look 'im in the face;
  Nine 'undred of 'is county an' the Regiment's disgrace,
  While they're hangin' Danny Deever in the mornin'.

"What's that so black agin the sun?" said Files-on-Parade.   25
"It's Danny fightin' 'ard for life," the Color-Sergeant said.
"What's that that whimpers over'ead?" said Files-on-Parade.
"It's Danny's soul that's passin' now," the Color-Sergeant said.
  For they're done with Danny Deever, you can 'ear the quickstep play,
  The Regiment's in column, an' they're marchin' us away;   30
Ho! the young recruits are shakin', an' they'll want their beer to-day,
  After hangin' Danny Deever in the mornin'!

Questions

1. This modern poem uses many of the devices we have observed in the traditional ballads. List them. What is the most important difference between the method of this poem and that of "Sir Patrick Spence"?

2. Do you think that "Danny Deever" would be more effective if the treatment were confined to dialogue? What are your arguments?

3. What facts do we have about Danny Deever? His relation to his comrades? Their attitude toward him? His crime? A possible justification

for the crime? What attitude does the poet expect us to take toward the event? Is there any relation between the dearth of actual information and the attitude the poet expects us to take?

4 In the second stanza, the Color-Sergeant says, first, that it is bitter cold, then that a man in the front rank has collapsed from a touch of the sun. Does this make sense?

5. Would you be satisfied if the name of the main character were Jackson Smithers? If not, why not? If so, why?

6. Try to feel the rhythm of the poem. Try to soak yourself in it. Do you perceive any relation between this rhythm and the subject matter and feeling of the poem?

Farewell to Barn and Stack and Tree

A. E. Housman [1859–1936]

Farewell to barn and stack and tree,
  Farewell to Severn shore.
Terence, look your last at me,
  For I come home no more.

"The sun burns on the half-mown hill,   5
  By now the blood is dried;
And Maurice amongst the hay lies still
  And my knife is in his side.

"My mother thinks us long away;
  'Tis time the field were mown.   10
She had two sons at rising day,
  To-night she'll be alone.

"And here's a bloody hand to shake,
  And oh, man, here's good-bye;
We'll sweat no more on scythe and rake,   15
  My bloody hands and I.

"I wish you strength to bring you pride,
  And a love to keep you clean,
And I wish you luck, come Lammastide,
  At racing on the green.   20

"Long for me the rick will wait,
  And long will wait the fold,
And long will stand the empty plate,
  And dinner will be cold."

The folk ballad, especially in its finest examples, powerfully impressed sophisticated literary men who attempted, particularly in the eighteenth and nineteenth centuries, to appropriate its special effects. So we get "literary" ballads of the sort printed above. Housman, a Cambridge don and professor of Classics, puts aside his sophistication in this and in many of his other poems, preferring to give a sense of simple narrative and of stark simplicity. Whether or not he has achieved these effects, it is interesting to see what he has attempted to do. The story he tells is one of conflict and death, the kind of story that is found in so many of the folk ballads. A young man has killed his brother. We are not told what the quarrel was about. The poet has limited his concern to suggesting the murderer's remorse at what he has done. The content of the ballad is the murderer's speech of farewell to a friend. But the speech is dramatic, and presents, among other things, several scenes in vivid detail.

Stanza 2, for example, describes the half-mown hill where Maurice's body lies with the death-dealing knife in his side. Stanza 6 describes what the speaker imagines the scene to be at home where his mother is preparing, or has just finished preparing, the evening meal. Eloquent of the speaker's remorse is this and an earlier reference to his mother, and his awareness of the worry that must now possess her at the failure of her boys to turn up now that the working day is over.

Questions

1. You may want to ask yourself about the last two stanzas. Are lines 17–20 in character? Would the murderer, under these circumstances, talk like this to his friend? What is accomplished by bringing the conversation into the poem? Does it give a hint of the quiet routine life of the village to which the murderer is still bound in sympathies and interests but which, as he now realizes, he has forfeited?

2. The last stanza is even more interesting in its possible effects upon the poem. In view of what has happened, why should the speaker refer to the relatively trivial matter of dinner's getting cold on the table at home? Is this a piece of pure bathos—a letdown—this unimportant little domestic item made the very climax of the poem and thus allowed to shoulder out of the way the big and bloody consequence of the day? Or is it actually a good dramatic detail and a powerful one on which to close? What does the detail do to focus the effect of the poem? On whose feelings does this poem formally focus?

Ten Days Leave

W. D. Snodgrass [1926–]

> He steps down from the dark train, blinking; stares
> At trees like miracles. He will play games
> With boys or sit up all night touching chairs.
> Talking with friends, he can recall their names.

Noon burns against his eyelids, but he lies   5
Hunched in his blankets; he is nalf awake
But still lacks nerve to open up his eyes;
Supposing it were just his old mistake?

But no; it seems just like it seemed. His folks
Pursue their lives like toy trains on a track.   10
He can foresee each of his father's jokes
Like words in some old movie that's come back.

He is like days when you've gone some place new
To deal with certain strangers, though you never
Escape the sense in everything you do,   15
"We've done this all once. Have I been here, ever?"

But no; he thinks it must recall some old film, lit
By lives you want to touch; as if he'd slept
And must have dreamed this setting, peopled it,
And wakened out of it. But someone's kept   20

His dream asleep here like a small homestead
Preserved long past its time in memory
Of some great man who lived here and is dead.
They have restored his landscape faithfully:

The hills, the little houses, the costumes: 25
How real it seems! But he comes, wide awake,
A tourist whispering through the priceless rooms
Who must not touch things or his hand might break

Their sleep and black them out. He wonders when
He'll grow into his sleep so sound again.   30

Questions

1. This poem describes the young soldier's coming home on ten days' leave. Having arrived, he finds the once familiar world of his youth strangely changed. What is this change? Why, for example, should the trees (line 2) look like "miracles"? Why (lines 7-8) does he now lack the nerve to open his eyes? What is this "old mistake" that presumably he has been making for some months past?

2. Why does it seem to the young soldier that his folks "pursue their lives like toy trains on a track" (line 10)?

3. Evidently the old familiar world has been pushed back so far from the soldier's life that having returned to it he is afraid that he will suddenly wake up and find that he has just been dreaming after all. How is this basic analogy worked out through the poem? Try to cite some particular instances.

4. In lines 27–28 how is it that the familiar rooms have become priceless, as in some great palace or museum?

5. In this poem the narrative elements may seem to have dwindled into the merest wisp of a story. Yet the narrative mode is important for

the presentation of the young soldier's experience. Why? As a matter of fact, narrative is very rarely used for its own sake. In most poems it is a vehicle—a way of presenting an experience that goes beyond a mere succession of events.

Waking in the Blue

Robert Lowell [*1917–*]

The night attendant, a B.U. sophomore,
rouses from the mare's-nest of his drowsy head
propped on *The Meaning of Meaning.*
He catwalks down our corridor.
Azure day   5
makes my agonized blue window bleaker.
Crows maunder on the petrified fairway.
Absence! My heart grows tense
as though a harpoon were sparring for the kill.
(This is the house for the "mentally ill.")   10

What use is my sense of humor?
I grin at Stanley, now sunk in his sixties,
once a Harvard all-American fullback,
(if such were possible!)
still hoarding the build of a boy in his twenties,   15
as he soaks, a ramrod
with the muscle of a seal
in his long tub,
vaguely urinous from the Victorian plumbing.
A kingly granite profile in a crimson golf-cap,   20
worn all day, all night,
he thinks only of his figure,
of slimming on sherbet and ginger ale—
more cut off from words than a seal.

This is the way day breaks in Bowditch Hall at McLean's;   25
the hooded night lights bring out "Bobbie,"
Porcellian '29,
a replica of Louis XVI
without the wig—
redolent and roly-poly as a sperm whale,   30
as he swashbuckles about in his birthday suit
and horses at chairs.

These victorious figures of bravado ossified young.

In between the limits of day,
hours and hours go by under the crew haircuts   35
and slightly too little nonsensical bachelor twinkle
of the Roman Catholic attendants.

(There are no Mayflower
screwballs in the Catholic Church.)

After a hearty New England breakfast,   40
I weigh two hundred pounds
this morning. Cock of the walk,
I strut in my turtle-necked French sailor's jersey
before the metal shaving mirrors,
and see the shaky future grow familiar   45
in the pinched, indigenous faces
of these thoroughbred mental cases,
twice my age and half my weight.
We are all old-timers,
each of us holds a locked razor.   50

In the 1940s Robert Lowell spent some time in a "house for the 'mentally ill'" (line 10). In this poem he has made his narrative conform rather specifically to the actual detail of his personal experience. "Bowditch Hall at McLean's," a sanitarium near Boston (line 25), is the real name of the place in which he stayed. A "B.U. sophomore" (line 1) is a sophomore from Boston University. This student is evidently working his way through college by serving in the sanitarium but finds time to do some of his required reading. *The Meaning of Meaning* is a book by C. K. Ogden and I. A. Richards, published in 1923. Nothing exciting happens on this typical day in the sanitarium: time has ceased to mean very much to the inmates. But one way to make that point is to use narrative as a kind of anti-narrative: nothing happens because nothing meaningful can happen.

Questions

1. We are told that Stanley was once a Harvard fullback and, since Porcellian is an exclusive Harvard club, "Bobbie" is obviously a Harvard alumnus too. Does the speaker regard himself, along with Bobbie and Stanley, as one of the Mayflower screwballs? Why should there be any connection between being a Mayflower descendant and being a screwball? Does having been brought up as a Roman Catholic tend to guard one's mental health? (Lowell attended Harvard, 1935–1937, and later became—for a time—a Roman Catholic.) Why the speaker's sardonic comments on this subject? What is the general tendency of his remark and how does it bear, if at all, on the *theme*—that is, the main idea—of the poem?

2. Later on in this book we shall be looking more closely at the poet's attitude toward the material and toward self-image, noting how these affect the *tone* of the poem. What is this poet's attitude toward himself? Toward the other inmates of this house for the mentally ill? Toward the civilization which has made such houses necessary? Such questions as these are worth pondering, for the poet's attitude toward the circumstances that have brought him to this pass could be essentially what this poem is "about."

3. Why are the shaving mirrors made of metal? Why are inmates' razors kept locked?

4. What is implied by the phrase "thoroughbred mental cases"? That this is an exclusive nursing home, open only to the thoroughbreds who have mental problems? That their problems come about because they are over-civilized, *i.e.,* too much the thoroughbreds of society? That their illness is a kind of distillation of the culture in which they have been bred, something bred in the bone? Or what?

5. We have seen earlier in this section of the book the value of with-holding some facts—of not telling all. Does this frankly "confessional" poem tell all? Or does it actually tell us very little about the author's personal problems? In any case, is the poem shockingly dramatic or is it finally undramatic?

6. To return to the fact that the book which the attendant is reading is *The Meaning of Meaning,* it is plausible that a student would be reading this particular book, and a real attendant observed by the patient might well have been reading it. But would just any book serve the poem quite as well? One of the novels of Sir Walter Scott or a history of England, perhaps?

Meeting at Night

Robert Browning [*1812–1889*]

The gray sea and the long black land:
And the yellow half-moon large and low;
And the startled little waves that leap
In fiery ringlets from their sleep,
As I gain the cove with pushing prow,   5
And quench its speed in the slushy sand.

Then a mile of warm sea-scented beach;
Three fields to cross till a farm appears;
Tap at the pane, the quick sharp scratch
And blue spurt of a lighted match,   10
And a voice less loud, thro' its joys and fears,
Than the two hearts beating each to each!

Parting at Morning

Robert Browning [*1812–1889*]

Round the cape of a sudden came the sea,
And the sun looked over the mountain's rim:
And straight was a path of gold for him,
And the need of a world of men for me.

Questions

1. How much story do we have in these two little poems? Do we need more?

2. If the human details of the story are so carefully withheld, why does the poet give so fully, in "Meeting at Night," the physical details of the approach—the "fiery ringlets," the "slushy sand," the number of fields, the scratch of the match? Wouldn't we expect to find the emphasis reversed? Or would we?

3. The occasion in the poem is a romantic one—the night meeting of two lovers. Why does the poet select, by and large, such matter-of-fact details to fill out his poem? Why do we not find the scent of blossoms, the song of the nightingale, the soft caress of the night breeze?

4. Consider the *image* (see pp. 68–70) in the first two lines of "Parting at Morning." How can the sea suddenly come round the cape? Literally? If not literally, how does the observer get that impression? What position of the observer might make such an impression possible? If the image is, at first glance, puzzling, why would the poet use it at all? And why would he start his poem with it?

5. Do you make sense of the last two lines of "Parting at Morning"? Are the two poems to be connected? If we try to relate them, what happens?

The Workbox

Thomas Hardy [*1840–1928*]

"See, here's the workbox, little wife,
    That I made of polished oak."
He was a joiner, of village life;
    She came of borough folk.

He holds the present up to her   5
    As with a smile she nears
And answers to the profferer,
    " 'Twill last all my sewing years!"

"I warrant it will. And longer too.
    'Tis a scantling that I got   10
Off poor John Wayward's coffin, who
    Died of they knew not what.

"The shingled pattern that seems to cease
    Against your box's rim
Continues right on in the piece   15
    That's underground with him.

"And while I worked it made me think
    Of timber's varied doom;
One inch where people eat and drink,
    The next inch in a tomb.   20

"But why do you look so white, my dear,
    And turn aside your face?
You knew not that good lad, I fear,
    Though he came from your native place?"

"How could I know that good young man,   25
    Though he came from my native town,
When he must have left far earlier than
    I was a woman grown?"

"Ah, no. I should have understood!
    It shocked you that I gave   30
To you one end of a piece of wood
    Whose other is in a grave?"

"Don't, dear, despise my intellect,
    Mere accidental things
Of that sort never have effect   35
    On my imaginings."

Yet still her lips were limp and wan,
    Her face still held aside,
As if she had known not only John,
    But known of what he died.   40

This poem is a vignette of nineteenth-century English village life. The husband, in presenting to his wife the workbox which he tells her was made of a scrap of wood left over from John Wayward's coffin, little realizes that his wife knew Wayward and that the mysterious malady of which he died was unrequited love for her. No wonder that "her lips were limp and wan." We as readers know why, though her husband does not.

Yet the little tale is almost conventionally melodramatic, and the dramatic shock it undertakes to give depends on a not wholly probable coincidence: that is, that in the rather small world which the characters inhabit, the husband knew Wayward but did not know of his passionate attachment to the woman now sitting beside him.

Questions

1. Where does the effective power of this poem lie—in the ironic disclosure of the last stanza or in the contrast so concisely put in lines 9–16? These lines are hair-raising in the way they juxtapose domestic coziness with the desolation of the grave—happy married life and the emptiness of the tomb. Perhaps the conjecture of the husband (lines 29–32) ought to be the correct surmise after all.

2. Whatever the student thinks of the general effectiveness of this story of unrequited love, the inept speech put into the mouth of the wife (lines 33–36) scarcely supports its plausibility. Do people—even Hardy characters —really talk this way? Or can you defend the speech?

3. Reread the poem and try to decide for yourself whether the narrative as developed here helps or hurts the poem. Take into account the notion voiced several times earlier (see pp. 23, 25–27, 29, 35) that not to tell all—deliberately to leave certain things out—oftentimes makes for dramatic power in a poem.

The Fall of Rome

W. H. Auden [1907–1973]

For Cyril Connolly

The piers are pummelled by the waves;
In a lonely field the rain
Lashes an abandoned train;
Outlaws fill the mountain caves.

Fantastic grow the evening gowns;   5
Agents of the Fisc[1] pursue
Absconding tax-defaulters through
The sewers of provincial towns.

Private rites of magic send
The temple prostitutes to sleep;   10
All the literati keep
An imaginary friend.

Cerebrotonic[2] Catos may
Extol the Ancient Disciplines,
But the muscle-bound Marines   15
Mutiny for food and pay.

Caesar's double-bed is warm
As an unimportant clerk
Writes I DO NOT LIKE MY WORK
On a pink official form.   20

Unendowed with wealth or pity,
Little birds with scarlet legs,
Sitting on their speckled eggs,
Eye each flu-infected city.

Altogether elsewhere, vast
Herds of reindeer move across   25
Miles and miles of golden moss,
Silently and very fast.

[1] treasury   [2] a quality of temperament correlated with ectomorphic bodily components; characteristic traits of the cerebrotonic temperament are restraint in posture, sensitivity, strong inhibitions, and difficulty in making adjustments with one's environment (see W. H. Sheldon, *The Varieties of Temperament*, Harper and Brothers, 1942)

The various happenings set forth here have to do with the fall of the Roman Empire—that is, we would presume so in view of the title. But though the Roman Empire had wharves and piers and there were in Roman times outlaws living in mountain caves, there were no railroad tracks; and though the Empire had a bureaucracy, the clerks certainly did not use modern "pink official form[s]." The poet is obviously generalizing his description to cover the circumstances of any highly developed culture tottering toward its fall. Thus he universalizes the poem by mingling items from the ancient world with items from the modern.

History is the realm of human beings. Flowers, birds, and animals have no history: they are so deeply immersed in nature that they are incapable of the artistic and imaginative endeavors of human beings, but they are also incapable of human imbecility and wickedness. The little birds described in the sixth stanza are completely indifferent—properly and necessarily indifferent—to what is happening in the cities of men. Empires rise and fall without affecting them.

Questions

1. Obviously the poet could have presented us with a merely descriptive poem in whch he glanced at the perversities, failures, obscenities, and follies characteristic of a dying empire. Does he gain something by using a historical-narrative frame? Would you undertake to state what he gains?

2. Note the diverse symptoms of a culture breaking down, the absurdities of *haute couture* (line 5); a technology in decay (line 3); cheating on taxes and civic corruption (lines 5–8); self-indulgent fantasies among the so-called upper classes; boredom among the middle classes; and strikes and mutinies among the workers and soldiers.

3. Discuss the effectiveness of the last stanza. It provides the same kind of contrast with history that stanza 6 provides, but what else does it do? Does it provide a proper climax to this poem? How is the annual migration of the reindeer related to human history? What light does it throw on human history?

Channel Firing

Thomas Hardy [*1840–1928*]

> That night your great guns, unawares,
> Shook all our coffins as we lay,
> And broke the chancel window-squares,
> We thought it was the Judgment-day
>
> And sat upright. While drearisome   5
> Arose the howl of wakened hounds:
> The mouse let fall the altar-crumb,
> The worms drew back into the mounds,

The glebe[1] cow drooled. Till God called, "No;   10
It's gunnery practice out at sea
Just as before you went below;
The world is as it used to be:

"All nations striving strong to make
Red war yet redder. Mad as hatters   15
They do no more for Christés sake
Than you who are helpless in such matters.

"That this is not the judgment-hour
For some of them's a blessed thing,
For if it were they'd have to scour   20
Hell's floor for so much threatening . . .

"Ha, ha. It will be warmer when
I blow the trumpet (if indeed
I ever do; for you are men,
And rest eternal sorely need)."

So down we lay again. "I wonder,   25
Will the world ever saner be,"
Said one, "than when He sent us under
In our indifferent century!"

And many a skeleton shook his head.
"Instead of preaching forty year,"   30
My neighbor Parson Thirdly said,
"I wish I had stuck to pipes and beer."

Again the guns disturbed the hour,
Roaring their readiness to avenge,
As far inland as Stourton Tower,[2]   35
And Camelot, and starlit Stonehenge.

This poem is not a folk ballad nor even a literary ballad. But it is strongly narrative in character, and, like a number of the poems in this section, it presents its story through a succession of dramatic scenes.

The poem literally begins with a bang. The first line tells us that someone has been awakened by the sound of cannonading, but we are shocked when we learn (in line 2) that the person awakened has been lying in a coffin, a dead man, long buried in a little churchyard near the English coast.

This situation is astonishing enough, but with line 9 comes a further jolt, for God himself speaks, telling the dead, so unceremoniously aroused from their dreamless sleep, that it's not the judgment day. He hasn't or-

[1] church land used for grazing   [2] commemorating King Alfred's victory over the Danes in 879 A.D.

dered them to wake: the horrendous sound is man-made. The British navy is simply at gunnery practice out in the English channel.

It is a wrathful God,* though He scarcely answers to the orthodox Christian conception. He speaks sardonically to the dead men. He even bursts into laughter † when He thinks of what He'd like to do to those who are the authors of "so much threatening." But then with a reversed twist of mood, He mutters darkly that perhaps He will never hold a judgment day at all. Instead of putting some men into hell for their sins, He may decide to let everyone sleep the final sleep with no bother about a resurrection into eternal bliss or eternal punishment. After all, God implies, what can you expect of men or how far hold them accountable for what they do? This is strange doctrine for the dead men to hear, buried as they are in a Christian churchyard. Parson Thirdly joins the rest in troubled wonder at what all this means.

The concluding stanza, however, conveys a different mood. The guns roar forth again, but this time we follow their reverberations farther and farther inland, past quiet English towns and ruined castles to prehistoric Stonehenge with its great stones standing under the starlit sky.

"Channel Firing" is a fantastic poem with some jarring collocations, and it makes its impact at once and emphatically, though some readers will wonder just how they are to "take it." Is it comic? Satiric? Tragic? Or what? These are matters that we shall return to consider later in this book, especially when we come to Section 3 on *tone*. At this point it may be sufficient to indicate how emphatically dramatic the poem is.

Questions

1. A familiar cliché, used to describe a very loud noise goes like this: "It was so loud you would have thought it would wake the dead." Is the opening of "Channel Firing" played off this cliché? Could one say that Hardy has improved on it by using it specifically? If you think so, discuss and illustrate. How much humor is involved here?

2. Discuss the appropriateness of the diction—particularly the kind of language that Hardy assigns to the dead men and to the Almighty. Why is the choice of the right diction particularly important in a poem like "Channel Firing"?

3. What and where are Camelot and Stonehenge? (If you aren't sure, look them up.) Suppose that Hardy had chosen the names of two English

---

* The special vehemence of His wrath may be accounted for by a close look at line 33. The guns roar their readiness to avenge but, as the Bible puts it, "Vengeance is mine; I will repay, saith the Lord." Man has seized upon the divine prerogative and this is a fine example of man's overweening pride as well as his savagery.

† In the Bible, God is made to use the exclamation "Ha ha" in only one place, Job 39:25. There Jehovah says of the horse: "He saith among the trumpets, Ha, ha: and he smelleth the battle afar off, the thunder of the captains, and the shouting." It is a resounding description of a war-horse, eager to get into the fray. Was Hardy remembering—or half-remembering—this passage? Just possibly, though in this poem he has completely inverted its meaning. Whereas the war-horse rejoiced at "the thunder of the captains," such thunder has here provoked the Almighty to bitter laughter.

cities on or near the south coast and made the last line read, "And Exeter, and gaslit Brighton." What would have been lost?

4. Compare the attitude expressed in this poem with that in Whitman's "Battle of the *Bonhomme Richard* and the *Serapis*."

Afterword

The seventeen poems we have been reading in this section represent a great variety of subject matters, themes, and modes of expression. But they all have one thing in common: they are all concerned with something other than providing information or stating some abstract moralization. All of them, whether realistic or fantastic, whether concerned with apparently trivial or highly important matters, arise out of, and "say" whatever they say through, a dramatic situation. In a sense, then, they are not accurately described as "statements" at all. They are dramatizations, and, as we have seen, some of the poems, such as "Sir Patrick Spence," break up into a series of dramatic scenes; others, such as Hardy's "The Workbox," simply explore one particular scene in which the husband presents his wife with a gift and the two people talk about it.

Though poems do, in their fashion, comment upon the world and involve "truths" that the poet has discovered about all human nature, and though they often make use of abstract concepts, nevertheless poems are incorrigibly concrete, making use of particular situations—all of which means that their method of presentation is finally dramatic. In fact, we can say that in every poem—even in the simplest and most abbreviated lyric—we find someone talking to someone (even if that someone is only another side of himself) and that his talk arises out of a concrete situation.

In the poems of this section we have stressed the element of narrative. Sometimes it is quite explicit, as in Whitman's account of a famous sea battle or Kipling's story of a British soldier's execution for murder. But sometimes the narrative is only implied, as for example in Browning's poem "Meeting at Night," where we have only hints of what has occasioned the night journey. In any case, in the poems of this group the narrative is not presented for its own sake but as a means to some larger consideration. What that consideration is and how best to describe it will be one of the things we shall be studying in this book as we gradually move toward a fuller conception of poetry. In doing so, we trust that we shall become better acquainted with the purpose of poetry as well as with the various means that it employs to realize its nature. Yet even on so early a page as this, one can make a number of suggestions for our later study. In the ballad of "Sir Patrick Spence," the seaman's manly and dignified acceptance of a commission which probably will lead to his death is not the whole of the matter related to us. Though Sir Patrick died some five hundred years ago, the essential "Sir Patrick" has existed in many guises and has appeared in many other centuries. He has gone to his death under all sorts of circumstances. But is alive today in the important sense that he represents a type of nobility and fidelity that is recurrent in history.

"The Demon Lover," which is a fantastic story—as if a ship with masts of beaten gold could sail the seas, or a demon could smash a ship into bits by the movement of one knee and the thrust of one hand—has its own "truth" nevertheless. The truth does not depend on the incredible detail but rather on the ways in which temptation often presents itself to us in almost unbelievably attractive guises and in the way in which the bad news about a particular choice often breaks in upon us: first the eerie sense of a wonderful adventure, really too good to be true, then the first premonition of alarm—which we put aside because it is simply too dreadful to be true—and finally the full and damning realization that disaster is actually at hand. In short, the "truth" that these poems in their varied ways have to tell is a truth about human nature, whether in the individual human psyche or as found in society and in history.

Poems do have their universal character as well as their particular details. They do point to matters of universal import. But this is *not at the expense of their particularity*. Thus, Hardy's comments on war through the centuries and, indeed, before the dawn of history, can best be presented through a particular happening, and, in this instance, through an event that never happened at all save in the imagination. Nevertheless, Hardy found the sources for his poem in the brute facts of history. Hardy appended the date "April 1914" to this poem, pointing to the fact that the gunnery practice was part of the arms race between England and Germany prior to World War I. The grotesqueries of the poem do not inhabit a separate world but are a reflection of the grotesqueries of history.

RHYTHM AND METER: 1

In "Poetry as a Way of Saying" we have remarked on the importance of rhythm as an element in poetry. Now, having become acquainted with the foregoing poems in this section, we may go back to consider more closely the part played by rhythm in the total effect—the part played, we may insist, in the total meaning of a poem.

The only way to grasp the significance of rhythm in a poem is to listen to it as an aspect of the total experience of reading. To get acquainted with a poem, you should read it several times aloud, opening yourself as fully as possible to the movement of the language, trying to discover its basic quality. One fact to be discovered in reading aloud is that you physically participate in the rhythm and other aspects of the sound the poem makes. Your lips and your tongue move and, however secretly or indirectly, your whole body shares in the experience; you are, as it were, an echo, an amplifier, a sounding board for the poem even as you intellectually and emotionally respond to it. (The implications of this fact will be discussed more fully later; see Appendix B, "Metrics.")

Since rhythm is not an isolated element but an aspect of a total and expressive whole, you should not feel that, having read a poem aloud a few times, you are through with that aspect of it. On the contrary, the more fully you get into the whole poem (into the dramatic situation, the implications of the metaphors, the ideas presented), the more fully you become aware of the significance of the rhythm and the more likely you are to modify your original notion of what the rhythm is and refine your response to it. You should, then, at this stage, not merely begin, but end, by reading a poem aloud. This does not mean that you should try to turn yourself into a performer, an elocutionist. What you are trying to do is, simply, to cultivate as fully as possible your awareness of the various aspects of language, from the strict denotation of words, at one end of the spectrum, to the muscular and nervous activity of utterance, at the other. The final "meaning" of the experience of the poem necessarily involves all the elements in such a spectrum, and our constant and underlying concern in this book is to explore the implications of this fact.

To read aloud is, simply, one of the ways of exploring the experience of a poem. In the end this process should make you capable of sensing more fully the range of language, and of the dimensions of the poetic experience, even when you read to yourself. Even without actual sound, the sense of full participation may be had. But remember that in reading silently you must take the time to open yourself to the experience of a poem in its various dimensions. There is no "rapid reading" of poetry *as* poetry. The poem is an experience, not a mere source of information.

The question of rhythm in poetry leads us naturally to that of *meter.* Even though all poetry is rhythmical, not all poetry is metrical. But most English poetry is and, even for nonmetrical poetry, an understanding is best based on a sense of the significance of meter. For a discussion of meter see Appendix B (pp. 493–506). Having read that section you are ready to deal with the following:

Questions

1. The first line of "The Fall of Rome" (p. 44) is clearly iambic tetrameter, even though line 2, *taken in isolation,* might be scanned as trimeter:

In a lone | -ly field | the rain.

But after reading the whole poem, would you scan it that way? If not, what would be your reasoning? If you have decided that, after all, the prevailing meter is tetrameter, locate other examples of tetrameter lines in which the first foot is defective.* What is the effect of the frequency of such feet? Does the frequency of such feet speed up the verse or retard it? Does it make the verse feel more crisp and sharp, or more blurred? You

* In | a lone | -ly field | the rain.

may more easily decide on an answer to these questions if we put all of stanza 1 into regular tetrameter with no defective feet:

> The piers are pummelled by the waves;
> And in a lonely field the rain
> Is lashing an abandoned train;
> And outlaws fill the mountain caves.

Do the rhythmic changes here seem to indicate some slight difference in attitude toward the collapse of civilization, which is the subject matter of the poem?

If we rewrite the stanza to change its basic rhythm even further from the original, the last question may be easier to answer:

> The crumbling piers are pummelled by the waves;
> And somewhere in a lonely field the rain
> In sharp gusts lashes an abandoned train;
> And outlaws fill the distant mountain caves.

2. "Meeting at Night" (p. 41) is prevailingly iambic tetrameter, but includes a number of metrical variations. In fact, there is only one line strictly in that meter. Which line? Scan lines 1, 2, 9, 10, and 12.

3. Read "Little Trotty Wagtail" by John Clare (p. 347) several times. Do you think the rhythm effective? Why?

Supplemental Poems

The Code

Robert Frost [*1874–1963*]

> There were three in the meadow by the brook
> Gathering up windrows, piling cocks of hay,
> With an eye always lifted toward the west
> Where an irregular sun-bordered cloud
> Darkly advanced with a perpetual dagger   5
> Flickering across its bosom. Suddenly
> One helper, thrusting pitchfork in the ground,
> Marched himself off the field and home. One stayed.
> The town-bred farmer failed to understand.
>
> 'What is there wrong?'
>   'Something you just now said.'   10
> 'What did I say?'
>   'About our taking pains.'

'To cock the hay?—because it's going to shower?
I said that more than half an hour ago.
I said it to myself as much as you.'

'You didn't know. But James is one big fool.   15
He thought you meant to find fault with his work.
That's what the average farmer would have meant.
James would take time, of course, to chew it over
Before he acted: he's just got round to act.'

'He is a fool if that's the way he takes me.'   20

'Don't let it bother you. You've found out something.
The hand that knows his business won't be told
To do work better or faster—those two things.
I'm as particular as anyone:
Most likely I'd have served you just the same.   25
But I know you don't understand our ways.

You were just talking what was in your mind,
What was in all our minds, and you weren't hinting.
Tell you a story of what happened once:
I was up here in Salem at a man's   30
Named Sanders with a gang of four or five
Doing the haying. No one liked the boss.
He was one of the kind sports call a spider,
All wiry arms and legs that spread out wavy
From a humped body nigh as big's a biscuit   35
But work! that man could work, especially
If by so doing he could get more work
Out of his hired help. I'm not denying
He was hard on himself. I couldn't find
That he kept any hours—not for himself.   40
Daylight and lantern-light were one to him:
I've heard him pounding in the barn all night.
But what he liked was someone to encourage.
Them that he couldn't lead he'd get behind
And drive, the way you can, you know, in mowing—   45
Keep at their heels and threaten to mow their legs off.
I'd seen about enough of his bulling tricks
(We call that bulling). I'd been watching him.
So when he paired off with me in the hayfield
To load the load, thinks I, Look out for trouble.   50
I built the load and topped it off; old Sanders
Combed it down with a rake and says, "O.K."
Everything went well till we reached the barn
With a big jag to empty in a bay.
You understand that meant the easy job   55
For the man up on top of throwing *down*
The hay and rolling it off wholesale
Where on a mow it would have been slow lifting.

You wouldn't think a fellow'd need much urging
Under those circumstances, would you now? 60

But the old fool seizes his fork in both hands.
And looking up bewhiskered out of the pit,
Shouts like an army captain, "Let her come!"
Thinks I, D'ye mean it? "What was that you said?"
I asked out loud, so's there'd be no mistake, 65
"Did you say, Let her come?" "Yes, let her come."
He said it over, but he said it softer.
Never you say a thing like that to a man,
Not if he values what he is. God, I'd as soon
Murdered him as left out his middle name. 70
I'd built the load and knew right where to find it.
Two or three forkfuls I picked lightly round for
Like meditating, and then I just dug in
And dumped the rackful on him in ten lots.
I looked over the side once in the dust 75
And caught sight of him treading-water-like,
Keeping his head above. "Damn ye," I says.
"That gets ye!" He squeaked like a squeezed rat.
That was the last I saw or heard of him.
I cleaned the rack and drove out to cool off. 80
As I sat mopping hayseed from my neck,
And sort of waiting to be asked about it,
One of the boys sings out, "Where's the old man?"
"I left him in the barn under the hay.
If ye want him, ye can go and dig him out." 85
They realized from the way I swabbed my neck
More than was needed something must be up.
They headed for the barn; I stayed where I was.
They told me afterward. First they forked hay,
A lot of it, out into the barn floor. 90
Nothing! They listened for him. Not a rustle.
I guess they thought I'd spiked him in the temple
Before I buried him, or I couldn't have managed.
They excavated more. "Go keep his wife
Out of the barn." Someone looked in a window, 95
And curse me if he wasn't in the kitchen
Slumped way down in a chair, with both his feet
Against the stove, the hottest day that summer.
He looked so clean disgusted from behind
There was no one that dared to stir him up, 100
Or let him know that he was being looked at.
Apparently I hadn't buried him
(I may have knocked him down); but my just trying
To bury him had hurt his dignity.
He had gone to the house so's not to meet me. 105
He kept away from us all afternoon.

We tended to his hay. We saw him out
After a while picking peas in his garden:
He couldn't keep away from doing something.'

'Weren't you relieved to find he wasn't dead?'   110

'No! and yet I don't know—it's hard to say.
I went about to kill him fair enough.'

'You took an awkward way. Did he discharge you?'

'Discharge me? No! He knew I did just right.'

Questions

1. Does the title of this poem help you to determine what the poem is about? Or, to reverse the question, does the action recounted in this poem indicate which of the several senses of the word *code* applies to this poem?

2. What is the character of the narrator? Why would James not have made a good narrator for this story? Merely because he is "one big fool"? What does he lack that the narrator does have? Would an objective third-person narration have served as well as the present method?

3. Comment on the "conversational" quality of this poem. Are the rhythms really like those of people talking to each other? Or do they merely suggest conversation? What other factors contribute to the tone of colloquial speech? Why are these matters particularly important in this poem?

The Three Ravens

Anonymous

There were three ravens sat on a tree,
    Downe a downe, hay downe, hay downe
There were three ravens sat on a tree,
    With a downe
There were three ravens sat on a tree,   5
They were as blacke as they might be.
    With a downe derrie, derrie, derrie, downe, downe.

The one of them said to his mate,
"Where shall we our breakfast take?"

"Downe in yonder greene field,   10
There lies a knight slain under his shield.

"His hounds they lie downe at his feete,
So well they can their master keepe.

"His haukes they flie so eagerly,
There's no fowle dare him come nie."   15

Downe there comes a fallow doe,
As great with yong as she might goe.

She lift up his bloudy hed,
And kist his wounds that were so red.

She got him up upon her backe,   20
And carried him to earthen lake.[1]

She buried him before the prime,
She was dead herselfe ere even-song time.

God send every gentleman,
Such haukes, such hounds, and such a leman.[2]   25

Questions

1. We are not told who killed the dead knight or what the fight was about. For our understanding of this poem, is it necessary to have such information? On what has the anonymous poet focused our attention?

2. In this poem the ravens are "bad." They see the dead knight as only so much food. The hawks are "good." Though they are also meat-eaters and get their food by preying on other birds, in this poem they loyally defend their dead master. Does the poet make plain what the difference between the birds is? Or is the matter unimportant?

3. At what point does the reader realize that the "doe" is not an animal but a human being—the "leman"? Why is the leman presented as a doe in the first place? What is implied here about love and fidelity—from hawk, hound, and human being in contrast to the ravens?

The Twa[1] Corbies

Anonymous

As I was walking all alane,[2]
I heard twa corbies making a mane;[3]
The tane[4] unto the t'other say,
"Where sall[5] we gang[6] and dine to-day?"

"In behint yon auld fail[7] dyke,   5
I wot there lies a new slain knight,
And naebody kens[8] that he lies there,
But his hawk, his hound, and lady fair.

"His hound is to the hunting gane,[9]
His hawk to fetch the wild-fowl hame,[10]   10
His lady's ta'en[11] another mate,
So we may mak our dinner sweet.

[1] pit [2] sweetheart or mistress
[1] two [2] alone [3] moan [4] one [5] shall [6] go [7] turf [8] knows [9] gone [10] home
[11] taken

"Ye'll sit on his white hause-bane,[12]
And I'll pike out his bonny blue een;[13]
Wi ae lock o his gowden[14] hair   15
We'll theek[15] our nest when it grows bare.

"Mony[16] a one for him makes mane,
But nane sall ken where he is gane;
Oer his white banes, when they are bare,
The wind sall blaw for evermair."   20

This poem reads almost as if it were a conscious answer to the preceding poem. *Corbie* is the Scottish word for raven, and as Francis James Childs wrote in his *English and Scottish Popular Ballads*, I, 253, "The Twa Corbies" sounds "something like a cynical variation of the tender little English ballad ["The Three Ravens"]."

Questions

1. Though we do not learn how the knight in "The Three Ravens" came to be killed, would you not say that in "The Twa Corbies" we are given a broad hint as to what happened?

2. "The Twa Corbies" seems to describe a dog-eat-dog world in which everyone tries to take care of his own interest and the devil can take the hindmost. Note in particular what the corbies say. Note further that in the last two stanzas their comments seem to go beyond the mere voicing of satisfaction at the prospect of an easy dinner.

3. Note that in "The Three Ravens" the carrion crows were denied their dinner. At the cost of her own life, the dead knight's leman gives him burial and thus saves his body from defilement. If the reader has not already picked up this implication from "The Three Ravens," a comparison of that poem with "The Twa Corbies" ought to make it clear. In general, does a reading of "The Twa Corbies" gain from a previous reading of "The Three Ravens"? Do the last lines thereby take on symbolic force?

The Cameo

Edna St. Vincent Millay   [*1892–1950*]

Forever over now, forever, forever gone
That day. Clear and diminished like a scene
Carven in cameo, the lighthouse, and the cove between
The sandy cliffs, and the boat drawn up on the beach;
And the long skirt of a lady innocent and young,   5
Her hand resting on her bosom, her head hung;
And the figure of a man in earnest speech.

---

[12] neck bone   [13] eyes   [14] golden   [15] thatch   [16] many

Clear and diminished like a scene cut in cameo
The lighthouse, and the boat on the beach, and the two shapes
Of the woman and the man; lost like the lost day   10
Are the words that passed, and the pain,—discarded, cut away
From the stone, as from the memory the heat of the tears escapes.

O troubled forms, O early love unfortunate and hard,
Time has estranged you into a jewel cold and pure;
From the action of the waves and from the action of sorrow forever
    secure,   15
White against a ruddy cliff you stand, chalcedony on sard.

Full comprehension of this poem requires some knowledge of how a genuine cameo is made. The precious stone usually employed (and that which the poet clearly has in mind) is sardonyx, which consists of alternate layers of white chalcedony and orange-red or reddish brown chalcedony (sard). The engraver carves the figures in the white chalcedony so as to show them in relief against the background of sard (line 16).

Questions

1. Is the poem about a literal cameo, or is the cameo a metaphor? Explain your choice.

2. If the cameo is metaphorical, justify the use here. Who, for instance, would be the engraver of the metaphorical jewel? What details in the scene suggest a cameo? Why a cameo here and not a painting?

3. Compare "The Cameo" with "The Last Ride Together" by Robert Browning (p. 397). What are the points of likeness? Of difference? Deal with such matters as imagery, rhythm, and tone—and whatever else seems relevant.

4. A story is implied in "The Cameo," but we know none of the details. Do we need such details to appreciate the emotion of the poem?

Ulysses

Alfred, Lord Tennyson   [*1809–1892*]

It little profits that an idle king,
By this still hearth, among these barren crags,
Matched with an agèd wife, I mete and dole
Unequal laws unto a savage race,
That hoard, and sleep, and feed, and know not me.   5
I cannot rest from travel: I will drink
Life to the lees: all times I have enjoyed
Greatly, have suffered greatly, both with those
That loved me, and alone; on shore, and when
Through scudding drifts the rainy Hyades   10

Vext the dim sea: I am become a name;
For always roaming with a hungry heart
Much have I seen and known; cities of men
And manners, climates, councils, governments,
Myself not least, but honored of them all;   15
And drunk delight of battle with my peers,
Far on the ringing plains of windy Troy.
I am a part of all that I have met;
Yet all experience is an arch wherethro'
Gleams that untraveled world, whose margin fades   20
For ever and for ever when I move.
How dull it is to pause, to make an end,
To rust unburnished, not to shine in use!
As though to breathe were life. Life piled on life
Were all too little, and of one to me   25
Little remains: but every hour is saved
From that eternal silence, something more,
A bringer of new things; and vile it were
For some three suns to store and hoard myself,
And this gray spirit yearning in desire   30
To follow knowledge like a sinking star,
Beyond the utmost bound of human thought.

This is my son, mine own Telemachus,
To whom I leave the scepter and the isle—
Well-loved of me, discerning to fulfill   35
This labor, by slow prudence to make mild
A rugged people, and through soft degrees
Subdue them to the useful and the good.
Most blameless is he, centered in the sphere
Of common duties, decent not to fail   40
In offices of tenderness, and pay
Meet adoration to my household gods,
When I am gone. He works his work, I mine.

There lies the port; the vessel puffs her sail:
There gloom the dark broad seas. My mariners,   45
Souls that have toiled, and wrought, and thought with me—
That ever with a frolic welcome took
The thunder and the sunshine, and opposed
Free hearts, free foreheads—you and I are old;
Old age hath yet his honor and his toil.   50
Death closes all: but something ere the end,
Some work of noble note, may yet be done,
Not unbecoming men that strove with Gods.
The lights begin to twinkle from the rocks;
The long day wanes: the slow moon climbs: the deep   55
Moans round with many voices. Come, my friends,
'Tis not too late to seek a newer world.
Push off, and sitting well in order smite

The sounding furrows; for my purpose holds
To sail beyond the sunset, and the baths   60
Of all the western stars, until I die.
It may be that the gulfs will wash us down:
It may be we shall touch the Happy Isles,
And see the great Achilles, whom we knew.
Though much is taken, much abides; and though   65
We are not now that strength which in old days
Moved earth and heaven, that which we are, we are;
One equal temper of heroic hearts,
Made weak by time and fate, but strong in will
To strive, to seek, to find, and not to yield.   70

Questions

1. Ulysses (Odysseus), the hero of Homer's *Odyssey,* after spending some ten years in the siege of Troy and another ten years of wandering and adventure, has at last succeeded in returning to his island home of Ithaca. Has he now become so habituated to wandering that home is a disappointment? Is this the point of the story? Or is the point other than this? Why has Ulysses resolved to leave the home to which, in spite of every kind of frustration, he had succeeded in returning?

2. Why does Ulysses say that his people "know not me"? How is he different from them?

3. Does Ulysses patronize his wife ("an agèd wife," line 3)? Does he patronize his son Telemachus? If you feel that such is an unfair charge, try to indicate, by reference to the text, why you feel that he does not dismiss them with a kind of contemptuous disdain.

4. What do you make of the last three lines of the poem? Does Ulysses resemble the American businessman who simply cannot think of retiring? Or the old Wild West Indian fighter who wants to die with his boots on? Or can you find more accurate analogies?

Hell Gate

A. E. Housman [*1859–1936*]

Onward led the road again
Through the sad uncolored plain
Under twilight brooding dim,
And along the utmost rim
Wall and rampart risen to sight   5
Cast a shadow not of night,
And beyond them seemed to glow
Bonfires lighted long ago.
And my dark conductor broke
Silence at my side and spoke,   10
Saying, "You conjecture well:
Yonder is the gate of hell."

Ill as yet the eye could see
The eternal masonry,
But beneath it on the dark   15
To and fro there stirred a spark.
And again the somber guide
Knew my question and replied:
"At hell gate the damned in turn
Pace for sentinel and burn."   20

Dully at the leaden sky
Staring, and with idle eye
Measuring the listless plain,
I began to think again.
Many things I thought of then,   25
Battle, and the loves of men,
Cities entered, oceans crossed,
Knowledge gained and virtue lost,
Cureless folly done and said,
And the lovely way that led   30
To the slimepit and the mire
And the everlasting fire.
And against a smolder dun
And a dawn without a sun
Did the nearing bastion loom,   35
And across the gate of gloom
Still one saw the sentry go,
Trim and burning, to and fro,
One for women to admire
In his finery of fire.   40
Something, as I watched him pace,
Minded me of time and place,
Soldiers of another corps
And a sentry known before.

Ever darker hell on high   45
Reared its strength upon the sky,
And our footfall on the track
Fetched the daunting echo back.
But the soldier pacing still
The insuperable sill,   50
Nursing his tormented pride,
Turned his head to neither side,
Sunk into himself apart
And the hell-fire of his heart.
But against our entering in   55
From the drawbridge Death and Sin
Rose to render key and sword
To their father and their lord.
And the portress foul to see

Lifted up her eyes on me   60
Smiling, and I made reply:
"Met again, my lass," said I.
Then the sentry turned his head,
Looked, and knew me, and was Ned.

Once he looked, and halted straight,   65
Set his back against the gate,
Caught his musket to his chin,
While the hive of hell within
Sent abroad a seething hum
As of towns whose king is come   70
Leading conquest home from far
And the captives of his war,
And the car of triumph waits,
And they open wide the gates.
But across the entry barred   75
Straddled the revolted guard,
Weaponed and accoutred well
From the arsenals of hell;
And beside him, sick and white,
Sin to left and Death to right   80
Turned a countenance of fear
On the flaming mutineer.
Over us the darkness bowed,
And the anger in the cloud
Clenched the lightning for the stroke;   85
But the traitor musket spoke.

And the hollowness of hell
Sounded as its master fell,
And the mourning echo rolled
Ruin through his kingdom old.   90
Tyranny and terror flown
Left a pair of friends alone,
And beneath the nether sky
All that stirred was he and I.

Silent, nothing found to say,   95
We began the backward way;
And the ebbing luster died
From the soldier at my side,
As in all his spruce attire
Failed the everlasting fire.   100
Midmost of the homeward track
Once we listened, and looked back;
But the city, dusk, and mute,
Slept, and there was no pursuit.

The story told here is obviously not realistic but fantastic, like a dream or a nightmare. But a narrative may be fantastic and nevertheless tell us a great deal about ourselves and the situations that human beings may actually encounter.

Questions

1. What is the literal story told in this poem? Is the "dark conductor" of line 9 a devil escorting the speaker to hell? What prevents the narrator's being incarcerated in hell? Who rescues him and how?

2. In spite of the fact that the poem begins by depicting hell as a place —a grim prison city—what does the poem imply that hell actually is? Even John Milton, in his *Paradise Lost,* indicates that hell is not merely a place but a state of mind. When Milton's Satan escapes from the burning pit and arrives on the newly created earth he exclaims: "Which way I flie is Hell; myself am Hell; . . ." Has Housman also treated hell as a mental state? What evidence for this view of hell do you find in this poem?

Proud Maisie

Sir Walter Scott   [*1771–1832*]

> Proud Maisie is in the wood,
>   Walking so early;
> Sweet Robin sits on the bush,
>   Singing so rarely.
>
> "Tell me, thou bonny bird,   5
>   When shall I marry me?"
> "When six braw[1] gentlemen
>   Kirkward[2] shall carry ye."
>
> "Who makes the bridal bed,
>   Birdie, say truly?"–   10
> "The gray-headed sexton
>   That delves the grave duly.
>
> "The glow-worm o'er grave and stone
>   Shall light thee steady;
> The owl from the steeple sing,   15
>   'Welcome, proud lady.' "

Questions

1. This poem evidently derives from the folk ballad. What are some of the specific ways in which it resembles the folk ballad?

2. The story, like that told in "Hell Gate," is a fantastic one: the robin, for example, is endowed with human speech. But does the fairy-tale qual-

[1] brave   [2] churchward

ity of the first stanza prevent the poem's becoming a thoroughly serious one?

3. Note that *carry* in line 8 may be used in the archaic sense of "escort," and does not necessarily mean "life up and transport." How does Maisie interpret the word in line 9?

4. Note that the funeral is consistently compared to a marriage, the six pallbearers becoming groomsmen, and so on. What is the poem, then, about? The expectations of a young girl unaware of the common human fate?

5. Give an account of the metrics of this poem.

La Belle Dame sans Merci

John Keats [*1795–1821*]

O what can ail thee, knight at arms,
    Alone and palely loitering?
The sedge has withered from the lake,
    And no birds sing!

O what can ail thee, knight at arms,   5
    So haggard and so woe-begone?
The squirrel's granary is full,
    And the harvest's done.

I see a lily on thy brow,
    With anguish moist and fever dew;   10
And on thy cheeks a fading rose
    Fast withereth too'.—

I met a lady in the meads,
    Full beautiful, a faery's child;
Her hair was long, her foot was light,   15
    And her eyes were wild.

I made a garland for her head,
    And bracelets, too, and fragrant zone;
She looked at me as she did love,
    And made sweet moan.   20

I set her on my pacing steed,
    And nothing else, saw all day long;
For sidelong would she bend, and sing
    A faery's song.

She found me roots of relish sweet,   25
    And honey wild, and manna dew;
And sure in language strange she said,
    "I love thee true."

She took me to her elfin grot
    And there she wept and sighed full sore;   30
And there I shut her wild, wild eyes
    With kisses four.

And there she lullèd me asleep,
    And there I dreamed, ah woe betide!
The latest dream I ever dreamt,   35
    On the cold hillside.

I saw pale kings, and princes too,
    Pale warriors, death-pale were they all,
Who cried, "La Belle Dame sans Merci
    Thee hath in thrall!"   40

I saw their starved lips in the gloam
    With horrid warning gaped wide—
And I awoke and found me here,
    On the cold hill's side.

And this is why I sojourn here,   45
    Alone and palely loitering;
Though the sedge is withered from the lake
    And no birds sing.

Questions

1. This poem, like "Farewell to Barn and Stack and Tree," "Danny Deever," and "Proud Maisie," clearly owes much to the method of the traditional ballad. What features in particular does it derive from the ballad? How does the meter compare with that of, for instance, "Sir Patrick Spence"? Is it accentual-syllabic or accentual?

2. "La Belle Dame sans Merci" is, of course, a "modern" poem by an extremely accomplished poet using the pretense of ballad simplicity. Suppose you came on this poem without knowing its authorship or anything about it. Could you fix on any features which might make you think it was not a true ballad? Language, for instance? Or rhythm? Or the attitude of the narrator? Or the method of developing the narrative?

3. Who is the knight? Who is La Belle Dame? If you can answer these two questions, you can state the theme of the poem. How might your answer to this question determine the answer to the second?

The Haunted Oak

Paul Laurence Dunbar   *[1872–1906]*

Pray why are you so bare, so bare,
    Oh, bough of the old oak-tree;
And why, when I go through the shade you throw,
    Runs a shudder over me?

My leaves were green as the best, I trow, 5
   And sap ran free in my veins,
But I saw in the moonlight dim and weird
   A guiltless victim's pains.

I bent me down to hear his sigh;
   I shook with his gurgling moan, 10
And I trembled sore when they rode away,
   And left him here alone.

They'd charged him with the old, old crime
   And set him fast in jail:
Oh, why does the dog howl all night long, 15
   And why does the night wind wail?

He prayed his prayer and he swore his oath,
   And he raised his hand to the sky;
But the beat of hoofs smote on his ear,
   And the steady tread drew nigh. 20

Who is it rides by night, by night,
   Over the moonlit road?
And what is the spur that keeps the pace,
   What is the galling goad?

And now they beat at the prison door, 25
   "Ho, keeper, do not stay!
We are friends of him whom you hold within,
   And we fain would take him away

"From those who ride fast on our heels
   With mind to do him wrong; 30
They have no care for his innocence,
   And the rope they bear is long."

They have fooled the jailer with lying words,
   They have fooled the man with lies;
The bolts unbar, the locks are drawn, 35
   And the great door open flies.

Now they have taken him from the jail,
   And hard and fast they ride,
And the leader laughs low down in his throat,
   As they halt my trunk beside. 40

Oh, the judge, he wore a mask of black,
   And the doctor one of white,
And the minister, with his oldest son,
   Was curiously bedight.

Oh, foolish man, why weep you now? 45
   'T is but a little space,

And the time will come when these shall dread
　　The mem'ry of your face.

I feel the rope against my bark,
　　And the weight of him in my grain,　　　　　　　　　　50
I feel in the throe of his final woe
　　The touch of my own last pain.

And never more shall leaves come forth
　　On a bough that bears the ban;
I am burned with dread, I am dried and dead,　　　　　55
　　From the curse of a guiltless man.

And ever the judge rides by, rides by,
　　And goes to hunt the deer,
And ever another rides his soul
　　In the guise of a mortal fear.　　　　　　　　　　　60

And ever the man he rides me hard,
　　And never a night stays he;
For I feel his curse as a haunted bough,
　　On the trunk of a haunted tree.

"The Haunted Oak," like "La Belle Dame sans Merci," "Farewell to Barn and Stack and Tree," and many other poems, is an imitation of the traditional ballad. The poem has, indeed, its virtues; it was written by a man of talent. But it also has certain defects and these result from the author's inability to work out a proper relation between his desire to imitate a traditional ballad and to treat contemporary material—"contemporary" meaning here the late nineteenth century and the "material" being a lynching in, presumably, one of the Southern States. For one thing, such lynchers would not say "Ho, keeper, do not stay," nor use the word *fain* (lines 26, 28). A spur may be the instrument that "keeps the pace" of horsemen but what of a "galling goad"? Goads are to be associated with oxen (lines 23–24). The line "the throe of his final woe" is a very fancy way to describe the effect of a noose (line 51). In the South deer are hunted on foot, unlike the deer in traditional English and Scots ballads (lines 57–58). None of these things taken individually might much matter, but the accumulated effect is destructive. In contrast, notice how in "Frankie and Johnny," a real American folk ballad, the language belongs to the world treated, as does that of "Jesse James."

It may be objected here that "La Belle Dame" uses a language associated with traditional balladry. This is true. But the point is that the language here is *not* inconsistent with the world presented; it is a world of fantasy, a world of fairy and legend, even if that world is used, in the end, symbolically. As for Housman's ballad, the language, again, does not violate the material.

Questions

1. What comparison would you make between "Mama and Daughter" by Langston Hughes and the present poem?

2. See "Kitchenette Building" by Gwendolyn Brooks (p. 158) and "Hard Rock Returns to Prison" by Etheridge Knight (p. 429), both poems by black writers, and compare the use of language and detail with the use in the present poem.

Description: Images, Moods, and Attitudes

2

Foreword

Poetry, as we have said on an earlier page, is incorrigibly particular and concrete—not general and abstract. It presents to us a world that appeals to our senses by giving us a more or less vivid and recognizable impression of some natural scene or natural object—a register, rendered as accurately as the poet could manage, of the impression received through the senses or through the imagination (remembering that to "imagine" is originally to *image* something). Such a lively sense of the perceptible world with its sights, sounds, smells, and sensations of taste and touch is fundamental to poetry. Poetry, we say, puts us back in touch with the freshness of things; and, for people living in an urbanized modern society, poetry becomes a means for, among other things, restoring our originally unprejudiced life of the senses.

This is not to say that poetry competes with the world of direct sensation. The odor of skunk at first hand is overpowering in a way in which no verbal description of that odor can be. The pain in a badly burned hand is more intense than the most vivid verbal account of burning one's hand. For poetry exists in words, not in direct sensations, and its true role is not to try to outdo the vividness of the world of sense impression, but to provide us with something else. In the pages that follow we shall have a great deal to say about what that something is. Here, let us simply say that the method that poetry uses is to stir our imaginations through a dramatic presentation of objects, persons, and events. This means that poetry cannot depart too much from the world of the senses. If it does so, it becomes abstract, talky, intellectualized, empty, and dull.

From time to time, the poetry of any given culture may lose its freshness and immediacy. When it does, sooner or later there will arise a generation of poets who feel impelled to rescue it from abstraction and return it to vividness by tying its meanings once more to images. Thus, early in our century a number of poets, tired of Victorian prolixity, worn conventions, and empty rhetoric, began to experiment with poems that concentrated on an image (or on a basic image about which are clustered subsidiary images) and who took care to let the reader make of the poem what he could, preferring not to interfere in the process.* The poets belonging to one offshoot of the Imagist movement actually called themselves "Objectivists," presumably to indicate their belief that the poem ought to be allowed to speak for itself.

The Imagists and their allies were much influenced by the poetry of the Far East, especially by the poetry that stressed one dominant image and made use of suggestion and implication, carefully avoiding direct statement. Here, for example, is a tiny Japanese poem:

> A crow is perched
> Upon a leafless withered bough—
> The autumn dusk.

Here is a somewhat longer poem by a fourteenth-century Japanese poet:

> Even in the flashing
> Of the lightning that does not linger
> Even for a moment,
> The very number of the drops of rain
> Could be counted on the leaves of plants.

Here is a third example from a Japanese poet of the twelfth century:

> For her straw-mat bedding
> The Lady of the Bridge of Uji now
> Spreads the moonlight out,
> And in the waiting autumn night
> Still lies there in the darkening wind.

All three poems insist on a dominant image, and each may be called a mood piece. Clearly the first and the third are. Most readers will find that the solitary crow perched in the dusk of autumn on a withered bough sug-

---

* They called themselves Imagists and included such poets as Ezra Pound, H.D., John Gould Fletcher, and Amy Lowell. Many another poet of the period experimented with Imagist poems or was influenced by the examples of the original Imagists.

gests loneliness, the pathos of the end of the season, or some related mood.

The third poem also suggests loneliness. The wind is up. The lady makes her bed on the bare ground with no bedding save the moonlight itself, and the autumn night is "waiting." Is the lady waiting too? Is her lover late to the tryst? Has he forgotten? Or is he dead? The poet does not tell us, and apparently is content to stir our imagination with possibilities and to conjure up a mood that accords with them.

The second of these poems is probably the most nearly objective of the three. The lightning flash during a thunder storm, though it seems blinding, doesn't really blind us, and in spite of its very brief duration it can reveal even minute things in sharp detail. But even this poem hints of an interpretation: a sudden and fleeting insight may provide a profound revelation.

To the poets who wrote them, these Japanese poems were probably less "objective" than they now appear to Westerners who read them in English translations. For, as the authorities on such poetry tell us, to the mind that is saturated with the rich symbolism of the East, the images in these poems are rich in special associations. Perhaps the translation of such poetry into English does less than justice to the oriental poet's "interpretation" through references to traditional meanings. Yet the loss of some of their traditional meanings was largely irrelevant to the twentieth-century Imagists, who cited these poems as proof of how fresh and moving poetry could be if the poet would only trust the images and keep down the chatter about what they meant. Images properly selected and presented would stir the reader's imagination and thus "say" more than an explicit statement.

Oriental poems of the sort that we have been discussing tend to make use of some natural object or scene. But the twentieth-century Imagists did not confine their subject matter to nature. They also offered vignettes of city life. For example, here is a short passage from John Gould Fletcher's poem "Irradiations."

> Flickering of incessant rain
> On flashing pavements;
> Sudden scurry of umbrellas;
> Bending recurved blossoms of the storm.

The scene is vividly rendered: apparently it is a day of sun and shower for the rain is "flickering" and the wetted pavements of the city streets are "flashing." Another shower has evidently just begun, for the street suddenly "blossoms" with umbrellas which go "scurrying" along the street— as if they moved under their own power.

The scene, though rather objectively presented, suggests an attitude as well. There is even a hint of gaiety and amusement at the scene presented. In part, this is effected by the witty comparison of umbrellas to blossoms. The umbrellas are "recurved," just the opposite of the corollas of natural flowers. For the stem of a flower ends in an open floral cup, whereas the "stems" of the umbrellas end in a "corolla" which is curved back upon itself—that is, "convex." Yet, in a sense the umbrellas can be fancifully compared to flowers, for the rain that brings up tulips or blue-bells from the flower bed brings up—quite suddenly—these grotesquely large black "blossoms" from the city pavement.

We shall later have a great deal more to say about metaphors and similes,* which may be defined as comparisons, either implied or explicit: "my love is a rose" (metaphor) or "a pretty girl is like a melody" (simile) will serve as examples. In the present section, however, we shall be primarily concerned, not with comparisons but with images as such. In fact, though the witty metaphor that turns umbrellas into flowers adds something important to the poem, even if the poet had not used it the poem produced would have been one kind of "Imagist" poem. Suppose the last line read: "Dark convex shields against the rain." The metaphor would have been eliminated,—or all but eliminated—but we would still have the images and an impression of a city street during a rain shower.

Ezra Pound, a poet very active in the development of the Imagist movement, was much influenced by Japanese and Chinese poetry. Here follows a tiny poem of nineteen syllables that resembles the Japanese *haiku* (a poem of precisely seventeen syllables, sometimes called a *hokku*).

In a Station of the Metro

Ezra Pound [*1885–1972*]

> The apparition of these faces in the crowd;
> Petals on a wet, black bough.

Pound has left a record of how he came to write the poem.

> I got out of a metro train at La Concorde, and saw suddenly a beautiful face, and then another beautiful woman, and I tried all that day to find words for what this had meant to me, and I could not find any words that seemed to me worthy, or as lovely as that sudden emotion. And that evening, as I went home, along the rue Raynouard, I was still trying and I found, suddenly, the expression. I do not mean that I found words, but there came an equation . . . not in speech, but in little splotches of colour. It was just that—a "pattern," or hardly a pattern, if by "pattern" you mean something with a "repeat" in it. But it was a word, the beginning, for me, of a language in colour. . . .
>
> That evening in the rue Raynouard, I realized quite vividly that if I were

---

* See particularly Section 4 (p. 196), though, of course, we have been encountering metaphors and similes all along: e.g., "true as the stars above" ("Frankie and Johnny"); "His folks / Pursue their lives like toy trains on a track" ("Ten Days Leave"); "rouses from the mare's-nest of his drowsy head" ("Waking in the Blue"), etc.

a painter, or if I had, often, *that kind* of emotion, or even if I had the energy to get paints and brushes and keep at it, I might found a new school of painting, of "non-representative" painting, a painting that would speak only by arrangements in colour.

And so, when I came to read Kandinsky's chapter on the language of form and colour, I found little that was new to me. I only felt that some one else understood what I understood, and had written it out very clearly. It seems quite natural to me that an artist should have just as much pleasure in an arrangement of planes or in a pattern of figures, as in painting portraits of fine ladies, or in portraying the Mother of God as the symbolists bid us. . . . That is to say, my experience in Paris should have gone into paint. If instead of colour I had perceived sound or planes in relation, I should have expressed it in music or in sculpture. Colour was, in that instance, the "primary pigment"; I mean that it was the first adequate equation that came into consciousness. . . . All poetic language is the language of exploration. Since the beginning of bad writing, writers have used images as ornaments. The point of Imagisme is that it does not use images *as ornaments*. The image is itself the speech. The image is the word beyond formulated language. . . . The "one-image poem" is a form of super-position, that is to say, it is one idea set on top of another. I found it useful in getting out of the impasse in which I had been left by my metro emotion. I wrote a thirty-line poem, and destroyed it because it was what we call work "of second intensity." Six months later I made a poem half that length; a year later I made the following *hokku*-like sentence: . . .*

The whole passage is interesting for several reasons: it suggests some of the ways in which Imagism is related to painting, an art in which the artist sets down literal images in line and color. It suggests further that Pound, in spite of all his insistence upon getting the exact image and the exact arrangement of words, was also concerned to express a personal emotion. What Pound tells us here about how he distilled into two lines the essence of a rich and complex experience constitutes a useful makeweight to any notion that the poet who insists on working through images is not concerned with expressing attitudes, moods, and even ideas. Pound's experience at the Metro station was obviously intensely meaningful for him. He was not simply a theorist having a game with images.

In fact, it may be well for us to disabuse ourselves, once and for all, of any notion that a poet's decision to refrain from any *direct* expression of attitudes and ideas denotes a lack of feelings and convictions. Genuine poets have them—after all, they are human beings—but their characteristic method is to stir our imaginations, and their prime way of doing this is to make use of concrete particulars—which means, at some level, the use of images. That is why even when poets make use of statement or develop a logical argument, they usually make it subordinate to an imaginative construction dominated by objects, scenes, and characters in action.

* *Gaudier-Brzeska: A Memoir*, New Directions, 1960.

If we compare Pound's account of how he wrote "In a Station of the Metro" with the poem itself, we see to what pains he has been to keep himself as observer out of the poem. But, of course, poets may place themselves in a poem, and their own observations and reactions may indeed become part of the poem.

Red Wheelbarrow

William Carlos Williams [*1883–1963*]

So much depends
upon

a red wheel
barrow

glazed with rain
water

beside the white
chickens.

We have said above that a relation exists between the poetry of Imagism and painting, an art involving literal images in line and color. Williams's "Red Wheelbarrow" seems, at first glance, to be an even more positive example of the relation than is Pound's "In a Station of the Metro." In Pound's little poem there is, at least, a metaphorical pairing of two images, while in "Red Wheelbarrow" there is the single image. On this image a strangely acute and puzzling sort of attention is brought to bear. Ordinarily in poetry we expect some awareness of the use of language—its being associated or fused, however marginally or even unconsciously, with the content of the poem, including imagery. Here it would appear that the writer has repudiated as far as possible the role of language in poetry and poetic method in general. What we seem to have is an ordinary prose sentence broken up in a peculiar way.*

The very arbitrariness of the slashing across the prose sentence may be important: the sentence is denied its own structure, and the reader is, as it were, left staring at the image. We have to focus our attention upon words, mere words, in a very special way, and the poem assumes a puzzling portentousness, the sort of portentousness that any object, even the simplest and most ordinary (in this case the wheelbarrow), assumes when we fix attention exclusively on it and cut it off from the rest of the world. Reading this poem is like peering at an ordinary object through a pin prick in a piece of cardboard. The fact that the tiny hole arbitrarily frames the

* In our discussion of Free Verse (pp. 565–566) we return to this poem.

object endows it with an exciting freshness that seems to hover on the verge of revelation.

And that is what the poem is actually about: "So much depends . . ." But what depends, we don't know. Or is it a way of saying that the act of experiencing the object is the very significance of this poem?

We began our comment on "Red Wheelbarrow" by remarking on the relation of Imagism and painting. But now we observe that even this poem is not objective in the sense that a painting is. Though the image seems to be all of the poem, the very first line is itself an interpretation; the image, after all, is declared to have consequences, and we are reminded of the fact that for Williams the essence of poetry was summed up in his declaration, "No ideas but in things." In other words, a human response is always implicit in the most objective—the most "imagistic"—poem.

Written in March

William Wordsworth   [1770–1850]

The cock is crowing,
The stream is flowing,
The small birds twitter,
The lake doth glitter,
The green field sleeps in the sun;   5
The oldest and youngest
Are at work with the strongest;
The cattle are grazing,
Their heads never raising;
There are forty feeding like one!   10

Like an army defeated
The snow hath retreated,
And now doth fare ill
On the top of the bare hill;
The plowboy is whooping—anon—anon: 15
There's joy in the mountains;
There's life in the fountains;
Small clouds are sailing,
Blue sky prevailing;
The rain is over and gone!   20

Wordsworth did not tell us how he wrote the foregoing poem—only that it was written "extempore." But his sister Dorothy gives us the circumstances in some detail in her *Journal* for April 16, 1802:

When we came to the foot of Brother's Water, I left William sitting on the bridge. . . . When I returned I found William writing a poem descriptive of the sights and sounds we saw and heard. There was the gentle flowing of the stream, the glittering, lively lake, green fields without a living creature to be seen on them; behind us, a flat pasture with forty-two cattle feeding . . . the people were at work ploughing, harrowing, and sowing; lasses working, a dog barking now and then; cocks crowing, birds twittering; the snow in patches at the top of the highest hills. . . . William finished his poem before we got to the foot of Pickstone.

In the first stanza the poet seems simply to be putting down what he could see, making no comment on it, explicit or implicit. In the second stanza (lines 11–12), however, he makes a comparison: the snow, like a defeated army, is in retreat; and (in lines 16–17) he does give us his own interpretation. It could be argued, of course, that line 17 is not really the poet's interpretation but a kind of metaphor. That is, if the fountains are flowing, which is what the poet literally alludes to, his metaphorical way of saying it is to suggest that their veins pulse with life.

There is certainly nothing amiss in a poet's giving us subjective interpretations of life experiences. In fact, it would be hardly possible (nor in every case desirable) to do otherwise, for we do not read poetry in order to obtain dry and clinical descriptions of the world about us. The point is that the good poet does observe the surrounding world and ultimately finds instances in it reflecting a personal interpretation of experienced reality. In any case, "Written in March" is an interesting example of where a poet's interpretation begins and, on occasion, how close it can remain to the kind of sensitive reporting of Dorothy Wordsworth in her *Journal*.

Questions

1. Do you see *any* relationship between this poem and the Imagist poems that we have been reading on earlier pages? If so, would this suggest that the Imagists were not so much making a discovery as making a recovery of poetic sources that had been lost or forgotten?

2. What images here strike you as fresh and effective? Why?

3. Does the word *whoop* surprise you?

4. The last line is an echo from the Bible.* What effect on the poem does this allusion have for you? How does this allusion strike you in relation to the word *whoop*?

5. Why does the poet point out the fact that the cattle are "feeding like one"? How does it relate to his assertion that all the people of the village are working as one? Does he suggest that there is zest and unanimity in both enterprises? That the spring stirs a related impulse in both beast and man?

6. Read the poem aloud several times, trying to surrender to its natural rhythm. Do you feel that the movement is suitable for the poem? Do you

---

* Song of Solomon 2:11, "For, lo, winter is past, the rain is over and gone."

find any places where the poet breaks the general movement? Do you think these places irritating—and the result of bad craftsmanship? Or do you find them interesting, and perhaps effective? Argue your case.

Pippa's Song

Robert Browning [*1812–1889*]

The year's at the spring,
And day's at the morn;
Morning's at seven;
The hillside's dew-pearled;
The lark's on the wing;   5
The snail's on the thorn:
God's in His Heaven—
All's right with the world!

from *Pippa Passes*

Usually, the poet does not leave us to interpret as we like the images of a poem. (We have noted that Wordsworth in "Written in March" did not quite do this.) "Pippa Passes" makes a firm interpretation of the meaning of the spring morning: that God is in his place of vantage in the universe and that since he is—as creator and governor—"All's right with the world!"

Yet it is only fair to point out that even here the poet has been less direct that it may first appear. Though Browning was an optimist and may very well have affirmed—at least in many of his moods—that all was well with this world, *he* does not sing Pippa's song as in his own voice. In the play from which this song is taken, Pippa is a poor young girl who works in the silk mills. She has been given a rare holiday and is up bright and early to enjoy it to the full. Thus, the poet has put the observer (and the interpreter) of the scene into the poem itself; indeed, her interpretation is a part of the poem.

Pippa presents three images to be seen on this fine spring morning. The poem might have ended with the last of these three images and would have registered its effect on us. But instead, the poet has Pippa add her own interpretation. That interpretation (in lines 7–8) does no violence to the effect that the poem might have made on us without this addition. In fact, if this interpretation did do violence to our previous feeling about the poem, we should say the poem was incoherent, that it didn't hang together, that it was bad. As things stand, the addition is, of course, consistent with the feeling of a fine spring morning when it seems that nothing can ever again go wrong; the addition merely makes the effect of the images more specific and forthright. All it does is to change our sense of the drift, the "feel" of the images, the mood created by them, into a general statement about the world.

This leads us to a most important consideration. In poetry (as in life) we make a very great error if we think of mood and thought as absolutely distinguishable. A mood implies a certain attitude toward the world and may shade over imperceptibly into thought, into general statement, into whole systems of philosophy. So, too, a general statement, or a system of philosophy, implies a certain drift of feeling. The ideas and imagery of a poem (since it is the imagery by which mood is in large part determined) are intimately and organically related—just as ideas and mood are in our ordinary process of living.

Questions

1. The first two of Browning's images are, in themselves, agreeable. Directly out of nature they bring, we may say, a "plus" value into the poem. But this is not true of the snail. It brings in a "minus" value—or at best a neutral element. We scarcely think of snails as being "poetic."

Let us make a revision:

> The bloom's on the thorn.

Do we now have a better poem? If so, why so? If not, why not?

2. At least one commentator finds the images in this poem, in spite of the presence of the snail, too obviously agreeable, and leading too readily to the general conclusion. As he puts it, "Six pretty, co-ordinate images are marched, like six little lambs to the slaughter, to a colon and a powerful text—namely, that God's in his heaven, and so on."* How do you feel about this? Does the commentator ask, by implication, too much of a very brief lyric?

Dust of Snow

Robert Frost [*1874–1963*]

> The way a crow
> Shook down on me
> The dust of snow
> From a hemlock tree
>
> Has given my heart
> A change of mood
> And saved some part
> Of a day I had rued.

Questions

1. Compare this poem with the Japanese three-line poem about a crow on p. 69. Comment on the place and importance of the observer in the two

---

* John Crowe Ransom, *The World's Body*, Charles Scribner's Sons, 1938, p. 121.

poems. As is "In a Station of the Metro," this poem is about a change of mood. What is the mood in the first poem? What do you think was the mood of the observer in Frost's poem before the crow shook snow on him?

2. Suppose "Dust of Snow" had been a poem in *free verse* (see Appendix B, pp. 560–575), taking this form:

A crow, black on snow-whitened hemlock, shook snow-dust on me,
     passing:
My heart's mood is changed, and some part of the day saved.

What this poem presumably states is substantially the same as what the Frost poem states. Do you sense any difference in general feeling—and hence about what the free-verse poem means? If so, try to put it into words.

3. Is the method of Frost's poem more like that of "Pippa's Song" or that of "In a Station of the Metro"?

November Cotton Flower

Jean Toomer [*1894–1967*]

> Boll-weevil's coming, and the winter's cold,
> Made cotton-stalks look rusty, seasons old,
> And cotton, scarce as any southern snow,
> Was vanishing; the branch, so pinched and slow,
> Failed in its function as the autumn rake;   5
> Drouth fighting soil had caused the soil to take
> All water from the streams; dead birds were found
> In wells a hundred feet below the ground—
> Such was the season when the flower bloomed.
> Old folks were startled, and it soon assumed   10
> Significance. Superstition saw
> Something it had never seen before:
> Brown eyes that loved without a trace of fear,
> Beauty so sudden for that time of year.

Questions

"November Cotton Flower" is primarily descriptive, but the last two lines turn toward interpretation. Define the interpretation. Do you feel that it arises naturally from the context?

Beloved, Let Us Once More Praise the Rain

Conrad Aiken [*1889–1973*]

> Beloved, let us once more praise the rain.
> Let us discover some new alphabet,
> For this, the often-praised; and be ourselves,
> The rain, the chickweed, and the burdock leaf,
> The green-white privet flower, the spotted stone,   5

And all that welcomes rain; the sparrow, too,—
Who watches with a hard eye, from seclusion,
Beneath the elm-tree bough, till rain is done.

There is an oriole who, upside down,
Hangs at his nest, and flicks an orange wing,—   10
Under a tree as dead and still as lead;
There is a single leaf, in all this heaven
Of leaves, which rain has loosened from its twig:
The stem breaks, and it falls, but it is caught
Upon a sister leaf, and thus she hangs;   15
There is an acorn cup, beside a mushroom
Which catches three drops from the stooping cloud.

The timid bee goes back to hive; the fly
Under the broad leaf of the hollyhock
Perpends stupid with cold; the raindark snail   20
Surveys the wet world from a watery stone . . .
And still the syllables of water whisper:
The wheel of cloud whirs slowly: while we wait
In the dark room; and in your heart I find
One silver raindrop,—on a hawthorn leaf,—   25
Orion in a cobweb, and the World.

Questions

1. We have commented on precision of observation in poetic effect, for instance the number of raindrops, so clearly visualized in a lightning flash that they might be counted, in the little poem from the Japanese (p. 69) or the description of the umbrellas in the little poem by John Gould Fletcher (p. 70). In the present poem, the body of the poem is a listing of such observed items. In each instance, specify the detail that makes for imaginative immediacy.

2. The body of this poem consists, as we have said, of a listing of observed items. The items themselves, in the general picture of a rain, evoke a general, pervasive mood. How would you describe this mood? But notice that the pervasive mood is not—as, for instance, in the little poems from the Japanese—the final effect of the poem. The observation involves the two lovers who are observing. So we are left with the question: what do the items observed, and the pervasive mood they evoke, signify for the lovers?

Two Voices in a Meadow

Richard Wilbur [*1921–*]

1. A MILKWEED

Anonymous as cherubs
Over the crib of God,
White seeds are floating

Out of my burst pod.
What power had I   5
Before I learned to yield?
Shatter me, great wind:
I shall possess the field.

2. A STONE

As casual as cow-dung
Under the crib of God,   10
I lie where chance would have me,
Up to the ears in sod.
Why should I move? To move
Befits a light desire.
The sill of Heaven would founder,   15
Did such as I aspire.

A milkweed plant yields feathery seeds that are blown about by the wind of autumn when the milkweed pods ripen and burst. It is a commonplace object, a plant that grows wild in waste places. Just as commonplace is the stone, outcropping from the turf in a meadow. Yet one notices that the poet makes both the milkweed plant and the stone speak of human concerns and actually with the voices of human beings.

Questions

1. If "up to the ears in sod" suggests that the stone is being compared to a human being, what kind of human being is it? How are you expected to feel toward this human being? Can you describe this human being's self-evaluation? How serious, or how humorous, is the effect of the comparison of stone to human being? What natural objects described in the preceding poems in Section 2 are described in human terms?

2. What does the human attitude implied in "A Milkweed" have in common with that in "A Stone"? The first poem deals with lightness, the second with heaviness. Does the contrast affirm what the two "meadow" poems have in common or does it cancel out the affinity? Are the poems better if taken individually or together, as parts of one double poem?

3. What is the "crib of God"? (Remember that the word *crib* can mean not only a child's bed but also a manger to hold food for cattle.) Why "cherubs," in connection with the child's crib in one poem and "cow-dung" in the other? Does the contrast between the two sets of associations shock you?

4. Look at the line "I shall possess the field." It literally means, of course, that the seed of the milkweed will take root all over the field. But is there a metaphor in this statement, a metaphor suggested by the phraseology?

5. Which object makes the better case for itself? Should one imitate the milkweed or the stone? Or should one refuse the option with the thought that fulfillment may be achieved in many ways?

6. How would you state, in general terms, the theme of this pair of poems as taken together? How do the "two voices" of the title relate to each other?

Cavalry Crossing a Ford

Walt Whitman [*1819–1892*]

A line in long array where they wind betwixt green islands,
They take a serpentine course, their arms flash in the sun—hark to
    the musical clank,
Behold the silvery river, in it the splashing horses loitering stop to drink,
Behold the brown-faced men, each group, each person a picture, the
    negligent rest on the saddles,
Some emerge on the opposite bank, others are just entering the ford—
    while,   5
Scarlet and blue and snowy white,
The guidon flags flutter gayly in the wind.

Is this a mere assemblage of details or is there some principle of organization? In the "serpentine course" between the green islands the command is seen as a unit, but the unity quickly dissolves into the details. The poet is quite consciously insisting on this fact; he says that each group, even each person, is a picture that can be regarded individually. Having fractured his general impression into these individual "pictures," he then begins to reassemble the whole. Again we begin to get a sense of the column as a unit, its head emerging on the far bank, the rear entering the stream. But still the scene has not come into sharp focus. It is only when our eyes fix on the guidons fluttering "gayly" that everything is drawn together.

Not only is the composition of the whole picture drawn together, but we get a feeling of how the men who, for a moment, had become individual, just men watering their horses as casually and lazily as a farmer after a day in the field, are jerked back into their places in the unit, losing their identity in the whole. So the mere matter of mechanical focus becomes, as it were, a lead to the human feeling of the poem.

Let us glance at another mechanical detail. Line 5 ends with the word *while,* preceded by a dash, followed by a comma, left hanging at the end. So we have a sense of suspense here; it is as though we are asking, "While what?" But the poet holds off the answer, and in the next line simply names three colors. This, too, gives suspense; for we do not know what the colors are to describe—they float vaguely, confusedly before us, qualities unattached to any object. Then, in the last line come the guidons, and after the two devices of suspense, our eye, and our curiosity, come to a rest, fulfilled. We have been made to "want" the guidons.

Questions

1. What is gained by the direct address used by the speaker of the poem? To whom is he speaking?

2. What view does the poet take toward the fact that the individual men, after the moment of pause, are drawn into the unit of the column? Does he seem to resent this or applaud it? How would you relate your answer to the last paragraph of the comment given above?

3. What is the effect of the word *gayly?* Is it to be taken in reference to your answer to the question above? Or is it to be taken as an ironical reference to the natural business of a military organization? Or to both? If to both, is there a necessary contradiction involved?

4. Who is the observer who describes this fording of a river? Is he an unobtrusive observer? Does he leave it up to the reader to make what he can of the incident? Or does he suggest the attitude that the reader is to take toward the event described?

5. Hunt up the word *guidon* in the dictionary. Have you enriched your sense of the poem?

Cuttings

Theodore Roethke   [*1908–1963*]

I

Sticks-in-a-drowse droop over sugary loam,
Their intricate stem-fur dries;
But still the delicate slips keep coaxing up water;
The small cells bulge;

One nub of growth   5
Nudges a sand-crumb loose,
Pokes through a musty sheath
Its pale tendrilous horn.

II

This urge, wrestle, resurrection of dry sticks,
Cut stems struggling to put down feet,
What saint strained so much,
Rose on such lopped limbs to a new life?

I can hear, underground, that sucking and sobbing,   5
In my veins, in my bones I feel it,—
The small waters seeping upward,
The tight grains parting at last.
When sprouts break out,
Slippery as fish,   10
I quail, lean to beginnings, sheath-wet.

Roethke's father operated a greenhouse. Apparently many of the poet's most vivid memories are of his life as a boy in the out of the greenhouse, and a good many of his poems, like the two that we have just read, have such a setting. In this instance, however, we are not interested in the light that these poems can throw on the poet's biography, but on the way in which he makes the reader see these "sticks-in-a-drowse" that are pushed down into the loam in the expectation that they will root themselves and begin to grow.

Questions

1. What do you think the poet means in line 1 by calling the loam "sugary"? What does he mean by the "stem-fur" of the cutting? In line 7, why does he set "musty sheath" in contrast with "pale tendrilous horn" in line 8? What is the deeper significance of "musty" and "tendrilous"?

2. What is the relation of the first "Cuttings" poem to the second? Would it be fair to say that the first is primarily concerned with providing a vivid description of the cuttings, whereas the second tends to relate the vegetable world to the human world? Point out some of the terms that apply literally to human beings but only by analogy to the cuttings.

3. Can you justify the poet's comparison of a cutting to a saint? The suggestion is that the saint has been martyred or at least mutilated for his faith, and so has to rise on "lopped limbs." What is the new life to which the cuttings, that now look so much like "dry sticks," aspire?

4. In the last line of Part II, why does the speaker say "I quail"? Why should he experience an awe that amounts to fear in the presence of the cuttings? What does he mean by "lean to beginnings"? Finally, why is "sheath-wet" a powerful word on which to conclude the poem? How does it apply literally to the cuttings? What is its emotional force?

Inversnaid

Gerard Manley Hopkins [*1844–1889*]

> This darksome burn, horseback brown,
> His rollrock highroad roaring down,
> In coop and in comb the fleece of his foam
> Flutes and low to the lake falls home.
>
> A windpuff-bonnet of fáwn-fróth 5
> Turns and twindles over the broth
> Of a pool so pitchblack, féll-frowning,
> It rounds and rounds Despair to drowning.
>
> Degged with dew, dappled with dew
> Are the groins of the braes that the brook treads through, 10
> Wiry heathpacks, flitches of fern,
> And the beadbonny ash that sits over the burn.

What would the world be, once bereft
Of wet and of wildness? Let them be left,
O let them be left, wildness and wet;   15
Long live the weeds and the wilderness yet.

Inversnaid is a Scottish town near Loch Lomond. As T. S. Eliot once remarked, a good poem can often communicate before it is fully understood, and so it is with "Inversnaid." It contains a good many words that are quite unfamiliar and that may not even occur in a small dictionary. Some of the comparisons used are curious, to say the least. What, for example, are "flitches of fern"? A flitch ordinarily means a side of bacon.* What is "fawn-froth"? Do fawns froth at the mouth when they run? Or is this bubbly froth floating on the roaring stream the color of a fawn's hide? And what color is "horse-back brown"? Wouldn't that depend on whether the horse was black, sorrel, roan, or simply the old gray mare? Or is the poet referring to the darker stain of sweat around the saddle after a brisk gallop?

Nevertheless, in spite of the puzzles to be found when we look hard at this or that term, the poem does convey the sense of a wild Scottish burn, pouring down a waterfall. The poem is richly concrete—excitingly circumstantial. Furthermore, the special rhythmic effects, the emphatic rhyming, and the strong alliteration (note, for example, the *d* consonant in "Degged with dew, dappled with dew") all have their effect on the reader. Later on (pp. 493–576) we shall consider in more detail the use of meter, rhyme, and alliteration. For our present purpose it is sufficient to acknowledge their special importance in this poem.

Questions

1. Examine the structure of the sentence which composes the first stanza. Why does the poet use this complicated and difficult structure to build up to the statement that the burn "falls home" to the lake? Would it have been better, as well as simpler, to start with the statement that the burn falls into the lake, and then attach the descriptive elements? If not, why not?

2. As we have seen, some of the images in this poem are difficult and some of the words are unusual. We want poetry to be immediate and vivid—we want the meaning embodied in, yet shining with exciting directness from, the images and language of the poem. But sometimes we have to make ourselves ready to receive that meaning. And sometimes looking up

---

* W. H. Gardner in *Gerard Manley Hopkins: A Study of Poetic Idiosyncrasy in Relation to Poetic Tradition* (London, 1944), p. 117, observes that "flitch . . . is related to *fleck* and probably also to *flake*. Thus, the combined meanings—feathery flakes, long stems, and clumps may justify our taking *flitches* to be a portmanteau word from *flake, switch,* and *patch*." In short, Hopkins's *flitch* is a "made-up word" from the three roots just mentioned. Perhaps so, since this meaning doesn't occur in any dictionary.

words in a dictionary and puzzling a little over the images are the simplest things that we have to do. (This is not to say that all such preparation can come from books. For some poems we can get ready only by living long enough and fully enough—by becoming more nearly emotionally mature —and by learning how to exercise our imaginations.)

Here are a few words that may puzzle the ordinary reader. In line 3, *coop* (on the analogy of a pen or small enclosure) is evidently a pothole or hollow in the stream bed; *comb* seems to mean here the "crest of a wave." In line 9 *degged* is a dialect word that means "sprinkled." In line 6 *twindles* (according to the *Oxford English Dictionary*) means "to bring forth twins"; that is, the bonnet of "fawn-froth" divides in two. But W. H. Gardner (see footnote above) thinks that "twindles" is another made-up word that Hopkins possibly coined from *twist, twiddle, sprinkle,* and *dwindle.* How do you respond to this idea?

3. In line 8 the word *rounds* would seem to mean "whisper," that is, in this instance, to whisper counsel or advice. See the *Oxford English Dictionary,* v. 2, 3-b.

4. The rhythms of Hopkins's poetry are often uncommon and sometimes even startling. (The accents here are provided by the poet to help the reader catch a movement that could ordinarily be missed.) How do Hopkins's unusual rhythms affect you? Do you detect any difference between the rhythm of the first three stanzas and that of the last stanza? What is the difference? What is its effect? Does its use make sense to you? In a later section we shall be dealing more specifically with metrical patterns and the various means by which a poet establishes or varies the rhythm. But it may be interesting here for the reader to consider the effects of varied and even violently deranged rhythms, even though metrical factors have not yet been discussed.

Spring

William Shakespeare [*1564–1616*]

> When daisies pied and violets blue,
>   And lady-smocks all silver-white,
> And cuckoo-buds of yellow hue,
>   Do paint the meadows with delight,
> The cuckoo then, on every tree,   5
> Mocks married men, for thus sings he—
>   "Cuckoo;
> Cuckoo, cuckoo"—O, word of fear,
> Unpleasing to a married ear!
>
> When shepherds pipe on oaten straws,   10
>   And merry larks are ploughmen's clocks,
> When turtles tread,[1] and rooks and daws,
>   And maidens bleach their summer smocks,

[1] mate

The cuckoo then, on every tree,
Mocks married men; for thus sings he—
 "Cuckoo;
Cuckoo, cuckoo"—O, word of fear,
Unpleasing to a married ear!   15

Love's Labour's Lost, V, ii

Winter

William Shakespeare   [*1564–1616*]

When icicles hang by the wall,
 And Dick the shepherd blows his nail,
And Tom bears logs into the hall,
 And milk comes frozen home in pail,
When blood is nipped and ways be foul,   5
Then nightly sings the staring owl—
 "To-who;
Tu-whit, to-who!" a merry note,
While greasy Joan doth keel[1] the pot.

When all aloud the wind doth blow,   10
 And coughing drowns the parson's saw,
And birds sit brooding in the snow,
 And Marian's nose looks red and raw
When roasted crabs[2] hiss in the bowl,
Then nightly sings the staring owl—   15
 "To-who;
Tu-whit, to-who!" a merry note,
While greasy Joan doth keel the pot.

Love's Labour's Lost, V, ii

These two contrasting songs are filled with images appropriate to the two seasons described. Lady-smocks and cuckoo-buds are flowers. Turtles, rooks, and daws are birds. This is the season in which birds mate ("tread"). In a celebrated poem, Wordsworth associates the cuckoo bird's call with springtime, but in the Elizabethan era the word "cuckoo" was associated with *cuckold* and the call of the bird could be regarded (as it is here) to be a taunt to a man whose wife had betrayed him.

  In the "Winter" song, modern English would require the poet to say that Dick blows "upon his nails"—that is, his fingernails—to warm them. The "parson's saw" is a homily or platitude, occurring in his sermon. Line 14 refers to the custom of roasting crabapples and using them to add flavor to a bowl of cider or ale.

[1] skim   [2] crabapples

Questions

1. Discuss the appropriateness of the images that the poet has selected to depict spring and winter. Do they suggest the speaker's attitudes toward those two seasons? What is the poet's attitude toward spring? Toward winter?

2. Is the cuckoo bird who "mocks" married men an appropriate image for the spring song? How can the owl's hooting possibly seem a merry song? Even if one could believe it was merry, does it accord with the other images that characterize the winter season?

3. Is it possible that the poet is suggesting that the gay and happy season is not necessarily gay for everyone, and that the wintry dismal season is not uniformly dismal in all respects? In short, do these songs make up a double poem in which we need both halves if we are to participate in the poet's attitude toward the world? How would this kind of pairing compare to that in Richard Wilbur's "Two Voices in a Meadow" (pp. 79–80)?

4. We notice that the agreeable—the "pretty"—images are in "Spring" while in "Winter" we find the shepherd blowing his nails, ways "foul," and Joan "greasy." Does this fact have any bearing on the goodness or badness of either poem? Try to state what is at stake in this question.

To Autumn

John Keats [*1795–1821*]

Season of mists and mellow fruitfulness,
  Close bosom-friend of the maturing sun;
Conspiring with him how to load and bless
  With fruit the vines that round the thatch-eaves run;
To bend with apples the mossed cottage-trees,   5
  And fill all fruit with ripeness to the core;
    To swell the gourd, and plump the hazel shells
With a sweet kernel; to set budding more,
  And still more, later flowers for the bees,
  Until they think warm days will never cease,   10
    For Summer has o'erbrimmed their clammy cells.

Who hath not seen thee oft amid thy store?
  Sometimes whoever seeks abroad may find
Thee sitting careless on a granary floor,
  Thy hair soft-lifted by the winnowing wind;   15
Or on a half-reaped furrow sound asleep,
  Drowsed with the fume of poppies, while thy hook
  Spares the next swath and all its twinèd flowers;
And sometimes like a gleaner thou dost keep
  Steady thy laden head across a brook;   20
  Or by a cider-press, with patient look,
    Thou watchest the last oozings, hours by hours.

Where are the songs of Spring? Ay, where are they?
Think not of them, thou hast thy music too,
While barrèd clouds bloom the soft-dying day, 25
And touch the stubble-plains with rosy hue;
Then in a wailful choir the small gnats mourn
Among the river sallows, borne aloft
Or sinking as the light wind lives or dies;
And full-grown lambs loud bleat from hilly bourn; 30
Hedge-crickets sing, and now with treble soft
The redbreast whistles from a garden-croft,
And gathering swallows twitter in the skies.

Questions

1. Note that after the predominantly visual imagery of the first two stanzas, the last stanza emphasizes auditory imagery. Why is this shift of imagery especially appropriate?

2. In this poem, Autumn is personified. What personality is indicated? What does descriptive detail in each of the three stanzas contribute to the definition of that personality? How is this personality related to the mood of the poem—and the theme?

3. In connection with the theme of the poem, read the following comment:

> The whole stanza presents the paradoxical qualities of autumn, its aspects of both lingering and passing. This is especially true of the final image of the stanza. Autumn is the season of dying as well as of fulfilling. Hence it is with "*patient* look" that she (or he?) watches "the last oozings hours by hours." Oozing, or steady dripping, is, of course, not unfamiliar as a symbol of the passing of time.
> It is in the last stanza that the theme emerges most conspicuously. . . .*

What elements in the last stanza continue the presentation of the paradoxical qualities of autumn? On what attitude may we say that the poem comes to rest?

4. Why, as a matter of fact, do swallows gather in the skies? What meaning does this have for the poem?

5. This poem has often been admired for its richness and appropriateness of rhythm. Get fully soaked in the poem and then discuss this topic.

6. The poem has also been admired for its precise and suggestive diction. Locate words and phrases which seem to justify this admiration. Or do you find any?

7. Compare "To Autumn" with Shakespeare's "Spring" and "Winter." Obviously, Keats's poem offers a much more massive and complex experience in its account of the autumnal season that Shakespeare's songs about the other seasons. But do these slighter poems have anything in common with Keats's great ode?

8. Who is the observer in Keats's poem? Let's not be content with saying

* Leonard Unger and William Van O'Connor, *Poems for Study*, Rinehart and Company, 1953, p. 455. See Appendix B, pp. 487–489.

that it is of course Keats himself who took a walk near Winchester and saw the warm stubble fields and set it all down. In some sense, of course, the whole poem comes out of Keats's experience as reworked through his imagination. But how has the artist suggested what attitude we ought to take toward the scene he described? He has moved the sensitive reader toward a particular attitude or set of attitudes, to be sure, but he has done it very subtly—so subtly that we are left to feel that it is the pattern of images itself that moves us toward the attitude. Does the pattern of images suggest more than a mood or an attitude? Perhaps an idea? If you think so, how would you formulate that idea? Is the clue in the first line of the last stanza?

Ode: Autumn

Thomas Hood [*1799–1845*]

> I saw old Autumn in the misty morn
> Stand shadowless like Silence, listening
> To silence, for no lonely bird would sing
> Into his hollow ear from woods forlorn,
> Nor lowly hedge nor solitary thorn;—   5
> Shaking his languid locks all dewy bright
> With tangled gossamer that fell by night,
>   Pearling his coronet of golden corn.
>
> Where are the songs of Summer?—With the sun,
> Oping the dusky eyelids of the south,   10
> Till shade and silence waken up as one,
> And Morning sings with a warm odorous mouth.
> Where are the merry birds? Away, away,
> On panting wings through the inclement skies,
>   Lest owls should prey   15
>   Undazzled at noonday,
> And tear with horny beak their lustrous eyes.
>
> Where are the blooms of Summer?—In the west,
> Blushing their last to the last sunny hours,
> When the mild Eve by sudden Night is prest   20
> Like tearful Proserpine snatch'd from her flow'rs
>   To a most gloomy breast.
> Where is the pride of Summer,—the green prime,—
> The many, many leaves all twinkling?—Three
>   On the moss'd elm, three on the naked lime   25
> Trembling,—and one upon the old oak tree!
>   Where is the Dryads' immortality?—
> Gone into mournful cypress and dark yew,
> Or wearing the long gloomy Winter through
>   In the smooth holly's green eternity.   30

The squirrel gloats on his accomplish'd hoard,
The ants have brimm'd their garners with ripe grain,
    And honey bees have stor'd
The sweets of Summer in their luscious cells;
The swallows all have wing'd across the main;   35
But here the Autumn melancholy dwells,
    And sighs her tearful spells
Amongst the sunless shadows of the plain.
    Alone, alone,
        Upon a mossy stone,   40
She sits and reckons up the dead and gone
With the last leaves for a love-rosary,
Whilst all the wither'd world looks drearily,
Like a dim picture of the drowned past
In the hush'd mind's mysterious far away,   45
Doubtful what ghostly thing will steal the last
Into that distance, gray upon the gray.

O go and sit with her, and be o'ershaded
Under the languid downfall of her hair:
She wears a coronal of flowers faded   50
Upon her forehead, and a face of care;—
There is enough of wither'd everywhere
To make her bower,—and enough of gloom;
There is enough of sadness to invite,
If only for the rose that died,—whose doom   55
Is Beauty's,—she that with the living bloom
Of conscious cheeks most beautifies the light;—
There is enough of sorrowing, and quite
Enough of bitter fruits the earth doth bear,—
Enough of chilly droppings form her bowl;   60
Enough of fear and shadowy despair,
To frame her cloudy prison for the soul!

Questions

1. See question 8 on Keats's poem (pp. 88-89). Try to apply the same question to this poem by Hood.

2. In line 9, Hood asks, "Where are the songs of Summer?" He implies an answer, just as Keats does when he asks, "Where are the songs of Spring?" Compare and contrast the implied answers.

3. Hood makes his Autumn melancholy and tearful (lines 36–37). Is Keats's Autumn primarily melancholy? What adjectives would you apply to Keats's Autumn?

4. Which poem would you say is more strongly unified and focused on a definite theme?

Composed upon Westminster Bridge
Sept. 3, 1803
William Wordsworth [1770–1850]

Earth has not anything to show more fair:
Dull would he be of soul who could pass by
A sight so touching in its majesty:
This city now doth like a garment wear
The beauty of the morning; silent, bare,   5
Ships, towers, domes, theaters, and temples lie
Open unto the fields, and to the sky;
All bright and glittering in the smokeless air.
Never did sun more beautifully steep
In his first splendor valley, rock, or hill;   10
Ne'er saw I, never felt, a calm so deep!
The river glideth at his own sweet will:
Dear God! the very houses seem asleep;
And all that mighty heart is lying still!

This poem ostensibly presents the speaker's view of London in the morning (line 5), presumably very early, for the inhabitants of the city are evidently still in their houses if not still in bed. The speaker is touched by the beauty of the scene and says so (lines 1–5).

Questions
1. Does the poem provide anything like a realistic view of the city? How strong is this poem on circumstantial detail? Does the poet pick out and mention particular church spires or public buildings?
2. Does the speaker content himself with expressing his pleasure in the beauty before his eyes? Does he indicate in any way that this particular scene has made a special and unexpected impression on him? (Note that he does indicate that he is surprised.) In what sense is this poem concerned with the relation of man and nature?

Preludes

T. S. Eliot [1888–1965]

I

The winter evening settles down
With smell of steaks in passageways.
Six o'clock.
The burnt-out ends of smoky days.
And now a gusty shower wraps   5

The grimy scraps
Of withered leaves about your feet
And newspapers from vacant lots;
The showers beat
On broken blinds and chimney-pots,   10
And at the corner of the street
A lonely cab-horse steams and stamps.
And then the lighting of the lamps.

II

The morning comes to consciousness
Of faint stale smells of beer   15
From the sawdust-trampled street
With all its muddy feet that press
To early coffee-stands.
With the other masquerades
That time resumes,   20
One thinks of all the hands
That are raising dingy shades
In a thousand furnished rooms.

III

You tossed a blanket from the bed,
You lay upon your back, and waited;   25
You dozed, and watched the night revealing
The thousand sordid images
Of which your soul was constituted;
They flickered against the ceiling.
And when all the world came back   30
And the light crept up between the shutters
And you heard the sparrows in the gutters,
You had such a vision of the street
As the street hardly understands;
Sitting along the bed's edge, where   35
You curled the papers from your hair,
Or clasped the yellow soles of feet
In the palms of both soiled hands.

IV

His soul stretched tight across the skies
That fade behind a city block,   40
Or trampled by insistent feet
At four and five and six o'clock;
And short square fingers stuffing pipes,
And evening newspapers, and eyes
Assured of certain certainties,   45
The conscience of a blackened street
Impatient to assume the world.

I am moved by fancies that are curled
Around these images, and cling:
The notion of some infinitely gentle   50
Infinitely suffering thing.

Wipe your hand across your mouth, and laugh;
The worlds revolve like ancient women
Gathering fuel in vacant lots.

This suite of poems represents the first poetry in this section in which the images are rather deliberately unbeautiful. In any case, few of them are taken from nature; they are almost aggressively urban—and urban without the elements of the beautiful that may be found in cities. This fact may disturb those who think that poetry somehow deals with beautiful objects and who do not understand that the "beauty" of poetry springs from the poet's ability to perceive meaning and significance even in scenes that are in themselves commonplace or ugly, in either city or country.

Eliot has told us that one of the things that he learned first from the French poet Baudelaire was the poetic possibility of "the more sordid aspects of the modern metropolis." He goes on to say that he found that "the sort of material that I had, the sort of experience that an adolescent had had, in an industrial city in America, could be the material for poetry; and that the source of new poetry might be found in what had been regarded hitherto as the impossible, the sterile, the intractably unpoetic."* Yet the reader must be warned not to mistake what is being said here: the point is not that one can prettify the sordid and dress it up, but rather that one can see the characteristically human in it and—to use a phrase from another essay of Eliot's—to be able to see the necessary interrelation of beauty and ugliness: "to see the boredom, and the horror, and the glory."† To state the matter another way, what is finally at stake here is the *expressiveness* of imagery—its function in the whole poem. The concern of poetry is *not* to present pictures; it is to dramatize human experience and human values. In these "Preludes" (which, incidentally, deny the meaning of the word since they look *forward* to nothing) we are presented mainly with the boredom and the horror, though the observer is stirred by the notion of "some infinitely gentle / Infinitely suffering thing," the victim of such an environment.

In line 27 the poet speaks of "The thousand sordid images" of which the soul of the "you" addressed in the poem is constituted. But are all the images in this poem "sordid"? None, to be sure, give us the sense of "glory," but do any bespeak tenderness or humanity?

---

* "What Dante Means to Me," *To Criticize the Critic*, Harcourt Brace Jovanovich, 1965, p. 126.
† *The Use of Poetry*, Harvard University Press, 1933, p. 106.

Questions

1. The first two sections of this poem describe a winter evening and a winter morning in a city. The description in these sections is objective, but it establishes a mood and attitude. Discuss the mood and attitude. What effect do the last three lines of the second section give?

2. In the third section, one of the people whose hand will raise dingy shades is addressed. Out of her own misery she has "a vision of the street" —an awareness of the general loneliness and defeat. Why does the poet say that "the street hardly understands" this vision? What is the implication of *masquerades* (section II) here?

3. In the fourth section another character is referred to, a man who is sensitive enough to be constantly affected by the life he sees around him —a life which appears to be dominated by a meaningless routine of satisfying animal requirements, the "certain certainties." Ironically, the poet calls the assurance of these certainties the only "conscience" that the street has; and the street seems to impose its own standards on the entire world. Then (in line 48) the poet announces himself as a commentator on the scenes he has presented. What attitude does he take? Whom is he addressing in the last three lines? How do the last two lines serve as a symbolic summary of the poem? Is the poet ready to wipe his own hand across his mouth—the gross gesture of satisfied appetite—and laugh at human suffering?

Blow, Bugle, Blow

Alfred, Lord Tennyson   [1809–1892]

> The splendor falls on castle walls
>   And snowy summits old in story:
> The long light shakes across the lakes
>   And the wild cataract leaps in glory.
> Blow, bugle, blow, set the wild echoes flying,   5
> Blow, bugle; answer, echoes, dying, dying, dying.
>
> O hark, O hear! how thin and clear,
>   And thinner, clearer, farther going!
> O sweet and far from cliff and scar
>   The horns of Elfland faintly blowing!   10
> Blow, let us hear the purple glens replying:
> Blow, bugle; answer, echoes, dying, dying, dying.
>
> O love, they die in yon rich sky,
>   They faint on hill or field or river:
> Our echoes roll from soul to soul,   15
>   And grow forever and forever.
> Blow, bugle, blow, set the wild echoes flying,
> And answer, echoes, answer, dying, dying, dying.

In one sense this poem reverses the method used in all the preceding poems. All of this poem except lines 15 and 16 develops the imagery, visual and aural, clustered around the sound of the bugle blowing at sunset. Through line 14 (as in "To Autumn," p. 87, and "The Main-Deep," p. 99), we find a poem in which the sense of ending, with its inevitable melancholy, is fused with a sense of vibrant beauty and fulfillment. If we rewrote lines 15 and 16, then, we might make this (even with our clumsy revision) the whole "idea" of the poem:

> O love, they die in yon rich sky,
>> They faint on hill or field or river;
> The echoes fade in the far glen's shade,
>> And farther, on the lake's gleam quiver.
> Blow, bugle blow, set the wild echoes flying,
> And answer, echoes, answer, dying, dying, dying.

With this revised version, as in all poems in this section, the method would be to develop a congruence between the imagery and the idea of the poem. For instance, in "To Autumn," the beauty of the imagery of the autumnal ending and the slow, rich rhythms embody the sense of satisfying fulfillment even with the overtone of melancholy. But in Tennyson's own version the method of congruence is reversed. The beauty and the sense of fulfillment are, of course, implicit in the imagery, but the poet is not satisfied with this in the context of the ending; he develops his poem not by congruence, but by saying that echoes of the human soul, *unlike* the echoes of the bugle, are outside of time and change, and do not fade but eternally continue.

Some critics have objected to lines 15 and 16 as an intrusion into the basic "feel" of the poem, as a piece of arbitrary editorializing. What do you think? But remember that with this question we are not interested in your personal views of the immortality of the soul or any belief—or disbelief—in some idea of the world as an infinite tissue of cause and effect in which nothing, however small, is irrelevant. We are concerned only with the quality of a poem.

"CHANNEL FIRING": A SECOND LOOK

We have discussed Hardy's "Channel Firing" (p. 45) under the rubric "Dramatic Situation," but it will be useful here to take up this poem again, with special emphasis on the imagery as such. Almost any poem, no matter how tiny, must involve all the aspects of poetry—imagery, rhythm, tone, theme, and so on. One way to emphasize this point is for us to return now, after our more concentrated discussion of imagery, and look at "Channel Firing" again, with special reference to Hardy's use of images.

Earlier we remarked on the highly dramatic and even shocking character of "Channel Firing." Though it seems to be an antiwar poem—

some might say also an antireligious poem—it is far from an abstract preachment or indictment. The force of the poem lies in its concreteness, and this inevitably means that its imagery is important and significant.

We have said that upon this peaceful scene, a churchyard in a Dorsetshire village on the south coast of England, there bursts the thunder of guns fired at sea. The hackneyed way to put it would be to say that the noise they made was loud enough to wake the dead. As we have observed earlier, what Hardy does here is to show us the dead being actually awakened.

The dramatic structure of the poem is, in fact, an exploration of the implications of this cliché. The poet takes it seriously enough to imagine what the scene would be like. Hardy has gone still further: he has tried to imagine what the Dread Judge himself would say on hearing this manmade imitation of the shock of Doom. How would He address the awakened dead? What could He say to those who had been buried in the Christian hope and who now have been startled out of their sleep prematurely by their fellowmen's devilish precocity in developing killing power?

All of this means that the poem abounds in concrete images. We have first a pastoral scene, complete with village church, church mouse, and chewing cow outside the churchyard—all representing an immemorially quiet and peaceful world that had changed little during the centuries. We have, breaking in upon this scene, the highly emotional speech of an anthropomorphic god who vents his irritation, sarcasm, and contemptuous pity on his creature, man.

Hardy also presents us with a concrete enactment of the effect of this angry god's words on the awakened dead. Even Parson Thirdly, who had been a priest in the service of the Christian God, wonders whether he shouldn't have cultivated at least a few mild vices in his earthly life. One notices that Hardy does not overdo such ironies; he doesn't have the parson wish that he had become a great Byronic lover or a dashingly romantic highwayman. Parson Thirdly thinks of vices appropriate to his his training and station—more beer and tobacco, less fasting, and fewer prayers.

Even the movement of the waves of sound through the English countryside is rendered concretely as Hardy portrays it pushing inland, past particular places on its way, farther and farther back from the south coast. But each place mentioned has its own aura of metaphoric association: we are moving back into history as well as across space—back into prehistory even, with Stonehenge—and this is a way of saying that with all of civilization and Christianity, man's old murderous heart has not fundamentally changed.

Questions

1. Review the poem, examining especially its concrete particularity. Thus, in line 29, what would a skeleton shaking its head look like? Would he have to be careful as he did so? Might he not topple it on the

floor? Would the action seem grotesquely funny or excruciatingly horrible, or both?

2. Why does Hardy give his dead parson the quite absurd name of "Thirdly"?

RHYTHM AND METER: 2

The student will certainly have noticed that in the discussion of meter in connection with Section 1, the principles presented would not accommodate certain poems there. For instance, the principles that provide a scansion for "Farewell to Barn and Stack and Tree" break down at certain points with "Sir Patrick Spence." Both this and Housman's poem are in what is called the *ballad measure,* an alternation of lines of four and three accents, but certain lines in the real ballad will not accept the accentual-syllabic scansion into the feet that we are now acquainted with. Line 3, for example, gives us this:

$$\acute{\text{O}}\ \text{whar will I get guid sailor,}$$

And line 27:

$$\text{And I feir, I feir, my deir master,}$$

We find similar problems in "The Demon Lover" and "Jesse James." These poems that cause difficulty are, in fact, examples of accentual (or *stress*) verse, not accentual-syllabic. See Appendix B, pp. 553–560, for a discussion of this topic.

Questions

1. Attempt a scansion of "Frankie and Johnny," which, like "Jesse James," is written in accentual verse. How many accents do you find in the first and second lines of each stanza? How many in the third line? How does this pattern differ from what we have in the so-called ballad measure?

2. Attempt a scansion of "Mama and Daughter." What seems to be the basic pattern: accentual or accentual-syllabic verse?

3. For the meter of "Danny Deever," see pp. 556–557. Try to state the general effect of the rhythm of the poem. What relation would you say it has to the event presented? Here we have the execution of a justly convicted criminal, a man who has killed a comrade in his sleep, a man for whom there is little extenuation; but the poem deals with the shock and horror of even this well-deserved execution. But this is a military execution, and the human quality is absorbed into, and overridden by, the military code and formality. How does this particular rhythm work in connection with this event? Think of the matter this way: If the event described were the equally horrible, or even more horrible, event of a man being torn to pieces by an enraged mob, would this meter give the same general effect?

4. Suppose that "'Out, Out—,'" "Battle of the *Bonhomme Richard* and the *Serapis,*" "Meeting at Night," or "Ten Days Leave" were written in the

meter of "Danny Deever." Would the change seriously affect their meanings? By asking this question we do not mean to imply that such metrical
and rhythmic effects are absolutely incompatible with the subject matter
of the poems just mentioned. Our point is simply to try to have our readers
imagine the kinds of effect that would result.

5. Scan and comment on the rhythm of "Inversnaid" (p. 83) by Gerard
Manley Hopkins. Comment on the relation of rhythm to the general effect
of the whole.

Supplemental Poems

from
The Palace of Art
Alfred, Lord Tennyson [*1809–1892*]

One seem'd all dark and red—a tract of sand,
  And some one pacing there alone,
Who paced for ever in a glimmering land,
  Lit with a low large moon.

One show'd an iron coast and angry waves. 5
  You seem'd to hear them climb and fall
And roar rock-thwarted under bellowing caves,
  Beneath the windy wall.

And one, a full-fed river winding slow
  By herds upon an endless plain, 10
The ragged rims of thunder brooding low,
  With shadow-streaks of rain.

And one, the reapers at their sultry toil.
  In front they bound the sheaves. Behind
Were realms of upland, prodigal in oil, 15
  And hoary to the wind.

And one a foreground black with stones and slags,
  Beyond, a line of heights, and higher
All barr'd with long white cloud the scornful crags,
  And highest, snow and fire. 20

And one, an English home—gray twilight pour'd
  On dewey pastures, dewey trees,
Softer than sleep—all things in order stored,
  A haunt of ancient Peace.

The stanzas printed above are excerpted from a much longer poem, "The Palace of Art," in which the poet describes the pleasant house of an elitist, and finally selfish, connoisseur of the arts. The thesis of the poem is that art is good but must be made available to the masses.

The stanzas quoted here describe a series of paintings in one gallery of the palace. We are told that the gallery contained landscapes "fit for every mood"—"gay, or grave, or sweet, or stern."

Questions

1. What are the moods presented in the six "landscapes" we have printed above?
2. Discuss the choice and patterning of the various descriptive details to establish each mood.

The Main-Deep

James Stephens [*1882–1950*]

> The long, rolling,
> Steady-pouring,
> Deep-trenchèd
> Green billow:
>
> The wide-topped, 5
> Unbroken,
> Green-glacid,
> Slow-sliding,
>
> Cold-flushing,
> On—on—on— 10
> Chill-rushing,
> Hush-hushing,
>
> Hush—hushing. . .

In Wordsworth's "Written in March" (p. 74) and in Browning's "Pippa's Song" (p. 76) we are aware of the presence of the poet between us and the scene in nature that he describes; that is, we are conscious that he is suggesting that we interpret the scene in a particular way.

In "The Main-Deep," however, we have a poem that seems to be purely objective—an immediate presentation of a natural object or process with the poet's implied license to the reader to interpret it as he will. How should we interpret it? Does it have a precise meaning of any kind? In order to try to answer these questions you might consider the following points·

We note that the poet has assumed a particular view of the sea—not just any view. For example, the sea here is not a stormy one.

The poet has been rigorously selective with the details that he puts into the poem. In short, the poet is using his details to create a particular impression, and this impression implies an interpretation of life—which we may say is the actual theme of the poem.

The poet concentrates his attention on one billow—not on the sea as a whole, but on the one billow that seems to rise above and then flow along the surface of the sea.

Questions

1. Though there is no direct reference to the fact that the one billow approaches the spectator (who is perhaps standing on the deck of a ship), yet we gather this from the nature of the billow's movement. Pick out the details that justify this interpretation.

2. Can it be said that we get an impression of increased speed in the movement of the billow, an impression gained not only from the words but from the additional accent and the line "On—on—on—"? Why has the poet gone to the trouble of suggesting to us the temperature of the sea water with words like "cold-flushing" and "chill-rushing"? What does the sensory detail add to the poem? Does it affect our attitude toward the billow? What do you make of the last line? It is an auditory, not a visual, image. Why does it seem—if it does seem—an appropriate ending to this poem? What does it suggest about the fulfillment of the billow's progress?

3. Could one say that part of the satisfaction that one gets from this poem is that we experience a process working itself out to a natural fulfillment? Out of the beautiful and splendid tumult of the billow comes a moment of poise when the process is completed. The billow has dissipated itself as an object of individual attention.

4. Is the idea behind this poem comparable in its own way to the idea behind Keats's "To Autumn"?

Pear Tree

H.D. (Hilda Doolittle)   [1886–1961]

> Silver dust
> lifted from the earth,
> higher than my arms reach,
> you have mounted.
> O silver,   5
> higher than my arms reach
> you front us with great mass;
> no flower ever opened
> so staunch a white leaf,
> no flower ever parted silver   10
> from such rare silver;

O white pear,
your flower-tufts,
thick on the branch,
bring summer and ripe fruits   15
in their purple hearts.

Heat

H.D. (Hilda Doolittle)   [1886–1961]

O wind, rend open the heat,
cut apart the heat,
rend it to tatters.

Fruit cannot drop
through this thick air—   5
fruit cannot fall into heat
that presses up and blunts
the points of pears
and rounds the grapes.

Cut through the heat—   10
plow through it,
turning it on either side
of your path.

Questions

1. Is "Pear Tree," like "The Main-Deep," to be regarded as a poem
about a natural process, working itself out to fulfillment? If you think so,
after a thoughtful reading, try to say why.

2. Read "Pear Tree" aloud several times and try to grasp its rhythm.
Be sure that you give some value to line units. How would you describe
the difference between the rhythm here and that of "The Main-Deep"?
Does the difference seem to you in any way appropriate?

3. Is "Heat" also a poem that celebrates the natural process? If you feel
that it is essentially such a poem, that is, if the poet celebrates fruition and
fulfillment, why does she call upon the wind to dissipate the fructifying
force—the heat? Is there a real contradiction or only an apparent one?

The Sun Has Set

Emily Brontë   [1818–1848]

The sun has set, and the long grass now
   Waves dreamily in the evening wind;
And the wild bird has flown from that old gray stone
   In some warm nook a couch to find.

In all the lonely landscape round   5
I see no light and hear no sound,
Except the wind that far away
Come sighing o'er the heathy sea.

Questions

1. Why do you suppose the editors have chosen to place this poem just here?

2. On what grounds may it be said that the phrase "heathy sea" makes this poem?

You Know

Jean Garrigue   [*1914–1972*]

You know those rose sherbets,
The gathering of evening around the leaves,
The suffusions of such tinctures of heavens
On the shorn meadows, the suèdes going gold,
And the delicious checkerboard squares   5
Taking on every strain of the light;
And you know how the shutters close,
How the rocks, wedged in between trees,
Turn rose,
And somebody blue in the grasses   10
Makes the gold leap, and how the washed skies
Glitter like scales.
So do cheeks, eyes, on fire
With the stilled clarity of the rose of air,
And we get on the bus,   15
Taking the last of it down with us.

Question

What difference in meaning would occur if the last two lines were omitted?

The Woodspurge

Dante Gabriel Rossetti   [*1828–1882*]

The wind flapped loose, the wind was still,
Shaken out dead from tree and hill:
I had walked on at the wind's will,—
I sat now, for the wind was still.

Between my knees my forehead was,—   5
My lips, drawn in, said not Alas!

My hair was over in the grass,
My naked ears heard the day pass.

My eyes, wide open, had the run
Of some ten weeds to fix upon;   10
Among those few, out of the sun,
The woodspurge flowered, three cups in one.

From perfect grief there need not be
Wisdom or even memory:
One thing then learnt remains to me,—   15
The woodspurge has a cup of three.

Questions

1. Can you characterize the speaker's grief as raging, passive, or suicidal? What descriptive details would you cite? How, for instance, does the description of the wind in stanza 1 suggest his mood?
2. "Naked ears" is an odd phrase. Is the intention of the adjective physical or psychological? In what way, specifically?
3. Why are the weeds "out of the sun"? Reread stanza 2.
4. What does "perfect grief" mean? The best he ever had?
5. Relate the rhyme scheme to the "monomania" of the final image.

The Geranium

Theodore Roethke [*1908–1963*]

When I put her out, once, by the garbage pail,
She looked so limp and bedraggled,
So foolish and trusting, like a sick poodle,
Or a wizened aster in late September,
I brought her back in again   5
For a new routine—
Vitamins, water, and whatever
Sustenance seemed sensible
At the time: she'd lived
So long on gin, bobbie pins, half-smoked cigars, dead beer,   10
Her shriveled petals falling
On the faded carpet, the stale
Steak grease stuck to her fuzzy leaves.
(Dried-out, she creaked like a tulip.)

The things she endured!   15
The dumb dames shrieking half the night
Or the two of us, alone, both seedy,
Me breathing booze at her,
She leaning out of her pot toward the window.

Near the end, she seemed almost to hear me—   20
And that was scary—

So when that snuffling cretin of a maid
Threw her, pot and all, into the trash-can,
I said nothing.

But I sacked the presumptuous hag the next week,   25
I was that lonely.

Questions

1. How does the description of the geranium give in capsule the quality of its owner's life?

2. Why do you think that the speaker attaches so much importance to the geranium? He could buy a healthy one for fifty cents.

3. Why does he refer to the geranium as "she"? Is there an implied comparison with a woman? Is the relationship romantic, marital, parental —or something so elusively particular that the comparison can only be implied?

4. In psychological lingo, one might say that the speaker "projects his feelings" onto the geranium. How does this compare with what the speaker in "The Woodspurge" did with the "cup of three"?

Separation on the River Kiang

Ezra Pound   [1885–1972]

Ko-Jin goes West from Ko-Keku-to,
The smoke-flowers are blurred over the river,
His lone sail blots the far sky,
And now I see only the river,
        The long Kiang, reaching heaven.

The River-Merchant's Wife: A Letter

Ezra Pound   [1885–1972]

While my hair was still cut straight across my forehead
Played I about the front gate, pulling flowers.
You came by on bamboo stilts, playing horse,
You walked about my seat, playing with blue plums.
And we went on living in the village of Chokan: 5
Two small people, without dislike or suspicion.

At fourteen I married My Lord you.
I never laughed, being bashful.
Lowering my head, I looked at the wall.
Called to, a thousand times, I never looked back.   10

At fifteen I stopped scowling,
I desired my dust to be mingled with yours

Forever and forever and forever.
Why should I climb the look out?

At sixteen you departed,   15
You went into far Ku-to-yen, by the river of swirling eddies,
And you have been gone five months.
The monkeys make sorrowful noise overhead.

You dragged your feet when you went out.
By the gate now, the moss is grown, the different mosses,   20
Too deep to clear them away!
The leaves fall early this autumn, in wind.
The paired butterflies are already yellow with August
Over the grass in the West garden;
They hurt me. I grow older.   25
If you are coming down through the narrows of the river Kiang,
Please let me know beforehand,
And I will come out to meet you
   As far as Cho-fu-Sa.

          by *Rihaku* *

Though Pound does not connect the two foregoing poems, it is not difficult to associate them, in both method and theme. The first short poem, as the title indicates, gives us some of the details of the parting of lovers, or a husband and wife. The man, presumably, is traveling up the Kiang River to the west, and his loved one watches as long as she can see the sail of the boat taking him away from her.

The second and longer poem suggests that this man, or someone like him, has indeed been away for a long time from his young wife, and that now she is writing him a letter in which she tells him—not so much by direct statement as by implication—how much she has missed him and how eager she is to learn of his return.

Questions

1. The first short poem "works" largely through the vivid presentation of a few details and what those details imply. Yet is there any *radical* difference in method employed in the longer poem? True, it leaves less to implication and it furnishes more details, but surely the method is basically the same?

2. What are some of the details in the longer poem that seem particularly suggestive? For example, what do you make of the image in line 20, or the image that dominates line 23?

3. Though the poet has been scrupulous in his general restraint and objectivity, he has certainly allowed the river merchant's wife to indicate how she interprets the various things that she sees, something that is likely to influence the attitudes of the sympathetic reader. For example, in line 18 she says that "The monkeys make sorrowful noise overhead." Is

* Pound's poem is a free "translation" of one by the Chinese poet Li Po, the Japanese form of whose name is Rihaku.

there any reason to believe that the monkeys in the trees overhead are literally sorrowful? Is there anything for them to be sorrowful about? Can you find other indications of the ways in which this young woman is interpreting what she hears and sees about her in terms of her own hopes, fears, and longings? What in the last four lines is gained by specifying the localities?

Rocky Acres

Robert Graves [*1895–*]

This is a wild land, country of my choice,
    With harsh craggy mountain, moor ample and bare.
Seldom in these acres is heard any voice
    But voice of cold water that runs here and there
    Through rocks and lank heather growing without care.   5
No mice in the heath run nor no birds cry
For fear of the dark speck that floats in the sky.

He soars and he hovers, rocking on his wings,
    He scans his wide parish with a sharp eye,
He catches the trembling of small hidden things,   10
    He tears them in pieces, dropping from the sky:
    Tenderness and pity the land will deny
Where life is but nourished from water and rock,
A hardy adventure, full of fear and shock.

Time has never journeyed to this lost land,   15
    Crakeberries and heather bloom out of date,
The rocks jut, the streams flow singing on either hand,
    Careless if the season be early or late.
    The skies wander overhead, now blue, now slate:
Winter would be known by his cold cutting snow   20
If June did not borrow his armor also.

Yet this is my country beloved by me best,
    The first land that rose from Chaos and the Flood,
Nursing no fat valleys for comfort and rest,
    Trampled by no hard hooves, stained with no blood.   25
    Bold immortal country whose hill-tops have stood
Strongholds for the proud gods when on earth they go,
Terror for fat burghers in far plains below.

Questions

1. What kind of man do you take the speaker to be? Does he seem to enjoy telling how the hawk (stanza 2) catches trembling "small hidden things" and "tears them in pieces"? If the reader regards him as a sadist, does he miss the point? In short, does the speaker love nature even if it is "red in tooth and claw," wanting it nevertheless to be preserved? Or does he love nature because he prefers it red in tooth and claw? Compare the meaning of this poem with that of "Inversnaid" (p. 83).

2. How do the "fat burghers" (line 28) come into the poem? Does their dislike for such a country as he chooses help define his choice?

3. Is line 25 inconsistent with lines 10–12, or is there an important distinction involved? How is this related to the distinction between man and nature implied in Wordsworth's "Composed upon Westminster Bridge"?

A Letter from the Caribbean

Barbara Howes [*1914–*]

Breezeways in the tropics winnow the air,
Are ajar to its least breath
But hold back, in a feint of architecture,
The boisterous sun
Pouring down upon   5

The island like a cloudburst. They
Slant to loft air, they curve, they screen
The wind's wild gaiety
Which tosses palm
Branches about like a marshal's plumes.   10

Within this filtered, latticed
World, where spools of shadow
Form, life and change,
The triumph of incoming air
Is that it is there,   15

Cooling and salving us. Louvers,
Trellises, vines—music also—
Shape the arboreal wind, make skeins
Of it, and a maze
To catch shade. The days   20

Are all variety, blowing;
Aswirl in a perpetual current
Of wind, shadow, sun,
I marvel at the capacity
Of memory   25

Which, in some deep pocket
Of my mind, preserves you whole—
As wind is wind, as the lion-taking
Sun is sun, you are, you stay:
Nothing is lost, nothing has blown away.   30

Questions

1. Is this poem about the architecture of a house on a Caribbean island? Or is it about the speaker's memory of what such a house was like? Or is it about memory itself?

2. What do you make of the concluding line: "Nothing is lost, nothing has blown away"?

The Yew in the Churchyard*

Alfred, Lord Tennyson [1809–1892]

Old Yew, which graspest at the stones
  That name the under-lying dead,
  Thy fibers net the dreamless head,
Thy roots are wrapped about the bones.

The seasons bring the flower again,   5
  And bring the firstling to the flock;
  And in the dusk of thee, the clock
Beats out the little lives of men.

O not for thee the glow, the bloom,
  Who changest not in any gale,   10
  Nor branding summer suns avail
To touch thy thousand years of gloom:

And gazing on thee, sullen tree,
  Sick for thy stubborn hardihood,
  I seem to fail from out my blood   15
And grow incorporate into thee.

The yew is the distinctive tree of the English churchyard, perhaps because it has immemorially signified eternity—as an evergreen and because of its remarkable longevity. Tennyson scarcely exaggerates when he speaks (line 12) of its "thousand years of gloom." Many yews are known to be centuries old.

Questions

1. The basic situation of the poem is this: a man oppressed by grief stares at the old yew in the churchyard and envies its "stubborn hardihood." What is this "hardihood"? In other words, what human attitude does the yew embody and why should a man envy it? What does the last line mean? Compare the theme of this poem with that of "The Woodspurge" and "Rocky Acres."

2. Suppose line 3 were changed to

  Thy fibers clasp the dreamless head.

* This poem is Section 2 of *In Memoriam*. Title by the editors.

What would be gained or lost? What would be the effect on the line that follows it?

3. Suppose line 6 were changed to

And bring the new lamb to the flock.

What difference do we have, not only in meaning and association, but in sound?

4. What does the word *branding* mean?

Yew-Trees

William Wordsworth   [*1770–1850*]

There is a Yew-tree, pride of Lorton Vale,
Which to this day stands single, in the midst
Of its own darkness, as it stood of yore:
Not loth to furnish weapons for the bands
Of Umfraville or Percy ere they marched   5
To Scotland's heaths; or those that crossed the sea,
And drew their sounding bows at Azincour,
Perhaps at earlier Crécy, or Poictiers.
Of vast circumference and gloom profound
This solitary Tree! a living thing   10
Produced too slowly ever to decay;
Of form and aspect too magnificent
To be destroyed. But worthier still of note
Are those fraternal Four of Borrowdale,
Joined in one solemn and capacious grove;   15
Huge trunks! and each particular trunk a growth
Of intertwisted fibers serpentine
Up-coiling, and inveterately convolved;
Nor uninformed with Phantasy, and looks
That threaten the profane;—a pillared shade,   20
Upon whose grassless floor of red-brown hue,
By sheddings from the pining umbrage tinged
Perennially—beneath whose sable roof
Of boughs, as if for festal purpose decked
With unrejoicing berries—ghostly Shapes   25
May meet at noontide; Fear and trembling Hope,
Silence and Foresight; Death the Skeleton
And Time the Shadow;—there to celebrate,
As in a natural temple scattered o'er
With altars undisturbed of mossy stone,   30
United worship; or in mute repose
To lie, and listen to the mountain flood
Murmuring from Glaramara's inmost caves.

The Percys were earls of Northumberland, and through the late Middle Ages they were engaged frequently in border warfare with the Scots. Umfraville, another member of the English nobility, took part in the Battle of Bannockburn (1314). At Crécy (1346), Poitiers (1356), and Agincourt (1415) the English won celebrated victories over the French.

Questions

1. Does this poem, in your opinion, go beyond a mere description of a clump of yew trees? Does it "say" anything? If so, what does it say?

2. A manuscript of "Yew-Trees" preserves the following additional lines which the poet decided to cancel before publication:

> Pass not the [? Place] unvisited—Ye will say
> That Mona's Druid Oaks composed a Fane
> Less awful than this grove: as Earth so long
> On its unwearied bosom has sustained
> The undecaying Pile: as Frost and Drought,
> The Fires of heaven have spared it, and the Storms,
> So for its hallowed uses may it stand
> For ever spared by Man!

Do these lines suggest that the poet himself at first thought his poem needed a more definite "conclusion" than the poem as published afforded? Is there any contradiction between what is said in these additional lines and in lines 10–13? Do the canceled lines add anything not already said in the poem?

3. Wordsworth dictated the following note on this poem:

> [Grasmere, 1803.] These yew-trees are still standing, but the spread of that at Lorton is much diminished by mutilation. I will here mention that a little way up the hill, on the road leading from Rosthwaite to Stonethwaite, lay the trunk of a yew-tree, which appeared as you approached, so vast was its diameter, like the entrance of a cave, and not a small one. Calculating upon what I have observed of the slow growth of this tree in rocky situations, and of its durability, I have often thought that the one I am describing must have been as old as the Christian era. The tree lay in the line of a fence. Great masses of its ruins were strewn about, and some had been rolled down the hillside and lay near the road at the bottom. As you approached the tree, you were struck with the number of shrubs and young plants, ashes, etc., which had found a bed upon the decayed trunk and grew to no inconsiderable height, forming, as it were, a part of the hedgerow. In no part of England, or of Europe, have I ever seen a yew-tree at all approaching this magnitude, as it must have stood. By the bye, Hutton, the old Guide, of Keswick, had been so impressed with the remains of this tree that he used gravely to tell strangers that there could be no doubt of its having been in existence before the flood.

Compare what is said in this note and what is said in lines 10–13. Is the contradiction important? In the light of it, can you justify lines 10–13? In what spirit are they to be read? Could the speaker of this poem state them with full dramatic propriety even though Wordsworth the man knew them to be false?

Pray to What Earth Does This Sweet Cold Belong

Henry David Thoreau [*1817–1862*]

Pray to what earth does this sweet cold belong,
Which asks no duties and no conscience?
The moon goes up by leaps her cheerful path
In some far summer stratum of the sky,
While stars with their cold shine bedot her way. 5
The fields gleam mildly back upon the sky,
And far and near upon the leafless shrubs
The snow dust still emits a silver light.
Under the hedge, where drift banks are their screen,
The titmice now pursue their downy dreams, 10
As often in the sweltering summer nights
The bee doth drop asleep in the flower cup,
When evening overtakes him with his load.
By the brooksides, in the still genial night,
The more adventurous wanderer may hear 15
The crystals shoot and form, and winter slow
Increase his rule by gentlest summer means.

Questions

This poem seems purely descriptive, but, as we have earlier insisted, the description represents a human perception and inevitably embodies a human attitude. Look back, for example, at "Dust of Snow" by Frost, "To Autumn" by Keats, "The Main-Deep" by Stephens, and "Rocky Acres" by Graves. Now try to frame, in writing, a brief statement of what attitude toward life may be implied in Thoreau's poem.

TONE

Foreword

The *tone* of a poem indicates the speaker's attitude toward his subject and toward his audience, and sometimes toward himself. The word is, strictly speaking, a metaphor, a metaphor drawn from the tone of voice in speech or song. In conversation we may imply our attitude—and hence our true meaning—by the tone in which we say something. The simple phrase, "Yes, indeed," may be made to mean, merely by alterations in the tone, anything from enthusiastic, or respectful, agreement to insolent denial. In ordinary life, a great part of our meaning—our basic attitude toward the *what* and the *who* of any transaction—is indicated by the tone. In a poem this is also true, but the poet must depend on the words on a page to take the place of his expressive human voice; he must choose and arrange his words so that the poem will dictate to the reader the desired tone, with all the subtle modifications of meaning. Our concern here will be to understand something of how this may be accomplished.

Tone, as we have said, expresses attitudes. And this leads us back to what we have also said earlier, that every poem is, in one sense, a little drama. A poem is an utterance. There is someone who utters. There is a provocation to utterance. There is an audience. This is clearly true of poems in which characters speak, but it is also true of the most lyrical piece. Even the song expresses a human response, and the response is provoked by something, and it implies a hearer—even if only the self.

This is true, even, of a poem like "The Main-Deep" (p. 99), which is about as objective and impersonal as a poem can be. But the poem inheres in words, and someone must have framed them. Further, they have been framed to express the reaction of the speaker—here presumably the poet himself—to an occasion. The occasion is simple: the speaker, staring at the movement of a wave, finds that the wave embodies his own feeling about the life process.

Where, however, is the audience? It is shadowy, not specified. The poet might, as it were, be talking to himself. As in a lyric, in a meditative poem —a poem in which the poet seems to be talking to himself, thinking out loud—what is of obvious importance is the attitude toward the subject, toward what has provoked the utterance. But even in this talking to one's self, there is a sense of audience, and a law imposed by this sense. One can express one's self to one's self, and thereby understand one's self, only by treating one's self as an audience—and that means by respecting the form of what is said so that anyone quite distinct from the self might be able to get the full force and implication of what is being expressed.

In some poems we are scarcely aware of the identity of the speaker— e.g., "The Main-Deep" or "In a Station of the Metro" (p. 71). In other poems, in varying degrees, a personality enters the poem—an "I"—and the attitude of the speaker becomes a very marked feature of the poem. In "Rocky Acres" by Robert Graves (p. 106), for instance, the "I" of the poem calls the wilderness the "country of my choice," and the description of the wilderness becomes, in an indirect fashion, a way of stating the attitude toward the world and other men held by the "I." Or in "Desert Places" by Robert Frost (p. 203), the form is focused on the "I" in a very personal way: without the challenge that the "I" makes to the snowy vacancy to do its worst, there would be no poem. Again, in "Preludes" (p. 91), at the very end we find the lines

> I am moved by fancies that are curled
> Around these images, and cling:
> The notion of some infinitely gentle
> Infinitely suffering thing.

The entrance of the "I" into the poem, here at the end, is a definite statement of the attitude that the poet takes toward the subject, and that, presumably, he expects us to take toward it.

How much are we to identify such an "I" with the personality of the poet? Is the poem to be taken as straight autobiography? In such a poem as "A Deep-Sworn Vow" by Yeats (p. 519), the poet presumably is speaking in his own person, autobiographically, to the woman with whom he had been in love for many years. We even know her name. She was Maud Gonne, the famous Irish beauty and patriot.

There are, however, many shadings off from this kind of literal identification to a merely fictitious "I," and for present purposes the degree of autobiographical identification is not *necessarily* important. We are concerned with the fact that the speaker of the poem, whether historical or fictional, is expressing an attitude through his particular use of language. This becomes clear as soon as we think of such poems as "Ulysses" by Tennyson (p. 57), or "Hell Gate" by Housman (p. 59), in which the "I" is obviously fictitious—in which there can only be an imaginative identification.

This is not to say that a poet may not speak his deepest convictions and reveal his deepest self through an imaginative identification. But if we are to say that Tennyson identified himself with Ulysses, we must also remember that, in some degree at least, he identified himself with the speaker of the poem "The Lotos-Eaters," in which a view exactly opposed to that in "Ulysses" is expressed, an attitude of self-indulgent and voluptuous world-weariness. Or we come to instances in which there is more than one speaker, where there is a dialogue as objective as that in a drama, poems like "The Canonization" (p. 134) or "Danny Deever" (p. 35). And this situation, in which there is a total distinction between the poet and the speaker, or speakers, in the poem, emphasizes the fact that the question of tone is *immediately* concerned with the speaker *in* the poem, in the situation *of* the poem, and not with degrees of identification of a speaker with any historical person, the poet or any other. The poem is, in this perspective, a drama.

Thus far we have been emphasizing the fact of the speaker. But there is always the audience, too, and the question of the attitude of the speaker to the audience. We began our discussion, in fact, by referring to the shadowy, unspecified audience in "The Main-Deep." Sometimes, however, a poem is addressed to a real person, as we have already pointed out in "A Deep-Sworn Vow," here the woman with whom Yeats had actually been in love. But there clearly does not have to be a particular person, historical or fictional, to whom a poem is directed. The reader himself may be the audience—not in the broad and inevitable sense in which the reader is always the eavesdropping audience, but in a specific sense, with the poet addressing him, the "you" of the poem, and adopting a clearly marked attitude toward him.

We have already pointed out how the "I" comes in at the end of "Preludes," and now let us remark how, just after that statement of pity, we find the "you" to whom the poem is addressed:

> Wipe your hand across your mouth and laugh;
> The worlds revolve like ancient women
> Gathering fuel in vacant lots.

In other words, the poet assumes that his audience will not sympathize with the attitude of pity, that the "you" may make the gross gesture of satisfied appetite and laugh at suffering—and may logically do so if we take the view that man is nothing but a mechanical detail in the great mechanism of the universe. The poet assumes this possible attitude on the part of his audience as a way of indicating, by ironical contrast,* the kind of response he does desire, and of indicating his own awareness of the difficulty of arriving substantially at that human sympathy. And the complication of this use of the "you" may indicate how important the role of the "you" as audience may be, and often is.

The audience, however, does not have to be a person at all. In "To Heaven" (p. 513), Ben Jonson is addressing God; in "Ah, Sunflower" (p. 514), Blake is addressing the flower; and in "To Autumn" (p. 87) and "Ode: Autumn" (p. 89), Keats and Hood are addressing the season. There are, too, many poems addressed to abstractions, like Fame or Fear. Sunflowers and seasons have no ears and, literally, cannot be audiences, but they serve in one way or another as a dramatic focus for the human attitude with which the poem is concerned. The tone which Shelley adopts in addressing the West Wind is very different from that which John Clare finds natural to use to the pert little bird in "Little Trotty Wagtail" (p. 347). To sum up: in one sense, the tone is an indication of the meaning of the poem.

We have just said: "the meaning of the poem." And here we must ask: "the meaning for *whom?*" Ultimately, for the reader, who is the final audience. Maud Gonne of "A Deep-Sworn Vow," the "I" and the "you" of "Preludes," the God of "To Heaven," the sunflower in Blake's poem, and the bird in Clare's—they are all part of the drama of the poem. That is, they are the audience *in* the poem, but not the audience *of* the poem.

---

* Contrast between what we expect and what we get, or between what we literally say and what we really mean, is the essential ingredient of an ironic effect. When the discrepancy occurs between the expected outcome and the real outcome, we have the irony of situation. A great ship whose builders have boasted that she is unsinkable goes to the bottom on her very first voyage. The boy who seemed to have all the gifts and the brightest future turns out to be a miserable failure.

One can find many poems that exploit irony of circumstance. Thomas Hardy wrote a whole series of such poems, entitled "Satires of Circumstance." But a much more important and general feature of poetry is the irony of statement, where literal statement stands in contrast to its true significance. Everyone knows that a word or phrase— "Very well," for example—can mean very different things when spoken in different tones of voice, everything from enthusiastic approval to emphatic disapproval. Many of the shadings of tone (though certainly not all) are to be regarded as ironic qualifications of the surface meaning. *Understatement* is closely related to irony since less is said on the subject than we might have expected. *Paradox* also has an ironic quality, for in paradox there is a discrepancy between the literal nonsense spoken and the actual truth that it conveys; for example, "The last shall be first."

A. THREE POEMS OF NATIONAL CELEBRATION

In 1887 Queen Victoria celebrated her golden jubilee marking the completion of the fiftieth year of her reign. As the poet laureate, Tennyson was expected to write a poem worthy of the occasion. We print below an excerpt of the poem that he did write. The note that he means to strike is one of formal eulogy.

from
On the Jubilee of Queen Victoria
Alfred, Lord Tennyson   *[1809–1892]*

I

Fifty times the rose has flower'd and faded,
Fifty times the golden harvest fallen,
Since our Queen assumed the globe, the sceptre.

II

She beloved for a kindliness
Rare in Fable or History,   5
Queen, and Empress of India,
Crown'd so long with a diadem
Never worn by a worthier,
Now with prosperous auguries
Comes at last to the bounteous   10
Crowning year of her Jubilee....

IX

Fifty years of ever-broadening Commerce!
Fifty years of ever-brightening Science!
Fifty years of ever-widening Empire!

X

You, the Mighty, the Fortunate,   15
You, the Lord-territorial,
You, the Lord-manufacturer,
You, the hardy, laborious,
Patient children of Albion,
You, Canadian, Indian,   20
Australasian, African,
All your hearts be in harmony,

All your voices in unison,
Singing 'Hail to the glorious
Golden year of her Jubilee!'   25

XI

Are there thunders moaning in the distance?
Are there spectres moving in the darkness?
Trust the Hand of Light will lead her people,
Till the thunders pass, the spectres vanish,
And the Light is Victor, and the darkness   30
Dawns into the Jubilee of the Ages.

The same occasion provided A. E. Housman with the subject of the
following poem:

1887

A. E. Housman [1859–1936]

From Clee to heaven the beacon burns,
    The shires have seen it plain,
From north and south the sign returns
    And beacons burn again.

Look left, look right, the hills are bright,   5
    The dales are light between,
Because 'tis fifty years tonight
    That God has saved the Queen.

Now, when the flame they watch not towers
    About the soil they trod,   10
Lads, we'll remember friends of ours
    Who shared the work with God.

To skies that knit their heartstrings right,
    To fields that bred them brave,
The saviors come not home tonight: 15
    Themselves they could not save.

It dawns in Asia, tombstones show
    And Shropshire names are read;
And the Nile spills his overflow
    Beside the Severn's dead.   20

We pledge in peace by farm and town
    The Queen they served in war,
And fire the beacons up and down
    The land they perished for.

"God save the Queen" we living sing,   25
   From height to height 'tis heard;
And with the rest your voices ring,
   Lads of the Fifty-third.

Oh, God will save her, fear you not:
   Be you the men you've been,   30
Get you the sons your fathers got,
   And God will save the Queen.

    The poem begins with a lilting rhythm appropriate to the joyful occasion. The beacons have been lighted up and down the land* in celebration of the half-century of order, prosperity, and power specified in Tennyson's "On the Jubilee," and far and wide people are singing the national anthem: "God Save the Queen." But something occurs in the second stanza of Housman's poem that provides a key to the attitude the poet really holds: it is the shift in feeling that occurs when we move from line 6 to lines 7 and 8:

    Because 'tis fifty years tonight
    That God has saved the Queen.

"God Save the Queen" is a phrase out of a ritual, a phrase gramatically petrified, as it were. We are, therefore, momentarily shocked to hear it suddenly fitted into a matter-of-fact statement, with the change of tense and the other syntactical adjustments that take it out of ritual and into commonplace statement. The effect is a little like that of seeing a priest, clad in his ritual garments, suddenly take the heavily embroidered maniple from his arm and begin to use it as if it were an ordinary towel—which it was originally before it was divorced from workaday chores and formalized into a band of embroidered cloth.

    The poet, of course, wants to give shock here, a shock which in this poem is not playful but sobering. Indeed, we could argue that the rest of the poem is devoted to working out the implications of this forcing of a ritual phrase into ordinary grammar. In short, the poem may be described as a realistic and ironic examination of the real meaning of "God Save the Queen"—words often uttered on such occasions glibly and without thought.

    God may indeed have saved the Queen, but He seems to have used ordinary human beings as His chosen instruments. The British infantryman, the lads of the Fifty-third Regiment (line 28), those who have not come home to celebrate the jubilee but lie in lonely graves in Africa or Asia, are, in their absence, mute testimony to this fact.

---

* Clee (a hill) and Severn (a river) are place names of the county of Shropshire, the region in which this, like almost all of Housman's poems, is localized. The title of his first volume (1896) was, in fact, *A Shropshire Lad.*

What Housman is doing in his jubilee poem comes out clearly when we compare it with Tennyson's straightforward praise of the Queen in his laureate poem. Tennyson, of course, would not have denied that Englishmen had perished to make Victoria empress, or that blood had been shed to build the empire and to guarantee the "ever-broadening Commerce" of which the poet laureate sings. But he evidently did not feel it appropriate to mention the fact on this occasion. Tennyson's tone in his jubilee poem is calm, deferential to the crown, even almost reverential, as he praises Victoria for what she has accomplished. To be sure, as the poem closes he does sound more ominous notes. He asks, "Are there thunders moaning in the distance?" But he expects these "thunders" to pass, and the ominous "spectres" to vanish.

Housman, on the other hand, has clearly abjured the laureate tone: he is realistic and ironic. Some readers might even regard him as irreverent. Notice lines 11–13, where he turns aside from the general celebration to say, "Lads, we'll remember friends of ours / Who shared the work [of saving the Queen] with God." The irreverence becomes even more pointed in the next stanza when the poet ironically echoes the words with which Christ was mocked on the cross: "He saved others, himself he cannot save." Are the young British soldiers who did not come back here being compared to Christ? In one sense, at least, they are: they gave themselves to save the Queen, and the ultimate terms of that service entailed not being able to save themselves.

Did Housman, then, regard the young British soldiers as innocent dupes? Did he deplore the wars in which they perished? He has left it on record* that he did not, and it is possible to read the last stanza of the poem, not as a bitter irony but as a genuine exhortation to the living Englishmen to beget the breed of men who, in spite of the human cost, will cheerfully, as their fathers did, serve the Queen in peace and war.

Nevertheless, the difference in tone between Tennyson's poem and Housman's is sharply defined. Tennyson pretty well confines himself to counting up the blessings that Victoria's reign has provided. Housman, on the other hand, makes his primary concern on this occasion honoring those who did not come back to join the other veterans now loyally singing "God Save the Queen." At the least, Housman's poem is aware of the bitter human cost of prosperity and glory.

---

* See Frank Harris, *Latest Contemporary Portraits,* Macaulay Company, 1927, p. 280. Harris said to Housman: " 'It stirs my blood to find an Englishman so free of the insensate snobbishness that corrupts all true value [in England]. I remember telling Kipling once that when he mixed his patriotism with snobbery it became disgusting to me; and here you have poked fun at the whole thing and made splendid mockery of it.'

"To my astonishment, Housman replied sharply: 'I never intended to poke fun, as you call it, at patriotism, and I can find nothing in the sentiment to make mockery of: I meant it sincerely: if Englishmen breed as good men as their fathers, then God will save their Queen.' His own words seemed to have excited him for he added precisely but with anger: 'I can only reject and resent your—your truculent praise.' "

We may get further help in defining the precise tone of Housman's "1887" by comparing it with another jubilee poem, that written by Rudyard Kipling on the occasion of Victoria's diamond jubilee, which was celebrated in 1897, the *sixtieth* year of her reign.

Recessional

Rudyard Kipling [*1865–1936*]

God of our fathers, known of old,
   Lord of our far-flung battle-line,
Beneath whose awful hand we hold
   Dominion over palm and pine—
Lord God of Hosts, be with us yet,   5
   Lest we forget—lest we forget!

The tumult and the shouting dies;
   The captains and the kings depart:
Still stands Thine ancient sacrifice,
   An humble and a contrite heart.   10
Lord God of Hosts, be with us yet,
   Lest we forget—lest we forget!

Far-called, our navies melt away;
   On dune and headland sinks the fire:
Lo, all our pomp of yesterday   15
   Is one with Nineveh and Tyre!
Judge of the Nations, spare us yet,
   Lest we forget—lest we forget!

If, drunk with sight of power, we loose
   Wild tongues that have not Thee in awe,   20
Such boastings as the Gentiles use,
   Or lesser breeds without the Law—
Lord God of Hosts, be with us yet,
   Lest we forget—lest we forget!

For heathen heart that puts her trust   25
   In reeking tube and iron shard,
All valiant dust that builds on dust,
   And, guarding, calls not Thee to guard,
For frantic boast and foolish word—
   Thy Mercy on Thy People, Lord!   30

The immediate occasion of this poem is the aftermath of the jubilee. The kings and commanders and high dignitaries have come and gone, and the speaker, as he reflects on the display of pomp and power that has just ended, is moved to utter a prayer that his countrymen may not fall into the sin of pride and overweening self-trust. Lines 9–10 refer, by the way, to Psalm 51, verse 17: "The sacrifices of God are a broken spirit: a broken and a contrite heart, O God, thou wilt not despise." Here follow a few notes: Line 16: Nineveh was a capital of the ancient empire of Assyria; Tyre, the capital of ancient Phoenicia, which, like Great Britain, was a great sea power; line 21: Gentiles means literally non-Jews; the suggestion here is that the British may feel themselves to be, like the Israelites, a chosen people.

Questions

1. What is the meaning of Kipling's title? What is the ecclesiastical meaning of a "recessional"?

2. What is suggested by the phrase "palm and pine" in line 4?

3. Since this poem is addressed to the Deity and is manifestly a prayer, that fact may seem to answer all questions about its tone. But there are prayers and prayers, and, in any case, some prayers ring true and others do not. What risks does the poet run in frankly making his poem a prayer? What does he gain, if anything? Try to define the special tone of this prayer.

4. The refrain of the first four stanzas is "Lest we forget—lest we forget!" What is it that "we" are not to forget? Try to find in the poem a specific statement of what that something is. (If you have difficulty in locating such a statement, it might prove helpful to note that this poem is a tissue of references to the Book of Psalms. For example, verse 7 of Psalm 20 reads: "Some trust in chariots, and some in horses; but *we will remember* [italics ours] the name of the Lord our God." Compare lines 25–28.

"Recessional" also leans heavily, it would appear, on Psalm 2, where Jehovah, the "Lord God of Hosts," mocks the heathen who "rage" (compare lines 19–21) and who "imagine a vain thing" (compare lines 25–26 and 29). But it is in vain that the heathen rage against the Lord and his chosen, for the Lord has set "His king upon [His] holy hill in Zion" and has given him "the heathen for [his] inheritance. Indeed the Lord promises that his chosen king will "break the [kings of the heathen] with a rod of iron."

Having in mind these echoes from Psalms 2 and 20—not to mention Psalm 51—one sees that Kipling is suggesting that the Lord regards the British as a Chosen People. Power has been given them—the sort of dominion prophesied in Psalm 2 to the King of Israel. Yet this dominion is contingent on their continuing to put their trust in the Lord of Hosts. God's mercy is asked (line 30) for those who, with "heathen heart," put their trust "in reeking tube and iron shard"—that is, in their rifles and cannon. For if the British people forget that their power ultimately comes from the

Lord, they are doomed. If they trust in their own powers and boast as the Gentiles—those who do not know the law of the Lord—do, then God will dash them to pieces just as surely as he has dashed to pieces the ancient pagan empires.

For the last half-century, Kipling has been much censured for speaking of "lesser breeds without the Law," as if he regarded people having other than white skins as inferior breeds. But, whatever were Kipling's views as a man and citizen, it is ironic that in this particular poem "lesser breeds without the Law" takes on a different and quite special meaning. In the context of Psalms 2 and 20, "lesser breeds without the Law" refers to those who do not acknowledge the Lord of Hosts and who stand outside His law. They are the Gentiles who, in their heathen delusions, trust in their own strength and in "frantic boast and foolish word" (line 29). The stress, in short, is not on race or any matter of mere biology, but on those who know and keep the divine law and those who do not.

To sum up, the point here is not to free Kipling from the charge of imperialism. He was an imperialist, as were most Europeans (and Americans) of his day. The point here is how the subject of imperialism—an inevitable aspect of the occasion he celebrates—is treated in the poem. And ultimately how, and in what degree, human attitudes and values in the poem involving imperialism may be applicable in other situations and contexts.

A brief summary of the likenesses and differences between the Housman and the Kipling poems might read something like this: the speaker of "Recessional" is evidently a believer in Jehovah, the Lord of Hosts; it is evident that the man who speaks in "1887" is not. But both are apparently patriotic Englishmen and neither poem is necessarily anti-empire. We have already noted that Housman the man, like Kipling, did not regard his poem of national celebration as mocking at patriotism. Kipling the man, like Housman, felt sympathy for the common soldiers who paid the highest price for maintaining the Empire.* Thus, "1887" and "Recessional" have much in common in subject matter and in general sympathy manifested for the rank and file of Britain's armies. But how different the poems are in many respects—and most of all in tone.

---

* In spite of his reputation for being a jingoistic imperialist, Kipling wrote a number of poems from the viewpoint of Tommy Atkins, the common soldier; and he was capable of referring to Queen Victoria as "The Widow at Windsor." Thus, he has Tommy Atkins warn the reader to

> Walk wide o' the Widow at Windsor,
>   For 'alf of Creation she owns!
> We 'ave bought 'er the same with the sword and the flame,
>   An' we've salted it down with our bones.
>   (Poor beggars!—it's blue with our bones!)

And Kipling was quite capable of celebrating the courage of the "lesser breeds without the Law," as in "Fuzzy-Wuzzy."

Question

Attempt to describe in some detail the tone of "Recessional," comparing and contrasting it with the tone of "1887" and "On the Jubilee of Queen Victoria."

B. DEATH IN BATTLE

Somebody's Darling

Marie Ravenel de la Coste   [*?1840s–?1909*]

Into a ward of the whitewashed walls,
    Where the dead and the dying lay
Wounded by bayonets, shells, and balls,
    Somebody's darling was borne one day.
Somebody's darling–so young and so brave   5
    Wearing still on his pale, sweet face–
Soon to be hid by the dust of the grave–
    The lingering light of his boyhood's grace.

Matted and damp are the curls of gold
    Kissing the snow of that fair young brow,   10
Pale are the lips of delicate mould–
    Somebody's darling is dying now.
Back from the beautiful, blue-veined face
    Brush every wandering silken thread,
Cross his hands as a sign of grace–   15
    Somebody's darling is still and dead.

Kiss him once for somebody's sake,
    Murmur a prayer, soft and low,
One bright curl from the cluster take–
    They were somebody's pride, you know.   20
Somebody's hand has rested there:
    Was it a mother's, soft and white?
And have the lips of a sister fair
    Been baptized in those waves of light?

God knows best. He was somebody's love: 25
    Somebody's heart enshrined him there:
Somebody wafted his name above,
    Night and morn, on the wings of prayer.
Somebody wept when he marched away,

Looking so handsome, brave and grand;   30
    Somebody's kiss on his forehead lay,
    Somebody clung to his parting hand.

Somebody's watching and waiting for him,
    Yearning to hold him again to her heart:—
There he lies—with the blue eyes dim,   35
    And smiling, child-like lips apart.
Tenderly bury the fair young dead,
    Pausing to drop on his grave a tear:
Carve on the wooden slab at his head
    Somebody's darling lies buried here.   40

The text of this poem, very popular in its day, is taken from *War Poetry of the South,* edited by William Gilmore Simms, New York, 1867. The speaker is evidently a visitor—perhaps a nurse or attendant—in a hospital in one of the Confederate states during the Civil War. At any rate she sees what a hospital attendant would see: the arrival of the wounded soldier and his death. She does not know the young man's name. This would account for the title and would explain her choice of the words that she thinks ought to be carved on his temporary headboard. (Presumably what would ordinarily be carved on the headboard would be some such description as "Unknown Soldier of the Third Alabama Infantry Regiment.")

The poet's attempt to intensify our sense of pity—not merely for the young man, but for his sweetheart and his mother or sisters—is obvious. Some of the devices used are gratuitous. For example, the phrase "soft and low" (line 18), which describes the prayer, is strictly unnecessary. If the prayer is murmured, then it is bound to be soft and low; the poet's motive in emphasizing the softness of the murmured prayer is to make it seem the more pathetic. So also in line 22, where the imagined mother's hand is described as "soft and white." The fact that the mother's hands are well tended (and in line 23, that the face of the imagined sister is "fair") has no real relation to the deathbed scene. In fact, one could argue that if the hands of the mother were red and raw from scrubbing, or the sister's face drawn and weary from anxiety, those details might actually evoke a more responsible sense of pathos. Again, the statement that the lips of the dying soldier's sister have been "baptized" in the young man's hair is a rather ridiculous straining for effect. Is the dying soldier being made a kind of martyr or saint? After all, could the young man's hair, by touching his sister's lips, confer a baptismal grace?

The death of a young man in battle is sad, and might well provide the subject for a poem; but quite another matter is at stake in our criticism of "Somebody's Darling": we are suggesting that in this instance, the poet, in her attempt to squeeze out of the presented situation every possible drop of sentiment, has actually hurt her own case. The poem is *sentimental.** A poem that showed more restraint and less obviously reached for the reader's heartstrings would be more moving in its effect.

A telltale sign of *sentimentality* in this poem is the poet's unwillingness to leave anything to our imagination. We are allowed no opportunity to develop a hint or work out an implication of the situation. We are forced to sit before the poem as completely passive as any viewer inert before the usual fare offered via the television set. *The imaginative involvement of the reader is essential to poetic effect.*

Compare the method of presentation in this poem with that of the poem that follows.

Inscription
For Marye's Heights, Fredericksburg

Herman Melville [*1819–1891*]

> To them who crossed the flood
> And climbed the hill, with eyes
>   Upon the heavenly flag intent,
>   And through the deathful tumult went
> Even unto death: to them this Stone—   5
> Erect, where they were overthrown—
>   Of more than victory the monument.

To understand the poem we need to know something about the circumstances. In 1862 the Confederates under General Lee were entrenched on Marye's Heights looking down on the town of Fredericksburg, Virginia, which is situated on the south bank of the Rappahannock River. General Burnside, the Union commander, got his troops across the Rappahannock (see line 1, "To them who crossed the flood") and attempted to storm the heights above the town. The Union forces fought bravely but suffered a bloody repulse, the victims of inept generalship.

What, then, does Melville commemorate? Not a victory, but the courage to go forward, even to death. In short, the inscription that the poet proposes for a stone to be erected on the heights was to celebrate not a military

---

* Sentimentality may be defined as emotion in excess of the occasion, whether as an overresponse on the part of the reader whose emotions are on hair trigger, or as an effect deliberately worked up by the poet who is willing to use illegitimate means. (Of course the poet need not be cold-blooded in his attempt: he may have taken in himself as well as any unwary reader. The author of "Somebody's Darling" probably emoted as powerfully as any of her readers.) We usually restrict the term *sentimentality* to an overexpression of the more tender emotions, but any emotion is subject to disproportionate emphasis. Jingoistic patriotism, for example, can be whipped up by the unscrupulous rhetorician pretending to be a true poet.

triumph but something that the poet regards as more precious and valuable than triumph.

Questions

1. Notice how quietly the poem begins: "crossed the flood" and "climbed the hill." The first clause is the sort that attracts no attention, and the second might, indeed, be used to describe a group of boys hunting for blackberries, and not a fierce rush up a height in the face of withering rifle fire.

2. How would you describe the tone of this poem? Before trying to find a single adjective or group of adjectives that describe it, note how carefully controlled the poem is, how tightly it is coiled on itself, and how it possesses something of the concision and authority of words to be engraved for a permanent record, on a memorial stone.

3. What is the effect of line 5? Note the contrast between the "Stone—/ Erect" and the men commemorated, who were "overthrown." Does this pointed contrast serve to sharpen the contrast between victory and that other thing which is "more than victory"?

4. This poem is certainly on the far side of sentimentality. Is it too tight-lipped? Too austere? Too much an "understatement"? To what degree, would you say, does the poet depend here on the reader's involvement or participation? How does he enlist that?

5. Compare the theme of this poem with that of "Sir Patrick Spence." With that of "The Battle of the *Bonhomme Richard* and the *Serapis.*"

With these two poems about death in battle, one might profitably compare another Civil War poem, Whitman's "Come Up from the Fields, Father."

Come Up from the Fields, Father

Walt Whitman [*1819–1892*]

> Come up from the fields father, here's a letter from our Pete,
> And come to the front door mother, here's a letter from thy dear son.
>
> Lo, 'tis autumn,
> Lo, where the trees, deeper green, yellower and redder,
> Cool and sweeten Ohio's villages with leaves fluttering in the moderate
>   wind,   5
> Where apples ripe in the orchards hang and grapes on the trellis'd
>   vines,
> (Smell you the smell of the grapes on the vines?
> Smell you the buckwheat where the bees were lately buzzing?)
> Above all, lo, the sky so calm, so transparent after the rain, and with
>   wondrous clouds,
> Below too, all calm, all vital and beautiful, and the farm prospers well. 10

Down in the fields all prospers well,
But now from the fields come father, come at the daughter's call,
And come to the entry mother, to the front door come right away.

Fast as she can she hurries, something ominous, her steps trembling,
She does not tarry to smooth her hair nor adjust her cap.   15

Open the envelope quickly,
O this is not our son's writing, yet his name is sign'd,
O a strange hand writes for our dear son, O stricken mother's soul!
All swims before her eyes, flashes with black, she catches the main
    words only,
Sentences broken, *gunshot wound in the breast, cavalry skirmish, taken
    to hospital,*   20
At present low, but will soon be better.

Ah now the single figure to me,
Amid all teeming and wealthy Ohio with all its cities and farms,
Sickly white in the face and dull in the head, very faint,
By the jamb of a door leans.   25

Grieve not so, dear mother, (the just-grown daughter speaks through
    her sobs,
The little sisters huddle around speechless and dismay'd)
See, dearest mother, the letter says Pete will soon be better.
Alas poor boy, he will never be better, (nor may-be needs to be better,
    that brave and simple soul,)
While they stand at home at the door he is dead already,   30
The only son is dead.

But the mother needs to be better,
She with thin form presently drest in black,
By day her meals untouch'd, then at night fitfully sleeping, often
    waking,
In the midnight waking, weeping, longing with one deep longing,   35
O that she might withdraw unnoticed, silent from life escape and
    withdraw,
To follow, to seek, to be with her dear dead son.

As in "Somebody's Darling," the stress in this poem is upon the mother and the sisters of the young soldier, now already dead, though the letter which the family have just received simply tells them that he has been wounded. In contrast to "Somebody's Darling," there is no attempt here to describe the young soldier's deathbed, his pallor, his blue-veined skin, his golden hair, and so on. Instead, what his death will mean is dramatized and given objective form through the reactions of the various members of his family. Their hurt is made the clearer by the way in which they clutch onto the hope that he will "soon be better."

The fact that the poem embodies a little drama (the reception of the letter, the calling of the father from the fields, the reaction of the mother and her daughters) provides a way of objectifying the situation so that it does not become simply an obvious play for our sympathy: the situation, faithfully presented, will require no help from a cheerleader.

The realism in this poem also serves the same end: these are simple farm people and there is no talk about "every wandering silken thread" of golden hair or of imagined kisses lying on the dead man's forehead. Finally, the poem is understated rather than overstated. We are told in lines 30–31, rather quietly, with no special fanfare, that "While they stand at home at the door he is dead already, / The only son is dead." One might well ask whether it would not have been better to end the poem just here rather than to carry it on through the last six lines. Could not the poet have relied on the reader's imagination to "fill out" the effect on this family of the subsequent news that the boy had died? But let us observe that in these last lines the poet does not insist on emotional effects. Even the mother's desire to withdraw and be with the dead son is given a tone of factuality; it is not poetically dressed up.

To repeat something pointed out earlier: it is not quite fair to assume that these three poems have the same subject matter and differ therefore only in their tonality. If we want to be accurate about it, no two genuine poems ever have precisely the same subject matter. The death of a young soldier can open out into very different themes. Yet, conceding all this, the three poems can help us to see differences in tone and how important the matter of tone is. For tone and theme are not absolutely different: the tone helps give shape to the particular theme. For tone also has much to do with the emotional power of the poem and its claim upon our sympathies. John Keats said that we resent a poem that has a special design on us. The disciplined reader probably resents most of all such a poem when the design is clearly to work upon our sympathies, especially our more tender sympathies, and when the poet is willing to make use of any device, however mawkish, insistent, or illegitimate, to effect this end. Which of the three poems of this group most obviously has a design upon us? Which of the three obviously risks falling into sentimentality?

There is nothing wrong, it should be emphasized, about emotional response as such. We want to feel deeply: this is one of the reasons why we read literature. But we want the claim on our sympathies to be a just claim, and we want our own emotional response to be "earned" by the poem. We resent being made the dupe of cheap and specious appeals to our response, like the canned laughter on a TV comedy show. The sentimental poem is irritating just here: we are asked to make full payment on a bogus check, to respond deeply to a piece of glib rhetoric—which is a very different thing from a full-bodied imaginative experience that provides adequate motivation for the response for which it asks.

Dulce et Decorum Est

Wilfred Owen   [*1893–1918*]

Bent double, like old beggars under sacks,
Knock-kneed, coughing like hags, we cursed through sludge,
Till on the haunting flares we turned our backs
And towards our distant rest began to trudge.
Men marched asleep. Many had lost their boots   5
But limped on, blood-shod. All went lame; all blind;
Drunk with fatigue; deaf even to the hoots
Of tired, outstripped Five-Nines that dropped behind.

Gas! Gas! Quick, boys! — An ecstasy of fumbling,
Fitting the clumsy helmets just in time;   10
But someone still was yelling out and stumbling
And flound'ring like a man in fire or lime . . .
Dim, through the misty panes and thick green light,
As under a green sea, I saw him drowning.

In all my dreams, before my helpless sight,   15
He plunges at me, guttering, choking, drowning.

If in some smothering dreams you too could pace
Behind the wagon that we flung him in,
And watch the white eyes writhing in his face,
His hanging face, like a devil's sick of sin;   20
If you could hear, at every jolt, the blood
Come gargling from the froth-corrupted lungs,
Obscene as cancer, bitter as the cud
Of vile, incurable sores on innocent tongues,—
My friend, you would not tell with such high zest   25
To children ardent for some desperate glory,
The old Lie: Dulce et decorum est
Pro patria mori.

The title is from the famous sentence in the *Odes* of Horace: "Dulce et decorum est pro patria mori" (It is sweet and fitting to die for the fatherland). The time is World War I; the scene is France. A contingent of British soldiers are on their way back from the trenches to a rest camp in the rear. The "Five-Nines" are artillery shells of a certain caliber that continue to fall, but now behind them. Suddenly there is a wave of poison gas.

Questions
1. Is this a poem with a "message"? If so, what is the message and to whom it is addressed?

2. Consider the phrase "smothering dreams" in line 17. Why is it particularly effective in this context?

3. The poet Yeats disliked Owens's poetry, calling it "all blood, dirt and sucked sugar stick." What do you suppose he meant? Would his judgment apply to this poem? Would it be fair?

4. Compare the tone of this poem with that of the two poems that immediately precede it. Also with Housman's "1887" (p. 117) and Kipling's "Recessional" (p. 120).

C. THE LOVERS GIVE UP THE WORLD

Let the Rest of the World Go By

J. Keirn Brennan [*1873–1948*]

Is the struggle and strife
We find in this life
Really worth while, after all?
I've been wishing today
I could just run away,   5
Out where the west winds call.

CHORUS
With someone like you, a pal good and true,
I'd like to leave it all behind, and go and find
Some place that's known to God alone,
Just a spot to call our own.   10
We'll find perfect peace, where joys never cease,
Out there beneath a kindly sky,
We'll build a sweet little nest, somewhere in the West,
And let the rest of the world go by.

Is the future to hold   15
Just struggles for gold
While the real world waits outside,
Away out on the breast
Of the wonderful West,
Across the great Divide?   20

This popular song of the 1920s, aided by its sentimental melody (by Ernest R. Ball), reinvoked for millions of hearers a daydream which has, for a long time, been fairly constant in universal human experience. The lovers will abandon this crass world, which probably doesn't understand them anyway, and live unto themselves, untroubled by the push and hurry of unfeeling men and women. They will find a sufficient society in themselves and in the beneficent nature that surrounds their idyllic retreat. And the poem also depends considerably on the sentimental myth of the "West"—a kindly and innocent environment.

The wish expressed is thoroughly human, and it is one that everyone has experienced at some time in his life. But it is a daydream, remote from reality, and it constitutes, in essence, a kind of sentimental indulgence. We could take the lovers' wish seriously only if we felt that they had taken fully into account the costs of their decision, were aware of the deprivations and difficulties entailed, and were willing to accept them. (The life of pioneers is notoriously hard.) Most of all, the discerning reader will respond only if these lovers retain a hold on reality, which means, among other things, retaining a sense of humor and an awareness of the absurdity—at least in others' eyes—of what they are proposing to do.

Questions

1. Do you find the first line of the chorus curious? Does the phrase "someone like you" impress you as an impassioned or even adequate description of the one person for whom the lover would abandon the world? The lover seems to be saying that a reasonable facsimile of "you" would do just as well. Or is the poet here merely the lazy victim of the need to pad out his line around the rhyme "you"–"true"?

2. What is the logical sequence of lines 9 and 10? If having a place to "call our own" is all that is required, does he have to seek it in a place known only to God? If, on the other hand, the crucial matter is to get completely away from civilization, won't it follow automatically that, through establishing squatter's rights on unknown and unoccupied land, he will acquire a place "to call our own"? The two lines don't really hang together logically or grammatically.

3. The vagueness of a daydream glimmers also through line 13: "somewhere in the West." Will just any place in the far West do? Will Death Valley do just as well as the shores of Lake Tahoe? The lover is rhapsodizing rather than talking sense. Is it really possible to take this bemused young man seriously?

Maesia's Song

Robert Greene [*1560?–1592*]

Sweet are the thoughts that savor of content;
    The quiet mind is richer than a crown;
Sweet are the nights in careless slumber spent;
    The poor estate scorns Fortune's angry frown.
Such sweet content, such minds, such sleep, such bliss,   5
Beggars enjoy, when princes oft do miss.

The homely house that harbors quiet rest;
  The cottage that affords no pride nor care;
The mean that 'grees with country music best;
  The sweet consort of mirth and music's fare;   10
Obscurèd life sets down a type of bliss:
A mind content both crown and kingdom is.

This song leans on the pastoral conventions* and gains some support from them. The pastoral poet describes life in a simpler world—typically it is a world of shepherds and shepherdesses or of goatherds and milk-maids. In this world, work and play are scarcely distinguishable: the shepherd plays on his pipes as he watches his sheep. Work is rarely drudgery, and the worries that accompany ambition are absent. It is a relaxed and honest world—not strained and tense. (The present-day communes indicate that the idea of the simple life lived close to nature exerts its appeal even today.)

"Let the Rest of the World Go By" belongs to a special tradition too, the notion that somewhere out in the West—west of Europe, or west of the Mississippi, but, in any case, west of wherever we are—life is simpler, happier, and peaceful. This dream has attracted mankind for a long time, just as the pastoral life has for a long time exerted its own spell on sophisticated city people. Actually, the two dreams have a good deal in common.

Why is "Maesia's Song," in its celebration of simple joys, effective, and "Let the Rest of the World Go By" not? Because the pastoral conventions disarm us and prevent our asking of "Maesia's Song" the realistic questions that expose the flimsiness of "Let the Rest of the World Go By"? This is not quite the answer. For the pastoral may also be attacked as giving a false view of life. Sir Walter Raleigh wrote a realistic "reply" to Christopher Marlowe's charming pastoral song "Come Live with Me and Be My Love" and Dr. Samuel Johnson condemned Milton's "Lycidas" (p. 334) out of hand because pastoral conventions were unnatural and artificial. But conventions are formalized and, in one sense or another, "unnatural" expressions—like the convention of shaking hands, or lifting a

* A convention is a technique, method, subject matter, or attitude that has become generally (and usually unconsciously) accepted. Just as we find social conventions (commonly accepted forms of address, manners, ceremonies, and so on) peculiar to a place and time, so with literary (or artistic) conventions. A convention arises as a vital expression or from an actual need and becomes formalized. When something, a poem for instance, seems to be *merely* an empty form, an echo, we say it is conventional. But conventions are a necessary part of society, as of art and literature, and in art and literature they provide the base from which originality and personal force may operate. The pastoral conventions go back as far as Greek literature. In these conventions a complex theme is treated in terms of a simpler and more primitive world, like that, for example, of the shepherds. This may be done ironically, sentimentally, comically, or seriously.

hat. *All* poetry is, in this sense, "conventionalized." The question is how consistently or expressively a convention is used. (See footnote on p. 132.)

A more adequate answer will concern what the poet actually does with his poem—whatever the tradition within which he writes or the conventions on which he depends. In the first place, "Maesia's Song" is thoroughly stylized, and this fact in itself discourages the raising of realistic questions of the sort that the less formal and more vernacular quality of the Brennan lyric tends to invite. In the second place, the twentieth-century writer has gone out of his way to emphasize the matter of place: the fact of living in the West will make all the difference to the lovers' lives, whereas in the Elizabethan lyric it is the mind itself that will make the difference. The "quiet mind"—regardless of place—will find "sweet content."

This is not to say that a good poet could not make a fine poem on the subject of man's desire to escape to some "West" of quiet and freedom. Poets can, and have. The point is that the writer of "Let the Rest of the World By" hasn't done so. He uses a trite idea and does nothing to renew it; he has merely propped it up by a set of clichés. "Maesia's Song," on the other hand, represents a traditional idea rather fully worked out. If the poem celebrates the joys of the simple life, the poem itself is not "simple," but, within its own rather narrow limits, rich and complex. Its use of language is interesting, and it reflects a quick intelligence and not vague daydreaming.

The last observation can be easily illustrated. In line 3, for example, *careless* means not only *easy, spontaneous,* but also *free from care.* In line 9, *mean* signifies the median quality or condition between extremes, but in Elizabethan times it could also signify the intermediate part in any harmonized composition such as that taken by the alto or tenor. In line 10 the word *consort* could in Greene's time mean not only accord or harmony but also *concert,* a word to which it was etymologically related. Thus, lines 9–10 can be read: the median condition (cf. happy mean) that agrees best with country music, the sweet harmony of mirth and the joy that music itself conveys. Thus, Greene's song is a richly organized descant on its theme: the quiet mind is richer than a king's, and the cottage happier than the palace. Lines 7–8 carry a mild paradox. The cottage "harbors" quiet rest because it does *not* have riches capable of sustaining those malcontents, pride and care. Only the wealthy can "afford" to entertain them as guests.

Questions

1. Try to describe the tone of this poem. Is there any development or complication of the tone?

2. Does this poem describe the cave or hut of a hermit? Or is the beloved companion here by implication? In Greene's poem, Maesia, who sings the song, is a woman.

It may be interesting to compare with the two poems just discussed a poem by John Donne, "The Canonization." It is a poem that combines the themes of the two poems we have just considered. The lovers will escape from the corrupting world of the courtier and the merchant to find their happiness in the more complete world of each other. They will, like hermits, live apart from the world, each becoming the other's "hermitage."

This poem does have its special complications, but it begins with a perfectly clear dramatic situation: the lover (who speaks the poem), in a fit of exasperation, is replying to a friend who had been trying to dissuade him from the folly of throwing over a promising career for something as unprofitable as romantic love.

The Canonization

John Donne [*1572–1631*]

For Godsake hold your tongue, and let me love,
  Or chide my palsie, or my gout,
My five gray haires, or ruin'd fortune flout,
With wealth your state, your minde with Arts improve,
    Take you a course, get you a place,   5
    Observe his honour, or his grace,
And the Kings reall, or his stamped face
    Contemplate; what you will, approve,
      So you will let me love.

Alas, alas, who's injur'd by my love?   10
  What merchants ships have my sighs drown'd?
Who saies my teares have overflow'd his ground?
When did my colds a forward spring remove?
    When did the heats which my veines fill
    Adde one man to the plaguie Bill?[1]   15
Soldiers finde warres, and Lawyers finde out still
    Litigious men, which quarrels move,
      Though she and I do love.

Call us what you will, wee'are made such by love;
  Call her one, mee another flye,   20
We'are Tapers too, and at our owne cost die,
And wee in us finde the'Eagle and the Dove;
    The Phoenix ridle hath more wit
    By us, we two being one, are it,
So, to one neutrall thing both sexes fit.   25
    Wee dye and rise the same, and prove
      Mysterious by this love.

[1] the printed list of those who had died each week of the plague in London

Wee can dye by it, if not live by love,
    And if unfit for tombes or hearse
Our legend bee, it will be fit for verse;   30
And if no peece of Chronicle wee prove,
    We'll build in sonnets pretty roomes;
    As well a well wrought urne becomes
The greatest ashes, as halfe-acre tombes,
    And by these hymnes, all shall approve   35
      Us *Canoniz'd* for Love.

And thus invoke us; You whom reverend love
    Made one anothers hermitage;
You, to whom love was peace, that now is rage;
Who did the whole worlds soule extract, and drove   40
    Into the glasses of your eyes,
    So made such mirrors, and such spies,
That they did all to you epitomize,
    Countries, Townes, Courts: Beg from above
    A patterne of your love!   45

First, we must notice that the dazzling display of metaphors, of witty comparisons, and of paradoxes prevents any sense of an indulgent daydream. But in spite of the swiftness of the movement of thought and the difficulties of some of the allusions, the poem makes full sense to a twentieth-century reader—common sense as well as uncommon sense.

The very title can tell us a good deal about the dramatic development of the poem. Saints are "canonized"—that is, the Church declares them to be saints—because of their extraordinary exemplification of Christian love—love of God and of their fellow human beings. The saint gives up the pursuit of wealth, secular ambitions, and everything else that might distract him from God's kingdom. He does so in his desire to devote himself completely to the service of God. The lovers in this poem, so its speaker prophesies, will be "canonized" too, because of their superlative love—though for romantic love, the love that unites a man and woman. Thus, in this poem sacred love becomes a metaphor for the transcendent quality of their human love.

Just as the Christian saint gives up the world of wealth and ambition, so too the lover in this poem abjures the world. In the first stanza the dedicated lover tells his listener to go ahead and run after the gauds of this world if he wants to, but to count the lover out of this self-seeking race. In line 7, the king's real face is the king as seen at court. The king is the fountainhead of social honor and political power, if one can sufficiently gain his favor. On the other hand, the king's stamped face is the sovereign's head as stamped on a coin and represents the world of wealth, for which most men strive.

Stanza 2 carries one stage farther the lover's protest to his friend. Why, he asks, should men enamored of the things of this world object to his love? How can it possibly hinder their pursuit of money, their filing of lawsuits, or their waging of war? The "sighs," "tears," "colds," and "heats" to which the lover refers were the conventional expressions of a passionate Elizabethan lover. (See *Hamlet,* II, scene i. We don't use these terms today, but we have our own twentieth-century variants of them: one is "crazy" about a girl; she leaves him "all shook up," and so on.) Notice that the lover does not play down the absurdity of such extreme expressions of his lovesickness. In fact, he almost jokingly and with ironic self-deprecation turns the absurdity to his own account: thus, if he sighs as a lover, that wind is scarcely enough to sink a ship, and, however much he has wept, it hasn't flooded anybody's farm. The expressions of his passion are personal and private: they do not have any effect on the public domain.

The poem is, we see, a kind of dramatic monologue. To the friend who is trying to convince him that his course is one of folly, the lover presents further arguments. Stanza 3 suggests that the friend has made some disparaging comparisons (hinted at in lines 19 and 20) that the lovers are like moths attracted to the candle's flame, and certain to perish by their own nonsensical conduct. The lover, instead of rejecting such analogies, devises more of them as the very substance of his argument. The lovers are well aware of how the great world regards them. They are not only like the moth about to singe its wings in the flame, but also like the candle itself, which is consumed in shedding light. Or the lover is like the eagle, an emblem of masculine strength, and his loved one, like the dove, type of feminine gentleness. Then the lover proceeds to combine two of the earlier-mentioned comparisons, those of birds and burning. The lovers are like that fabulous bird the phoenix which, when it comes to the time of its death, builds itself a nest, which it then sets on fire, burning itself to ashes, out of which a new phoenix arises. In line 26 he declares, "Wee dye and rise the same." This last figure has an additional significance. The phoenix combines masculine and feminine qualities (i.e., eagle and dove), for it propagates itself, not as other birds do, but by renewing itself through fire and making its death the occasion for its rebirth.

In saying that "Wee dye and rise the same," the lover draws one further inference from his comparison of the lovers to the phoenix. In the Renaissance, "to die," when used in certain contexts, carried a sexual meaning: it meant to experience the climax of the sexual act. Thus the lovers are like the "mysterious" and supernatural phoenix. Their love, which is more than mere sexual appetite, does not exhaust itself in the satisfaction of appetite so that they turn away from the bed of love in listlessness, having gratified the flesh. They "rise the same," as much in love as ever.

The next stanza is connected with the preceding by a repetition of the word *die*. If they cannot live by love—"on love," in the modern idiom—in the thriving and competitive world, they can die by it and are willing to do so. Like the Christian martyr, they embrace death (an elaboration of the sexual meaning of the word), and through it they will win their place in the canon as saints of love. True, they will figure in no "Chronicle," for chronicles record great historical events and matters of secular importance. But they will leave a legend. (A "legend" was originally the story of a saint's life.) Their story will be recorded in "sonnets"—that is, love poetry—and it is better to have one's ashes preserved in such a receptacle—the well wrought sonnet or the well wrought urn—than to be entombed in some vulgar and monstrous building that covers half an acre.

The last stanza treats of their future as saints of love. All lovers will invoke their prayers as two saints who, in giving up the world of affairs, found a better and more complete world. The lovers will be revered as those who found in each other an appropriate hermitage and found, paradoxically, in retiring from the world, the very "soul" of the world. Looking into each other's eyes, they look upon all that they had abandoned, for the very essence of the living world is epitomized in their relation to each other.

The reader may question the propriety of comparing this massive poem with the flimsy little lyric from Tin Pan Alley quoted above on page 130. Surely one does not need to bring up a howitzer in order to annihilate a gnat. Yet it may be important, at this stage of our discussion, to make as emphatically as possible certain important distinctions. John Donne, in imagining his lover's rejection of the world in order to devote himself to one person, felt no need to turn off his intellect or to erase from his consciousness what the world would think of the divine absurdity of what he proposed to do. For Donne, the contemplation of the lovers' retreat from the world does not require putting the mind to sleep but actually entails a heightened consciousness. Here the poet does not ignore or flee from the hard realistic context of the lovers' situation: he recognizes it, and actually exploits it.

By contrast, the tone of "Let the Rest of the World Go By" is all too simply that of sentimental reverie. Any old cliché will do to describe the details—such as there are—of the reverie. The word "nest" (for the house that the lovers will build) carries little more meaning than that of unpretentious coziness. If it suggests that the occupants are really "lovebirds," that association is unimportant and is certainly not developed by the writer of the lyric. Compared with the place of retreat described in "The Canonization," the modern lovers' abode does little more than satisfy the need for a rhyming word (nest : west).

D. A GARLAND OF LOVE POEMS

What has been said about Donne's "Canonization" does *not* mean, of course, that an authentic love poem must have a complex structure or a complicated development. Consider, for example, the following poem:

Western Wind

Anonymous

> Western wind, when wilt thou blow,
> The[1] small rain down can[2] rain?
> Christ, if my love were in my arms
> And I in my bed again!

This poem is often praised as uttering the pure lyric cry, the naked expression of feeling. But under the apparent simplicity, the poem may not be so simple after all, and the hint of complexity may be what establishes the sense of full emotional expression, not in having denied certain aspects of experience, but in having absorbed them.

Let us call attention to a contrast in tone between the first two lines and the fourth line, with the third line as a kind of transition between them. The first two lines give the pure romantic cry, the appeal to the wind and the rain that they come to relieve the aridity and deadness of the lover's loneliness. This is expansive; it would involve all nature in a response to the lover's plight. Even the third line continues something of this expansive treatment; that is, the exclamation "Christ" continues the excitement of the earlier part, and, too, the phrase "in my arms" has a romantic implication. But with the last line a change occurs. The generalized romantic excitement, with its expansiveness and vagueness, is all at once brought down to the realistic and literal, with all the realistic and literal implications:

> And I in my bed again!

The tone of the last line works to make the whole poem more credible and acceptable. It gives a context—a hint of the full human and physical context—for the romantic cry. Therefore, we "believe" the cry. Aware-

---

[1] i.e., "that the"   [2] i.e., "can begin to"

ness of context: that is another way of saying what we usually suggest when we use the phrase "poetic sincerity," as contrasted with personal sincerity? In that case, "Western Wind" would represent a small-scale example of poetic sincerity; "The Canonization," a large-scale instance.

Questions

1. Do you find any other realistic detail that we have not mentioned?
2. Suppose the last line read:

Then my soul might bloom again.

What difference would this make to you?

3. Compare the tone of this poem with that of "Let the Rest of the World Go By."

When Love Meets Love

Thomas Edward Brown [*1830–1897*]

When love meets love, breast urged to breast,
God interposes,
An unacknowledged guest,
And leaves a little child among our roses.

We love, God makes: in our sweet mirth   5
God spies occasion for a birth.
Then is it His, or is it ours?
I know not—He is fond of flowers.

O, gentle hap!
O, sacred lap!   10
O, brooding dove!
But when he grows
Himself to be a rose,
God takes him—where is then our love?
O, where is all our love?   15

Questions

1. In this poem does God become a "guest," though entertained unawares, or does the poet seem to make of Him a Peeping Tom?
2. What is the—effect of "spies" (line 6)? What is the effect of line 8?
3. Is it reasonable to suppose that the author was here trying to give some complexity of tone, but simply was not aware of some of the absurd or comic implications? (This is not to say, of course, that comic implications may not be used for serious effects; see p. 189, "Mr. Flood's Party.")
4. Conceding that the idea behind this poem is a serious and profound one (the idea of love as a sacramental act), does the poem render the idea

worthily, or does it debase the idea? In other words, is the poem incoherent and sentimental?

5. Notice that in Donne's "The Canonization" the idea of love as a sacramental act is also present. But Donne, though he makes the lovers' abandonment of the world for each other really an analogue of the saints' rejection of the world, nevertheless does not fall into incoherence, but works out the analogy with full logic. Would you agree? If not, why not?

Fatima

Alfred, Lord Tennyson [1809–1892]

O Love, Love, Love! O withering might!
O sun, that from thy noonday height
Shudderest when I strain my sight,
Throbbing thro' all thy heat and light,
   Lo, falling from my constant mind,   5
   Lo, parch'd and wither'd, deaf and blind,
   I whirl like leaves in roaring wind.

Last night I wasted hateful hours
Below the city's eastern towers:
I thirsted for the brooks, the showers: 10
I roll'd among the tender flowers:
   I crush'd them on my breast, my mouth:
   I look'd athwart the burning drouth
   Of that long desert to the south.

Last night, when some one spoke his name,   15
From my swift blood that went and came
A thousand little shafts of flame
Were shiver'd in my narrow frame.
   O Love, O fire! once he drew
   With one long kiss my whole soul thro'   20
   My lips, as sunlight drinketh dew.

Before he mounts the hill, I know
He cometh quickly: from below
Sweet gales, as from deep gardens, blow
Before him, striking on my brow.   25
   In my dry brain my spirit soon,
   Down-deepening from swoon to swoon,
   Faints like a dazzled morning moon.

The wind sounds like a silver wire,
And from beyond the noon a fire   30
Is pour'd upon the hills, and nigher
The skies stoop down in their desire;
   And isled in sudden seas of light,

My heart, pierced thro' with fierce delight,
Bursts into blossom in his sight.   35

My whole soul waiting silently,
All naked in a sultry sky,
Droops blinded with his shining eye:
I *will* possess him or will die.
    I will grow round him in his place,   40
    Grow, live, die looking on his face,
    Die, dying clasp'd in his embrace.

Questions

1. Fatima is presumably a Moorish maiden longing for the return of her lover. Her passion is a burning flame. Note how many images of intense heat and light as from a blazing sun are to be found in this poem.

2. Is this source of light and heat, however, always treated as beneficent and life-giving ("Bursts into blossom," line 35)? What do you make of such expressions as "withering might" (line 1), "faints like a dazzled morning moon" (line 28), "fierce delight" (line 34), "sultry sky" (line 37), and "Droops blinded" (line 38)?

3. Fatima is obviously completely committed to her lover. But is she a victim, a woman suffering and perhaps likely to suffer more? Or is she a happy prospective bride?

4. The second stanza (with its reference to the coolness of "brooks" and "showers") was added later, as an afterthought. Why do you think the poet chose to add it?

5. As first published, this poem had as a Greek epigraph a quotation from Sappho, which might be translated: "This man to me seems equal to the gods." Does the epigraph fit the poem?

6. Notice the emphatic and insistent use of rhyme throughout the poem. Suppose the poem were without rhyme, for example, in the first stanza:

O Love, Love, Love! O withering might
O sun, that from thy very zenith
Shudderest when I strain my eyes,
Throbbing through all thy heat and brilliance,
    Lo, falling from my constant mind,
    Lo, parched and withered, deaf and dumb,
    I whirl like leaves in a roaring blast.

What difference would this make in the effect of the poem? Relate this question to Fatima's attitude.

Let Me Not to the Marriage of True Minds

William Shakespeare [*1564-1616*]

Let me not to the marriage of true minds
Admit impediments. Love is not love

Which alters when it alteration finds,
Or bends with the remover to remove:
O, no! it is an ever-fixèd mark   5
That looks on tempests and is never shaken;
It is the star to every wandering bark,
Whose worth's unknown, although his height be taken.
Love's not Time's fool, though rosy lips and cheeks
Within his bending sickle's compass come;   10
Love alters not with his brief hours and weeks,
But bears it out even to the edge of doom.
If this be error and upon me proved,
I never writ, nor no man ever loved.

Questions

1. Work out in detail the implied as well as the developed images. What
is the relation among the various images? Is the imagery inconsistent or
confused?

2 What is the meaning of "Love's not Time's fool"? And of "bending
sickle's compass"?

3. What is the tone of the poem? How does the poet avoid a tone of
extravagant protestation?

If Thou Must Love Me

Elizabeth Barrett Browning   [*1806–1861*]

If thou must love me, let it be for nought
Except for love's sake only. Do not say,
"I love her for her smile—her look—her way
Of speaking gently,—for a trick of thought
That falls in well with mine, and certes brought   5
A sense of pleasant ease on such a day,"—
For these things in themselves, Belovèd, may
Be changed, or change for thee,—and love so wrought
May be unwrought so. Neither love me for
Thine own dear pity's wiping my cheeks dry: 10
A creature might forget to weep, who bore
Thy comfort long, and lose thy love thereby.
But love me for love's sake, that evermore
Thou mayst love on through love's eternity.

Questions

1. Try to state exactly what is being said here. What is loving "for love's
sake"? The previous sonnet has spoken of love's permanence, but is that
the same thing as loving for love's sake? Or does it assume some basis for
love that is not assumed here? We are familiar with the remark that some
young person is "in love with love" (that is, with the experience of love)

and not with some actual person. Such a lover creates the beloved from imagination, not facts. Can you distinguish the love "for love's sake only" in the poem here from the adolescent's dream love?

2. Try to describe the tone of this poem in comparison with that of the previous one and with that of "Western Wind."

Lullaby

W. H. Auden [1907–1973]

Lay your sleeping head, my love,
Human on my faithless arm;
Time and fevers burn away
Individual beauty from
Thoughtful children, and the grave   5
Proves the child ephemeral:
But in my arms till break of day
Let the living creature lie,
Mortal, guilty, but to me
The entirely beautiful.   10

Soul and body have no bounds:
To lovers as they lie upon
Her tolerant enchanted slope
In their ordinary swoon,
Grave the vision Venus sends   15
Of supernatural sympathy,
Universal love and hope;
While[1] an abstract insight wakes
Among the glaciers and the rocks
The hermit's carnal ecstasy.   20

Certainty, fidelity
On the stroke of midnight pass
Like vibrations of a bell,
And fashionable madmen raise
Their pedantic boring cry: 25
Every farthing of the cost,
All the dreaded cards foretell,
Shall be paid, but from this night
Not a whisper, not a thought,
Not a kiss nor look be lost.   30

Beauty, midnight, vision dies:
Let the winds of dawn that blow
Softly round your dreaming head
Such a day of sweetness show
Eye and knocking heart may bless,   35

[1] i.e., "Whereas an abstract," etc.

Find the mortal world enough;
Noons of dryness see you fed
By the involuntary powers,
Nights of insult let you pass
Watched by every human love.   40

In "Western Wind" the lover aches to be once more beside the loved one.
Only in that relationship will he find fulfillment and peace; but he does not
lie beside her now. In "Lullaby" the two lovers do lie beside one another
and there is fulfillment, but the lover who speaks the poem looks on beyond
this present experience of joy and wonder.

The subtitle of the poem might well be "Love without Illusions," for the
loved one (lines 1–2) is not really "divine," but "human," and the lover's
arm on which the sleeping head lies is, as the speaker too well knows,
"faithless" (line 2). Human beings grow old, lose their beauty, as do their
fellow mammals, and eventually die.

Questions

1. Is the speaker, then, disillusioned and cynical? Does he say that the
vision of "supernatural sympathy, Universal love and hope" sent by the
sensual experience of sexual love is merely an illusion to be dismissed?
If you think such would be a wrong interpretation, indicate why.

2. What is the point of bringing in the reference to the "hermit's carnal
ecstasy" in the second stanza? Does this reference help explain the
speaker's attitude toward love?

3. The poem asserts that love is little more than a fleeting illusion in
contrast to the hard actualities of life. How does this idea find expression in
the poem?

4. Can one realize the flimsiness of the human base on which an experience of transcendence rests, and yet believe that the transcendence is
authentic and the experience one of priceless value? Explain your view.

5. In the last stanza, the speaker seems to be uttering a prayer for the
loved one. Is the prayer, do you feel, a sincere one? In this connection discuss the meaning of the two phrases "Find the mortal world enough"—
enough for what?—and "by every human love."

6. In a footnote to the poem (line 18) we have called attention to the
meaning "whereas" of the word *while*. But it can be argued that the
notion of simultaneity is also significant here. The sense of "whereas" is,
shall we say, basic, but both processes are always going on, at the same
time, in the world. Furthermore, images as given in the poem coexist
in the imagination, like figures on a fresco.

7. The poet, as we have pointed out, realizes that love is subject to all
the accidents of human nature and human life. If this is the realistic context of the "human love," why does the poet use such a lyrical style, a style
marked by verbal flow and musicality? What does this contrast have to do
with setting a tone for the poem? Try to imagine what the difference would

be if the poet had used a rather hard and prosaic style in, perhaps free verse.

8. "Western Wind" and "Fatima" deal with love as an immediate passion. The sonnets by Shakespeare and Elizabeth Barrett Browning deal with it as an enduring force—a spiritual force, shall we say. The poem by Auden assumes passion but a passion naturally transitory and known by the lover to be transitory but nevertheless having a spiritual component. Does the attitude of a particular poem here determine the value of that poem? There is no ready and easy and "correct" answer for such a question. But it is a constantly recurring one.

E. THE MISER AND THE SPENDTHRIFT

Lord Byron's satire, *Don Juan,* held up to varying degrees of scorn a great many aspects of the early nineteenth century, both in Great Britain and on the Continent. Some of the best sections constitute an attack on the British Establishment in the period 1818–1824, some fifteen to twenty years before Victoria ascended the throne. The following section (lines 49–88 of Canto XII) deals with a variety of topics, but the primary emphasis of the verses here is on money and the love of wealth.

from

Don Juan

George Gordon, Lord Byron [*1788–1824*]

> Why call the miser miserable? as
>   I said before: the frugal life is his,
> Which in a saint or cynic ever was
>   The theme of praise: a hermit would not miss
> Canonization for the self-same cause.   5
>   And wherefore blame gaunt wealth's austerities?
> Because, you'll say, nought calls for such a trial;—
> Then there's more merit in his self-denial.
>
> He is your only poet;—passion, pure
>   And sparkling on from heap to heap, displays,   10
> *Possess'd,* the ore, of which *mere hopes* allure
>   Nations athwart the deep: the golden rays
> Flash up in ingots from the mine obscure;
>   On him the diamond pours its brilliant blaze;
> While the mild emerald's beam shades down the dyes   15
> Of other stones, to soothe the miser's eyes.

The lands on either side are his; the ship.
   From Ceylon, Inde, or far Cathay, unloads
For him the fragrant produce of each trip;
   Beneath his cars of Ceres[1] groan the roads,   20
And the vine blushes like Aurora's[2] lip;
   His very cellars might be kings' abodes;
While he, despising every sensual call,
Commands—the intellectual lord of all.

Perhaps he hath great projects in his mind,   25
   To build a college, or to found a race,
A hospital, a church—and leave behind
   Some dome surmounted by his meagre face:
Perhaps he fain would liberate mankind
   Even with the very ore which makes them base;   30
Perhaps he would be wealthiest of his nation,
Or revel in the joys of calculation.

But whether all, or each, or none of these
   May be the hoarder's principle of action,
The fool will call such mania a disease:—   35
   What is his *own?* Go—look at each transaction,
Wars, revels, loves—do these bring men more ease
   Than the mere plodding through each "vulgar fraction"?
Or do they benefit mankind? Lean miser!
Let spendthrifts' heirs inquire of yours—who's wiser?   40

In his own life, Byron scarcely practiced what he seems to preach in these verses that praise the miser. But this is perhaps a way of saying that the verses are not a "preachment" at all, but a witty descant on the power of money, a commentary in which his mock-serious celebration of the miser's virtues is a way of needling all sorts of people: the stern moralist, the sentimentalist, and in general the habits and practices of the bourgeois citizen. In line 1 Byron's word-play on "miser" and "miserable" has a sound etymological basis. Both words come from the same Latin root, and a miser was originally a miserable person, "a wretch."

Questions

1. What is the speaker's real belief? From what moral base does he direct his commendations and his censures? If his proof that the miser is really better than the saint or the poet is spoken tongue-in-cheek, what is the true target of his satirical shots? Or does the speaker occupy any stable moral or intellectual base? Is his merely a free-wheeling satire?

2. Try to define the tone of this passage. The student ought to take into account the general high spirits of the passage, the sometimes forced and amusing rhymes, the *pot pourri* of the diction, the sudden digressions,

[1] Roman goddess of grain   [2] goddess of the dawn

the slap-dash quality, and even the rhythmical pattern. All of these have their effect in telling us how we are to "take" the sentiments expressed.

Here follows another poem about money and property. It also has a satiric tone, and here too the speaker indulges in some mock serious commendation, though Johnson's mock-commendation is addressed, not to the miser but to his opposite, the profligate: more particularly, to a young heir who has just come into his fortune. (Incidentally, Lord Byron, especially in his younger years, might almost have served, had he flourished in Johnson's lifetime, for a model of the conduct of a young heir. He ran into debt quite promptly after coming of age and later had to sell the ancestral seat, Newstead Abbey.)

To a Young Heir

Samuel Johnson [*1709–1784*]

Long-expected one-and-twenty,
   Ling'ring year, at length is flown:
Pride and pleasure, pomp, and plenty,
   Great * * * * * * *, are now your own.

Loosened from the minor's tether,   5
   Free to mortgage or to sell,
Wild as wind, and light as feather,
   Bid the sons of thrift farewell.

Call the Betsies, Kates, and Jennies,
   All the names that banish care;   10
Lavish of your grandsire's guineas,
   Show the spirit of an heir.

All that prey on vice and folly
   Joy to see their quarry fly:
There the gamester, light and jolly,   15
   There the lender, grave and sly.

Wealth, my lad, was made to wander,
   Let it wander as it will:
Call the jockey, call the pander,
   Bid them come and take their fill.   20

When the bonny blade carouses,
   Pockets full, and spirits high—
What are acres? What are houses?
   Only dirt, or wet or dry.

Should the guardian friend or mother   25
   Tell the woes of willful waste,
Scorn their counsel, scorn their pother;—
   You can hang or drown at last!

Questions

1. Here, under the guise of sympathetic advice, Johnson says what to the "Young Heir"?

2. How much does Johnson identify himself with the attitude of the heir? The heir is a "bonny blade"—a gay dashing young fellow, above such vulgar considerations as property—and generous, even generous to a fault. Take the phrase "Wild as wind." Isn't there some hint of approbation in this—applause at the sense of freedom and strength? Even if it is made ambiguous by the phrase "light as feather"? Ambiguity of attitude—an irony that pretends to give approbation, praise, and sympathy even while it condemns—is at the very center of the poem. It sets the tone of the poem. What other examples of this ironical tone can you isolate in the poem?

3. What is the tone of the last line? Does it differ from that of the body of the poem?

4. How would you characterize the rhythm of the poem? How would you describe the relation of this rhythm to the tone of the poem?

5. Compare and contrast as fully as you can the tone of this poem with that of the excerpt from "Don Juan" which precedes it.

Provide, Provide

Robert Frost [*1874–1963*]

> The witch that came (the withered hag)
> To wash the steps with pail and rag,
> Was once the beauty Abishag.[1]
>
> The picture pride of Hollywood.
> Too many fall from great and good   5
> For you to doubt the likelihood.
>
> Die early and avoid the fate.
> Or if predestined to die late,
> Make up your mind to die in state.
>
> Make the whole stock exchange your own!   10
> If need be occupy a throne,
> Where nobody can call *you* crone.
>
> Some have relied on what they knew;
> Others on being simply true.
> What worked for them might work for you.   15
>
> No memory of having starred
> Atones for later disregard,
> Or keeps the end from being hard.

[1] the name of the beautiful maiden whom the Hebrew elders put into bed with old King David when he was feeble and ill; when, though "covered . . . with clothes . . . [he] gat no heat"; see 1 Kings, 1:1–4.

Better to go down dignified
With boughten friendship at your side   20
Than none at all. Provide, provide!

Questions

1. This poem is also about money and, as the title indicates, the necessity of holding on to our money with which we are enjoined to provide ourselves. Johnson ironically consoles the profligate heir by telling him that even if he has thrown his money away, he doesn't have to live in penury. He can always "hang or drown at last!" In Frost's poem the advice, ostensibly at least, takes a very different form. It amounts to this: for goodness' sake, hold on to enough money to allow you to die in comfort and in state. But what is the tone of the poem? Are we here also being offered only mock-serious advice?

2. What is the relation of lines 13–15 to the rest of the poem? These lines have the air of having been almost casually interpolated—as if they constituted an aside that interrupts only momentarily the main argument of the poem. What is their importance in the poem? How do they qualify the general tone of the poem—if at all?

F. AGAINST THE ESTABLISHMENT

London

William Blake [*1757–1827*]

I wander through each chartered street,
Near where the chartered Thames does flow
And mark in very face I meet
Marks of weakness, marks of woe.

In every cry of every man,   5
In every infant's cry of fear,
In every voice; in every ban,
The mind-forged manacles I hear:

How the chimney-sweeper's cry
Every blackening church appalls,   10
And the hapless soldier's sigh
Runs in blood down palace-walls.

But most, through midnight streets I hear
How the youthful harlot's curse
Blasts the new-born infant's tear,   15
And blights with plagues the marriage-hearse.

Questions

1 What is the meaning of *chartered* in lines 1 and 2? What does the poet gain by repeating *mark* in lines 3 and 4? Does it have the effect of childish repetition? Or what?

2. In the eighteenth century, children were employed as chimney-sweepers. Does this help account for the fact that the chimney-sweeper's cry appalls the church?

3. The speaker says that he hears the "mind-forged manacles" in every cry. In what sense do the various cries mentioned come under this description? Does the youthful harlot's voice serve as a climax to these cries? How?

4. How would you describe the tone of this poem?

from
Beppo
George Gordon, Lord Byron   [*1788–1824*]

"England! with all thy faults I love thee still,"
    I said at Calais,[1] and have not forgot it;
I like to speak and lucubrate my fill;
    I like the government (but that is not it);
I like the freedom of the press and quill;   5
    I like the Habeas Corpus (when we've got it);[2]
I like a parliamentary debate,
Particularly when 'tis not too late;

I like the taxes, when they're not too many;
    I like a seacoal fire, when not too dear;   10
I like a beef-steak, too, as well as any;
    Have no objection to a pot of beer;
I like the weather, when it is not rainy,
    That is, I like two months of every year,
And so God save the Regent, Church, and King!   15
Which means that I like all and everything.

Our standing army, and disbanded seamen,
    Poor's rate, Reform, my own, the nation's debt,
Our little riots just to show we are free men,
    Our trifling bankruptcies in the Gazette,   20
Our cloudy climate, and our chilly women,
    All these I can forgive, and those forget,
And greatly venerate our recent glories,
And wish they were not owing to the Tories.

[1] on his final departure from England, Byron had landed in Calais, France   [2] the writ of habeas corpus allows an indicted man to be set free on a bail bond before his trial; Byron hints that the writ was frequently suspended at the pleasure of the government

Byron wrote "Beppo: A Venetian Story" in 1817. The stanzas quoted represent one of the several digressions from the tale, a personal aside in which he pays his respects to the England he had left a year before as a man self-exiled after the breakup of his marriage.

Questions

1. Line 1 is a quotation from a poem by William Cowper, a heartfelt utterance. In what tone of voice does Byron speak it?

2. What is the tone of the whole passage? Savage irony? Bitter sarcasm? Playful banter? Or what? Try to describe the tone and give your reasons for your way of characterizing it.

England in 1819

Percy Bysshe Shelley [*1792–1822*]

> An old, mad, blind, despised and dying king;
> Princes, the dregs of their dull race, who flow
> Through public scorn—mud from a muddy spring;
> Rulers, who neither see, nor feel, nor know,
> But leech-like to their fainting country cling,   5
> Till they drop, blind in blood, without a blow;
> A people starved and stabbed in the untilled field;
> An army which liberticide and prey
> Makes as a two-edged sword to all who wield;
> Golden and sanguine laws which tempt and slay;   10
> Religion Christless, Godless—a book sealed;
> A Senate—Time's worst statute unrepealed,
> Are graves from which a glorious Phantom may
> Burst to illumine our tempestuous day.

Questions

1. The England that is described in this poem is basically the England that Byron described in the preceding poem. The old, mad, and dying king of line 1 is George III, soon to be succeeded by his son, the Regent. The two poets pretty well agree on what the situation is, but their attitudes toward it—at least as reflected in their two poems—are vastly different. Try to describe the difference.

2. Shelley seems more bitter than Byron, yet at the same time more optimistic. What are the grounds for this optimism? Does the comparison of England's rulers to leeches reflect this optimism? If so, how?

3. What is the tone of Shelley's sonnet? Is the tone consistent? In short, is the poem all of a piece?

4. Unlike Byron, Shelley depends fundamentally here on imagery to convey his attitude. How does the imagery relate to the tone?

An Elementary School Classroom in a Slum

Stephen Spender [*1909–*]

Far far from gusty waves, these children's faces,
Like rootless weeds the torn hair round their paleness.
The tall girl with her weighed-down head. The paper-
Seeming boy with rat's eyes. The stunted unlucky heir
Of twisted bones, reciting a father's gnarled disease,   5
His lesson from his desk. At back of the dim class
One unnoted, mild and young: his eyes live in a dream
Of squirrels' game, in tree room, other than this.

On sour cream walls, donations. Shakespeare's head
Cloudless at dawn, civilized dome riding all cities.   10
Belled, flowery, Tyrolese valley. Open-handed map
Awarding the world its world. And yet, for these
Children, these windows, not this world, are world,
Where all their future's painted with a fog,
A narrow street sealed in with a lead sky,   15
Far far from rivers, capes, and stars of words.

Surely Shakespeare is wicked, the map a bad example
With ships and sun and love tempting them to steal—
For lives that slyly turn in their cramped holes
From fog to endless night? On their slag heap, these children   20
Wear skins peeped through by bones, and spectacles of steel
With mended glass, like bottle bits in slag.
Tyrol is wicked; map's promising a fable:
All of their time and space are foggy slum,
So blot their maps with slums as big as doom.   25

Unless, governor, teacher, inspector, visitor,
This map becomes their window and these windows
That open on their lives like crouching tombs
Break, O break open, till they break the town
And show the children to the fields and all their world   30
Azure on their sands, to let their tongues
Run naked into books, the white and green leaves open
The history theirs whose language is the sun.

Questions

1. Why does the poet say that "Surely Shakespeare is wicked" (line 17)?

2. In what sense can the boy be said to be "reciting a father's gnarled disease" (line 5)? How are the windows of the classroom related to the pictures and maps on the classroom wall? Examine the imagery of the slag heap in stanza 3.

3. How is the last stanza related to the rest of the poem? Is it a preachment, direct and explicit? Is the tone closer to Byron's or Shelley's, in the previous examples? What about general method?

4. Compare the theme of this poem with that of Blake's "London." Both poems (not to mention Wordsworth's "Westminster Bridge," p. 91) deal with one city, though in different ages, and involve the same or closely related themes. Compare the tone of this poem with that of Blake's and Wordsworth's poems.

Joe Hill

Alfred Hayes [*1911–*]

I dreamed I saw Joe Hill last night
Alive as you and me.
Says I, "But Joe you're ten years dead."
"I never died," says he.
"I never died," says he. 5

"In Salt Lake, Joe," says I to him,
Him standing by my bed,
"They framed you on a murder charge."
Says Joe, "But I ain't dead."
Says Joe, "But I ain't dead." 10

"The copper bosses killed you, Joe,
They shot you, Joe," says I.
"Takes more than guns to kill a man,"
Says Joe, "I didn't die,"
Says Joe, "I didn't die." 15

And standing there as big as life
And smiling with his eyes,
Joe says, "What they forgot to kill
Went on to organize,
Went on to organize." 20

"Joe Hill ain't dead," he says to me,
"Joe Hill ain't never died.
Where working men are out on strike
Joe Hill is at their side,
Joe Hill is at their side." 25

"From San Diego up to Maine,
In every mine and mill,
Where workers strike and organize,"
Says he, "You'll find Joe Hill,"
Says he, "You'll find Joe Hill." 30

I dreamed I saw Joe Hill last night,
Alive as you or me.
Says I, "But Joe, you're ten years dead,"
"I never died," says he,
"I never died," says he.   35

Joseph Hillstrom emigrated from Sweden to the United States in 1902 and, after bumming around the country for several years, became a member of the radical labor organization called the Industrial Workers of the World (the "Wobblies"). He actually composed one of their more famous songs, a parody of the Salvation Army song "In the Sweet Bye and Bye." In 1914, still a drifter, Hill was indicted and convicted of robbery and murder. Innocent or guilty, Hill's trial was a legal farce, and in spite of a number of protests, including two telegrams from President Wilson, he was executed by firing squad on November 19, 1915, and became a hero of American labor under the name of Joe Hill.

Questions

1. What is the effect of the ballad conventions here? Suppose the first stanza ran as follows and set a pattern for the whole:

I dreamed I saw Joe Hill alive last night,
In all the flush of health and manhood's might.
"But, Joe, you're dead!" in my surprise I cried.
And he: "Death was but your dream, I've never died!"

What difference would the change of form make?

2. Describe the tone of the poem.

Sam Hall

Anonymous

Oh, my name it is Sam Hall,
Oh, my name it is Sam Hall,
Oh, my name it is Sam Hall, and I hate you one and all,
You're a bunch of muckers all,
Damn your eyes, damn your eyes.   5

Oh, I killed a man 'tis said, so 'tis said,
Oh, I killed a man 'tis said, and I bashed his bloody head,
And I left him there for dead,
    (And I kicked him where he bled).

Oh, they took me to the quad, to the quad,   10
Oh, they took me to the quad,
    and they left me there, by God,
With a ball and chain and rod,

Now the preacher he did come, he did come,
Now the preacher he did come,   15
   and he looked so God-damn glum,
As he talked of Kingdom Come,
   (He can kiss my ruddy bum).

Oh, the sheriff he come too, he come too,
Oh, the sheriff he come too, with his little boys in blue,   20
Sayin', "Sam, we'll see you through,"

Oh, it's up the rope I go, up I go,
Oh, it's up the rope I go, with those bastards down below,
Sayin', "Sam, we told you so,"

I saw Nellie in the crowd, in the crowd,   25
I saw Nellie in the crowd,
   and she looked so stooped and bowed,
That I hollered right out loud,
   ("Hey Nellie! Ain't you proud!")
(Like to see her in her shroud.)   30

Let this be my parting knell, parting knell,
Let this be my parting knell, hope to see you all in Hell,
Hope to hell you sizzle well,

It's in Heaven now I dwell, now I dwell,
It's in Heaven now I dwell, and it is a bloody cell,   35
All the whores are down in Hell,
Damn their eyes, damn their eyes,
All the whores are down in Hell, God damn their eyes.

"Sam Hall" was originally an English ballad, springing from the hanging of one Jack Hall, a chimney sweep, in 1701. The first Sam Hall
version was composed and sung by a comic minstrel in London about
1850. The song then became widely popular in the cowboy culture of
the American West with various folk modifications, often obscene.

Questions
In "Joe Hill," what is the grievance against society? What is Hill's
role? What is Sam Hall's grievance? In what sense, if any, can he be
said to demand admiration? Connect the answer to that question with
your description of the tone of the poem.

For the Union Dead
Robert Lowell [*1917–*]

Relinquunt Omnia Servare Rem Publicam

The old South Boston Aquarium stands
in a Sahara of snow now. Its broken windows are boarded.

The bronze weathervane cod has lost half its scales.
The airy tanks are dry.

Once my nose crawled like a snail on the glass;   5
my hand tingled
to burst the bubbles
drifting from the noses of the cowed, compliant fish.

My hand draws back. I often sigh still
for the dark downward and vegetating kingdom   10
of the fish and reptile. One morning last March,
I pressed against the new barbed and galvanized

fence on the Boston Common. Behind their cage,
yellow dinosaur steamshovels were grunting
as they cropped up tons of mush and grass   15
to gouge their underworld garage.

Parking spaces luxuriate like civic
sandpiles in the heart of Boston.
A girdle of orange, Puritan-pumpkin colored girders
braces the tingling Statehouse,   20

shaking over the excavations, as it faces Colonel Shaw
and his bell-cheeked Negro infantry
on St. Gaudens' shaking Civil War relief,
propped by a plank splint against the garage's earthquake.

Two months after marching through Boston,   25
half the regiment was dead;
at the dedication,
William James could almost hear the bronze Negroes breathe.

Their monument sticks like a fishbone
in the city's throat.   30
Its Colonel is as lean
as a compass-needle.

He has an angry wrenlike vigilance,
a greyhound's gentle tautness;
he seems to wince at pleasure,   35
and suffocate for privacy.

He is out of bounds now. He rejoices in man's lovely,
peculiar power to choose life and die—
when he leads his black soldiers to death,
he cannot bend his back.   40

On a thousand small town New England greens,
the old white churches hold their air
of sparse, sincere rebellion; frayed flags
quilt the graveyards of the Grand Army of the Republic.

The stone statues of the abstract Union Soldier   45
grow slimmer and younger each year—
wasp-waisted, they doze over muskets
and muse through their sideburns . . .

Shaw's father wanted no monument
except the ditch,   50
where his son's body was thrown
and lost with his "niggers."

The ditch is nearer.
There are no statues for the last war here;
on Boylston Street, a commercial photograph   55
shows Hiroshima boiling

over a Mosler Safe, the "Rock of Ages"
that survived the blast. Space is nearer.
When I crouch to my television set,
the drained faces of Negro school-children rise like balloons.   60

Colonel Shaw
is riding on his bubble,
he waits
for his blessèd break.

The Aquarium is gone. Everywhere,   65
giant finned cars nose forward like fish;
a savage servility
slides by on grease.

The Latin epigraph may be translated "They gave up everything to serve the Republic." Colonel Robert Gould Shaw (1837–1863) commanded a regiment of black troops in the Civil War. He was killed at the head of his troops in an assault on Fort Wagner in South Carolina. When it was proposed that Shaw's body be recovered and buried in Boston, Shaw's father refused, deeming it proper that he should be buried in the common grave with his troops. William James (1842–1910), the philosopher and psychologist, and Booker T. Washington (1856–1915) spoke at the Boston ceremony at which a sculptured relief by Augustus Saint-Gaudens (1848–1907) was dedicated in Shaw's memory.

Questions

1. Two mementoes of wars fought by the United States are described in this poem: the relief in bronze showing Colonel Shaw riding at the head of his troops and a picture of the atomic bomb exploding over Hiroshima. The two representations are contrasted for what purpose and with what effect?

2. What is the poet's implied criticism of modern America?

3. What is the tone of this poem? Righteous indignation? Scathing indictment? Sorrowful resignation? Or what?

Puzzled

Langston Hughes [*1902–1967*]

Here on the edge of hell
Stands Harlem—
Remembering the old lies,
The old kicks in the back,
The old, *Be patient,*   5
They told us before.

Sure, we remember.
Now, when the man at the corner store
Says sugar's gone up another two cents,
And bread one,   10
And there's a new tax on cigarettes—
We remember the job we never had,
Never could get,
And can't have now
Because we're colored.   15

So we stand here
On the edge of hell
In Harlem
And look out on the world
And wonder   20
What we're gonna do
In the face of
What we remember.

Questions

1. Does this poem voice a threat to American society? Or make a plea for better treatment? Or does the poem, formally at least, simply put a question to the victims of the society? Is the title of the poem relevant to such questions?

2. Compare and contrast this poem in the matter of tone with Blake's "London" (p. 149) and Shelley's "England in 1819" (p. 151).

Kitchenette Building

Gwendolyn Brooks [*1917–*]

We are things of dry hours and the involuntary plan,
Grayed in, and gray. "Dream" mate, a giddy sound, not strong
Like "rent," "feeding a wife," "satisfying a man."

But could a dream send up through onion fumes
Its white and violet, fight with fried potatoes   5

And yesterday's garbage ripening in the hall,
Flutter, or sing an aria down these rooms,

Even if we were willing to let it in,
Had time to warm it, keep it very clean,
Anticipate a message, let it begin?   10

We wonder. But not well! not for a minute!
Since Number Five is out of the bathroom now,
We think of lukewarm water, hope to get in it.

Questions

1. Who are the "we" in this poem? How do they regard themselves?
With contempt? Pity? Or what?
2. Note lines 8–13. How do you "warm" a dream? Or "keep it very
clean"? What is meant? Can you connect line 3 with line 9?
3. Describe the tone of this poem.

If We Must Die

Claude McKay [*1890–1948*]

If we must die—let it not be like hogs
Hunted and penned in an inglorious spot,
While round us bark the mad and hungry dogs,
Making their mock at our accursed lot.
If we must die—oh, let us nobly die,   5
So that our precious blood may not be shed
In vain; then even the monsters we defy
Shall be constrained to honor us though dead!
Oh, Kinsmen! We must meet the common foe;
Though far outnumbered, let us show us brave,   10
And for their thousand blows deal one death-blow!
What though before us lies the open grave?
Like men we'll face the murderous, cowardly pack,
Pressed to the wall, dying, but fighting back!

Question

Write a brief commentary on the tone of this poem, making specific
references to details in it.

A Supermarket in California

Allen Ginsberg [*1926–*]

What thoughts I have of you tonight, Walt Whitman, for I walked
on the sidestreets under the trees with a headache self-conscious
looking at the full moon.

In my hungry fatigue, and shopping for images, I went into the neon fruit supermarket, dreaming of your enumerations!

What peaches and what penumbras! Whole families shopping at night! Aisles full of husbands! Wives in the avocados, babies in the tomatoes!—and you, García Lorca,[1] what were you doing down by the watermelons?

I saw you, Walt Whitman, childless, lonely old grubber, poking among the meats in the refrigerator and eyeing the grocery boys.

I heard you asking questions of each: Who killed the pork chops? What price bananas? Are you my Angel?   9

I wandered in and out of the brilliant stacks of cans following you, and followed in my imagination by the store detective.

We strode down the open corridors together in our solitary fancy tasting artichokes, possessing every frozen delicacy, and never passing the cashier.

Where are we going, Walt Whitman? The doors close in an hour. Which way does your beard point tonight?

(I touch your book and dream of our odyssey in the supermarket and feel absurd.)

Will we walk all night through solitary streets? The trees add shade to shade, lights out in the houses, we'll both be lonely.   10

Will we stroll dreaming of the lost America of love past blue automobiles in driveways, home to our silent cottage?

Ah, dear father, graybeard, lonely old courage-teacher, what America did you have when Charon[2] quit poling his ferry and you got out on a smoking bank and stood watching the boat disappear on the black waters of Lethe?[3]

Berkeley 1955

Questions

1. Is this poem about Walt Whitman or about modern America? Does Ginsberg use one to make a criticism of the other? If so, what is his criticism?

2. Why do you suppose the poet presents Whitman as lonely, solitary, and childless? Could Whitman, if alive today, be expected to frequent supermarkets? Why?

3. What is the point of Ginsberg's referring to "the lost America of love" (line 11)?

4. What is the poet's attitude toward modern America? Indifference? Contempt? Scorn? Sorrowful regret? Or what?

[1] Federico García Lorca, a Spanish poet murdered by Rightists in 1936, during the Spanish Civil War   [2] in Greek mythology, the boatman who ferried the souls of the dead across the river Styx to begin their life in Hades, the underworld   [3] another river of the underworld, the river of forgetfulness

5. To what extent do you think the historical contrast between the old America and the new justifies Ginsberg's attitude?

Afterword

In this section we have thus far considered thirty poems (in whole or in part) and we have found that there are as many varieties of tone as there are poems, for, as even a little consideration makes plain, the tone of a poem is an aspect of its individual quality.

From this perspective, the rubrics under which we have grouped these thirty poems are obviously very general labels. They have, for our purposes, a certain convenience, but they really tell us very little about the poems grouped under them. They do not, for instance, tell us much about the precise theme, and they tell us nothing at all about what the poet in question does with his theme.

In working through this section, we have seen how the poet's mastery of tone can give depth and authority to sentiments that might otherwise be merely vapid, or can give amplitude and resonance to statements which as naked assertions would be only banal truisms.

Though in the interests of clarity and clear definition most of our examples are meant to illustrate one fairly simple tonal quality, we have included a number of poems that show a complex development of tone or abrupt shifts in tone. In "The Canonization" (p. 134), for example, the tone shifts from one of exasperation (or at least mock-exasperation) in the first two stanzas to something very close to exultation in the last two stanzas. The prayer with which the poem ends—the invocation that the speaker imagines future lovers will use to address himself and his loved one as saints of love—has been all but drained of irony. If it is in some sense a parody of the invocation of two literal saints, it is a serious invocation in its own right.

Lines 13–15 of "Provide, Provide" (p. 148) demand a very different tone of voice from those that precede and those that follow. The abruptness of the shift is, to be sure, somewhat disguised. The lines are spoken almost as an aside, but only a very careless reading will dismiss the tonal change as unimportant. It has everything to do with the true import of the poem.

For a striking example of an abrupt change in tone, the reader might look at "A Litany" (p. 185). Here we find in the last stanza a complete reversal of that of the opening stanza.

Since tone is an important aspect of all poetry, the reader will do well to apply to the poems that follow all that he has learned thus far in reading the poems in this section. He might find it well to turn back to poems read earlier in this text and see how a focus of attention on tone and attitude can enrich his understanding of poems previously studied under the more general rubrics of dramatic situation and description.

RHYTHM AND METER: 3

In Section 1 you have already encountered several poems in free verse* and have, no doubt, considered the question of what principles of form, if any, might be relevant to them. Furthermore, in Section 2 the first five selections and two others in the main group are in free verse, with six more in the Supplemental Poems. See Appendix B, pp. 560–575, for a discussion of form in free verse.

Questions

1. Comment on the principle of the rhythmical composition manifested in "Waking in the Blue," by Robert Lowell (p. 39).

2. Turn to Whitman's "Battle of the *Bonhomme Richard* and the *Serapis*" (p. 31). Mark the accents, primary and secondary, of the first twenty lines. Are these accents basically rhetorical or metrical? What is the basis of the divisions of the poem into stanzas, or sections? Comment on the choice of descriptive detail throughout the poem.

3. How would you help an inexperienced reader to grasp the form of Ammons's "Hardweed Path Going" (p. 407)?

4. Here is the opening passage from Allen Ginsberg's "Howl." Compare the rhythms of this with those of "Battle of the *Bonhomme Richard* and the *Serapis*" and Williams's "By the Road to the Contagious Hospital" (p. 570).

> I saw the best minds of my generation destroyed by madness, starving
>   hysterical naked,
> dragging themselves through the negro streets at dawn looking for an
>   angry fix,
> angelheaded hipsters burning for the ancient heavenly connection to the
>   starry dynamo in the machinery of night,
> who poverty and tatters and hollow-eyed and high sat up smoking in the
>   supernatural darkness of cold-water flats floating across the tops
>   of cities contemplating jazz,
> who bared their brains to Heaven under the El and saw Mohammedan
>   angels staggering on tenement roofs illuminated,
> who passed through universities with radiant cool eyes hallucinating
>   Arkansas and Blake-light tragedy among the scholars of war,
> who were expelled from the academies for crazy & publishing obscene odes
>   on the windows of the skull,
> who cowered in unshaven rooms in underwear, burning their money in
>   wastebaskets and listening to the Terror through the wall,
> who got busted in their pubic beards returning through Laredo with a
>   belt of marijuana for New York,

5. Describe the technical aspects of "A Supermarket in California." How would you state the difference in rhythmic effect in "A Supermarket . . ." and Whitman's "Come Up from the Fields, Father"?

6. Choose a stanza from Keats's "To Autumn" and recast it into free verse.

* "Mama and Daughter," "Battle of the *Bonhomme Richard* and the *Serapis*," and "Waking in the Blue."

7. Find a passage of prose that seems to have some poetic quality and transpose it into free verse.

8. Reread Tennyson's "Blow, Bugle, Blow" (p. 94) and the commentary. We have said that the basic tension of the poem, as in "To Autumn" (p. 87), is between the melancholy of the passing of time and yet the sense of vibrant beauty that comes with it. Take line 3:

> ⌣ / // / ⌣ / ⌣ /
> The long | light shakes | across | the lakes.

Here, with the secondary accent inserted, the massing of accents in the first two feet and the alliteration give an emphasis and a focus for the visual imagery.

To take line 4:

> / ⌣ // / ⌣⌣ / ⌣ / ⌣
> ∧ And | the wild cat | aract leaps | in glo | ry*

Thus far we have been dealing with the relation of the metrics to the sense of vitality and excitement in the beauty of the scene. Up to this point in the first stanza, and indeed through line 5, there has been a prevailingly *rising rhythm,* even though lines 2, 4, and 5 have feminine endings. It is true, too, that line 5 opens with a trochee, as we see if we scan it:

> / // ⌣ / / ⌣ // / ⌣ / ⌣
> Blow, bu | gle, blow, |∧ set | the wild ech | oes fly | ing †

Here, though the first foot is trochaic, the falling effect is largely negated by the strong secondary accent on the second syllable (bú-) and the rising rhythm that sets in almost immediately after it.

But let us look at line 6. It is the nature of all pattern, including of course metrical pattern, to set up expectation of repetition, and since we expect line 6 to repeat line 5, we may scan it thus:

> / // ⌣ / ⌣ / ⌣ / ⌣ / ⌣ / ⌣
> Blow, bu | gle, an | swer, ech | oes, dy | ing, dy | ing, dy | ing

---

* There are possible variations in the scansion here. For example.

> ⌣ ⌣ / / ⌣⌣ / ⌣ / ⌣
> And the wild |∧ cat | aract leaps | in glor | y

But for our purposes here the difference is not crucial. The big difference lies in the accent on *And* in our first version. See the discussion of "Rose Aylmer," pp. 517–519, particularly Question 2 on p. 519. Can you think of other reasonable scansions? It is possible, in fact, that Tennyson would have used:

> ⌣ ⌣ / / ⌣ ⌣ / ⌣ / ⌣
> And the wild |∧ cata | ract leaps | in glo | ry

† Or possibly:

> / ⌣ // / ⌣ / ⌣
> . . . | set the | wild ech | oes fly | ing

But this difference would not effect our point.

This scansion, abstractly* considered, is acceptable, but every word except *blow* itself (which even so appears in a trochaic foot) is a word which, taken in itself, constitutes a trochee, and furthermore a trochee set off by commas to emphasize its individual rhythm; so, in spite of the metrical pattern, there is a strong rhetorical pull toward a falling rhythm, a situation that is emphasized by the fact that the length of the line, with six, not five, feet, makes it easier for the falling movement to establish itself.

To sum up, the stanza opens and proceeds for some lines with a strong rising movement with exciting dramatic variations. Then, in contrast to this, a positive falling rhythm sets in, most marked in the last, fading-away line. This contrast supports the contrast in feeling and idea in the poem.

9. Return to "The Echoing Green" (p. 30) and the commentary. There are some general similarities between the general idea of this poem and those of "To Autumn" and "Blow, Bugle, Blow." But comment on any differences that strike you. Comment on technique in relation to the idea and the "feel" of the poem. Look especially at the last line of the poem. Suppose it were changed to read:

> In the dark of the Green.

Would this alter the effect in any way? After all, the word *darkening* has, taken in isolation, a falling rhythm.

10. What rhythmic qualities are shown by "Somebody's Darling" and "Let the Rest of the World Go By"?

11. Compare the tone of "To a Young Heir" with the tone of "Provide, Provide."

Supplemental Poems

G. EVE IN THE GARDEN

Eve

Ralph Hodgson [*1872–1962*]

> Eve, with her basket, was
> Deep in the bells and grass,
> Wading in bells and grass
> Up to her knees,
> Picking a dish of sweet   5

---

* As we have said, meter, in one sense, is always abstract. But it does affect the rhythmic experience. See Appendix B, p. 503.

Berries and plums to eat,
Down in the bells and grass
Under the trees.

Mute as a mouse in a
Corner the cobra lay,   10
Curled round a bough of the
Cinnamon tall. . . .
Now to get even and
Humble proud heaven and
Now was the moment or   15
Never at all.

"Eva!" Each syllable
Light as a flower fell,
"Eva!" he whispered the
Wondering maid,   20
Soft as a bubble sung
Out of a linnet's lung,
Soft and most silverly
"Eva!" he said.

Picture that orchard sprite,   25
Eve, with her body white,
Supple and smooth to her
Slim finger tips,
Wondering, listening,
Listening, wondering,   30
Eve with a berry
Half-way to her lips.

Oh had our simple Eve
Seen through the make-believe!
Had she but known the   35
Pretender he was!
Out of the boughs he came,
Whispering still her name.
Tumbling in twenty rings
Into the grass.   40

Here was the strangest pair
In the world anywhere,
Eve in the bells and grass
Kneeling, and he
Telling his story low. . . .   45
Singing birds saw them go
Down the dark path to
The Blasphemous Tree.

Oh, what a clatter when
Titmouse and Jenny Wren   50

Saw him successful and
Taking his leave!
How the birds rated him,
How they all hated him!
How they all pitied   55
Poor motherless Eve!

Picture her crying
Outside in the lane,
Eve, with no dish of sweet
Berries and plums to eat,   60
Haunting the gate of the
Orchard in vain. . . .
Picture the lewd delight
Under the hill tonight—
"Eva!" the toast goes round,   65
"Eva!" again.

Questions

1. How would you describe the tone of Hodgson's poem? Or if you prefer to put the question as one of attitude, how would you characterize the poet's attitude toward Eve? Toward the whole episode? What are the indications of his attitude? Is there a development or a complication of the attitude, or does it remain fairly simple?

2. In attempting to describe the tone of this poem, what weight do you give the poet's calling his heroine "our simple Eve" (line 33)? Or his referring to her as "poor motherless Eve!" (line 56)? Or his having the birds chatter at the serpent in excited scolding (lines 53–54)? (For the latter item there is justification in actuality. Birds, with good warrant, are afraid of snakes and scream at, sometimes attack, them.) What effect on the tone, if any, is provided by the indignation of the birds and their sympathy for Eve?

3. What is the force of the last stanza? Does it act to modernize the situation? Does it make Eve a girl of our own day? Is this poem about the fall of man at all? Or is it about the loss of one girl's innocence? Or about neither subject, in the last analysis?

Eve

Arthur J. Bull   [*1903–*   ]

There was great beauty by the Tree,
Less sense, I fear, and wit;
She showed herself a harlotry,
And did as she thought fit.
The knees uncrossed in Paradise   5
Were fatal to our kind—
O that the Boss had given her
More brain and less behind!

If she had not opened up 10
To Adam her man, and made
Men, there would have been no
Strife, and sparring with spade;
And all our piling woes
Stopped at the very Spring—
Innocent as the rose 15
Then, each rejoicing Spring.

This poem is a piece of conscious irreverence. God becomes "the Boss"; Eve is pictured as a rather brainless sex object; and Eve's fall something other than a matter of the seduction of a guileless girl.

Milton in his *Paradise Lost* was very careful to indicate that there was sexual love between Adam and Eve before the Fall had occurred. In fact, Milton introduces into his poem a hymn to married love, in which he proclaims it pure and holy. In Bull's poem, Eve's fall seems to consist entirely in her coupling with Adam. Had she not done so, strife, hard work, and the other woes that afflict mankind would not have come into being, for the good reason that there would have been no mankind to cause such trouble, and only nature, innocent as the rose, would have revived with each new spring season.

Questions

1. What is the poet's attitude toward Eve? Toward sex? And toward the human race? Is the poem simply an innocent *jeu d'esprit*—a twitting of Milton and of the Genesis story? Or is it something else?

2. What is the difference between Hodgson's calling Eve "our simple Eve" and Bull's noting that she could have used "more brain"? What are the associations of "simple"? Of "brainless"? Does the emphasis on brain or lack of it make Eve's fall a matter of sheer intelligence? Or of calculation? For example, a cynical gold-digger could lose out because she didn't have enough intelligence. Is intelligence, "wit," lack of brains, the pivotal matter in the story as Hodgson tells it? Was Eve's fall or the Fall of Man primarily a matter of simplicity and ignorance?

In the passage from *Paradise Lost* (Book IX) that follows, Eve has bade Adam farewell and has departed to work by herself in the garden. The human pair have so much to do "to dress [the garden] and to keep it," as God had commanded, that Eve proposes that they separate. She feels that they spend so much time in talk and dalliance that the growth is getting ahead of them. Adam hesitates to accept her proposal, but is finally won over and bids her goodbye. As someone has remarked, when specialization of work comes into being, work is separated off from play, and the possibility of drudgery is introduced. When all this happens, the Fall of Man is imminent. It does come speedily enough, as Milton tells the story.

from
Paradise Lost

John Milton [*1608–1674*]

Her long with ardent look his Eye pursu'd
Delighted, but desiring more her stay.
Oft he to her his charge of quick returne
Repeated, shee to him as oft engag'd
To be returnd by Noon amid the Bowre,   5
And all things in best order to invite
Noontide repast, or Afternoons repose.
O much deceav'd, much failing, hapless *Eve,*
Of thy presum'd return! event perverse!
Thou never from that houre in Paradise   10
Foundst either sweet repast, or sound repose;
Such ambush hid among sweet Flours and Shades
Waited with hellish rancor imminent
To intercept thy way, or send thee back
Despoild of Innocence, of Faith, of Bliss.   15
For now, and since first break of dawne the Fiend,
Meer Serpent in appearance, forth was come,
And on his Quest, where likeliest he might finde
The onely two of Mankinde, but in them
The whole included Race, his purposd prey.   20
In Bowre and Field he sought, where any tuft
Of Grove or Garden-Plot more pleasant lay,
Thir tendance or Plantation for delight,
By Fountain or by shadie Rivulet
He sought them both, but wish'd his hap might find   25
Eve separate, he wish'd, but not with hope
Of what so seldom chanc'd, when to his wish,
Beyond his hope, *Eve* separate he spies,
Veild in a Cloud of Fragrance, where she stood,
Half spi'd, so thick the Roses bushing round   30
About her glowd, oft stooping to support
Each Flour of slender stalk, whose head though gay,
Carnation, Purple, Azure, or spect with Gold,
Hung drooping unsustain'd, them she upstaies
Gently with Mirtle band, mindless the while,   35
Her self, though fairest unsupported Flour,
From her best prop so farr, and storm so nigh.
Neerer he drew, and many a walk travers'd
Of stateliest Covert, Cedar, Pine, or Palme,
Then voluble and bold, now hid, now seen   40
Among thick-wov'n Arborets and Flours
Imborderd on each Bank, the hand of *Eve:*
Spot more delicious then those Gardens feign'd

Or of reviv'd *Adonis,* or renownd
Alcinous, host of old *Laertes* Son,   45
Or that, not Mystic, where the Sapient King
Held dalliance with his faire *Egyptian* Spouse.
Much hee the Place admir'd, the Person more.
As one who long in populous City pent,
Where Houses thick and Sewers annoy the Aire,   50
Forth issuing on a Summers Morn to breathe
Among the pleasant Villages and Farmes
Adjoynd, from each thing met conceaves delight,
The smell of Grain, or tedded Grass, or Kine,
Or Dairie, each rural sight, each rural sound;   55
If chance with Nymphlike step fair Virgin pass,
What pleasing seemd, for her now pleases more,
She most, and in her look summs all Delight.
Such Pleasure took the Serpent to behold
This Flourie Plat, the sweet recess of Eve   60
Thus earlie, thus alone; her Heav'nly forme
Angelic, but more soft, and Feminine,
Her graceful Innocence, her every Aire
Of gesture or lest action overawd
His Malice, and with rapine sweet bereav'd   65
His fierceness of the fierce intent it brought:
That space the Evil one abstracted stood
From his own evil, and for the time remaind
Stupidly good, of enmitie disarm'd,
Of guile, of hate, of envie, of revenge;   70
But the hot Hell that alwayes in him burnes,
Though in mid Heav'n, soon ended his delight,
And tortures him now more, the more he sees
Of pleasure not for him ordain'd.

The poet wishes to emphasize Eve's beauty and her innocence, but he never forgets that she is at this point in the poem still unfallen, perfect woman, the mother of the human race; and so he invests her with dignity and a certain stateliness. Thus, if she is like a wood nymph as imagined in the old pagan times, she is also like Pomona, the Roman goddess of fruits, or Ceres, the august Roman goddess of grain. Indeed, Milton tries in this passage to strike some sort of balance between her innate dignity and the pathos of her unprotected innocence. Thus, in lines 29–37 she is likened to the very flowers that she is tending in the paradisiacal garden. She "upstaies" the drooping flowers "Gently with Mirtle band," but is "mindless the while" that she "Her self, though fairest unsupported Flour," is "From her best prop so farr, and storm so nigh."

Then, shifting the angle of vision, the poet lets us see Eve through the eye of Lucifer as, concealed within the serpent, he lurks in the pleasant garden. In lines 49–58 he is like a person who has been long shut up in the polluted air of a city but who now is taking a walk on a summer morning "Among the pleasant Villages and Farmes," enjoying the smell of grain or grass cut for hay, and sees passing some fair virgin who "in her look summs all Delight"—that is, all his sense of freshness and natural beauty and burgeoning fertility. Indeed, the poet says, her "graceful Innocence" actually overawed the devil's malice, so that "the Evil one abstracted stood / From his own evil, and for the time remain'd / Stupidly good."

If Milton has associated Eve first with pagan goddesses and wood nymphs, he goes on to humanize her by likening her to an English village girl whose very innocence and country grace captures the fancy of a sophisticated man of the city—in this case, the newly arrived citizen of Hell.

Questions

1. Which of these three poems is the most "puritanical" in your opinion? What attitude toward sex is implied in each poem?

2. Would you say that Hodgson and Milton are perhaps closer in their attitudes toward Eve than one might have thought possible? Has Hodgson borrowed from Milton? If you think so, indicate what.

3. Look up the word "stupid" in a large dictionary. What is the etymological meaning? With this in mind, reflect on the meaning of Milton's desciption of Lucifer as "Stupidly good" (line 69).

4. Write a brief comparison of the attitudes taken toward Eve in the three poems.

H. MODERN WAR

A Utilitarian View of the Monitor's *Fight*

Herman Melville [*1819–1891*]

> Plain be the phrase, yet apt the verse,
>   More ponderous than nimble;
> For since grimed War here laid aside
> His Orient pomp, 'twould ill befit
>   Over much to ply   5
>   The rhyme's barbaric cymbal.
>
> Hail to victory without the gaud
>   Of glory; zeal that needs no fans
> Of banners; plain mechanic power

Plied cogently in War now placed—   10
    Where War belongs—
Among the trades and artisans.

Yet this was battle, and intense—
    Beyond the strife of fleets heroic;
Deadlier, closer, calm 'mid storm;   15
No passion; all went on by crank,
    Pivot, and screw,
And calculations of caloric.

Needless to dwell; the story's known.
    The ringing of those plates on plates   20
Still ringeth round the world—
The clangor of that blacksmiths' fray.
    The anvil-din
Resounds this message from the Fates:

War shall yet be, and to the end;   25
    But war-paint shows the streaks of weather;
War yet shall be, but warriors
Are now but operatives; War's made
    Less grand than Peace,
And a singe runs through lace and feather.   30

It was on March 9, 1862, that the *Monitor* slugged it out to a draw
with the *Virginia,* which the Confederates had rebuilt as an ironclad
from the captured Federal frigate *Merrimac.* The arrival of the *Monitor*
saved the Federal fleet, for, the day before, the *Virginia* had begun to
play havoc with the wooden ships of the Federal navy. This first battle
of armored craft thus marked a turning point in naval warfare.

Questions
    1. Why does Melville demand a "plain" phrase for this poem?
    2. Metrically (except for lines 2, 6, and 21), this poem is consistent in
the stanza pattern. But the rhythmical effect is very different in, for example, the first and second stanzas. Can you see a reason for the difference?
Do subsequent stanzas follow, in general, the rhythmical effect of the
first stanza or of the second?

The Death of the Ball Turret Gunner
Randall Jarrell [*1914–1965*]

From my mother's sleep I fell into the State
And I hunched in its belly till my wet fur froze.
Six miles from earth, loosed from its dream of life,
I woke to black flak and the nightmare fighters.
When I died they washed me out of the turret with a hose.   5

Questions

1. Try to characterize the tone of this poem. Is it ragingly bitter? Or coldly sarcastic? Or what?

2. Who is speaking the poem? What is his implied attitude toward war? Toward his death? Toward other men?

3. What are the implications of the first two lines? How does one "fall" into the "State"? How can the ball turret be called the State's "belly"? What is the meaning of "my mother's sleep"? Is this poem *merely* about war?

The Fury of Aerial Bombardment

Richard Eberhart   [*1904–*   ]

You would think the fury of aerial bombardment
Would rouse God to relent; the infinite spaces
Are still silent. He looks on shock-pried faces.
History, even, does not know what is meant.

You would feel that after so many centuries   5
God would give man to repent; yet he can kill
As Cain could, but with multitudinous will,
No farther advanced than in his ancient furies.

Was man made stupid to see his own stupidity?
Is God by definition indifferent, beyond us all?   10
Is the eternal truth man's fighting soul
Wherein the Beast ravens in its own avidity?

Of Van Wettering I speak, and Averill,
Names on a list, whose faces I do not recall
But they are gone to early death, who late in school   15
Distinguished the belt feed lever from the belt holding pawl.

Questions

1. This poem invites comparison with Hardy's "Channel Firing" (p. 45). Compare and contrast the poems in their attitudes toward war, in their attitudes toward God, and in their attitudes toward ordinary men.

2. Why, in the last stanza, does the poet use such technical terms as "belt feed lever" or mention the names of his students who went into the war? Does such precision have an influence on the tone? If so, how?

3. What is the meter of this poem? Note the many extra syllables that have to be absorbed in the line (for example, lines 7, 10, and 15). What is the effect of these variations?

4. Is there a difference in tone between the first three quatrains and the last? Discuss this point.

Naming of Parts

Henry Reed [*1914–*]

Today we have naming of parts. Yesterday,
We had daily cleaning. And tomorrow morning,
We shall have what to do after firing. But today,
Today we have naming of parts. Japonica
Glistens like coral in all of the neighboring gardens,   5
    And today we have naming of parts.

This is the lower sling swivel. And this
Is the upper sling swivel, whose use you will see,
When you are given your slings. And this is the piling swivel,
Which in your case you have not got. The branches   10
Hold in the gardens their silent, eloquent gestures,
    Which in our case we have not got.

This is the safety-catch, which is always released
With an easy flick of the thumb. And please do not let me
See anyone using his finger. You can do it quite easy   15
If you have any strength in your thumb. The blossoms
Are fragile and motionless, never letting anyone see
    Any of them using their finger.

And this you can see is the bolt. The purpose of this
Is to open the breech, as you see. We can slide it   20
Rapidly backwards and forwards: we call this
Easing the spring. And rapidly backwards and forwards
The early bees are assaulting and fumbling the flowers:
    They call it easing the Spring.

They call it easing the Spring: it is perfectly easy   25
If you have any strength in your thumb: like the bolt,
And the breech, and the cocking-piece, and the point of balance,
Which in our case we have not got; and the almond-blossom
Silent in all of the gardens and the bees going backwards and forwards,
    For today we have naming of parts.   30

Question

  Is the tone of this poem more like that in Whitman (pp. 31, 126), Owen (p. 129), Melville, Jarrell, or Eberhart?

The Leg

Karl Shapiro [*1913–*]

Among the iodoform, in twilight-sleep,
What have I lost? he first inquires,
Peers in the middle distance where a pain,

Ghost of a nurse, hastily moves, and day,
Her blinding presence pressing in his eyes   5
And now his ears. They are handling him
With rubber hands. He wants to get up.

One day beside some flowers near his nose
He will be thinking, *When will I look at it?*
And pain, still in the middle distance, will reply,   10
At what? and he will know it's gone,
O where! and begin to tremble and cry.
He will begin to cry as a child cries
Whose puppy is mangled under a screaming wheel.

Later, as if deliberately, his fingers   15
Begin to explore the stump. He learns a shape
That is comfortable and tucked in like a sock.
This has a sense of humor, this can despise
The finest surgical limb, the dignity of limping,
The nonsense of wheel-chairs. Now he smiles to the wall: 20
The amputation becomes an acquisition.

For the leg is wondering where he is (all is not lost)
And surely he has a duty to the leg;
He is its injury, the leg is his orphan,
He must cultivate the mind of the leg,   25
Pray for the part that is missing, pray for peace
In the image of man, pray, pray for its safety,
And after a little it will die quietly.

The body, what is it, Father, but a sign
To love the force that grows us, to give back   30
What in Thy palm is senselessness and mud?
Knead, knead the substance of our understanding
Which must be beautiful in flesh to walk,
That if Thou take me angrily in hand
And hurl me to the shark, I shall not die!   35

Questions

1. This poem could be said to trace an amputee's "adjustment" to the loss of his leg. But is the tone of the last stanza consonant with what "adjustment" usually implies? What is the tone of the last stanza? What is the tone of the first?

2. What is the tone of the fourth stanza? Serious whimsy? Self-irony? What can the poet possibly mean by writing "He must cultivate the mind of the leg"? Is this part of the poem a piece of nonsense? If not, what is the poet up to here?

I. DEATH AND MOURNING

After the Burial

James Russell Lowell   [*1819–1891*]

Yes, faith is a goodly anchor;
  When skies are sweet as a psalm,
At the bows it lolls so stalwart,
  In its bluff, broad-shouldered calm.

And when over breakers to leeward   5
  The tattered surges are hurled,
It may keep our head to the tempest,
  With its grip on the base of the world.

But, after the shipwreck, tell me
  What help in its iron thews,   10
Still true to the broken hawser,
  Deep down among sea-weed and ooze?

In the breaking gulfs of sorrow,
  When the helpless feet stretch out
And find in the deeps of darkness   15
  No footing so solid as doubt,

Then better one spar of Memory,
  One broken plank of the Past,
That our human heart may cling to,
  Though hopeless of shore at last!   20

To the spirit its splendid conjectures,
  To the flesh its sweet despair,
Its tears o'er the thin-worn locket
  With its anguish of deathless hair!

Immortal? I feel it and know it,   25
  Who doubts it of such as she?
But that is the pang's very secret—
  Immortal away from me.

There's a narrow ridge in the graveyard
  Would scarce stay a child in his race,   30
But to me and my thought it is wider
  Than the star-sown vague of Space.

Your logic, my friend, is perfect,
  Your moral most drearily true;
But, since the earth clashed on *her* coffin,   35
  I keep hearing that, and not you.

Console if you will, I can bear it;
   'Tis a well-meant alms of breath;
But not all the preaching since Adam
   Has made Death other than Death.   40

It is pagan; but wait till you feel it,—
   That jar of our earth, that dull shock
When the plowshare of deeper passion
   Tears down to our primitive rock.

Communion in spirit! Forgive me,   45
   But I, who am earthly and weak,
Would give all my incomes from dreamland
   For a touch of her hand on my cheek.

That little shoe in the corner,
   So worn and wrinkled and brown,   50
With its emptiness confutes you,
   And argues your wisdom down.

This poem raises some difficult problems—in particular, the problem of whether deep personal sincerity can validate and guarantee poetry. We know, for example, that Lowell's poem was written as the expression of deep personal grief. Yet many readers, including sensitive and intelligent readers, have indicated that they believed it to be a bad poem, inauthentic, full of banalities and sentimentalities. Is it possible, however, for evident sincerity to contrive poetry that is hollow and false, or pretentious and cheap? In order to deal with this general question, let us put some specific questions about this poem.

Questions

1. The poem insists over and over again on the difficulty of accepting consolation. And the point is well taken: it may be very difficult where the loss is great and the wound to the spirit fresh. But is this insistence simply mechanical? Does the poem seem to go anywhere? Does the experience show any development? Or control? Does it resemble a child in a tantrum of hurt feelings rather than a person of some maturity trying to make sense of a deeply shocking experience?

2. No poem can be as immediate in its intensity as a child's wail or a grown man's bitter sobbing. But then a poem does not compete with such immediate intensity—such animal "sincerity." A poem is not a matter of instinctive cries. It is made of words. Words are more reflective than cries. If we want poetry at all, as opposed to the expression of raw emotion, we have to accept the fact of words, and this means that an attitude has moved into the realm of interpretation and even of a certain mastery of the emotion of grief. How are the words used in this poem? Do they give us items of experience freshly perceived, or are they closer to the lingo of the popular song and the advertising agency? For example,

what about "thin-worn locket," the "anguish of deathless hair," "incomes from dreamland," or the "worn and wrinkled and brown" child's shoe?

3. Read Landor's "Rose Aylmer" (p. 517). The situation portrayed there is different from that treated in Lowell's poem. Rose Aylmer is presumably the sweetheart of the speaker, not his little daughter. Nevertheless, "Rose Aylmer" will show what may be gained—even in poignance and emotional intensity—through form, control, and a sense of restraint. State in your own words the general difference in method between that poem and Lowell's.

4. It has been asserted that this poem represents a crude assault on our human sympathies, a kind of emotional bullying. What, if anything, can be said for this view? Can you point out examples from the text of the poem?

5. What lines or passages in this poem do you find most effective?

A Refusal to Mourn the Death, by Fire, of a Child in London

Dylan Thomas   [*1914–1953*]

> Never until the mankind making
> Bird beast and flower
> Fathering and all humbling darkness
> Tells with silence the last light breaking
> And the still hour   5
> Is come of the sea tumbling in harness
>
> And I must enter again the round
> Zion of the water bead
> And the synagogue of the ear of corn
> Shall I let pray the shadow of a sound   10
> Or sow my salt seed
> In the least valley of sackcloth to mourn
>
> The majesty and burning of the child's death.
> I shall not murder
> The mankind of her going with a grave truth   15
> Nor blaspheme down the stations of the breath
> With any further
> Elegy of innocence and youth.
>
> Deep with the first dead lies London's daughter,
> Robed in the long friends,   20
> The grains beyond age, the dark veins of her mother
> Secret by the unmourning water
> Of the riding Thames.
> After the first death, there is no other.

Questions

1. To begin, consider the contrast between the insistence on inconsolable grief in Lowell's poem and the "refusal" of grief in this. Why does the speaker refuse to mourn the death of the child? How does the fact of refusal set the tone of this poem?

2. The first sentence might perhaps be paraphrased as follows: "Never until the darkness that begets and humbles all tells me that hour of my own death will I utter any prayer or weep any tear to mourn the majesty of this child's death." How accurate is the paraphrase? Indicate why the poet has chosen his much more involved and intricate sentence.

3. It might be said that the last line of "A Refusal to Mourn" sums up the difference between this poem and Lowell's. Explain.

Luke Havergal

Edwin Arlington Robinson [*1869–1935*]

Go to the western gate, Luke Havergal,
There where the vines cling crimson on the wall,
And in the twilight wait for what will come.
The leaves will whisper there of her, and some,
Like flying words, will strike you as they fall;   5
But go, and if you listen, she will call.
Go to the western gate, Luke Havergal—
Luke Havergal.

No, there is not a dawn in eastern skies
To rift the fiery night that's in your eyes;   10
But there, where western glooms are gathering
The dark will end the dark, if anything:
God slays Himself with every leaf that flies,
And hell is more than half of paradise.
No, there is not a dawn in eastern skies—   15
In eastern skies.

Out of a grave I come to tell you this,
Out of a grave I come to quench the kiss
That flames upon your forehead with a glow
That blinds you to the way that you must go.   20
Yes, there is yet one way to where she is,
Bitter, but one that faith may never miss.
Out of a grave I come to tell you this—
To tell you this.

There is the western gate, Luke Havergal,   25
There are the crimson leaves upon the wall.
Go, for the winds are tearing them away,—
Nor think to riddle the dead words they say,

Nor any more to feel them as they fall;
But go, and if you trust her she will call.   30
There is the western gate, Luke Havergal—
Luke Havergal.

Questions

1. Note that this poem in certain aspects resembles "Ulalume" (p. 507). It depends heavily on its "music" (i.e., metrical and rhythmic effects), on a mood, and even a certain vagueness. We may have some difficulty in deciding, for example, what "the western gate" (line 25) really signifies, or the identity of the person in line 18 who says "Out of a grave I come to tell you this." Is this poem more or less successful than is "Ulalume"? Is there a core of realistic drama in it?

2. What is the mood of this poem? Can you distinguish the mood from the tone of the poem? What is the attitude of the speaker toward Luke? (The tone of the poem is the reflex of that attitude.) What is Luke's attitude toward the dead beloved?

3. What effect do you find in the rhyme scheme here—the protracted runs on a single rhyme? How does this relate to the mood of the poem? How would you compare it, on this count, with "Fatima" (p. 140)?

At the Slackening of the Tide

James Wright [*1927–*   ]

Today I saw a woman wrapped in rags
Leaping along the beach to curse the sea.
Her child lay floating in the oil, away
From oarlock, gunwale, and the blades of oars.
The skinny lifeguard, raging at the sky,   5
Vomited sea, and fainted on the sand.

The cold simplicity of evening falls
Dead on my mind.
And underneath the piles the water
Leaps up, leaps up, and sags down slowly, farther   10
Than seagulls disembodied in the drag
Of oil and foam.

Plucking among the oyster shells a man
Stares at the sea, that stretches on its side.
Now far along the beach, a hungry dog   15
Announces everything I knew before:
Obliterate naiads weeping underground,
Where Homer's tongue thickens with human howls.
I would do anything to drag myself
Out of this place: 20

Root up a seaweed from the water,
To stuff it in my mouth, or deafen me,
Free me from all the force of human speech;
Go drown, almost.

Warm in the pleasure of the dawn I came   25
To sing my song
And look for mollusks in the shallows,
The whorl and coil that pretty up the earth,
While far below us, flaring in the dark,
The stars go out.   30

What did I do to kill my time today,
After the woman ranted in the cold,
The mellow sea, the sound blown dark as wine?
After the lifeguard rose up from the waves
Like a sea-lizard with the scales washed off?   35
Sit there, admiring sunlight on a shell?

Abstract with terror of the shell, I stared
Over the waters where
God brooded for the living all one day.
Lonely for weeping, starved for a sound of mourning,   40
I bowed my head, and heard the sea far off
Washing its hands.

Question

Explain the metaphorical force of the last line. To do this you must
read the account of Jesus before Pilate, "who washed his hands before
the multitude, saying, 'I am innocent of the blood of this just person.'"
(See Matthew 27.) What change of tone concludes the poem?

Bells for John Whiteside's Daughter

John Crowe Ransom [*1888–1974*]

There was such speed in her little body,
And such lightness in her footfall,
It is no wonder her brown study
Astonishes us all.

Her wars were bruited in our high window.   5
We looked among orchard trees and beyond,
Where she took arms against her shadow,
Or harried unto the pond

The lazy geese, like a snow cloud
Dripping their snow on the green grass,   10

Tricking and stopping, sleepy and proud,
Who cried in goose, Alas,

For the tireless heart within the little
Lady with rod that made them rise
From their noon apple-dreams, and scuttle   15
Goose-fashion under the skies!

But now go the bells, and we are ready;
In one house we are sternly stopped
To say we are vexed at her brown study,
Lying so primly propped.   20

The first stanza is based on two clichés: first, "Heavens, won't that child ever be still, she is driving me distracted"; and second, "She was such an active child, who would have thought she would just up and die?" In fact, the whole poem develops these clichés and depends on the irony created by putting them side by side: the child you wished would be still just for a minute is now very still, and for good.

Questions

1. Consider the word *vexed* in line 19. The poet's choice of this word may provide the key to the attitude that the speaker brings to this occasion.

2. The usual associations of the phrase "brown study" (lines 3 and 19) are with the scholar or the philosopher, oblivious to the world about him as he meditates some abstruse problem. The term can certainly be applied to a child caught up in a particular mood or motionless in deep reverie. But the usual associations of the phrase may give it, as in this application to a child, a special tinge of humor or irony or even a wry whimsy. What is the effect of the phrase as applied to the little girl? (Note that the poet applies it to her twice.)

3. Write a short essay in which you try to define as precisely as you can the quality of the irony in this poem. Concentrate on the effect of the irony on the reader's attitude. Cite elements of diction, rhythm, and descriptive detail that substantiate your case.

Epitaph on Salomon Pavy

Ben Jonson   [1573?–1637]

Weepe with me all you that read
   This little storie:
And know, for whom a teare you shed,
   Death's self is sorry.

'Twas a child, that so did thrive
    In grace, and feature,
As Heaven and Nature seem'd to strive
    Which own'd the creature.   5
Yeeres he numbred scarse thirteene
    When Fates turn'd cruell,   10
Yet three fill'd Zodiackes had he beene
    The stages jewell;
And did act (what now we mone)
    Old men so duely,
As, sooth, the Parcae[1] thought him one,   15
He plai'd so truly.
So by error, to his fate
    They all consented;
But viewing him since (alas, too late)
    They have repented.   20
And have sought (to give new birth)
    In bathes to steepe him;
But, being so much too good for earth,
    Heaven vowes to keepe him.

[1] the Greek Fates

   Salomon Pavy was a boy actor in plays such as *Cynthia's Revels* and
The Poetaster, which Jonson wrote for performance by the Children of
Queen Elizabeth's Chapel. In modern times the child actor's name has
usually been printed as Salathiel Pavy, but Professor Gerald E. Bentley
has shown that he was actually named for Solomon—Salomon is a regular Elizabethan form of Solomon—and how the mistaken expansion of
Sal. (as Salomon was often abbreviated) to Salathiel came about.

Questions
   1. This poem does not pretend that Pavy's death was a personal loss
or that it is occasioned by some outpouring of grief. Is the poem, however,
devoid of all emotion? What is the note that is struck?
   2. The speaker says that Death himself is sorry for the boy's death.
Does this seem a fulsome and exaggerated statement? If not, what keeps
it from seeming so?
   3. What is the speaker's attitude toward Pavy's death? What is the
tone of the poem?

J. A SECOND GARLAND OF LOVE POEMS

Winter Remembered

John Crowe Ransom [*1888–1974*]

Two evils, monstrous either one apart,
Possessed me, and were long and loath at going:
A cry of Absence, Absence, in the heart,
And in the wood the furious winter blowing.

Think not, when fire was bright upon my bricks,   5
And past the tight boards hardly a wind could enter,
I glowed like them, the simple burning sticks,
Far from my cause, my proper heat and center.

Better to walk forth in the murderous air
And wash my wound in the snows; that would be healing;   10
Because my heart would throb less painful there,
Being caked with cold, and past the smart of feeling.

And where I went, the hugest winter blast
Would have this body bowed, these eyeballs streaming,
And though I think this heart's blood froze not fast   15
It ran too small to spare one drop for dreaming.

Dear love, these fingers that had known your touch,
And tied our separate forces first together,
Were ten poor idiot fingers not worth much,
Ten frozen parsnips hanging in the weather.   20

Questions

1. The lover, now at last restored to his beloved after a time of wintry absence, in this poem tells her quite flatly that she must not suppose that he spent much time dreaming of her. Such a declaration seems to be an odd thing for a fervent lover to say. Yet he claims to be her devoted lover. Is there a contradiction?

2. How does this apparent contradiction affect the tone of the poem?

3. The comparison (in lines 19–20) of the lover's fingers to "frozen parsnips" will seem to be an absurd—a ridiculous—comparison. Does the comparison ruin the poem? Or does it "make" the poem? Explain your judgment.

4. In what sense can it be argued that the use of the parsnip image in lines 19–20 works in a way very similar to that of the word *vexed* in "Bells for John Whiteside's Daughter"?

5. The poet revised line 9 to read ". . . in the frozen air," and line 13 to read "And where I walked, the murderous winter blast." Do you

regard the revisions as improvements? Why do you think the poet made
these changes?

La Figlia che Piange

T. S. Eliot [1888–1965]

O quam te memorem virgo

Stand on the highest pavement of the stair—
Lean on a garden urn—
Weave, weave the sunlight in your hair—
Clasp your flowers to you with a pained surprise—
Fling them to the ground and turn   5
With a fugitive resentment in your eyes:
But weave, weave the sunlight in your hair.

So I would have had him leave,
So I would have had her stand and grieve,
So he would have left   10
As the soul leaves the body torn and bruised,
As the mind deserts the body it has used.
I should find
Some way incomparably light and deft,
Some way we both should understand,   15
Simple and faithless as a smile and shake of the hand.

She turned away, but with the autumn weather
Compelled my imagination many days,
Many days and many hours:
Her hair over her arms and her arms full of flowers.   20
And I wonder how they should have been together!
I should have lost a gesture and a pose.
Sometimes these cogitations still amaze
The troubled midnight and the noon's repose.

Questions

1. What is this scene that is being rehearsed in memory? One of
estrangement, hurt, and misunderstanding? What would you say is the
relation of the man to the woman whose gestures are described?

2. Is the speaker the man who bade the girl goodbye? Or is he simply
an outside observer? Someone who happened on the scene and was impressed by it?

3. Whatever your answer to the preceding question, the sense of
detachment is stressed. The speaker might almost be a movie director
coaching an actress on how she is to play a scene. Yet he seems to indicate (in the closing lines) that the scene made a deep and troubling
impression upon him. Is there a contradiction here between his apparent
detachment and his deep emotional involvement?

4. The poet has left on record that the inspiration for his poem was a piece of statuary that he once saw in Italy.* Does this information lessen your sense of a poignant emotional experience? Or is the precise experience that led to the poet's writing the poem irrelevant to its meaning and effect? In short, how do you determine the emotional power of such a dramatization—by whether you think it reflects a personal experience of the author or by something else? In any case, a carved figure cannot weave sunlight in its hair or turn away. What of this fact?

A Litany

Sir Philip Sidney [*1554–1586*]

Ring out your bells, let mourning shows be spread;
For Love is dead.
  All Love is dead, infected
With plague of deep disdain;
    Worth, as nought worth, rejected,   5
And Faith fair scorn doth gain.
  From so ungrateful fancy,
  From such a female franzy,
    From them that use men thus,
    Good Lord, deliver us!   10

Weep, neighbors, weep! do you not hear it said
That Love is dead?
  His death-bed, peacock's folly;
His winding-sheet is shame;
    His will, false-seeming holy;   15
His sole executor, blame.
  From so ungrateful fancy,
  From such a female franzy,
    From them that use men thus,
    Good Lord, deliver us!   20

Let dirge be sung and trentals rightly read,
For Love is dead.
  Sir Wrong his tomb ordaineth
My mistress Marble-heart,
    Which epitaph containeth,   25

---

* "While Eliot was traveling in Europe in 1911, he visited a museum in Northern Italy possessing a *stele* designated, according to a friend who suggested that he take a look at it, 'La Figlia che Piange' ('young girl weeping'). For some reason, when he searched for this tablet, he was unable to find it. The subject of his resulting lines being nameless, he understandably in reprinting the poem used as an epigram the phrase from Aeneas' address to Venus: 'Maiden, by what name shall I know you?' (*Aeneid*, i., 327.)" Grover Smith, *T. S. Eliot's Poetry and Plays,* University of Chicago Press, 1956, p. 27.

"Her eyes were once his dart."
  From so ungrateful fancy,
  From such a female franzy,
    From them that use men thus,
  Good Lord, deliver us!   30

Alas! I lie, rage hath this error bred;
Love is not dead.
  Love is not dead, but sleepeth
In her unmatchèd mind,
  Where she his counsel keepeth,   35
Till due desert she find.
  Therefore from so vile fancy,
  To call such wit a franzy,
    Who Love can temper thus,
  Good Lord, deliver us!   40

A litany is a form of liturgical prayer, with invocations, supplications, and responses. "Good Lord, deliver us" is one of the reiterated responses in the Litany that is printed in the Book of Common Prayer, with which, of course, Sir Philip Sidney was familiar. And so Sidney's references to it here help to define the special tone of the poem. The death of Love is being treated as if it were a kind of public calamity, one such as the outbreak of the dreaded plague, that might properly call for a recital of the Litany. Indeed, there is more than a hint of this in the first stanza with its call for ringing the church bells, its reference to mourning shows, and its remark that Love is dead, having been "infected / With plague." A very private matter, the ill fortune of the speaker's love affair, is being treated as if it were a matter of public concern.

Such may at first glance appear to be a dangerous strategy for a poet to employ, embodying the worst features of what today we call "confessional" poetry. Thus the problem of tone in this poem is readily seen to be crucial.

Perhaps a few notes on certain words and spellings in this Elizabethan poem may be useful. *Fancy* in its first three occurrences in this poem means *love* (or *loved one*). We still use the word in this sense in the phrase "fancy-free." But in line 37 *fancy* has its present meaning: a supposition or *imagined idea*. *Franzy* (in line 8 and elsewhere) is simply our modern word *frenzy*. A *dirge* (line 21) is a funeral hymn (or, by extension, the whole funeral service). *Trentals* (line 21) are masses for the dead.

In the third stanza, the expression is somewhat elliptical. We venture to expand it thus: "Sir Wrong ordaineth (that is, solemnly proclaims) my mistress's Marble-heart as his (love's) tomb which containeth (the) epitaph 'Her (the mistress's) eyes were once his (love's) dart.' " The irony of this last clause would be more apparent to a reader of Sidney's own time than perhaps to a modern reader, for in Elizabethan time certain mannerisms of love poetry were flourishing. These mannerisms grew from the tradition of Petrarch, the Italian poet of the fourteenth century who first popularized the love sonnet. In what came to be known as the Petrarchan tradition, the lover's mistress was often ridiculously idolized.

The imagery used here in the description of Love's tomb is Petrarchan; princely tombs were made of marble, and the hardness of the lady's heart, its marblelike quality, makes it appropriate that it should be Love's tomb. She once furnished Love with his darts, supplying him with the bright beams of her eyes (with an allusion to the belief that love flashed from a beautiful woman's eyes). But the imagery here is plainly mock-heroic. Sidney has used these clichés ironically, expecting the reader to recognize their stereotyped quality. They help define the appropriate tone.

Questions

1. What is the poet's *real* attitude toward his plight? How seriously does he take himself? Does the poem develop a sufficient make-weight of self-irony? If you think it does, produce your evidence from the text of the poem.

2. What is the poet's attitude toward his sweetheart? Exasperation? Rage at unfair treatment? Fury at her fatuous notion of how a fine lady ought to act when courted by an ardent lover? Or what?

3. What is the shift in tone that occurs in the last stanza? Describe it. What is its psychological and dramatic basis? How is the shift in tone reflected in the metrical situation itself? Scan this stanza and see how it deviates from the others.

Cynara

Ernest Dowson [*1867–1900*]

> Last night, ah, yesternight, betwixt her lips and mine
> There fell thy shadow, Cynara! thy breath was shed
> Upon my soul between the kisses and the wine;
> And I was desolate and sick of an old passion,
>   Yea, I was desolate and bowed my head: 5
> I have been faithful to thee, Cynara! in my fashion.
>
> All night upon mine heart I felt her warm heart beat,
> Night-long within mine arms in love and sleep she lay;
> Surely the kisses of her bought red mouth were sweet;
> But I was desolate and sick of an old passion,   10
>   When I awoke and found the dawn was gray:
> I have been faithful to thee, Cynara! in my fashion.

I have forgot much, Cynara! gone with the wind,
Flung roses, roses, riotously with the throng,
Dancing, to put thy pale, lost lilies out of mind;   15
But I was desolate and sick of an old passion,
    Yea, all the time, because the dance was long:
I have been faithful to thee, Cynara! in my fashion.

I cried for madder music and for stronger wine,
But when the feast is finished and the lamps expire,   20
Then falls thy shadow, Cynara! the night is thine;
And I am desolate and sick of an old passion,
    Yea, hungry for the lips of my desire:
I have been faithful to thee, Cynara! in my fashion.

This poem, like "A Litany" by Sidney, deals with the subject of lost love. Dowson centers his poem on a paradox: "I have been faithful to thee, Cynara! in my fashion." Presumably, he felt that the use of this paradox would lend a sharpness, a sense of precise statement, and a toughness that would help him to avoid the sentimental and trite in treating his subject.

Questions

1. Assuming that there is an element of truth in the paradox, and that a successful poem might be based upon it, the question remains: Is this a successful poem?

2. Does the speaker seem to enjoy feeling sorry for himself? Does he enjoy recalling what a sad dog he has been? In this connection, consider how much of the poem is taken up with recounting his past exploits.

3. How well (or ill) do the "pale, lost lilies" (in contrast with the riotous roses) suggest the personality of Cynara?

4. Does the paradox develop as the poem proceeds? Does repetition enrich its meaning or weaken it? Suppose that we reversed the order of the last three stanzas. Would transposing them make any difference?

5. How would you characterize the rhythmic effect?

I Knew a Woman

Theodore Roethke [*1908–1963*]

I knew a woman, lovely in her bones,
When small birds sighed, she would sigh back at them;
Ah, when she moved, she moved more ways than one:
The shapes a bright container can contain!
Of her choice virtues only gods should speak,   5
Or English poets who grew up on Greek
(I'd have them sing in chorus, cheek to cheek).

How well her wishes went! She stroked my chin,
She taught me Turn, and Counter-turn, and Stand;
She taught me Touch, that undulant white skin;   10
I nibbled meekly from her proffered hand;
She was the sickle; I, poor I, the rake,
Coming behind her for her pretty sake
(But what prodigious mowing we did make).

Love likes a gander, and adores a goose: 15
Her full lips pursed, the errant note to seize;
She played it quick, she played it light and loose;
My eyes, they dazzled at her flowing knees;
Her several parts could keep a pure repose,
Or one hip quiver with a mobile nose   20
(She moved in circles, and those circles moved).

Let seed be grass, and grass turn into hay:
I'm martyr to a motion not my own;
What's freedom for? To know eternity.
I swear she cast a shadow white as stone.   25
But who would count eternity in days?
These old bones live to learn her wanton ways:
(I measure time by how a body sways).

Question

Develop a set of exercises based on the striking and significant features of this poem, and directed toward a description of the tone of the poem and a statement of its theme.

K. FOUR NEW ENGLAND POEMS

Mr. Flood's Party

Edwin Arlington Robinson [*1869–1935*]

Old Eben Flood, climbing alone one night
Over the hill between the town below
And the forsaken upland hermitage
That held as much as he should ever know
On earth again of home, paused warily.   5
The road was his with not a native near;
And Eben, having leisure, said aloud,
For no man else in Tilbury Town to hear:

"Well, Mr. Flood, we have the harvest moon
Again, and we may not have many more;   10

The bird is on the wing, the poet says,
And you and I have said it here before.
Drink to the bird." He raised up to the light
The jug that he had gone so far to fill,
And answered huskily: "Well, Mr. Flood,   15
Since you propose it, I believe I will."

Alone, as if enduring to the end
A valiant armor of scarred hopes outworn,
He stood there in the middle of the road
Like Roland's ghost winding a silent horn.   20
Below him, in the town among the trees,
Where friends of other days had honored him,
A phantom salutation of the dead
Rang thinly till old Eben's eyes were dim.

Then, as a mother lays her sleeping child   25
Down tenderly, fearing it may awake,
He set the jug down slowly at his feet
With trembling care, knowing that most things break;
And only when assured that on firm earth
It stood, as the uncertain lives of men   30
Assuredly did not, he paced away,
And with his hand extended paused again:

"Well, Mr. Flood, we have not met like this
In a long time; and many a change has come
To both of us, I fear, since last it was   35
We had a drop together. Welcome home!"
Convivially returning with himself,
Again he raised the jug up to the light;
And with an acquiescent quaver said:
"Well, Mr. Flood, if you insist, I might.   40

"Only a very little, Mr. Flood—
For auld lang syne. No more, sir; that will do."
So, for the time, apparently it did,
And Eben evidently thought so too;
For soon amid the silver loneliness   45
Of night he lifted up his voice and sang,
Secure, with only two moons listening,
Until the whole harmonious landscape rang—

"For auld lang syne." The weary throat gave out,
The last word wavered; and the song being done,   50
He raised again the jug regretfully
And shook his head, and was again alone.
There was not much that was ahead of him,
And there was nothing in the town below—
Where strangers would have shut the many doors   55
That many friends had opened long ago.

Questions

1. Mr. Flood, a drunken derelict, an outcast, a disgrace to the community, a friendless and poverty-bit old nuisance, has a night out—not on the town, but outside the town, a binge in which he is the only participant. He doesn't, we soon gather, really like to drink alone, but having no one to drink with, he makes the best of the situation.

The poem almost at once reveals the pathos of his situation. Is the poem sentimental, an invitation to have our heart-strings pulled? If it is not, then what has the poet done to keep the poem from becoming a lachrymose self-indulgence? Give your reasons. Be specific. Cite the text.

2. Is the poem funny? Can the poem be funny and pathetic at the same time? If you think so, explain.

3. Comment upon lines 25–28. Is the comparison there an obvious bid for sympathy? Or is it comic? Why should Mr. Flood lay down his jug with such loving care? And of what kind of human care can it be taken as a parody? How does this accent his loneliness?

4. Stanza 3 would seem to be a direct attempt to connect the old drunkard with valiant, defeated heroes of the romantic past. Thus, Mr. Flood is literally compared to Roland, the hero of the Old French epic *The Song of Roland,* the nephew of Charlemagne, who, as commander of the rear guard of the Emperor's army in the mountains of Spain, held off an overwhelming force of the Moors and refused, until the very end, to blow his famous horn for help. Do you feel that the association of the village drunk with Roland is too romantic, too obviously and arrantly a bid for our sympathy: as Roland called for help to his far-off friends, so Mr. Flood summons up the old days of friendship and dignity?

Is there any realistic basis for the comparison? Does a man lifting a horn to his lips look like a man drinking out of a jug? Is there a comic element here which prevents mere sentimentality?

5. In a short paragraph, try to describe the tone of the poem as a whole.

Stopping by Woods on a Snowy Evening

Robert Frost [*1874–1963*]

> Whose woods these are I think I know.
> His house is in the village though;
> He will not see me stopping here
> To watch his woods fill up with snow.
>
> My little horse must think it queer   5
> To stop without a farmhouse near
> Between the woods and frozen lake
> The darkest evening of the year.
>
> He gives his harness bells a shake
> To ask if there is some mistake.   10

The only other sound's the sweep
Of easy wind and downy flake.

The woods are lovely, dark and deep.
But I have promises to keep,
And miles to go before I sleep,   15
And miles to go before I sleep.

Questions

1. Why does the speaker stop by the woods? (The horse thinks it queer that he stops; the owner of the woods, it is implied, would also think it queer if he could see him.)

2. Does the speaker drive on with reluctance? What does this implied reluctance tell us about the motive for stopping?

3. What attitude toward nature is implied in this little poem? The woods are "lovely, dark, and deep" and make some deep appeal to the speaker. Note that it is not an appeal that is felt by the horse or presumably would be felt by the owner of the woods, and that it is an appeal that is finally resisted by even the speaker himself.

4. What is the speaker's attitude toward himself? Self-congratulation for being superior to the brute or for having a finer aesthetic sense than the man who owns the woods, or for being moral and punctual and keeping his promises? What kind of person do you suppose the speaker to be? Are there any hints in the poem?

Father

John Wheelwright   [*1897–1940*]

An East Wind asperges Boston with Lynn's sulphurous brine.
Under the bridge of turrets my father built,—from turning sign
of CHEVROLET, out-topping our gilt State House dome
to burning sign of CARTER'S INK,—drip multitudes
of checker-board shadows. Inverted turreted reflections   5
sleeting over axle-grease billows, through all directions
cross-cut parliamentary gulls, who toss like gourds.

Speak. Speak to me again, as fresh saddle leather
(Speak; talk again) to a hunter smells of heather.
Come home. Wire a wire of warning without words.   10
Come home and talk to me again, my first friend. Father,
come home, dead man, who made your mind my home.

Questions

1. Look up *asperges* in the dictionary (the poet was a Roman Catholic). How does the poet's choice of this word set the tone for lines 1–7? How is the tone amplified and developed?

2. What is the meaning of *parliamentary* as applied to gulls? Look up *parliamentary* in the *Oxford English Dictionary*. Does meaning 1.d fit best? What does the choice of this word contribute to the tone?

3. What change in tone occurs with line 8? Characterize the tone of lines 8–12. What effect does the shift in tone (of the latter lines) contribute to the meaning of the whole poem?

Tell All the Truth

Emily Dickinson [*1830–1886*]

Tell all the Truth but tell it slant—
Success in Circuit lies
Too bright for our infirm Delight
The Truth's superb surprise
As Lightning to the Children eased   5
With explanation kind
The Truth must dazzle gradually
Or every man be blind—

Questions

1. This poem takes the form of an admonition or perhaps a warning. But is this the "tone" of the poem? Is the flavor of the poem didactic— that of a preachment or a lecture?

2. Isn't to "dazzle gradually" a contradiction in terms? Aren't we always dazzled immediately by a flash like that of an explosion or a lightning bolt? If there is a contradiction, does it reduce the poem to nonsense?

3. Would it be fair to say that this poem is in part whimsical—even playful? But in that case, how playful or how serious is the closing line?

4. How can the first line be understood as a description of the method of all successful poetry?

RHYTHM AND METER: 4

The art of poetry, like any art, is full of subtleties and complications, and our present topic, "Tone," invites the special consideration of certain technical questions not yet considered. See Appendix B, pp. 506–525.

Questions on Tone

1. Reread "The Canonization" (p. 134). In the attached comment we have remarked on the relation of the logicality to the emotional attitude that it defends and on the resulting tone—the disinfecting of sentimentality.

(a) But we have not remarked on the tone of the poem in relation to the critical friend to whom it is addressed. There is, in fact, not one tone but several, the tone changing as the poem proceeds. With the first line—and first stanza—there is a burst of vexation—even if, perhaps, a sort of half-humorous vexation—with the friend, in effect, and paraphrased: "For God's sake, get on with your concerns and let me get on with mine." Then the poet gives a humorously satirical view of what the friend's concerns are. With each stanza the poem becomes more serious. Try to define the tone of each stanza.

(b) Scan stanza 1, indicating all secondary accents and pauses. Then do a rhetorical graph (as on p. 504 of Appendix B) superimposed on the scansion. We have said above that the tone in this stanza is conversational and familiar, not formal. How do the scansion and the rhetorical variation relate to this fact?

(c) Scan and make a rhetorical chart of the first line of each of the following stanzas: 2, 3, and 4. Do you find that these first lines are more difficult—that is, show more tension between meter and rhetoric—than most subsequent lines in a stanza? If so, would you surmise that, in each stanza, the first line sets the dramatic tone against which the more regular lines are played off? In this connection turn back to " 'Out, Out—' " (p. 18) and to the comment on the first few lines of the poem.

(d) Mark the pauses in stanzas 2 and 3. Do you find that the placement sets up a dramatic tension with the elaborately formal stanza—that is, that the pauses give another rhetorical tension to the overall form?

(e) Examine the last stanza. Here the first line is, in contrast to the opening lines of the preceding stanzas, remarkably regular; and in fact the whole of the last stanza is extremely easy in its metrics. The poem, then, seems to end on a quiet tone, with a sense of completion and fulfillment. (In this connection we may notice that the short last line of each stanza has the same quietening effect; and that, significantly, each stanza ends with the word *love,* as does the first line of each stanza, *love* being, we may say, the key rhyme word of the poem.*) If the whole of the last stanza offers such a quietening effect, what is the effect, and significance, of the very different next-to-last line? Scan it, remembering that, according to the pattern of the stanza, the line is tetrameter.

2. Turn to "Why So Pale and Wan?" (p. 508). Study the exercises there on the relation of metrics to tone.

3. Reread "Inscription for Marye's Heights" (p. 125) and the commentary. Consider the placement of the pauses and the fact that three of the first four lines are run on. In other words, there is a strong forward thrust, tending to break out of the pattern of line, with, actually, only a light pause (a comma) at the end of line 3, after the word *intent* (gaze "intent" on the advancing flag), after which the thrust resumes to spill over from line 4 to the caesura in line 5, the stop coming after the word *death.* How does this situation support the meaning of the poem?

What is the effect of the abrupt early placement of the caesura in line 6? What is gained by the interpolation of line 6 between the word

---

* The other most frequent rhyme word is *prove,* in one form or another. After all, the poem is, as we have said, an argument moving toward a "proof."

stone (which ends line 5) and the word's modifying phrase which constitutes 7? What is the effect of the two metrical accents in the word *victory?* On the word *monument?* In fact, the two words balanced here constitute most of the entire line, and certainly have its metrical weight. How would you relate such factors to the tone of the poem? Remember that the battle was, for the Federal army, a stunning defeat, and that Melville was a Unionist.

Analogical Language: Metaphor and Symbol

4

Foreword

Concreteness—the image of person, scene, action, or object—is, as we have earlier insisted, at the very heart of poetry. But we have also insisted that the image, in poetry, is never present *merely* as description, as report, as documentation; it has, at the very least, some aura of significance (pp. 68–71), and it may have, as we have already seen, rather complex meanings (p. 77). A poet, it is sometimes said, "thinks" by means of his images, or in his images. It might be said, too, that he feels by means of them and in them. This density, this interpenetration, this fusion of thought, feeling, image, and, as we must add, rhythm and verbal texture, is of the essence of poetry and is the source of its power.

We now turn to explore some instances more complex and subtle than most of those that have engaged us thus far; or at least, we now bring more concentrated attention to bear on their qualities as imagery. What function, we must ask ourselves in each case, is being served by imagery? And in what particular fashion?

A. ATMOSPHERE TO SYMBOL

Mariana

Alfred, Lord Tennyson [*1809–1892*]

"Mariana in the moated grange."—*Measure for Measure*

With blackest moss the flower-pots
   Were thickly crusted, one and all;
The rusted nails fell from the knots
   That held the pear to the gable-wall.
The broken sheds looked sad and strange: 5
   Unlifted was the clinking latch;
   Weeded and worn the ancient thatch
Upon the lonely moated grange.
     She only said, "My life is dreary,
       He cometh not," she said;   10
     She said, "I am aweary, aweary,
       I would that I were dead!"

Her tears fell with the dews at even;
   Her tears fell ere the dews were dried;
She could not look on the sweet heaven,   15
   Either at morn or eventide.
After the flitting of the bats,
   When thickest dark did trance the sky,
   She drew her casement-curtain by,
And glanced athwart the glooming flats.   20
     She only said, "The night is dreary,
       He cometh not," she said;
     She said, "I am aweary, aweary,
       I would that I were dead!"

Upon the middle of the night,   25
   Waking she heard the night-fowl crow;
The cock sung out an hour ere light;
   From the dark fen the oxen's low
Came to her; without hope of change,
   In sleep she seemed to walk forlorn,   30
   Till cold winds woke the gray-eyed morn
About the lonely moated grange.
     She only said, "The day is dreary,
       He cometh not," she said;
     She said, "I am aweary, aweary,   35
       I would that I were dead!"

About a stone-cast from the wall
  A sluice with blackened waters slept,
And o'er it many, round and small,
  The clustered marish-mosses crept.   40
Hard by a poplar shook alway,
  All silver-green with gnarlèd bark:
  For leagues no other tree did mark
The level waste, the rounding gray.
    She only said, "My life is dreary,   45
      He cometh not," she said;
    She said, "I am aweary, aweary,
      I would that I were dead!"

And ever when the moon was low,
  And the shrill winds were up and away,   50
In the white curtain, to and fro,
  She saw the gusty shadow sway.
But when the moon was very low,
  And wild winds bound within their cell,
  The shadow of the poplar fell   55
Upon her bed, across her brow.
    She only said, "The night is dreary,
      He cometh not," she said;
    She said, "I am aweary, aweary,
      I would that I were dead!"   60

All day within the dreamy house,
  The doors upon their hinges creaked;
The blue fly sung in the pane; the mouse
  Behind the moldering wainscot shrieked,
Or from the crevice peered about.   65
  Old faces glimmered thro' the doors,
  Old footsteps trod the upper floors,
Old voices called her from without.
    She only said, "My life is dreary,
      He cometh not," she said;   70
    She said, "I am aweary, aweary,
      I would that I were dead."

The sparrow's chirrup on the roof,
  The slow clock ticking, and the sound
Which to the wooing wind aloof   75
  The poplar made, did all confound
Her sense; but most she loathed the hour
  When the thick-moted sunbeam lay
  Athwart the chambers, and the day
Was sloping toward his western bower.   80
    Then said she, "I am very dreary,
      He will not come," she said;
    She wept, "I am aweary, aweary,
      O God, that I were dead!"

In Shakespeare's play *Measure for Measure,* Mariana is the young woman betrothed to Angelo. But Angelo has refused to marry her and she lives far away from the gay life of the capital, in the country at a "moated grange." In this poem Tennyson has tried to imagine her situation of lonely desperation. In describing the physical background of her *isolation,* he has enlarged on the hint afforded by the phrase "moated grange." A moated grange would be a large farmhouse fortified against attack by being enclosed within a moat. Many castles in the Middle Ages had moats, but few granges were moated unless they were in hard-to-defend flat country. The moated grange of the poem is surrounded by such a "level waste" marked by only a single tree, with dark fens all about it and with marsh vegetation filling up the disused moat.

Clearly Tennyson's larger purpose in choosing this particular landscape was to find a physical counterpart to the jilted woman's state of mind. For this poem has to do finally with the depiction of an interior, not an exterior, state of affairs. The refrain with its repetitions and its rhymed insistence upon the girl's weariness and her wish for death tell us that. Doubtless Mariana's state of frustration and depression could occur to a person living on a mountaintop or in a luxury hotel, but the gray, monotonous countryside does accord with her condition of spirit and embodies it.

To sum up, we may say that in this poem the imagery creates an atmosphere, but an atmosphere which, grounded in a psychological situation, has a symbolic aura.

Questions

1. "Mariana" is a poem that obviously might have been studied in Section 2 under the rubric "Description." But from the foregoing paragraphs it is plain that it might also have been reasonably placed among the poems of Section 3, those that offer special problems in tone. What is the tone of this poem? What attitude are we to take toward Mariana? The situation invites pity and might seem to justify self-pity. But can it be said that self-pity is the dominant feeling here? Does the sense of precision in the objectification of the woman's feeling in the external world do anything to reduce the effect of self-pity?

2. Compare the use of imagery here with that in Rossetti's "The Woodspurge" (p. 102). To what extent do the two poems have the same psychological base?

3. On what basis do the auditory images in "Mariana" appear to be selected?

4. Why could Mariana "not look on the sweet heaven"?

5. Is there some development or progression in the poem? In this connection, note the change in refrain in the last stanza. What image represents the climactic horror? Comment on its meaning.

6. What elements in the poem in addition to imagery may be said to fuse with the general effect? In connection with this topic, it may be

useful to inspect the "Choric Song" from Tennyson's "The Lotus Eaters," a stanza of which is on p. 542.

Anecdote of the Jar

Wallace Stevens [1879–1955]

I placed a jar in Tennessee,
And round it was, upon a hill.
It made the slovenly wilderness
Surround that hill.

The wilderness rose up to it,   5
And sprawled around, no longer wild.
The jar was round upon the ground
And tall and of a port in air.

It took dominion everywhere.
The jar was gray and bare.   10
It did not give of bird or bush,
Like nothing else in Tennessee.

The jar, whose image is at the center of the poem, is a very ordinary one, it would seem, "gray and bare," a crock jar presumably. But the poem is rather odd, and the oddness begins with the first line. One might say, "In Tennessee, one time, on a hill, I set a jar down on the ground." Factually, this is what the speaker here does say, but in a very twisted way that distorts any ordinary meaning. What does the first line imply? One puts a jar on the second shelf instead of on the third, on the table, on the doorstep—and implied in such a statement is a choice: on the table instead of on the second shelf, and so on. But if the speaker says "I placed a jar in Tennessee," we have the vague notion of a hand holding a jar moving, in a very extraordinary fashion, across Kentucky, or Virginia, perhaps, as though across a map, and then finding, in Tennessee, a real hill to set the jar on. But to say you have placed a jar on a hill is an odd way to talk. A jar is small; you set it on the ground or on a stump or rock; you don't "place" it "upon a hill." The stump or rock may be on a hill, but that is another matter. This jar is somehow made to loom up like a tree, or a great boulder, or a monument. The jar has some mysterious quality.

Questions

1. The jar stands in contrast to the wilderness. What is the basis of the contrast? Why is the wilderness "slovenly"? Then, why "no longer wild"?

2. What does the word *port* mean here? Consult an unabridged dictionary. Is the word a common word in this sense? Why would Stevens use this word in this connection? How "tall" would a jar have to be to have a "port," would you think? What kind of image are we actually seeing here? Has the jar changed size before our eyes? What about the word *dominion*? Is this an unexpected word here? How would you justify it in relation to the poem?

3. Interpret the last two lines.

4. If the poem can be said to be about man in contrast to nature, what is implied in the image of the jar? How does the wrenching of language and imagery connect with the meaning?

5. Do the red wheelbarrow in Williams's poem (p. 73) and the jar have similar significance? If not, why not?

Having considered such questions as appear in the list above, we realize that there is a distinction to be made between the function of the imagery in "Mariana" and that in Stevens's poem. The imagery in "Mariana" is diffuse. Its relation to the meaning of the poem is very general. The image of the jar, however, is *focal* for the meaning of "Anecdote of the Jar." In Stevens's poem it is a diffuse meaning, rather than a diffuse imagery, that has to be brought to focus. The jar is a symbol; that is to say, an image which in itself embodies—or "stands for"—a complex of emotion and idea.

The Lamb

William Blake [*1757–1827*]

> Little Lamb, who made thee?
> Dost thou know who made thee?
> Gave thee life, and bid thee feed,
> By the stream and o'er the mead;
> Gave thee clothing of delight,   5
> Softest clothing, woolly, bright;
> Gave thee such a tender voice,
> Making all the vales rejoice?
> Little Lamb, who made thee?
> Dost thou know who made thee?   10
>
> Little Lamb, I'll tell thee,
> Little Lamb, I'll tell thee:
> He is callèd by thy name,
> For he calls himself a Lamb.
> He is meek, and he is mild;   15
> He became a little child.
> I a child, and thou a lamb,
> We are callèd by his name.
> Little Lamb, God bless thee!
> Little Lamb, God bless thee!   20

This poem, from Blake's *Songs of Innocence*, should be compared with "The Tiger," from his *Songs of Experience*.

Questions

1. Does this poem describe a lamb? Or does it describe the mind of the child who is speaking to the lamb? Is it important to choose between these two emphases?

2. The child speaks to the lamb as if it were another human being— perhaps the speaker's younger brother or sister. How does this device of presentation support the meaning of the poem? What is the relation of the lamb and the child to God (as incarnate in Christ, the Second Person of the Trinity)? What facts seem to constitute for the child the basis of the relationship? (For further questions see those on "The Tiger.")

3. Try to state briefly what the lamb "stands for."

The Tiger

William Blake [*1757–1827*]

Tiger! Tiger! burning bright
In the forests of the night,
What immortal hand or eye
Could frame thy fearful symmetry?

In what distant deeps or skies   5
Burnt the fire of thine eyes?
On what wings dare he aspire?
What the hand dare seize the fire?

And what shoulder, and what art,
Could twist the sinews of thy heart?   10
And when thy heart began to beat,
What dread hand? and what dread feet?

What the hammer? what the chain?
In what furnace was thy brain?
What the anvil? what dread grasp   15
Dare its deadly terrors clasp?

When the stars threw down their spears,
And watered heaven with their tears,
Did he smile his work to see?
Did he who made the Lamb make thee?   20

Tiger! Tiger! burning bright
In the forests of the night,
What immortal hand or eye,
Dare frame thy fearful symmetry?

Questions

1. Like "The Lamb," this poem is concerned with creation. Lamb and Tiger symbolize, as it were, opposite poles in creation. But does this mean that the two poems—or the two principles symbolized here—cancel out each other? Or do they illuminate each other? Do they complete each other? Could one be conceivable without the other?

2. Can you see how the idea involved in the questions above might be said to apply to the reader's attitude in confronting, in general, poems that contradict each other, directly or by implication, or that offer competing values or moods?

3. Can you see how it might be said that the principle behind Blake's pair of poems applies to artistic creation or authorship as well as to God's creation of the world?

4. Note the abrupt phrases and unfinished sentences in stanzas 3, 4, and 5. Can this relative disorder be said to reflect the agitation of the speaker? Who is the speaker?

5. Does the poem contain a realistic description of the tiger? Does it stress the tiger's terrible power? In this description does the tiger become more than a literal animal? If more, then what more? And to what end? What does the tiger ultimately come to stand for? What does it symbolize?

6. Attempt to say what "The Tiger" is "about." What "The Lamb—The Tiger" (considered as a double poem) is "about."

7. Compare this poem with "The Eagle," by Tennyson (p. 361). In which poem is the thing signified by the image made more specific? But what qualities, objectively considered, do the images share? If the poem about the lamb did not exist, would "The Tiger" seem more like "The Eagle"? Why?

B. IMAGE TO METAPHOR

Desert Places

Robert Frost [*1874–1963*]

Snow falling and night falling fast oh fast
In a field I looked into going past,
And the ground almost covered smooth in snow,
But a few weeds and stubble showing last.

The woods around it have it—it is theirs.   5
All animals are smothered in their lairs.
I am too absent-spirited to count;
The loneliness includes me unawares.

And lonely as it is that loneliness
Will be more lonely ere it will be less—   10

A blanker whiteness of benighted snow
With no expression, nothing to express.

They cannot scare me with their empty spaces
Between stars—on stars where no human race is.
I have it in me so much nearer home   15
To scare myself with my own desert places.

Questions

1. What is the difference in the speaker's attitude toward his or her personal condition in "Mariana" and "Desert Places"?

2. Return to Ransom's "Bells for John Whiteside's Daughter" (p. 180) and consider the effect on tone of the word *vexed* in line 19. Compare the effect of *vexed* in setting the tone of Ransom's poem with the effect here of the word *scare* in lines 13 and 16. Would either word be natural for Mariana to use? If not, why not? Suppose we substitute the word *appall* for *scare*. What difference in the meaning of the poem would result?

3. How would you compare (or contrast) Frost's attitude toward nature in "Desert Places" with Keats's in "To Autumn" (p. 87)? With Stevens's in "Anecdote of the Jar"?

4. If this poem ended with line 12, what would it mean? How would you compare its meaning with that of "Mariana"? How would you compare the method in using imagery in the two instances?

"Desert Places" does not, however, end with line 12. The next four lines involve a special shift in the tone. Moreover, they have much to do with developing and defining the theme embodied in the total poem. How the shift in tone is effected (in part, at least) by Frost's choice of diction and how the theme is made to emerge are matters with which the four preceding questions are concerned.

The last four lines, however, may be used to illustrate something else of importance: the difference between a symbol and a metaphor. The poet does not use his imagery in these last four lines to create atmosphere or to *symbolize* a state of mind. Indeed, the basic image in the last stanza takes on metaphoric quality.

What are the differences among symbol, metaphor, and simile? In calling Stevens's jar a symbol, we said (p. 201) that it "stands for" something beyond itself, a "complex of emotion and idea." But metaphors may also be said to "stand for" things beyond themselves. Still earlier, we have cited a number of metaphors that occur in earlier poems in this book: umbrellas described as "recurved blossoms of the storm," a young man in a mental hospital waking up and in doing so rousing from "the mare's nest of his drowsy head." (We may need to remind ourselves here that a mare's nest is a hoax or a fraud.) On the same page, we also cited some comparisons such as "true as the stars above" and "His folks / Pursue their lives like toy trains on a track." Explicit comparisons such as these two last are called *similes*. Metaphors are often defined as *implied* comparisons, and this view has its element of truth, though some authorities see an essential difference in that metaphors boldly assert an *identity:* e.g., umbrellas *are* blossoms; whereas similes simply point to resemblances. In any case, symbols, metaphors, and similes are related in the fact that they all have an analogical function. (Analogy means correspondence between things usually thought of as quite unlike.) All state or imply that this "particular" signifies something other than itself, or that this "particular" is like that other thing (or state of being or action), or that this thing *is* that other thing. Analogy is the great human process by which we orient ourselves in the confusing world in which we live, and through which we make many of the discoveries about that world and about ourselves.

Though it is easy, on a grammatical basis, to distinguish *similes* from *symbols* and *metaphors,* since similes make use of *like* or *as* or some such word, symbols and metaphors are not so easily distinguished from each other. A simple practical test, however, is available: the term or phrase in question is a metaphor *if it cannot be taken literally.* Suppose we apply this test to "Desert Places."

The images in lines 1–12 are basically descriptive. (This is not, of course, to say that they are *merely* descriptive.) As the context of the poem develops, a mood and an implied attitude toward reality are built up. That is, the landscape pictured begins to acquire symbolic force. But the images can be taken literally—even the words "benighted snow / With no expression, nothing to express." *Benighted,* to be sure, is often applied to human beings living in ignorance, and a phrase such as "no expression" has powerful human associations; e.g., a bemused or be-numbed person whose face wears no expression. These human associations are subtly but powerfully used by the poet to develop his symbolic effect: they are indeed important for the poem. Even so, these items of description can be taken quite literally. "Benighted snow" is snow over-taken by darkness—snow under a night sky. The "blanker whiteness" of such snow does indeed literally have "no expression."

But "my own desert places" in line 16 cannot be taken literally. "Empty spaces" such as occur between the stars are not to be found inside the human head or the human body. The phrase makes sense only analogi-cally or, as we would say here, "metaphorically." The word *metaphor,* by the way, comes from a Greek verb meaning "to transfer," and a transfer occurs here: by a process of analogy the terrifying loneliness that shook Pascal as he thought of the silence of the inhuman emptiness of outer space is transferred from that context to a very different one—to the inner being of the speaker. In sum, "my own desert places" does not mean literally that great hole in my head, but that sense of terrifying emptiness that I find within my own spiritual being—that lonely void in my own psyche.

In her *Grammar of Metaphor* (London, 1958), Christine Brooke-Rose defines metaphor as "any replacement of one word by another, or any identification of one thing, concept, or person with any other." In this instance one could say that "my own desert places" *replaces* some such phrase as "the terrifying lonely emptiness that I find within my own spiritual being."

For another illustration of the distinction between symbol and metaphor, consider "Anecdote of the Jar." In this poem the jar does stand for something, but it doesn't "replace" any other word or phrase. It can be taken quite literally. It is true, as we have pointed out, that the way in which the poet describes his placing of the jar on a hill "is an odd way to talk" and invites symbolic interpretation; yet the "transfer" typical of metaphor does not occur. The jar was literally "gray and bare" and it was "round." "It did not give of bird or bush."

There are, to be sure, subsidiary expressions in the poem that show something of the character of metaphor—or at least such could be reasonably argued. For example, can a wilderness be literally "slovenly"? This adjective is associated with human behavior. By straining a point one might make out a kind of metaphor: Nature has in this instance been a poor housekeeper. Again, can a static object, whether a jar or a power-line pylon, make a wilderness "surround" anything? Only, one would say, in the human imagination—hence a hint of metaphor.

Thus, we would concede that in some of the related detail of this "Anecdote of the Jar" there are metaphoric relationships, though the principal strategy in the poem is that of symbolism. That symbol and metaphor should occur together is not surprising. Poets do not work by arbitrary rules, but according to the broad principles of analogy; and symbol, metaphor, and simile may, as we have earlier suggested, occur together in one and the same poem. In fact, they often do.

Here is another question that calls for an honest answer. Does it really matter whether the reader can discriminate between a metaphor and a symbol? We think it does, but not because failure to do so is a hanging offense. As we have remarked several times earlier, the modes tend at places to overlap, and one can sometimes argue the case either way. Yet a discussion of how symbols are developed and how they "work," and of the sense in which metaphors "transfer" from one context to another and often strike us forcefully and immediately as the symbol usually does not—such discussions can throw considerable light on the poetic process and perhaps help us to understand how poems come about and how they work on our sensibility. (For further discussion of the differences between symbol and metaphor, see Appendix C, p. 577.

Further Questions

1. Reread "The Lamb." Why may we say that the lamb is used in this poem as a symbol rather than as a metaphor?

2. In "Anecdote of the Jar" the jar is described as "tall and of a port in air." Could it be argued that in this instance "tall" is not being used literally but primarily metaphorically? As we indicated (pp. 200–201), the tallness of the jar suggests something more than a matter of feet and inches. How, in this instance, would you apply the test suggested on pp. 205–206? Would you say that though "tall" is here more than literal, it still can be applied literally? Or would you say that it is metaphorical? In that case, what is the "transfer"?

The Song of the Smoke

W. E. B. Du Bois [*1868–1963*]

I am the smoke king,
I am black.
I am swinging in the sky,
I am ringing worlds on high:
I am the thought of the throbbing mills,   5
I am the soul toil kills,
I am the ripple of trading rills.

Up I'm curling from the sod,
I am whirling home to God.
I am the smoke king,   10
I am black.

I am the smoke king,
I am black.
I am wreathing broken hearts,
I am sheathing devils' darts;   15
Dark inspiration of iron times,
Wedding the toil of toiling climes
Shedding the blood of bloodless crimes.

Down I lower in the blue,
Up I tower toward the true,   20
I am the smoke king,
I am black.

I am the smoke king,
I am black.

I am darkening with song,   25
I am hearkening to wrong;
I will be black as blackness can,
The blacker the mantle the mightier the man,
My purpl'ing midnights no day dawn may ban.

I am carving God in night,   30
I am painting hell in white.
I am the smoke king,
I am black.

I am the smoke king,
I am black.   35

I am cursing ruddy morn,
I am nursing hearts unborn;
Souls unto me are as mists in the night.
I whiten my blackmen, I beckon my white,
What's the hue of a hide to a man in his might!   40

Sweet Christ, pity toiling lands!
Hail to the smoke king,
Hail to the black!

Questions

1. Is any other aspect of smoke beyond its color involved here?
2. Do you find any individual images worthy of comment because
very effective or very inept?
3. Which predominates here, symbol or metaphor? Explain your choice.

The Windhover [1]

Gerard Manley Hopkins [1844–1889]

To Christ our Lord

I caught this morning morning's minion,[2] king-
    dom of daylight's dauphin, dapple-dawn-drawn Falcon, in his riding
    Of the rolling level underneath him steady air, and striding
High there, how he rung upon the rein[3] of a wimpling[4] wing
In his ecstasy! then off, off forth on swing,   5
    As a skate's heel sweeps smooth on a bow-bend: the hurl and
        gliding
    Rebuffed the big wind. My heart in hiding
Stirred for a bird,—the achieve of, the mastery of the thing!

Brute beauty and valour and act, oh, air, pride, plume here
    Buckle![5] and the fire that breaks from thee then, a billion   10
Times told lovelier, more dangerous, O my chevalier!

    No wonder of it; sheer plod makes plough down sillion[6]
Shine, and blue-bleak embers, ah my dear,
    Fall, gall themselves, and gash gold-vermilion.

[1] the kestrel, a small European hawk, somewhat resembling the American sparrow-
hawk [2] darling [3] "to ring on the rein," a term from the riding school meaning to
guide a horse in a circle at the end of a long rein [4] rippling [5] obviously a key term
for the poem; but what meaning (or meanings) of *buckle* applies to this context, (1)
putting on battle dress? (2) bringing together into unity? (3) giving way, crumpling
under pressure? or some other meaning? (Consult the *Oxford English Dictionary* for
the many divergent meanings of this term) [6] ridge left between two ploughed furrows; also spelled *selion*

Questions

1. We have here the literal image of a falcon in flight. Why, in the light of the treatment of the image in the poem, would you say that the poem is dedicated "To Christ our Lord"? In what sense is the poem symbolic? (It is important, in thinking of this question, not to try to work out strict parallels in details, as one would in dealing with allegory.)

2. Perhaps the following exercise should precede the first, for it involves elements that may well be said to bear on the symbolic force of the poem. In any case, examine the rhythms here, and the imagery as affecting the general tone of the poem. In the light of this matter, what would you say was Hopkins's feeling toward his religion? Try to be as specific as possible. For instance, do you think he would regard it as a religion of restrictions? Use possible examples.

The Goat Paths

James Stephens [*1882–1950*]

The crooked paths go every way
Upon the hill—they wind about
Through the heather in and out
Of the quiet sunniness.
And there the goats, day after day,   5

Stray in sunny quietness,
Cropping here and cropping there,
As they pause and turn and pass,
Now a bit of heather spray,
Now a mouthful of the grass.   10

In the deeper sunniness,
In the place where nothing stirs,
Quietly in quietness,
In the quiet of the furze,
For a time they come and lie   15
Staring on the roving sky.

If you approach they run away,
They leap and stare, away they bound,
With a sudden angry sound,
To the sunny quietude;   20
Crouching down where nothing stirs
In the silence of the furze,
Crouching down again to brood
In the sunny solitude.

If I were as wise as they,   25
I would stray apart and brood,

I would beat a hidden way
Through the quiet heather spray
To a sunny solitude;

And should you come I'd run away,   30
I would make an angry sound,
I would stare and turn and bound
To the deeper quietude,
To the place where nothing stirs
In the silence of the furze.   35

In that airy quietness
I would think as long as they;
Through the quiet sunniness
I would stray away to brood
By a hidden, beaten way   40
In the sunny solitude,

I would think until I found
Something I can never find,
Something lying on the ground,
In the bottom of my mind.   45

Questions

1. In regard to the way in which imagery is used here, would you say that "The Goat Paths" more nearly resembles "Mariana," "Anecdote of the Jar," or "Desert Places"?

2. If we take the attitude toward life expressed in "Desert Places" to be one of stoic courage in the face of blankness and meaninglessness, and that in Keats's "To Autumn" to be one of calm fulfillment in the life process, with which poet, Frost or Keats, would you say that Stephens (as represented here) would be more congenial? This is not to say, of course, that Stephens might not be different even from the poet he found more congenial. How would you define his attitude? What is he seeking for in the "bottom" of his "mind"? If he has not found it, is he bitter, resigned, content? Or what? In answering this question, be sure to consider the general tone of the poem.

3. Note the various repetitions of words and phrases, especially rhyme words, and the hypnotic effect this gives. How do these matters relate to the tone of the poem? In this connection, what about the falling rhythm frequent in the poem?

4. Compare this poem with "The Main-Deep," also by Stephens (p. 99), on the ground of metaphorical method.

5. Compare the attitudes and meanings in "The Goat Paths" with those in "Rocky Acres" (p. 106), "Nightingales" (p. 366), and "Composed upon Westminster Bridge" (p. 91).

6. Here are some possible revisions for "The Goat Paths." What differences would such changes make?

> *line 6:* Stray in sunny quietness
> *to:* Walk in sunny peace and calm

line 9: Now a bit of heather spray
to: Now a bit of heather leaf

line 16: Staring on the roving sky
to: Watching the bright sunlit sky

line 30: And should you come I'd run away
to: And should you come I'd rise and flee.

Consider various aspects of the revisions. For instance, does one lose a rhyme? Does one change a rhythm? What is the difference in tone? Has precision of imagery been lost or gained? Consider the general context in each instance.

A City Shower
In Imitation of Virgil's Georgics
Jonathan Swift [*1667–1745*]

Careful observers may foretell the hour
(By sure prognostics) when to dread a shower.
While rain depends, the pensive cat gives o'er
Her frolics, and pursues her tail no more;
Returning home at night, you'll find the sink   5
Strike your offended sense with double stink.
If you be wise, then, go not far to dine:
You'll spend in coach-hire more than save in wine.
A coming shower your shooting corns presage,
Old aches will throb, your hollow tooth will rage.   10
Sauntering in coffee-house is Dulman seen;
He damns the climate, and complains of spleen.
　Meanwhile, the south, rising with dabbled wings,
A sable cloud athwart the welkin flings,
That swilled more liquor than it could contain,   15
And, like a drunkard, gives it up again.
Brisk Susan whips her linen from the rope,
While the first drizzling shower is borne aslope:
Such is that sprinkling which some careless quean
Flirts on you from her mop, but not so clean: 20
You fly, invoke the gods; then, turning, stop
To rail; she, singing, still whirls on her mop.
Not yet the dust had shunned th'unequal strife,
But aided by the wind, fought still for life;
And, wafted with its foe by violent gust,   25
'Twas doubtful which was rain and which was dust.
Ah! where must needy poet seek for aid,
When dust and rain at once his coat invade?
Sole coat! where dust cemented by the rain
Erects the nap, and leaves a cloudy stain!   30

Now in contiguous drops the rain comes down,
Threatening with deluge this devoted town.
To shops in crowds the daggled females fly,
Pretend to cheapen goods but nothing buy.
The templar spruce, while every spout's abroach,   35
Stays till 'tis fair, yet seems to call a coach.
The tucked up seamstress walks with hasty strides,
While streams run down her oiled umbrella's sides.
Here various kinds, by various fortunes led,
Commence acquaintance underneath a shed.   40
Triumphant Tories and desponding Whigs
Forget their feuds, and join to save their wigs.
Boxed in a chair, the beau impatient sits,
While spouts run clattering o'er the roof by fits,
And ever and anon with frightful din   45
The leather sounds; he trembles from within.
So when Troy chairmen bore the wooden steed,
Pregnant with Greeks impatient to be freed
(Those bully Greeks, who, as the moderns do,
Instead of paying chairmen, ran them through),   50
Laocoön struck the outside with his spear,
And each imprisoned hero quaked for fear.
Now from all parts the swelling kennels flow,
And bear their trophies with them as they go:
Filths of all hues and odor seem to tell   55
What street they sailed from by their sight and smell.
They, as each torrent drives with rapid force,
From Smithfield or St. 'Pulchre's shape their course,
And in huge confluence joined at Snowhill ridge,
Fall from the conduit prone to Holborn bridge.   60
Sweepings from butchers' stalls, dung, guts, and blood,
Drowned puppies, stinking sprats, all drenched in mud,
Dead cats, and turnip tops, come tumbling down the flood.

Questions

1. At one level this poem is the description of a literal rainstorm in eighteenth-century London. At this literal level what details do you find striking and well-observed? But as the poem proceeds we find more and more details that have to do with filth, until the climax in lines 53 to 63. Can you correlate this fact with a view of human nature that is being developed in the poem?

2. In contrast to the realistic detail we find such language as

A sable cloud athwart the welkin flings

or

You fly, invoke the gods.

And we find the beau trapped in his sedan chair by the rain compared to the Greeks in the wooden horse craftily introduced into Troy, and the poet using the elevated language and the long simile modeled on Homer. This, of course, is the mock-heroic method. But why is it used here? To deflate what pretensions? What relation does this tone have to the filth?

3. In line 63 why does Swift use the word *flood* instead of *stream, gutter, sewer,* or *torrent?* (Rhyme cannot be taken as the reason here; any competent poet can use rhyme for his purposes and is not "used" by rhyme.) How significant here would be the reminder of the Biblical deluge?

4. What is the effect of the three rhyming lines here instead of the expected two?

5. If the Biblical deluge is implied here, why doesn't Swift dwell on the real vices, evils, and general wickedness of the city instead of drowned puppies and garbage?

6. Who is the "you" of the poem? What is Swift's attitude toward the "you"? That is, what is his tone?

7. How would you describe the use of imagery in this poem?

Go, Lovely Rose

Edmund Waller [*1606–1687*]

    Go, lovely Rose,
Tell her that wastes her time and me,
    That now she knows,
When I resemble her to thee,
How sweet and fair she seems to be.   5

    Tell her that's young,
And shuns to have her graces spied,
    That hadst thou sprung
In deserts where no men abide,
Thou must have uncommended died.   10

    Small is the worth
Of beauty from the light retir'd:
    Bid her come forth,
Suffer herself to be desir'd,
And not blush so to be admir'd.   15

    Then die, that she
The common fate of all things rare
    May read in thee,
How small a part of time they share,
That are so wondrous sweet and fair.   20

Here, a lover, whose suit has been rejected, is about to send a rose to his lady, and addresses the flower, the poem being the development of the ways in which the rose and the lady are parallels. The logic of the analogy, then, provides the framework of the poem, and the analogy is coterminous with the poem. We can even say that it constitutes the envelope of the poem.

Waller's working out of the analogies is, to be sure, not pedantic and heavy-handed. Quite the contrary—it is most deft and graceful. On one level the poem is a beautifully turned compliment to the lady to whom he sends the rose. But how tactful he is. His praise never becomes fulsome. Indeed, the lover never addresses his sweetheart directly, but simply allows her to overhear, as it were, the message that he confides to the rose and that he expects the rose to transmit to her in the flower's own wordless way.

Such a method of presentation has several obvious advantages, but its success depends on our acceptance of the poet's unargued assumption of a real likeness between rose and woman—a relationship that is ultimately as "natural" as anything in a poem by Wordsworth. Like the rose, the lady is "sweet and fair"; like the beauties of the rose, the lady's beauties will die "uncommended" if she modestly "shuns to have her graces spied." Finally, the lady is enjoined to remember that, like the rose's time of blossom, her own time is short, for all lovely things must fade and die. Youth must gather its rosebuds while it may, and the lady must suffer herself to be gathered; otherwise, her beauty has blossomed for nothing.

Much of the charm of Waller's poem, then, derives from his adroit use of a cliché—that of the basic analogy between rose and woman. The reader is delighted to see how eloquently he can make his mute offering speak to his shy mistress and how lightly and gracefully he freights the delicate flower with his love plea. That is to say, Waller's control of tone is masterly: on the surface this is a piece of *vers de société*—the graceful, witty, mannered verse of polite compliment—but the warning that lurks beneath the surface is urgent and, furthermore, touches on fundamental aspects of life.

Vers de société is often dismissed as too mannered and "artificial" to count as serious poetry. But the poets of the seventeenth century frequently converted it into work of deep feeling and power. We may glance at the way in which such qualities are here manifested. The first two stanzas constitute, indeed, merely an elegantly turned example of the complimentary style, its distinction being primarily one of rhythmic expertness and a skill in threading the syntactical structure through the stanza form. The third stanza begins, again, with the conventional tone of compliment—that is, through lines 11 to 13. And except for the word "suffer," the stanza continues in this vein. "To suffer" commonly meant, in Waller's time, "to permit"—as when, in the Bible, Jesus says, "Suffer little children to come unto me" (Luke 18:16). At the surface level, line 14 merely means "allow herself to be desired." But the word *suffer* also had its present meaning, and so, coupled with the secondary sexual meaning of *desir'd,* a secondary meaning is hinted at—to experience the strenuousness, even the pain, of sexual embrace, and not "blush" at it, but accept it.

This secondary meaning continues into line 16 with the word *die,* which meant, in addition to its obvious literal meaning, to come to sexual climax (as a play on words, in poem after poem of the period). It is true that the word *die* appears, strictly speaking, as a command to the rose, but it also can be absorbed into the word-order of lines 13 to 15: "Bid her come forth, / Suffer herself . . . not blush . . . Then die. . . ." This as referring to the lady. So the two ideas get interfused, and the sense is that the rose is ordered to die, literally, as a warning to the lady that she may literally die without having died in the secondary sense, that is, without fulfillment in nature. We may notice, too, how in the structure of the last stanza the word *die* gets a dramatic emphasis. This is established by the heavy caesura after *die*—a pause that gets unusual weight when followed by two run-on lines (16 and 17) together in a poem which is so prevailingly of end-stop lines. Notice, too, how the last two lines of the poem, which constitute a rhymed couplet, settle back into a conventional, almost pattering movement, in marked contrast to the rhetorical openness of the first three lines of the stanza. We may even suggest that the force of the poem—the seriousness itself—would scarcely be possible if it were not played off as a contrast in tone against the temper of *vers de société.* And this contrast is focused on the handling of the image of the rose.

Follow Thy Fair Sun, Unhappy Shadow

Thomas Campion [*1567–1620*]

Follow thy fair sun, unhappy shadow,
Though thou be black as night,
And she made all of light,
Yet follow thy fair sun, unhappy shadow.

Follow her whose light thy light depriveth, 5
Though here thou liv'st disgraced,
And she in heaven is placed,
Yet follow her whose light the world reviveth.

Follow those pure beams whose beauty burneth,
That so have scorchèd thee, 10
As thou still black must be,
Till her kind beams thy black to brightness turneth.

Follow her while yet the glory shineth:
There comes a luckless night,
That will dim all her light; 15
And this the black unhappy shade divineth.

Follow still since so thy fates ordainèd;
The sun must have his shade,
Till both at once do fade,
The sun still proud, the shadow still disdainèd.   20

As we have observed earlier, in a poem such as "Mariana" the imagery has a general atmospheric function, but in a poem such as "Yew-Trees" (p. 109) the poet has concentrated his description on two basic images, the lone yew tree and then the group of four, in the course of his description developing a weight of symbolic meaning. His method is essentially that of suggestion: through it, the image becomes more and more massive, acquiring reverberations of meaning, but the meanings are never analyzed nor even brought to specific focus. To go further, we have seen more specific functions of imagery in poems such as "Go, Lovely Rose."

With "Follow Thy Fair Sun," we find another example of the method found in "Go, Lovely Rose." Here, as before, we have one basic image—the sun and a shadow—but the process is, we may say, analytical, as it is in Waller's poem. That is, the poet does not work primarily by suggestion, but by listing and explicating quite systematically the ways in which the image becomes a metaphor; that is, the ways in which the image can be made to apply to the subject of the poem, here the relation of a lover and his beloved. Thus we have, very tidily, a series of statements, one to a stanza:

1. Though you are "black" (unhappy, unbeautiful), follow (as a shadow must follow the sun) your mistress (who is beautiful, powerful, free).
2. Though the light (beauty) of your mistress puts out your own (by contrast with her brilliance, by the fact that you are subordinate to her power), you must follow her whose power revives the world around her (at your cost, as it were).
3. Though her force has "scorched" you to blackness (as in stanza 3), she may yet turn your darkness to light (as she "revives" the world in stanza 2).
4. Follow her now, for even her beauty and power are not eternal, as you (being a "shadow") might, from your own unhappiness, guess.
5. It is natural and inevitable (ordained by fate) that you should follow your mistress (as the shadow follows the sun) until death ends the story, with, very probably, your mistress still disdaining you.

In such a method the poet commits himself to precision in the working out of the metaphorical implications of his basic image. He may work with a far-fetched comparison—much more far-fetched than the present one—but he must, point by point, "prove" its final aptness. The poet must be consistent in developing his image, *if he has once committed himself to this method.* The commitment a poet makes is the important thing here, and there are various kinds of commitments. This is not to say that one method is better or worse than another, for great triumphs have been scored in all kinds of poetic styles. It is only to say that each method implies its own logic, and we should try to understand that logic.

Questions

1. Compare the tone of this poem with that of "A Litany" (p. 185) and "I Knew a Woman" (p. 188).

2. Let us not forget that the handling of the imagery is only one factor in a poem. What other factors here, do you think, contribute to the success of "Follow Thy Fair Sun"?

Blame Not My Cheeks

Thomas Campion [*1567–1620*]

> Blame not my cheeks, though pale with love they be;
> The kindly heat unto my heart is flown,
> To cherish it that is dismaid by thee,
> Who art so cruel and unsteadfast grown:
> For nature, called for by distressèd hearts,   5
> Neglects and quite forsakes the outward parts.
>
> But they whose cheeks with careless blood are stained,
> Nurse not one spark of love within their hearts,
> And, when they woo, they speak with passion feigned,
> For their fat love lies in their outward parts: 10
> But in their breasts, where love his court should hold,
> Poor Cupid sits and blows his nails for cold.

Questions

1. Lines 3 and 4 with the "dismayed" lover and the "cruel and unsteadfast" mistress state the Petrarchan cliché. Scan these lines. How many secondary accents are there? What is the effect of this weighty rhythm in conjunction with the staleness—the ironic staleness, we might say—of the content of the lines? Is there a hint of reality introduced into the clichés?

2. Let us take a series of items, and examine as fully as we may their range of possible meanings in the poem: *parts, careless, stained, fat love.* Notice how if the first impressioin of meaning is literal (as with *stained*—the flush of health), the meaning moves over into a metaphoric (morally stained), or how, if the first impression is metaphoric (as with *fat love*), we move over to various possible literal applications. Do not these words, the more we dwell on their meanings and references in the poem, fortify the impression of grossness, fleshiness, sensuality? If this is true, does this work toward an acceptance, because of a sudden burst of realism, of the Petrarchan distinction between the true and the false lover?

3. Look at the word *lies*. What do you make of it?

4. How is the speaker's attitude toward himself, the subject, and the audience addressed reflected in the closing image of the poor, naked little Cupid shivering beside a fireless hearth? Is this supposed to be pathetic, ridiculous, or what?

My Springs

Sidney Lanier [*1842–1881*]

In the heart of the Hills of Life, I know
Two springs that with unbroken flow
Forever pour their lucent streams
Into my soul's far Lake of Dreams.

Not larger than two eyes, they lie   5
Beneath the many-changing sky
And mirror all of life and time,
—Serene and dainty pantomime.

Shot through with lights of stars and dawns,
And shadowed sweet by ferns and fawns,   10
—Thus heaven and earth together vie
Their shining depths to sanctify.

Always when the large Form of Love
Is hid by storms that rage above,
I gaze in my two springs and see
Love in his very verity.   15

Always when Faith with stifling stress
Of grief hath died in bitterness,
I gaze in my two springs and see
A faith that smiles immortally.   20

Always when Charity and Hope,
In darkness bounden, feebly grope,
I gaze in my two springs and see
A Light that sets my captives free.

Always when Art on perverse wing   25
Flies where I cannot hear him sing,
I gaze in my two springs and see
A charm that brings him back to me.

When Labor faints, and Glory fails,
And coy Reward in sighs exhales,   30
I gaze in my two springs and see
Attainment full and heavenly.

O Love, O Wife, thine eyes are they
—My springs from out whose shining gray
Issue the sweet celestial streams   35
That feed my life's bright Lake of Dreams.

Oval and large and passion-pure
And gray and wise and honor-sure;
Soft as a dying violet-breath
Yet calmly unafraid of death;   40

Thronged, like two dove-cotes of gray doves,
With wife's and mother's and poor-folk's loves,
And home-loves and high glory-loves
And science-loves and story-loves,

And loves for all that God and man   45
In art and nature make or plan,
And lady-loves for spidery lace
And broideries and supple grace

And diamonds and the whole sweet round
Of littles that large life compound,   50
And loves for God and God's bare truth,
And loves for Magdalen and Ruth,

Dear eyes, dear eyes and rare complete—
Being heavenly-sweet and earthly-sweet,
—I marvel that God made you mine,   55
For when He frowns, 'tis then ye shine!

Questions

1. The first nine stanzas are built on one basic image, that of the springs; the next four, on that of doves in a dove-cote. What is the pattern of imagery developed in each instance? Does it have any basis of consistency?

2. For example, the poet says that his beloved's eyes, the springs, are located in the Hills of Life and that their overflow keeps full the Lake of Dreams in his own soul. But an overflow of these eye-springs is surely weeping. Yet, does the poet mean that his wife's weeping keeps his Lake of Dreams replenished? How many other elements inconsistent with the poet's obvious purpose do you find?

3. Would it be fair to say that Campion's developed imagery works with a fine consistency, whereas Lanier's images are always threatening to betray and confuse, or become irrelevant to, the poet's purpose?

C. IMAGE IN THE DISCOURSE OF A POEM

She Dwelt Among the Untrodden Ways

William Wordsworth [*1770–1850*]

> She dwelt among the untrodden ways
>   Beside the springs of Dove,
> A Maid whom there were none to praise
>   And very few to love:
>
> A violet by a mossy stone   5
>   Half hidden from the eye!
> Fair as a star, when only one
>   Is shining in the sky.
>
> She lived unknown, and few could know
>   When Lucy ceased to be;   10
> But she is in her grave, and oh,
>   The difference to me!

In all the poems in Division B in this section, we have seen a single image developed, in one way or another, as the basic envelope, or structure, of a poem. In the present poem, the basic structure is a discourse; the poet tells us various things about Lucy, but no image appears until the second stanza. To understand the importance of imagery here we may try the experiment of omitting the second stanza. What have we left? The "poem" remaining (stanzas 1 and 3) tells us that since Lucy lived remote from the great world, her death passed unnoticed. Few people knew her, and anyway they were simple, unlettered folk who lacked the means to set forth to the world the tributes due her. Yet, though Lucy's passing made no difference to the great world, it has made all the difference to her lover, who speaks the poem.

So much for a summary of the content of stanzas 1 and 3. But isn't this all the poem has to say anyway? What is lost if we leave out the images of the violet and the evening star? We may be tempted to answer: just some ornamentation—two comparisons that are meant to enhance Lucy's charm by associating her with such attractive objects as flowers and stars.

Yet, if this is all the imagery does, one might properly wonder why the poem wouldn't be just as valuable (or vapid) if Wordsworth had never written stanza 2. Or if we feel that the poem would seem intolerably bare if it contained no comparisons at all, wouldn't another flower have done just as well? For example, the poet might have written:

> A full-blown rose of glorious hue,
> Bright'ning a garden wall.

Clearly, the rose will not do—and the fact that it will not proves that the imagery in stanza 2 does more than supply a vague enhancement to the girl. Lucy's natural charm, like that of the violet, was derived from her modesty. She, too, was "half-hidden from the eye," obscure and unnoticed. Yet, if this is really the point the poet has attempted to make with his violet-comparison, then doesn't another problem arise? Doesn't the poet confuse matters by offering the star-comparison that immediately follows? Doesn't his emphasis on the prominence of the star—it must almost certainly be Venus as evening star, normally the first star to shine forth after sunset—involve a contradiction? How can Lucy be at once too easily overlooked and yet impossible to miss?

There is, of course, no contradiction. The second stanza enacts through its imagery the very "statement" made in the third stanza—and it is a somewhat paradoxical statement: though Lucy was, to the world, as completely obscure as the modest flower in the shadow of the mossy stone, to the eye of her lover she was the only star in his heaven, shining like the planet of love itself.

We are perhaps now ready to answer the question asked earlier: what is the importance of the imagery in this poem? In an important sense the imagery *is* the poem. It is not simply a fancy way of illustrating what the poet might have said in abstract terms; that is, the imagery is not something "additional"—merely decorative. If poetry does bring together idea and emotion, rendering an experience dramatically in concrete terms (see pp. 9, 14), then stanza 2 is the core—the very heart—of the poem.

Questions

1. The fact that in "She Dwelt Among the Untrodden Ways" the poet compares the girl to a violet, not a rose, suggests some comparison between this poem and Waller's. What is the difference between the worlds the two poets are writing about? Which is the simpler, the more natural, the more unsophisticated? Which poet depends on the natural suggestion in his images, and which intellectualizes, as it were, and analyzes his images? How would the world of a poem and its method be related? Whatever the answers to these questions, observe that the two poems, in spite of their differences, rely fundamentally on their images.

2. Return to Wordsworth's "Composed upon Westminster Bridge" (p. 91). If it were shorn of its imagery, what would it say? What would it "feel like"?

The Definition of Love
Andrew Marvell [*1621–1678*]

My love is of a birth as rare
As 'tis for object strange and high:
It was begotten by Despair
Upon Impossibility.

Magnanimous Despair alone   5
Could show me so divine a thing,
Where feeble Hope could ne'er have flown
But vainly flapped its tinsel wing.

And yet I quickly might arrive
Where my extended soul is fixed,   10
But Fate does iron wedges drive,
And always crowds itself betwixt.

For Fate with jealous eye does see
Two perfect loves, nor lets them close:
Their union would her ruin be,   15
And her tyrannic power depose.

And therefore her decrees of steel
Us as the distant poles have placed,
(Though love's whole world on us doth wheel)
Not by themselves to be embraced,   20

Unless the giddy heaven fall,
And earth some new convulsion tear,
And, us to join, the world should all
Be cramped into a planisphere.

As lines, so loves oblique may well   25
Themselves in every angle greet;
But ours, so truly parallel,
Though infinite, can never meet.

Therefore the love which us doth bind,
But fate so enviously debars,   30
Is the conjunction of the mind,
And opposition of the stars.

We place this poem just after "She Dwelt Among the Untrodden Ways" because it illustrates in a more complex and extended form the method used by Wordsworth. In "The Definition of Love," as in Wordsworth's poem, a discourse provides the envelope for the poem. The discourse in Wordsworth's poem is basically narrative, and here it is logical, analytical, and abstract; but the important fact is that in both instances a discourse provides the frame, the structure, the envelope of the poem, and the images (which are not related to one another) appear along the way to support, develop, or interpret the discourse.

These introductory remarks may make the poem seem dull and pedantic, but it is, on the contrary, generally regarded as one of the finer and more famous poems in our language, and one that has, ultimately, a strong emotional aura. Our remarks may be useful only to give some orientation for the reader to whom the method may, at first, seem strained.

The poem is built upon a paradox: the very fact that his love cannot be consummated makes it somehow more rare and precious than a love that can be fulfilled and may be subject to routine, boredom, and the casual problems of life. The shock of the paradox—the sharp break it makes with the stale and conventional in general—allows him to state with no sense of overfacile, glib exaggeration that

> My love is of a birth as rare
> As 'tis for object strange and high.

The first word of the second stanza enforces the paradox. It lets us know that the poet is going to stand by his paradox. Despair is not *grim* or *harsh* or *cruel,* as one would anticipate, but *magnanimous.* His love is too divine to have been hoped for—it could only have been shown to him by Despair itself. Already the paradox has done something more than startle us out of an accustomed attitude; it helps us grasp the poet's attitude, one complex enough to perceive a magnanimity in the very hopelessness of attaining his love since only that hopelessness allows him to see its true and ideal character.

The poet now proceeds to develop this paradox through images. It is nothing less than fate that separates him from his love. Fate drives iron wedges between them. And the poet, having personified fate—having turned it into a person—provides the person with a motive. Fate itself would cease to exist if any complete perfection might be attained. Their love is so perfect that its consummation would be incompatible with a world ruled over by fate. That this should be prevented from happening is therefore not the result of one of fate's malicious caprices—the character of the love itself determines the "fate."

Notice at this point that the poet's attitude toward fate is not that of hysterical outrage. There is a calm reasoned tone here such as we have already found in the ability to see despair as "magnanimous." And yet this sense of reasonableness has been achieved *in the process* of making statements that ordinarily would seem the most outrageous exaggerations. His love is the highest possible; his love is too divine to be even hoped for. The result is that the statements are felt, not as outrageous statements to be immediately discounted, but as having the weight of reasoned truth.

In the fifth stanza the major paradox is given a decisive statement through an unusually fine figure. Fate has placed the two lovers as far apart as "the distant poles." This seems at first merely the conventional expression which we use to indicate great distance apart. But the poet immediately seizes on the implied figure and develops it for us. The two lovers are, like the poles of the earth, unable to touch each other; but though they are separated by the distance of the entire globe, they are the focal points in determining the rotation of the earth. Thus, the lovers, though separated, define the ideal nature of love. The world of love, like a globe, turns on the axis of their relationship. The exactness of the comparison gives force to his statement, and Marvell further stresses the exactness of the relationship between his own situation and the figure which he uses to illustrate it by going on to state the only condition on which the poles might be united. The poles might be united only if the earth were suddenly compressed into a two-dimensional disc which would have no thickness at all—that is, into a *planisphere*. The associations of a technical word again support the sense of exact, calculated statement in the poem. The poet continues to expound the incredible nature of his love with the poise of a mathematician. Therefore we are more readily inclined to accept the statement.

The technical word also prepares somewhat for the figure that the poet uses in the seventh stanza. Loves "oblique," the loves of those who are not in perfect accord, are like lines which cross each other at an angle. Their very lack of parallelism forms the possibility of their meeting. His own love and that of his mistress accord with each other so perfectly that, though stretched to infinity, they could draw no nearer together. In this image, then, the poet finds exactly the illustration of the paradoxical relationship of which he is writing. The application of this image is made easier by the ordinary association of the idea of infinity with the idea of love; it is a conventional association in love poetry. But Marvell has taken the conventional association and, by developing it, has derived a renewed life and freshness.

The poem closes with another paradox, this time drawn from astrology. We say that stars are in *conjunction* when they are seen in the sky very close together; that they are in *opposition* when they are situated in opposite parts of the sky. According to astrology, planets in conjunction unite their influences. In opposition they fight against each other. Here the lovers' minds are in conjunction. They are united, but their stars (fate) are against them. This concluding comparison, then, combines the idea of the third and fourth stanzas with that of the fifth and sixth. In a way, it epitomizes the whole poem.

Is the poem merely an ingenious bundle of paradoxes? Some readers may dislike the very active play of the mind here and will dislike also the exactness of the diction and the imagery drawn from mathematics and kindred subjects. But does this ingenuity and exactness make the poem insincere? Does it not have indeed the opposite effect? The lover protesting his love is too often vague and rhetorical. He gives a sense of glibness and effusiveness. The effect of Marvell's imagery is not only one of freshness as opposed to stale conventionality—it is also one of calculation as opposed to one of unthinking excitement.

There is another aspect of the kind of imagery characteristic of this poem—of what is called "metaphysical poetry" (illustrated most famously by John Donne, pp. 134, 240, 243, 330, 529. As we have seen, some poets—often some of the finest poets—may use imagery that is in itself charming, beautiful, or "poetical"; for example, John Keats in "To Autumn" (p. 87), or Tennyson in his "Choric Song" (p. 542). This kind of imagery is not, however, characteristic of Marvell, nor of the metaphysical poets in general. Though here we do find Hope's "tinsel wing" (which is a pretty or poetical thing, presumably), the other images (iron wedges, a planisphere, and parallel lines) are what may be called "neutral"—that is, they come into a poem with no particular emotional charge, no association of the "poetic" or agreeable. The poet, in other words, is working here by repudiating such adjuncts to poetry, and thus emphasizes the precision of his metaphysical practice, its expressive function.

Questions

1. Would you say that "The Definition of Love" has any qualities of *vers de société*? Think of "Go, Lovely Rose" and "Blame Not My Cheeks." By the way, what other poems read thus far have some relation to that genre?

2. As we have said, this poem is built on a paradox. Is this paradox merely a piece of glittering rhetoric but finally specious? Or does it embody a truth?

3. Return to "Channel Firing" (p. 45), which, like this poem, is written in iambic tetrameter, rhymed *abab*. What differences do you observe between Hardy's and Marvell's use of the form? In run-on lines? In run-on stanzas? In the use of caesura? In regularity of meter? Having distinguished the differences, try to relate them to other aspects of the two poems. For instance, which poem makes freer use of realistic detail? Which poem exploits shocking shifts in tone?

You're the Top

Cole Porter   [*1893–1964*]

> At words poetic
> I'm so pathetic
> that I always have found it best,
> instead of getting them off my chest,
> to let 'em rest   5
> unexpressed.

I hate parading
my serenading
as I'll probably miss a bar,
but if this ditty   10
is not so pretty
at least it'll tell you how great you are.

You're the top,
you're the Colosseum,
you're the top,   15
you're the Louvre Museum,
you're a melody
from a symphony
by Strauss,
you're a Bendel bonnet,   20
a Shakespeare sonnet,
you're Mickey Mouse.

You're the Nile,
You're the Tower of Pisa,
you're the smile,   25
on the Mona Lisa.
I'm a worthless check,
a total wreck,
a flop,
but if, baby, I'm the bottom, you're the top.   30

You're the top,
you're Mahatma Gandhi,
you're the top,
you're Napoleon brandy,
you're the purple light   35
of a summer night
in Spain,
you're the National Gallery,
you're Garbo's salary,
you're cellophane.   40

You're sublime,
you're a turkey dinner,
you're the time
of the Derby winner.
I'm a toy balloon   45
that's fated soon
to pop,
but if, baby, I'm the bottom, you're the top.

You're the top,
you're an Arrow collar,   50
you're the top,
you're a Coolidge dollar,

you're the nimble tread
of the feet of Fred
Astaire,   55
you're an O'Neill drama,
you're Whistler's mama,
you're Camembert.

You're repose,
you're *Inferno's* Dante,   60
you're the nose
on the Great Durante.
I'm just in the way—
as the French would say,
"*de trop*"—   65
but if, baby, I'm the bottom, you're the top.

You're the top,
you're a Waldorf salad,
you're the top,
you're a Berlin ballad,   70
you're the baby grand
of a lady and
a gent,
you're an Old Dutch Master,
you're Mrs. Astor,   75
you're Pepsodent.

You're romance,
you're the steppes of Russia,
you're the pants
on a Roxy usher.   80
I'm a lazy lout
that's just about
to stop,
but if, baby, I'm the bottom, you're the top.

This song was written for the 1934 Broadway musical *Anything Goes*.
Obviously, the song is a kind of period piece. Nobody wears an Arrow
collar anymore, and the youngest generation has probably never heard
of one; as for cellophane, it's no longer a novelty but as common as
newsprint, and therefore will make the young reader wonder why a lover
ever thought of comparing his sweetheart to *that*. Yet this period piece
can serve our purposes here. A great deal of its ebullience and verve
and enthusiasm still comes through, the unexpected rhymes are delightful,
and, most important for our purposes, the poem provides an elaborate
exercise in the ways in which analogies can be used—comparisons that
are humorous, fulsome, exuberant, far-fetched, even ridiculous.

Questions

1. The associations of the various items to which the lover's sweetheart are compared range from the grand and sublime to the pedestrian and the trivial. The only quality that these items have in common is that, like the girl, they are the "top"—the best in their class. How many comparisons are actually made tongue-in-cheek? In other words, do a series of tonal shifts have something to do with the verve and ebullience of the piece?

2. How "sincere" is the poem? Is it just an exercise in ingenuity? Or does it manage to convey a quality of genuine feeling? Compare the feeling here with that of "The Definition of Love" and that of "Go, Lovely Rose." How would you describe the "speaker" of this poem in comparison with those of the other two poems?

3. We have remarked in connection with several poems (pp. 187, 217) on the Petrarchan convention of the self-abasing lover. How is it used here? With what tonal quality? Compare the tone here to that of "Follow Thy Fair Sun" (p. 215).

Cleopatra's Lament

William Shakespeare [*1564–1616*]

> *Cleopatra.* I dreamed there was an Emperor Antony:
> O! such another sleep, that I might see
> But such another man.
> > *Dolabella.*   If it might please ye,—
> *Cleopatra.* His face was as the heavens, and therein stuck   5
> A sun and moon, which kept their course, and lighted
> The little O, the earth.
> > *Dolabella.*   Most sovereign creature,—
> *Cleopatra.* His legs bestrid the ocean; his reared arm
> Crested the world; his voice was propertied   10
> As all the tunèd spheres, and that to friends;
> But when he meant to quail and shake the orb,
> He was as rattling thunder. For his bounty,
> There was no winter in 't, an autumn 'twas
> That grew the more by reaping; his delights   15
> Were dolphin-like, they showed his back above
> The element they lived in; in his livery
> Walked crowns and crownets, realms and islands were
> As plates dropped from his pocket.
> > *Dolabella.*   Cleopatra,—   20
> *Cleopatra.* Think you there was, or might be, such a man
> As this I dreamed of?
> > *Dolabella.*   Gentle madam, no.

Antony and Cleopatra V, ii

We have seen in "Follow Thy Fair Sun" and other poems, how a poet makes a commitment to develop consistently one basic image, which becomes the sensuous envelope of the work. But, of course, this is not the only kind of method available for the use of imagery. We may observe, for instance, that in a poem such as Wordsworth's "Yew-Trees" (p. 109) a scene may be the sensuous envelope or an event may be, as in "Sir Patrick Spence" (p. 23) or "Danny Deever" (p. 35). We observe, too, that in "The Definition of Love," the envelope is not sensuous at all, but is a discourse, with various sensuous elements—images—attached to it, as it were, to develop or enrich meaning.

In "Cleopatra's Lament," we find another, and very different, use of imagery. We should begin our consideration of the speech by reminding ourselves that it is from a play and by reconstructing the circumstances of its utterance. Antony is recently dead, and nothing now stands between the Egyptian queen and the vengeance of the conquering Octavius. Dolabella, the emissary of Octavius, has appeared before Cleopatra to arrange what amounts to the terms of surrender. As he tries to introduce himself, her mind leaps back to the days of her happiness. It is a "dream"—in shocking contrast to the present reality; and the image of Antony, now godlike in her recollection, is in shocking contrast to what any human being might be.

Cleopatra begins with a comparison so extreme as to break any ordinary logic—Antony's face as the very heavens, with eyes like sun and moon lighting the little earth. But the violation of logic is an index to the force of her emotion, which now breaks out. We feel a dramatic grounding for the violence and elevation of the utterance—with its sense of dream-like release and apocalyptic grandeur—which is not unlike the language of, let us say, the Book of Revelation, another attempt to utter the unutterable. Note that Dolabella three times (lines 3, 6, and 17) attempts to break in. His is the voice of realism demanding to be heard in the midst of the rapture of the vision.

With the next section Cleopatra begins what seems to be a systematic description of the creature whose improbable face she has just sketched—how "his legs bestrid the ocean," how his arm was lifted to crest the world, how his voice affected others. But this systematic description soon breaks into a series of images which have no consistent relation to the main image with which the passage begins, or with each other. Here again we feel that the breaking away from the systematic description is, like the violation of ordinary logic in the first big image, an index to the dramatic urgency, the power of the queen's feeling. Then, with the last image, we return to the first, the image of the godlike creature bestriding the world, with realms and islands like gold or silver "plates" dropped from his pockets in careless generosity. So the main image serves as a kind of envelope to hold the other inconsistent and unrelated images. Then, as further rounding out and tightening of the passage, the whole speech is again defined as a dream; the voice of everyday realism speaks.

Though, as we have pointed out, there is a sort of inclusive image in this passage, what we want to stress is the way imagery is used within that frame (or, as we shall see, without reference to any frame). In the central part of the passage we have what is called mixed metaphor: the bounty like an autumn, delights with dolphin backs, and so on. But here we not only find the images acceptable, we find them grandly expressive. We accept them because, on one level, we sense the dramatic urgency from which they spring, spilling over one another, and because, on another, we recognize the kind of commitment the poet is making. He does not pretend to give a system, as does the poet of "Follow Thy Fair Sun"; the very violence of his general style and the exaggerated differences between one image and another declare this. We refer each image back to the central intent, the central drift of the passage, the controlling emotion of the passage, and accept or reject it by this reference. The images may, as is the case here with the return to the godlike figure in the end, be enclosed in some general image, but that is not our point. Our point is the very *discontinuity* of the individual images.

We have, then, two basic kinds of commitment in the use of images. In the first, as in "Follow Thy Fair Sun," the poet undertakes to give a series of images related to each other to form a consistent series—the image of the shadow following the sun. This development of an image in a series of consistent manifestations carries the idea, the "argument," of the poem, which may or may not be actually stated. Let us make a little chart of this:

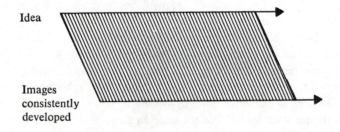

Idea

Images
consistently
developed

The progression of the idea, we may say, is totally projected into the imagery, and the imagery is as consistent as the argument it embodies. Continuity is the earmark of this method, and self-consistency in the use of imagery.

For the kind of commitment we find in "Cleopatra's Lament," we may make another chart:

Antony's godlike qualities, power, grandeur, bounty, etc.

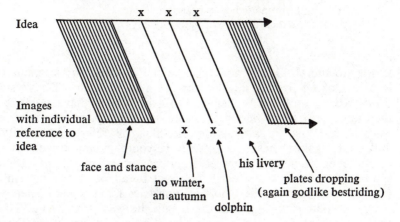

As we have said, the very point of this style is the discontinuity of the images. Each image must be guaranteed by its individual reference to the line of idea, of argument.

We might add that each image must be validated by its reference to the line of feeling, too—to the tone of the poem. We have indicated how the passion of Cleopatra breaks out in the intrinsic violence of her imagery as well as in the discontinuity. This kind of commitment in the use of imagery, however, is useful not only with poetry of high dramatic tension; it has other uses, as we saw in "The Definition of Love," by Andrew Marvell, where the leap from one image to the next is not an indication of a driving, overwhelming feeling, but of an alert, probing intellectuality trying to understand a feeling. But in Marvell's poem, we remember, the discourse would be logically coherent, on the whole, *without* some of the imagery; in "Cleopatra's Lament" it is the *imagery that actually embodies the idea.*

Questions

1. Look at the word *crested* in line 10. The word itself is, clearly, a metaphor, condensed or submerged. But what is the image in the metaphor? The arm crests the world—an orb with a bent shape above. By reason of the word *crested,* and the warlike and chivalric temper of the passage, we are led to some sense of helmet with plume, perhaps mailed arm bent above the plume, or some other heraldic device. In any case, the word carries a weight of possibility which affects the hearer *as possibility,* the speed and depth of mental association being what it is, even when we do not rationalize the metaphor. What do you make of the dolphinlike delights? Can we say that the image is basically sexual?

2. An example of mixed metaphor sometimes given in handbooks of rhetoric is: "Mr. Speaker, I smell a rat. Shall I nip him in the bud?" How does this differ from Cleopatra's "mixed" metaphors?

3. Here is a passage from one of Shakespeare's sonnets:

O how shall summer's honey breath hold out
Against the wreckful siege of battering days.

Sonnet 65

If we are literal-minded and mistake the kind of commitment the poet is here making for his images, we get a mere hash. "Days" stands for Time, which, as René Wellek and Austin Warren have pointed out, "is then metaphorized as besieging a city and attempting, by battering-rams, to take it. What is attempting—city-like, or ruler of the city-like—to 'hold out' against these assaults? It is youth, metaphorized as summer, or more exactly, as the sweet fragrance of summer: the fragrance of summer flowers is to the earth as sweet breath is to the human body, a part of or adjunct of the whole. If one tries to fit together neatly in one image the battering siege and the breath, he gets jammed up. The figurative movement is rapid and hence elliptical."* The point these critics are making is that the reader should not try to fit the separate items neatly into one image. He should accept the rapid and elliptical reference to the line of idea and/or emotion.

Macbeth Thinks of Murdering the King
William Shakespeare [1564–1616]

If it were done when 'tis done, then 'twere well
It were done quickly, if the assassination
Could trammel up the consequence, and catch,
With his surcease, success; that but this blow
Might be the be-all and the end-all here,   5
But here, upon this bank and shoal of time,—
We'd jump the life to come. But in these cases
We still have judgment here; that we but teach
Bloody instructions, which, being taught, return
To plague the inventor: this even-handed justice   10
Commends the ingredients of our poison'd chalice
To our own lips. He's here in double trust;
First, as I am his kinsman and his subject,
Strong both against the deed; then, as his host,
Who should against his murderer shut the door,   15
Not bear the knife myself. Besides, this Duncan
Hath borne his faculties so meek, hath been
So clear in his great office, that his virtues
Will plead like angels, trumpet-tongued, against
The deep damnation of his taking-off;   20

* René Wellek and Austin Warren, *Theory of Literature*, Harcourt, Brace, 1949, p. 208.

And pity, like a naked new-born babe,
Striding the blast, or heaven's cherubim, hors'd
Upon the sightless couriers of the air,
Shall blow the horrid deed in every eye,
That tears shall drown the wind.—I have no spur   25
To prick the sides of my intent, but only
Vaulting ambition, which o'er-leaps itself,
And falls on the other.

Macbeth I, vii

In this speech, Macbeth contemplates the murder of Duncan, the king, who is his kinsman, and who has just that day bestowed honors upon him. The king is spending the night in Macbeth's castle. There is opportunity; and Lady Macbeth has urged her husband to murder the king and seize the crown for himself.

Questions

1. Do lines 1–4 convey the sense of excitement and conspiratorial whispering? How?

2. What is the meaning of lines 2–7? What is the proviso that appeals to Macbeth—that would decide him if he could but be sure of it? ("Trammel" means to entangle as in a kind of net: cf. modern *trammel net*. "Jump," line 7, is interpreted by *A Shakespeare Glossary* to mean "risk," "hazard." But does this sense of "jump" necessarily exclude the other?) What image or images are to be found in these lines?

3. Pick out the various images that occur in the rest of the passage. How are the images related to each other? Do you find any mixed metaphors? Can you or can you not justify them?

4. Consider in particular the metaphors that occur in lines 21–28. Babes, angels, horses, tears, and the wind occur in a remarkable mixture in these lines. What does the passage mean? How are the images interrelated? Is the poet confused? Or does the passage constitute great poetry?

At Melville's Tomb

Hart Crane [*1899–1932*]

Often beneath the wave, wide from this ledge
The dice of drowned men's bones he saw bequeath
An embassy. Their numbers as he watched,
Beat on the dusty shore and were obscured.

And wrecks passed without sound of bells,   5
The calyx of death's bounty giving back
A scattered chapter, livid hieroglyph,
The portent wound in corridors of shells.

Then in the circuit calm of one vast coil,   10
Its lashings charmed and malice reconciled,
Frosted eyes there were that lifted altars;
And silent answers crept across the stars.

Compass, quadrant and sextant contrive
No farther tides . . . High in the azure steeps   15
Monody shall not wake the mariner.
This fabulous shadow only the sea keeps.

This poem is an elegy on Herman Melville, the author of *Moby Dick,* the great American novel of the sea and whaling. The general meaning of the poem is easy enough. The poet says that the spirit of the writer whose imagination was so vividly engaged by the sea, and who saw such grandeur in man's struggle with it, though his body might be buried on land, would find its real abiding place in the sea:

> This fabulous shadow only the sea keeps.

This poem gives a clear example in modern poetry of the method used in "Cleopatra's Lament" and in part of Macbeth's speech. It is interesting to observe that the editor who first published the poem was as puzzled by it as though Crane had just invented the method. Here are some of the questions she asked Crane in a letter:

> Take me for a hard-boiled unimaginative reader, and tell me how *dice can bequeath an embassy* (or anything else); and how a calyx (of *death's bounty* or anything else) can give back *a scattered chapter, livid hieroglyph;* and how, if it does, such a *portent* can be *wound in corridors* (of shells or anything else).
> And so on. I find your image of *frosted eyes lifting altars* difficult to visualize.* Nor do compass, quadrant, and sextant *contrive* tides, they merely record them, I believe.
> All this may seem impertinent, but is not so intended. Your ideas and rhythms interest me, and I am wondering by what process of reasoning you would justify this poem's succession of champion mixed metaphors, of which you must be conscious. The packed line should pack its phrases in orderly relation, it seems to me, in a manner tending to clear confusion instead of making it worse confounded.†

The first part of the poet's reply to the editor's letter was concerned with a general justification of comparisons that are not scientifically and logically exact. (This general question has already emerged in connection with various poems. See pp. 3–9.) Then the poet undertook to answer the editor's specific objections:

---

* The editor here falls into a not uncommon error, that of assuming that all imagery is visual.
† Harriet Monroe, editor, *Poetry: A Magazine of Verse,* to Hart Crane.

. . . I'll . . . come at once to the explanations you requested on the Melville poem:

> "The dice of drowned men's bones he saw bequeath
> An embassy."

Dice bequeath an embassy, in the first place, by being ground (in this connection only, of course) in little cubes from the bones of drowned men by the action of the sea, and are finally thrown up on the sand, having "numbers" but no identification. These being the bones of dead men who never completed their voyage, it seems legitimate to refer to them as the only surviving evidence of certain messages undelivered, mute evidence of certain things, experiences that the dead mariners might have had to deliver. Dice as a symbol of chance and circumstance is also implied.

> "The calyx of death's bounty giving back," etc.

This calyx refers in a double ironic sense both to a cornucopia and the vortex made by a sinking vessel. As soon as the water has closed over a ship this whirlpool sends up broken spars, wreckage, etc., which can be alluded to as *livid hieroglyphs,* making a *scattered chapter* so far as any complete record of the recent ship and her crew is concerned. In fact, about as much definite knowledge might come from all this as anyone might gain from the roar of his own veins, which is easily heard (haven't you ever done it?) by holding a shell close to one's ear.

> "Frosted eyes lift altars"

refers simply to a conviction that a man, not knowing perhaps a definite god yet being endowed with a reverence for deity—such a man naturally postulates a deity somehow, and the altar of that deity by the very *action* of the eyes *lifted* in searching.

> "Compass, quadrant and sextant contrive
> No farther tides."

Hasn't it often occurred that instruments originally invented for record and computation have inadvertently so extended the concepts of the entity they were invented to measure (concepts of space, etc.) in the mind and imagination that employed them, that they may metaphorically be said to have extended the original boundaries of the entity measured? This little bit of "relativity" ought not to be discredited in poetry now that scientists are proceeding to measure the universe on principles of pure *ratio,* quite as metaphorical, so far as previous standards of scientific methods extended. . . .

Questions

1. What elements that might be thought puzzling are not mentioned by the editor or by Crane? What would you say about them?

2. Can it be said that there is a sort of general frame that helps the understanding of the individual images? Explain your idea.

D. IMAGE AS SUMMARY

Sylvester's Dying Bed

Langston Hughes [1902–1967]

I woke up this mornin'
'Bout half-past three.
All the womens in town
Was gathered round me.

Sweet gals was a-moanin', 5
"Sylvester's gonna die!"
And a hundred pretty mamas
Bowed their heads to cry.

I woke up little later
'Bout half-past fo', 10
The doctor 'n' undertaker's
Both at ma do'.

Black gals was a-beggin',
"You can't leave us here!"
Brown-skins cryin', "Daddy! 15
Honey! Baby! Don't go, dear!"

But I felt ma time's a-comin',
And I know'd I's dyin' fast.
I seed the River Jerden,
A-creepin' muddy past— 20
But I's still Sweet Papa 'Vester,
Yes, sir! Long as life do last!

So I hollers, "Com'ere, babies,
Fo' to love yo' daddy right!"
And I reaches up to hug 'em— 25
When the Lawd put out the light.

Then everything was darkness
In a great . . . big . . . night.

Questions

1. The focal image of the poem, the image that summarizes the whole, is a very simple and obvious one, but it is very effective. Try to imagine the poem with images used freely along the way. What effect would such use have on this final image?

2. Return to Keats's ode "To Autumn" (p. 87). That poem is very rich in imagery; in fact, it is a series of images, the last of which serves

as a fine conclusion for the poem—a summarizing image. What accounts for its effectiveness after that rich series of images, in contrast to the dramatic isolation of the final image in "Sylvester's Dying Bed"?

3. Suppose this poem were written in the third person and in a less colloquial style. What difference would this make?

4. On what basis may it be thought that the matter at issue in Question 1 and that in Question 2 are closely related?

Dark House*

Alfred, Lord Tennyson [*1809–1892*]

> Dark house, by which once more I stand
> Here in the long unlovely street,
> Doors where my heart was used to beat
> So quickly, waiting for a hand,
>
> A hand that can be clasp'd no more—   5
> Behold me, for I cannot sleep,
> And like a guilty thing I creep
> At earliest morning to the door.
>
> He is not here; but far away
> The noise of life begins again,   10
> And ghastly thro' the drizzling rain
> On the bald street breaks the blank day.

In Memoriam, vii

With "Dark House" we have, it seems, gone back to the kind of simple use of imagery with which we opened this section—or even have gone back to Section 2. That is true, but we have made such a return with a purpose. In this poem and the two that follow, we illustrate how the single image may be used to summarize and focus the idea and emotion of a poem. Here, the image of the drizzling dawn summarizes the sense of bleakness and loss which the bereaved speaker feels. The fact that the poem is peculiarly bare of imagery sets off the concluding image with special force.

Questions

1. Suppose the last stanza were revised to read as follows:

> He is not here; but far away
> He lies and will not come again,
> And ghastly thro' the drizzling rain
> On the bald street breaks the blank day.

What has been lost or gained?

* Title by the editors.

2. Comment on the technical features of the last line. Suppose it ran:
On the empty street now breaks the day.

Then what?

Commemorative of a Naval Victory

Herman Melville [*1819–1891*]

Sailors there are of gentlest breed,
    Yet strong, like every goodly thing;
The discipline of arms refines,
    And the wave gives tempering.
    The damasked blade its beam can fling;   5
It lends the last grave grace:
The hawk, the hound, and sworded nobleman
    In Titian's picture for a king,
Are of hunter or warrior race.

In social halls a favored guest   10
    In years that follow victory won,
How sweet to feel your festal fame
    In woman's glance instinctive thrown:
    Repose is yours—your deed is known,
It musks the amber wine;   15
It lives, and sheds a light from storied days
    Rich as October sunsets brown,
Which make the barren place to shine.

But seldom the laurel wreath is seen
    Unmixed with pensive pansies dark;   20
There's a light and a shadow on every man
    Who at last attains his lifted mark—
    Nursing through night the ethereal spark.
Elate he never can be;
He feels that spirits which glad had hailed his worth,   25
    Sleep in oblivion.—The shark
Glides white through the phosphorous sea.

"Commemorative of a Naval Victory" is a much more complicated poem than "Dark House," more complicated in idea, with a more elaborate development of theme and emotion; but it, too, comes to focus on a single image that summarizes the whole, and on which the point of the poem finally depends.

We may say, too, that the whole poem is a preparation for the image. Let us inspect the poem in some detail with this in mind. In the first stanza, against the background of an unspecified naval victory in the

American Civil War, there is the comment on the gentleness mixed with strength in the "sailors." They are, the poet says, like a well-tempered steel blade that gives off a gleam and illuminates the place where it lies. In the last three lines of the stanza the description of the painting by Titian serves as another image for the sailor; the rich lordliness of the Renaissance figure is absorbed, as it were, into the modern hero. We realize, however, that the organization here is not very clear, the logical continuity is faulty. But do we make the leaps necessary to follow Melville despite his poor organization? Or can we say that the poor organization and loose syntax have a virtue of their own in this instance? In any case, we follow the drift of the stanza, and understand the kind of praise that Melville would give his sailors.

The second stanza is addressed to the hero himself, the "you," who now, long after his great moment, still enjoys his "festal fame," the respect of men and the glances of women as a tribute to his now storied bravery that shines over his later life like rich October light. The hero deserves his fame; Melville is paying him an honest compliment. There is no hint of irony, even if the hero may seem to bask somewhat complacently in the old glory. His is an earned "repose."

But, as the last stanza puts it, the hero cannot enjoy his fame fully and easily. There is an irony after all: even success has a shadow on it. The last three lines explain the nature of this shadow. Those who generously would best have appreciated his bravery are dead. Not only are they dead, but they died, we suddenly realize, in the naval battle for which the "you" now enjoys the fame. How do we know this? There is the image of the white shark that suddenly appears like a shocking vision across the scene of "festal fame," the savage creature drawn to the bleeding bodies of the wounded and dying in the sea, the image of evil.

There is one more step to take, one more question to ask. Does Melville mean the poem to apply merely to the naval hero? Or is he writing, finally, about all success, and the shadow over all success? Does he mean to imply that any successful man, if he is honest and has humanity, will understand that others as worthy as he have failed, and sleep in oblivion? That, in a way, he lives off of their virtue and their generosity, for they would "glad" have "hailed his worth," and perhaps even by their death or failure have prepared the way for his success?

Questions

1. In each stanza of the poem we find an image of light. In the first, the finely tempered blade gives off a beam. In the second, the October light makes a barren landscape shine. In the third, there is light and shadow on every man, even in success. Interpret these three images as closely as possible. Is there any continuity of meaning among them? What do they imply about heroism and fame?

2. What is the meaning of the word *elate?* How does it apply here?

3. In the last two lines, we notice that "The shark" ends a line and is set off from the rest of the sentence to which it belongs and which composes the last line: "Glides white through the phosphorous sea." Is this arrangement effective?

4. To return to the import of the image of the shark: clearly there is the contrast between the scene of festivity and the human cost. But can it be said that those who now celebrate the victory and the hero's fame are, themselves, somehow like the shark, drawn to the taint of blood? How much irony—and what kind—would thus appear in the last image?

5. What would the poem be without the shark?

6. Is the shark here used as a metaphor, or could you make out a case for Melville's having used it symbolically? (Note that this distinction is *ultimately* unimportant: the important thing is to see what happens, not to classify it.)

A Valediction: Forbidding Mourning

John Donne [*1572–1631*]

As virtuous men pass mildly away,
　　And whisper to their souls, to go,
Whilst some of their sad friends do say,
　　The breath goes now, and some say, no:

So let us melt, and make no noise,　　　　　　　　　　5
　　No tear-floods, nor sigh-tempests move.
'Twere profanation of our joys
　　To tell the laity our love.

Moving of th' earth brings harms and fears,[1]
　　Men reckon what it did and meant.　　　　　　　　10
But trepidation of the spheres,
　　Though greater far, is innocent.

Dull sublunary lovers' love
　　(Whose soul is sense) cannot admit
Absence, because it doth remove　　　　　　　　　　15
　　Those things which elemented it.

But we by a love, so much refined,
　　That our selves know not what it is,
Inter-assurèd of the mind,
　　Care less, eyes, lips, and hands to miss.　　　　　20

---

[1] the imagery of stanzas 3 and 4 refers to the Ptolemaic system: the earth is at the center of the universe and the moon, sun, planets, and stars—all fixed in their own spheres—revolve around it; a movement of the relatively tiny earth ("an earthquake") terrifies human beings, but the "trepidation" (shaking, quivering movement) of the much vaster crystalline sphere is not even perceived

Our two souls therefore, which are one,
  Though I must go, endure not yet
A breach, but an expansion,
  Like gold to airy thinness beat.[2]

If they be two, they are two so   25
  As stiff twin compasses[3] are two,
Thy soul the fixed foot, makes no show
  To move, but doth, if th' other do.

And though it in the center sit,
  Yet when the other far doth roam,   30
It leans, and hearkens after it,
  And grows erect, as that comes home.

Such wilt thou be to me, who must
  Like th' other foot, obliquely run;
Thy firmness makes my circle just,   35
  And makes me end, where I begun.

In this poem Donne uses a peculiarly complex method of handling his imagery. If the poem ended with line 24, it would be complete—and good. Up to that point it would exhibit the method characteristic of "The Definition of Love" (p. 222)—that is, it could be described as a logical discourse from which certain images are developed metaphorically. But with line 25 the method changes; from this line to the end, the image of the compasses dominates the poem and is analytically worked out in the way we find in, for instance, "Follow Thy Fair Sun" (p. 215).

Our point here is this: Donne has begun with a diversity of images, and now in closing he fixes on a single image. But the concluding single image is not like the street on a drizzly morning in "Dark House" (p. 237) or the shark in "Commemorative of a Naval Victory" (p. 238). The effect is not, therefore, quite the same as in the poems by Tennyson and Melville. In those poems, the effect is of a sudden, intense illumination, one that depends on an unexpected emotional realization. The final image in Donne's poem, with its full elaboration, does not aim at a sudden emotional impact; it aims, rather, at another kind of climax, a sense of the total validation of what has gone before—a logical focus (which is dependent not on abstract logic but on the impression of logicality with which the image is worked out).

Questions

1. What is the tone of the first two stanzas?
2. If the poem ended with line 24, what would it mean? How would it differ from the total version?

[2] students who have any difficulty with stanza 6 should look up the term "gold-leaf" and perhaps consult an encyclopedia to learn how it is made [3] with reference to stanzas 7–9: the compass referred to is not the mariner's compass, which indicates north, but the geometer's compass, with which one draws circles

3. Comment on the relation of the various images to one another. Is there a development of some kind?

4. Comment on the metrics of lines 19–20 and 25–26. On the enjambment in lines 22 and 25, see Appendix B, p. 511.

E. COMBINATION AND VARIATION

Tears, Idle Tears

Alfred, Lord Tennyson [*1809–1892*]

Tears, idle tears, I know not what they mean,
Tears from the depth of some divine despair
Rise in the heart, and gather to the eyes,
In looking on the happy Autumn-fields,
And thinking of the days that are no more.   5

Fresh as the first beam glittering on a sail,
That brings our friends up from the underworld,
Sad as the last which reddens over one
That sinks with all we love below the verge;
So sad, so fresh, the days that are no more.   10

Ah, sad and strange as in dark summer dawns
The earliest pipe of half-awakened birds
To dying ears, when unto dying eyes
The casement slowly grows a glimmering square;
So sad, so strange, the days that are no more.   15

Dear as remembered kisses after death,
And sweet as those by hopeless fancy feigned
On lips that are for others; deep as love,
Deep as first love, and wild with all regret;
O Death in Life, the days that are no more!   20

The Princess

This poem at first reading may appear to have little in common with the vigorous thinking through images that we associate with poets like Marvell and Donne. We find here no witty turns or plays on the meaning of certain words, and certainly no bold leaping from image to image or involved elaborations of some central analogy. Instead, the poet seems to be intent on building up a mood of vague melancholy, partly by repetition, partly by associating the melancholy with special scenes of sadness and loss—the last glimpse of the ship carrying a loved one away to some distant land or a dying man's last vision of the light of day.

There are no sharply disparate materials, no images that clash violently in their association.

Moreover, the tears that engender the poem are confessed by the poet himself to be "idle," that is, not to be accounted for by any special circumstance. Even if they are possibly the overflowing of "some divine despair" (line 2), the poet confesses that he really doesn't know what they mean. The poet therefore may seem to have been bent on making a virtue out of the very vagueness of his sense of loss.

Yet the reader will do well to look deeper into the poem. Though the poet begins by saying that he does not know why he is weeping, perhaps he finds out as he lives through the experience and perhaps he has actually succeeded in telling the reader what the tears *do,* in fact, mean—through his choice and handling of images. At any rate, the reader must not conclude in advance that the strategy of poets so different as Tennyson and Marvell are in complete opposition. They need not be. Tennyson's attempt to define what overcame him as a fit of unmotivated melancholy may in fact exhibit a real thinking through images.

Questions

1. The days that are no more are called "sad" and "fresh" in stanza 2; and in stanza 3, "sad" and "strange." Why are they *fresh* and *strange?* Does the imagery of stanzas 2 and 3 throw any light on their freshness and strangeness? On their "wildness" (see line 19)?

2. How can the poet say that the days that are no more are "deep as love, / Deep as first love, and wild with all regret" (lines 18–19)? How can days be *deep* and *wild?* What do these words come to mean in the context of the poem? Has their application to "days" been prepared for? How?

3. What do the poet's images tell us about "the days that are no more"? We often regard the past as sad. Is it possible to regard it also as strange and even fresh—as if we were discovering it for the first time? Can it be said that we carry our past within us, that the past is not at all dead, but very much alive, and as we sometimes discover, strange—really not understood by us? What, for example, do some of the great twentieth-century psychologists say with regard to this matter?

4. Consider the matter of tone. Is this a weepy, sentimental poem? Or is it in reality something quite different?

A Lecture upon the Shadow

John Donne [*1572–1631*]

> Stand still, and I will read to thee
>   A Lecture, Love, in loves philosophy.
> These three houres that we have spent,

Walking here, two shadowes went
Along with us, which we our selves produc'd;   5
But, now the Sunne is just above our head,
   We doe those shadowes tread;
And to brave clearenesse all things are reduc'd.
   So whilst our infant loves did grow,
   Disguises did, and shadowes, flow   10
From us, and our care; but, now 'tis not so.

That love hath not attain'd the high'st degree,
Which is still diligent lest others see.

   Except our loves at this noone stay,
We shall new shadowes make the other way.   15
   As the first were made to blinde
   Others; these which come behinde
Will worke upon our selves, and blind our eyes.
If our loves faint, and westwardly decline;
   To me thou, falsly, thine,   20
And I to thee mine actions shall disguise.
   The morning shadowes weare away,
   But these grow longer all the day,
But oh, loves day is short, if love decay.

Love is a growing, or full constant light;   25
And his first minute, after noone, is night.

Question

Work out for yourself the sun-shadow image through the second half
of the poem. What is meant in line 15 by "new shadows make the other
way"? These shadows, we are told in line 17, are "those which come
behinde." Helen Gardner* interprets "come behinde" as "come later";
and she points out that to interpret the new shadows otherwise would
imply that the lovers "had spent three hours walking steadily in one direction,† which is absurd . . . since they have in fact simply been strolling
to and fro, with their shadows sometimes behind them, sometimes in
front."

How, then, should we interpret "We shall new shadowes make the
other way" (line 15)? Does the poet's elaborate figure here become confused? What is the significance, if any, of "westwardly" (line 19)? How
can shadows "blind *our* eyes" (line 18)? Can you make out a consistent
relationship among the aspects of the poet's complicated figure?

   * *The Elegies and Songs and Sonnets of John Donne,* Oxford University Press, 1965,
p. 208.
   † It would also imply that their direction had been steadily west—if we have to conceive of the morning shadows having stretched before them and those of afternoon as
having to stretch behind them.

As I Walked Out One Evening

W. H. Auden [*1907–1973*]

As I walked out one evening,
   Walking down Bristol Street,
The crowds upon the pavement
   Were fields of harvest wheat.

And down by the brimming river   5
   I heard a lover sing
Under an arch of the railway:
   "Love has no ending.

I'll love you, dear, I'll love you
   Till China and Africa meet,   10
And the river jumps over the mountain
   And the salmon sing in the street.

I'll love you till the ocean
   Is folded and hung up to dry,
And the seven stars go squawking   5
   Like geese about the sky.

The years shall run like rabbits,
   For in my arms I hold
The Flower of the Ages,
   And the first love of the world."   20

But all the clocks in the city
   Began to whirr and chime:
"O let not Time deceive you,
   You cannot conquer Time.

In the burrows of the Nightmare   25
   Where Justice naked is,
Time watches from the shadow
   And coughs when you would kiss.

In headaches and in worry
   Vaguely life leaks away,   30
And Time will have his fancy
   Tomorrow or today.

Into many a green valley
   Drifts the appalling snow;
Time breaks the threaded dances   35
   And the diver's brilliant bow.

O plunge your hands in water,
   Plunge them in up to the wrist;
Stare, stare in the basin
   And wonder what you've missed.   40

The glacier knocks in the cupboard,
   The desert sighs in the bed,
And the crack in the tea-cup opens
   A lane to the land of the dead.

Where the beggars raffle the banknotes   45
   And the Giant is enchanting to Jack,
And the Lily-white Boy is a Roarer,
   And Jill goes down on her back.

O look, look in the mirror,
   O look in your·distress;   50
Life remains a blessing
   Although you cannot bless.

O stand, stand at the window
   As the tears scald and start;
You shall love your crooked neighbor   55
   With your crooked heart."

It was late, late in the evening,
   The lovers they were gone;
The clocks had ceased their chiming,
   And the deep river ran on.   60

Questions

Line 46 is a reference to the story of Jack the Giant Killer. The Lily-white Boy, line 47, is a reference to the song "Green Grow the Rushes O" (the Dorsetshire version of which is also included by Auden in his *Oxford Book of Light Verse*): "Two, two for the lily-white boys." Compare also line 15, "And the seven stars go squawking," to line 9 of "Green Grow the Rushes O"—"Seven for the seven stars in the sky." Jill in line 48 is the companion of Jack in the nursery rhyme which tells how they went to fetch a pail of water.

1. What use is made of these allusions?

2. What is the tone of this poem? Is it one of quiet moralizing, or of heavy-handed sermonizing? Of bitter mockery, or of cynical disillusion, or what?

3. Though the imagery used in lines 41–46 seems to be just as extravagant as that used in lines 9–20, what is the difference in effect? Or do you sense any difference in effect?

4. Why are the clocks, the means by which time is measured, chosen by the poet to voice the warning against time? Time is often treated as a flowing stream. Is the brimming river in this poem related to the problem of time? If so, how? What is its relation to the clocks?

After Great Pain, a Formal Feeling Comes—*

Emily Dickinson   [1830–1886]

After great pain, a formal feeling comes—
The Nerves sit ceremonious, like Tombs—
The stiff Heart questions was it He, that bore,
And Yesterday, or Centuries before?

The Feet, mechanical, go round—   5
Of Ground, or Air, or Ought—
A Wooden way
Regardless grown,
A Quartz contentment, like a stone—

This is the Hour of Lead—   10
Remembered, if outlived,
As Freezing persons, recollect the Snow—
First—Chill—then Stupor—then the letting go—

Questions

1. Some of the imagery used in this poem is very bold. What, for
example, do you make of line 2? How can nerves be said to *sit?* What
is meant by *ceremonious?* Why like *tombs?* What is the total image?
Comment upon it.

2. Who is "He"?

3. What is meant by a "Quartz contentment"? Why "Quartz" and not
some other stone? Can this figure be related to "Wooden way" and "Hour
of Lead"?

4. The experience of deep grief in stanza 3 is compared to death by
freezing. What are the steps of this process? How carefully is the analogy
worked out? What is the force of "Remembered, if outlived"?

Evening Song

Sidney Lanier   [1842–1881]

Look off, dear Love, across the sallow sands,
   And mark yon meeting of the sun and sea,
How long they kiss in sight of all the lands.
      Ah! longer, longer, we.

Now in the sea's red vintage melts the sun,   5
   As Egypt's pearl dissolved in rosy wine,

* The capitalization in this poem follows the poet's practice.

And Cleopatra night drinks all. 'Tis done,
   Love, lay thine hand in mine.

Come forth, sweet stars, and comfort heaven's heart;
   Glimmer, ye waves, round else unlighted sands.   **10**
O night! divorce our sun and sky apart
   Never our lips, our hands.

In some of the poems that we have been reading, we find imagery aimed at intellectual precision (as in Donne's "Valediction"); in some, imagery as a means of development of idea or feeling (as in "Cleopatra's Lament" or "Tears, Idle Tears"); in some, as a focus for the general meaning of a poem (as in "Commemorative of a Naval Victory"). In a good poem of any of these types, the imagery is under control; that is, it does not introduce or suggest ideas or feelings that are not coherent with the main impulse (idea and/or feeling) of the poem. Furthermore, even if an image at first seems shocking or irrelevant, the poet ends by justifying its inclusion—according to his purposes and without distractions from his purposes.

In the poem just presented we find a very strained and irresponsible use of imagery. The poet, writing a love poem, hits on images that, in general, seem to be relevant. The sun kisses the sea. Then we have the reference to the anecdote of Cleopatra's dissolving a pearl in wine and drinking it—we all know her great love story; so we have love here, too. Next the stars come out to comfort heaven's heart. Everything is directed toward creating a poetical atmosphere around the notion of love. But the poet has neglected either to observe his images or to think through their implications for his poem.

To take the sun kissing the sea: true, the sun does touch the horizon, but in this contact there is very little natural suggestion of a kiss. Conceivably a poet might make it pass muster. But not if he makes that kiss last a long time. As a matter of fact, the one situation when we can literally see the motion of the sun is when it touches and sinks below the horizon. Here the poet just thinks that a long kiss would be nice for his poem, and so slams it in.

To continue our nagging at the poem, why is the kiss "in sight of all the lands"? What is involved here? Are the lands supposed to be waiting around to spy on the marathon kiss, which isn't such a marathon kiss, after all? Or indeed did the poet get himself stuck with the word *lands* merely to get an easy rhyme? The plural form, to begin with, is strained. We think of lands as great units, such as Egypt, Mexico, or Canada, not such limited areas as would be involved here. This is not very important, but it signifies a general slackness in thinking and perception.

The second stanza starts well enough. We might think of the sunset sea as resembling wine—though it would be an enormous amount of wine and the color suggested isn't exactly right; but the sun is even redder than the sea is, and by no stretch of the imagination can the red sun be said to resemble a pearl, which is white, or whitish. How, to continue, can the night be said to drink the sea? By the same token, and even-handedly, it must eat the land. What a monster this "Cleopatra night" must be, and what an appetite! To wind up the stanza, what is the connection between watching this "Cleopatra night" drink the sea and taking the literal beloved's hand?

In the last stanza, what is being suggested by sweet stars coming out to comfort heaven's heart? Because the sun is gone? What has this to do with the poem except to "prettify" it? In line 11 we must remind ourselves that "night"—here addressed as a person—cannot well be "Cleopatra night," but some other creature who can "divorce" the "sun and sky apart." As for the last line, it follows from the stanza only by negation, as it were; this in itself might, again, be made to pass muster (Tennyson uses this weak device in "Blow, Bugle, Blow," p. 94). But insofar as the poet has insisted on literal kissing by the lovers and literal hand-holding, the last line of the poem doesn't follow the pattern or make much sense. The longest kisses don't last forever.

The poem is both logically and imagistically a kind of hash. The poet evidently thought that if enough generally "poetic" stuff and pretty atmosphere gets dragged in, nothing else matters. Atmosphere is very important in poetry and imagery is often very important in establishing it (as in Keats's "To Autumn"), but atmosphere itself is not enough to support a poem—and certainly not atmosphere that is not derived from valid observation combined with an act of imagination. In this poem there is only one valid observation combined with an act of imagination—in the second line of the last stanza: the glimmer of waves, and the whiteness of foam does seem, sometimes, to give a false light.

Questions

1. Reread Keats's "To Autumn" (p. 87) and read Joyce's "All Day I Hear" (p. 552). Each of these poems does create a special atmosphere, but in each case the atmosphere is absorbed into a meaning. Try to justify this remark. How is the atmosphere, in each case, created? Discuss the imagery. Is any other factor than imagery involved?

2. What is the importance of atmosphere in Wordsworth's "Yew-Trees" (p. 109)?

3. Return to Cole Porter's "You're the Top" (p. 225). Why, do you think, does the strained and arbitrary imagery work here and not in Lanier's poem?

On the Founding of Liberia

Melvin Tolson   [*1898–1966*]

Liberia?
No micro-footnote in a bunioned book
Homed by a pedant
With a gelded look:
You are   5
The ladder of survival dawn men saw
In the quicksilver sparrow that slips
The eagle's claw!

Liberia?
No side-show barker's bio-accident,   10
No corpse of a soul's errand
To the Dark Continent:
You are
The lightning rod of Europe, Canaan's key,
The rope across the abyss,   15
Mehr licht[1] for the Africa-To-Be!

Liberia?
No haply black man's X
Fixed to a Magna Charta without a magic-square
By Helon's[2] leprous hand, to haunt and vex: 20
You are
The Orient of Colors everywhere,
The oasis of Tahoua,[3] the salt bar of Harrar,[4]
To trekkers in saharas, in sierras, with Despair!

Liberia?   25
No oil-boiled Barabas,
No Darwin's bulldog for ermined flesh,
No braggart Lamech,[5] no bema's[6] Ananias:[7]
You are
Libertas flayed and naked by the road   30
To Jericho, for a people's five score years
Of bones for manna, for balm an alien goad!

---

[1] "more light," exclaimed by Goethe as he was dying; i.e., more knowledge, more understanding   [2] an Old Testament character mentioned in Numbers, though there is no reference to any "leprous hand"   [3] in French West Africa, just northwest of Nigeria   [4] Harar (if this word is meant) is a province and a city of Ethiopia   [5] in the genealogy of Genesis 4:17–24, a descendant of Cain, with three sons, Jabal, Jubal, and Tubal (originators of pastoral society, music, and metal-working); Lamech's exultation on possessing a new weapon (Genesis 4:23–24), the "sword song," must be the boast referred to here   [6] a space, sometimes enclosed, before the altar of a cathedral   [7] a character in the Old Testament struck down by God for lying

Liberia?
No pimple on the chin of Africa,
No brass-lipped cicerone of Big Top democracy,   35
No lamb to tame a lion with a baa:
You are
Black Lazarus risen from the White Man's grave,
Without a road to Downing Street,
Without a hemidemisemiquaver in an Oxford stave!   40

Liberia?
No Cobra Pirate of the Question Mark,
No caricature with a mimic flag
And golden joys to fat the shark:
You are   45
American genius uncrowned in Europe's charnel-house.
Leave fleshpots for the dogs and apes; for Man
The books whose head is golden espouse!

Liberia?
No waste land yet, nor yet a destooled elite,   50
No merry-andrew, an Ed-dehebi[8] at heart,
With St. Paul's[9] root and Breughel's[10] cheat:
You are
The iron nerve of lame and halt and blind,
Liberia and not Liberia,   55
A moment of the conscience of mankind!

from *Libretto for the Republic of Liberia*

Liberia was established in 1822 as a home for freed American slaves. Tolson, a black American poet, was invited by the Liberian government to write the ode in celebration from which these lines are drawn. (The title of this section is by the editors.)

RHYTHM AND METER: 5

This section is specifically concerned with imagery, and we naturally think of imagery as an evocation in the imagination of some literal sense perception. But we must remember that not only things visually perceived give rise to imagery. Though visual imagery is the most common sort in poetry, there are also images of touch, temperature, smell, and sound, as, for instance, in the following passage from Keats's "The Eve of St. Agnes," which describes the heroine's preparation for bed:

Of all its wreathed pearls her hair she frees;
Unclasps her warmed jewels one by one;
Loosens her fragrant bodice; by degrees
Her rich attire creeps rustling to her knees.

[8] unidentified   [9] see Romans 11:16–24   [10] famous sixteenth-century Flemish painter, whose work sets the stupidity and brutality of men against natural grandeur; it is this view of humanity that may be the "cheat" intended here

Here the whole constitutes a visual image, but in the second line we find "warmed" jewels; in the third the "fragrant" bodice; and in the fourth, the "rustling" dress. The tactile sense is strong: she "frees," "unclasps," "loosens."

Whatever we can become physically aware of may provide imagery, and often the poetic image comes, as things come in ordinary experience, as a bundle of almost undifferentiated awarenesses absorbed into a unity of effect. To quote Keats again, take this line from "Ode to Psyche" in which several kinds of imagery are fused in one perception:

> Mid hush'd, cool-rooted flowers fragrant-eyed.

Thus far we have been talking of the image as a reproduction of the natural event—the "thing" as experienced in nature. But it cannot be stressed too emphatically that, in poetry, the image comes to us in words and that words themselves intrinsically afford special sensory experiences (including various muscular and nervous sensations) and that, in fact, each word offers a unique experience. To pursue this idea, the words not only evoke an image, *but provide a new image,* what may be called a secondary image, that of the sensory experience of the words themselves, to be fused with the primary image evoked.

In all our discussion of rhythm and meter, we have, of course, been referring to such a fusion and to its effects. Now, however, as we more specifically deal with imagery and how imagery works in poetry, we may appropriately consider aspects other than rhythm and meter that enter into the fusion with the primary image reported from nature. With this in mind, see Appendix B, pp. 495 (footnote), 525–541.

Questions

1. Reread "Inversnaid" by Gerard Manley Hopkins (p. 83). It is composed of four tetrameter quatrains, rhymed *aabb.* In other words, the quatrain is composed of two couplets, and if the stanza divisions were abolished, we would have another very common form, that of rhymed tetrameter couplets, the form used in "Hell Gate" by A. E. Housman (p. 59). Can you see a reason why Hopkins uses the quatrain unit and Housman does not?

To answer the question above consider the following facts. Housman, though he does not use a fixed stanza form, does break the mass of his poem into sections. This is a narrative poem, and the sections are determined by narrative considerations, stages in development and dramatic effects. What principle of progression, then, appears in Hopkins's poem? What logic determines the stages?

We may regard the matter from yet another angle. Housman, we observe, uses many run-on lines, and among those that are not run-on, many are stopped very lightly, as elements in a continuing sentence. That is, the flux and flow of the sentence is natural to narrative, and the verse line tends to be used primarily as a kind of punctuation played against the form of the sentence.* Notice that the lines (and the syntactical units within lines) are much more emphatic in Hopkins's poem—and we may say, too, that the individual phrase, the unusual vocabulary and striking imagery, stand out more sharply here. Can you imagine a narrative poem in the style of "Inversnaid"? Wouldn't it tend to explode into brilliant fragments? Why doesn't it "explode" here?

Make a comparison of "Inversnaid" with "Channel Firing" (p. 45) in regard to the use of the stanza. Both, you notice, are in iambic tetrameter. Reread "The Fall of Rome" (p. 44). Which poem, "Inversnaid" or "Channel Firing," does it more nearly resemble? But, in spite of resemblances, how is it different in method? Why?

2. Suppose Johnson's "To a Young Heir" (p. 147), which is also in tetrameter quatrains, had been composed with a number of run-on lines and internal stops, as in the revision that follows:

> Long-expected one-and-twenty
>   Comes at last. So, time now flown,
> All the promised pomp and plenty
>   Are, at last, your very own.

What difference in tone would result?

3. Examine Auden's "Lullaby" (p. 143). Is there a rhyme scheme here, however recessive? If there is such a recessive scheme, why do you think the poet would bother to use one at all? Elsewhere can you find examples of recessive rhyming?

4. In "Mama and Daughter" (p. 29) there are five quatrains, the first four rhymed *xaxa,* and the last *axxa.* But it should be noticed that the quatrain form is not insisted upon, is not, in the first two instances, even set up in the format of a quatrain; and there is, too, a dead line between the fourth and the last quatrains. Why do you think Hughes here treats the quatrain form so recessively? In the same general connection, what sense do you make of the stanza form in "A Letter from the Caribbean" (p. 107)?

5. Examine "The Canonization" (p. 134). Notice the different ways in which sentence and clause units are played against the stanza pattern. For instance, in the first six lines (10–15) of the second stanza, five lines end in question marks—that is, stand as complete sentences. The remaining three lines of the stanza belong to a single sentence. Or take the last stanza, which is essentially one long sentence (with certain heavy stops, indeed), that is drawn in a most complicated manner through the rhyme pattern. Can you comment on the different effects in such instances? Differences in tone would be involved here, wouldn't they? If so, wouldn't this be fused with the primary imagery of the poem?

6. In "To Autumn" (p. 87) remark on the quantitative factor in the effect of the verse. To what extent are secondary accents used to support the effect? How do this various factors relate to the atmosphere —and to the meaning—of the poem? In other words, how do the atmosphere and meaning coalesce here?

---

* This is, of course, true of all verse but, in narrative, the forward thrust is, generally speaking, more pronounced.

7. After reading Gerard Manley Hopkins's "God's Grandeur" (Appendix B, p. 537), write a commentary on the meter and verse texture of "The Windhover" (p. 208).

8. Comment on the use of stanza and verbal factors in "The Goat Paths" (p. 209).

9. Scan the first six lines of "Macbeth Thinks of Murdering the King" (p. 232), marking all secondary accents, caesuras, and secondary pauses. Study the verbal quality. Look especially at the clause beginning "if the assassination" and ending with "success." Is there a sense of accelerated pace here? What is the effect of the prevalence of front vowels (see Appendix B, pp. 537, footnote, 542, footnote) and of the general sibilance?

10. Discuss the metrical and verbal effects in (a) the first three stanzas of the selection from "The Palace of Art" (p. 98); (b) the last stanza of "Channel Firing" (p. 45); (c) "At Melville's Tomb" (p. 233); (d) "Dark House" (p. 237); (e) the last two lines of "Commemorative of a Naval Victory" (p. 238); and (f) lines 23–24 of "A Valediction: Forbidding Mourning" (p. 240).

11. What examples of onomatopoeia do you find in (a) " 'Out, Out—' " (p. 18); (b) "Channel Firing" (p. 45); and (c) "Mariana" (p. 197)?

Supplemental Poems

F. LOVE AND TIME

Sonnet 65

William Shakespeare [*1564–1616*]

Since brass, nor stone, nor earth, nor boundless sea,
But sad mortality o'ersways their power,
How with this rage shall beauty hold a plea,
Whose action is no stronger than a flower?
O, how shall summer's honey breath hold out   5
Against the wrackful siege of battering days,
When rocks impregnable are not so stout,
Nor gates of steel so strong, but Time decays?
O fearful meditation! Where, alack,
Shall Time's best jewel from Time's chest lie hid?   10
Or what strong hand can hold his swift foot back?
Or who his spoil of beauty can forbid?
   O, none, unless this miracle have might,
   That in black ink my love may still shine bright.

Questions

1. The lover's desperate question is how something so weak and delicate of beauty shall withstand the overwhelmingly destructive power of time. But the poet uses a variety of images to body forth the frailty of one and the brutal force of the other. What is the relation among these images?

2. Are some of the images given a particular elaboration? If so, describe the particular elaboration.

3. In line 6 "the wrackful siege of battering days" suggests a battering ram attempting to breach the wall of a fortified town. Do you find any other such sequences? (See page 232.)

To His Coy Mistress

Andrew Marvell   [*1621–1678*]

Had we but world enough, and time,
This coyness, Lady, were no crime.
We would sit down and think which way
To walk and pass our long love's day.
Thou by the Indian Ganges' side   5
Shouldst rubies find; I by the tide
Of Humber would complain. I would
Love you ten years before the Flood,
And you should, if you please, refuse
Till the conversion of the Jews.   10
My vegetable love should grow
Vaster than empires, and more slow;
An hundred years should go to praise
Thine eyes and on thy forehead gaze;
Two hundred to adore each breast,   15
But thirty thousand to the rest;
An age at least to every part,
And the last age should show your heart.
For, Lady, you deserve this state,
Nor would I love at lower rate.   20
  But at my back I always hear
Time's wingèd chariot hurrying near;
And yonder all before us lie
Deserts of vast eternity.
Thy beauty shall no more be found,   25
Nor, in thy marble vault, shall sound
My echoing song; then worms shall try
That long preserved virginity.
And your quaint honor turn to dust,
And into ashes all my lust: 30
The grave's a fine and private place,

But none, I think, do there embrace.
    Now therefore, while the youthful hue
Sits on thy skin like morning lew[1]
And while thy willing soul transpires   35
At every pore with instant fires,
Now let us sport us while we may,
And now, like amorous birds of prey,
Rather at once our time devour
Than languish in his slow-chapt power.   40
Let us roll all our strength and all
Our sweetness up into one ball,
And tear our pleasures with rough strife
Thorough[2] the iron gates of life:
Thus, though we cannot make our sun   45
Stand still, yet we will make him run.

Questions

1. Distinguish the three divisions of the logical structure to the poem. Comment upon the tone of each division.

2. Someone has said that the imagery in the first part of the poem is playful, conversational, and absurd; that of the second section, grand; and that of the third section, exciting. Can you justify this characterization? Or is there too much interpenetration among the parts to justify the remark?

3. What does the poet mean by "amorous birds of prey"? Does this figure carry over into "tear our pleasures" (line 43)?

4. Define the attitude presented in the passage comprising lines 25 to 32.

5. What range of imagery do you find here—little or considerable variety?

Because I Could Not Stop for Death—

Emily Dickinson [*1830–1886*]

Because I could not stop for Death—
He kindly stopped for me—
The Carriage held but just Ourselves—
And Immortality.

We slowly drove—He knew no haste   5
And I had put away
My labor and my leisure too,
For His Civility—

---

[1] warmth (conjectured by H. M. Margoliouth; the 1681 text reads *glew;* other conjectured readings are "dew" and "glow")   [2] through

We passed the School, where Children strove
At Recess—in the Ring—   10
We passed the Fields of Gazing Grain—
We passed the Setting Sun—

Or rather—He passed Us—
The Dews drew quivering and chill—
For only Gossamer, my Gown—   15
My Tippet—only Tulle—

We paused before a House that seemed
A Swelling of the Ground—
The Roof was scarcely visible—
The Cornice—in the Ground—   20

Since then—'tis Centuries—and yet
Feels shorter than the Day
I first surmised the Horses' Heads
Were toward Eternity—

Questions

1. Look at the word *stop* in line 1. Does it mean the same thing here as in line 2? How does the word in line 1 relate to the meaning of line 7?

2. What is the tone of stanza 1? Why didn't the lady refuse Death's invitation? Particularly in view of the fact that she wasn't really expecting Death to call for her and didn't look forward to taking a ride with him? Because she was afraid to refuse? Because he was so polite about it? Because a well-bred lady must not be rude when she is given the very special attention that she has been given in not being summoned but marked out for special favor? Or why?

3. Though the lady sits in the carriage of Death (stanza 3), the activity of the world goes on. Does the lady seem surprised at that fact? What is implied about her attitude?

4. Consider carefully the last stanza. Does the lady speak from Heaven? Or from the grave? Or is she alive but thoroughly conscious of the fact that she, being human, is going to die? What can she mean by saying that the centuries that have passed seem shorter than "the Day" on which she first surmised that she was leaving the world of time?

5. What would you say is the poet's concept of "Immortality" (line 4)? Christian? Non-Christian? Or what? What do the concrete images that she uses imply with reference to her attitude?

6. To return to certain details: Explain the word "Civility" (line 8). What is suggested in the phrase "Gazing Grain" (line 11)? What kind of relation, if any, does this have to the school children in line 9?

7. Comment on technical features of this poem. Consider the use of run-on lines. Can you see any reason in their disposition here—for instance, none in stanza 3 and three in the last stanza. What about the placement of caesuras?

Envoi (1919)

Ezra Pound   [1885–1972]

Go, dumb-born book,
Tell her that sang me once that song of Lawes:
Hadst thou but song
As thou hast subjects known,
Then were there cause in thee that should condone   5
Even my faults that heavy upon me lie,
And build her glories their longevity.

Tell her that sheds
Such treasure in the air,
Recking naught else but that her graces give   10
Life to the moment,
I would bid them live
As roses might, in magic amber laid,
Red overwrought with orange and all made
One substance and one color   15
Braving time.

Tell her that goes
With song upon her lips
But sings not out the song, nor knows
The maker of it, some other mouth,   20
May be as fair as hers,
Might, in new ages, gain her worshippers,
When our two dusts with Waller's shall be laid,
Siftings on siftings in oblivion,
Till change hath broken down   25
All things save Beauty alone.

Questions

Waller's "Go, Lovely Rose" (p. 213) was set to music by Henry Lawes,
the seventeenth-century musician and friend of Milton.

1. Compare the theme of this poem with that of Waller's "Go,
Lovely Rose."

2. Comment upon the importance of the roses-in-amber image of lines
13–16. Is it successful? What does it accomplish?

3. Does an appreciation of "Envoi" depend upon a knowledge of
Waller's "Go, Lovely Rose"? What are the principal differences between
the two poems in the matter of imagery and tone?

Empty Bed Blues

Bessie Smith   [*1895–1937*]

I woke up this morning with an awful aching head,
I woke up this morning with an awful aching head,
My new man had left me just a room and an empty bed.

Bought me a coffee grinder, got the best one I could find,
Bought me a coffee grinder, got the best one I could find.   5
So he could grind me coffee, cause he had a brand new grind.

He's a deep-sea diver with a stroke that can't go wrong.
He's a deep-sea diver with a stroke that can't go wrong.
He can touch the bottom, and his wind holds out so long.

He knows how to thrill me, and he thrills me night and day,   10
He knows how to thrill me, and he thrills me night and day,
He's got a new way of loving, almost takes my breath away.

He's got that sweet something, and I told my gal-friend Lou,
He's got that sweet something, and I told my gal-friend Lou,
'Cause the way she's raving, she must have gone and tried it too.   15

When my bed gets empty, makes me feel awful mean and blue,
When my bed gets empty, makes me feel awful mean and blue,
'Cause my springs getting rusty, sleepin' single the way I do.

Bought him a blanket, pillow for his head at night,
Bought him a blanket, pillow for his head at night,   20
Then I bought him a mattress so he could lay just right.

He came home one evening with his fair head way up high,
He came home one evening with his fair head way up high,
What he had to give me made me wring my hands and cry.

He give me a lesson that I never had before,   25
He give me a lesson that I never had before,
When he got through teaching me, from my elbows down was sore.

He boiled my first cabbage, and he made it awful hot,
He boiled my first cabbage, and he made it awful hot,
Then he put in the bacon and it overflowed the pot.   30

When you get good lovin' never go and spread the news,
When you get good lovin' never go and spread the news,
They'll double-cross you and leave you with them empty bed blues.

Questions

1. This poem (the lyric of a famous "blues") springs from the world of "Frankie and Johnny" and like that poem tells a story of love betrayed. Both, in a sense, are ballads. There is a fundamental difference in the

handling of the two stories, however. In "Frankie and Johnny" the narrative is objective, told by a third person, and the pathos and irony of the poem lie in the story itself, or rather, the feelings of the characters come to us primarily in the action. In "Empty Bed Blues" the action is essential—the fact of the desertion by the lover—but the substance of the poem is in the woman's backward-looking at her happiness, and her attempt to recreate that experience. Here, then, the descriptive detail and the vigor of metaphor (the imagery of description and metaphor comes primarily from the literal world of the speaker*) carry the emotion of the poem. Select a poem about love that you have already encountered in this book (for instance, "Cleopatra's Lament," p. 228), and write a comparison on the grounds of tone and imagery of it and "Empty Bed Blues." The point here is not to decide on better or worse, but the matter of evaluation is not, of course, ruled out.

2. "Empty Bed Blues" is certainly not to be scanned as accentual-syllabic verse. Does it contain five or six accents in a line? Try to work out a pattern. If possible, get a recording of Bessie Smith singing the song and see what this indicates about the rhythmic structure.

The Last Days of Alice

Allen Tate [*1899–*]

> Alice grown lazy, mammoth but not fat,
> Declines upon her lost and twilight age,
> Above in the dozing leaves the grinning cat
> Quivers forever with his abstract rage;
>
> Whatever light swayed on the perilous gate   5
> Forever sways, nor will the arching grass
> Caught when the world clattered undulate
> In the deep suspension of the looking-glass.
>
> Bright Alice! always pondering to gloze
> The spoiled cruelty she had meant to say   10
> Gazes learnedly down her airy nose
> At nothing, nothing thinking all the day:
>
> Turned absent-minded by infinity
> She cannot move unless her double move,
> The All-Alice of the world's entity   15
> Smashed in the anger of her hopeless love,
>
> Love for herself who as an earthly twain
> Pouted to join her two in a sweet one:
> No more the second lips to kiss in vain
> The first she broke, plunged through the glass alone—   20

* The exceptions are in the metaphor in lines 7 to 9, and in the adjective "fair" in lines 22 and 23. "Fair" is an echo of traditional balladry.

Alone to the weight of impassivity
Incest of spirit, theorem of desire
Without will as chalky cliffs by the sea
Empty as the bodiless flesh of fire;

All space that heaven is a dayless night   25
A nightless day driven by perfect lust
For vacancy, in which her bored eyesight
Stares at the drowsy cubes of human dust.

—We too back to the world shall never pass
Through the shattered door, a dumb shade-harried crowd,   30
Being all infinite, function, depth and mass
Without figure, a mathematical shroud

Hurled at the air—blessèd without sin!
O God of our flesh, return us to Your wrath
Let us be evil could we enter in   35
Your grace, and falter on the stony path!

Questions

1. The "Alice" referred to in this poem is the heroine of *Alice's Adventures in Wonderland* and *Through the Looking-Glass*. How much of the imagery of the first five stanzas is derived from these two books?

2. What does Alice stand for in this poem? What does the absurdly but inhumanly logical world of the Looking-Glass (or of her Wonderland) stand for? Why is *our* plight (see line 29) like that of Alice? (Note how many figures suggest that the Alice of this poem has hypnotized herself—has locked herself into the world spun out of her own head.)

3. Comment on the meaning of such phrases as "Incest of spirit," "mathematical shroud," and "blessèd without sin." What is this poem about? The poem may be said to end with a prayer. How is the prayer related to the rest of the poem?

Voyages

Hart Crane [*1899–1932*]

II

And yet this great wink of eternity,
Of rimless floods, unfettered leewardings,
Samite sheeted and processioned where
Her undinal vast belly moonward bends,
Laughing the wrapt inflections of our love;   5

Take this Sea, whose diapason knells
On scrolls of silver snowy sentences,
The sceptered terror of whose sessions rends
As her demeanors motion well or ill,
All but the pieties of lovers' hands.   10

And onward, as bells off San Salvador
Salute the crocus lusters of the stars,
In these poinsettia meadows of her tides,—
Adagios of islands, O my Prodigal,
Complete the dark confessions her veins spell.   15

Mark how her turning shoulders wind the hours,
And hasten while her penniless rich palms
Pass superscription of bent foam and wave,—
Hasten, while they are true,—sleep, death, desire,
Close round one instant in one floating flower.   20

Bind us in time, O seasons clear, and awe.
O minstrel galleons of Carib fire,
Bequeath us to no earthly shore until
Is answered in the vortex of our grave
The seal's wide spindrift gaze toward paradise.   25

VI

Where icy and bright dungeons lift
Of swimmers their lost morning eyes,
And ocean rivers, churning, shift
Green borders under stranger skies,

Steadily as a shell secretes   5
Its beating leagues of monotone,
Or as many waters trough the sun's
Red kelson past the cape's wet stone;

O rivers mingling toward the sky
And harbor of the phoenix' breast—   10
My eyes pressed black against the prow,
—Thy derelict and blinded guest

Waiting, afire, what name, unspoke,
I cannot claim: let thy waves rear
More savage than the death of kings,   15
Some splintered garland for the seer.

Beyond siroccos harvesting
The solstice thunders, crept away,
Like a cliff swinging or a sail
Flung into April's inmost day—   20

Creation's blithe and petaled word
To the lounged goddess when she rose
Conceding dialogue with eyes
That smile unsearchable repose—

Still fervid covenant, Belle Isle,   25
—Unfolded floating dais before
Which rainbows twine continual hair—
Belle Isle, white echo of the oar!

The imaged Word, it is, that holds
Hushed willows anchored in its glow.   30
It is the unbetrayable reply
Whose accent no farewell can know.

These two poems make use of a very rich and perhaps tangled imagery. Try to determine whether the imagery is confused or whether it hangs together; and then, on what principle the images are interrelated. Before beginning this examination, you might well reread what Crane has to say about the imagery used in "At Melville's Tomb" (see p. 235).

Questions

1. What aspects of the sea are pictured by the imagery? Suggested by the imagery?

2. In the first of these two poems the sea is addressed as if it were a goddess; in the second, the goddess Aphrodite (who was the Greek goddess of love and who was fabled to have been born of the seafoam) is directly referred to. What does the sea come to symbolize in these poems?

3. Look back at the several general strategies for handling imagery discussed on pages 199–201, 204–206, 213–217, 220–225, 229–232, 234–235, 238–239, 241–243, 248–249. Which strategy is dominant here? Or is it possible to say that any is dominant?

Night

Louise Bogan   [*1897–1970*]

The cold remote islands
And the blue estuaries
Where what breathes, breathes
The restless wind of the inlets,
And what drinks, drinks   5
The incoming tide;

Where shell and weed
Wait upon the salt of the sea,
And the clear nights of stars
Swing their lights westward   10
To set behind the land;

Where the pulse clinging to the rocks
Renews itself forever;
Where, again on cloudless nights,
The water reflects   15
The firmament's partial setting;

—O remember
In your narrowing dark hours
That more things move
Than blood in the heart.   20

Questions

1. To whom is this poem addressed?
2. What is the relevance of the images in this poem?
3. What is this poem about? Does it come to sufficient focus for you to say?

The Goldfish Wife

Sandra Hochman [1936–   ]

It is Monday morning
And the goldfish wife
Comes out with her laundry
To shout her message.
There! Her basket glistens   5
In the sun and shines—
A wicker O. And see how
The goldfish wife touches
The clothes, her fingers
Stretching toward the starch,   10
The wind beating her hair
As though all hair
Were laundry. Come,
Dear fishwife, golden
In your gills, come tell   15
Us of your life and be
Specific. Come into our lives—
Where no sun shines and no
Winds spill
The laundry from the rope—   20
Come on the broomstick of a
Widow-witch, fly
From the empty clotheslines
Of the poor
And teach us now to air   25
Our lives again.

Love Calls Us to the Things of This World

Richard Wilbur [1921–   ]

The eyes open to a cry of pulleys,
And spirited from sleep, the astounded soul
Hangs for a moment bodiless and simple
As false dawn.
          Outside the open window   5
The morning air is all awash with angels.

Some are in bed-sheets, some are in blouses,
Some are in smocks: but truly there they are.
Now they are rising together in calm swells
Of halcyon feeling, filling whatever they wear   10
With the deep joy of their impersonal breathing;

Now they are flying in place, conveying
The terrible speed of their omnipresence, moving
And staying like white water, and now of a sudden
They swoon down into so rapt a quiet   15
That nobody seems to be there.
                                        The soul shrinks

From all that it is about to remember,
From the punctual rape of every blessèd day,
And cries,   20
               "Oh, let there be nothing on earth but laundry,
Nothing but rosy hands in the rising steam
And clear dances done in the sight of heaven."

Yet, as the sun acknowledges
With a warm look the world's hunks and colors,   25
The soul descends once more in bitter love
To accept the waking body, saying now
In a changed voice as the man yawns and rises,
      "Bring them down from their ruddy gallows;
Let there be clean linen for the backs of thieves;   30
Let lovers go fresh and sweet to be undone,
And the heaviest nuns walk in a pure floating
Of dark habits,
                keeping their difficult balance."

Question

Both "The Goldfish Wife" and "Love Calls Us" depend on the image
of laundry. Compare method and meaning with reference to this image
in the two poems.

Theme, Meaning, and Dramatic Structure

Foreword

In earlier sections of this book the reader has encountered references to themes common to various series of poems. For example, the celebration of Queen Victoria's jubilee year (whether her golden or her diamond jubilee) provides the occasion for the three poems discussed on pages 116–122. Many readers would accordingly be inclined to say that these poems share a common theme. But if we consider the poems in any detail, we see that each is "saying" something quite different from the other two. Tennyson's poem provides what amounts to a eulogy of the queen; Kipling is concerned to issue a warning against overweening national pride and makes no reference to the queen at all; Housman reminds his friends of the human cost incurred in the process of "saving the queen" —and incidentally, in promoting the growth of the empire. Tennyson's "On the Jubilee of Queen Victoria" might be called a patriotic speech; Kipling's, a prayer; and Housman's, an ironic (though not unpatriotic) examination of what the phrase "God Save the Queen," so often uttered glibly, actually entails. And also, it should be clear from the various groupings already set up that one "love poem," for example, may have a very different meaning from another "love poem."

The total meaning of a poem, then, is to be carefully distinguished from the event, real or imagined, that occasions the poem, as well as from the material of the poem or even from particular statements in the poem. Nor is the basic meaning necessarily the topic that first catches the eye. The ostensible theme of Frost's "Provide, Provide" (p. 148) is that one should provide enough income for one's self so that when the end comes one can "die in state." But in its full meaning the poem actually exposes the poor second best of having "boughten friendship" at one's side when one lies on the deathbed. What the poet clearly believes to be the best defense against a miserable ending is stated almost offhand in lines 13–15. The rest of the poem is there to provide the right kind of context for these three lines. In short, when we talk about the theme of a poem we must be careful to distinguish between the ostensible topic or even the statements of a poem and the basic attitude and idea implied by a poem when it is understood as a whole. A corollary observation is that no two poems have precisely the same tone. (Tone has its special and important effect on the theme. Say the poem in a somewhat different tone of voice, and the meaning is appreciably changed.)

In view of what has been said above, it is plain that the total meaning of a poem can never be fully summed up in a "statement." *The meaning is the special import of the dramatization of a situation.* In sum, a poem, being a kind of drama that embodies a human situation, implies an attitude toward that situation. It is we, the readers, who often abstract the "theme" and express it as a statement. Thus, we might say that the theme of "Somebody's Darling" (p. 123) and "Come Up from the Fields, Father" (p. 126) is "the tragic waste of war," which is a statement. Yet how different the two poems are in their values and in what they really "say." In short, poems do not so much "state" themes as "test" ideas and attitudes by putting those ideas and attitudes into dramatic situations, by dramatizing human concerns and interests. In fact, we may think of a poem, in one sense, as an experiment in living—that is, as an imaginative enactment. That is why the theme as *mere* statement is always an abstraction from the poem as a realized human experience. Discussion of the theme of a poem may be useful, but only as a tool is useful—to get a job done: and *the job is to achieve both an imaginative and an intellectual grasp of the drama that is the poem.*

A poet such as Longfellow may try to build his poems directly on the "statement of a theme." His "Psalm of Life" insists that

> Life is real! Life is earnest!
>   And the grave is not its goal;
> Dust thou art, to dust returneth,
>   Was not spoken of the soul.

But this comes close to a flat didacticism that kills the drama and turns the poem into moralistic advice. To build on a "statement," the poet must convert "statement" into "experience"—into drama and feeling. For instance, Donne's "If Poisonous Minerals" (p. 330) involves ideas that might well be put into statements, but those ideas are passionately felt in the poem.

Are we to conclude, then, that there is no profit in talking about the theme of a poem? Or, more drastically still, are we to conclude that poems have nothing to say about actuality? Not at all. The argument that poems are dramas and do not traffic in naked propositions must not be taken to mean that in poetry ideas are trivial or nonexistent. In talking seriously about poems, we shall not be able to avoid talking about ideas. For one thing, poetry exists in the medium of words, and, as the philosopher George Santayana* says, words inevitably carry with them some weight of idea; "the detail of things and the detail of ideas pass equally into his [the poet's] verse," and "it is only by the net of new connections which words throw over things, in recalling them, that poetry arises at all." A poem, then, even when presumably it is aiming at a direct expression of feeling or the direct presentation of an object, can only give what Santayana calls "an echo of crude experience," and "a theoretic vision of things at arm's length." The theme, however indirectly it is presented, is as inevitable to poetry as are words.

Or, to look at the matter another way, we can remember that a mood implies an idea, as an idea implies a mood. The human being is a unity, and the slightest shift in feeling implies some new interpretation of things—which is susceptible of being stated as an idea. Or, conversely, the slightest shift in our ideas implies some new stance of feeling, however minimal. To take this in relation to poetry, we may recall Keats's "To Autumn" (p. 87), in which there is no statement of an idea, but in which the general mood, built up by the rhythm and imagery, leads us inevitably to a certain attitude toward life—that is, to an idea, a theme. And such a relation between mood and idea is at the root of all poetry.

All of this is a way of saying again what was said at the beginning of this book, that a poem, insofar as it is a good poem, is an organic unity in which all the elements are vitally interfused. We may abstract rhythm, or imagery, for discussion, but we know that we are making an abstraction, and that the thing we abstract is really an aspect of a whole. We make the abstraction, we study the aspect, merely in order to understand better the whole in its complex interrelations—to experience more deeply the whole in its wholeness.

In this connection we may remind ourselves of what we said earlier in this Foreword: that what we want from poetry is not the idea as such —the theme as a slogan, a poster, or a piece of sampler work to hang on the wall. As far as poetry is concerned, an idea is worthless unless it is dramatized in the poem, unless it seems to grow out of the poem.

* Three Philosophical Poets, Doubleday, 1953, p. 114.

Early in this book we said that every poem is a little drama, and we may now say that the theme of a poem is what the little drama amounts to. The theme embodies the attitude toward life that grows out of the little drama—the evaluation of human experience, but evaluation in relation to the intensities of human experience.

This kind of talk may sound very heavy and sober-sided when we put it over against the lightness, brightness, deftness, or even comedy of such poems as "You're the Top" (p. 225) or "Blame Not My Cheeks" (p. 217). But not all themes are somber—"Life is a jest," one poet wrote. Besides, even the lighthearted poem may have grown out of the confrontation of the deeper realities. It is even possible to argue that comedy, however lighthearted, is possible only because there is some urgency in the world which it treats lightheartedly; and humor and poetry have much in common, including the warmth of feeling and the leap of imagination.

The theme of a poem, then, amounts to a comment on human values, an interpretation of life. But what are we to make of poems in which the theme does not accord with our own feelings about life? * This is a constant question, and one that can hardly be settled once and for all, but it may help us to think of our estimates of poems (or poets) as we think of our estimates of other people. We associate, more or less happily, with a great number of people, and with most of them we have, on some point or other, serious differences of opinion, taste, and values. But we manage to be friendly with most of them. We manage to recognize in many of them certain qualities which, despite our disagreements, can be valued and enjoyed. In people whom we respect we recognize some underlying good will, some attempt to make sense of things and deal honestly with them. In recognizing this fact about others, we discover in ourselves some tolerance and some power of sympathetic imagination that enables us to feel ourselves into another person's skin and to understand how the world looks to him. In this process of imaginative sympathy we realize that the world is complicated and the richer for its complications. We realize, too, that opinions, tastes, and values, which are in some sense opposed to one another, may each have a place, that to many questions there may be more than one answer, and that our own private convictions and dogmatic beliefs may have to be modified. In other words, imagination may teach us a little humility.

Indeed, no attitude or interpretation will invalidate a poem if it is an attitude or interpretation that can conceivably be held by a serious and intelligent person in the dramatic situation stated or implied in the poem. Obviously, words like *serious* and *intelligent* do not mean the same thing to all people, and consequently there is a margin for disagreement in estimating poetry. But such disagreements, taken by and large over a

---

* In recent years this question is often referred to as "the problem of belief."

long sweep of time, after contemporary prejudices have died, are relatively infrequent where first-rate work—or really poor work—is concerned.

The fact that no serious and intelligent attitude will in itself invalidate a poem is not to be taken as saying that one thing is as good as another. Ultimately, we each have to work out our own scale of values and try to justify it and live by it. But it does mean that when we encounter differences, we must try to understand their nature and try to find the underlying common ground that makes respect and appreciation possible.

What, then, is this common ground in poetry? The common ground is the understanding of the fact that, insofar as a theme is coherently developed through a poem, insofar as it actually flowers from the whole process of the poem, *we are witnessing and taking part in the great human effort to achieve meaning through experience.* It is only when the attitude involved in the poem comes as an over-simplified, and unvalidated, generalization, when the response that the poem demands is not warranted by the dramatic situation, when, to sum up, the poem is incoherent—it is only in these cases that we ordinarily reject a poem.

If we find the poem coherent—that is, dramatically significant—we tend to take the leap of sympathetic imagination. We can appreciate it for the sense of the conquest over disorder and meaninglessness that it gives us. Perhaps this sense may be the very basis of the exhilaration we find in poetry—just as it may be the basis for the pleasure we take in watching the clean drive of an expert golfer or the swoop of a hawk, as contrasted with the accidental tumbling of a stone downhill. The sense of order and control in the vital act—that is what in a successful poem confirms us in the faith that experience itself may be made meaningful. *A poem is, in this sense, an image of our life process—and in being that, an enlightening image of ourselves.*

In reading the poems that follow in this section (or in rereading those in earlier sections) we are not to think of ourselves as indulging in message-hunting. We do want to be able to state to ourselves as clearly as possible the theme of a poem, but we must be aware of the fact that our statement will always be little more than a brutal paraphrase. We must make our statement, but we make it in order to appreciate more keenly the modifications and extensions of meaning that the texture—the rhythm, the tone, the imagery—of the poem imposes.

A. DEATH AND RENOWN

Death the Leveler

James Shirley   [*1596–1666*]

> The glories of our blood and state
>> Are shadows, not substantial things;
> There is no armor against Fate;
>> Death lays his icy hand on kings:
>>> Sceptre and Crown   5
>>> Must tumble down,
> And in the dust be equal made
> With the poor crooked scythe and spade.
>
> Some men with swords may reap the field,
>> And plant fresh laurels where they kill: 10
> But their strong nerves[1] at last must yield;
>> They tame but one another still:
>>> Early or late
>>> They stoop to fate,
> And must give up their murmuring breath   15
> When they, pale captives, creep to death.
>
> The garlands wither on your brow;
>> Then boast no more your mighty deeds!
> Upon Death's purple altar now
>> See where the victor-victim bleeds.   20
>>> Your heads must come
>>> To the cold tomb:
> Only the actions of the just
> Smell sweet and blossom in their dust.

In this poem we are told that the king is ultimately conquered by death just as certainly as is the peasant. Though the man with the sword (line 9) may, in "blood" (that is, in lineage and pride of birth) and in "state" (that is, in terms of prestige), far outrank the man who swings his scythe as he reaps the wheatfield, in the end death (line 7) reduces them both to dust.

Is the theme of this poem the wickedness of power? Is this an antiwar poem? Is it an antiaristocratic poem? Does it say that the humble tiller of the soil is a better man than the knight or the king? If the reader is

---

[1] muscles or tendons

inclined to say yes to these questions, then perhaps he had better read the poem again and more carefully.

In order to come to terms with the essential theme of this poem, the reader should pay careful attention to the imagery. He should notice, in particular, the way in which the peasant and the king are defined by their implements, by the sword on the one hand, and by the scythe and spade on the other. (The poet emphasizes this point by describing the warrior's action as a kind of planting and reaping—activities like the peasant's. The warriors "reap the field" of battle and, in achieving fame, they "plant fresh laurels," the trees from whose leaves the garlands for the victor were woven).

Questions

1. Note the related imagery of blossoming and withering that is developed in the last stanza. How is this imagery related to the theme?

2. What is meant by "victor-victim" (line 20)? Has the poet in earlier lines prepared for our accepting this paradox? Indicate how.

3. In line 17 the adjective "your" is used. Who is the "you" implied, to whom the poet addresses himself? Does the poet confuse or strengthen matters by addressing his poem, as it closes, to a particular person or persons?

4. What is the reference of "their" in line 24?

5. Attempt to state the theme of this poem.

6. What is the tone of the last two lines? Can you relate the tone to any technical factors? Compare the tone of these lines to that of the last five lines of "Go, Lovely Rose" (p. 213).

When I Have Fears

John Keats [*1795–1821*]

> When I have fears that I may cease to be
>   Before my pen has glean'd my teeming brain,
> Before high-pilèd books, in charact'ry,
>   Hold like rich garners the full-ripen'd grain;
> When I behold, upon the night's starr'd face,   5
>   Huge cloudy symbols of a high romance,
> And think that I may never live to trace
>   Their shadows, with the magic hand of chance;
> And when I feel, fair creature of an hour,
>   That I shall never look upon thee more,   10
> Never have relish in the faery power
>   Of unreflecting love!—then on the shore
> Of the wide world I stand alone, and think
> Till Love and Fame to nothingness do sink.

This is a poem addressed by a young poet to an imagined love. Keats died early, before he could marry the actual girl with whom he was in love and before he could be sure that he could realize his ambition to be "among the English poets after my death." He asked that on his tombstone should be inscribed: "Here lies one whose name was writ in water."

Questions

1. Notice that one sentence makes up the whole sonnet. What effect, if any, does this have on the concluding lines?

2. What is the point of his calling the girl a "creature of an hour"? In contrast to any living human being, great poems may live on for centuries. Does the poet value the girl more than the great poem, or less? Love more than fame, or less? Or is this issue relevant here?

3. Why does he call love "unreflecting"?

4. Why does he stand on the "shore" of the wide world? What is the meaning of this concluding rhetorical figure? What does it "say"?

Elegy
Written in a Country Churchyard
Thomas Gray [*1716–1771*]

The Curfew tolls the knell of parting day,
    The lowing herd wind slowly o'er the lea,
The plowman homeward plods his weary way,
    And leaves the world to darkness and to me.

Now fades the glimmering landscape on the sight,   5
    And all the air a solemn stillness holds,
Save where the beetle wheels his droning flight,
    And drowsy tinklings lull the distant folds;

Save that from yonder ivy-mantled tower
    The moping owl does to the moon complain   10
Of such, as wandering near her secret bower,
    Molest her ancient solitary reign.

Beneath those rugged elms, that yew-tree's shade,
    Where heaves the turf in many a mould'ring heap,
Each in his narrow cell for ever laid,   15
    The rude Forefathers of the hamlet sleep.

The breezy call of incense-breathing Morn,
    The swallow twitt'ring from the straw-built shed,
The cock's shrill clarion, or the echoing horn,
    No more shall rouse them from their lowly bed.   20

For them no more the blazing hearth shall burn,
    Or busy housewife ply her evening care:
No children run to lisp their sire's return,
    Or climb his knees the envied kiss to share.

Oft did the harvest to their sickle yield,   25
    Their furrow oft the stubborn glebe has broke;
How jocund did they drive their team afield!
    How bowed the woods beneath their sturdy stroke!

Let not Ambition mock their useful toil,
    Their homely joys, and destiny obscure;   30
Nor Grandeur hear with a disdainful smile
    The short and simple annals of the poor.

The boast of heraldry, the pomp of power,
    And all that beauty, all that wealth e'er gave,
Awaits alike th' inevitable hour.   35
    The paths of glory lead but to the grave.

Nor you, ye Proud, impute to These the fault,
    If Memory o'er their Tomb no Trophies raise,
Where through the long-drawn aisle and fretted vault
    The pealing anthem swells the note of praise.   40

Can storied urn or animated bust
    Back to its mansion call the fleeting breath?
Can Honor's voice provoke the silent dust,
    Or Flattery sooth the dull cold ear of Death?

Perhaps in this neglected spot is laid   45
    Some heart once pregnant with celestial fire;
Hands, that the rod of empire might have swayed,
    Or waked to ecstasy the living lyre.

But Knowledge to their eyes her ample page
    Rich with the spoils of time did ne'er unroll;   50
Chill Penury repressed their noble rage,
    And froze the genial current of the soul.

Full many a gem of purest ray serene,
    The dark unfathomed caves of ocean bear:
Full many a flower is born to blush unseen,   55
    And waste its sweetness on the desert air.

Some village-Hampden, that with dauntless breast
    The little Tyrant of his fields withstood;
Some mute inglorious Milton here may rest,
    Some Cromwell guiltless of his country's blood.   60

Th' applause of list'ning senates to command
    The threats of pain and ruin to despise,
To scatter plenty o'er a smiling land,
    And read their history in a nation's eyes,

Their lot forbade: nor circumscribed alone   65
    Their growing virtues, but their crimes confined;
Forbade to wade through slaughter to a throne,
    And shut the gates of mercy on mankind,

The struggling pangs of conscious truth to hide,
    To quench the blushes of ingenuous shame,   70
Or heap the shrine of Luxury and Pride
    With incense kindled at the Muse's flame.

Far from the madding crowd's ignoble strife,
    Their sober wishes never learned to stray;
Along the cool sequestered vale of life   75
    They kept the noiseless tenor of their way.

Yet ev'n these bones from insult to protect,
    Some frail memorial still erected nigh,
With uncouth rhymes and shapeless sculpture decked,
    Implores the passing tribute of a sigh.   80

Their name, their years, spelt by th' unlettered muse,
    The place of fame and elegy supply:
And many a holy text around she strews,
    That teach the rustic moralist to die.

For who to dumb Forgetfulness a prey,   85
    This pleasing anxious being e'er resigned,
Left the warm precincts of the cheerful day,
    Nor cast one longing ling'ring look behind?

On some fond breast the parting soul relies,
    Some pious drops the closing eye requires;   90
Ev'n from the tomb the voice of Nature cries,
    Ev'n in our Ashes live their wonted Fires.

For thee, who mindful of th' unhonored Dead
    Dost in these lines their artless tale relate,
If chance, by lonely contemplation led,   95
    Some kindred Spirit shall inquire thy fate,

Haply some hoary-headed Swain may say,
    "Oft have we seen him at the peep of dawn
Brushing with hasty steps the dews away
    To meet the sun upon the upland lawn.   100

"There at the foot of yonder nodding beech
    That wreathes its old fantastic roots so high,
His listless length at noontide would he stretch,
    And pore upon the brook that babbles by.

"Hard by yon wood, now smiling as in scorn,   105
    Mutt'ring his wayward fancies he would rove,
Now drooping, woeful wan, like one forlorn,
    Or crazed with care, or crossed in hopeless love.

"One morn I missed him on the customed hill,
   Along the heath and near his favorite tree;   110
Another came; nor yet beside the rill,
   Nor up the lawn, nor at the wood was he;

"The next with dirges due in sad array
   Slow through the church-way path we saw him borne.
Approach and read (for thou can'st read) the lay,   115
   Graved on the stone beneath yon agèd thorn."

THE EPITAPH

Here rests his head upon the lap of earth
   A youth to fortune and to fame unknown.
Fair Science frowned not on his humble birth,
   And Melancholy marked him for her own.   120

Large was his bounty, and his soul sincere,
   Heaven did a recompense as largely send:
He gave to Misery all he had, a tear,
   He gained from Heaven ('twas all he wished) a friend.

No farther seek his merits to disclose,   125
   Or draw his frailties from their dread abode,
(There they alike in trembling hope repose)
   The bosom of his Father and his God.

This celebrated poem incorporates topics and situations found in the two poems that precede it. The man who speaks this poem at dusk, as he stands near the churchyard of an English village, meditates on the lives of the people buried here, all of them, presumably, simple farming folk. These dead have no claim to fame. Their lot was simply to endure as "Dynasties pass." In contemplating the meaning of their lives, the observer contrasts this rural churchyard with its frail memorials bearing epitaphs displaying "uncouth rhymes" and "shapeless sculpture" with other burial places—the magnificent tombs of the men and women who could indeed lay claim to "the glories of our blood and state" and whose bodies lie under the pavement of some great abbey church or cathedral. But the famous and the powerful found, like the men and women in Shirley's poem, that they had no "armor against Fate" and had been laid in the dust as low as those that wielded the "crooked scythe and spade."

In Gray's "Elegy," of course, the primary emphasis is on those whose implements were the scythe and the spade. (In the first quatrain the poet tells us that the "plowman homeward plods his weary way.") In this poem the splendid tombs of the "Proud" are described primarily for the purpose of contrast: to set off the lot of those whose graves are not sheltered beneath the "fretted vault" of a great church but lie under the open sky and are exposed to the elements.

Before taking up the matter of the specific theme (or perhaps the bundle of related themes) to be found in this poem, the reader ought to be alerted to several details in the text of the poem. Lines 56–60 refer to three Englishmen who, in the seventeenth century, won their fame in politics or in letters. John Hampden (1594–1643) distinguished himself by opposing on constitutional grounds the king's attempt to raise funds without the authorization of Parliament. He later died fighting in the Parliamentary army in the English Civil War. In that war his cousin Oliver Cromwell (1599–1658) emerged as the leader of the victorious Parliamentary forces that captured, tried, and finally, in 1649, executed the king. Cromwell took over the executive power and until his death was the virtual dictator of the Commonwealth. John Milton (1608–1674), the great English poet, the author of *Paradise Lost,* was involved in the struggle against the royal power, as a pamphleteer and later as Cromwell's Latin Secretary. Thus Gray has chosen as his examples of famous men three who were connected with the great political upheaval that took place in Britain about a century before he wrote the "Elegy."

The reader should observe that the speaker of this poem, who has through lines 1–92 been concerned to relate the "artless tale" of the "unhonored Dead," evidently means to practice what he preaches; that is, he means to eschew ambition, to give himself up to a quiet life of contemplation and meditation, and envisages his own eventual burial in this very churchyard. The poem in fact concludes with the epitaph that he expects to have carved on his own headstone and that, of course, he has himself composed.

Questions

1. What is an "animated bust" (line 41)? A marble bust is by definition "inanimate." What does the speaker mean to imply? If the phrase carries some note of irony, what is the special nature of the irony? And is it justified here? In this general connection, consider "pleasing anxious being" (line 86), "artless tale" (line 94), and "shapeless sculpture" (line 79).

2. What is the special force of "homely joys" (line 30)? Look up the word *homely* in a large dictionary. Can you justify the phrase "noble rage" (line 51)? Just what is meant? What is the meaning of "genial" in line 52? Consult a good dictionary.

3. Is the speaker saying in the "Elegy" that the villagers buried in the churchyard lacked all vanity? Does he sentimentalize their innocence? Is his attitude toward them patronizing in any degree? If you are inclined to answer no to all of these questions, indicate your reasons, with specific reference to the text of the poem.

4. This poem makes a number of general statements about life. Are these statements insisted upon in isolation? Or do they grow out of the dramatic context of the poem?

5. How would you state the theme of this poem? You may prefer to work out your account of the theme by indicating how it combines or builds upon or develops a theme already discussed in "Death the Leveler."

In Memory of W. B. Yeats*

W. H. Auden [1907–1973]

I

He disappeared in the dead of winter: [1]
The brooks were frozen, the airports almost deserted,
And snow disfigured the public statues;
The mercury sank in the mouth of the dying day.
O all the instruments agree   5
The day of his death was a dark cold day.

Far from his illness
The wolves ran on through the evergreen forests,
The peasant river was untempted by the fashionable quays;
By mourning tongues   10
The death of the poet was kept from his poems.

But for him it was his last afternoon as himself,
An afternoon of nurses and rumors;
The provinces of his body revolted,
The squares of his mind were empty,   15
Silence invaded the suburbs,
The current of his feeling failed: he became his admirers.

Now he is scattered among a hundred cities
And wholly given over to unfamiliar affections;
To find his happiness in another kind of wood   20
And be punished under a foreign code of conscience.
The words of a dead man
Are modified in the guts of the living.

But in the importance and noise of tomorrow
When the brokers are roaring like beasts on the floor of the Bourse, 25
And the poor have the sufferings to which they are fairly accustomed,
And each in the cell of himself is almost convinced of his freedom;
A few thousand will think of this day
As one thinks of a day when one did something slightly unusual.
O all the instruments agree   30
The day of his death was a dark cold day.

* The text used here is from *Collected Poems,* 1945; the text of *Selected Poetry,*
1958, omits lines 47–58 and reads for lines 5 and 30: "What instruments we have
agree."

[1] Yeats's death, January 28, 1939

II

You were silly like us: your gift survived it all;
The parish[2] of rich women, physical decay,
Yourself; mad Ireland hurt you into poetry.
Now Ireland has her madness and her weather still,   35
For poetry makes nothing happen: it survives
In the valley of its saying where executives
Would never want to tamper; it flows south
From ranches of isolation and the busy griefs,
Raw towns that we believe and die in; it survives,   40
A way of happening, a mouth.

III

Earth, receive an honored guest;
William Yeats is laid to rest:
Let the Irish vessel lie
Emptied of its poetry.   45

Time that is intolerant
Of the brave and innocent,
And indifferent in a week
To a beautiful physique,

Worships language and forgives   50
Everyone by whom it lives;
Pardons cowardice, conceit,
Lays its honors at their feet.

Time that with this strange excuse
Pardoned Kipling and his views,   55
And will pardon Paul Claudel,[3]
Pardons him for writing well.

In the nightmare of the dark
All the dogs of Europe bark,
And the living nations wait,   60
Each sequestered in its hate;[4]

Intellectual disgrace
Stares from every human face,
And the seas of pity lie
Locked and frozen in each eye.   65

Follow, poet, follow right
To the bottom of the night,
With your unconstraining voice
Still persuade us to rejoice;

[2] use of "parish" here not literal but quasi-metaphorical, meaning "congregation" of rich women, a rather local and smug community, parochial in its interests and range of vision   [3] Paul Claudel (1868–1955), French poet and diplomat, whose outlook was extremely conservative   [4] Auden's poem first printed on March 8, 1939; to the thoughtful observer, outbreak of World War II was clearly imminent

With the farming of a verse　　　　　　　　　　　　70
Make a vineyard of the curse,
Sing of human unsuccess
In a rapture of distress;

In the deserts of the heart
Let the healing fountain start,　　　　　　　　　　75
In the prison of his days
Teach the free man how to praise.

Questions

1. What are the relations to each other of the three divisions?
2. What is the poem really "about"? Yeats? War? The function of poetry? The responsibilities of the poet? Or what?

The Country Wedding

A Fiddler's Story

Thomas Hardy [1840–1928]

Little fogs were gathered in every hollow,
But the purple hillocks enjoyed fine weather
As we marched with our fiddles over the heather
—How it comes back!—to their wedding that day.

Our getting there brought our neighbours and all, O!　　　5
Till, two and two, the couples stood ready.
And her father said: "Souls, for God's sake, be steady!"
And we strung up our fiddles, and sounded out "A."

The groomsman he stared, and said, "You must follow!"
But we'd gone to fiddle in front of the party,　　　　　10
(Our feelings as friends being true and hearty)
And fiddle in front we did—all the way.

Yes, from their door by Mill-tail-Shallow,
And up Styles-Lane, and by Front-Street houses,
Where stood maids, bachelors, and spouses,　　　　　15
Who cheered the songs that we knew how to play.

I bowed the treble before her father,
Michael the tenor in front of the lady,
The bass-viol Reub—and right well played he!—
The serpent Jim; ay, to church and back.　　　　　20

I thought the bridegroom was flurried rather,
As we kept up the tune outside the chancel,
While they were swearing things none can cancel
Inside the walls to our drumstick's whack.

"Too gay!" she pleaded. "Clouds may gather,　　　　25
And sorrow come." But she gave in, laughing,

And by supper-time when we'd got to the quaffing
Her fears were forgot, and her smiles weren't slack.

A grand wedding 'twas! And what would follow
We never thought. Or that we should have buried her   30
On the same day with the man that married her,
A day like the first, half hazy, half clear.

Yes: little fogs were in every hollow,
Though the purple hillocks enjoyed fine weather,
When we went to play 'em to church together,   35
And carried 'em there in an after year.

Thomas Hardy rejoiced in the local customs and the folkways of England's "West Country," describing them in his many novels and in a great many of his poems. The following are a few brief notes that bear on these customs.

The musical instruments mentioned in this poem consist of a treble and a tenor violin (we would today call them the first and second violins), a bass-viol (that is, in modern nomenclature, a double-bass), and a serpent, a deep-voiced wind instrument of serpentine shape, made of brass or wood. Line 24 indicates that there was also a drum.

An engaged pair walked to their wedding along with their friends and the musicians, who, in this instance at least, and evidently over the protest of the groomsman, led the procession rather than walked behind the bridegroom and bride. The music was apparently kept up outside the chancel of the church (see lines 21–24) while the ceremony was going on inside.

The custom of the country was also to have the funeral procession march to the churchyard to music. The musical note A (line 8) is still the note usually sounded when a concert group or orchestra is tuning up.

The subtitle of this poem is important. The poem does tell a "story." The teller is a fiddler who played with the rest of his group for the couple's wedding, and then, later on, played for their funeral. It is also important that in this poem, in contrast to the preceding poem, the narrator is not a person who has any strong emotional attachment to either of those who died. The narrator of "The Country Wedding" therefore speaks with some detachment about the two most important occasions of the couple's lives, and his detachment has an important bearing, not only on the tone of the poem, but on the theme as well.

Questions

1. What does the bride's father's exclamation (line 7) tell us about the importance on this occasion of music fittingly rendered?

2. Is the bride (lines 25–28) apprehensive about the future or merely nervous? Is there any importance to the meaning of the poem that she was worried at this time that the music might be "too gay"?

3. Why aren't we told the circumstances that accounted for the fact that both husband and wife were buried on the same day? Did they die of the same disease? Were they killed together in an accident? How does the fiddler's lack of any concern to tell us about the manner of their dying indicate what the reminiscence of their funeral essentially meant to him?

4. One would expect the fiddler to make something of the coincidence that he had played for the couple on their wedding day and again on their funeral day, but hardly of the fact that the weather on both these crucial days was strangely similar. Though the fiddler doesn't indicate why he thinks the state of the weather was important, do you believe it has any significance for the meaning of the poem? For the theme?

5. Attempt to state the theme of this poem. (In doing so, compare it with the theme of "Death the Leveler" and "Elegy Written in a Country Churchyard.") What kind of "moral weather" do the lives of most ordinary folk show? Sunshine? Gloom? Or what?

B. THE JOYS OF THE SIMPLE LIFE

Under the Greenwood Tree

William Shakespeare [1564–1616]

Under the greenwood tree
Who loves to lie with me,
And turn his merry note
Unto the sweet bird's throat,
Come hither, come hither, come hither!   5
  Here shall he see
  No enemy
But winter and rough weather.

Who doth ambition shun,
And loves to live i' the sun,   10
Seeking the food he eats,
And pleased with what he gets,
Come hither, come hither, come hither!
  Here shall he see
  No enemy   15
But winter and rough weather.

This song occurs in Shakespeare's play *As You Like It*. The rightful duke has been deposed by his wicked younger brother and now lives in exile in the Forest of Arden. One of his retainers, Amiens, sings this song in praise of life in the forest, away from the sophisticated court.

The gist of his song is clearly that it is much easier to bear the hardships imposed by nature—winter and rough weather—than the cruelty and wickedness that all too frequently are found in human society. This basic interpretation seems to be clinched by the fact that Amiens later on in the play sings another song that makes just this point:

> Blow, blow, thou winter wind!
> Thou art not so unkind
>   As man's ingratitude;
> Thy tooth is not so keen,
> Because thou'rt not seen,
>   Although thy breath be rude.

The special twist given to the sentiment expressed in these songs is supplied by the man who sings them: Amiens is a courtier who, though accustomed to the luxury of a court, now sings in praise of honest simplicity found in the life in the forest. There, one can take for his pitch pipe the spontaneous and natural notes of the bird. He can lie at full length and soak up the sunshine. He "seeks" the food he eats—the duke and his retainer, we learn from the play, go hunting for deer in the forest —and does not have it provided by someone else. Moreover, he is content with what he manages to procure, whatever it may be. Such a life, Amiens insists, is better than the sheltered life at court, and, though nature may not always be kind, one can put up with winter and rough weather better than with some other things.

Later in the play, Corin, no courtier but an old shepherd, makes the same claim, stating it in forthright prose. He says: "Sir, I am a true laborer: I earn that I eat, get that I wear; owe no man hate, envy no man's happiness; glad of other men's good, content with my harm; and the greatest of my pride is, to see my ewes graze and my lambs suck."

One must not conclude that such was necessarily Shakespeare's conception of the good life, or of the proper relation of man to nature and to society. But what Amiens sings and what Corin speaks in prose represent a view of reality with which not only Shakespeare but all the Elizabethans were perfectly well acquainted. Indeed, this praise of the simple life together with a depreciation of the sophisticated life to be found at court was a traditional (and even stock) truism of the period, as we have seen in connection with "Maesia's Song," by Robert Greene (p. 131). The Elizabethans were an active, aggressive, and litigious breed, constantly seeking to acquire wealth and power, but in their songs and plays they never tired of expressing the wish that they might live close to nature and enjoy the carefree life of the shepherd or the peasant. (The contradiction is, of course, thoroughly human: For example, landscape painting is born only when men begin to shut themselves up in cities.) We may also remark here a deeper paradox, not unrelated to this one, in Elizabethan life. It was, relatively speaking, an "open" period, in which a person of ability or cunning might readily rise to power, but the vice most greatly rebuked in Elizabethan tragedy is ambition.

Questions

1. What is the theme of "Under the Greenwood Tree"? Is it too simple in this poem, too nakedly stated, to take on dramatic interest? If you answer no to this question, then what factors—of tone, imagery, metrical arrangement—give it the complication necessary to engage the reader's interest?

2. If you are to be fair to the aesthetic merit of this song, should you consider it in pure isolation? Or are you required to see the song as part of a larger context, that of the play as a whole? In short, do we need to take into account the character of the singer and the situation that conditions his song? (Actually, in our brief preliminary discussion of the poem we found it necessary to touch on these matters. In any case, an experienced reader immediately recognizes the genre of the pastoral and would accept the poem with the special limitations of the genre and without a specified context or dramatic background.)

Art Thou Poor, Yet Hast Thou Golden Slumbers?

[possibly by]   Thomas Dekker   [c. 1572–1632]

Art thou poor, yet hast thou golden slumbers?
    Oh sweet content!
Art thou rich, yet is thy mind perplexed?
    Oh punishment!
Dost thou laugh to see how fools are vexed   5
To add to golden numbers, golden numbers?[1]
Oh sweet content! Oh sweet, oh sweet content!
    Work apace, apace, apace, apace;
    Honest labor bears a lovely face;
Then hey nonny nonny, hey nonny nonny!   10

Canst drink the waters of the crispèd spring?
    Oh sweet content!
Swimm'st thou in wealth, yet sink'st in thine own tears?
    Oh punishment!
Then he that patiently want's burden bears   15
No burden bears, but is a king, a king!
Oh sweet content! Oh sweet, oh sweet content!
    Work apace, apace, apace, apace;
    Honest labor bears a lovely face;
Then hey nonny nonny, hey nonny nonny!   20

[1] numbers of golden coins

This poem provides another example of praise for the simple life, and, in conjunction with "Under the Greenwood Tree," can help us test the limits (or something approaching the limits) of simplicity in the matter of theme. The case for a sufficient complexity to be interesting in these poems might begin with the observation that neither claims too much: The person who sings the joy of living under the greenwood tree doesn't forget the inconveniences in such an abode. In fact, he emphasizes at the end of both stanzas: "winter and rough weather." The greenwood tree, once it has shed its leaves, provides a very thin and leaky roof against the snow and rain. His point is that it does have its summer delights and that there are worse discomforts than winter and rough weather. The person happy in the Forest of Arden will only be that person who is "pleased with what he gets." (The implication is clear: "pleased with whatever he gets"—which may in some instances amount to very little.)

Dekker's song exhibits the same realism. As does "Under the Greenwood Tree," it firmly locates the contentment within the contented person's own mind—not in his possession of goods usually acquired only after anxious care, which, once obtained, still beget anxious care lest they be lost. In sum, neither poem offers a self-indulgent fancy, a daydream of happiness. Both poems, simple though they be, suggest that a realistic contentment costs something—has to be earned.

We may use "Under the Greenwood Tree" and "Art Thou Poor" to raise another issue. These two poems, and many others like them, associate honest work, modest requirements, and a contented mind with a life lived close to nature.* The tradition that associates the shepherd or the husbandman with the healthy joys of the simple life is still very much alive today. But what if the poet tries to find this life of healthy-minded and cheerful poverty within the city? Does the altered circumstance make a different demand on our credibility? Does such a shift engage a very different theme?

Questions

1. Compare these two poems, on as many points as possible, with "Let the Rest of the World Go By" (p. 130).

2. Can you say that there are pastoral elements suggested in Spender's "An Elementary School Classroom in a Slum" (p. 152)?

---

* This is not to say, of course, that hurt and loss cannot be found in the village and on the farm. Wordsworth himself, the poet who celebrates the calming and beneficent power of nature, gives us poems of rural life that do show hurt and loss. A contemporary of his, George Crabbe (1754–1832) exhibits extreme instances in his poetry. In fact, there is a whole body of literature that is "anti-pastoral," that sets out to show the misery and cramping limitations of life on farm or in village. But the pastoral and the anti-pastoral do not cancel out, as it were: they represent two fundamental views about life; we find both views current in our own time.

To the Four Courts, Please
James Stephens [*1882–1950*]

The driver rubbed at his nettly chin
With a huge, loose forefinger, crooked and black,
And his wobbly, violet lips sucked in,
And puffed out again and hung down slack:
One fang shone through his lop-sided smile,   5
In his little pouched eye flickered years of guile.

And the horse, poor beast, it was ribbed and forked,
And its ears hung down, and its eyes were old,
And its knees were knuckly, and as we talked
It swung the stiff neck that could scarcely hold   10
Its big, skinny head up—then I stepped in,
And the driver climbed to his seat with a grin.

God help the horse and the driver too,
And the people and beasts who have never a friend,
For the driver easily might have been you,   15
And the horse be me by a different end.
And nobody knows how their days will cease,
And the poor, when they're old, have little of peace.

The Four Courts is a building near the center of Dublin. It was seized by Irish revolutionists in 1922 and burned during the fighting with the British army. The title, of course, represents the speech of a man who is giving a street address to the driver of a cab.

In this poem we encounter once more a poor man, who is driving a horse as poor as himself, but he is no plowman homeward plodding "his weary way." The driver is a city man and his horse is pulling, one supposes, a hansom cab. The driver, much the worse for wear, is described very realistically in the first stanza, a battered man, out of whose "little pouched eye flickered years of guile."

Questions

1. Why does the poet describe the horse in such detail? Is he particularly interested in horses? Or does he carefully describe the horse in order to tell us something about the horse's owner and about the situation in which both horse and driver find themselves?

2. What is the speaker's attitude toward the horse and the driver? Does he have any illusions about the innocence or the genuine simplicity of the driver? Is he sincere in his statement in line 13 "God help the horse, and the driver too"?

3. What is the theme of this poem? In this connection, what is the meaning of line 17 and of line 18?

4. Is the poem sentimental? Or does it express a responsible pity? To

put the question a little differently, is the poet realistic in his view of man
and beast and the plight of the poor?

5. Does the fact that the poor man and his poor horse are transferred
from a country setting onto the paved streets of a modern city make the
situation more pathetic or not? How does it affect what the poem is saying
—the theme of the poem?

6. Compare the theme of this poem with that of "Preludes" (p. 91).

Two Songs from Sweeney Agonistes

T. S. Eliot [*1888–1965*]

In this unfinished play, one of the characters, Sweeney, a rather raffish
urban Irishman, is exchanging some banter with a girl by the name of
Doris. They are at a party and he laughingly threatens to carry her off
to a "cannibal isle." He says to her:

SWEENEY: You'll be my little seven stone[1] missionary!
            I'll gobble you up. I'll be the cannibal.
DORIS: You'll carry me off? To a cannibal isle?
SWEENEY: I'll be the cannibal.
DORIS: I'll be the missionary.   5
            I'll convert you!
SWEENEY: I'll convert *you!*
            Into a stew.
            A nice little, white little, missionary stew.

Sweeney then proceeds to tell Doris what life is like on a "crocodile
isle." There are no telephones, motorcars, or any of the rest of the
paraphernalia of civilization. On the island there is nothing to see "but
the palms one way / And the sea the other way, / Nothing to hear but
the sound of the surf." But the island really offers everything, for Sweeney
declares that there are in fact only three things in life, and when Doris
asks him what they are, Sweeney answers: "Birth, and copulation, and
death, / That's all, that's all, that's all, that's all, / Birth, and copulation,
and death." Then comes the following song:

SONG BY WAUCHOPE AND HORSFALL
    Snow as Tambo. Swarts as Bones.[2]

Under the bamboo
Bamboo bamboo
Under the bamboo tree
Two live as one
One live as two   5

---

[1] stone (British measure): fourteen pounds   [2] "Tambo" and "Bones," from the traditional black-face minstrel show, are the "end men," Tambo playing the tambourine
and Bones (or Mr. Bones, as he is usually called) clicking the "bones," the two bits of
wood or bone that are sounded somewhat like Spanish castanets

Two live as three
Under the bam
Under the boo
Under the bamboo tree.
  Where the breadfruit fall   10
And the penguin call
And the sound is the sound of the sea
Under the bam
Under the boo
Under the bamboo tree.   15

  Where the Gauguin maids
In the banyan shades
Wear palmleaf drapery
Under the bam
Under the boo   20
Under the bamboo tree.

  Tell me what part of the wood
Do you want to flirt with me?
Under the breadfruit, banyan, palmleaf
Or under the bamboo tree?   25
Any old tree will do for me
Any old wood is just as good
Any old isle is just my style
Any fresh egg
Any fresh egg   30
And the sound of the coral sea.

DORIS: I don't like eggs; I never liked eggs;
  And I don't like life on your crocodile isle.

SONG BY KLIPSTEIN AND KRUMPACKER
  Snow and Swarts as before.

My little island girl
My little island girl
I'm going to stay with you
And we won't worry what to do
We won't have to catch any trains   5
And we won't go home when it rains
We'll gather hibiscus flowers
For it won't be minutes but hours
For it won't be hours but years
And the morning   10
And the evening
And noontime
And night
Morning   [diminuendo]
Evening   15
Noontime
Night

DORIS: That's not life, that's no life
    Why I'd just as soon be dead.
SWEENEY: That's what life is. Just is   20
DORIS: What is?
    What's that life is?
SWEENEY: Life is death.

This account of life on a South Sea island is a rather jumbled affair—and one supposes that the poet satirically meant it to be so. The people singing about the delights of this simple life have evidently never been in the South Sea islands themselves, and they have added to the clichés of the earthly paradise some details that don't quite fit. For example, there are in fact no penguins found on a South Sea island and probably no banyan trees. One element in this muddled, composite picture comes from the old-fashioned cartoon of lugubrious white missionaries sitting in great iron pots over a fire while the cannibal chef stands over them with a huge ladle. Another element is derived from pictures of the South Sea islands done by Paul Gauguin (1848–1903), who left his native France to live in Tahiti. His paintings of Polynesian life adorn many galleries in the United States and in Europe.

An even more obvious source was a popular song by James Weldon Johnson and his brother (for the words) and Bob Cole (for the music). The song was entitled "Under the Bamboo Tree" and was the great hit of 1902.

Questions

1. What is the tone of the first song? Is the tone of the second song noticeably different? Are the singers singing with carefree abandon? Are they celebrating the delights of a life close to nature? Or are they really mocking it?

2. Compare nature and the simple life, as described in this poem, with nature and the simple life in the poems on page 282 and page 284 above. How does life "Under the Greenwood Tree" differ from life "Under the Bamboo Tree"?

3. What is the theme of these songs? That a life with no worries about catching trains is heavenly? Or that it is boring? Could Doris's last statement be translated: "Why, I'd be bored to death"? If it can be adequately so translated, why has the poet put it as he has?

4. What is the poet's intent in offering Sweeney's defense of his "pastoral"—that is, that the island really affords the only three things in life?

C. THE BREAKUP OF A CIVILIZATION

The Unknown Citizen

W. H. Auden   [1907–1973]

(To JS/07/M/378
This Marble Monument
Is Erected by the State)

He was found by the Bureau of Statistics to be
One against whom there was no official complaint,
And all the reports on his conduct agree
That, in the modern sense of an old-fashioned word, he was a saint,
For in everything he did he served the Greater Community.   5
Except for the War till the day he retired
He worked in a factory and never got fired,
But satisfied his employers, Fudge Motors Inc.
Yet he wasn't a scab or odd in his views,
For his Union reports that he paid his dues,   10
(Our report on his Union shows it was sound)
And our Social Psychology workers found
That he was popular with his mates and liked a drink.
The Press are convinced that he bought a paper every day
And that his reactions to advertisements were normal in every way. 15
Policies taken out in his name prove that he was fully insured,
And his Health-card shows he was once in hospital but left it cured.
Both Producers Research and High-Grade Living declare
He was fully sensible to the advantages of the Instalment Plan
And had everything necessary to the Modern Man,   20
A phonograph, a radio, a car and a frigidaire.
Our researchers into Public Opinion are content
That he held the proper opinions for the time of year;
When there was peace, he was for peace; when there was war, he went.
He was married and added five children to the population,   25
Which our Eugenist says was the right number for a parent of his
          generation,
And our teachers report that he never interfered with their education.
Was he free? Was he happy? The question is absurd:
Had anything been wrong, we should certainly have heard.

Several nations have honored a representative dead soldier by creating
a monument to him. Since he is to be truly representative, they have
buried beneath the monument an unidentified corpse, the body of a man
whose name is unknown, or, as the formal description usually puts it, a
soldier "Known Only to God." The Unknown Citizen whose life is being
commemorated in this monument seems to lack a name too: see the

second half of the title, which is printed within parentheses. But the unknown citizen, though he lacks a name, quite clearly does have a number, and in knowing his number, the state knows all that it needs to know about him. If he is not John Smith or Charles Baker or Joe Doakes, he is something more important, a midpoint on the statistical chart, and thus truly representative of the vast horde of faceless citizenry. In this poem we have not the short and simple annals of the poor, as Gray described them, but the computerized facts about the not-so-divine average. The simple life here has become the very negation of life.

Questions

1. What would you say is the "modern sense" of sainthood (line 4)?
2. Why are the questions in line 28 "absurd"?
3. In what sense is the citizen "unknown"?
4. What is the theme of the poem? Compare it with that of "Death the Leveler" (p. 271) and that of Gray's "Elegy" (p. 273).
5. Do we hear the clank of the "mind-forged manacles" in this poem as in Blake's "London" (p. 149)?

Shine, Perishing Republic

Robinson Jeffers [*1887–1961*]

> While this America settles in the mold of its vulgarity, heavily
> thickening to empire,
> And protest, only a bubble in the molten mass, pops and sighs out,
> and the mass hardens,
>
> I sadly smiling remember that the flower fades to make fruit, the
> fruit rots to make earth.
> Out of the mother; and through the spring exultances, ripeness and
> decadence; and home to the mother.
>
> You make haste on decay: not blameworthy; life is good, be it
> stubbornly long or suddenly   5
> A mortal splendor: meteors are not needed less than mountains:
> shine, perishing republic.
>
> But for my children, I would rather have them keep their distance from
> the thickening center; corruption
> Never has been compulsory, when the cities lie at the monster's feet
> there are left the mountains.
>
> And boys, be in nothing so moderate as in love of man, a clever
> servant, insufferable master.
> There is the trap that catches noblest spirits, that caught—they say—
> God, when he walked on earth.   10

Questions

1. Does this poet "hate" America? Is he trying to admonish his country? What does he mean by asking it to "shine"? Is he saying that America's

course of action is "not blameworthy" (line 5)? Does he love the "perishing republic"?

2. To whom are the last two lines addressed? How do these lines relate to the first four stanzas of the poem?

3. Compare and contrast the theme of this poem with that of Ginsberg's "A Supermarket in California" (p. 159).

4. What theory of history is implied in this poem?

from

Hugh Selwyn Mauberley
(Life and Contacts) I–V

Ezra Pound [1885–1972]

E. P. Ode Pour l'Election de Son Sepulchre[1]

I

For three years, out of key with his time,
He strove to resuscitate the dead art
Of poetry; to maintain "the sublime"
In the old sense. Wrong from the start—

No, hardly, but seeing he had been born   5
In a half savage country, out of date;
Bent resolutely on wringing lilies from the acorn;[2]
Capaneus;[3] trout for factitious bait;

Ἴδμεν γάρ τοι πάνθ', ὅσ' ἐνὶ Τροίῃ[4]
Caught in the unstopped ear;
Giving the rocks small lee-way
The chopped seas held him, therefore, that year.

His true Penelope was Flaubert,
He fished by obstinate isles;
Observed the elegance of Circe's[5] hair   15
Rather than the mottoes on sun-dials.[6]

---

[1] "Ezra Pound's Ode on the Choice of His Tomb"; in sections I and II, Pound writes about himself as he feels he must have appeared to the London literary world of the first decades of the century: wrong-headed, obstinate, a literary failure—"Wrong from the start—" [2] Pound ironically regarded as a kind of poetic Luther Burbank (the expert on plants), but a Burbank silly enough to believe that he could breed lilies from acorns [3] a prince in the Greek myth of the Seven against Thebes, regarded as a type of arrogance and overweening pride [4] from the *Odyssey*: "for we know all the things that [are] in Troy," a fragment of the song of the Sirens who tried to tempt the vessel of Odysseus (Ulysses) onto the rocks; Odysseus, returning from Troy, was trying to get home to Ithaca and his faithful wife, Penelope; Pound is also a voyager, but his goal is Gustave Flaubert, the great nineteenth-century French novelist; Flaubert stood for perfection in his art, but he also insisted on exposing the shams of the age in which he lived [5] an enchantress who also tried to detain Odysseus [6] such mottoes usually urge the view that time passes and one mustn't waste it

Unaffected by "the march of events,"
He passed from men's memory in *l'an trentiesme*
De son âge;[7] the case presents
No adjunct to the Muses' diadem.   20

II

The age demanded an image
Of its accelerated grimace,
Something for the modern stage,
Not, at any rate, an Attic grace;

Not, not certainly, the obscure reveries   25
Of the inward gaze;
Better mendacities
Than the classics in paraphrase!

The "age demanded" chiefly a mould in plaster,
Made with no loss of time,   30
A prose kinema, not, not assuredly, alabaster
Or the "sculpture" of rhyme.

III

The tea-rose tea-gown, etc.
Supplants the mousseline of Cos,[8]
The pianola "replaces"   35
Sappho's barbitos.[9]

Christ follows Dionysus,
Phallic and ambrosial
Made way for macerations;
Caliban casts out Ariel.   40

All things are a flowing,
Sage Heracleitus says;
But a tawdry cheapness
Shall outlast our days.

Even the Christian beauty   45
Defects—after Samothrace;
We see τὸ καλόν[10]
Decreed in the market place.

Faun's flesh is not to us,
Nor the saint's vision.
We have the press for wafer;[11]   50
Franchise for circumcision.

All men, in law, are equals.
Free of Pisistratus,[12]

[7] the opening line of the *Grand Testament* of the great medieval poet, François Villon: in "the thirtieth year of his age" he had drunk all his shames; when Pound published this poem he was himself 35   [8] the Latin poet refers to the muslin ("mousseline") of the Greek island of Cos   [9] Shappho of Lesbos: the celebrated Greek poet of the seventh century B.C.; barbitos: a kind of lyre or lute   [10] "the beautiful"   [11] wafer: consecrated bread offered in the Eucharist   [12] "free of dictatorship"; Pisistratos: a celebrated Athenian tyrant

We choose a knave or an eunuch   55
To rule over us.

O bright Apollo,
τίν' ἄνδρα, τίν' ἤρωα, τίνα θεόν,[13]
What god, man, or hero
Shall I place a tin wreath upon!   60

IV

These fought in any case,[14]
and some believing,
                    pro domo,[15] in any case . . .

Some quick to arm,   65
some for adventure,
some from fear of weakness,
some from fear of censure,
some for love of slaughter, in imagination,
learning later . . .
some in fear, learning love of slaughter;   70

Died some, pro patria, non "dulce" non "et decor"[16] . . .
walked eye-deep in hell
believing in old men's lies, then unbelieving
came home, home to a lie,
home to many deceits,   75
home to old lies and new infamy;
usury age-old and age-thick
and liars in public places.

Daring as never before, wastage as never before.
Young blood and high blood,   80
fair cheeks, and fine bodies;

fortitude as never before,

frankness as never before,
disillusions as never told in the old days,
hysterias, trench confessions,   85
laughter out of dead bellies.

V

There died a myriad,
And of the best, among them

---

[13] somewhat misquoted from Pindar's Second Olympian Ode: "What man, what hero, what god [shall we praise]?"; "tin," line 60: a scornful play on the Greek word τίν', "what"   [14] from here through line 94 Pound refers to World War I, in which many of the brightest and best of the young men of Europe were killed; several of them, including some fine artists and poets, were close friends of Pound   [15] "for home" [16] Horace: "Dulce et decorum est pro patria mori," that is, "It is sweet and fitting to die for one's native land" (cf. Owen's poem, p. 129)

For an old bitch gone in the teeth,
For a botched civilization,   90

Charm, smiling at the good mouth,
Quick eyes gone under earth's lid,

For two gross of broken statues,
For a few thousand battered books.

Questions

1. In Section I of the poem Pound is clearly referring to the poor reception his own work received. Is his indictment of the taste of the public an attempt to justify himself? Is the tone one of personal complaint? Or is he using his personal case as a means for getting into a general indictment of the culture? Before you try to answer these questions, examine carefully the sequence I through V.

2. What is the tone of I? Of II and III? Of III and IV?

3. Does Pound establish any relation between the deterioration of taste for the arts and literature and the deterioration of society, government, and international relations? He could scarcely say that a breakdown of proper appreciaton of the arts brought on World War I. What do you think he could justifiably say in regard to this subject? What do you think he does say in this poem?

4. Do you think that Pound sentimentalizes the young men who fought in World War I? Is he fair to the complex motives that brought them into the war?

5. If Pound loved the artist and his work, how could he write lines 93–94? How do you interpret these lines in the context into which Pound has put them?

6. Are the editors justified in putting this work among the poems having to do with "The Breakup of a Civilization"? In short, what do you make out to be Pound's theme?

The Second Coming

William Butler Yeats   [*1865–1939*]

Turning and turning in the widening gyre
The falcon cannot hear the falconer;
Things fall apart; the center cannot hold;
Mere anarchy is loosed upon the world,
The blood-dimmed tide is loosed, and everywhere   5
The ceremony of innocence is drowned;
The best lack all conviction, while the worst
Are full of passionate intensity.
Surely some revelation is at hand;
Surely the Second Coming is at hand.   10
The Second Coming! Hardly are those words out

When a vast image out of *Spiritus Mundi*
Troubles my sight: somewhere in sands of the desert
A shape with lion body and the head of a man,
A gaze blank and pitiless as the sun,   15
Is moving its slow thighs, while all about it
Reel shadows of the indignant desert birds.
The darkness drops again; but now I know
That twenty centuries of stony sleep
Were vexed to nightmare by a rocking cradle,   20
And what rough beast, its hour come round at last,
Slouches towards Bethlehem to be born?

The "Second Coming" of the title alludes to the second coming of Christ to usher in the millennium. But as Yeats uses the term in this poem, it alludes not to the end of human history, but to the end of the 2000-plus years of Christian culture and the coming of the new supernatural force that will inaugurate the next 2000-year cycle, which will supersede the Christian era. (See W. B. Yeats, *A Vision,* Macmillan, 1938.)

Whereas the generating force of the Christian era was a divine child born in a cattle shed and laid in a manager at Bethlehem, the generating force of the era to come will be a supernatural creature, the "rough beast" of line 21. The speaker sees this creature in a momentary glimpse of an image out of *Spiritus Mundi* (the spirit of the world), which—to use the Jungian terminology—would be something like the collective unconscious.

Questions

1. What do you make of the first two lines? That power (the falcon) has now broken loose from all control?

2. Why, at the stage of affairs described in this poem, should the "best lack all conviction"? If such was the state of affairs at the breakdown of classical civilization when the barbarian hordes began to overrun the Roman empire, how much evidence do you see that something of the same situation may prevail now?

3. How could a "rocking cradle" vex "to nightmare" "twenty centuries of stony sleep"? Is the poet here implying a repetition of this process in his own time? Is he saying that he has been vouchsafed a glimpse of this nightmare?

4. What do you take to be the theme of this poem? Try to state it as fully as possible.

5. Compare this poem with "Shine, Perishing Republic" by Jeffers (p. 291).

The Waste Land

T. S. Eliot [*1888–1965*]

"Nam Sibyllam quidem Cumis ego ipse oculis meis
vidi in ampulla pendere, et cum illi pueri dicerent:
Σίβυλλα τί θέλεις; respondebat illa: ἀποθανεῖν θέλω."[1]

For Ezra Pound
il miglior fabbro[2]

I. THE BURIAL OF THE DEAD

April is the cruelest month, breeding
Lilacs out of the dead land, mixing
Memory and desire, stirring
Dull roots with spring rain.
Winter kept us warm, covering   5
Earth in forgetful snow, feeding
A little life with dried tubers.
Summer surprised us, coming over the Starnbergersee
With a shower of rain; we stopped in the colonnade,
And went on in sunlight, into the Hofgarten,   10
And drank coffee, and talked for an hour.
Bin gar keine Russin, stamm' aus Litauen, echt deutsch.[3]
And when we were children, staying at the arch-duke's,
My cousin's, he took me out on a sled,
And I was frightened. He said, Marie,   15
Marie, hold on tight. And down we went.
In the mountains, there you feel free.
I read, much of the night, and go south in the winter.

What are the roots that clutch, what branches grow
Out of this stony rubbish? Son of man,   20
You cannot say, or guess, for you know only
A heap of broken images, where the sun beats,
And the dead tree gives no shelter, the cricket no relief,
And the dry stone no sound of water. Only
There is shadow under this red rock,   25
(Come in under the shadow of this red rock),
And I will show you something different from either
Your shadow at morning striding behind you
Or your shadow at evening rising to meet you;
I will show you fear in a handful of dust.   30

---

[1] "For with my own eyes I saw the Sibyl of Cumae hanging in a cage, and when the boys cried to her, 'Sibyl, what do you want?' she answered, 'I want to die'" (from Petronius' *Satyricon*); the Sibyl, a prophetic old woman, was supposed to be about a thousand years old [2] "the superior maker" [3] "I'm by no means a Russian, I come from Lithuania—pure German"

Frisch weht der Wind
Der Heimat zu
Mein Irisch Kind,
Wo weilest du?[4]

"You gave me hyacinths first a year ago;   35
"They called me the hyacinth girl."
—Yet when we came back, late, from the hyacinth garden,
Your arms full, and your hair wet, I could not
Speak, and my eyes failed, I was neither
Living nor dead, and I knew nothing,   40
Looking into the heart of light, the silence.
Oed' und leer das Meer.[5]

Madame Sosostris, famous clairvoyante,
Had a bad cold, nevertheless
Is known to be the wisest woman in Europe,   45
With a wicked pack of cards. Here, said she,
Is your card, the drowned Phoenician Sailor,
(Those are pearls that were his eyes. Look!)
Here is Belladonna, the Lady of the Rocks,
The lady of situations.   50
Here is the man with three staves, and here the Wheel,
And here is the one-eyed merchant, and this card,
Which is blank, is something he carries on his back,
Which I am forbidden to see. I do not find
The Hanged Man. Fear death by water.   55
I see crowds of people, walking around in a ring.
Thank you. If you see dear Mrs. Equitone,
Tell her I bring the horoscope myself:
One must be so careful these days.

Unreal City,   60
Under the brown fog of a winter dawn,
A crowd flowed over London Bridge, so many,
I had not thought death had undone so many.
Sighs, short and infrequent, were exhaled,
And each man fixed his eyes before his feet.   65
Flowed up the hill and down King William Street,
To where Saint Mary Woolnoth kept the hours
With a dead sound on the final stroke of nine.
There I saw one I knew; and stopped him, crying: "Stetson!
"You who were with me in the ships at Mylae!   70
"That corpse you planted last year in your garden,
"Has it begun to sprout? Will it bloom this year?
"Or has the sudden frost disturbed its bed?
"Oh keep the Dog far hence, that's friend to men,
"Or with his nails he'll dig it up again!   75
"You! hypocrite lecteur!—mon semblable,—mon frère!"[6]

[4] "A fresh wind blows toward the homeland; my Irish child, where are you lingering?" (*Tristan und Isolde*, I, 5–8)   [5] "Wide and empty is the sea" (*Tristan und Isolde*, III, 24)   [6] "hypocritical reader!—my likeness,—my brother!" (Baudelaire, preface to *Fleurs de Mal*); here the reader is suddenly addressed directly

II. A GAME OF CHESS

The chair she sat in, like a burnished throne,
Glowed on the marble, where the glass
Held up by standards wrought with fruited vines
From which a golden Cupidon peeped out   80
(Another hid his eyes behind his wing)
Doubled the flames of sevenbranched candelabra
Reflecting light upon the table as
The glitter of her jewels rose to meet it,
From satin cases poured in rich profusion;   85
In vials of ivory and colored glass
Unstoppered, lurked her strange synthetic perfumes,
Unguent, powdered, or liquid—troubled, confused
And drowned the sense in odors; stirred by the air
That freshened from the window, these ascended   90
In fattening the prolonged candle-flames,
Flung their smoke into the laquearia,
Stirring the pattern on the coffered ceiling.
Huge sea-wood fed with copper
Burned green and orange, framed by the colored stone,   95
In which sad light a carvèd dolphin swam.
Above the antique mantel was displayed
As though a window gave upon the sylvan scene
The change of Philomel, by the barbarous king
So rudely forced; yet there the nightingale   100
Filled all the desert with inviolable voice
And still she cried, and still the world pursues,
"Jug Jug" to dirty ears.
And other withered stumps of time
Were told upon the walls; staring forms   105
Leaned out, leaning, hushing the room enclosed.
Footsteps shuffled on the stair.
Under the firelight, under the brush, her hair
Spread out in fiery points
Glowed into words, then would be savagely still.   110

"My nerves are bad tonight. Yes, bad. Stay with me.
"Speak to me. Why do you never speak. Speak.
    "What are you thinking of? What thinking? What?
"I never know what you are thinking. Think."

I think we are in rats' alley   115
Where the dead men lost their bones.

"What is that noise?"
              The wind under the door.

"What is that noise now? What is the wind doing?"
              Nothing again nothing.   120
                    "Do

"You know nothing? Do you see nothing? Do you remember
"Nothing?"
     I remember
Those are pearls that were his eyes.   125
"Are you alive or not? Is there nothing in your head?"
                                                     But

O O O O that Shakespeherian Rag—
It's so elegant
So intelligent   130
"What shall I do now? What shall I do?"
"I shall rush out as I am, and walk the street
"With my hair down, so. What shall we do tomorrow?
"What shall we ever do?"
                    The hot water at ten.   135
And if it rains, a closed car at four.
And we shall play a game of chess,
Pressing lidless eyes and waiting for a knock upon the door.

When Lil's husband got demobbed, I said—
I didn't mince my words, I said to her myself,   140
HURRY UP PLEASE ITS TIME
Now Albert's coming back, make yourself a bit smart.
He'll want to know what you done with that money he gave you
To get yourself some teeth. He did, I was there.
     You have them all out, Lil, and get a nice set,   145
He said, I swear, I can't bear to look at you.
And no more can't I, I said, and think of poor Albert
He's been in the army four years, he wants a good time,
And if you don't give it him, there's others will, I said.
Oh is there, she said, Something o'that, I said.   150
Then I'll know who to thank, she said, and give me a straight look.
HURRY UP PLEASE ITS TIME
If you don't like it you can get on with it, I said.
Others can pick and choose if you can't.
But if Albert makes off, it won't be for lack of telling.   155
You ought to be ashamed, I said, to look so antique.
(And her only thirty-one.)
I can't help it, she said, pulling a long face,
It's them pills I took, to bring it off, she said.
(She's had five already, and nearly died of young George.)   160
The chemist said it would be all right, but I've never been the same.
You *are* a proper fool, I said.
Well, if Albert won't leave you alone, there it is, I said,
What you get married for if you don't want children?
HURRY UP PLEASE ITS TIME   165
Well, that Sunday Albert was home, they had a hot gammon,
And they asked me in to dinner, to get the beauty of it hot—
HURRY UP PLEASE ITS TIME
HURRY UP PLEASE ITS TIME

Goonight Bill. Goonight Lou. Goonight May. Goonight.   170
Ta ta. Goonight. Goonight.
Good night, ladies, good night, sweet ladies, good night, good night.

III. THE FIRE SERMON

The river's tent is broken: the last fingers of leaf
Clutch and sink into the wet bank. The wind
Crosses the brown land, unheard. The nymphs are departed.   175
Sweet Thames, run softly, till I end my song.
The river bears no empty bottles, sandwich papers,
Silk handkerchiefs, cardboard boxes, cigarette ends
Or other testimony of summer nights. The nymphs are departed.
And their friends, the loitering heirs of city directors;   180
Departed, have left no addresses.
By the waters of Leman I sat down and wept . . .
Sweet Thames, run softly till I end my song,
Sweet Thames, run softly, for I speak not loud or long.
But at my back in a cold blast I hear   185
The rattle of the bones, and chuckle spread from ear to ear.
A rat crept softly through the vegetation
Dragging its slimy belly on the bank
While I was fishing in the dull canal
On a winter evening round behind the gashouse   190
Musing upon the king my brother's wreck
And on the king my father's death before him.
White bodies naked on the low damp ground
And bones cast in a little low dry garret,
Rattled by the rat's foot only, year to year.   195
But at my back from time to time I hear
The sound of horns and motors, which shall bring
Sweeney to Mrs. Porter in the spring.
O the moon shone bright on Mrs. Porter
And on her daughter   200
They wash their feet in soda water
Et O ces voix d'enfants, chantant dans la coupole![7]
Twit twit twit
Jug jug jug jug jug jug
So rudely forc'd.   205

Tereu

Unreal City
Under the brown fog of a winter noon
Mr. Eugenides, the Smyrna merchant
Unshaven, with a pocket full of currants   210
C. i. f. London: documents at sight,
Asked me in demotic French
To luncheon at the Cannon Street Hotel
Followed by a weekend at the Metropole.

---

[7] "And O these children's voices, singing in the cupola!" (Verlaine, *Parsifal*)

At the violet hour, when the eyes and back   215
Turn upward from the desk, when the human engine waits
Like a taxi throbbing waiting,
I Tiresias, though blind, throbbing between two lives,
Old man with wrinkled female breasts, can see
At the violet hour, the evening hour that strives   220
Homeward, and brings the sailor home from sea,
The typist home at teatime, clears her breakfast, lights
Her stove, and lays out food in tins.
Out of the window perilously spread
Her drying combinations touched by the sun's last rays,   225
On the divan are piled (at night her bed)
Stockings, slippers, camisoles, and stays.
I Tiresias, old man with wrinkled dugs
Perceived the scene, and foretold the rest—
I too awaited the expected guest.   230
He, the young man carbuncular, arrives,
A small house agent's clerk, with one bold stare,
One of the low on whom assurance sits
As a silk hat on a Bradford millionaire.
The time is now propitious, as he guesses,   235
The meal is ended, she is bored and tired,
Endeavors to engage her in caresses
Which still are unreproved, if undesired.
Flushed and decided, he assaults at once;
Exploring hands encounter no defense;   240
His vanity requires no response,
And makes a welcome of indifference.
(And I Tiresias have foresuffered all
Enacted on this same divan or bed;
I who have sat by Thebes below the wall   245
And walked among the lowest of the dead.)
Bestows one final patronizing kiss,
And gropes his way, finding the stairs unlit . . .

She turns and looks a moment in the glass,
Hardly aware of her departed lover;   250
Her brain allows one half-formed thought to pass:
"Well now that's done: and I'm glad it's over."
When lovely woman stoops to folly and
Paces about her room again, alone,
She smooths her hair with automatic hand,   255
And puts a record on the gramophone.

"This music crept by me upon the waters"
And along the Strand, up Queen Victoria Street.
O City city, I can sometimes hear
Beside a public bar in Lower Thames Street,   260

The pleasant whining of a mandolin
And a clatter and a chatter from within
Where fishmen lounge at noon: where the walls
Of Magnus Martyr hold
Inexplicable splendor of Ionian white and gold.   265

    The river sweats
    Oil and tar.
    The barges drift
    With the turning tide
    Red sails   270
    Wide
    To leeward, swing on the heavy spar.
    The barges wash
    Drifting logs
    Down Greenwich reach   275
    Past the Isle of Dogs.
        Weialala leia
        Wallala leialala
    Elizabeth and Leicester
    Beating oars   280
    The stern was formed
    A gilded shell
    Red and gold
    The brisk swell
    Rippled both shores   285
    Southwest wind
    Carried down stream
    The peal of bells
    White towers
        Weialala leia   290
        Wallala leialala
"Trams and dusty trees.
Highbury bore me. Richmond and Kew
Undid me. By Richmond I raised my knees
Supine on the floor of a narrow canoe."   295

"My feet are at Moorgate, and my heart
Under my feet. After the event
He wept. He promised 'a new start.'
I made no comment. What should I resent?"

"On Margate Sands.   300
I can connect
Nothing with nothing
The broken fingernails of dirty hands.
My people humble people who expect
Nothing."   305
      la la

> To Carthage then I came
> Burning burning burning burning
> O Lord Thou pluckest me out
> O Lord Thou pluckest   310
>
> burning

IV. DEATH BY WATER

Phlebas the Phoenician, a fortnight dead,
Forgot the cry of gulls, and the deep sea swell
And the profit and loss.
                    A current under sea   315
Picked his bones in whispers. As he rose and fell
He passed the stages of his age and youth
Entering the whirlpool.
                    Gentile or Jew
O you who turn the wheel and look to windward,   320
Consider Phlebas, who was once handsome and tall as you.

V. WHAT THE THUNDER SAID

After the torchlight red on sweaty faces
After the frosty silence in the gardens
After the agony in stony places
The shouting and the crying   325
Prison and palace and reverberation
Of thunder of spring over distant mountains
He who was living is now dead
We who were living are now dying
With a little patience   330

Here is no water but only rock
Rock and no water and the sandy road
The road winding above among the mountains
Which are mountains of rock without water
If there were water we should stop and drink   335
Amongst the rock one cannot stop or think
Sweat is dry and feet are in the sand
If there were only water amongst the rock
Dead mountain mouth of carious teeth that cannot spit
Here one can neither stand nor lie nor sit   340
There is not even silence in the mountains
But dry sterile thunder without rain
There is not even solitude in the mountains
But red sullen faces sneer and snarl
From doors of mudcracked houses   345
                    If there were water
    And no rock
    If there were rock
    And also water
    And water   350

A spring
A pool among the rock
If there were the sound of water only
Not the cicada
And dry grass singing   355
But sound of water over a rock
Where the hermit-thrush sings in the pine trees
Drip drop drip drop drop drop drop
But there is no water

Who is the third who walks always beside you?   360
When I count, there are only you and I together
But when I look ahead up the white road
There is always another one walking beside you
Gliding wrapped in a brown mantle, hooded
I do not know whether a man or a woman   365
—But who is that on the other side of you?

What is that sound high in the air
Mumur of maternal lamentation
Who are those hooded hordes swarming
Over endless plains, stumbling in cracked earth   370
Ringed by the flat horizon only
What is the city over the mountains
Cracks and reforms and bursts in the violet air
Falling towers
Jerusalem Athens Alexandria   375
Vienna London
Unreal

A woman drew her long black hair out tight
And fiddled whisper music on those strings
And bats with baby faces in the violet light   380
Whistled, and beat their wings
And crawled head downward down a blackened wall
And upside down in air were towers
Tolling reminiscent bells, that kept the hours
And voices singing out of empty cisterns and exhausted wells.   385

In this decayed hole among the mountains
In the faint moonlight, the grass is singing
Over the tumbled graves, about the chapel
There is the empty chapel, only the wind's home.
It has no windows, and the door swings,   390
Dry bones can harm no one.
Only a cock stood on the rooftree
Co co rico co co rico
In a flash of lightning. Then a damp gust
Bringing rain   395

Ganga was sunken, and the limp leaves
Waited for rain, while the black clouds

Gathered far distant, over Himavant.
The jungle crouched, humped in silence.
Then spoke the thunder   400
DA
Datta:[8] what have we given?
My friend, blood shaking my heart
The awful daring of a moment's surrender
Which an age of prudence can never retract   405
By this, and this only, we have existed
Which is not to be found in our obituaries
Or in memories draped by the beneficent spider
Or under seals broken by the lean solicitor
In our empty arms   410
DA
Dayadhvam: I have heard the key
Turn in the door once and turn once only
We think of the key, each in his prison
Thinking of the key, each confirms a prison   415
Only at nightfall, ethereal rumors
Revive for a moment a broken Coriolanus
DA
Damyata: The boat responded
Gaily, to the hand expert with sail and oar   420
The sea was calm, your heart would have responded
Gaily, when invited, beating obedient
To controlling hands

              I sat upon the shore
Fishing, with the arid plain behind me   425
Shall I at least set my lands in order?
London Bridge is falling down falling down falling down
Poi s'ascose nel foco che gli affina
Quando fiam uti chelidon[9]—O swallow swallow
Le Prince d'Aquitaine à la tour abolie[10]   430
These fragments I have shored against my ruins
Why then Ile fit you. Hieronymo's mad againe.
Datta. Dayadhvam. Damyata.
        Shantih shantih shantih [11]

The Waste Land is a poem totally concerned with the breakup of a civilization—not, to be sure, the physical breakup, with buildings crashing into the street or government offices burning, but a spiritual breakup—the loss of meaning, significance, and purpose. Because it is a poem about the crack-up of Western civilization—about the disorientation of

---

[8] *datta, dayadhvam, damyata:* "give, sympathize, control"   [9] "Then he hid him in the flame that refines them / When shall I become as the swallow?"   [10] "The Prince of Aquitaine at the ruined tower"   [11] when repeated, a formal ending equivalent to "the Peace which passeth understanding"

modern man—it is not strange that it is filled with references to the history of Western culture or that it alludes to the great documents, literary and religious, that have shaped that culture, or that it makes use of some of the great myths and archetypes that have in the past embodied salient features of the culture.

Yet there is a danger that the reader, encountering the poem for the first time, may be overwhelmed by the allusions and, in trying to run them down, may miss the poetry altogether. It may be well, therefore, for you to make your first reading(s) of the poem relatively open, naive, and "innocent." There will be time later—if you become interested in the poem through its powerful scenes, its haunting images, and its compulsive rhythms—to deal with the literary and historical allusions. To this end Eliot himself provided notes, which are here combined with other information concerning allusions.

Yet, though we recommend initially a relatively innocent reading, no reading can ever be literally that. Besides, we have already made some comments about the kinds of thematic material to be found in this poem. So it may be profitable to enlarge a bit upon this material and even to suggest the *general* use the poet makes of traditional literary and religious materials—how, for example, he deals with the Bible and Dante's *Divine Comedy*. All of us are—or ought to be—more than vaguely familiar with these documents at least.

The legend from which the title of the poem derives has to do with the parched land ruled over by a maimed and impotent king. His castle stands on the banks of a river and he is called the Fisher King. The fate of the land is bound up with the fate of its lord. Until he is healed, the land will remain under the curse: cattle will not breed; the crops will not grow. The curse may be removed only if a knight is bold enough to make his way to the castle and inquire about the meanings of the various objects that will be shown to him.

In her book *From Ritual to Romance*,* Jessie Weston argued that the Fisher King was originally the vegetation god whose death was mourned in the dying year, but whose triumphant return as expressed in the renewed life of nature was celebrated in the spring. According to Weston this fertility cult was widely disseminated through Europe, and the principal carriers of its mysteries were soldiers and Syrian merchants. The story of the Fisher King was later Christianized in the Grail legends which are reminiscent of an initiation rite. The candidate's courage was tested by making a journey to the Perilous Chapel, around which demons seemed to howl. Moreover, when the candidate arrived at the Castle of the Fisher King, he had to take the initiative in seeking the truth—had to demand the meaning of the

---

* In his notes on the poem, Eliot writes: "Not only the title, but the plan and a good deal of the symbolism of the poem were suggested by" this book. "I recommend it . . . to any who think . . . elucidation of the poem worth the trouble."

various symbols, if the secret doctrine was to be revealed. What was then disclosed to him was the interrelation of death and birth, with its corollary truth that the way into life was through death.

References to characters and events of the waste-land legend are to be found throughout the poem, but the characters have usually become degraded and the events have lost their original meaning. For example, Madame Sosostris employs the Tarot pack of cards (probably used in ancient Egypt to predict the rise of the waters upon which the prosperity of a whole people depended) for vulgar and specious "fortune-telling" (lines 43–59).

Mr. Eugenides (line 209) is a modern descendant of the Syrian merchants who, like Phlebas the Phoenician (section 4), once brought the mysteries to faraway Britain. "Eugenides" means "son of the well born," but his function is now degraded. His invitation to a "weekend at the Metropole" does not promise initiation into the secret of life but into a cult of empty, and perhaps perverted, pleasure. The agonized journey to the chapel (section 5) alludes to the journey to the Perilous Chapel, which was part of the initiation ceremony.

For the reader of this poem, the waste-land legend has a special relevance. The poet is attempting to dramatize for us what it feels like to live in a world emptied of religious meaning. But the prime difficulty for the modern reader is that he may be himself so thoroughly numbed by secularization that he cannot see what the poet is talking about. The poet has therefore adopted the device of putting the reader into something of the position of the knight in the Grail legends. The knight in the story was able to remove the curse only if he questioned what he saw—only if he demanded meanings of the symbols shown to him. If he merely marveled at them, the truth was not revealed to him. If we are to experience the poem—as opposed to being merely "told" about the theme—we must be alert for the significance of what we see. Otherwise we shall find a mere jumble of fragments that can be tied together as an abstract and arbitrary scheme, but that never unite in felt significance.

Eliot finds in the Bible and in Dante further analogues for what he considers to be the state of the contemporary world. He takes the phrase "Son of man" (line 20) from Ezekiel 2. The relevant passage reads:

> 1. And he said unto me, Son of man, stand upon thy feet, and I will speak unto thee. 2. And the spirit entered into me when he spake unto me, and set me upon my feet, that I heard him that spake unto me. 3. And he said unto me, Son of man, I send thee to the children of Israel, to a rebellious nation that hath rebelled against me: they and their fathers have transgressed against me, even unto this very day.

Though Eliot in the notes he appended to *The Waste Land* does not refer to Ezekiel 37, it too bears upon the poem, for there the prophet describes his vision of a waste land—a valley of dry bones. He is asked (verse 3),

"Son of man can these bones live? And I answered, O Lord God, thou knowest"; (verse 4), "Again he said unto me, Prophesy upon these bones, and say unto them, O ye dry bones, hear the word of the Lord."

Ecclesiastes 12 (to which Eliot's note on line 23 refers) also describes a parched and nightmare world:

1. Remember now thy Creator in the days of thy youth, while the evil days come not, nor the years draw nigh, when thou shalt say, I have no pleasure in them; 2. While the sun, or the light, or the moon, or the stars, be not darkened, nor the clouds return after the rain; 3. In the day when the keepers of the house shall tremble, and the strong men shall bow themselves, and the grinders cease because they are few, and those that look out of the windows be darkened, 4. And the doors shall be shut in the streets, when the sound of the grinding is low, and he shall rise up at the voice of the bird, and all the daughters of musick shall be brought low; 5. Also when they shall be afraid of that which is high, and fears shall be in the way, and the almond tree shall flourish, and the grasshopper shall be a burden, and desire shall fail: because man goeth to his long home, and the mourners go about the streets; 6. Or ever the silver cord be loosed, or the golden bowl be broken, or the pitcher be broken at the fountain, or the wheel broken at the cistern. 7. Then shall the dust return to the earth as it was: and the spirit shall return unto God who gave it. 8. Vanity of vanities, saith the preacher; all is vanity.

This vision matches the landscape described in section 5 of *The Waste Land*, and various details of the poem seem to have been drawn from it.

The modern waste land also resembles Dante's Hell. Eliot's notes on line 63 refer us to Canto 3 of the *Inferno;* his note on line 64, to Canto 4. Canto 3 describes the place of those who on earth had "lived without praise or blame." They share this antechamber of hell with the angels "who were not rebels, nor were faithful to God, but were for themselves." These then are the "trimmers," those who make no commitment. Now they bewail the fact that they "have no hope of death." But though they may not hope for death,* Dante scornfully calls them "these unfortunate who never were alive." To have real life demands a kind of commitment which men too fearful of death can never make.†

* This is the hopeless wish of the Sibyl in the epigraph at the beginning of the poem. The Sibyl was a prophetess to whom the god Apollo had granted a thousand years of life, but she had forgotten to ask for youth as well.

† The following passage from the work of a modern psychiatrist bears on this point. He writes: "During the last war I had frequent occasion to note that those who vegetate more than they live [see lines 1–6 of *The Waste Land*] were the most afraid and the first to run for the shelters during air raids. Panic was always greatest in hospitals for incurable cases and homes for old people." So writes Ignace Lepp, in *Death and Its Mysteries* (1968, pp. 38–39). He goes on to tell of a house servant in his employ whose life was miserable. Her drunkard husband beat her and she suffered from a terminal disease. Yet she was the first to race for the shelter, for the thought of death terrified her, and especially the thought of a violent death.

Keeping in mind the three realms of negation and sterility (as described in the Grail legend, the Bible, and Dante), let us see how Eliot has developed his poem. In section 1, there pass through the speaker's mind glimpses of a world that is tired and timid, bored and yet uneasy, preferring the half-life of winter to the violent renewal of the energies of spring. It is a world that fears death as the greatest evil, but is disturbed by the idea of birth, and certainly sees birth and death as utterly distinct. There are reflections of the character of this world (lines 1–7; 20–30) intermingled with memories of specific scenes (lines 8–18; 35–41). These are interspersed with scraps of song or remembered bits of poetry.

It is a world apprehensive of the future and eager for signs and portents, even though it cannot believe in them. The hero has his fortune told, and in contrast to the almost prophetic injunction of line 30, "I will show you fear in a handful of dust," is admonished by the fortune-teller to "Fear death by water."

The crowds going over London Bridge on their way to work in the foggy winter dawn remind the protagonist of the multitude of the dead whom Dante saw in his vision of Hell. These people in their meaningless activity are dead, not really alive.

The theme of death, sterility, and meaninglessness receives a more complicated treatment in the closing lines of section 1. In the age of the fertility cults, the ritual burial of the god was undertaken in the confidence that his energies, like those of nature, would revive again. The life of nature was not only dependent on the god's powers: it offered a specific example of his powers. Bury the seed of corn and the corn would spring up again. But now the burial of the dead is without hope. The jeering question about the possibilities of the sprouting of that "corpse you planted in your garden" implies its answer.

Questions

1. Who is the person who speaks this poem? Is he entirely impersonal, simply a voice? Or does one gain some sort of notion about what kind of man he is?

2. Do you find any thematic resemblances between this poem and the other poems in Subsection C ("The Breakup of a Civilization") or "The Fall of Rome" (p. 44)?

3. Though this poem is a tissue of literary allusions and historical references, it establishes its own symbolism. What, for example, do you take to be the meaning of water in the poem? Rock? Circular motion (of all kinds)?

Afterword

Much the same observation that we made in the Afterword of Section 3 is appropriate here. The three rubrics we have used to make rough classifications are indeed rough. In fact, our best justification for employing them is their very imprecision. When we examine the individual poems in any of our three categories, we find that they not only differ widely in theme but often seem to contradict the rubric under which they are placed. Thus, Eliot's "Songs from *Sweeney Agonistes*" suggest that what are at least generally advertised as the joys of the simple life are usually anything but joyful. Moreover the same poem could be placed under more than one rubric. We have, for example, put Auden's "The Unknown Citizen" in with other poems about "The Break-up of a Civilization," but it could also be regarded as a sardonic comment on "The Joys of the Simple Life." In the kind of civilization in which the Unknown Citizen lived, an ordinary and average life is not joyful and not truly simple. The Citizen's life would seem to be complicated, harried, and desperate.

Our classification headings, then, are not so much statements of themes as topics under which, in a rough and ready way, we may assemble poems for closer examination. What is a theme, then? It is what the poem "says." It is, as we have said earlier, the *total meaning* of a poem. But a careful reading of the preceding twenty-odd poems should have made it plain that even this definition cannot be pressed very far. For if we take "total" seriously, we see that the total meaning of the poem resists being reduced to a statement, even a considered and carefully thought-out statement. For poems are not statements at all, but significant dramatizations of a situation, experiences that are concrete embodiments, not abstractions. Thus, the images, the tone, even the metrical patterning can qualify the meaning significantly. If we come to know a poem well and are asked what it "means," we may well be hesitant about answering the question with a statement that attempts to paraphrase the total meaning. If we are serious and the question demands a responsible answer, we may have to say: Read the poem. Take time to learn to read it properly. Then read it again. For what it says is so rich and so precise with its shadings and qualifications that the poet apparently found no simpler way to say what he wanted to say except through the very words of this poem, patterned just as he patterned them. Had he found a simpler, shorter way that could convey his total meaning without distortion or diminution, surely he would have presented us with that and saved some forty—or maybe a hundred —words.

All of this is not to say that talk about themes does not have its utility— that it is not even necessary. It is to say that authentic poems do not have any superfluous parts. They are not concise statements that have been bloated with figures of speech and fancy diction and then metrified. They are totally meaningful, and the themes that we talk about are finally abstractions—abstractions that are justified by usefulness and convenience, and harmless as long as we recognize them for the abstractions that they are. But we must not forget what they are: we must not confuse them with the total meaning of the poem. They are guides, we may say, to meaning—projections of meaning. And our discussions are merely ways to bring us a little closer to the *experience* of meaning, not the *statement* of meaning.

RHYTHM AND METER: 6

In one sense, we instinctively feel that the theme of a poem and its musicality (insofar as a poem in question does possess that quality) are antithetical, or at least refer to very different dimensions of poetry. In connection with this topic, see Appendix B (pp. 542–553), but remember that the topic of musicality is simply an extension of all previous considerations of rhythm, meter, and verbal quality. *Musicality is—or should be—an aspect of meaning—a component of meaning.*

Questions

1. Comment on musicality in (a) "Grapes Making" (p. 393); (b) "If Poisonous Minerals" (p. 330); (c) "Fatima" (p. 140); (d) "All Day I Hear" (p. 552); (e) "On the Late Massacre in Piedmont" (p. 526); (f) "Tears, Idle Tears" (p. 242); (g) "The Unknown Citizen" (p. 290). Make comparisons of the themes.

2. Contrast the musicality in the two villanelles "Missing Dates" by William Empson and "Do Not Go Gentle into That Good Night" by Dylan Thomas (pp. 532, 533).

3. Here are two versions of the same passage (the original by Keats). Which do you prefer? Why?

> (a) The tunes you hear are sweet, but the ones unheard
> Are sweeter; therefore, you gentle pipes, play on;
> Not to the physical ear, but more endeared
> To the deep heart, make a music of no tone.

> (b) Heard melodies are sweet, but those unheard
> Are sweeter; therefore, ye soft pipes, play on;
> Not to the sensual ear, but more endeared,
> Pipe to the spirit ditties of no tone.

4. Comment on the musicality in "Art Thou Poor" (p. 284).

5. "To the Four Courts, Please" (p. 286) is certainly not "musical," but is it expressive?

6. Reread pp. 545-548 of Appendix B, then turn to "Cynara" by Ernest Dowson (p. 187). Would this poem invite parody? Why? Try a few lines in the same style.

7. What contrast between musicality and nonmusicality do you find in "Desert Places" (p. 203)? How do these differences relate to changes in tone?

8. Both "Inversnaid" (p. 83) and "Elegy Written in a Country Churchyard' (p. 273) are musical. Explain and comment on the differences in musicality in relation to attitude and theme.

Supplemental Poems

D. MAN AND NATURE

After Apple-Picking

Robert Frost [*1874–1963*]

My long two-pointed ladder's sticking through a tree
Toward heaven still,
And there's a barrel that I didn't fill
Beside it, and there may be two or three
Apples I didn't pick upon some bough.   5
But I am done with apple-picking now.
Essence of winter sleep is on the night,
The scent of apples: I am drowsing off.
I cannot rub the strangeness from my sight
I got from looking through a pane of glass   10
I skimmed this morning from the drinking trough
And held against the world of hoary grass.
It melted, and I let it fall and break.
But I was well
Upon my way to sleep before it fell,   15
And I could tell
What form my dreaming was about to take.
Magnified apples appear and disappear,
Stem end and blossom end,
And every fleck of russet showing clear.   20
My instep arch not only keeps the ache,
It keeps the pressure of a ladder-round.
I feel the ladder sway as the boughs bend.
And I keep hearing from the cellar bin
The rumbling sound   25
Of load on load of apples coming in.
For I have had too much
Of apple-picking: I am overtired
Of the great harvest I myself desired.
There were ten thousand thousand fruit to touch,   30
Cherish in hand, lift down, and not let fall.
For all
That struck the earth,
No matter if not bruised or spiked with stubble,
Went surely to the cider-apple heap   35

As of no worth.
One can see what will trouble
This sleep of mine, whatever sleep it is.
Were he not gone,
The woodchuck could say whether it's like his   40
Long sleep, as I describe its coming on,
Or just some human sleep.

Questions

1. Is this poem no more than a piece of description—a vignette of New England farm life? Does it suggest an attitude toward life itself? What theme do you find here?
2. What is the tone of the poem? Is it solemn? Whimsical? Serious? Playful? Try to define the tone of this poem.
3. Can you state the theme of this poem apart from considerations of tone? Does the tone in fact almost define the theme?
4. How would you compare the theme of this poem with Keats's "To Autumn" (p. 87)? What is the role of the woodchuck here?

The Miracle

Walter de la Mare   [*1873–1956*]

Who beckons the green ivy up
  Its solitary tower of stone?
What spirit lures the bindweed's cup
      Unfaltering on?
Calls even the starry lichen to climb   5
By agelong inches endless Time?

Who bids the hollyhock uplift
  Her rod of fast-sealed buds on high;
Fling wide her petals—silent, swift,
      Lovely to the sky?   10
Since as she kindled, so she will fade.
Flower above flower in squalor laid.

Ever the heavy billow rears
  All its sea-length in green, hushed wall;
But totters as the shore it nears,   15
      Foams to its fall;
Where was its mark? on what vain quest
Rose that great water from its rest?

So creeps ambition on; so climb
  Man's vaunting thoughts. He, set on high,   20
Forgets his birth, small space, brief time,
      That he shall die;
Dreams blindly in his stagnant air;
Consumes his strength, strips himself bare;

Rejects delight, ease, pleasure, hope,   25
  Seeking in vain, but seeking yet,
Past earthly promise, earthly scope,
      On one aim set:
As if, like Chaucer's child, he thought
All but "O Alma!" nought.   30

Questions

1. "After Apple-Picking" makes a few observations, whimsical and serious, about man's relation to nature. What does this poem say about man's relation to nature?

2. Lines 29–30 refer to Chaucer's "Prioress' Tale." In that story, the little choir-boy sings his hymn to the Virgin, "O Alma Redemptoris," in spite of threats and, miraculously, even after his throat has been cut. How does this comparison qualify what the poet has to say about man's ambition? In what sense is the word *ambition* used here? To get rich? To be elected mayor? To have military command? To be among the best-dressed women of the year? How does it contrast with (or perhaps support) the images drawn from the blind motion of the billow or of the blind life-force in plants?

The Force That Through the Green Fuse

Dylan Thomas [*1914–1953*]

The force that through the green fuse drives the flower
Drives my green age; that blasts the roots of trees
Is my destroyer.
And I am dumb to tell the crooked rose
My youth is bent by the same wintry fever.   5

The force that drives the water through the rocks
Drives my red blood; that dries the mouthing streams
Turns mine to wax.
And I am dumb to mouth unto my veins
How at the mountain spring the same mouth sucks.   10

The hand that whirls the water in the pool
Stirs the quicksand; that ropes the blowing wind
Hauls my shroud sail.
And I am dumb to tell the hanging man
How of my clay is made the hangman's lime.   15

The lips of time leech to the fountain head;
Love drips and gathers, but the fallen blood
Shall calm her sores.
And I am dumb to tell a weather's wind
How time has ticked a heaven round the stars.   20

And I am dumb to tell the lover's tomb
How at my sheet goes the same crooked worm.

Questions

1. Compare and contrast the theme of this poem with that of "The Miracle."

2. What is the speaker's attitude toward his kinship with plant and water and wind? Does he exult in the kinship? Or commiserate, as with fellow victims? Or what? Compare and contrast the tone of this poem with that of "The Miracle."

3. How do the last two lines sum up the poem? How do they bear upon the tone of the poem?

A Slumber Did My Spirit Seal

William Wordsworth [*1770–1850*]

> A slumber did my spirit seal;
>   I had no human fears—
> She seemed a thing that could not feel
>   The touch of earthly years.
>
> No motion has she now, no force;   5
>   She neither hears nor sees;
> Rolled round in earth's diurnal course,
>   With rocks, and stones, and trees.

Questions

1. What in this poem is the relation of the human being to nature and natural things? Is the speaker made calm and reconciled by the thought that the dead woman is companioned by "rocks, and stones, and trees" or does he feel an anguished grief that this should be so?

2. Why does the speaker say in line 1 that a slumber sealed *his* spirit, when the shocking event is now that a slumber has sealed *her* spirit? Why does he call her a "thing" (line 3) when she was still alive rather than reserving this term for her present state, in which she is as inert as a stone? Do these inversions suggest careless and inept writing? Or can we say that the poem deals with a difference (and an identity) in nature and human nature—with man as part of nature?

The Eagle and the Mole

Elinor Wylie [*1885–1928*]

> Avoid the reeking herd,
> Shun the polluted flock,
> Live like that stoic bird,
> The eagle of the rock.

The huddled warmth of crowds 5
Begets and fosters hate;
He keeps above the clouds
His cliff inviolate.

When flocks are folded warm,
And herds to shelter run, 10
He sails above the storm,
He stares into the sun.

If in the eagle's track
Your sinews cannot leap,
Avoid the lathered pack, 15
Turn from the steaming sheep.

If you would keep your soul
From spotted sight or sound,
Live like the velvet mole;
Go burrow underground. 20

And there hold intercourse
With roots of trees and stones,
With rivers at their source,
And disembodied bones.

Question

In the poem by Wordsworth just presented, the grief of the bereaved lover is accentuated by the fact that the dead girl has become a "thing"—an object rolled round in the earth's motion with "rocks and stones and trees." In the present poem the poet advises that one avoid human contact and seek "roots of trees and stones" and "disembodied bones"—whatever "things" remain of human bodies. In other words, the same objects are used in quite different relations to the theme in these two poems. Explain the relation in both cases. Are both justified?

Brahma

Ralph Waldo Emerson   [*1803–1882*]

If the red slayer think he slays,
  Or if the slain think he is slain,
They know not well the subtle ways
  I keep, and pass, and turn again.

Far or forgot to me is near; 5
  Shadow and sunlight are the same;
The vanished gods to me appear;
  And one to me are shame and fame.

They reckon ill who leave me out;
    When me they fly, I am the wings;
I am the doubter and the doubt,
    And I the hymn the Brahmin sings.

10

The strong gods pine for my abode,
    And pine in vain the sacred Seven;
But thou, meek lover of the good!
    Find me, and turn thy back on heaven.

15

Brahma, in philosophic Hinduism, is the impersonal supreme being, the primal source and the ultimate goal of all that exists.

Questions

1. Does the poem give vitality and power to this concept?
2. Does the poem state meaningless contradictions or meaningful paradoxes?
3. What is the implied relation of man to nature in this poem?

Kubla Khan

Samuel Taylor Coleridge   [1772–1834]

In Xanadu did Kubla Khan
A stately pleasure-dome decree:
Where Alph, the sacred river, ran
Through caverns measureless to man
    Down to a sunless sea.

5

So twice five miles of fertile ground
With walls and towers were girdled round:
And here were gardens bright with sinuous rills,
Where blossomed many an incense-bearing tree,
And here were forests ancient as the hills,

10

Enfolding sunny spots of greenery.

But oh! that deep romantic chasm which slanted
Down the green hill athwart a cedarn cover!
A savage place! as holy and enchanted
As e'er beneath a waning moon was haunted

15

By woman wailing for her demon-lover!
And from this chasm, with ceaseless turmoil seething,
As if this earth in fast thick pants were breathing,
A mighty fountain momently was forced,
Amid whose swift half-intermitted burst

20

Huge fragments vaulted like rebounding hail,
Or chaffy grain beneath the thresher's flail:
And 'mid these dancing rocks at once and ever
It flung up momently the sacred river.

Five miles meandering with a mazy motion   25
Through wood and dale the sacred river ran,
Then reached the caverns measureless to man,
And sank in tumult to a lifeless ocean:
And 'mid this tumult Kubla heard from far
Ancestral voices prophesying war!   30

    The shadow of the dome of pleasure
    Floated midway on the waves;
    Where was heard the mingled measure
    From the fountain and the caves.
It was a miracle of rare device,   35
A sunny pleasure-dome with caves of ice!

    A damsel with a dulcimer
    In a vision once I saw:
    It was an Abyssinian maid,
    And on her dulcimer she played,   40
    Singing of Mount Abora.
    Could I revive within me
    Her symphony and song,
    To such a deep delight 't would win me,
That with music loud and long,   45
I would build that dome in air,
That sunny dome! those caves of ice!
And all who heard should see them there,
And all should cry, Beware! Beware!
His flashing eyes, his floating hair!   50
Weave a circle round him thrice,
And close your eyes with holy dread,
For he on honey-dew hath fed,
And drunk the milk of Paradise.

Questions

1. This poem also, in one dimension at least, concerns itself with the relation of man to nature. Lines 1–36 describe how an oriental potentate chose a propitious place (holy, life-giving, numinous) to build his "dome of pleasure." The palace was a "miracle of rare device," but its having been built beside a "sacred river," with gardens and "forests ancient as the hills" is obviously most important too. The Khan did not simply impose his will on nature but placed his palace in a special relationship to nature. Note the details of the setting so carefully described and ponder their possible significance. For example, what might the river Alph stand for?

2. The rest of the poem asserts that the speaker could build that palace with music if he could revive in himself the deep delight that he felt at visions that he once beheld. Notice that the speaker is unlike the great Khan who could literally plant the sunny dome on this earth. The speaker, even if won to his visionary delight, could build the dome only in his imagination. Note also that he says that his fervent creativity would fill the

people around him with dread—"holy dread," to be sure, but dread never-theless. Why should this be so? Is some connection hinted at between the "holiness" of the place of the pleasure dome and the "holy dread" evoked by the singer?

3. What is the relation—if any—between the two parts of the poem? Could it be said that the poem is concerned with the plight of the poet in our day? Does it make a comment on the modern world and its separation of head and heart, action and contemplation, the quotidian world and the realm of the imagination? Would you attempt to describe the theme of the poem?

Ode on a Grecian Urn

John Keats [*1795–1821*]

Thou still unravished bride of quietness,
  Thou foster-child of silence and slow time,
Sylvan historian, who canst thus express
  A flowery tale more sweetly than our rime:
What leaf-fringed legend haunts about thy shape   5
  Of deities or mortals, or of both,
    In Tempe or the dales of Arcady?
What men or gods are these? What maidens loth?
  What mad pursuit? What struggle to escape?
    What pipes and timbrels? What wild ecstasy?   10

Heard melodies are sweet, but those unheard
  Are sweeter; therefore, ye soft pipes, play on;
Not to the sensual ear, but, more endeared,
  Pipe to the spirit ditties of no tone:
Fair youth, beneath the trees, thou canst not leave   15
  Thy song, nor ever can those trees be bare;
    Bold Lover, never, never canst thou kiss,
Though winning near the goal—yet, do not grieve;
  She cannot fade, though thou hast not thy bliss,
    Forever wilt thou love, and she be fair!   20

Ah, happy, happy boughs! That cannot shed
  Your leaves, nor ever bid the Spring adieu:
And, happy melodist, unwearièd,
  Forever piping songs forever new;
More happy love! more happy, happy love!   25
  Forever warm and still to be enjoy'd,
    Forever panting, and forever young;
All breathing human passion far above,
  That leaves a heart high-sorrowful and cloyed,
    A burning forehead, and a parching tongue.   30

Who are these coming to the sacrifice?
　To what green altar, O mysterious priest,
Lead'st thou that heifer lowing at the skies,
　And all her silken flanks with garlands drest?
What little town by river or sea shore, 35
　Or mountain-built with peaceful citadel,
　　Is emptied of this folk, this pious morn?
And, little town, thy streets for evermore
　Will silent be; and not a soul to tell
　　Why thou art desolate, can e'er return. 40

O Attic shape! Fair Attitude! with brede
　Of marble men and maidens overwrought,
With forest branches and the trodden weed;
　Thou, silent form, dost tease us out of thought
As doth eternity: Cold Pastoral! 45
　When old age shall this generation waste,
　　Thou shalt remain, in midst of other woe
Than ours, a friend to man, to whom thou sayst,
　Beauty is Truth,—Truth Beauty,—that is all
　　Ye know on earth, and all ye need to know.[1] 50

Questions

1. In what sense is the urn a "sylvan historian" (line 3)? What are some of the "flowery tales" that it expresses to the observer?

2. Does the ideal life depicted in the scenes wrought upon the urn leave out of account the disappointments of actual life? If so, has the poet played fair by presenting these scenes as lifeless and cold? Is an ironic counterpoise thus maintained in the poem?

3. What is the force of the phrase "Cold Pastoral" (line 45)? How does it gather up and summarize the relation of the ideal to the actual?

4. Is the famous concluding passage (lines 49–50) insisted upon as a philosophic generalization in its own right? Does it represent the theme of the poem? Is it to be regarded as a dramatic utterance spoken by the urn? The poet has said that the urn "tease[s] us out of thought / As doth eternity." Do the last two lines develop the same idea? If so, how? Is the timeless ideal world of the urn as enigmatic as eternity? It bewilders our time-ridden human minds: it teases us. Are the last two lines a teasing utterance or not? What is their truth? Do the preceding forty-eight lines serve to define it?

---

[1] In lines 49–50, the editors follow the punctuation of four extant manuscripts of the poem made by Keats's friends, "all unquestionably not far removed from the original, and all [of which] agree." See Alvin Whitley, "The Message of the Grecian Urn," *Keats-Shelley Memorial Bulletin*, V (1953), pp. 2–3.

E. THE FALSE LOVER OR INDIFFERENT LOVER

Careless Love

Anonymous

It's on this railroad bank I stand,
It's on this railroad bank I stand,
It's on this railroad bank I stand,
All for the love of a railroad man.
How I wish that train would come,   5
How I wish that train would come,
How I wish that train would come,
And take me back where I come from.

CHORUS

Love, oh, love, oh, careless love,
Love, oh, love, oh, careless love,   10
Love, oh, love, oh, careless love,
See what careless love has done.

When my apron string will bow,
When my apron string will bow,
When my apron string will bow,   15
You'll pass my door an' say "hello."
But when my apron string won't pin,
When my apron string won't pin,
When my apron string won't pin,
You'll pass my door an' won't come in.   20

It's caused me to weep, it's caused me to mourn,
It's caused me to weep, it's caused me to mourn,
It's caused me to weep, it's caused me to mourn,
It's caused me to leave my happy home.
What do you reckon my mama'll say,   25
What do you reckon my mama'll say,
What do you reckon my mama'll say,
When she hears I've gone astray.

"Careless Love" is an American folksong that tells of love betrayed. The girl who speaks in the poem waits for the train that will take her home: see lines 25–28. She has evidently been seduced by a railroad man (line 4). She has left her "happy home" to be with him and now she waits, with some anxiety about her reception there, upon her return.

Questions

1. Can you make out her attitude toward her false lover? Is she still in love with him? Is she angry with him? Do we gain any hint of the nature of the girl herself? Is she silly? Pitiable? Both? Neither? Or is it impossible to say? Does the refrain help you to answer such questions?

2. Is this poem a conscious bid for sympathy? To whom does the girl address herself?

Before making up your mind about this poem, you may prefer to look at some of the poems that follow.

Ye Flowery Banks

Robert Burns [*1759–1796*]

Ye flowery banks o' bonie[1] Doon,
    How can ye blume sae[2] fair?
How can ye chant, ye little birds,
    And I sae fu'[3] o' care?

Thou'll break my heart, thou bonie bird,   5
    That sings upon the bough:
Thou minds me o' the happy days
    When my fause[4] Luve was true.

Thou'll break my heart, thou bonie bird,
    That sings beside thy mate: 10
For sae I sat, and sae I sang,
    And wist na[5] o' my fate.

Aft hae I rov'd by bonie Doon
    To see the woodbine twine,
And ilka[6] bird sang o' its luve,   15
    And sae did I o' mine.

Wi' lightsome heart I pu'd[7] a rose
    Frae aff[8] its thorny tree,
And my fause luver staw[9] my rose,
    But left the thorn wi' me.   20

Note that in this poem the girl specifically describes her lover as false. Evidently she entertains no hope that he will return.

Questions

1. How does this girl differ, if she does differ, from the girl who speaks the preceding poem? Is she still in love with the false lover?

[1] bonny or handsome   [2] so   [3] full   [4] false   [5] had no knowledge of   [6] every
[7] pulled   [8] from off   [9] stole

2. This poem is, in spite of its dialect and its apparent simplicity, more "literary" and has a more careful formal organization than "Careless Love." What does it gain, if anything, by this formal quality? Does it lose anything?

3. Does the poem make too obvious a bid for our sympathy for the girl?

4. The poem begins with a reference to the flowers and the birds of the spring season. How does the poet use images of the birds and the flowers to provide concrete images of the girl's state of mind?

When Lovely Woman Stoops to Folly

Oliver Goldsmith [*1728–1774*]

When lovely woman stoops to folly,
   And finds too late that men betray,
What charm can sooth her melancholy,
   What art can wash her guilt away?

The only art her guilt to cover,   5
   To hide her shame from every eye,
To give repentance to her lover,
   And wring his bosom—is to die.

Note that in this poem the betrayed woman does not tell her story. Her plight is observed and commented on by a rather detached observer.

Questions

1. What is the tone of this poem as compared with the tone of the two preceding poems?

2. Does this poem, with its third-person speaker, its relative detachment, and its formality, avoid the sentimental person's bid for sympathy? Or does it succeed in this less well than the more naive ballads? Or is this poem, written in the eighteenth century, simply too far removed from our world to appeal to us?

3. Return to lines 215–256 of "The Waste Land." Note that the passage ends in a parody of this poem. What is the purpose of the parody?

The Dark-Eyed Gentleman

Thomas Hardy [*1840–1928*]

I

I pitched my day's leazings[1] in Crimmercrock Lane,
   To tie up my garter and jog on again,

[1] bundle of gleaned wheat

When a dear dark-eyed gentleman passed there and said,
In a way that made all o' me colour rose-red,
　　"What do I see—　　　　　　　　　　　　　　5
　　O pretty knee!"
And he came and he tied up my garter for me.

II

'Twixt sunset and moonrise it was, I can mind:
Ah, 'tis easy to lose what we nevermore find!—
Of the dear stranger's home, of his name, I knew nought,　　10
But I soon knew his nature and all that it brought.
　　Then bitterly
　　Sobbed I that he
Should ever have tied up my garter for me!

III

Yet now I've beside me a fine lissom lad,　　　　　15
And my slip's nigh forgot, and my days are not sad;
My own dearest joy is he, comrade, and friend,
He it is who safe-guards me, on him I depend;
　　No sorrow brings he,
　　And thankful I be　　　　　　　　　　　　20
That his Daddy once tied up my garter for me!

The situation described in this poem has certain resemblances to that explored in Hardy's novel, *Tess of the D'Urbervilles;* yet how different is the treatment of this poem.

Questions

1. What is the tone of this poem? Is the girl making a bid for sympathy? Is she consciously defying the Victorian conventions, which at worst condemned her and at best pitied her as a creature hopelessly stained? Is she serious in the third stanza?

2. On reflection, however, we can't answer questions about what the girl's attitude is toward her seduction and its outcome until we have the answer to a prior question: what kind of person is the girl? A remarkably naive young woman? A bitter and defiant young woman? A woman who is resigned to what has happened to her and is cheerfully making the best of it?

3. Can you make out a consistent view of the young woman's character? Is she being ironic in stanza 2 when she refers to her seducer as the "dear stranger"? Or does she still regard him as dear though indeed he has been a "careless lover"?

4. How would you justify putting this poem in Section 3 under the heading "Against the Establishment"? Or how would it go under the heading "Man and Nature"? In this last connection, how would you compare it with Goldsmith's poem above?

My Silks and Fine Array

William Blake [*1757–1827*]

My silks and fine array,
My smiles and languish'd air,
By love are driv'n away;
And mournful lean Despair
Brings me yew to deck my grave: 5
Such end true lovers have.

His face is fair as heav'n
When springing buds unfold
O why to him was't giv'n
Whose heart is wintry cold?   10
His breast is love's all worship'd tomb,
Where all love's pilgrims come.

Bring me an axe and spade,
Bring me a winding sheet;
When I my grave have made   15
Let winds and tempests beat:
Then down I'll lie as cold as clay.
True love doth pass away!

If we are to appreciate this poem, we shall have to take account of a number of literary conventions. In this instance, more is involved than simply certain conventions dear to Blake's own century, for in this poem an eighteenth-century poet is quite deliberately using literary conventions borrowed from the Elizabethan period of a century and a half before. We know, for example, that he has borrowed some of his terms from a sixteenth-century poem by Lord Vaux entitled "The Aged Lover Renounceth Love." The borrowings and imitations, however, have to do with the manner of the poem, for the speaker in Blake's poem is a young woman not a man, as in Vaux's poem, and in this poem she is certainly not renouncing love.

Some of the terms and conventions used in this poem are the following: the yew (as we have indicated earlier) is the tree especially associated with English graveyards. Graves were sometimes decorated with branches of yew. The heart of the man loved by the young woman is really a cold tomb, but, like the tomb of a saint in the Middle Ages, it attracts pilgrims who visit it as a holy place. The young woman who speaks the poem sees herself as such a pilgrim. In the Middle Ages, moreover, it was counted a privilege to be interred near a saint's grave or even near some relic of the saint. Since her love for him is unrequited, there is nothing left for the young woman except to die. Thus she prepares to make her grave near

"His breast," which she regards as "love's all worship'd tomb," for she venerates it even though it offers only death to her fervent love.

Questions

1. What is meant by "languish'd air" in line 2? Is there a contradiction here? If the girl is truly languishing even unto death because of unrequited love, why are we told that love has driven her languished air *away*?

2. What is the girl's attitude toward her cold lover? Is she convincing in her praise of him, even though he has given her no encouragement? Does she seem to blame him for his indifference, or is she so passionately in love with him that she forgives all? How seriously can the reader take her protestations?

3. Consider the last four lines. Is the speaker being petulant in calling on the winds and tempests now to do their worst since she, being dead, can no longer feel them? Does she really want to be buried in a storm? Note that she says *"Then* down I'll lie" (italics ours).

4. Could it be argued that Blake's echoing of the locutions and phrasings of an earlier and more august age should warn the reader not to regard the poem as simply a piece of extravagant claptrap; that is, does Blake's way of suggesting the manners and ideas of an earlier age caution us against taking the lady's protestations literally? Could it even be argued that the woman in her broken-hearted grief is not so much preparing actually to set to work with a pickaxe and spade, but rather attempting to find fit images in which to express her genuine desolation?

I Shall Go Back

Edna St. Vincent Millay [*1892–1950*]

I shall go back again to the bleak shore
And build a little shanty on the sand
In such a way that the extremest band
Of brittle seaweed will escape my door
But by a yard or two, and nevermore   5
Shall I return to take you by the hand.
I shall be gone to what I understand
And happier than I ever was before.
The love that stood a moment in your eyes,
The words that lay a moment on your tongue   10
Are one with all that in a moment dies,
A little under-said and over-sung,
But I shall find the sullen rocks and skies
Unchanged from what they were when I was young.

Here again, as in "My Silks and Fine Array," the lover is not necessarily false, but unloving and indifferent. But this lady has no idea of digging her grave; instead she means to go away, and the poem is presumably her farewell speech.

Two poets who have commented on this poem express their doubts about whether the lady really expects to "be happier than [she] ever was before." They write:

> . . . we are not convinced that she really loves the sea or living in a shanty on the seashore. . . . What she seems to want is to be thoroughly miserable, so miserable that she'll make him sorry, and repentant; and perhaps he will come back. Our little lady, we begin to feel, is just playing a game. She is teasing; she will build her shanty so near the sea that she will always be on the verge of being washed away, yet always there the next morning to go on teasing. And the nasty sandfleas that breed in the seaweed will come right in at her front door and make her more miserable and him sorrier. . . .*

Questions

1. Does the passage just quoted count as a fair reading of the poem?
2. What about the lady in Blake's poem—is she simply teasing? If you think she isn't, indicate why.
3. What would be wrong if we assume that the lady *is* teasing? Will the text of the poem accommodate that kind of interpretation?

Early Evening Quarrel

Langston Hughes [*1902–1967*]

Where is that sugar, Hammond,
I sent you this morning to buy?
I say, where is that sugar
I sent you this morning to buy?
Coffee without sugar   5
Makes a good woman cry.

  I ain't got no sugar, Hattie,
  I gambled your dime away.
  Ain't got no sugar, I
  Done gambled that dime away.   10
  If you's a wise woman, Hattie,
  You ain't gonna have nothin to say.

I ain't no wise woman, Hammond.
I am evil and mad.
Ain't no sense in a good woman   15
Bein' treated so bad.

---

* Laura Riding and Robert Graves, *A Pamphlet Against Anthologies,* New York, 1928, p. 120.

I don't treat you bad, Hattie,
Neither does I treat you good.
But I reckon I could treat you
Worser if I would.   20

Lawd, these things we women
Have to stand!
I wonder is there nowhere a
Do-right man?

Questions

To whom are the last four lines of this poem addressed? To Hammond? To herself? To the world in general?

F. BELIEF (INCLUDING THE PROBLEMS IN BELIEVING)

The Scoffers

William Blake [*1757–1827*]

Mock on, mock on, Voltaire, Rousseau,
    Mock on, mock on; 'tis all in vain;
You throw the sand against the wind
    And the wind blows it back again.

And every sand becomes a gem   5
    Reflected in the beams divine;
Blown back, they blind the mocking eye,
    But still in Israel's paths they shine.

The atoms of Democritus
    And Newton's particles of light   10
Are sands upon the Red Sea shore,
    Where Israel's tents do shine so bright.

The speaker begins abruptly by addressing two of the Scoffers, Voltaire and Rousseau. (It does not matter, insofar as the merit of the poem is concerned, whether or not we regard the historical Voltaire and Rousseau—or, for that matter, Newton and Democritus—as really scoffers against the things of the spirit. The important matter is that Blake should have felt them to be so and should have been able to make poetry out of his indignation against them.) He taunts the Scoffers with the futility of their actions and uses a vivid figure with which to make his point: they are throwing sand against the wind. Such would be the action of a madman: though endlessly repeated, it is performed in vain.

The second stanza gives a further extension of meaning (though the development of the idea is made through the development of the figure). "To throw dust into a person's eyes" is a proverbial image for an attempt at deception. Blake freshens and sharpens the conventional figure by having the wind blow the sand back into the eyes of the would-be deceivers. Blake makes further extensions of the meaning by stating that every "sand" (that is, grain of sand) becomes a gem, and by making the momentarily puzzling statement that the grains of sand shine in *Israel's* path.

The third stanza develops and extends the reference to Israel, by an allusion to Israel's journey out of Egyptian bondage to the Promised Land.

Questions

1. In your opinion, is Blake's image of the flung grains of sand becoming gems strained and forced? Or is it successful?

2. Democritus is alluded to as the founder of the atomic theory in ancient times, and Newton as an exponent of the theory in more modern times. What is the connection, if any, between the atoms (particles of matter), the particles of light, and the grains of sand? Is there sufficient consistency of imagery? What is implied here about the meaning of science?

3. Attempt to state the theme of his poem. Does the presentation of it gain by the use of vivid images? Does it lose in clarity by being presented through images?

4. Would you try to do a prose paraphrase of Blake confronting modern science? What do you think modern science (insofar as you are acquainted with its views) would make of Blake's poems?

If Poisonous Minerals

John Donne [*1573–1631*]

If poisonous minerals, and if that tree
Whose fruit threw death on else immortal us,
If lecherous goats, if serpents envious
Cannot be damned, Alas! why should I be?
Why should intent or reason, born in me,   5
Make sins, else equal, in me more heinous?
And mercy being easy, and glorious
To God, in his stern wrath why threatens he?
But who am I, that dare dispute with thee,
O God? O! of thine only worthy blood,   10
And my tears, make a heavenly Lethean flood,
And drown in it my sins' black memory;
That thou remember them, some claim as debt,
I think it mercy, if thou wilt forget.

Questions

1. Here the contrast between man and nature is the key to the poem. Explain the relation of this fact to the theme.

2. Consider what may be called the exclamatory effects. Does the poet overwork the use of such exclamations as "Alas" and "O God"? If you think that they are used properly and heighten the dramatic effect of the poem, try to show how they do.

3. Discuss the series of contrasts in which the basic argument is worked out. For example, the lower creation is contrasted with the higher creation (that is, man) on the grounds of relative guilt. What are some of the other contrasts? Though there are few actual metaphors and similes, note the number of vivid concrete instances and details. What are some of them?

4. Make a careful scansion of the poem. Having done so, would you agree that Donne's handling of the metrical situation serves powerfully to add proper pause and emphasis to the sonnet—indeed, makes it difficult for any sensitive reader not to feel the urgency of the poet's prayer? Write a short essay on these metrical effects. Would you say that this poem is deficient in musicality? Discuss the question.

Church Going

Philip Larkin [*1922–*]

Once I am sure there's nothing going on
I step inside, letting the door thud shut.
Another church: matting, seats, and stone,
And little books; sprawlings of flowers, cut
For Sunday, brownish now; some brass and stuff   5
Up at the holy end; the small neat organ;
And a tense, musty, unignorable silence,
Brewed God knows how long. Hatless, I take off
My cycle-clips in awkward reverence,

Move forward, run my hand around the font.   10
From where I stand, the roof looks almost new—
Cleaned or restored? Someone would know: I don't.
Mounting the lectern, I peruse a few
Hectoring large-scale verses, and pronounce
"Here endeth" much more loudly than I'd meant.   15
The echoes snigger briefly. Back at the door
I sign the book, donate an Irish sixpence,
Reflect the place was not worth stopping for.

Yet stop I did: in fact I often do,
And always end much at a loss like this,   20
Wondering what to look for; wondering, too,
When churches fall completely out of use

What we shall turn them into, if we shall keep
A few cathedrals chronically on show,
Their parchment, plate, and pyx in locked cases,   25
And let the rest rent-free to rain and sheep.
Shall we avoid them as unlucky places?

Or, after dark, will dubious women come
To make their children touch a particular stone;
Pick simples for a cancer; or in some   30
Advised night see walking a dead one?
Power of some sort or other will go on
In games, in riddles, seemingly at random;
But superstition, like belief, must die,
And what remains when disbelief has gone?   35
Grass, weedy pavement, brambles, buttress, sky,

A shape less recognizable each week,
A purpose more obscure. I wonder who
Will be the last, the very last, to seek
This place for what it was; one of the crew   40
That tap and jot and know what rood-lofts were?
Some ruin-bibber, randy for antique,
Or Christmas-addict, counting on a whiff
Of gown-and-bands and organ-pipes and myrrh,
Or will he be my representative,   45

Bored, uninformed, knowing the ghostly silt
Dispersed, yet tending to this cross of ground
Through suburb scrub because it held unspilt
So long and equably what since is found
Only in separation—marriage, and birth,   50
And death, and thoughts of these—for whom was built
This special shell? For, though I've no idea
What this accoutred frowsty barn is worth,
It pleases me to stand in silence here;

A serious house on serious earth it is,   55
In whose blent air all our compulsions meet,
Are recognized, and robed as destinies.
And that much never can be obsolete,
Since someone will forever be surprising
A hunger in himself to be more serious,   60
And gravitating with it to this ground,
Which, he once heard, was proper to grow wise in,
If only that so many dead lie round.

Questions

1. Why does the speaker enter this church?
2. Why does the speaker end his visit to the church "much at a loss"
(line 20)?

3. What has spread a "pall" over this church (cf. Blake's "London," line 10)? The chimney-sweeper's cry? The hapless soldier's sigh? The harlot's curse? Or what?

Dover Beach

Matthew Arnold [*1822–1888*]

The sea is calm tonight,
The tide is full, the moon lies fair
Upon the straits;—on the French coast the light
Gleams and is gone; the cliffs of England stand,
Glimmering and vast, out in the tranquil bay.   5
Come to the window, sweet is the night-air!
Only, from the long line of spray
Where the sea meets the moon-blanched land,
Listen! you hear the grating roar
Of pebbles which the waves draw back, and fling,   10
At their return, up the high strand,
Begin, and cease, and then again begin,
With tremulous cadence slow, and bring
The eternal note of sadness in.

Sophocles long ago   15
Heard it on the Aegean, and it brought
Into his mind the turbid ebb and flow
Of human misery; we
Find also in the sound a thought,
Hearing it by this distant northern sea.   20

The Sea of Faith
Was once, too, at the full, and round earth's shore
Lay like the folds of a bright girdle furled.
But now I only hear
Its melancholy, long, withdrawing roar,   25
Retreating, to the breath
Of the night-wind, down the vast edges drear
And naked shingles of the world.

Ah, love, let us be true
To one another! for the world, which seems   30
To lie before us like a land of dreams,
So various, so beautiful, so new,
Hath really neither joy, nor love, nor light,
Nor certitude, nor peace, nor help for pain;
And we are here as on a darkling plain   35
Swept with confused alarms of struggle and flight,
Where ignorant armies clash by night.

Questions

1. To whom is the poem addressed? What relation in regard to theme do you find between "Dover Beach" and Eliot's "Preludes" (p. 91)? And Tate's "The Last Days of Alice" (p. 260)? What differences strike you?

2. By using the last figure (lines 35–37) does the poet make an abrupt and unjustified shift in imagery? If not, how do you justify the figure?

3. Compare this poem with Larkin's "Church-Going." How do the speakers of these poems differ in their attitudes toward their loss of faith?

Lycidas

John Milton [*1608–1674*]

```
Yet once more, O ye Laurels, and once more,
Ye Myrtles brown, with Ivy never sere,
I come to pluck your berries harsh and crude,
And with forced fingers rude
Shatter your leaves before the mellowing year.          5
Bitter constraint and sad occasion dear
Compels me to disturb your season due;
For Lycidas is dead, dead ere his prime,
Young Lycidas, and hath not left his peer.
Who would not sing for Lycidas? he knew               10
Himself to sing, and build the lofty rhyme.
He must not float upon his wat'ry bier
Unwept, and welter to the parching wind.
Without the meed of some melodious tear.
    Begin, then, Sisters of the Sacred Well           15
That from beneath the seat of Jove doth spring,
Begin, and somewhat loudly sweep the string.
Hence with denial vain and coy excuse:
So may some gentle Muse
With lucky words favor my destined urn,               20
And, as he passes, turn,
And bid fair peace be to my sable shroud!
For we were nursed upon the self-same hill,
Fed the same flocks, by fountain, shade, and rill;
    Together both, ere the high lawns appeared        25
Under the opening eyelids of the Morn,
We drove a-field, and both together heard
What time the gray-fly winds her sultry horn,
Battening our flocks with the fresh dews of night,
Oft till the star that rose at evening bright         30
Towards Heaven's descent had sloped his westering wheel.
Meanwhile the rural ditties were not mute,
Tempered to the oaten flute,
Rough Satyrs danced, and Fauns with cloven heel
From the glad sound would not be absent long;         35
```

And old Damætas loved to hear our song.
  But, O the heavy change, now thou art gone,
Now thou art gone, and never must return!
Thee, Shepherd, thee the woods and desert caves,
With wild thyme and the gadding vine o'ergrown,   40
And all their echoes mourn.
The willows, and the hazel copses green,
Shall now no more be seen
Fanning their joyous leaves to thy soft lays.
As killing as the canker to the rose,   45
Or taint-worm to the weanling herds that graze,
Or frost to flowers, that their gay wardrobe wear
When first the white thorn blows;
Such, Lycidas, thy loss to shepherd's ear.
  Where were ye, Nymphs, when the remorseless deep   50
Closed o'er the head of your loved Lycidas?
For neither were ye playing on the steep
Where your old bards, the famous Druids, lie,
Nor on the shaggy top of Mona high,
Nor yet where Deva spreads her wizard stream.   55
Ay me! I fondly dream!
Had ye been there—for what could that have done?
What could the Muse herself that Orpheus bore,
The Muse herself, for her enchanting son,
Whom universal Nature did lament,   60
When, by the rout that made the hideous roar,
His gory visage down the stream was sent,
Down the swift Hebrus to the Lesbian shore?
  Alas! what boots it with uncessant care
To tend the homely, slighted, shepherd's trade,   65
And strictly meditate the thankless Muse?
Were it not better done, as others use,
To sport with Amaryllis in the shade,
Or with the tangles of Neæra's hair?
Fame is the spur that the clear spirit doth raise   70
(That last infirmity of noble mind)
To scorn delights and live laborious days;
But the fair guerdon when we hope to find,
And think to burst out into sudden blaze,
Comes the blind Fury with the abhorrèd shears,   75
And slits the thin-spun life. "But not the praise,"
Phœbus replied, and touched my trembling ears:
"Fame is no plant that grows on mortal soil,
Nor in the glistering foil
Set off to the world, nor in broad Rumor lies,   80
But lives and spreads aloft by those pure eyes
And perfect witness of all-judging Jove;
As he pronounces lastly on each deed,
Of so much fame in Heav'n expect thy meed."

O fountain Arethuse, and thou honored flood,   85
Smooth-sliding Mincius, crowned with vocal reeds,
That strain I heard was of a higher mood:
But now my oat proceeds.
And listens to the Herald of the Sea,
That came in Neptune's plea.   90
He asked the waves, and asked the felon winds,
What hard mishap hath doomed this gentle swain?
And questioned every gust of rugged wings
That blows from off each beakèd promontory:
They knew not of his story;   95
And sage Hippotadés their answer brings,
That not a blast was from his dungeon strayed:
The air was calm, and on the level brine
Sleek Panopé with all her sisters played.
It was that fatal and perfidious bark,   100
Built in the eclipse, and rigged with curses dark,
That sunk so low that sacred head of thine.
    Next, Camus, reverend sire, went footing slow,
His mantle hairy, and his bonnet sedge,
Inwrought with figures dim, and on the edge   105
Like to that sanguine flower inscribed with woe.
"Ah! who hath reft," quoth he, "my dearest pledge?"
Last came, and last did go,
The pilot of the Galilean lake;
Two massy keys he bore of metals twain   110
(The golden opes, the iron shuts amain).
He shook his mitered locks, and stern bespake:—
"How well could I have spared for thee, young Swain,
Enow of such, as for their bellies' sake,
Creep, and intrude, and climb into the fold!   115
Of other care they little reckoning make
Than how to scramble at the shearers' feast,
And shove away the worthy bidden guest.
Blind mouths! that scarce themselves know how to hold
A sheep-hook, or have learned aught else the least   120
That to the faithful herdsman's art belongs!
What recks it them? What need they? they are sped;
And, when they list, their lean and flashy songs
Grate on their scrannel pipes of wretched straw;
The hungry sheep look up, and are not fed,   125
But, swollen with wind and the rank mist they draw,
Rot inwardly, and foul contagion spread;
Besides what the grim wolf with privy paw
Daily devours apace, and nothing said;
But that two-handed engine at the door   130
Stands ready to smite once, and smite no more."
    Return, Alphéus; the dread voice is past
That shrunk thy streams; return, Sicilian Muse,

And call the vales, and bid them hither cast
Their bells and flowerets of a thousand hues.   135
Ye valleys low, where the mild whispers use
Of shades, and wanton winds, and gushing brooks,
On whose fresh lap the swart star sparely looks,
Throw hither all your quaint enameled eyes,
That on the green turf suck the honied showers,   140
And purple all the ground with vernal flowers.
Bring the rathe primrose that forsaken dies,
The tufted crow-toe, and pale jessamine,
The white pink, and the pansy freaked with jet,
The glowing violet,   145
The musk-rose, and the well-attired woodbine,
With cowslips wan that hang the pensive head,
And every flower that sad embroidery wears;
Bid Amaranthus all his beauty shed,
And daffadillies fill their cups with tears,   150
To strew the laureate hearse where Lycid lies.
For so, to interpose a little ease,
Let our frail thoughts dally with false surmise,
Ay me! whilst thee the shores and sounding seas
Wash far away, where'er thy bones are hurled;   155
Whether beyond the stormy Hebrides,
Where thou, perhaps, under the whelming tide
Visit'st the bottom of the monstrous world;
Or whether thou, to our moist vows denied,
Sleep'st by the fable of Bellerus old,   160
Where the great Vision of the guarded mount
Looks toward Namancos and Bayona's hold:
Look homeward, angel, now, and melt with ruth;
And, O ye Dolphins, waft the hapless youth.
    Weep no more, woeful shepherds, weep no more,   165
For Lycidas, your sorrow, is not dead,
Sunk though he be beneath the watery floor:
So sinks the day-star in the ocean bed
And yet anon repairs his drooping head,
And tricks his beams, and with new-spangled ore   170
Flames in the forehead of the morning sky:
So Lycidas sunk low, but mounted high,
Through the dear might of Him that walked the waves,
Where other groves and other streams along,
With nectar pure his oozy locks he laves,   175
And hears the unexpressive nuptial song,
In the blest kingdoms meek of Joy and Love.
There entertain him all the Saints above,
In solemn troops, and sweet societies,
That sing, and singing in their glory move,   180
And wipe the tears forever from his eyes.
Now, Lycidas, the shepherds weep no more;

Henceforth thou art the Genius of the shore,
In thy large recompense, and shalt be good
To all that wander in that perilous flood.   185

    Thus sang the uncouth swain to the oaks and rills,
While the still Morn went out with sandals gray;
He touched the tender stops of various quills,
With eager thought warbling his Doric lay:
And now the sun had stretched out all the hills,   190
And now was dropped into the western bay.
At last he rose, and twitched his mantle blue:
Tomorrow to fresh woods and pastures new.

Questions

1. This is a pastoral elegy written at the death of one of Milton's friends, Edward King, a young scholar who was drowned in the Irish Sea. At this time Milton was a relatively young man already engaged in his pursuit of literary fame. Is the poem merely a compliment to King and an expression of grief at his death? What is the real theme of the poem? How is the theme related to the fact of the death of King? What is the relation of the apparently irrelevant passages (lines 64–84, lines 103–131) to the theme as you see it?

2. Dr. Samuel Johnson criticized this poem adversely in the following terms:

One of the poems on which much praise has been bestowed is *Lycidas* of which the diction is harsh, the rhymes uncertain, and the numbers unpleasing. What beauty there is we must therefore seek in the sentiments and images. It is not to be considered as the effusion of real passion; for passion runs not after remote allusions and obscure opinions. Passion plucks no berries from the myrtle and ivy, nor calls Arethuse and Mincius, nor tells of rough *satyrs* and *fauns with cloven heel.* Where there is leisure for fiction there is little grief.

In this poem there is no nature, for there is no truth; there is no art, for there is nothing new. Its form is that of a pastoral, easy, vulgar, and therefore disgusting; whatever images it can supply are long ago exhausted, and its inherent improbability always forces dissatisfaction on the mind. When Cowley [a poet who was the contemporary of Milton] tells of Hervey, that they studied together, it is easy to suppose how much he must miss the companion of his labors, and the partner of his discoveries; but what image of tenderness can be excited by these lines?—

We drove a-field, and both together heard
What time the gray-fly winds her sultry horn,
Batt'ning our flocks with the fresh dews of night.

We know that they never drove a-field, and that they had no flocks to batten; and though it be allowed that the representation may be allegorical, the true meaning is so uncertain and remote that it is never sought because it cannot be known when found. . . . He who thus grieves will excite no sympathy; he who thus praises will confer no honor.

from "John Milton," in *Lives of the English Poets*

Dr. Johnson, to sum up, attacks the poem for awkward technique and for insincerity. What do you make of these two charges?

In regard to the first, scan lines 1–4 and 64–84, and comment on the rhythm, verse texture, alliteration, consonance, and other technical factors.

3. In regard to the second charge, is the pastoral convention *necessarily* more artificial than the fiction indulged in by Keats in calling his urn the "foster-child of silence and slow time" (p. 320)? What do you mean by "insincerity" in poetry?

Note, further, that the speaker of the poem acknowledges the difficulty in maintaining a pastoral note. Apollo was one of the high gods, and his pronouncement is acknowledged as a strain of "higher mood" as the speaker tries to resume the humbler pastoral note. After St. Peter's scathing comment on the unworthy shepherds, the speaker calls back the Sicilian muse (the muse of pastoral poetry) as if she had been frightened away. Do these admissions weaken the poem? Or strengthen it? How do they bear on the charge by Dr. Johnson that the pastoral was by Milton's time a worn-out and artificial form?

4. Discuss the shifts in tone of this poem. How are they marked? What do they indicate about the narrative element in the poem? What do the last eight lines do for the tone as a whole? (Note that we have a third-person ending, though the poem begins in the first person, with the swain speaking. Can you justify this lack of symmetry?)

5. Dr. Johnson objected to the mixture of pagan and Christian elements in this poem. Can you justify it? Is there evidence that the poet mixed them consciously and for a purpose?

6. Note the water imagery. Why is there so much of it? Does it develop into a symbolism?

7. What is the significance of allusion in "Lycidas"? Do you see any difference between the use here and that in Wordsworth's "Yew-Trees" (p. 109)?

8. For an interpretation of "Lycidas," see E. M. W. Tillyard's *Milton* (Macmillan, 1930, pp. 80–85). What bearing does this interpretation have on the whole question of sincerity and convention?

The Day After Sunday

Phyllis McGinley [*1905–*]

> Always on Monday, God's name is in the morning papers,
>   His name is a headline, His Works are rumored abroad.
> Having been praised by men who are movers and shakers,
>   From prominent Sunday pulpits, newsworthy is God.
>
> On page 27, just opposite Fashion Trends,   5
>   One reads at a glance how He scolded the Baptists a little,
> Was firm with the Catholics, practical with the Friends,
>   To Unitarians pleasantly noncommittal.

In print are His numerous aspects, too; God smiling,
God vexed, God thunderous, God whose mansions are pearl,   10
Political God, God frugal, God reconciling
Himself with science, God guiding the Camp Fire Girl.

Always on Monday morning the press reports
God as revealed to His vicars in various guises—
Benevolent, stormy, patient, or out of sorts.   15
God knows which God is the God God recognizes.

Questions

At first glance we recognize that the tone of this poem is very different
from that of any other in this group. It is humorous, amusingly satirical.
But is there a serious question underlying the poem? Toward what is the
satire directed? Do you think a believer would be offended by this poem?

Applications: The Poet Looks at a Bird

6

Foreword

Here we have collected a group of poems that deal directly or indirectly with birds. Many other subjects might serve our purpose as well—flowers, stars, sea, or sun—for the point is simply that there is sometimes a practical advantage in having a common objective element in poems to be discussed. Such an element offers a ready means for comparing and contrasting the different uses of images or the different shadings of tone or the different theme to be met with.

Yet perhaps the bird will prove a happier choice than most. The bird is a winged creature, not earthbound as man is. Thus, the Psalmist cries out: "Oh that I had wings like a dove, for then would I fly away and be at rest" (55:6). Man has also long been fascinated by the songs and even the call of birds. The croak of a raven has been immemorially associated with the ominous; the warbling of the lark has suggested a perpetual happiness to which man can only partly attain. Most of all, birds are closely associated with nature, especially in their spontaneous and joyous activity. Because the bird seems to have a special relation to nature the poet sometimes uses it as a symbol of nature itself. Of course, man also is a natural creature and his kinship with other natural creatures is obvious. But his consciousness allows him to transcend nature.

341

The power of transcendence can be interpreted as guaranteeing man's lordship and dominance over the rest of the creatures, since he is far less than they subject to immediate sensations, instincts, and blind urgencies. But his transcendence of nature can also be interpreted as a tragic alienation from nature. By contrast, the bird seems at home in nature—unhampered by the burden of consciousness—and, for this reason, he sometimes becomes the object of man's envy. But in either case, the bird's relation to nature has often been seized on by poets as a way of defining man's special position in the universe.

Hawk Roosting

Ted Hughes [*1930–*]

I sit in the top of the wood, my eyes closed.
Inaction, no falsifying dream
Between my hooked head and hooked feet:
Or in sleep rehearse perfect kills and eat.

The convenience of the high trees!   5
The air's buoyancy and the sun's ray
Are of advantage to me;
And the earth's face upward for my inspection.

My feet are locked upon the rough bark.
It took the whole of Creation   10
To produce my foot, my each feather:
Now I hold Creation in my foot

Or fly up, and revolve it all slowly—
I kill where I please because it is all mine.
There is no sophistry in my body: 15
My manners are tearing off heads—

The allotment of death.
For the one path of my flight is direct
Through the bones of the living.
No arguments assert my right: 20

The sun is behind me.
Nothing has changed since I began.
My eye has permitted no change.
I am going to keep things like this.

Questions

1. To what kind of human being is the hawk being compared?

2. We are told in line 2 that there is no "falsifying dream" to get in the way of the perfect articulation of the "hooked head" and the "hooked feet." (Compare "crooked hands" in Tennyson's "The Eagle," p. 361.)

Certain kinds of men are made indecisive simply by seeing the complexities of the problem presented. The hawk experiences no trouble of this sort. Yet could it be said that, though Hughes makes use of human terms, what he has his hawk say comes close to making the hawk utterly "inhuman," and that is the poet's intention?

3. Hughes's hawk is represented as a kind of solipsist: that is, he sees the world purely in his own terms and cannot get outside his own subjectivity. What lines in the poem support this interpretation?

4. What attitude does the poet expect us to take toward this proud, self-confident, and aggressive bird? Envy? Contempt? Horror? Or what? What is the tone of the poem?

5. In one of his poems, Tennyson described nature as "red in tooth and claw." Is such a fair description of the character of nature implied in "Hawk Roosting"? Or not?

Hurt Hawks

Robinson Jeffers [*1887–1962*]

I

The broken pillar of the wing jags from the clotted shoulder,
The wing trails like a banner in defeat,
No more to use the sky forever but live with famine
A few days: cat nor coyote
Will shorten the week of waiting for death, there is game without
      talons.   5
He stands under the oak-bush and waits
The lame feet of salvation; at night he remembers freedom
And flies in a dream, the dawns ruin it.
He is strong and pain is worse to the strong, incapacity is worse.
The curs of the day come and torment him   10
At distance, no one but death the redeemer will humble that head,
The intrepid readiness, the terrible eyes.
The wild God of the world is sometimes merciful to those
That ask mercy, not often to the arrogant.
You do not know him, you communal people, or you have fogotten
      him;   15
Intemperate and savage, the hawk remembers him;
Beautiful and wild, the hawks, and men that are dying, remember
      him.

II

I'd sooner, except the penalties, kill a man than a hawk; but the
      great redtail
Had nothing left but unable misery
From the bone too shattered for mending, the wing that trailed under
      his talons when he moved.   20
We had fed him six weeks, I gave him freedom,

He wandered over the foreland hill and returned in the evening,
    asking for death,
Not like a beggar, still eyes with the old
Implacable arrogance. I gave him the lead gift in the twilight. What
    fell was relaxed,
Owl-downy, soft feminine feathers; but what   **25**
Soared: the fierce rush: the night-herons by the flooded river cried
    fear at its rising
Before it was quite unsheathed from reality.

Questions

In their two poems Ted Hughes and Robinson Jeffers look at the same creature, with the same qualities, but the attitudes expressed are very nearly antithetical. Forgetting the object they regard, what human values are esteemed by Hughes, what by Jeffers? Do you feel that you must definitively choose between the two sets of values? Do you feel that you choose between the two poems primarily on account of the differing values implied? If you do not feel this choice necessary, how would you explain your position?

The Owl

Edward Thomas [1878–1917]

Down hill I came, hungry, and yet not starved;
Cold, yet had heat within me that was proof
Against the North wind; tired, yet so that rest
Had seemed the sweetest thing under a roof.

Then at the inn I had food, fire, and rest,   **5**
Knowing how hungry, cold, and tired was I.
All of the night was quite barred out except
An owl's cry, a most melancholy cry

Shaken out long and clear upon the hill,
No merry note, nor cause of merriment,   **10**
But one telling me plain what I escaped
And others could not, that night, as in I went.

And salted was my food, and my repose,
Salted and sobered, too, by the bird's voice
Speaking for all who lay under the stars,   **15**
Soldiers and poor, unable to rejoice.

The dramatic situation presented by this poem can be put briefly. A man arrives at night at an inn, cold, hungry, and quite tired. The warm comfort of the inn bars out all of the hardships of the night except one thing: the speaker can still hear the cry of an owl on the hills outside.

Questions

1. To the man, now warm and under shelter, what does the cry of the owl signify? Note that in this poem we are not concerned with either a fairly objective description of a bird (see pp. 343–344) or with a bird's arrogant and inhuman self-absorption and complacency (p. 342). The owl in this poem stands for something else. In this context, what does its cry come to mean? Can you give a precise paraphrase of what is said in stanza 3?

2. Why does the poet not end the poem with stanza 3? What, if anything, does the last stanza contribute to the total meaning of the poem?

3. Note the repetition of "salted." How can the bird's voice be said to *salt* anything? What is the relation of "salted" to "sobered"? What would be lost if the poet had preferred to have line 14 read "sweetened and sobered, too, by the bird's voice"?

4. The last two lines state that the owl is "Speaking for all . . . unable to rejoice." Does this assertion run counter to common sense and scientific fact? How would you defend the poet's making the owl the spokesman for "all who lay under the stars"?

5. Would a nightingale have served the poet equally well here?

The Darkling[1] Thrush

Thomas Hardy [*1840–1928*]

I leant upon a coppice gate[2]
    When Frost was specter-gray,
And Winter's dregs made desolate
    The weakening eye of day.
The tangled bine-stems[3] scored the sky   5
    Like strings of broken lyres,
And all mankind that haunted nigh
    Had sought their household fires.

The land's sharp features seemed to be
    The Century's corpse[4] outleant,   10
His crypt the cloudy canopy,
    The wind his death-lament.
The ancient pulse of germ and birth
    Was shrunken hard and dry,
And every spirit upon earth   15
    Seemed fervorless as I.

At once a voice arose among
    The bleak twigs overhead
In a fullhearted evensong
    Of joy illimited;   20

[1] in the dark   [2] gate leading to a small wood or thicket   [3] twining stems of shrubs
[4] this poem was written on December 31, 1900, the last day of the nineteenth century

An aged thrush, frail, gaunt, and small,
   In blast-beruffled plume,
Had chosen thus to fling his soul
   Upon the growing gloom.

So little cause for carolings   25
   Of such ecstatic sound
Was written on terrestrial things
   Afar or nigh around,
That I could think there trembled through
   His happy good-night air   30
Some blessed Hope, whereof he knew
   And I was unaware.

The man who speaks this poem feels lost and desolate. The world on which he looks out is "specter-gray." It is nature, but a nature that is hostile and unpitying. The joyful nature of which so many poets sing has been abolished.

The bird seems unaware of the hostility of nature, which the man feels so keenly. Indeed, he sings so happily that the man can fancy that the bird possesses some superior wisdom which he, as a human being, lacks.

This poem, we may observe, is as much a poem of the twentieth century as Robert Burns's poem about the "bonie bird" (p. 323) was of the Romantic outburst at the beginning of the nineteenth century. Between Burns and Hardy there had appeared Charles Darwin and Thomas Huxley, whose universe was without concern for human values. It is nature blindly devoted to the survival of the species most fit to survive.

Questions

1. What is Hardy's attitude toward the thrush? Does he feel for it a pitying contempt? A kind of awe for its joyous vitality and its sense of well-being under the most trying circumstances? Anguish at its misplaced optimism? Or what?

2. Does the human observer *really* believe that the thrush is aware of some blessed hope?

3. Note the force of the phrase "fullhearted evensong" in line 19. In the Anglican church service, evensong is the evening service that comes shortly before sunset each day. (There is a reference to evensong in "The Three Ravens," p. 54). Evensong is essentially a service of thanksgiving for the day and a prayer for protection and quiet repose through the night. Does a knowledge of this meaning lend any special poignance to the thrush's evening song? Does an awareness of the meaning of evensong add resonance to the phrase used in the last stanza, "His happy good-night air"?

4. How would you compare this poem with "Pippa's Song" (p. 76)? With "Hell Gate" (p. 59)?

Bantams in Pine-Woods

Wallace Stevens [*1879–1955*]

Chieftain Iffucan of Azcan in caftan
Of tan with henna hackles, halt!

Damned universal cock, as if the sun
Was blackamoor to bear your blazing tail.

Fat! Fat! Fat! Fat! I am the personal.   5
Your world is you. I am my world.

You ten-foot poet among inchlings. Fat!
Begone! An inchling bristles in these pines,

Bristles, and points their Appalachian tangs,
And fears not portly Azcan nor his hoos.   10

In this poem Stevens is evidently having some fun—with word sounds and word associations. The bantam rooster that disputes his path as the poet walks through the woods is addressed as if he were an Indian (perhaps an Aztec Indian) chief. He is made a "portly" bird—that is, stately and dignified—though the repeated "fat" perhaps hints at another associated meaning of "portly." Most important of all, the author makes the bantam cock a "ten-foot poet."

Questions

1. In what ways does the bird represent a poet? Do other lines in the poem suggest why?
2. Iffucan and Azcan are transparent syncopations of "If you can" and "As [you] can." Do these meanings suggest that the poet is doing more than simply playing with the syllable "can" in this first pair of lines?
3. Write a short paragraph attempting to describe the tone of the poem.
4. In what way may the attitude attributed to the little bantam rooster resemble that of the hawk? That of the thrush? Whatever the resemblances in a general sense, the tone of "Bantams . . ." is vastly different from that of either of the previous poems; and this makes a vast difference in the meanings. Explain.

Little Trotty Wagtail

John Clare [*1793–1864*]

Little trotty wagtail, he went in the rain,
And tittering, tottering sideways he ne'er got straight again,

He stooped to get a worm, and looked up to get a fly,
And then he flew away ere his feathers they were dry.

Little trotty wagtail, he waddled in the mud,   5
And left his little footmarks, trample where he would.
He waddled in the water-pudge, and waggle went his tail,
And chirrup up his wings to dry upon the garden rail.

Little trotty wagtail, you nimble all about,
And in the dimpling water-pudge you waddle in and out;   10
Your home is nigh at hand, and in the warm pigsty,
So, little Master Wagtail, I'll bid you a good-bye.

The wagtail—a bird not found in the United States—belongs to the *Motacillidae* family (the Latin word means "tail wagglers"). Because of its love for water, in England the bird is sometimes called a "water wagtail."

The author of this poem was a Northamptonshire peasant poet, and in the poem he makes use of obsolete and dialect forms of speech drawn from the Northamptonshire countryside. Thus a "trotty" (line 1) is "a little toddling child." "Tittering" (line 2) does not mean "giggling," but is a dialect word meaning "tottering" or "reeling." "Water-pudge" (line 7), another dialect word, means a "puddle." "Nimble" (line 9) is used here as a verb meaning "to move quickly" and is probably also a dialect form. "Chirrup" (line 8) is more difficult to account for. Since the line says literally that the bird "chirrup up his wings to dry," we probably ought to regard it as a kind of condensed expression for "with a chirp brings up his wings to dry."

Questions

1. Does the poet manage to give a vivid sense of the movements of the bird? What descriptive details do you find particularly effective?

2. What is the poet's attitude toward the bird? Does he find it cute, charming, funny, foolish? Or what? Try to determine what part is played in defining the poet's attitude by the realistic and humorous detail.

3. Does the poet's use of dialect forms like *tittering, trotty,* etc., play any part in conveying the poet's attitude? Would a more formal and indeed a more nearly standard diction suggest a rather different attitude?

4. In the first two stanzas the poet refers to the bird as "he." But in the last stanza the poet addresses him as "you." What is the effect of this shift upon the tone of the poem?

5. Read the poem aloud a number of times and try to catch the rhythm. Would you say that the basic foot is the iamb or the anapest? How many feet are there in the line? Or is the meter too irregular for you to be certain? You may find it more satisfactory to regard the poem as written in accentual verse (see pp. 553–560). In any case, does the highly irregular and "unpolished" metrical pattern have any effect on the tone of the poem?

Philomela

Matthew Arnold [*1822–1888*]

Hark! ah, the nightingale—
The tawny-throated!
Hark, from that moonlit cedar what a burst!
What triumph! hark!—what pain!

O wanderer from a Grecian shore,   5
Still, after many years, in distant lands,
Still nourishing in thy bewilder'd brain
That wild, unquench'd, deep-sunken, old-world pain—
Say, will it never heal?
And can this fragrant lawn   10
With its cool trees, and night,
And the sweet, tranquil Thames,
And moonshine, and the dew,
To thy rack'd heart and brain
Afford no balm?   15

Dost thou to-night behold,
Here, through the moonlight on this English grass,
The unfriendly palace in the Thracian wild?
Dost thou again peruse
With hot cheeks and sear'd eyes   20
The too clear web, and thy dumb sister's shame?
Dost thou once more assay
Thy flight, and feel come over thee,
Poor fugitive, the feathery change
Once more, and once more seem to make resound   25
With love and hate, triumph and agony,
Lone Daulis, and the high Cephissian vale?
Listen, Eugenia—
How thick the bursts come crowding through the leaves!
Again—thou hearest?   30
Eternal passion!
Eternal pain!

To understand this poem fully, the reader should know the story that the ancient Greeks told of Philomela and her sister Procne. Procne married Tereus, the King of Thrace. He became enamored of his sister-in-law, Philomela, raped her, and then cut out her tongue to prevent her telling anyone of his crime. He hid her away and told Procne that Philomela had died. But Philomela wove into a tapestry the story of her wrongs and managed to have it secretly conveyed to her sister. Procne then sought her out and the two sisters conferred on how to punish Tereus. They decided that Procne would kill Itylus, her son by Tereus, and serve up his flesh to his unsuspecting father. This they did at Daulis (line 27). Procne told her husband on what food he had dined, and at that instant Philomela rushed in with the severed head of Itylus to offer proof that what Procne had said was true. Tereus snatched up his sword to kill the sisters, but the gods intervened and changed them all into birds: Tereus into a hoopoe, Itylus into a sandpiper, Procne into a swallow, and Philomela into a nightingale. The "Cephissian vale" (line 27) was the valley of the river Cephissus which flowed near Daulis.

According to Arnold's poem, Philomela has made her way from Greece to England, but even in this far-off island and after thousands of years, she is still repeating her sad story in melodious song.

Questions

1. Does the foregoing note account for the fact that the listener hears "triumph" in the nightingale's song as well as love, hate, and agony? How?

2. Arnold, as a modern man, knows, of course, that the nightingale he hears singing by the Thames is not the woman of the Greek legend, transformed into a bird. How, then, justify what he has his listener say in this poem? How is he using the Greek story here? What is the transformation wrought of the brutal story?

3. Who is Eugenia? Does it matter that the poet does not tell us who she is? What function is served by intruding her name into the poem?

4. Compare the relation of human being to bird in this poem with that found in the six poems that immediately precede "Philomela."

The Need of Being Versed in Country Things

Robert Frost [*1874–1963*]

The house had gone to bring again
To the midnight sky a sunset glow.
Now the chimney was all of the house that stood,
Like a pistil after the petals go.

The barn opposed across the way,   5
That would have joined the house in flame
Had it been the will of the wind, was left
To bear forsaken the place's name.

No more it opened with all one end
For teams that came by the stony road   10
To drum on the floor with scurrying hoofs
And brush the mow with the summer load.

The birds that came to it through the air
At broken windows flew out and in,
Their murmur more like the sigh we sigh   15
From too much dwelling on what has been.

Yet for them the lilac renewed its leaf,
And the aged elm, though touched with fire;
And the dry pump flung up an awkward arm;
And the fence post carried a strand of wire.   20

For them there was really nothing sad.
But though they rejoiced in the nest they kept,
One had to be versed in country things
Not to believe the phoebes wept.

Questions

1. Compare "The Need of Being Versed" with Hardy's "The Darkling Thrush." Hardy says the thrush is not mournful but joyous. Does Frost say much the same thing about the phoebes? Where do the two poems differ in this matter?

2. Are the details of the scene as presented by Frost—"the dry pump flung up an awkward arm," "the fence post carried a strand of wire," etc. —used to make the scene of desolation more vivid? Or are they also related to the theme of the poem? If so, how?

3. Would Frost quarrel with the Romantic poets in their interpretation of nature? How radically does his interpretation differ from theirs? Would you say that he deliberately fashions his poem so as to lead us to expect a Romantic response to nature and then abruptly shifts from that response? If such is not the ground plan of his poem, then what is the plan?

4. What is the tone of this poem? Do you note any changes in tone as the poem develops? By what details is such a change, if any, developed? And why are such changes important?

The Wild Swans at Coole

William Butler Yeats   [*1865–1939*]

The trees are in their autumn beauty,
The woodland paths are dry,
Under the October twilight the water
Mirrors a still sky;
Upon the brimming water among the stones   5
Are nine-and-fifty swans.

The nineteenth autumn has come upon me
Since I first made my count;
I saw, before I had well finished,
All suddenly mount   10
And scatter wheeling in great broken rings
Upon their clamorous wings.

I have looked upon those brilliant creatures,
And now my heart is sore.
All's changed since I, hearing at twilight,   15

The first time on this shore,
The bell-beat of their wings above my head,
Trod with a lighter tread.

Unwearied still, lover by lover,
They paddle in the cold   20
Companionable streams or climb the air;
Their hearts have not grown old;
Passion or conquest, wander where they will,
Attend upon them still.

But now they drift on the still water,   25
Mysterious, beautiful;
Among what rushes will they build,
By what lake's edge or pool
Delight men's eyes when I awake some day
To find they have flown away?   30

Coole was the estate of Lady Augusta Gregory, Yeats's friend and patron, who encouraged the young poet and made her house a second home to him. As line 7 indicates, the man who speaks this poem had first come to Coole some nineteen years before. Those years have left the swans apparently unchanged, but the man who has watched them through the years knows that he has greatly changed.

Questions

1. How central are the swans to the meaning of this poem? What do they represent? What do they stand for in the observer's experience? As a mere mark of unchangeableness against his changes? Or more?

2. In attempting an answer to the question just raised, it may be useful to compare the role of the swans in this poem with that of the hawk in "Hawk Roosting," or that of the "aged thrush" in Hardy's "The Darkling Thrush." For example, is Hardy's thrush a brave little stoic, or simply a high-hearted but ignorant child, able to endure with equanimity a world that the human observer regards as cold, bleak, and heartless? Or is he really the recipient of a revelation of some sort that is not available to the poet? What kind of world do the swans inhabit and what is their relation to it?

3. What is the force of lines 20–21: "They paddle in the cold / Companionable streams or climb the air"? Is "companionable" a normal adjective for a cold stream? Not from the human standpoint, surely?

4. Contrast this poem with "The Need of Being Versed in Country Things." Compare the roles of the phoebes in Frost's poem with that of the swans in Yeats's.

5. Try to sum up in one or two paragraphs the theme of this poem. Does it involve the relation of man to nature? If so, how does the speaker in the poem conceive that relationship?

Wild Swans

Edna St. Vincent Millay   [1892–1950]

I looked in my heart while the wild swans went over;—
  And what did I see I had not seen before?
  Only a question less or a question more;
Nothing to match the flight of wild birds flying.
Tiresome heart, forever living and dying!   5
  House without air! I leave you and lock your door!
Wild swans, come over the town, come over
The town again, trailing your legs and crying.

Questions

1. Compare this with Yeats's poem on the basis of tone. Be as specific
as possible in sorting out your evidence in both cases.

2. Can you relate differences in tone here to differences in theme?

Sailing to Byzantium

William Butler Yeats   [1865–1939]

That is no country for old men. The young
In one another's arms, birds in the trees
—Those dying generations—at their song,
The salmon-falls, the mackerel-crowded seas,
Fish, flesh, or fowl, commend all summer long   5
Whatever is begotten, born, and dies.
Caught in that sensual music all neglect
Monuments of unaging intellect.

An aged man is but a paltry thing,
A tattered coat upon a stick, unless   10
Soul clap its hands and sing, and louder sing
For every tatter in its mortal dress,
Nor is there singing school but studying
Monuments of its own magnificence;
And therefore I have sailed the seas and come   15
To the holy city of Byzantium.

O sages standing in God's holy fire
As in the gold mosaic of a wall,
Come from the holy fire, perne in a gyre,[1]
And be the singing-masters of my soul.   20
Consume my heart away; sick with desire

[1] spin off in a spiral

And fastened to a dying animal
It knows not what it is; and gather me
Into the artifice of eternity.

Once out of nature I shall never take   25
My bodily form from any natural thing,
But such a form as Grecian goldsmiths make
Of hammered gold and gold enameling
To keep a drowsy Emperor awake;
Or set upon a golden bough to sing   30
To lords and ladies of Byzantium
Of what is past, or passing, or to come.

The city of Byzantium was for centuries the capital of the Eastern
Roman Empire. Its period of greatest power and glory was that of the
Emperor Justinian the Great, who reigned 527–565. For what Byzantium
meant to Yeats one might consult Yeats's *A Vision* (1938 edition, pp.
279–280). Yeats associated it with an intellectual, non-representational art.
Such art did not imitate nature; it went beyond nature.

Though Yeats never visited Byzantium (modern Istanbul), he was acquainted with the great Byzantine mosaics in Italy—at Ravenna and at
Monreale. The sages mentioned in stanza 3 are probably drawn directly
from Yeats's memory of the procession of martyrs done in mosaic on the
north wall of San Appolinaire Nuovo, at Ravenna. In this connection, and
generally for Yeats's poetry, the reader might consult A. Norman Jeffares's
A Commentary on the Collected Poems of W. B. Yeats, 1968.

Questions

1. Why does the poet abandon Ireland for Byzantium? Is he leaving
"nature" or is "nature" abandoning him? What symbolism is here involved?

2. Work out the relation in this poem between the "birds in the trees
. . . at their song" (lines 2–3) and the bird fashioned by "Grecian goldsmiths" (line 27). What is the speaker's present relation to the birds of
nature (see line 10) and to the bird made of metal by clever artificers?

3. What does the golden bird stand for? Contrast its meaning with that
of the wild swans (pp. 351, 353).

4. What is the tone of stanza 2? Self-pity? Playful self-deprecation?
Stoic resignation? Or what? Against what standard is the human entrap-
ment in time set in this poem? Compare the situation here with that in
"The Wild Swans at Coole."

5. Try to state the theme of this poem and compare it with certain
other poems in this section that have to do with man's relation to nature
and "the burden of consciousness" that distinguishes man from other
natural creatures.

Ode to a Nightingale

John Keats [*1795–1821*]

My heart aches, and a drowsy numbness pains
  My sense, as though of hemlock I had drunk,
Or emptied some dull opiate to the drains
  One minute past, and Lethe-wards had sunk:
'Tis not through envy of thy happy lot,   5
  But being too happy in thy happiness,—
    That thou, light-wingèd Dryad of the trees,
      In some melodious plot
  Of beechen green, and shadows numberless,
    Singest of summer in full-throated ease.   10

O for a draught of vintage! that hath been
  Cooled a long age in the deep-delvèd earth,
Tasting of Flora and the country-green,
  Dance, and Provençal song, and sunburnt mirth!
O for a beaker full of the warm South,   15
  Full of the true, the blushful Hippocrene,
    With beaded bubbles winking at the brim,
      And purple-stainèd mouth;
  That I might drink, and leave the world unseen,
    And with thee fade away into the forest dim: 20

Fade far away, dissolve, and quite forget
  What thou among the leaves hast never known,
The weariness, the fever, and the fret
  Here, where men sit and hear each other groan;
Where palsy shakes a few, sad, last gray hairs,   25
  Where youth grows pale, and spectre-thin, and dies;
    Where but to think is to be full of sorrow
      And leaden-eyed despairs,
  Where Beauty cannot keep her lustrous eyes,
    Or new Love pine at them beyond tomorrow.   30

Away! away! for I will fly to thee,
  Not charioted by Bacchus and his pards,
But on the viewless wings of Poesy,
  Though the dull brain perplexes and retards:
Already with thee! tender is the night,   35
  And haply the Queen-Moon is on her throne,
    Clustered around by all her starry Fays;
      But here there is no light,
  Save what from heaven is with the breezes blown
    Through verdurous glooms and winding mossy ways.   40

I cannot see what flowers are at my feet,
    Nor what soft incense hangs upon the boughs,
But, in embalmèd darkness, guess each sweet
    Wherewith the seasonable month endows
The grass, the thicket, and the fruit-tree wild;   45
    White hawthorn, and the pastoral eglantine;
    Fast-fading violets covered up in leaves;
        And mid-May's eldest child,
    The coming musk-rose, full of dewy wine,
        The murmurous haunt of flies on summer eves.   50

Darkling I listen; and, for many a time
    I have been half in love with easeful Death,
Called him soft names in many a musèd rhyme,
    To take into the air my quiet breath;
Now more than ever seems it rich to die,   55
    To cease upon the midnight with no pain,
        While thou art pouring forth thy soul abroad
            In such an ecstasy!
    Still wouldst thou sing, and I have ears in vain—
        To thy high requiem become a sod.   60

Thou wast not born for death, immortal Bird!
    No hungry generations tread thee down;
The voice I hear this passing night was heard
    In ancient days by emperor and clown:
Perhaps the self-same song that found a path   65
    Through the sad heart of Ruth, when, sick for home,
        She stood in tears amid the alien corn;
            The same that oft-times hath
    Charmed magic casements, opening on the foam
        Of perilous seas, in faery lands forlorn.   70

Forlorn! the very word is like a bell
    To toll me back from thee to my sole self!
Adieu! the fancy cannot cheat so well
    As she is famed to do, deceiving elf.
Adieu! adieu! thy plaintive anthem fades   75
    Past the near meadows, over the still stream,
        Up the hill-side; and now 'tis buried deep
        In the next valley-glades:
Was it a vision, or a waking dream?
Fled is that music:—Do I wake or sleep?   80

In "Sailing to Byzantium" the speaker, an aging man, yearns to leave
the world of nature, the world of whatever is "begotten, born, and dies,"
and enter into a world of changeless forms. In "Ode to a Nightingale," the
speaker, a young man, yearns to free himself from the burden of human
cares and anxieties and to immerse himself in the world of nature (lines

20–30). As the speaker listens to the bird singing out of the darkness, he tries through an act of sympathetic imagination to enter the world that the nightingale inhabits (lines 31–34). It is a peaceful realm, without anxiety or competition, a realm of fruition, fulfillment, and perfect harmony (lines 35–50).

Midway in the poem the speaker has told us that what makes difficult his joining the nightingale in its realm of happiness is the "dull brain [that] perplexes and retards" (line 34). Moreover, in the last two lines of stanza 2 and the first two lines of stanza 3, his wish to join the nightingale is expressed in a rather significant way. He wishes, he says, to "leave the world unseen, / And with thee fade away into the forest dim: / Fade far away, dissolve, and quite forget / What thou among the leaves hast never known." It is his anxiety about the future, his memories of the past, his consciousness itself that he would be rid of, and must be rid of if he is to inhabit the nightingale's world. Significantly, the very process of moving into the nightingale's world is described as a fading into nature.

The emphasis on *unseen, fade,* and *dim* is appropriate and full of meaning. The nightingale characteristically sings in darkness, and the poet not only stresses this fact of natural history, but fills the whole ode with darkness: "shadows numberless" (line 9), "verdurous glooms" (line 40), and images of fading and dissolving. The word *fade* ("fades," "fading") occurs four times in the poem.

The poet seems to suggest that the discrete objects and separated "things" into which the world of our daylight experience is fragmented become merged in the darkness. They become unified and unperplexing. The poet says he "cannot see what flowers are at [his] feet," (line 41). From them arises a "soft incense," but he is left to "guess each sweet/ Wherewith the seasonable month endows/The grass" (lines 43–45). He seems to have merged into the world of natural things but in line 43 he refers to the darkness in which he stands as "embalmèd"* as if he were entombed rather than enwombed in nature.

Yet the reader is probably not shocked by the word "embalmed," for if darkness is associated with the womb, it is also associated with death. Only a few lines later the speaker will make this hint of death quite explicit with his confession that "for many a time/I have been half in love with easeful Death," and his statement that "Now more than ever seems it rich to die, . . ." In the third and fourth stanzas, as we have seen, the listener expressed his yearning to enter into the world of the nightingale, which is harmonious, natural, and free of anxiety and "leaden-eyed despairs." He wished to throw off the burden of human self-consciousness. But to subside

---

* The etymology of the word suggests the ease with which the poet can move from his sense of darkness sweet with the incense of flowers to a body prepared for the grave, for to *embalm* is to anoint a body with fragrant perfumes and aromatic gums.

completely into nature and to free oneself from *all* human consciousness is to die.

To be sure, in this setting and at this moment, death seems not a dreadful deprivation, but rich, a kind of fulfillment—something very different from the way it had appeared in stanzas 1 and 3. But Keats does not delude himself. He knows what death entails. Because of his medical training, he knew, more than most young men, the nature of the body and what happens to it when the heart ceases to beat. He is fully aware that to die to the "high requiem" (line 60) of the nightingale's song would entail losing the very richness of the nightingale's world and becoming deaf to its "high requiem." For to "dissolve" into nature is to become insensate, to become part of the blind and deaf world into which the human body—and the nightingale's body too—will ultimately be merged.

Yet, doesn't Keats in the very next line call the nightingale immortal? He does; but in no sense contradicting what has just been said. He addresses the nightingale thus: "Thou wast not born for death, immortal Bird!" (line 61). But surely the context of the poem makes plain in what way the nightingale is immortal: it does not live under the shadow of death; no "hungry generations" tread it down (line 62) as they threaten to tread down the anxious human being. The nightingale has almost no prevision of the future and almost no memory of the past. It lives in a kind of timeless present, and it has no intimation that its timeless present will ever flow away. All of this is a way of saying that the nightingale's immortality resides in the fact that it does not bear the burden of consciousness that every human being is forced to bear.

This great ode, then, is not merely a piece of intricate verbal tapestry nor merely a rich froth of emotion. It is a profound statement about the human predicament. Though man possesses a consciousness that for him endows the nightingale's song with a multiplicity of significances that make it infinitely rich and poignant, man yearns at times to be freed of the burden of consciousness. But man cannot have it both ways, and the last stanza of the poem reveals the speaker's sorrowful acceptance of the situation. The listener, who at the beginning of the poem had wished to "fade away" into the nightingale's world, now hears the nightingale's song, no longer as a high requiem, but as a "plaintive anthem," which "fades" away, "Past the near meadows, over the still stream,/Up the hill-side" until it is finally "buried deep/In the next valley-glades" (lines 75–78).

Questions

1. The phrase "alien corn" (line 67) comes with special poignance. Why would "alien trees" or "alien hills"—apart from the loss of the rhyme—be less moving?

2. What changes in the meaning of the word *forlorn* occur between lines 70 and 71?

3. This poem has been justly celebrated for its evocative quality, for

its scenes that shimmer with the magic of the imagination, and for the richness of its sensual imagery. But could one also argue that, along with the aforementioned qualities, it is essentially a very hard-headed and tough-minded account of the human predicament as many a modern poet sees it? Do you agree, and if you do, how would you justify this claim for the poem's modernity? Does the poet provide an easy—and sentimental—solution for the problem described, or does he leave the reader to confront it with his own resources of self-understanding and moral strength?

4. Compare the nightingale as Keats treats it in this poem with Hardy's thrush (p. 345) or Yeats's wild swans (p. 351). The attraction of the golden bird of Byzantium (p. 353) is that it is not subject to time. Keats makes a like claim for his nightingale. How does its immortality differ from that of the golden bird?

Afterword

In this section of our book we have limited ourselves to poems in which birds figure, but, as we have said, only in the interest of providing a device that may make it easier to compare significant differences among them. Within the poems we have studied, however, there is a very wide range in the use of the bird in developing the theme. In some of these poems the bird is little more than a part of the natural landscape; in other poems, its voice seems to become the very voice of nature itself. Sometimes the bird is almost peripheral to the scene, amounting to little more than an illustration or an ornament; but on occasion the bird becomes the central symbol.

Some of the birds are described in human terms and become almost caricatures of types of human beings. But others are separated from humanity by a great chasm. They inhabit a world to which the suffering mortal can never attain, as, for example, Keats's nightingale does. Or they may exhibit nature's indifference to man, as do Frost's phoebes, for whom men are an irrelevance. Indeed, the poet often uses the bird to depict—by negatives, by contrast—what man is and how he is situated with reference to the nature that surrounds him, and of which, in some sense, he is a part.

Yet, important as the thematic material is, and as useful for the study of man in relation to nature and the natural world that he inhabits, in the poems of this section we have been primarily interested in studying another matter—or rather, a series of other matters. For the poems that we have been reading are not little essays on the relation of man to nature. They are poems, and that means that they present their themes through poetic means. The poetic methods and techniques are a very important part of what we have been studying here.

Two matters might be selected for particular emphasis. In the first place, we have been engaged in this section of the book in a study of how a poet uses images, how they aid in the presentation of the theme, and, in many specific instances, what the poet has been able to do with them. They range from fairly simple images presented as part of the natural scene, images that are incidental to the dramatic presentation of the theme, on up to central symbols that constitute the very core of the presentation. The images become the primary element in functional metaphors, or else are turned into massive symbols.

Though some of the critics of the neoclassical age tended to dismiss the function of metaphor as mere embellishment or illustration, we shall find in the poems of this section very few instances of images with so minimal a function. The comparison of the Solitary Reaper's song (p. 363) to that of the nightingale and the cuckoo could tempt the casual reader to say that the birds are used here merely to associate natural beauty with the Highland girl's song, or to associate it with a romantic scene; but, as we shall see, the bird-girl comparisons do far more than that, and in Wordsworth's poem they prove to be the most delicate and yet forceful way in which the poet could describe the precise effect of the girl's song.

To take an instance from an earlier section, Shakespeare's mention of the cuckoo and the owl in his "Spring" and "Winter" songs (pp. 85, 86) may seem casual and incidental; and yet the two birds, as he has used them, turn out to be important for the theme. The easiest way to prove this would be to have the cuckoo in the "Spring" song do the expected thing and sing a merry note, and to have the owl in the "Winter" song pronounce a note of warning and fear. The view of life presented would then be reduced to banality.

Often in these poems the bird is, as one would expect, a representative of nature itself, but nature can be seen by the human observer in many lights, and the birds as actually used in the poems represent a great many aspects of nature that have, throughout the ages, tantalized man. There are Frost's phoebes, whose song seems plaintive to the man coming upon the abandoned barn in which they rest; there is Hardy's thrush, whose song seems joyful, though the natural scene seems to the poet black and melancholy. There are Yeats's swans, whose power and elegance and apparent imperviousness to time provoke the envy of the sorrowful human being. There is the nightingale of Keats, whose joy and happy accommodation to nature—and apparent imperviousness to time—are so attractive to the young poet, who cannot forget that love wanes, that beautiful women become old and ugly, and that all human beings are attacked by disease and die. Indeed, in certain respects, the Yeats and Keats poems are remarkably alike. One could actually argue that Yeats has made his swans "immortal birds" for the same reason that Keats regarded his nightingale as "immortal." And yet how different are the birds, and how different the poems! And granted the thematic likenesses between the poems, how different they are in mood and tone—in, we might say, their feeling, their life-sense.

The second poetic element that we have been studying in working through this group of poems is the matter of tone. The poems we have been studying range from gay to grave, from melancholy to playful, from ironic to exalted. Most of all, it should be apparent by now that the very thing the poet is saying in these poems is qualified by the tone of voice in which it is said. A whole attitude toward the bird, toward the natural scene, and toward the speaker is implied in the poem. It may actually become the central fact of the poem.

The richest and most powerful of the poems in this section show not only a masterful control of tone, they exhibit complexity of tone and, through the development of the poem, shifts of tone. If readers can see the importance of tone and learn to discriminate with some sensitivity among the various kinds of tone, they will have gone a long way toward appreciating and evaluating poetry, whether it concerns birds or gods or men.

The following group of supplemental poems will provide opportunities for students to test for themselves how much they have learned about poetic technique and in particular about how much they have learned about the poet's handling of imagery and control of tone. We present them with a minimum of commentary. We have supplied some notes having to do with unusual words, biographical facts about the author, or historical setting. We have also supplied a few questions mainly to suggest some of the areas worth exploration.

Supplemental Poems

The Eagle

Alfred, Lord Tennyson [*1809–1892*]

> He clasps the crag with crooked hands;
> Close to the sun in lonely lands,
> Ringed with the azure world he stands.
>
> The wrinkled sea beneath him crawls;
> He watches from his mountain walls,   5
> And like a thunderbolt he falls.

Questions

1. What does the poet accomplish by giving the eagle "crooked hands" (line 1) rather than, say, the "hooked feet" of "Hawk Roosting" (p. 342)? What does he imply by referring to the eagle's "mountain walls" (line 5) rather than, perhaps, "mountain peaks"?

2. What are the implications of "Close to the sun" (line 2) and "Ringed with the azure world" (line 3)? Why "azure"? If the poet had simply written "quite high up on the crags" what would be lost?

3. Can it be said that the poet gives us an eagle's eye view of the world in lines 3 and 4? Why does he call the sea "wrinkled"? What is suggested by saying that the sea "crawls"?

4. Does the last line provide a kind of climax to the poem? How does it do so?

5. It may be said that in "Hawk Roosting" the poet is actually writing an ironic, or even satirical, comment on certain aspects of human nature—at least a "critical" view of it. Could this be said of Tennyson's poem?

Gamecock

James Dickey [*1923*–]

Fear, jealousy and murder are the same
When they put on their long reddish feathers,
Their shawl neck and moccasin head
In a tree bearing levels of women.
There is yet no thread   5

Of light, and his scabbed feet tighten,
Holding sleep as though it were lockjaw,
His feathers damp, his eyes crazed
And cracked like the eyes
Of a chicken head cut off or wrung-necked   10

While he waits for the sun's only cry
All night building up in his throat
To leap out and turn the day red,
To tumble his hens from the pine tree,
And then will go down, his hackles   15

Up, looking everywhere for the other
Cock who could not be there,
Head ruffed and sullenly stepping
As upon his best human-curved steel:
He is like any fierce   20

Old man in a terminal ward:
There is the same look of waiting
That the sun prepares itself for;
The enraged, surviving-
another-day blood,   25

And from him at dawn comes the same
Cry that the world cannot stop.
In all the great building's blue windows
The sun gains strength; on all floors, women
Awaken—wives, nurses, sisters and daughters—   30

And he lies back, his eyes filmed, unappeased,
As all of them, clucking, pillow-patting,
Come to help his best savagery blaze, doomed, dead-
game, demanding, unreasonably
Battling to the death for what is his.   35

This poem begins with a morning scene in which the gamecock sits guarding his hens (referred to as "women" in line 4), who are roosting in the pine tree on a branch of which he sits. He is waiting for the first dawning of light to release from his throat the cockcrow that is at once a challenge and a cry of triumph.

Questions

1. Have you ever seen a gamecock? If not, a picture—especially a picture of gamecocks fighting—may help you to appreciate such descriptive touches as "shawl neck" and "moccasin head" (line 3), the cock's "crazed eyes" (lines 8–9), his "hackles" (lines 15–16), his "ruffed" head (line 18) and his gait (lines 18–19).

2. In lines 20–21 the poet begins a long simile by saying that the gamecock "is like any fierce / Old man in a terminal ward: . . ." The rest of the poem develops this long simile with a detailed description of the old man, obviously dying, who still seems to dominate and lord it over the "wives, nurses, sisters, and daughters" that hover about him in the hospital. But which is being compared to which: the gamecock to the fierce old man? Or the man to the gamecock? Does it make any difference? Would it surprise you to be told that the poet's father died of cancer in such a "terminal ward"? What is the attitude toward the dying man? Is this poem, which stresses the old man's fierceness and his "unreasonable" fight for his life, actually tender and admiring?

The Solitary Reaper

William Wordsworth [*1770–1850*]

Behold her, single in the field,
Yon solitary Highland Lass!
Reaping and singing by herself;
Stop here, or gently pass!
Alone she cuts and binds the grain,   5
And sings a melancholy strain;
O listen! for the Vale profound
Is overflowing with the sound.

No Nightingale did ever chaunt
More welcome notes to weary bands   10
Of travelers in some shady haunt,
Among Arabian sands:

A voice so thrilling ne'er was heard
In spring-time from the Cuckoo-bird,
Breaking the silence of the seas   15
Among the farthest Hebrides.

Will no one tell me what she sings?—
Perhaps the plaintive numbers flow
For old, unhappy, far-off things,
And battles long ago: 20
Or is it some more humble lay,
Familiar matter of today?
Some natural sorrow, loss, or pain,
That has been, and may be again?

Whate'er the theme, the Maiden sang   25
As if her song could have no ending;
I saw her singing at her work,
And o'er the sickle bending;—
I listened, motionless and still;
And, as I mounted up the hill,   30
The music in my heart I bore,
Long after it was heard no more.

This poem is deceptively simple. The plot of the little incident is told rather straightforwardly in stanzas 1, 3, and 4. The traveler cannot make out the words of the song, because, presumably, they are in Gaelic, the native language of the Scottish Highlands.

Stanza 2, with its comparison of the girl's song to those of the cuckoo and the nightingale may easily be dismissed as vaguely ornamental comparisons. But we suggest that they are much more than that and that the answer to why the girl's singing made such an impression on the traveler is told us through these comparisons. With that possibility in mind, the reader might ponder the following questions.

Questions

1. A bird sings for no audience—is merely overheard. Like the peasant girl's song, it is without intelligible words. Could one say that, furthermore, the bird sings as if its "song could have no ending" (line 26)? What, then, are some of the other ways in which the girl's song resembles no song of art but of nature?

2. If, on hearing a bird sing, we sometimes feel that we are hearing the voice of nature itself, could we, in overhearing the girl's song (under the circumstances described), feel that we were overhearing the voice of *human* nature itself? In this connection, remember that human beings can sophisticate their utterances, but bird's cannot. They are always sincere. Are those elements active here in the girl-bird comparisons?

3. Comment on the poignance of lines 15–16. Where are the Hebrides? Who is imagined to be hearing the cuckoo's song in this instance?

Lady Lost

John Crowe Ransom [*1888–1974*]

This morning, flew up the lane
A timid lady bird to our birdbath
And eyed her image dolefully as death;
This afternoon, knocked on our windowpane
To be let in from the rain.   5

And when I caught her eye
She looked aside, but at the clapping thunder
And sight of the whole world blazing up like tinder
Looked in on us again so miserably
It was as if she would cry.   10

So I will go out into the park and say,
"Who has lost a delicate brown-eyed lady
In the West End section? Or has anybody
Injured some fine woman in some dark way
Last night, or yesterday?   15

"Let the owner come and claim possession,
No questions will be asked. But stroke her gently
With loving words, and she will evidently
Return to her full soft-haired white-breasted fashion
And her right home and her right passion."   20

Questions

1. Lines 12–15 evidently glance at the Philomela legend, but at the end the poet seems to allude to one of several fairy tales in which a human being has been turned through enchantment into a bird or animal, and may, with the right spell, be restored to human form. How seriously are we to regard the injury dealt to the woman-bird? Surely, she has not suffered at the hands of a modern-day Tereus? How would you describe the tone of lines 13–15?

2. In discussing "Gamecock" (p. 362), we asked whether the poem was primarily about a bird or a man. Is this poem primarily about a bird or a woman?

3. What is the tone of this poem? Obviously the tone has everything to do with whether the reader will dismiss it as fanciful nonsense or accept it as delightful whimsy of the sort that may give an insight into human affairs.

Nightingales

Robert Bridges   [*1844–1930*]

Beautiful must be the mountains whence ye come,
And bright in the fruitful valleys the streams wherefrom
    Ye learn your song:
Where are those starry woods? O might I wander there,
  Among the flowers, which in that heavenly air   5
    Bloom the year long!

Nay, barren are those mountains and spent the streams:
Our song is the voice of desire, that haunts our dreams,
    A throe of the heart,
Whose pining visions dim, forbidden hopes profound,   10
  No dying cadence nor long sigh can sound,
    For all our art.

Alone, aloud in the raptured ear of men
We pour our dark nocturnal secret; and then,
    As night is withdrawn   15
From these sweet-springing meads and bursting boughs of May,
  Dream, while the innumerable choir of day
    Welcome the dawn.

Clearly Robert Bridges in writing this poem was not interested in whether the nightingale, as a matter of natural fact, sings out of joy or of sorrow. To approach his basic concern, let us compare Bridges's poem with Shelley's "To a Skylark." Because Shelley believes that the beauty of the skylark's song must issue from an intense joy, he asks the bird to say "What objects are the fountains / Of thy happy strain? / What fields, or waves, or mountains? / What shapes of sky or plain?" Shelley goes on to say that "Our sweetest songs" (that is, the songs of mortal men) are so different. "Our sweetest songs are those that tell of saddest thought." The questioner in "Nightingales" starts from the same premise: because the song of the nightingales is so beautiful, they must inhabit a kind of paradise. But the nightingales reject his assumption and make it plain that their song springs from deprivation and loss.

Questions

1. Would Bridges, do you suppose, put Shelley's skylark in with the more trivial singers that make up the "choir of day" (line 17)?

2. What is the meaning of "dark nocturnal secret" (line 14)? It is a rich and evocative phrase. What does it imply? Does Keats's nightingale also utter a "dark nocturnal secret"? Or would the quality of its song

have to be expressed in different terms? What about the "secret" of
Arnold's nightingale?

3. Is this poem really about nature or about art? About birds or
about poets and musicians? Or about general human experience?

No Swan So Fine

Marianne Moore [*1887–1972*]

> "No water so still as the
>   dead fountains of Versailles." No swan,
> with swart blind look askance
> and gondoliering legs, so fine
>   as the chintz china one with fawn-   5
> brown eyes and toothed gold
> collar on to show whose bird it was.
>
> Lodged in the Louis Fifteenth
>   candelabrum-tree of cockscomb-
> tinted buttons, dahlias,   10
> sea urchins, and everlastings,
>   it perches on the branching foam
> of polished sculptured
> flowers—at ease and tall. The king is dead.

Marianne Moore supplies two notes on this poem: the first tells us that
she has in mind a Louis XV candelabrum ornamented with Dresden china
figures of swans. It had come into the possession of Lord Balfour. The
second note identifies the quotation in lines 1 and 2. It is from an article
by Percy Phillip in *The New York Times Magazine* for May 10, 1931.
This quotation provides the "text," as it were, upon which the poet develops her commentary. But only insofar as we explore the poem itself
shall we be able to see how it constitutes the text.

Questions

1. What is the poet's attitude toward art versus nature? Does she
opt for the permanence of art at any cost, and so assume that the porcelain swan is really finer than the living swan? Or is her attitude more
complicated than that?

2. Are we forced to choose between art and nature—between the
thing that was never alive but may endure for centuries and the live and
vital creature that is doomed to old age and death? Surely we want
both. Is there any real competition between them? Yet, people are constantly comparing one with the other and forcing themselves to say that

the one is more "lifelike" or more "valuable" than the other. In saying that the live swan is not so "fine" as the porcelain swan, is the poet here making such a choice? If you say that she is not, justify your statement.

3. Can you see now the bearing of the passage quoted in lines 1 and 2 on the theme of the poem? If you think you can, try to put it in a brief statement.

POEMS FOR STUDY

7

The poems in this section, which are from the late nineteenth and the twentieth centuries, are presented without comments or questions. We feel that there may be, at this point in the book, positive advantages, in fact, a liberating experience, in offering an immediate and naked confrontation with the particular poem. In any case, it will give you a chance to discover what a first, innocent reading may yield; and if you sense that there remain in the poem further meanings and resonances to be explored, the poem will provide you with an opportunity to test how much you have learned about how to conduct such explorations.

A Grave

Marianne Moore [1887–1972]

    Man looking into the sea
    taking the view from those who have as much right to it as you
        have to it yourself,
    it is human nature to stand in the middle of a thing,

but you cannot stand in the middle of this;
the sea has nothing to give but a well excavated grave.   5
The firs stand in a procession, each with an emerald turkey-foot at
        the top,
reserved as their contours, saying nothing;
repression, however, is not the most obvious characteristic of the sea;
the sea is a collector, quick to return a rapacious look.
There are others besides you who have worn that look—   10
Whose expression is no longer a protest; the fish no longer investigate
        them
for their bones have not lasted:
men lower nets, unconscious of the fact that they are desecrating a
        grave,
and row quickly away—the blades of the oars
moving together like the feet of water-spiders as if there were no
        such thing as death.   15
The wrinkles progress among themselves in a phalanx—beautiful
        under networks of foam,
and fade breathlessly while the sea rustles in and out of the seaweed;
the birds swim through the air at top speed, emitting cat-calls as
        heretofore—
the tortoise-shell scourges about the feet of the cliffs, in motion
        beneath them;
and the ocean, under the pulsation of lighthouses and noise of
        bell-buoys,   20
advances as usual, looking as if it were not that ocean in which
        dropped things are bound to sink—
into which if they turn and twist, it is neither with volition nor
        consciousness.

Little Exercise

Elizabeth Bishop [*1911–*]

Think of the storm roaming the sky uneasily
like a dog looking for a place to sleep in,
listen to it growling.

Think how they must look now, the mangrove keys   5
lying out there unresponsive to the lightning
in dark, coarse-fibered families,

where occasionally a heron may undo his head,
shake up his feathers, make an uncertain comment
when the surrounding water shines.

Think of the boulevard and the little palm trees   10
all stuck in rows, suddenly revealed
as fistfuls of limp fish-skeletons.

It is raining there. The boulevard
and its broken sidewalks with weeds in every crack,
are relieved to be wet, the sea to be freshened.   15

Now the storm goes away again in a series
of small, badly lit battle-scenes,
each in "Another part of the field."

Think of someone sleeping in the bottom of a row-boat
tied to a mangrove root or the pile of a bridge;   20
think of him as uninjured, barely disturbed.

The Snow-Storm

Ralph Waldo Emerson [*1803–1882*]

Announced by all the trumpets of the sky,
Arrives the snow, and, driving o'er the fields,
Seems nowhere to alight: the whited air
Hides hills and woods, the river, and the heaven,
And veils the farm-house at the garden's end.   5
The sled and traveller stopped, the courier's feet
Delayed, all friends shut out, the housemates sit
Around the radiant fireplace, enclosed
In a tumultous privacy of storm.

   Come see the north wind's masonry.   10
Out of an unseen quarry evermore
Furnished with tile, the fierce artificer
Curves his white bastions with projected roof
Round every windward stake, or tree, or door.
Speeding, the myriad-handed, his wild work   15
So fanciful, so savage, nought cares he
For number or proportion. Mockingly,
On coop or kennel he hangs Parian wreaths;
A swan-like form invests the hidden thorn;
Fills up the farmer's lane from wall to wall,   20
Maugre the farmer's sighs; and at the gate
A tapering turret overtops the work.
And when his hours are numbered, and the world
Is all his own, retiring, as he were not,
Leaves, when the sun appears, astonished Art   25
To mimic in slow structures, stone by stone,
Built in an age, the mad wind's night-work,
The frolic architecture of the snow.

Snow-Flakes

Henry Wadsworth Longfellow   [*1807–1882*]

Out of the bosom of the Air,
  Out of the cloud-folds of her garments shaken,
Over the woodlands brown and bare,
  Over the harvest-fields forsaken,
    Silent, and soft, and slow   5
    Descends the snow.

Even as our cloudy fancies take
  Suddenly shapes in some divine expression,
Even as the troubled heart doth make
  In the white countenance confession,   10
    The troubled sky reveals
    The grief it feels.

This is the poem of the air,
  Slowly in silent syllables recorded;
This is the secret of despair,   15
  Long in its cloudy bosom hoarded,
    Now whispered and revealed
    To wood and field.

The Season 'Tis, My Lovely Lambs

E. E. Cummings   [*1894–1962*]

the season 'tis, my lovely lambs,

of Sumner Volstead Christ and Co.
the epoch of Mann's righteousness
the age of dollars and no sense.
Which being quite beyond dispute   5

as prove from Troy (N. Y.) to Cairo
(Egypt) the luminous dithyrambs
of large immaculate unmute
antibolshevistic gents
(each manufacturing word by word   10
his own unrivalled brand of pyro
-technic blurb anent the (hic)
hero dead that gladly (sic)
in far lands perished of unheard
of maladies including flu)   15

my little darlings, let us now
passionately remember how—

braving the worst, of peril heedless,
each braver than the other, each
(a typewriter within his reach)   20
upon his fearless derrière
sturdily seated—Colonel Needless
To Name and General You know who
a string of pretty medals drew

(while messrs jack james john and jim   25
in token of their country's love
received my dears the order of
The Artificial Arm and Limb)

—or, since bloodshed and kindred questions
inhibit unprepared digestions,   30
come: let us mildly contemplate
beginning with his wellfilled pants
earth's biggest grafter, nothing less;
the Honorable Mr. (guess)
who, breathing on the ear of fate,   35
landed a seat in the legislat-
ure whereas tommy so and so
(an erring child of circumstance
whom the bulls nabbed at 33rd)

pulled six months for selling snow   40

Epitaph on an Army of Mercenaries
A. E. Housman   [1859–1936]

These, in the day when heaven was falling,
  The hour when earth's foundations fled,
Followed their mercenary calling
  And took their wages and are dead.

Their shoulders held the sky suspended;   5
  They stood, and earth's foundations stay;
What God abandoned, these defended,
  And saved the sum of things for pay.

Ode to the Confederate Dead
Allen Tate   [1899–   ]

Row after row with strict impunity
The headstones yield their names to the element,
The wind whirrs without recollection;
In the riven troughs the splayed leaves

Pile up, of nature the casual sacrament 5
To the seasonal eternity of death;
Then driven by the fierce scrutiny
Of heaven to their election in the vast breath,
They sough the rumor of mortality.

Autumn is desolation in the plot 10
Of a thousand acres where these memories grow
From the inexhaustible bodies that are not
Dead, but feed the grass row after rich row.
Think of the autumns that have come and gone!—
Ambitious November with the humors of the year, 15
With a particular zeal for every slab,
Staining the uncomfortable angels that rot
On the slabs, a wing chipped here, an arm there:
The brute curiosity of an angel's stare
Turns you, like them, to stone, 20
Transforms the heaving air
Till plunged to a heavier world below
You shift your sea-space blindly
Heaving, turning like the blind crab.

   Dazed by the wind, only the wind 25
   The leaves flying, plunge

You know who have waited by the wall
The twilight certainty of an animal,
Those midnight restitutions of the blood
You know—the immitigable pines, the smoky frieze 30
Of the sky, the sudden call: you know the rage,
The cold pool left by the mounting flood,
Of muted Zeno and Parmenides.
You who have waited for the angry resolution
Of those desires that should be yours tomorrow, 35
You know the unimportant shrift of death
And praise the vision
And praise the arrogant circumstance
Of those who fall
Rank upon rank, hurried beyond decision— 40
Here by the sagging gate, stopped by the wall.

   Seeing, seeing only the leaves
   Flying, plunge and expire

Turn your eyes to the immoderate past,
Turn to the inscrutable infantry rising 45
Demons out of the earth—they will not last.
Stonewall, Stonewall, and the sunken fields of hemp,
Shiloh, Antietam, Malvern Hill, Bull Run.
Lost in that orient of the thick-and-fast
You will curse the setting sun. 50

Cursing only the leaves crying
Like an old man in a storm

You hear the shout, the crazy hemlocks point
With troubled fingers to the silence which
Smothers you, a mummy, in time.   55

        The hound bitch
Toothless and dying, in a musty cellar
Hears the wind only.

        Now that the salt of their blood
Stiffens the saltier oblivion of the sea,   60
Seals the malignant purity of the flood,
What shall we who count our days and bow
Our heads with a commemorial woe
In the ribboned coats of grim felicity,
What shall we say of the bones, unclean,   65
Whose verdurous anonymity will grow?
The ragged arms, the ragged heads and eyes
Lost in these acres of the insane green?
The gray lean spiders come, they come and go;
In a tangle of willows without light   70
The singular screech-owl's tight
Invisible lyric seeds the mind
With the furious murmur of their chivalry.

    We shall say only the leaves
    Flying, plunge and expire   75

We shall say only the leaves whispering
In the improbable mist of nightfall
That flies on multiple wing:
Night is the beginning and the end
And in between the ends of distraction   80
Waits mute speculation, the patient curse
That stones the eyes, or like the jaguar leaps
For his own image in a jungle pool, his victim.
What shall we say who have knowledge
Carried to the heart? Shall we take the act   85
To the grave? Shall we, more hopeful, set up the grave
In the house? The ravenous grave?

        Leave now
The shut gate and the decomposing wall:
The gentle serpent, green in the mulberry bush,   90
Riots with his tongue through the hush—
Sentinel of the grave who counts us all!

The Heron

Vernon Watkins [*1906–1967*]

The cloud-backed heron will not move:
He stares into the stream.
He stands unfaltering while the gulls
And oyster-catchers scream.
He does not hear, he cannot see   5
The great white horses of the sea,
But fixes eyes on stillness
Below their flying team.

How long will he remain, how long
Have the gray woods been green?   10
The sky and the reflected sky,
Their glass he has not seen,
But silent as a speck of sand
Interpreting the sea and land,
His fall pulls down the fabric   15
Of all that windy scene.

Sailing with clouds and woods behind,
Pausing in leisured flight,
He stepped, alighting on a stone,
Dropped from the stars of night.   20
He stood there unconcerned with day,
Deaf to the tumult of the bay,
Watching a stone in water,
A fish's hidden light.

Sharp rocks drive back the breaking waves,   25
Confusing sea with air.
Bundles of spray blown mountain-high
Have left the shingle bare.
A shipwrecked anchor wedged by rocks,
Loosed by the thundering equinox,   30
Divides the herded waters,
The stallion and his mare.

Yet no distraction breaks the watch
Of that time-killing bird.
He stands unmoving on the stone;   35
Since dawn he has not stirred.
Calamity about him cries,
But he has fixed his golden eyes
On water's crooked tablet,
On light's reflected word.   40

The Gallows

Edward Thomas [*1878–1917*]

There was a weasel lived in the sun
With all his family,
Till a keeper shot him with his gun
And hung him up on a tree,
Where he swings in the wind and rain,   5
In the sun and in the snow,
Without pleasure, without pain,
On the dead oak tree bough.

There was a crow who was no sleeper,
But a thief and a murderer   10
Till a very late hour; and this keeper
Made him one of the things that were,
To hang and flap in rain and wind
In the sun and in the snow.
There are no more sins to be sinned   15
On the dead oak tree bough.

There was a magpie, too,
Had a long tongue and a long tail;
He could both talk and do—
But what did that avail?   20
He, too, flaps in the wind and rain
Alongside weasel and crow,
Without pleasure, without pain,
On the dead oak tree bough.

And many other beasts   25
And birds, skin, bone, and feather,
Have been taken from their feasts
And hung up there together.
To swing and have endless leisure
In the sun and in the snow,   30
Without pain, without pleasure,
On the dead oak tree bough.

The Cottage Hospital

John Betjeman [*1906–*]

At the end of a long-walled garden
   in a red provincial town,
A brick path led to a mulberry
   scanty grass at its feet.

I lay under blackening branches   5
    where the mulberry leaves hung down
Sheltering ruby fruit globes
    from a Sunday-tea-time heat.
Apple and plum espaliers
    basked upon bricks of brown;   10
The air was swimming with insects,
    and children played in the street.

Out of this bright intentness
    into the mulberry shade
Musca domestica (housefly)   15
    swung from the August light
Slap into slithery rigging
    by the waiting spider made
Which spun the lithe elastic
    till the fly was shrouded tight.   20
Down came the hairy talons
    and horrible poison blade
And none of the garden noticed
    that fizzing, hopeless fight.

Say in what Cottage Hospital   25
    whose pale green walls resound
With the tap upon polished parquet
    of inflexible nurses' feet
Shall I myself be lying
    when they range the screens around?   30
And say shall I groan in dying,
    as I twist the sweaty sheet?
Or gasp for breath uncrying,
    as I feel my senses drown'd
While the air is swimming with insects   35
    and children play in the street?

The Groundhog

Richard Eberhart [*1904–*]

In June, amid the golden fields,
I saw a groundhog lying dead.
Dead lay he; my senses shook,
And mind outshot our naked frailty.
There lowly in the vigorous summer   5
His form began its senseless change,
And made my senses waver dim
Seeing nature ferocious in him.
Inspecting close his maggots' might
And seething cauldron of his being,   10

Half with loathing, half with a strange love,
I poked him with an angry stick.
The fever arose, became a flame
And Vigor circumscribed the skies,
Immense energy in the sun,   15
And through my frame a sunless trembling.
My stick had done nor good nor harm.
Then stood I silent in the day
Watching the object, as before;
And kept my reverence for knowledge   20
Trying for control, to be still,
To quell the passion of the blood;
Until I had bent down on my knees
Praying for joy in the sight of decay.
And so I left; and I returned   25
In Autumn strict of eye, to see
The sap gone out of the groundhog,
But the bony sodden hulk remained.
But the year had lost its meaning,
And in intellectual chains   30
I lost both love and loathing,
Mured up in the wall of wisdom.
Another summer took the fields again
Massive and burning, full of life,
But when I chanced upon the spot   35
There was only a little hair left,
And bones bleaching in the sunlight
Beautiful as architecture;
I watched them like a geometer,
And cut a walking stick from a birch.   40
It has been three years, now.
There is no sign of the groundhog.
I stood there in the whirling summer,
My hand capped a withered heart,
And thought of China and of Greece,   45
Of Alexander in his tent;
Of Montaigne in his tower,
Of Saint Theresa in her wild lament.

The Heavy Bear Who Goes with Me

Delmore Schwartz   [*1913–1966*]

"the withness of the body"—Whitehead

The heavy bear who goes with me,
A manifold honey to smear his face,
Clumsy and lumbering here and there,

The central ton of every place,
The hungry beating brutish one   5
. In love with candy, anger, and sleep,
Crazy factotum, dishevelling all,
Climbs the building, kicks the football,
Boxes his brother in the hate-ridden city.

Breathing at my side, that heavy animal,   10
That heavy bear who sleeps with me,
Howls in his sleep for a world of sugar,
A sweetness intimate as the water's clasp,
Howls in his sleep because the tight-rope
Trembles and shows the darkness beneath.   15
—The strutting show-off is terrified,
Dressed in his dress-suit, bulging his pants,
Trembles to think that his quivering meat
Must finally wince to nothing at all.

That inescapable animal walks with me,   20
Has followed me since the black womb held,
Moves where I move, distorting my gesture,
A caricature, a swollen shadow,
A stupid clown of the spirit's motive,
Perplexes and affronts with his own darkness,   25
The secret life of belly and bone,
Opaque, too near, my private, yet unknown,
Stretches to embrace the very dear
With whom I would walk without him near,
Touches her grossly, although a word   30
Would bare my heart and make me clear,
Stumbles, flounders, and strives to be fed
Dragging me with him in his mouthing care.
Amid the hundred million of his kind,
The scrimmage of appetite everywhere.   35

Thou Art Indeed Just, Lord

Gerard Manley Hopkins [1844–1889]

Justus quidem tu es, Domine, si disputem tecum:
verumtamen justa loquar ad te: Quare via impiorum
prosperatur?[1]

Thou art indeed just, Lord, if I contend
With thee; but, sir, so what I plead is just.
Why do sinners' ways prosper? And why must
Disappointment all I endeavor end?
Wert thou my enemy, O thou my friend,   5

[1] Jeremiah 12:1; translated in lines 1–3

How wouldst thou worse, I wonder, than thou dost
Defeat, thwart me? Oh, the sots and thralls of lust
Do in spare hours more thrive than I that spend,
Sir, life upon thy cause. See, banks and brakes
Now, leavèd how thick! lacèd they are again   10
With fretty chervil, look, and fresh wind shakes
Them; birds build—but not I build; no, but strain,
Time's eunuch, and not breed one work that wakes.
Mine, O thou lord of life, send my roots rain.

Lucifer in Starlight

George Meredith   [*1828–1909*]

On a starred night Prince Lucifer uprose.
Tired of his dark dominion swung the fiend
Above the rolling ball in cloud part screened,
Where sinners hugged their specter of repose.
Poor prey to his hot fit of pride were those.   5
And now upon his western wing he leaned,
Now his huge bulk o'er Afric's sands careened,
Now the black planet shadowed Arctic snows.
Soaring through wider zones that pricked his scars
With memory of the old revolt from Awe,   10
He reached a middle height, and at the stars,
Which are the brain of heaven, he looked, and sank.
Around the ancient track marched, rank on rank,
The army of unalterable law.

The Visitant

Theodore Roethke   [*1908–1963*]

1

A cloud moved close. The bulk of the wind shifted.
A tree swayed overwater.
A voice said:
Stay. Stay by the slip-ooze. Stay.

Dearest tree, I said, may I rest here?   5
A ripple made a soft reply.
I waited, alert as a dog.
The leech clinging to a stone waited;
And the crab, the quiet breather.

2

Slow, slow as a fish she came,   10

Slow as a fish coming forward,
Swaying in a long wave;
Her skirts not touching a leaf,
Her white arms reaching towards me.

She came without sound,   15
Without brushing the wet stones,
In the soft dark of early evening,
She came,
The wind in her hair,
The moon beginning.   20

3
I woke in the first of morning.
Staring at a tree, I felt the pulse of a stone.
Where's she now, I kept saying.
Where's she now, the mountain's downy girl?

But the bright day had no answer.   25
A wind stirred in a web of appleworms;
The tree, the close willow, swayed.

Piano

D. H. Lawrence [1885–1930]

Softly, in the dusk, a woman is singing to me;
Taking me back down the vista of years, till I see
A child sitting under the piano, in the boom of the tingling strings
And pressing the small, poised feet of a mother who smiles as she
    sings.

In spite of myself, the insidious mastery of song   5
Betrays me back, till the heart of me weeps to belong
To the old Sunday evenings at home, with winter outside
And hymns in the cozy parlor, the tinkling piano our guide.

So now it is vain for the singer to burst into clamor
With the great black piano appassionato. The glamor   10
Of childish days is upon me, my manhood is cast
Down in the flood of remembrance, I weep like a child for the past.

Losses

Randall Jarrell [1914–1965]

It was not dying: everybody died.
It was not dying: we had died before
In the routine crashes—and our fields

Called up the papers, wrote home to our folks,
And the rates rose, all because of us.   5
We died on the wrong page of the almanac,
Scattered on mountains fifty miles away;
Diving on haystacks, fighting with a friend,
We blazed up on the lines we never saw.
We died like ants or pets or foreigners.   10
(When we left high school nothing else had died
For us to figure we had died like.)

In our new planes, with our new crews, we bombed
The ranges by the desert or the shore,
Fired at towed targets, waited for our scores—   15
And turned into replacements and woke up
One morning, over England, operational.
It wasn't different: but if we died
It was not an accident but a mistake
(But an easy one for anyone to make).   20
We read our mail and counted up our missions—
In bombers named for girls, we burned
The cities we had learned about in school—
Till our lives wore out; our bodies lay among
The people we had killed and never seen.   25
When we lasted long enough they gave us medals;
When we died they said, "Our casualties were low."
They said, "Here are the maps"; we burned the cities.

It was not dying—no, not ever dying;
But the night I died I dreamed that I was dead,   30
And the cities said to me: "Why are you dying?
We are satisfied, if you are; but why did I die?"

Song for the Last Act

Louise Bogan [1897–1970]

Now that I have your face by heart, I look
Less at its features than its darkening frame
Where quince and melon, yellow as young flame,
Lie with quilled dahlias and the shepherd's crook.
Beyond, a garden. There, in insolent ease   5
The lead and marble figures watch the show
Of yet another summer loath to go
Although the scythes hang in the apple trees.

Now that I have your face by heart, I look.

Now that I have your voice by heart, I read   10
In the black chords upon a dulling page
Music that is not meant for music's cage,

Whose emblems mix with words that shake and bleed.
The staves are shuttled over with a stark
Unprinted silence. In a double dream   15
I must spell out the storm, the running stream.
The beat's too swift. The notes shift in the dark.

Now that I have your voice by heart, I read.

Now that I have your heart by heart, I see
The wharves with their great ships and architraves;   20
The rigging and the cargo and the slaves
On a strange beach under a broken sky.
O not departure, but a voyage done!
The bales stand on the stone; the anchor weeps
Its red rust downward, and the long vine creeps   25
Beside the salt herb, in the lengthening sun.

Now that I have your heart by heart, I see.

The Soul Selects

Emily Dickinson [*1830–1886*]

The soul selects her own society,
Then shuts the door;
On her divine majority
Obtrude no more.

Unmoved, she notes the chariot's pausing   5
At her low gate;
Unmoved, an emperor is kneeling
Upon her mat.

I've known her from an ample nation
Choose one;   10
Then close the valves of her attention
Like stone.

Love in Vain

Robert Johnson [*c. 1898–1937*]

I followed her to the station, with her suitcase in my hand.
And I followed her to the station, with her suitcase in my hand.
Well, it's hard to tell, it's hard to tell, when all your love's in vain,
    All my love's in vain.

When the train rolled up to the station, I looked her in the eye. 5
When the train rolled up to the station, I looked her in the eye.

Well I was lonesome, I felt so lonesome, and I could not help but cry.
   All my love's in vain.

When the train left the station, with two lights on behind,
When the train left the station, with two lights on behind,   10
Well the blue light was my blues, and the red light was my mind.
   All my love's in vain.

I Shall Not Care

Sara Teasdale   *[1884–1933]*

When I am dead and over me bright April
   Shakes out her rain-drenched hair,
Though you should lean above me broken-hearted,
   I shall not care.

I shall have peace, as leafy trees are peaceful   5
   When rain bends down the bough;
And I shall be more silent and cold-hearted
   Than you are now.

My Father Moved Through Dooms of Love

E. E. Cummings   *[1894–1962]*

my father moved through dooms of love
through sames of am through haves of give,
singing each morning out of each night
my father moved through depths of height

this motionless forgetful where   5
turned at his glance to shining here;
that if(so timid air is firm)
under his eyes would stir and squirm

newly as from unburied which
floats the fist who, his april touch   10
drove sleeping selves to swarm their fates
woke dreamers to their ghostly roots

and should some why completely weep
my father's fingers brought her sleep:
vainly no smallest voice might cry   15
for he could feel the mountains grow.

Lifting the valleys of the sea
my father moved through griefs of joy;
praising a forehead called the moon
singing desire into begin   20

joy was his song and joy so pure
a heart of star by him could steer
and pure so now and now so yes
the wrists of twilight would rejoice

keen as midsummer's keen beyond   25
conceiving mind of sun will stand,
so strictly(over utmost him
so hugely)stood my father's dream

his flesh was flesh his blood was blood:
no hungry man but wished him food;   30
No cripple wouldn't creep one mile
uphill to only see him smile.

Scorning the pomp of must and shall
my father moved through dooms of feel;
his anger was as right as rain   35
his pity was as green as grain

septembering arms of year extend
less humbly wealth to foe and friend
than he to foolish and to wise
offered immeasurable is   40

proudly and(by octobering flame
beckoned)as earth will downward climb,
so naked for immortal work
his shoulders marched against the dark

his sorrow was as true as bread: 45
no liar looked him in the head;
if every friend became his foe
he'd laugh and build a world with snow.

My father moved through theys of we,
singing each new leaf out of each tree   50
(and every child was sure that spring
danced when she heard my father sing)

then let men kill which cannot share,
let blood and flesh be mud and mire,
scheming imagine, passion willed,   55
freedom a drug that's bought and sold

giving to steal and cruel kind,
a heart to fear, to doubt a mind,
to differ a disease of same,
conform the pinnacle of am   60

though dull were all we taste as bright,
bitter all utterly things sweet,
maggoty minus and dumb death
all we inherit, all bequeath

and nothing quite so least as truth   65
—i say though hate were why men breathe—
because my father lived his soul
love is the whole and more than all

Frescoes for Mr. Rockefeller's City

Archibald MacLeish [*1892–*]

I. LANDSCAPE AS A NUDE

She lies on her left side her flank golden:
Her hair is burned black with the strong sun:
The scent of her hair is of rain in the dust on her shoulders:
She has brown breasts and the mouth of no other country:

Ah she is beautiful here in the sun where she lies: 5
She is not like the soft girls naked in vineyards
Nor the soft naked girls of the English islands
Where the rain comes in with the surf on an east wind:

Hers is the west wind and the sunlight: the west
Wind is the long clean wind of the continents—   10
The wind turning with earth: the wind descending
Steadily out of the evening and following on:

The wind here where she lies is west: the trees
Oak ironwood cottonwood hickory: standing in
Great groves they roll on the wind as the sea would: 15
The grasses of Iowa Illinois Indiana.

Run with the plunge of the wind as a wave tumbling:

Under her knees there is no green lawn of the Florentines:
Under her dusty knees is the corn stubble:
Her belly is flecked with the flickering light of the corn: 20

She lies on her left side her flank golden:
Her hair is burned black with the strong sun:
The scent of her hair is of dust and of smoke on her shoulders:
She has brown breasts and the mouth of no other country:

II. WILDWEST

There were none of my blood in this battle: 25
There were Minneconjous: Sans Arcs: Brules:
Many nations of Sioux: they were few men galloping:

This would have been in the long days in June:
They were galloping well deployed under the plum-trees:
They were driving riderless horses: themselves they were few: 30

Crazy Horse had done it with few numbers:
Crazy Horse was small for a Lakota:
He was riding always alone thinking of something:

He was standing alone by the picket lines by the ropes:
He was young then: he was thirty when he died: 35
Unless there were children to talk he took no notice:

When the soldiers came for him there on the other side
On the Greasy Grass in the villages we were shouting
"Hoka Hey! Crazy Horse will be riding!"

They fought in the water: horses and men were drowning: 40
They rode on the butte: dust settled in sunlight:
Hoka Hey! they lay on the bloody ground:

No one could tell of the dead which man was Custer . . .
That was the end of his luck: by that river:
The soldiers beat him at Slim Buttes once: 45

They beat him at Willow Creek when the snow lifted:
The last time they beat him was the Tongue:
He had only the meat he had made and of that little:

Do you ask why he should fight? It was his country:
My God should he not fight? It was his: 50
But after the Tongue there were no herds to be hunting:

He cut the knots of the tails and he led them in:
He cried out "I am Crazy Horse! Do not touch me!"
There were many soldiers between and the gun glinting. . . .

And a Mister Josiah Perham of Maine had much of the   55
land Mister Perham was building the Northern Pacific
railroad that is Mister Perham was saying at lunch that

forty say fifty million of acres in gift and
government grant outright ought to be worth a
wide price on the Board at two-fifty and   60

later a Mister Cooke had relieved Mister Perham and
later a Mister Morgan relieved Mister Cooke:
Mister Morgan converted at prices current:

It was all prices to them: they never looked at it:
why should they look at the land: they were Empire Builders: 65
it was all in the bid and the asked and the ink on their books . . .

When Crazy Horse was there by the Black Hills
His heart would be big with the love he had for that country
And all the game he had seen and the mares he had ridden
And how it went out from you wide and clean in the sunlight   70

III. BURYING GROUND BY THE TIES

Ayee! Ai! This is heavy earth on our shoulders:
There were none of us born to be buried in this earth:
Niggers we were Portuguese Magyars Polacks:

We were born to another look of the sky certainly:
Now we lie here in the river pastures: 75
We lie in the mowings under the thick turf:

We hear the earth and the all-day rasp of the grasshoppers.
It was we laid the steel on this land from ocean to ocean:
It was we (if you know) put the U. P. through the passes

Bringing her down into Laramie full load   80
Eighteen mile on the granite anticlinal
Forty-three foot to the mile and the grade holding:

It was we did it: hunkies of our kind:
It was we dug the caved-in holes for the cold water:
It was we built the gully spurs and the freight sidings: 85

Who would do it but we and the Irishmen bossing us?
It was all foreign-born men there were in this country:
It was Scotsmen Englishmen Chinese Squareheads Austrians. . . .

Ayee! but there's weight to the earth under it:
Not for this did we come out—to be lying here   90
Nameless under the ties in the clay cuts:

There's nothing good in the world but the rich will buy it:
Everything sticks to the grease of a gold note—
Even a continent—even a new sky!

Do not pity us much for the strange grass over us: 95
We laid the steel to the stone stock of these mountains:
The place of our graves is marked by the telegraph poles!

It was not to lie in the bottom we came out
And the trains going over us here in the dry hollows. . . .

IV. OIL PAINTING OF THE ARTIST AS THE ARTIST

The plump Mr. Pl'f is washing his hands of America: 100
The plump Mr. Pl'f is in ochre with such hair:

America is in blue-black-grey-green-sandcolor:
America is a continent—many lands:

The plump Mr. Pl'f is washing his hands of America:
He is pictured at Pau on the *place* and his eyes glaring: 105

He thinks of himself as an exile from all this:
As an émigré from his own time into history—

(History being an empty house without owners
A practical man may get in by the privy stones—

The dead are excellent hosts: they have no objections—   110
And once in he can nail the knob on the next one

Living the life of a classic in bad air with
Himself for the Past and his face in the glass for Posterity)

The Cinquecento is nothing at all like Nome
Or Natchez or Wounded Knee or the Shenandoah: 115

Your vulgarity Tennessee: your violence Texas:
The rocks under your fields Ohio Connecticut:

Your clay Missouri your clay: you have driven him out:
You have shadowed his life Appalachians purple mountains:

There is much too much of your flowing Mississippi: 120
He prefers a tidier stream with a terrace for trippers and

Cypresses mentioned in Horace or Henry James:
He prefers a country where everything carries the name of a

Countess or real king or an actual palace or
Something in Prose and the stock prices all in Italian: 125

There is more shade for an artist under a fig
Than under the whole damn range (he finds) of the Big Horns.

V. EMPIRE BUILDERS
   The Museum Attendant:

This is *The Making of America in Five Panels:*

This is Mister Harriman making America:
Mister-Harriman-is-buying-the-Union-Pacific-at-Seventy:
The Sante Fe is shining on his hair: 130

This is Commodore Vanderbilt making America:
Mister-Vanderbilt-is-eliminating-the-short-interest-in-Hudson:
Observe the carving on the rocking chair:

This is J. P. Morgan making America:
(The Tennessee Coal is behind to the left of the Steel Company:)   135
Those in mauve are braces he is wearing:

This is Mister Mellon making America:
Mister-Mellon-is-represented-as-a-symbolical-figure-in-aluminum-
Strewing-bank-stocks-on-a-burnished-stair:

This is the Bruce is the Barton making America: 140
Mister-Barton-is-selling-us-Doctor's-Deliciousest-Dentifrice:
This is he in beige with the canary:

You have just beheld the Makers making America:
This is *The Making of America in Five Panels:*
America lies to the west-southwest of the Switch-Tower: 145
There is nothing to see of America but land:

The Original Document under the Panel Paint:

"To Thos. Jefferson Esq. his obd't serv't
M. Lewis: captain: detached:
$\qquad\qquad$ Sir:
Having in mind your repeated commands in this matter:$\qquad\qquad$150
And the worst half of it done and the streams mapped:

And we here on the back of this beach beholding the
Other ocean—two years gone and the cold

Breaking with rain for the third spring since St. Louis:
The crows at the fishbones on the frozen dunes:$\qquad\qquad$155

The first cranes going over from south north:
And the river down by a mark of the pole since the morning:

And time near to return, and a ship (Spanish)
Lying in for the salmon: and fearing chance or the

Drought or the Sioux should deprive you of these discoveries—$\qquad$160
Therefore we send by sea in this writing:
$\qquad\qquad\qquad\qquad$Above the

Platte there were long plains and a clay country:
Rim of the sky far off: grass under it:

Dung for the cook fires by the sulphur licks:
After that there were low hills and the sycamores:$\qquad\qquad$165

And we poled up by the Great Bend in the skiffs:
The honey bees left us after the Osage River:

The wind was west in the evenings and no dew and the
Morning Star larger and whiter than usual—

The winter rattling in the brittle haws:$\qquad\qquad$170
The second year there was sage and the quail calling:

All that valley is good land by the river:
Three thousand miles and the clay cliffs and

Rue and beargrass by the water banks
And many birds and the brant going over and tracks of$\qquad$175

Bear elk wolves marten: the buffalo
Numberless so that the cloud of their dust covers them:

The antelope fording the fall creeks: and the mountains and
Grazing lands and the meadow lands and the ground

Sweet and open and well-drained:
$\qquad\qquad\qquad\qquad$We advise you to$\qquad\qquad$180
Settle troops at the forks and to issue licenses:

Many men will have living on these lands:
There is wealth in the earth for them all and the wood standing

And wild birds on the water where they sleep:
There is stone in the hills for the towns of a great people . . ."   185

You have just beheld the Makers making America:

They screwed her scrawny and gaunt with their seven-year panics:
They bought her back on their mortgages old-whore-cheap:
They fattened their bonds at her breasts till the thin blood ran from them:

Men have forgotten how full clear and deep   190
The Yellowstone moved on the gravel and grass grew
When the land lay waiting for her westward people!

VI. BACKGROUND WITH REVOLUTIONARIES

And the corn singing Millennium!
Lenin! Millennium Lennium!

When they're shunting the cars on the Katy a mile off   195
When they're shunting the cars when they're shunting the cars on the Katy
You can hear the clank of the couplings riding away

Also Comrade Devine who writes of America
Most instructively having in 'Seventy-four
Crossed to the Hoboken side on the Barclay Street Ferry   200

She sits on a settle in the State of North Dakota
O she sits on a settle in the State of North Dakota
She can hear the engines whistle over Iowa and Idaho

Also Comrade Edward Remington Ridge
Who has prayed God since the April of 'Seventeen   205
To replace in his life his lost (M.E.) religion.

And The New York Daily Worker *goes a'blowing over Arkansas*
The New York Daily Worker *goes a'blowing over Arkansas*
The grasses let it go along the Ozarks over Arkansas

Even Comrade Grenadine Grilt who has tried since   210
August tenth for something to feel about strongly in
Verses—his personal passions having tired

I can tell my land by the jays in the apple-trees
Tell my land by the jays in the apple-trees
I can tell my people by the blue-jays in the apple-trees   215

Aindt you read in d'books you are all brudders?
D' glassic historic objective broves you are brudders!
You and d'Wops and d'Chinks you are all brudders!
Havend't you got it d' same ideology? Havend't you?

When it's yesterday in Oregon it's one A M in Maine   220
And she slides: and the day slides: and it runs: runs over us:
And the bells strike twelve strike twelve strike twelve

In Marblehead in Buffalo and Cheyenne in Cherokee
Yesterday runs on the states like a crow's shadow

For Marx has said to us Workers what do you need?   225
And Stalin has said to us Starvers what do you need?
You need the Dialectical Materialism!

She's a tough land under the corn mister:
She has changed the bone in the cheeks of many races:
She has winced the eyes of the soft Slavs with her sun on them: 230
She has tried the fat from the round rumps of Italians:
Even the voice of the English has gone dry
And hard on the tongue and alive in the throat speaking:

She's a tough land under the oak-trees mister:
It may be she can change the word in the book   235
As she changes the bone of a man's head in his children:
It may be that the earth and the men remain. . . .

There is too much sun on the lids of my eyes to be listening

Grapes Making
Léonie Adams [1899–   ]

Noon sun beats down the leaf; the noon
Of summer burns along the vine
And thins the leaf with burning air,
Till from the underleaf is fanned,
And down the woven vine, the light.   5
Still the pleached leaves drop layer on layer
To wind the sun on either hand,
And echoes of the light are bound,
And hushed the blazing cheek of light,
The hurry of the breathless noon,   10
And from the thicket of the vine
The grape has pressed into its round.

The grape has pressed into its round,
And swings, aloof chill green, clean won
Of light, between the sky and ground;   15
Those hid, soft-flashing lamps yet blind,
Which yield an apprehended sun,
Fresh triumph in a courteous kind,
Having more ways to be, and years,
And easy, countless treasuries,   20
You whose all-told is still no sum,
Like a rich heart, well-said in sighs,
The careless autumn mornings come,
The grapes drop glimmering to the shears.

Now shady sod at heel piles deep,   25
An overarching shade, the vine
Across the fall of noon is flung;
And here beneath the leaves is cast
A light to color noonday sleep,
While cool, bemused the grape is swung   30
Beneath the eyelids of the vine;
And deepening like a tender thought
Green moves along the leaf, and bright
The leaf above, and leaf has caught,
And emerald pierces day, and last   35
The faint leaf vanishes to light.

The Quaker Graveyard in Nantucket

Robert Lowell [*1917–*]

For Warren Winslow, Dead at Sea[1]

Let men have dominion over the fishes of the sea and the fowls of the air and
the beasts and the whole earth, and every creeping creature that moveth upon
the earth.

I

A brackish reach of shoal off Madaket,—
The sea was still breaking violently and night
Had steamed into our North Atlantic Fleet,
When the drowned sailor clutched the drag-net. Light
Flashed from his matted head and marble feet,   5
He grappled at the net
With the coiled, hurdling muscles of his thighs:
The corpse was bloodless, a botch of reds and whites,
Its open, staring eyes
Were lusterless dead-lights   10
Or cabin-windows on a stranded hulk
Heavy with sand. We weight the body, close
Its eyes and heave it seaward whence it came,
Where the heel-headed dogfish barks its nose
On Ahab's void and forehead; and the name   15
Is blocked in yellow chalk.
Sailors, who pitch this portent at the sea
Where dreadnaughts shall confess
Its hell-bent deity,
When you are powerless   20
To sand-bag this Atlantic bulwark, faced
By the earth-shaker, green, unwearied, chaste
In his steel scales: ask for no Orphean lute
To pluck life back. The guns of the steeled fleet
Recoil and then repeat   25
The hoarse salute.

[1] Warren Winslow, the poet's cousin, drowned at sea during World War II

II

Whenever winds are moving and their breath
Heaves at the roped-in bulwarks of this pier,
The terns and sea-gulls tremble at your death
In these home waters. Sailor, can you hear   30
The Pequod's sea wings, beating landward, fall
Headlong and break on our Atlantic wall
Off 'Sconset, where the yawing S-boats splash
The bellbuoy, with ballooning spinnakers,
As the entangled, screeching mainsheet clears   35
The blocks: off Madaket, where lubbers lash
The heavy surf and throw their long lead squids
For blue-fish? Sea-gulls blink their heavy lids
Seaward. The wind's wings beat upon the stones,
Cousin, and scream for you and the claws rush   40
At the sea's throat and wring it in the slush
Of this old Quaker graveyard where the bones
Cry out in the long night for the hurt beast
Bobbing by Ahab's whaleboats in the East.

III

All you recovered from Poseidon died   45
With you, my cousin, and the harrowed brine
Is fruitless on the blue beard of the god,
Stretching beyond us to the castles in Spain,
Nantucket's westward haven. To Cape Cod
Guns, cradled on the tide,   50
Blast the eelgrass about a waterclock
Of bilge and backwash, roil the salt and sand
Lashing earth's scaffold, rock
Our warships in the hand
Of the great God, where time's contrition blues   55
Whatever it was these Quaker sailors lost
In the mad scramble of their lives. They died
When time was open-eyed,
Wooden and childish; only bones abide
There, in the nowhere, where their boats were tossed   60
Sky-high, where mariners had fabled news
Of IS, the whited monster. What it cost
Them is their secret. In the monster's slick
I see the Quakers drown and hear their cry:
"If God himself had not been on our side,   65
"If God himself had not been on our side,
When the Atlantic rose against us, why
Then it had swallowed us up quick."

IV

This is the end of the whaleroad and the whale
Who spewed Nantucket bones on the thrashed swell   70
And stirred the troubled waters to whirlpools

To send the Pequod packing off to hell:
This is the end of them, three-quarters fools,
Snatching at straws to sail
Seaward and seaward on the turntail whale,   75
Spouting out blood and water as it rolls,
Sick as a dog to these Atlantic shoals:
Clamavimus,[2] O depths. Let the sea-gulls wail

For water, for the deep where the high tide
Mutters to its hurt self, mutters and ebbs.   80
Waves wallow in their wash, go out and out,
Leave only the death-rattle of the crabs,
The beach increasing, its enormous snout
Sucking the ocean's side.
This is the end of running on the waves;   85
We are poured out like water. Who will dance
The mast-lashed master of Leviathans
Up from this field of Quakers in their unstoned graves?

V

When the whale's viscera go and the roll
Of its corruption orerruns this world   90
Beyond tree-swept Nantucket and Woods Hole
And Martha's Vineyard, Sailor, will your sword
Whistle and fall and sink into the fat?
In the great ash-pit of Jehoshaphat
The bones cry for the blood of the white whale,   95
The fat flukes arch and whack about its ears,
The death-lance churns into the sanctuary, tears
The gun-blue swingle, heaving like a flail,
And hacks the coiling life out: it works and drags
And rips the sperm-whale's midriff into rags,   100
Gobbets of blubber spill to wind and weather,
Sailor, and gulls go round the stoven timbers
Where the morning stars sing out together
And thunder shakes the white surf and dismembers
The red flag hammered in the mast-head. Hide,   105
Our steel, Jonas Messias, in Thy side.

VI

OUR LADY OF WALSINGHAM

There once the penitents took off their shoes
And then walked barefoot the remaining mile;
And the small trees, a stream and hedgerows file
Slowly along the munching English lane,   110
Like cows to the old shrine, until you lose
Track of your dragging pain.
The stream flows down under the druid tree,

2 "We have cried out"

Shiloah's whirlpool gurgle and make glad
The castle of God. Sailor, you were glad 115
And whistled Sion by that stream. But see:

Our Lady, too small for her canopy,
Sits near the altar. There's no comeliness
At all or charm in that expressionless
Face with its heavy eyelids. As before, 120
This face, for centuries a memory,
Non est species, neque decor,[3]
Expressionless, expresses God: it goes
Past castled Sion. She knows what God knows,
Not Calvary's Cross nor crib at Bethlehem 125
Now, and the world shall come to Walsingham.

VII

The empty winds are creaking and the oak
Splatters and splatters on the cenotaph,
The boughs are trembling and a gaff
Bobs on the untimely stroke 130
Of the greased wash exploding on a shoal-bell
In the old mouth of the Atlantic. It's well;
Atlantic, you are fouled with the blue sailors,
Sea-monsters, upward angel, downward fish:
Unmarried and corroding, spare of flesh 135
Mart once of supercilious, wing'd clippers,
Atlantic, where your bell-trap guts its spoil
You could cut the brackish winds with a knife
Here in Nantucket, and cast up the time
When the Lord God formed man from the sea's slime 140
And breathed into his face the breath of life,
And blue-lung'd combers lumbered to the kill.
The Lord survives the rainbow of His will.

The Last Ride Together

Robert Browning [*1812–1889*]

I

I SAID—Then, dearest, since 'tis so,
Since now at length my fate I know,
Since nothing all my love avails,
Since all, my life seemed meant for, fails,
    Since this was written and needs must be— 5
My whole heart rises up to bless
Your name in pride and thankfulness!
Take back the hope you gave,—I claim
Only a memory of the same,

---

[3] "He hath no form nor comeliness" (Isaiah 53:2)

—And this beside, if you will not blame,
   Your leave for one more last ride with me.   10

II

My mistress bent that brow of hers;
Those deep dark eyes where pride demurs
When pity would be softening through,
Fixed me a breathing-while or two   15
   With life or death in the balance: right!
The blood replenished me again;
My last thought was at least not vain:
I and my mistress, side by side
Shall be together, breathe and ride,   20
So, one day more am I deified.
   Who knows but the world may end to-night?

III

Hush! if you saw some western cloud
All billowy-bosomed, over-bowed
By many benedictions—sun's   25
And moon's and evening-stars at once—
   And so, you, looking and loving best,
Conscious grew, your passion drew
Cloud, sunset, moonrise, star-shine too,
Down on you, near and yet more near,   30
Till flesh must fade for heaven was here!—
Thus leant she and lingered—joy and fear!
   Thus lay she a moment on my breast.

IV

Then we began to ride, My soul
Smoothed itself out, a long-cramped scroll   35
Freshening and fluttering in the wind.
Past hopes already lay behind.
   What need to strive with a life awry?
Had I said that, had I done this,
So might I gain, so might I miss.   40
Might she have loved me? just as well
She might have hated, who can tell!
Where had I been now if the worst befell?
   And here we are riding, she and I.

V

Fail I alone, in words and deeds?   45
Why, all men strive and who succeeds?
We rode; it seemed my spirit flew,
Saw other regions, cities new,
   As the world rushed by on either side.

I thought,—All labor, yet no less 50
Bear up beneath their unsuccess.
Look at the end of work, contrast
The petty done, the undone vast,
This present of theirs with the hopeful past!
    I hoped she would love me; here we ride. 55

VI

What hand and brain went ever paired?
What heart alike conceived and dared?
What act proved all its thought had been?
What will but felt the fleshly screen?
    We ride and I see her bosom heave. 60
There's many a crown for who can reach.
Ten lines, a statesman's life in each!
The flag stuck on a heap of bones,
A soldier's doing! what atones?
They scratch his name on the Abbey-stones. 65
    My riding is better, by their leave.

VII

What does it all mean, poet? Well,
Your brains beat into rhythm, you tell
What we felt only; you expressed
You hold things beautiful the best, 70
    And pace them in rhyme so, side by side.
'Tis something, nay 'tis much: but then,
Have you yourself what's best for men?
Are you—poor, sick, old ere your time—
Nearer one whit your own sublime 75
Than we who never have turned a rhyme?
    Sing, riding's a joy! For me, I ride.

VIII

And you, great sculptor—so, you gave
A score of years to Art, her slave,
And that's your Venus, whence we turn 80
To yonder girl that fords the burn!
    You acquiesce, and shall I repine?
What, man of music, you grown gray
With notes and nothing else to say,
Is this your sole praise from a friend, 85
"Greatly his opera's strains intend,
But in music we know how fashions end!"
    I gave my youth; but we ride, in fine.

IX

Who knows what's fit for us? Had fate
Proposed bliss here should sublimate 90

My being—had I signed the bond—
Still one must lead some life beyond,
   Have a bliss to die with, dim-descried.
This foot once planted on the goal,
This glory-garland round my soul,   95
Could I descry such? Try and test!
I sink back shuddering from the quest.
Earth being so good, would Heaven seem best?
   Now, Heaven and she are beyond this ride.

X

And yet—she has not spoke so long!   100
What if heaven be that, fair and strong
At life's best, with our eyes upturned
Whither life's flower is first discerned,
   We, fixed so, ever should so abide?
What if we still ride on, we two   105
With life for ever old yet new,
Changed not in kind but in degree,
The instant made eternity,—
And heaven just prove that I and she
   Ride, ride together, forever ride?   110

The Going

Thomas Hardy [1840–1928]

Why did you give no hint that night
That quickly after the morrow's dawn,
And calmly, as if indifferent quite,
You would close your term here, up and be gone
   Where I could not follow   5
   With wing of swallow
To gain one glimpse of you ever anon!

   Never to bid good-bye,
   Or lip me the softest call,
Or utter a wish for a word, while I   10
Saw morning harden upon the wall,
   Unmoved, unknowing
   That your great going
Had place that moment, and altered all.

Why do you make me leave the house   15
And think for a breath it is you I see
At the end of the alley of bending boughs
Where so often at dusk you used to be;
   Till in darkening dankness
   The yawning blankness   20
Of the perspective sickens me!

You were she who abode
By those red-veined rocks far West,
You were the swan-necked one who rode
Along the beetling Beeny Crest, 25
 And, reining nigh me,
 Would muse and eye me,
While Life unrolled us its very best.

Why, then, latterly did we not speak,
Did we not think of those days long dead, 30
And ere your vanishing strive to seek
That time's renewal? We might have said,
 "In this bright spring weather
 We'll visit together
Those places that once we visited." 35

 Well, well! All's past amend,
 Unchangeable. It must go.
I seem but a dead man held on end
To sink down soon. . . . O you could not know
 That such swift fleeing 40
 No soul foreseeing—
Not even I—would undo me so!

O Black and Unknown Bards

James Weldon Johnson [*1871–1938*]

O black and unknown bards of long ago,
How come your lips to touch the sacred fire?
How, in your darkness, did you come to know
The power and beauty of the minstrel's lyre?
Who first from midst his bonds lifted his eyes? 5
Who first from out the still watch, lone and long,
Feeling the ancient faith of prophets rise
Within his dark-kept soul, burst into song?

Heart of what slave poured out such melody
As "Steal Away to Jesus"? On its strains 10
His spirit must have nightly floated free,
Though still about his hands he felt his chains.
Who heard great "Jordan roll"? Whose starward eye
Saw chariot "swing low"? And who was he
That breathed that comforting, melodic sigh, 15
"Nobody Knows de Trouble I See"?

What merely living clod, what captive thing,
Could up toward God through all its darkness grope,
And find within its deadened heart to sing
These songs of sorrow, love, and faith, and hope? 20

How did it catch that subtle undertone,
That note in music heard not with the ears?
How sound the elusive reed so seldom blown,
Which stirs the soul or melts the heart to tears?

Not that great German master in his dream   25
Of harmonies that thundered amongst the stars
At the creation, ever heard a theme
Nobler than "Go Down, Moses." Mark its bars,
How like a mighty trumpet-call they stir
The blood. Such are the notes that men have sung   30
Going to valorous deeds; such tones there were
That helped make history when Time was young.

There is a wide, wide wonder in it all,
That from degraded rest and servile toil
The fiery spirit of the seer should call   35
These simple children of the sun and soil.
O black slave singers, gone, forgot, unfamed,
You—you alone, of all the long, long line
Of those who've sung untaught, unknown, unnamed,
Have stretched out upward, seeking the divine.   40

You sang not deeds of heroes or of kings;
No chant of bloody war, no exulting paean
Of arms-won triumphs; but your humble strings
You touched in chord with music empyrean.
You sang far better than you knew; the songs   45
That for your listeners' hungry hearts sufficed
Still live—but more than this to you belongs:
You sang a race from wood and stone to Christ.

We Wear the Mask

Paul Laurence Dunbar [*1872–1906*]

We wear the mask that grins and lies,
It hides our cheeks and shades our eyes,
This debt we pay to human guile;
With torn and bleeding hearts we smile,
And mouth with myriad subtleties.   5

Why should the world be overwise,
In counting all our ears and sighs?
Nay, let them only see us, while
    We wear the mask.

We smile, but, O great Christ, our cries   10
To thee from tortured souls arise.
We sing, but oh, the clay is vile

Beneath our feet, and long the mile;
But let the world dream otherwise,
   We wear the mask.

Swing Low, Sweet Chariot

Anonymous

Swing low, sweet chariot, comin' fer to carry me home.
Swing low, sweet chariot, comin' fer to carry me home.

   I looked over Jordan, an' what did I see,
   Comin' fer to carry me home?
   A band of angels comin' after me,   5
   Comin' fer to carry me home.

Swing low, *etc.*

   If you get a dere befo' I do,
   Comin' fer to carry me home,
   Tell all my friends I'm comin' too,
   Comin' fer to carry me home.   10

Swing low, *etc.*

I Know Moonrise

Anonymous

   I know moonrise, I know starrise,
   Lay dis body down.
   I walk in de moonlight, I walk in de starlight,
   To lay dis body down.

   I walk in de graveyard, I walk through de graveyard,   5
   To lay dis body down.
   I'll lie in de grave and stretch out my arms,
   To lay dis body down.

   I go to de judgment in de evenin' of de day,
   When I lay dis body down;   10
   And my soul and yore soul will meet in de day
   When I lay dis body down.

Upon a Dying Lady

William Butler Yeats   *[1865–1939]*

I. HER COURTESY

With the old kindness, the old distinguished grace,
She lies, her lovely piteous head amid dull red hair
Propped upon pillows, rouge on the pallor of her face.

She would not have us sad because she is lying there,
And when she meets our gaze her eyes are laughter-lit, 5
Her speech a wicked tale that we may vie with her,
Matching our broken-hearted wit against her wit,
Thinking of saints and of Petronius Arbiter.

II. CERTAIN ARTISTS BRING HER DOLLS AND DRAWINGS

Bring where our Beauty lies
A new modeled doll, or drawing, 10
With a friend's or an enemy's
Features, or maybe showing
Her features when a tress
Of dull red hair was flowing
Over some silken dress 15
Cut in the Turkish fashion,
Or, it may be, like a boy's.
We have given the world our passion,
We have naught for death but toys.

III. SHE TURNS THE DOLLS, FACES TO THE WALL

Because to-day is some religious festival 20
They had a priest say Mass, and even the Japanese,
Heel up and weight on toe, must face the wall
—Pedant in passion, learned in old courtesies,
Vehement and witty she had seemed—; the Venetian lady
Who had seemed to glide to some intrigue in her red shoes, 25
Her domino, her panniered skirt copied from Longhi;
The meditative critic; all are on their toes,
Even our Beauty with her Turkish trousers on.
Because the priest must have like every dog his day
Or keep us all awake with baying at the moon, 30
We and our dolls being but the world were best away.

IV. THE END OF DAY

She is playing like a child
And penance is the play,
Fantastical and wild
Because the end of day 35
Shows her that some one soon
Will come from the house, and say—
Though play is but half done—
"Come in and leave the play."

V. HER RACE

She has not grown uncivil 40
As narrow natures would
And called the pleasures evil
Happier days thought good;

She knows herself a woman,   45
No red and white of a face,
Or rank, raised from a common
Unreckonable race;
And how should her heart fail her
Or sickness break her will
With her dead brother's valor   50
For an example still?

VI. HER COURAGE

When her soul flies to the predestined dancing-place
(I have no speech but symbol, the pagan speech I made
Amid the dreams of youth) let her come face to face,
Amid that first astonishment, with Grania's shade,   55
All but the terrors of the woodland flight forgot
That made her Diarmuid dear, and some old cardinal
Pacing with half-closed eyelids in a sunny spot
Who had murmured of Giorgione at his latest breath—
Aye, and Achilles, Timor, Babar, Barhaim, all   60
Who have lived in joy and laughed into the face of Death.

VII. HER FRIENDS BRING HER A CHRISTMAS TREE

Pardon, great enemy,
Without an angry thought
We've carried in our tree,
And here and there have bought   65
Till all the boughs are gay,
And she may look from the bed
On pretty things that may
Please a fantastic head.
Give her a little grace,   70
What if a laughing eye
Have looked into your face?
It is about to die.

REPRESENTATIVE POEMS
of OUR TIME

8

Earlier in this book we have presented a large number of writers, British and American, both living and dead, whose work is characteristic of this century and whose reputations have long since become established. They are: Léonie Adams, Conrad Aiken, W. H. Auden, John Betjeman, Louise Bogan, Robert Bridges, Gwendolyn Brooks, Hart Crane, E. E. Cummings, Walter de la Mare, James Dickey, Hilda Doolittle, W. E. B. Du Bois, Richard Eberhart, T. S. Eliot, William Empson, Robert Frost, Jean Garrigue, Allen Ginsberg, Robert Graves, Thomas Hardy, Ralph Hodgson, Barbara Howes, Langston Hughes, Ted Hughes, Randall Jarrell, Robinson Jeffers, James Weldon Johnson, James Joyce, Philip Larkin, D. H. Lawrence, Robert Lowell, Archibald MacLeish, Phyllis McGinley, Edna St. Vincent Millay, Marianne Moore, Ogden Nash, Wilfred Owen, Ezra Pound, John Crowe Ransom, Henry Reed, Theodore Roethke, Delmore Schwartz, Karl Shapiro, W. D. Snodgrass, James Stephens, Wallace Stevens, Allen Tate, Sara Teasdale, Dylan Thomas, Edward Thomas, Melvin Tolson, Jean Toomer, Vernon Watkins, John Wheelwright, Richard Wilbur, William Carlos Williams, James Wright, Elinor Wylie, and W. B. Yeats. We have also presented a few younger poets whose reputations remain to be established.

The poems that follow in this section have been selected to give an impression of work especially characteristic of the time in which we now live. Though poems by certain poets, for instance, James Dickey, Allen Ginsberg, W. D. Snodgrass, and James Wright, have appeared in earlier sections of this book, it is fitting to give them representation also in this collection of rather recent poetry to which their work essentially belongs.

Hardweed Path Going

A. R. Ammons   [1926–   ]

                    Every evening, down into the hardweed
          going,
          the slop bucket heavy, held-out, wire handle
          freezing in the hand, put it down a minute, the jerky
          smooth unspilling levelness of the knees,   5
                    meditation of a bucket rim,
          lest the wheat meal,
          floating on clear greasewater, spill,
          down the grown-up path:

                    don't forget to slop the hogs,   10
                    feed the chickens,
                    water the mule,
                    cut the kindling,
                    build the fire,
                    call up the cow: 15

                    supper is over, it's starting to get
          dark early,
          better get the scraps together, mix a little meal in,
          nothing but swill.

                    The dead-purple woods hover on the west.   20
          I know those woods.
          Under the tall, ceiling-solid pines, beyond the edge of
          field and brush, where the wild myrtle grows,
                    I let my jo-reet loose.
          A jo-reet is a bird. Nine weeks of summer he   25
          sat on the well bench in a screened box,
          a stick inside to walk on,
                    "jo-reet," he said, "jo-reet."
                    and I
          would come up to the well and draw the bucket down   30
          deep into the cold place where red and white marbled
          clay oozed the purest water, water celebrated
          throughout the county:
                    "Grits all gone?"
                    "jo-reet."   35

Throw a dipper of cold water on him. Reddish-black
flutter.
        "reet, reet, reet!"

        Better turn him loose before
cold weather comes on.   40
        Doom caving in
        inside
        any pleasure, pure
        attachment
        of love.   45

Beyond the wild myrtle away from cats I turned him loose
and his eye asked me what to do, where to go;
he hopped around, scratched a little, but looked up at me.
Don't look at me. Winter is coming.
Disappear in the bushes. I'm tired of you and will   50
be alone hereafter. I will go dry in my well.
        I will turn still.
Go south. Grits is not available in any natural form.
Look under leaves, try mushy logs, the floors of pinywoods.
South into the dominion of bugs.   55

        They're good woods.
But lay me out if a mourning dove far off in the dusky pines
        starts.

        Down the hardweed path going,
leaning, balancing, away from the bucket, to   60
Sparkle, my favorite hog, sparse, fine black hair,
grunted while feeding if rubbed,
scratched against the hair, or if talked to gently:
got the bottom of the slop bucket:
        "Sparkle . . .   65
        You hungry?
        Hungry, girly?"
blowing, bubbling in the trough.

        Waiting for the first freeze:

"Think it's going to freeze tonight?" say the neighbors,   70
the neighbors, going by.

        Hog-killing.

Oh, Sparkle, when the axe tomorrow morning falls
and the rush is made to open your throat,
I will sing, watching dry-eyed as a man, sing my   75
        love for you in the tender feedings.

        She's nothing but a hog, boy.

Bleed out, Sparkle, the moon-chilled bleaches
        of your body hanging upside-down
hardening through the mind and night of the first freeze.   80

These Lacustrine Cities

John Ashbery   [*1927–*   ]

These lacustrine cities grew out of loathing
Into something forgetful, although angry with history.
They are the product of an idea: that man is horrible, for instance.
Though this is only one example.

They emerged until a tower   5
Controlled the sky, and with artifice dipped back
Into the past for swans and tapering branches,
Burning, until all that hate was transformed into useless love.

Then you are left with an idea of yourself
And the feeling of ascending emptiness of the afternoon   10
Which must be charged to the embarrassment of others
Who fly by you like beacons.

The night is a sentinel.
Much of your time has been occupied by creative games
Until now, but we have all-inclusive plans for you.   15
We had thought, for instance, of sending you to the middle of the
                desert,

To a violent sea, or of having the closeness of the others be air
To you, pressing you back into a startled dream
As sea-breezes greet a child's face.
But the past is already here, and you are nursing some private project.   20

The worst is not over, yet I know
You will be happy here. Because of the logic
Of your situation, which is something no climate can outsmart.
Tender and insouciant by turns, you see

You have built a mountain of something,   25
Thoughtfully pouring all your energy into this single monument,
Whose wind is desire starching a petal,
Whose disappointment broke into a rainbow of tears.

Sand Creek

Charles Ballard

Wild bird singer, sing on!

Nothing lives long
But the earth and the mountain
What remains in the fire, in the flames
Becomes the final song   5

Listen hard to the words
From the winter's whiteness they come
And on this day too old to run am I
Too old for the land of the young

Black Kettle raised the flag   10
The air is crisp and cold
Here is my home I sing
Nothing lives long
But the earth and the mountain

White Antelope is my name   15

Poem for HalfWhite College Students

Imamu Amiri Baraka (LeRoi Jones)   [*1934–*   ]

Who are you, listening to me, who are you
listening to yourself? Are you white or
black, or does that have anything to do
with it? Can you pop your fingers to no
music, except those wild monkies go on   5
in your head, can you jerk, to no melody,
except finger poppers get it together
when you turn from starchecking to checking
yourself. How do you sound, your words, are they
yours? The ghost you see in the mirror, is it really   10
you, can you swear you are not an imitation greyboy,
can you look right next to you in that chair, and swear,
that the sister you have your hand on is not really
so full of Elizabeth Taylor, Richard Burton is
coming out of her ears. You may even have to be Richard   15
with a white shirt and face, and four million negroes
think you cute, you may have to be Elizabeth Taylor, old lady,
if you want to sit up in your crazy spot dreaming about dresses,
and the sway of certain porters' hips. Check yourself, learn who it is
speaking, when you make some ultrasophisticated point, check
        yourself,   20
when you find yourself gesturing like Steve McQueen, check it out, ask
in your black heart who it is you are, and is that image black or white,
you might be surprised right out the window, whistling dixie
        on the way in.

from
Eleven Addresses to the Lord
John Berryman [*1914–1972*]

1

Master of beauty, craftsman of the snowflake,
inimitable contriver,
endower of Earth so gorgeous & different from the boring Moon,
thank you for such as it is my gift.

I have made up a morning prayer to you   5
containing with precision everything that most matters.
According to Thy will' the thing begins.
It took me off & on two days. It does not aim at eloquence.

You have come to my rescue again & again
in my impassable, sometimes despairing years.   10
You have allowed my brilliant friends to destroy themselves
and I am still here, severely damaged, but functioning.

Unknowable, as I am unknown to my guinea pigs:
how can I 'love' you?
I only as far as gratitude & awe   15
confidently & absolutely go.

I have no idea whether we live again.
It doesn't seem likely
from either the scientific or the philosophical point of view
but certainly all things are possible to you,   20

and I believe as fixedly in the Resurrection-appearances to Peter & to Paul

as I believe I sit in this blue chair.
Only that may have been a special case
to establish their initiatory faith.

Whatever your end may be, accept my amazement.   25
May I stand until death forever at attention
for any your least instruction or enlightenment.
I even feel sure you will assist me again, Master of insight & beauty.

3

Sole watchman of the flying stars, guard me
against my flicker of impulse lust: teach me   30
to see them as sisters & daughters. Sustain
my grand endeavours: husbandship & crafting.

Forsake me not when my wild hours come;
grant me sleep nightly, grace soften my dreams;
achieve in me patience till the thing be done,   35
a careful view of my achievement come.

Make me from time to time the gift of the shoulder.
When all hurt nerves whine shut away the whiskey.
Empty my heart toward Thee.
Let me pace without fear the common path of death.   40

Cross am I sometimes with my little daughter:
fill her eyes with tears. Forgive me, Lord.
Unite my various soul,
sole watchman of the wide & single stars.

The Figures

Robert Creeley   [1926–   ]

The stillness
of the wood,
the figures formed

by hands so still   5
they touched it
to be one

hand holding one
hand, faces
without eyes,

bodies of wooden   10
stone, so still
they will not move

from that quiet
action ever
again. Did the man   15

who made them find
a like quiet? In
the act of making them

it must have been
so still he heard the wood   20
and felt it with his hands

moving into
the forms
he has given them,

one by singular   25
one, so quiet,
so still.

Bed Time

Peter Davison [*1928–*]

Few beds are stonier than one shared by a sleeper
and a waker who stares into the dark
listening to the house breathe. Children
sigh, dogs snore, clocks tick, radiators mutter.
Love past, he lies vacant. Bed carries him   5
to countries that his body will never visit,
regions where his mind cannot drink the water.

Feet up. Blood trickles through his head
to pass between Horn Gate and Ivory Gate.
Sleep pilot, dreamer, flying Dutchman,   10
he steers his ticktock course between chills and fever
bound out of Birthport for Lovepool and Death Haven.

Love past! Clandestine beds in borrowed apartments.
Fern beds, pine needles, beds for *porcheria.*
Beds whose springs have crumpled from exuberance   15
or rattled with anger. Beds whose backs have bent
from nightly throes of union and reunion.
'Oh bed, where first I loosed my virgin girdle . . .'
She fell upon her knees and kissed the bed.

As in a hospital where he awaits in bed   20
the next day's condescension of doctors,
he bleeds broken promises. Is it sailing time
for the ship of fools, the ship of the dead?
Pain lightning flickers and spatters
the four-cornered flatland of his life,   25
but what else is there to fall back on?
In bed we depend on nothing but bed.

Faces Seen Once

James Dickey [*1923–*]

Faces seen once are seen

To fade from around one feature,
Leaving a chin, a scar, an expression

Forever in the air beneath a streetlight,
Glancing in boredom from the window
Of a bus in a country town,
Showing teeth for a moment only,
All of which die out of mind, except
One silver one.

Who had the dog-bitten ear?   10
The granulated lids? The birthmark?

Faces seen once change always

Into and out of each other:
An eye you saw in Toulon
Is gazing at you down a tin drainpipe   15
You played with as a dull child
In Robertstown, Georgia.
There it is April; the one eye

Concentrates, the rusty pipe

Is trembling; behind the eye   20
Is a pine tree blurring with tears:

You and someone's blue eye
Transforming your boyhood are weeping
For an only son drowned in warm water
With the French fleet off Senegal.   25
Soon after, the cancer-clamped face
Of your great-grandfather relaxes,

Smiles again with the lips of a newsboy.
Faces seen once make up

One face being organized   30

And changed and known less all the time,
Unsexed, amorphous, growing in necessity
As you deepen in age.
The brow wrinkles, a blind, all-knowing
Questioning look comes over it,   35
And every face in the street begins

To partake of the look in the eyes,

Every nose is part of that nose
And changes the nose; every innocence and every

Unspoken-of guilt goes into it,   40
Into the face of the one
Encountered, unknowable person who waits
For you all over the world
In coffee shops, filling stations, bars,
In mills and orphan asylums,   45

In hospitals, prisons, at parties,
Yearning to be one thing.

At your death, they—it is there,

And the features congeal,
Having taken the last visage in,   50

Over you, pretesting its smile,
The skin the indwelling no
Color of all colors mingled,
The eyes asking all there is.

Composed, your own face trembles near   55

Joining that other, knowing
That finally something must break

Or speak. A silver tooth gleams;
You mumble, whispering "You
Are human, are what I have witnessed.   60
You are all faces seen once."
Through the bent, staring, unstable dark
Of a drainpipe, Unity hears you—

A God-roar of hearing—say only
"You are an angel's too-realized   65

Unbearable memoryless face."

My Sad Self

Allen Ginsberg [*1926–*]

to Frank O'Hara

Sometimes when my eyes are red
I go up on top of the RCA Building
        and gaze at my world, Manhattan—
            my buildings, streets I've done feats in,
                lofts, beds, coldwater flats   5
—on Fifth Ave below which I also bear in mind,
        its ant cars, little yellow taxis, men
            walking the size of specks of wool—
        Panorama of the bridges, sunrise over Brooklyn machine,
            sun go down over New Jersey where I was born   10
                & Paterson where I played with ants—
my later loves on 15th Street,
        my greater loves of Lower East Side,
            my once fabulous amours in the Bronx
                    faraway—   15
paths crossing in these hidden streets,
        my history summed up, my absences
                and ecstasies in Harlem—
        —sun shining down on all I own
            in one eyeblink to the horizon   20
                in my last eternity—
                    matter is water.

Sad,
    I take the elevator and go
        down, pondering,   25
and walk on the pavements staring into all man's
                  plateglass, faces,
      questioning after who loves,

    and stop, bemused
        in front of an automobile shopwindow   30
    standing lost in calm thought,
        traffic moving up & down 5th Avenue blocks
          behind me
        waiting for a moment when. . . .

Time to go home & cook supper & listen to   35
        the romantic war news on the radio

              . . . all movement stops
& I walk in the timeless sadness of existence,
    tenderness flowing thru the buildings,
        my fingertips touching reality's face,   40
    my own face streaked with tears in the mirror
    of some window—at dusk—
        where I have no desire—
for bonbons—or to own the dresses or Japanese
    lampshades of intellection—   45

Confused by the spectacle around me,
    Man struggling up the street
        with packages, newspapers,
            ties, beautiful suits

        toward his desire   50
    Man, woman, streaming over the pavements
        red lights clocking hurried watches &
        movements at the curb—

And all these streets leading
    so crosswise, honking, lengthily,   55
        by avenues

    stalked by high buildings or crusted into slums
        thru such halting traffic
            screaming cars and engines
so painfully to this   60
    countryside, the graveyard
        this stillness
            on deathbed or mountain
  once seen
        never regained or desired   65
          in the mind to come
where all Manhattan that I've seen must disappear.

Mothers

Nikki Giovanni [*1943–*]

the last time i was home
to see my mother we kissed
exchanged pleasantries
and unpleasantries pulled a warm
comforting silence around   5
us and read separate books

i remember the first time
i consciously saw her
we were living in a three room
apartment on burns avenue   10

mommy always sat in the dark
i don't know how i knew that but she did

that night i stumbled into the kitchen
maybe because i've always been
a night person or perhaps because i had wet   15
the bed
she was sitting on a chair
the room was bathed in moonlight diffused through
those thousands of panes landlords who rented
to people with children were prone to put in windows   20
she may have been smoking but maybe not
her hair was three-quarters her height
which made me a strong believer in the samson myth
and very black

i'm sure i just hung there by the door   25
i remember thinking: what a beautiful lady

she was very deliberately waiting
perhaps for my father to come home
from his night job or maybe for a dream
that had promised to come by   30
"come here" she said "i'll teach you
a poem: *i see the moon*
> *the moon sees me*
> *god bless the moon*
> *and god bless me"*   35
i taught it to my son
who recited it for her
just to say we must learn
to bear the pleasures
as we have borne the pains   40

For My Mother

Louise Glück   [1943–   ]

It was better when we were
together in one body.
Thirty years. Screened
through the green glass
of your eye. moonlight   5
filtered into my bones
as we lay
in the big bed, in the dark,
waiting for my father.
Thirty years. He closed   10
your eyelids with
two kisses. And then spring
came and withdrew from me
the absolute
knowledge of the unborn,   15
leaving the brick stoop
where you stand, shading
your eyes, but it is
night, the moon
is stationed in the beech tree,   20
round and white among
the small tin markers of the stars:
Thirty years. A marsh
grows up around the house.
Schools of spores circulate   25
behind the shades, drift through
gauze flutterings of vegetation.

Christmas Eve in Whitneyville, 1955

Donald Hall   [1928–   ]

to my father

December, and the closing of the year;
The momentary carolers complete
Their Christmas Eves, and quickly disappear
Into their houses on each lighted street.

Each car is put away in each garage;   5
Each husband, home from work to celebrate,
Has closed his house around him like a cage,
And wedged the tree until the tree stood straight.

Tonight you lie in Whitneyville again,
Near where you lived, and where the woods or farms   10
Which Eli Whitney settled with the men
Who worked at mass-producing firearms.

The main-street, which was nothing after all
Except a school, a stable, and two stores,
Was improvised and individual,   15
Picking its way alone, until the wars.

Not Whitneyville is like the other places,
Ranch-houses stretching flat beyond the square,
Same stores and movie, same composite faces
Speaking the language of the public air.   20

Old buildings loiter by the cemetery.
When you were twelve they dressed you up in black
With five companions from the class, to carry
The body of a friend. Now you are back,

Beside him, but a man of fifty-two.   25
Talk to the boy. Tell him about the years
When Whitneyville quadrupled, and how you
And all his friends went on to make careers,

Had cars as long as hayricks, flew in planes,
And took vacation trips across the sea.   30
Like millionaires. Tell him how yearly gains,
Profit and volume built the company.

"The things you had to miss," you said last week,
"Or thought you had to, take your breath away."
You propped yourself on pillows, where your cheek   35
Was hollow, stubbled lightly with new gray

This love is jail; another sets us free.
Tonight the houses and their noise distort
The thin rewards of solidarity.
The houses lean together for support.   40

The noises fail. Now lights go on upstairs.
The men and women are undressing now
To go to sleep. They put their clothes on chairs
To take them up again. I think of how,

Across America, when midnight comes,   45
They lie together and are quieted,
To sleep as children sleep, who suck their thumbs,
Cramped in the narrow rumple of each bed.

They will not have unpleasant thoughts tonight.
They make their houses jails, and they will take   50
No risk of freedom for the appetite,
Or knowledge of it, when they are awake.

The light go out and it is Christmas Day.
The stones are white, the grass is black and deep;
I will go back and leave you here to stay,   55
While the dark houses harden into sleep.

Those Winter Sundays

Robert Hayden   [1918–   ]

Sundays too my father got up early
and put his clothes on in the blueblack cold,
then with cracked hands that ached
from labor in the weekday weather made
banked fires blaze. No one ever thanked him.   5

I'd wake and hear the cold splintering, breaking.
When the rooms were warm, he'd call,
and slowly I would rise and dress,
fearing the chronic angers of that house,

Speaking indifferently to him,   10
who had driven out the cold
and polished my good shoes as well.
What did I know, what did I know
of love's austere and lonely offices?

"More Light! More Light!"

Anthony Hecht   [1923–   ]

Composed in the Tower before his execution
These moving verses, and being brought at that time
Painfully to the stake, submitted, declaring thus:
"I implore my God to witness that I have made no crime."

Nor was he forsaken of courage, but the death was horrible,   5
The sack of gunpowder failing to ignite.
His legs were blistered sticks on which the black sap
Bubbled and burst as he howled for the Kindly Light.

And that was but one, and by no means one of the worst;
Permitted at least his pitiful dignity;   10
And such as were by made prayers in the name of Christ,
That shall judge all men, for his soul's tranquility.

We move now to outside a German wood.
Three men are there commanded to dig a hole
In which the two Jews are ordered to lie down   15
And be buried alive by the third, who is a Pole.

Not light from the shrine at Weimar beyond the hill
Nor light from heaven appeared. But he did refuse.
A Lüger settled back deeply in its glove.
He was ordered to change places with the Jews.   20

Much casual death had drained away their souls.
The thick dirt mounted toward the quivering chin.
When only the head was exposed the order came
To dig him out again and to get back in.

No light, no light in the blue Polish eye.   25
When he finished a riding boot packed down the earth.
The Lüger hovered lightly in its glove.
He was shot in the belly and in three hours bled to death.

No prayers or incense rose up in those hours
Which grew to be years, and every day came mute   30
Ghosts from the ovens, sifting through crisp air,
And settled upon his eyes in a black soot.

The Center of Attention

Daniel Hoffman   [1928–   ]

As grit swirls in the wind the word spreads.
On pavements approaching the bridge a crowd
Springs up like mushrooms.
They are hushed at first, intently

Looking. At the top of the pylon   5
The target of their gaze leans toward them.
The sky sobs
With the sirens of disaster crews

Careening toward the crowd with nets,
Ladders, resuscitation gear, their First   10
Aid attendants antiseptic in white duck.
The police, strapped into their holsters,

Exert themselves in crowd-control. They can't
Control the situation
Atop the pylon there's a man who threatens   15
Violence. He shouts, *I'm gonna jump—*

And from the river of upturned faces
—Construction workers pausing in their construction work,
Shoppers diverted from their shopping,
The idlers relishing this diversion   20

In the vacuity of their day—arises
A chorus of cries—*Jump!*

Jump! and *No—*
Come down! Come down! Maybe, if he can hear them,

They seem to be saying *Jump down!* The truth is,   25
The crowd cannot make up its mind.
This is a tough decision. The man beside me
Reaches into his lunchbox and lets him have it,

Jump! before he bites his sandwich,
While next to him a young blonde woman clutches   30
Her handbag to her breasts and moans
Don't Don't Don't so very softly

You'd think she was afraid of being heard.
The will of the people is divided.
Up there he hasn't made his mind up either.   35
He has climbed and climbed on spikes imbedded in the pylon

To get where he has arrived at.
Is he sure now that this is where he was going?
He looks down one way into the river.
He looks down the other way into the people.   40

He seems to be looking for something
Or for somebody in particular.
Is there anyone here who is that person
Or can give him what it is that he needs?

From the back of a firetruck a ladder teeters.   45
Inching along, up, up up up up, a policeman
Holds on with one hand, sliding it on ahead of him.
In the other, outstretched, a pack of cigarettes.

Soon the man will decide between
The creature comfort of one more smoke   50
And surcease from being a creature.
Meanwhile the crowd calls *Jump!* and calls *Come down!*

Now, his cassock billowing in the bulges of Death's black flag,
A priest creeps up the ladder too.
What will the priest and the policeman together   55
Persuade the man to do?

He has turned his back to them.
He has turned away from everyone.
His solitariness is nearly complete.
He is alone with his decision.   60

No one on the ground or halfway into the sky can know
The hugeness of the emptiness that surrounds him.
All of his senses are orphans.
His ribs are cold andirons.

Does he regret his rejection of furtive pills,   65
Of closet noose or engine idling in closed garage?
A body will plummet through shrieking air,
The audience dumb with horror, the spattered street . . .

The world he has left is as small as toys at his feet.
Where he stands, though nearer the sun, the wind is chill.   70
He clutches his arms—a caress, or is he trying
Merely to warm himself with his arms?

The people below, their necks are beginning to ache.
The are getting impatient for this diversion
To come to some conclusion. The priest   75
Inches further narrowly up the ladder.

The center of everybody's attention
For some reason has lit up a butt. He sits down.
He looks down on the people gathered, and sprinkles
Some of his ashes upon them.   80

Before he is halfway down
The crowd is half-dispersed.
It was his aloneness that clutched them together.
They were spellbound by his despair

And now each rung brings him nearer,   85
Nearer to their condition
Which is not sufficiently interesting
To detain them from business or idleness either,

Or is too close to a despair
They do not dare   90
Exhibit before a crowd
Or admit to themselves they share.

Now the police are taking notes
On clipboards, filling the forms.
He looks round as though searching for what he came down for.   95
Traffic flows over the bridge.

The Curse

John Hollander   [*1929*–   ]

Outside, a delicate arch
Of steel rises above
The desolate streets, and westward,
The river's long-since-fallen
Water lies darkly quiet,   5
Holding in its broad lap
Golden lights from rewarding

Shores, showered in payment;
Slowly the moon-tied flow tugs
Downward; everything runs   10
Unstopped out of the bay.

Inside, the yellow lights
Of the hopeless IRT
Die for a second, as car
By car, the train blacks out,   15
Moment echoing moment.
They stand at the front window
Watching the opening tunnel
That crashes into their faces.
She is a week late.   20
They are waiting to stop waiting
For something inside to happen.

On the surface of it,
A blessing will come in time,
Falling on her one morning   25
When they are separate;
When they meet that evening
She will tell him sweetly,
On the wide street, in the spill
Of fluorescence from the grocer's: 30
"It's all right now." "I thought so."
Blessed in the change, they scamper
Uptown toward a shining corner.

Blessed? Cursed? or merely
Commanded to be? To issue   35
Forth from love's subway
Is to reclaim a world
Not lost, but checked at an entrance:
Their fear's sole issue only
The delayed mundane omen,   40
They move from depth to surface,
Over the skin-deep avenues
Then, along and across them.
And so on. And so forth.

But, at bottom, that light   45
Will again be revoked.
As when the moon's dark falls
Across the tar of rooftops,
Gathering the pale shadows
Of a fortnight past,   50
There in the wheal and flare
Of another underground
Tube, the shadows of coming
Shadows mold their cheeks,
Their bright, unhollowed eyes.   55

A Far Cry After a Close Call

Richard Howard [*1929*–   ]

> For if they do these things in a green tree what
> shall be done in the dry?—*Luke 23:31*

Nuns, his nieces, bring the priest in the next
Bed pralines, not prayers for the next world,
    But I've had one look myself
      At *that* one (looking

Back now, crammed in the convalescent ward,   5
With the invisible man opposite
    Sloshing most of the Black Sea
      Around in his lungs,

While the third patient coughs and borrows *Time*).
No one turned over when I was wheeled in;   10
    The efficient British nurse
      Snipped off my soggy

Trousers and put me right, "sure as Bob's your
Uncle." The water roared and ran away,
    Leaving only words to stock   15
      My mind like capsules

Crowding a bottle. Then the lights blew up,
Went out, someone was going through My Things
    While I rowed—rowed for my life
      Down the rubber floor—   20

But the waves failed me. The hallway heaved where I
Foundered and turned in my doctor's dry hands
    To sovereign selflessness:
      Meaning had melted.

"*Mon corps est moi*," Molière said. They're more than that,   25
This monster the body, this miracle
    Its pain—when was I ever
      Them, when were they me?

At thirty-three, what else is there to do
But wait for yet another great white moth   30
    With eager, enlarging eyes
      To land on my chest.

Slowly, innocently choking me off?
The feelers stir while I lie still, lie here
    (Where on earth does it come from,   35
      That wind, that wounding

Breath?), remembering the future now,
Foreseeing a past I shall never know,
    Until the little crisis
        Breaks, and I wake.   40

For as Saint Paul sought deliverance from
The body of this death, I seek to stay—
    Man is mad as the body
        Is sick, by nature.

Graves at Elkhorn

Richard Hugo [*1923–*]

for Joe Ward

'Eighty-nine was bad. At least a hundred
children died, the ones with money planted
in this far spot from town. The corn
etched in these stones was popular that year.
'Our dearest one is gone.' The poorer ones   5
used wood for markers. Their names
got weaker every winter. Now gray wood
offers a blank sacrifice to rot.

The yard and nearly every grave are fenced.
Something in this space must be defined—   10
where the lot you paid too much for ends
or where the body must not slide beyond.
The yard should have a limit like the town.
The last one buried here: 1938. The next
to the last: 1911 from a long disease.   15

The fence around the yard is barbed, maintained
by men, around the graves, torn down
by pines. Some have pines for stones.
The yard is this far from the town because
when children die the mother should repeat   20
some form of labor, and a casual glance
would tell you there could be no silver here.

Europe and America

David Ignatow [*1914–*]

My father brought the emigrant bundle
of desperation and worn threads,
that in anxiety as he stumbles
tumble out distractedly;

while I am bedded upon soft green money   5
that grows like grass. Thus,
between my father who lives on a bed of anguish
for his daily bread, and I who tear money
at leisure by the roots,
where I lie in sun or shade,   10
a vast continent of breezes, storms to him,
shadows, darkness to him, small lakes,
difficult channels to him, and hills,
mountains to him, lie between us.

My father comes of a hell   15
where bread and man have been kneaded
and baked together. You have heard the scream
as the knife fell; while I have slept
as guns pounded on the shore.

How You Get Born

Erica Jong   [1942–   ]

One night, your mother is listening to the walls.
The clock whirrs like insect wings.
The ticking says lonely lonely lonely.

In the living room, the black couch swallows her.
She trusts it more than men,   5
but no one will ever love her
enough.

She doesn't yet know you
so how can she love you?
She loves you like God or Shakespeare.   10
She loves you like Mozart.

You are trembling in the walls like music.
You cross the ceiling in a phantom car of light.

Meanwhile unborn,
you wait in a heavy rainsoaked cloud   15
for your father's thunderbolt.
Your mother lies in the living room dreaming your hands.
Your mother lies in the living room dreaming your eyes.

She awakens & a shudder shakes her teeth.
The world is beginning again after the flood.   20

She slides into bed beside that gray-faced man,
your father.
She opens her legs to your coming.

Counting the Mad

Donald Justice [*1925–*]

This one was put in a jacket,
This one was sent home,
This one was given bread and meat
But would eat none,
And this one cried No No No No   5
All day long.

This one looked at the window
As though it were a wall,
This one saw things that were not there,
And this one cried No No No No   10
All day long.

This one thought himself a bird,
This one a dog,
And this one thought himself a man,
An ordinary man,   15
And cried and cried No No No No
All day long.

Getting the Mail

Galway Kinnell [*1927–*]

I walk back
toward the frog pond, carrying
the one letter, a few wavy lines
crossing the stamp: tongue-streaks
from the glue   5
and spittle beneath: my sign.

The frogs'
eyes bulge toward the visible, suddenly
an alderfly glitters past, declining
to die: her third giant step   10
into the world.

And touching
the name stretched over the letter
like a blindfold, I wonder,
what did *getting warm* used to mean? And tear   15

open the words,
to the far-off, serene
groans of a cow
a farmer is milking in the August dusk
and the Kyrie of a chainsaw drifting down off Wheelock Mountain.   20

Hard Rock Returns to Prison
from the Hospital for the Criminal Insane

Etheridge Knight [*1933–*]

Hard Rock was "known not to take no shit
From nobody," and he had the scars to prove it:
Split purple lips, lumped ears, welts above
His yellow eyes, and one long scar that cut
Across his temple and plowed through a thick   5
Canopy of kinky hair.

The WORD was that Hard Rock wasn't a mean nigger
Anymore, that the doctors had bored a hole in his head,
Cut out part of his brain, and shot electricity
Through the rest. When they brought Hard Rock back,   10
Handcuffed and chained, he was turned loose,
Like a freshly gelded stallion, to try his new status.
And we all waited and watched, like indians at a corral,
To see if the WORD was true.

As we waited we wrapped ourselves in the cloak   15
Of his exploits: "Man, the last time, it took eight
Screws to put him in the Hole." "Yeah, remember when he
Smacked the captain with his dinner tray?" "He set
The record for time in the Hole—67 straight days!"
"Ol Hard Rock! man, that's one crazy nigger."   20
And then the jewel of a myth that Hard Rock had once bit
A screw on the thumb and poisoned him with syphilitic spit.

The testing came, to see if Hard Rock was really tame.
A hillbilly called him a black son of a bitch
And didn't lose his teeth, a screw who knew Hard Rock   25
From before shook him down and barked in his face.
And Hard Rock did *nothing*. Just grinned and looked silly,
His eyes empty like knot holes in a fence.

And even after we discovered that it took Hard Rock
Exactly 3 minutes to tell you his first name,   30
We told ourselves that he had just wised up,
Was being cool; but we could not fool ourselves for long,
And we turned away, our eyes on the ground. Crushed.
He had been our Destroyer, the doer of things
We dreamed of doing but could not bring ourselves to do,   35
The fears of years, like a biting whip,
Had cut grooves too deeply across our backs.

I think of Housman who said the poem
is a morbid secretion, like the pearl

Judith Kroll   [1943–   ]

You are the grain
of sand in my side.
I cover you over
with layers and layers
of papery pearl. Poems,   5
there are hundreds,
microscope-thin.

Their ink is all invisible, is not
the important part as each
addition wraps around.   10
It has got so big
I cannot hear
my heart through the mountain.
The grain is far away,
like a childhood myth,   15
the good angel
who changes dimes for teeth.

Where does it all come from?

Doctor,

what does it mean to have   20
a white stone of considerable size
growing beneath one's
skin?

I see.

The Testing-Tree

Stanley Kunitz   [1905–   ]

1

On my way home from school
       up tribal Providence Hill
              past the Academy ballpark
where I could never hope to play
       I scuffed in the drainage ditch   5
              among the sodden seethe of leaves
hunting for perfect stones
       rolled out of glacial time

into my pitcher's hand;
then sprinted lickety-   10
split on my magic Keds
from a crouching start,
scarcely touching the ground
with my flying skin
as I poured it on   15
for the prize of the mastery
over that stretch of road,
with no one no where to deny
when I flung myself down
that on the given course   20
I was the world's fastest human.

2

Around the bend
that tried to loop me home
dawdling came natural
across a nettled field   25
riddled with rabbit-life
where the bees sank sugar-wells
in the trunks of the maples
and a stringy old lilac
more than two stories tall   30
blazing with mildew
remembered a door in the
long teeth of the woods.
All of it happened slow:
brushing the stickseed off, 35
wading through jewelweed
strangled by angel's hair,
spotting the print of the deer
and the red fox's scats.

Once I owned the key   40
to an umbrageous trail
thickened with mosses
where flickering presences
gave me right of passage
as I followed in the steps 45
of straight-backed Massassoit
soundless heel-and-toe
practicing my Indian walk.

3

Past the abandoned quarry
where the pale sun bobbed 50
in the sump of the granite,

past copperhead ledge,
    where the ferns gave foothold,
        I walked, deliberate,
on to the clearing,   55
    with the stones in my pocket
        changing to oracles
and my coiled ear tuned
    to the slightest leaf-stir.
        I had kept my appointment.   60
There I stood in the shadow,
    at fifty measured paces,
        of the inexhaustible oak,
tyrant and target,
    Jehovah of acorns,   65
        watchtower of the thunders,
that locked King Philip's War
    in its annulated core
        under the cut of my name.
Father wherever you are   70
    I have only three throws
        bless my good right arm.
In the haze of afternoon,
    while the air flowed saffron,
        I played my game for keeps—   75
for love, for poetry,
    and for eternal life—
        after the trials of summer.

4

In the recurring dream
    my mother stands   80
        in her bridal gown
under the burning lilac,
    with Bernard Shaw and Bertie
        Russell kissing her hands;
the house behind her is in ruins;   85
    she is wearing an owl's face
        and makes barking noises.
Her minatory finger points.
    I pass through the cardboard doorway
        askew in the field   90
and peer down a well
    where an albino walrus huffs.
        He has the gentlest eyes.
If the dirt sifting in,
    staining the water yellow,   95
        why should I be blamed?
Never try to explain.

That single Model A
    sputtering up the grade
unfurled a highway behind   100
    where the tanks maneuver,
       revolving their turrets.
In a murderous time
    the heart breaks and breaks
       and lives by breaking.   105
It is necessary to go
    through dark and deeper dark
       and not to turn.
I am looking for the trail.
    Where is my testing-tree?   110
       Give me back my stones!

The Old Adam

Denise Levertov [*1923–*   ]

A photo of someone else's childhood,
a garden in another country—world
he had no part in and has no power to imagine:

yet the old man who has failed his memory
keens over the picture—'Them happy days—   5
gone—gone for ever!'—glad for a moment to suppose

a focus for unspent grieving, his floating
sense of loss.
He wanders

asking the day of the week, the time,   10
over and over the wrong questions.
Missing his way in the streets

he acts out
the bent of his life,
the lost way   15

never looked for, life
unlived, of which he is dying
very slowly.

'A man,'
says his son, 'who never   20
made a right move in all his life.' A man

who thought the dollar was sweet and
couldn't make a buck, riding the subway
year after year to untasted sweetness,

loving his sons obscurely, incurious   25
who they were, these men, his sons—
a shadow of love, for love longs

to know the beloved, and a light goes with it
into the dark mineshafts of feeling . . . A man
who now, without knowing,   30

in endless concern for the smallest certainties,
looking again and again at a paid bill,
inquiring again and again, 'When was I here last?'

asks what it's too late to ask:
'Where is my life? Where is my life?   35
What have I done with my life?'

The Open Sea

William Meredith   [*1919–*   ]

We say the sea is lonely; better say
Ourselves are lonesome creatures whom the sea
Gives neither yes nor no for company.

Oh, there are people, all right, settled in the sea;
It is as populous as Maine today,   5
But no one who will give you the time of day.

A man who asks there of his family
Or a friend or teacher gets a cold reply
Or finds him dead against that vast majority.

Nor does it signify that people who stay   10
Very long, bereaved or not, at the edge of the sea
Hear the drowned folk call: that is mere fancy,

They are speechless. And the famous noise of sea
Which a poet has beautifully told us in our day
Is hardly a sound to speak comfort to the lonely.   15

Although not yet a man given to prayer, I pray
For each creature lost since the start at sea,
And give thanks it was not I, nor yet one close to me.

Thistledown

James Merrill   [*1926–*   ]

First clan of autumn, thistleball on a stem
Between forefinger and thumb,
Known for the seeds

That make a wish come true when the light last of them
Into air blown subsides, 5

Feathery sphere of seeds, frail brain
On prickly spine,
I feared their dissipation, deeds of this crown aspin,
Words from a high-flown talker, pale brown
Thistledown. 10

Yet when, bewildered what to want
Past the extravagant
Notion of wanting, I puffed
And the soft cluster broke and spinning went
More channels than I knew, aloft 15

In the wide air to lift its lineage
Ha! how the Scotch flower's spendthrift
Stars drifted down
Many to tarn or turf, but ever a canny one
On the stem left 20

To remind me of what I had wished:
That none should have clung, lest summer, thistle-bewitched,
Dry up, be done
—And the whole of desire not yet into watched
Air at a breath blown! 25

The Widow

W. S. Merwin [1927–]

How easily the ripe grain
Leaves the husk
At the simple turning of the planet

There is no season
That requires us 5

Masters of forgetting
Threading the eyeless rocks with
A narrow light

In which ciphers wake and evil
Gets itself the face of the norm 10
And contrives cities

The widow rises under our fingernails
In this sky we were born we are born

And you weep wishing you were numbers
You multiply you cannot be found 15

You grieve
Not that heaven does not exist but
That it exists without us

You confide
In images in things that can be   20
Represented which is their dimension you
Require them you say This
Is real and you do not fall down and moan

Not seeing the irony in the air

Everything that does not need you is real   25

The Widow does not
Hear you and your cry is numberless

This is the waking landscape
Dream after dream after dream walking away through it
Invisible invisible invisible   30

Earth and I Gave You Turquoise

N. Scott Momaday   [*1934–*   ]

Earth and I gave you turquoise
    when you walked singing
We lived laughing in my house
    and told old stories
You grew ill when the owl cried   5
We will meet on Black Mountain

I will bring you corn for planting
    and we will make fire
Children will come to your breast
    You will heal my heart   10
I speak your name many times
The wild cane remembers you

My young brother's house is filled
    I go there to sing
We have not spoken of you   15
    but our songs are sad
When the Moon Woman goes to you
I will follow her white way

Tonight they dance near Chinle
    by the seven elms   20
There your loom whispered beauty
    They will eat mutton
and drink coffee till morning
You and I will not be there

I saw a crow by Red Rock   25
   standing on one leg
It was the black of your hair
   The years are heavy
I will ride the swiftest horse
You will hear the drumming of hooves   30

I Saw My Darling

Frederick Morgan   [*1922–*   ]

I saw my darling on the street
walking home with clothes in her arms—
clothes from the cleaners—she walked along
past where the school was being built

on the next block. I called to her—   5
shouting "Paula!" out my window.
Shouted twice, three times. A black
construction worker grinned at me

from the unfinished roof. My dear one
turned, looked back the way she'd passed,   10
then—as I called again—looked up,
saw me, and smiled, and called: "I'm coming!"

Earlier on the telephone
we had spoken to a dying friend
in a suburban hospital.   15
A loving voice, but very faint.

God takes our friends in death. He gives
us pains to match (at least) our joys.
But gives, too, moments in each day
in which the heart may find itself   20

and learn its freedom in the vaster
gift of love in which it breathes.
Just as my heart is learning now—
my heart in which her smile still blooms.

Long Island Springs

Howard Moss   [*1922–*   ]

Long Island springs not much went on,
Except the small plots gave their all
In weeds and good grass; the mowers mowed

Up to the half-moon gardens crammed
With anything that grew. Our colored maid 5

Lived downstairs in a room too small
To keep a bird in, or so she claimed;
She liked her drinks, sloe-gin, gin-and . . .
When she was fired, my grandma said,
"Give them a finger, they'll take your hand." 10

So much for the maid. My grandma lived
In a room almost as small. She gave
Bread to the birds, saved bits of string,
Paper, buttons, old shoelaces, thread . . .
Not peasant stock but peasant—the real thing. 15

What stuff we farmed in our backyard!
Horseradish that my grandma stained beet-red—
Hot rouge for fish—her cosmos plants
With feathery-fine carrot leaves, and my
Poor vegetables, no first class restaurant's 20

Idea of France. "Your radishes are good,"
My sister said, who wouldn't touch the soil.
My mother wouldn't either. "Dirt, that's all."
Those afternoons of bridge and mah-jongg games,
Those tournaments! Click-click went forty nails 25

That stopped their racket for the candy dish.
"Coffee, girls?" came floating up the stairs.
Our house was "French Provincial." Chinese mirrors
Warred against the provinces. The breakfast nook
Had a kind of style. But it wasn't ours. 30

I'd walk down to the bay and sit alone
And listen to the tide chew gum. There was
An airport on the other shore. Toy-like,
It blew toy moths into the air. At night,
We'd hear the distant thunder of New York. 35

Grandpa, forgive me. When you called for me
At school in a sudden rain or snow, I was
Ashamed that anyone would see your beard
Or hear you talk in broken English. You
Would bring a black umbrella, battle-scarred, 40

And walk me home beneath it through the lots,
Where seasonal wild roses took a spill
And blew their cups, and sumac bushes grew
Up from the sand, attached to secret springs,
As I was secretly attached to you. 45

Friday night. The Bible. The smell of soup,
Fresh bread in the oven, the mumbling from

The kitchen where my grandma said her prayers.
Reading the Bible, she kept one finger under
Every line she read. Alone, upstairs,   50

The timelessness of swamps came over me,
A perpetual passing of no time, it seemed,
Waiting for dinner, waiting to get up
From dinner, waiting, waiting all the time.
For what? For love, as longed-for as a trip   55

A shut-in never takes. It came to me.
But what Proust said is true: If you get
What you want in life, by the time you do,
You no longer want it. But that's another
Story, or stories, I should say, much too   60

Pointless to go into now. For what
Matters to me are those lifelong two
Transplanted figures in a suburb who
Loved me without saying, "I love you."
Grandpa, tonight, I think of you.   65

ENVOI

Grandma, your bones lie out in Queens.
The black funeral parlor limousines
Just make it up the narrow aisles.
When flowers on your headstone turn to moss,
Russian cossack horses leap across
The stone, the stone parentheses of years.   70

from

Life on Earth

Frank O'Hara   [*1928–1966*]

I

Shine, "O world!" don't weary the gulping Pole
deep in drinking this night his mighty syrup of aches.
His song will be calmer when the laughing birds settle on his soul
        and cling.
When calmness is near, he will lie with his breast on the fountain
        and scream
"Walking behind me and distributing my joys is a goose!   5
My darling is a leaf! My leaf is a toad!"
Hearing this echoed, he burns the air with sobs.

Night is knelling her platitudes and tearing his garments of feeling.
"Here am I! these cries are nearly mine!

their loudness is possessing me, I am becoming a leer, the very glass   10
of millions of things that find me disgusting.
I have thrown myself from the Bridge of Richness throughout the
    world!"

Misery has always reached itself a helping hand on the river bed,
the sky burgeons with aspirations as the years exhale and inhale.
It is a great feast! those blossoms which are like the Lives of the
    Saints.   15
And must he, then, die of longing in his sty?
He has already forgotten the nearness of his youth, its whiteness
in the morbid dances and truncated limbs of the yards.

See yourself then! in the skeleton of moonlight
you are spending your blood like so many ribbons in a tornado,   20
your desperate remedies are wildly murmuring curses in your mouth,
hear them thrashing in the dusts and the fears!
Yet choose yourself. The great open stare of unconsciousness is a
    crystal ball.
Your life is pushing us to our feet, O leaf!

The Quiet Fog

Marge Piercy [*1934–*]

The pitch pines fade
into a whiteness
that has blotted the marsh.

Beyond
starts ten feet   5
outside the magic circle
of lit house.

The hill has dissolved.
The road ends
under a soft wall   10
that creeps.

Why am I happy?
I cradle my elbows
corners of a mirror
tall as childhood   15
reflecting
nothing.

Daddy

Sylvia Plath [*1932–1963*]

You do not do, you do not do
Any more, black shoe
In which I have lived like a foot
For thirty years, poor and white,
Barely daring to breathe or Achoo.   5

Daddy, I have had to kill you.
You died before I had time——
Marble-heavy, a bag full of God,
Ghastly statue with one grey toe
Big as a Frisco seal   10

And a head in the freakish Atlantic
Where it pours bean green over blue
In the waters off beautiful Nauset.
I used to pray to recover you.
Ach, du.   15

In the German tongue, in the Polish town
Scraped flat by the roller
Of wars, wars, wars.
But the name of the town is common.
My Polack friend   20

Says there are a dozen or two.
So I never could tell where you
Put your foot, your root,
I never could talk to you:
The tongue stuck in my jaw.   25

It stuck in a barb wire snare.
Ich, ich, ich, ich,
I could hardly speak.
I thought every German was you.
And the language obscene   30

An engine, an engine
Chuffing me off like a Jew.
A Jew to Dachau, Auschwitz, Belsen.
I began to talk like a Jew.
I think I may well be a Jew.   35

The snows of the Tyrol, the clear beer of Vienna
Are not very pure or true.
With my gypsy ancestress and my weird luck
And my Taroc pack and my Taroc pack
I may be a bit of a Jew.   40

I have always been scared of *you,*
With your Luftwaffe, your gobbledygoo.
And your neat moustache
And your Aryan eye, bright blue.
Panzer-man, panzer-man, O You——   45

Not God but a swastika
So black no sky could squeak through.
Every woman adores a Fascist,
The boot in the face, the brute
Brute heart of a brute like you.   50

You stand at the blackboard, daddy,
In the picture I have of you,
A cleft in your chin instead of your foot
But no less a devil for that, no not
Any less the black man who   55

Bit my pretty red heart in two.
I was ten when they buried you.
At twenty I tried to die
And get back, back, back to you.
I thought even the bones would do.   60

But they pulled me out of the sack,
And they stuck me together with glue.
And then I knew what to do.
I made a model of you,
A man in black with a Meinkampf look   65

And a love of the rack and the screw,
And I said I do, I do.
So daddy, I'm finally through.
The black telephone's off at the root,
The voices just can't worm through.   70

I've killed one man, I've killed two——
The vampire who said he was you
And drank my blood for a year,
Seven years, if you want to know.
Daddy, you can lie back now.   75

There's a stake in your fat black heart
And the villagers never liked you.
They are dancing and stamping on you.
They always *knew* it was you.
Daddy, daddy, you bastard, I'm through.   80

The Feral Pioneers

Ishmael Reed   [*1938–*   ]

for Dancer

I rise at 2 a.m. these mornings, to
polish my horns; to see if the killing
has stopped. It is still snowing outside;
it comes down in screaming white
clots.   5

We sleep on the floor. I popped over
the dog last night & we ate it with
roots & berries.

The night before, lights of a
wounded coyote I found in   10
the pass.
(The horse froze weeks ago)

Our covered wagons be trapped
in strange caverns of the world.
Our journey, an entry in the thirty-   15
year old Missourian's '49 Diary.
    'All along the desert road from the
    very start, even the wayside was strewed
    with dead bodies of oxen, mules & horses
    & the stench was horrible.'   20

America, the mirage of a
naked prospector, with sand
in the throat, crawls thru
the stink.
Will never reach the Seven Cities.   25
Will lie in ruins of
once great steer.

I return to the cabin's
warmest room; Pope Joan is
still asleep. I lie down, my hands   30
supporting my head.

Living in Sin

Adrienne Rich   [*1929–*   ]

She had thought the studio would keep itself;
no dust upon the furniture of love.
Half heresy, to wish the taps less vocal,

the panes relieved of grime. A plate of pears,
a piano with a Persian shawl, a cat   5
stalking the picturesque amusing mouse
had risen at his urging.
Not that at five each separate stair would writhe
under the milkman's tramp; that morning light
so coldly would delineate the scraps   10
of last night's cheese and three sepulchral bottles;
that on the kitchen shelf among the saucers
a pair of beetle-eyes would fix her own—
envoy from some black village in the mouldings . . .
Meanwhile, he, with a yawn,   15
sounded a dozen notes upon the keyboard,
declared it out of tune, shrugged at the mirror,
rubbed at his beard, went out for cigarettes;
while she, jeered by the minor demons,
pulled back the sheets and made the bed and found   20
a towel to dust the table-top,
and let the coffee-pot boil over on the stove,
By evening she was back in love again,
though not so wholly but throughout the night
she woke sometimes to feel the daylight coming   25
like a relentless milkman up the stairs.

Poem (I Lived in the First Century)

Muriel Rukeyser [*1913–*]

I lived in the first century of world wars.
Most mornings I would be more or less insane,
The newspapers would arrive with their careless stories,
The news would pour out of various devices
Interrupted by attempts to sell products to the unseen.   5
I would call my friends on other devices;
They would be more or less mad for similar reasons.
Slowly I would get to pen and paper,
Make my poems for others unseen and unborn.
In the day I would be reminded of those men and women   10
Brave, setting up signals across vast distances,
Considering a nameless way of living, of almost unimagined values.
As the lights darkened, as the lights of night brightened,
We would try to imagine them, try to find each other.
To construct peace, to make love, to reconcile   15
Waking with sleeping, ourselves with each other,
Ourselves with ourselves. We would try by any means
To reach the limits of ourselves, to reach beyond ourselves,
To let go the means, to wake.
I lived in the first century of these wars.   20

Summer Words for a Sister Addict

Sonia Sanchez   [*1935–*   ]

the first day i shot dope
was on a sunday.
                       i had just come
home from church
                       got mad at my mother   5
cuz she got mad at me.   u dig?
                       went out. shot up
behind a feeling against her.
                       it felt good.
goodeɪ than dooing it.   yeah   10
                       it was nice.
i did it.   uh. huh.   i did it.   uh. huh.
i want to do it again.   it felt so gooooood.
                       and as the sister
                       sits in her silent/   15
                       remembered/high
                       someone leans for
                       ward gently asks her:
                           sister.
                               did u   20
                           finally
                       learn how to hold yr/mother?
and the music of the day
                       drifts in the room
to mingle with the sister's young tears.   25
                   and we all sing.

from

The Modes of Vallejo Street
San Diego Los Angeles

Hugh Seidman   [*1940–*   ]

for Laurie

3

He imagines her
a sister of her generation
passing thru Taos or the Badlands

searching in her Saab for the communes
blue eye intent on the desert   5

driving to an ocean
because she is no longer his

where he walks at night
in the white foam
of the spotlight on the cliff   10
where the lights of La Jolla lie south

where he knows
that five hundred miles from him
she will hear
the ocean that he hears   15

to know he is in this place
that the stars have not lied

that when he lay upon the beach
she was inside him still

that he shivered in her power   20
driving him
blue eye intent on the desert

9

He knows he must explain this
how they had eaten dinner
had eaten with others   25
her good friends

and how he had been angered
by the red-haired woman
and by the man that she lived with
who were *her* friends   30

how at that time he had told himself
he was angered by the beauty of this woman
that he, himself, could not have

but later he saw that what he hated
was the fact of their love   35

the love that he wanted from her
that she would not give
would not under any circumstances

so that they went to the house of these people
and he felt himself ruined   40
a marked man

in the light of a black and shrunken sun
that was charring him
with silence and with blame

and it came upon him   45
and would not relinquish him
so that the whole of the world was filled with it

and afterwards, in his house
before they took their clothes off
she yelled at him   50

she accused him
and he curled away from her
he let her judge him

and he claimed
that Hamlet was more than his sickness   55
and said this to defend himself

to save himself, instead of fighting her
instead of screaming back at her
that he was right

for finally she had said: 60
but I love those people
as if to say she had chosen them

and he wanted to cry, to cry out
to hold and to choke her with the knowledge
that it was he, he was the one who loved her   65
and not *those* people

and by what right
had she the power to choose them over him
by what right in this world
had she that power   70

but he could not do this
or did not know how

because clearly she had tried to want him
had tried deeply but could not
so that that was why   75

For My Lover, Returning to His Wife

Anne Sexton   [1928–1974]

She is all there.
She was melted carefully down for you
and cast up from your childhood,
cast up from your one hundred favorite aggies.

She has always been there, my darling.   5
She is, in fact, exquisite.

Fireworks in the dull middle of February
and as real as a cast-iron pot.

Let's face it, I have been momentary.
A luxury. A bright red sloop in the harbor.   10
My hair rising like smoke from the car window.
Littleneck clams out of season.

She is more than that. She is your have to have,
has grown you your practical, your tropical growth.
This is not an experiment. She is all harmony.   15
She sees to oars and oarlocks for the dinghy,

has placed wild flowers at the window at breakfast,
sat by the potter's wheel at midday,
set forth three children under the moon,
three cherubs drawn by Michelangelo,   20

done this with her legs spread out
in the terrible months in the chapel.
If you glance up, the children are there
like delicate balloons resting on the ceiling.

She has also carried each one down the hall   25
after supper, their heads privately bent,
two legs protesting, person to person,
her face flushed with a song and their little sleep.

I give you back your heart.
I give you permission—   30

for the fuse inside her, throbbing
angrily in the dirt, for the bitch in her
and the burying of her wound—
for the burying of her small red wound alive—

for the pale flickering flare under her ribs,   35
for the drunken sailor who waits in her left pulse,
for the mother's knee, for the stockings,
for the garter belt, for the call—

the curious call
when you will burrow in arms and breasts   40
and tug at the orange ribbon in her hair
and answer the call, the curious call.

She is so naked and singular.
She is the sum of yourself and your dream.
Climb her like a monument, step after step.   45
She is solid.

As for me, I am a watercolor.
I wash off

Love Poem

Leslie Marmon Silko   [*1948–*   ]

Rain smell comes with the wind
                out of the southwest.
Smell of the sand dunes
         tall grass glistening
              in the rain.   5
Warm raindrops that fall easy
           (this woman)
The summer is born.
Smell of her breathing new life
            small gray toads on damp sand.   10
(this woman)
       whispering to dark wide leaves
       white moon blossoms dripping
               tracks in the sand
Rain smell   15
      I am full of hunger
      deep and longing to touch
wet tall grass, green and strong beneath.
This woman loved a man
and she breathed to him   20
        her damp earth song.

I am haunted by this story
I remember it in cottonwood leaves
          their fragrance in the shade.
I remember it in the wide blue sky   25
when the rain smell comes with the wind.

Stumpfoot on 42nd Street

Louis Simpson   [*1923–*   ]

1

A Negro sprouts from the pavement like an asparagus.
One hand beats a drum and cymbal;
He plays a trumpet with the other.

He flies the American flag;
When he goes walking, from stump to stump,   5
It twitches, and swoops, and flaps.

Also, he has a tin cup which he rattles;
He shoves it right in your face.
These freaks are alive in earnest.

He is not embarrassed.   10
It is for you to feel embarrassed,
Or God, or the way things are.

Therefore he plays the trumpet
And therefore he beats the drum.

2

I can see myself in Venezuela,   15
With flowers, and clouds in the distance.
The mind tends to drift.

But Stumpfoot stands near a window
Advertising cameras, trusses, household utensils.
The billboards twinkle. The time   20
Is 12 26.

O why don't angels speak in the infinite
To each other? Why this confusion,
These particular bodies—
Eros with clenched fists, sobbing and cursing?   25

The time is 12:26.
The streets lead on in burning lines
And giants tremble in electric chains.

3

I can see myself in the middle of Venezuela
Stepping in a nest of ants.   30
I can see myself being eaten by ants.

My ribs are caught in a thorn bush
And thought has no reality.
But he has furnished his room

With a chair and table.   35
A chair is like a dog, it waits for man.
He unstraps his apparatus,

And now he is taking off his boots.
He is easing his stumps,
And now he is lighting a cigar.   40

It seems that a man exists
Only to say, Here I am in person.

Mementos, 1

W D. Snodgrass [*1926–*   ]

Sorting out letters and piles of my old
   Canceled checks, old clippings, and yellow note cards

That meant something once, I happened to find
    Your picture. *That* picture. I stopped there cold,
Like a man raking piles of dead leaves in his yard   5
    Who has turned up a severed hand.

Still, that first second, I was glad: you stand
    Just as you stood—shy, delicate, slender,
In that long gown of green lace netting and daisies
    That you wore to our first dance. The sight of you stunned   10
Us all. Well, our needs were different, then,
    And our ideals came easy.

Then through the war and those two long years
    Overseas, the Japanese dead in their shacks
Among dishes, dolls, and lost shoes; I carried   15
    This glimpse of you, there, to choke down my fear,
Prove it had been, that it might come back.
    That was before we got married.

—Before we drained out one another's force
    With lies, self-denial, unspoken regret   20
And the sick eyes that blame; before the divorce
    And the treachery. Say it: before we met. Still,
I put back your picture. Someday, in due course,
    I will find that it's still there.

All the Spirit Powers Went to Their Dancing Place

Gary Snyder [*1930–*]

Floods of men
    on foot, fighting and starving, cans rusted
    by the roadside

Clouds swirling and spiralling up the sky,
    men fighting with scythes.   5

Wild beings sweeping on cities—spirits and ghosts—
    cougar, eagle, grizzly bear, coyote, hummingbird
    intelligences
    directing   destructing   instructing;   us all
    as through music: 10
    songs filling the sky.

The earth lifting up and flying like millions of birds
    into dawn.

Hills rising and falling as music, long plains and deserts
    as slow quiet chanting,   15

Swift beings, green beings, all beings—all persons;
  the two-legged beings
  shine in smooth skin and their furred spots

Drinking clear water together
  together   turning and dancing
  speaking   new words
  the first time, for

Air, fire, water, and
  Earth is our dancing place now.

20

In Time of Need

William Stafford   [1914-   ]

We out our hands on the window—cold:
less of a world out there but more of its plain
hard shell. That scene is the still landscape
carved out of our days, a place time needed.

A time of need: we will drive over
the mountains. Whatever we find, it is
away from home. The years have drifted
wrong, and we are afraid, looking elsewhere.

Time to move—I walk through the empty house,
let the rooms flood still after me. I
pick up a picture. It curls, and the turning events
caught on the surface bend into themselves.

My still hand closes outside it, folds down while
the years flow together. I put the picture
into my mouth and run the long going away,
holding a calm face against the opening world.

5

10

15

from
Elegy for My Father
(Robert Strand, 1908–1968)

Mark Strand   [1934-   ]

1 THE EMPTY BODY
The hands were yours, the arms were yours,
But you were not there.
The eyes were yours, but they were closed and would not open.
The distant sun was there.

The moon poised on the hill's white shoulder was there.   5
The wind on Bedford Basin was there.
The pale green light of winter was there.
Your mouth was there,
But you were not there.
When somebody spoke, there was no answer.   10
Clouds in the blind air came down
And buried the buildings along the water,
And the water was silent.
The gulls stared.
The years, the hours, that would not find you   15
Turned in the wrists of others.
There was no pain. It had gone.
There were no secrets. There was nothing to say.
The shade scattered its ashes.
The body was yours, but you were not there.   20
The air shivered against its skin.
The dark leaned into its eyes.
But you were not there.

6 THE NEW YEAR

It is winter and the new year.
Nobody knows you.   25
Away from the stars, from the rain of light,
You lie under the weather of stones.
There is no thread to lead you back.
Your friends doze in the dark
Of pleasure and cannot remember.   30
Nobody knows you. You are the neighbor of nothing.
You do not see the rain falling and the man walking away,
The soiled wind blowing its ashes across the city.
You do not see the sun dragging the moon like an echo.
You do not see the bruised heart go up in flames,   35
The skulls of the innocent turn into smoke.
You do not see the scars of plenty, the eyes without light.
It is over. It is winter and the new year.
The meek are hauling their skins into heaven.
The hopeless are suffering the cold with those who have nothing
        to hide.   40
It is over and nobody knows you.
There is starlight drifting on the black water.
There are stones in the sea no one has seen.
There is a shore and people are waiting.
And nothing comes back.   45
Because it is over.
Because there is silence instead of a name.
Because it is winter and the new year.

How to Be Old

May Swenson [*1909–*]

It is easy to be young. (Everybody is,
at first.) It is not easy
to be old. It takes time.
Youth is given; age is achieved.
One must work a magic to mix with time   5
in order to become old.

Youth is given. One must put it away
like a doll in a closet,
take it out and play with it only
on holidays. One must have many dresses   10
and dress the doll impeccably
(but not to show the doll, to keep it hidden.)

It is necessary to adore the doll,
to remember it in the dark on the ordinary
days, and every day congratulate   15
one's aging face in the mirror.

In time one will be very old.
In time, one's life will be accomplished.
And in time, in time, the doll—
like new, though ancient—will be found.   20

The Lost Pilot

James Tate [*1943–*]

for my father, 1922–1944

Your face did not rot
like the others—the co-pilot,
for example, I saw him

yesterday. His face is corn-
mush: his wife and daughter,   5
the poor ignorant people, stare

as if he will compose soon.
He was more wronged than Job.
But your face did not rot

like the others—it grew dark,   10
and hard like ebony;
the features progressed in their

distinction. If I could cajole
you to come back for an evening,
down from your compulsive 15

orbiting, I would touch you,
read your face as Dallas,
your hoodlum gunner, now,

with the blistered eyes, reads
his braille editions. I would 20
touch your face as a disinterested

scholar touches an original page.
However frightening, I would
discover you, and I would not

turn you in; I would not make 25
you face your wife, or Dallas,
or the co-pilot, Jim. You

could return to your crazy
orbiting, and I would not try
to fully understand what 30

it means to you. All I know
is this: when I see you,
as I have seen you at least

once every year of my life,
spin across the wilds of the sky 35
like a tiny, African god,

I feel dead. I feel as if I were
the residue of a stranger's life,
that I should pursue you.

My head cocked toward the sky, 40
I cannot get off the ground,
and, you, passing over again,

fast, perfect, and unwilling
to tell me that you are doing
well, or that it was mistake 45

that placed you in that world,
and me in this; or that misfortune
placed these worlds in us.

In the Churchyard

Eleanor Ross Taylor   [*1920–*   ]

In the churchyard I hear them hammering
On the new roof of my new house
A hundred years old.
Cupped acorns glut the walks,
The greenish nuts crushed in.   5
Cupped earths hold up the bright memorial ferns.
They're gone!
Down over Mamma's face
They nailed, we nailed, I nailed the lid.
And there was Uncle Risdon.   10
Married a Miss Catherine Tye. Aunt Catherine
Somehow I can't now call her full name.
She took a galloping consumption
After she let the baby catch on fire.
Aunt Oratha despised the coat   15
That Uncle bought her. She died of pride.
Pride knoweth neither hot nor cold
But hers knew both.
They die of fleshly pride.
And Cousin Mazeppa took laudanum.   20
"Why did you do it, Zeppie, girl?
Wa'n't Daddy good to you?"
"Pray, let me sleep!"

Child, brave it to blind-out the fur
Of the evergreens in sun above: 25
They are too far;
Shade has rinsed out their sun,
Hushed up their green.
They'll dizzy one.

There's the rattat of the hammers—   30
The nails, the little nails,
The nirds eat out one's hands!

The Gardener to His God

Mona Van Duyn   [*1921–*   ]

Amazing research proves simple prayer makes flowers
grow many times faster, stronger, larger.
              —Advertisement in *The Flower Grower*

I pray that the great world's flowering stay as it is,
that larkspur and snapdragon keep to their ordinary size,

and bleedingheart hang in its old way, and Judas tree
stand well below oak, and old oaks color the fall sky.
For the myrtle to keep underfoot, and no rose   5
to send up a swollen face, I pray simply.

There is no disorder but the heart's. But if love goes leaking
outward, if shrubs take up its monstrous stalking,
all greenery is spurred, the snapping lips are overgrown,
and over oaks red hearts hang like the sun.   10
Deliver us from its giant gardening, from walking
all over the earth with no rest from its disproportion.

Let all flowers turn to stone before ever they begin to share
love's spaciousness, and faster, stronger, larger
grow from a sweet thought, before any daisy   15
turns, under love's gibberellic wish, to the day's eye.
Let all blooms take shape from cold laws, down from a cold air
let come their small grace or measurable majesty.

For in every place but love the imagination lies
in its limits. Even poems draw back from images   20
of that one country, on top of whose lunatic stemming
whoever finds himself there must sway and cling
until the high cold God takes pity, and it all dies
down, down into the great world's flowering.

In the Badlands

David Wagoner   [*1926–*]

When we fell apart in the Badlands and lay still
As naked as sunlight
On the level claybed among the broken buttes,
We were ready for nothing—
The end of the day or the end of our quick breathing,   5
The abolishment of hearts—
And saw in the sky a dozen vultures sailing
With our love as the pivot.
They had come in our honor, invited by what could pass
In their reckoning   10
For the thresh and crux and sprawled languor of death,
Too much pale skin
In that burning bed where we lay at our own banquet,
Being taken in
As thoroughly as the fossils under us   15
When they lay down;
And the sea that once was there welled up in our eyes
For the sake of the sun.

Placing a $2 Bet for a Man Who Will Never Go to the Horse Races Any More

Diane Wakoski   [1937–   ]

for my father

There is some beauty in sorrow
and the sorrowing,
perhaps not beauty
perhaps dignity
would be a better word   5
which communicates
life
beyond just what the body dictates
            food
                clothing   10
                shelter.
It is nothing that lasts.
It quickly turns into gloom, hate, resentment,
a burdening apathy
sometimes severity towards others;   15
but like a scarlet bird
from the tropics
suddenly seen flying in a New York City park,
so unexpected,
so unexplainable,   20
there,
different from its surroundings.

Caliente,
the poor man's race track,
in Tijuana, Mexico,   25
where I met my real father,
an old retired sailor
after 14 years of separation
and learned that the real pleasures of gambling
are knowing how   30
to lose.

Old man,
I place a bet for you
now that you're dead
and I am still living.   35
It is on a horse called, "The Man I Love."
Gamblers are sentimental
so you will forgive me
living now
and giving away my love.   40

Win or lose
you played the races every day.
A certain spirit
I hope
you've passed on to me.   45

A Far Cry from Africa

Derek Walcott   [*1930–*   ]

A wind is ruffling the tawny pelt
Of Africa. Kikuyu, quick as flies,
Batten upon the bloodstreams of the veldt.
Corpses are scattered through a paradise.
Only the worm, colonel of carrion, cries: 5
'Waste no compassion on these separate dead!'
Statistics justify and scholars seize
The salients of colonial policy.
What is that to the white child hacked in bed?
To savages, expendable as Jews?   10

Threshed out by beaters, the long rushes break
In a white dust of ibises whose cries
Have wheeled since civilization's dawn
From the parched river or beast-teeming plain.
The violence of beast on beast is read   15
As natural law, but upright man
Seeks his divinity by inflicting pain.
Delirious as these worried beasts, his wars
Dance to the tightened carcass of a drum,
While he calls courage still that native dread   20
Of the white peace contracted by the dead.

Again brutish necessity wipes its hands
Upon the napkin of a dirty cause, again
A waste of our compassion, as with Spain,
The gorilla wrestles with the superman.   25
I who am poisoned with the blood of both,
Where shall I turn, divided to the vein?
I who have cursed
The drunken officer of British rule, how choose
Between this Africa and the English tongue I love?   30
Betray them both, or give back what they give?
How can I face such slaughter and be cool?
How can I turn from Africa and live?

Birth of Love

Robert Penn Warren   [*1905–*   ]

Season late, day late, sun just down, and the sky
Cold gunmetal but with a wash of live rose, and she,
From water the color of sky except where
Her motion has fractured it to shivering splinters of silver,
Rises. Stands on the raw grass. Against   5
The new-curdling night of spruces, nakedness
Glimmers and, at bosom and flank, drips
With fluent silver. The man,

Some ten strokes out, but now hanging
Motionless in the gunmetal water, feet   10
Cold with the coldness of depth, all
History dissolving from him, is
Nothing but an eye. Is an eye only. Sees

The body that is marked by his use, and Time's,
Rise, and in the abrupt and unsustaining element of air,   15
Sway, lean, grapple the pond-bank. Sees
How, with that posture of female awkwardness that is,
And is the stab of, suddenly perceived grace, breasts bulge down in
The pure curve of their weight and buttocks
Moon up and, in that swelling unity,   20
Are silver, and glimmer. Then

The body is erect, she is herself, whatever
Self she may be, and with an end of the towel grasped in each hand,
Slowly draws it back and forth across back and buttocks, but
With face lifted toward the high sky, where   25
The over-wash of rose color now fails. Fails, though no star
Yet throbs there. The towel, forgotten,
Does not move now. The gaze
Remains fixed on the sky. The body,

Profiled against the darkness of spruces, seems   30
To draw to itself, and condense in its whiteness, what light
In the sky yet lingers or, from
The metallic and abstract severity of water, lifts. The body,
With the towel now trailing loose from one hand, is
A white stalk from which the face flowers gravely toward the high sky.   35
This moment is non-sequential and absolute, and admits
Of no definition, for it
Subsumes all other, and sequential, moments, by which
Definition might be possible. The woman,

Face yet raised, wraps,   40
With a motion as though standing in sleep,

The towel about her body, under the breasts, and,
Holding it there hieratic as lost Egypt and erect,
Moves up the path that, stair-steep, winds
Into the clamber and tangle of growth. Beyond   45
The lattice of dusk-dripping leaves, whiteness
Dimly glimmers, goes. Glimmers and is gone, and the man,

Suspended in his darkling medium, stares
Upward where, though not visible, he knows
She moves, and in his heart he cries out that, if only   50
He had such strength, he would put his hand forth
And maintain it over her to guard, in all
Her out-goings and in-comings, from whatever
Inclemency of sky or slur of the world's weather
Might ever be. In his heart   55
He cries out. Above

Height of the spruce-night and heave of the far mountain, he sees
The first star pulse into being. It gleams there.

I do not know what promise it makes to him.

The Minneapolis Poem

James Wright   [*1927–*   ]

1

I wonder how many old men last winter
Hungry and frightened by namelessness prowled
The Mississippi shore
Lashed blind by the wind, dreaming
Of suicide in the river.   5
The police remove their cadavers by daybreak
And turn them in somewhere.
Where?
How does the city keep lists of its fathers
Who have no names?   10
By Nicollet Island I gaze down at the dark water
So beautifully slow.
And I wish my brothers good luck
And a warm grave.

2

The Chippewa young men   15
Stab one another shrieking
Jesus Christ.
Split-lipped homosexuals limp in terror of assault.
High school backfields search under benches

Near the Post Office. Their faces are the rich   20
Raw bacon without eyes.
The Walker Art Center crowd stare
At the Guthrie Theater.

3

Tall Negro girls from Chicago
Listen to light songs.   25
They know when the supposed patron
Is a plainclothesman.

A cop's palm
Is a roach dangling down the scorched fangs
Of a light bulb.   30
The soul of a cop's eyes
Is an eternity of Sunday daybreak in the suburbs
Of Juárez, Mexico.

4

The legless beggars are gone, carried away
By white birds.   35
The Artificial Limbs Exchange is gutted
And sown with lime.
The whalebone crutches and hand-me-down trusses
Huddle together dreaming in a desolation
Of dry groins.   40
I think of poor men astonished to waken
Exposed in broad daylight by the blade
Of a strange plough.

5

All over the walls of comb cells
Automobiles perfumed and blindered   45
Consent with a mutter of high good humor
To take their two naps a day.
Without sound windows glide back
Into dusk.
The sockets of a thousand blind bee graves tier upon tier   50
Tower not quite toppling.
There are men in this city who labor dawn after dawn
To sell me my death.

6

But I could not bear
To allow my poor brother my body to die   55
In Minneapolis.
The old man Walt Whitman our countryman
Is now in America our country

Dead.   60
But he was not buried in Minneapolis
At least.
And no more may I be
Please God.

7

I want to be lifted up
By some great white bird unknown to the police,   65
And soar for a thousand miles and be carefully hidden
Modest and golden as one last corn grain,
Stored with the secrets of the wheat and the mysterious lives
Of the unnamed poor.

How Poems Come About: Intention and Meaning

Appendix A

Why are we, or why should we be, interested in how poems come about? A historian or biographer might be intensely interested in the materials that got into a poem—the personal experiences or observations of the poet, or ideas current in his time. Or a psychologist might equally well be interested in the mental process of creation that gave us the poem. But the historian or psychologist, strictly as historian or psychologist, would not be interested in the quality of the poem. For his interests, the bad poem might be as useful as the good poem. But our present concern is different from that of the historian or psychologist. We are primarily interested in the nature of the poem and its quality.

If the poem itself is our primary interest, we may say that there is no good reason why we should investigate the origins of the poem, and that a knowledge of the materials that went into the poem or of the process by which it came to be, cannot change the nature of the poem itself. Many people take the view that we have no proper concern with the private lives of writers even if the lives do provide material for the work. Wordsworth says in a letter to James Gray, a friend of Robert Burns:

> Our business is with their books,—to understand and to enjoy them. And, of poets more especially, it is true—that, if their works be good, they contain within themselves all that is necessary to their being comprehended and relished.

464

And Charles Lamb was shocked when he saw the manuscript of Milton's "Lycidas" (p. 334), as he reports in his essay "Oxford in the Vacation":

> I had thought of the Lycidas as a full-grown beauty—as springing up with all its parts absolute—till, in an evil hour, I was shown the original copy of it, together with the other minor poems of the author, in the library of Trinity, kept like some treasure to be proud of. I wish they had thrown them in the Cam, or sent them after the latter Cantos of Spenser, into the Irish Channel. How it staggered me to see the fine things in their ore! interlined, corrected! as if their words were mortal, alterable, displaceable at pleasure! as if they might have been otherwise, and just as good! as if inspiration were made up of parts, and these fluctuating, successive, indifferent! I will never go into the workshop of any great artist again.

In one sense, Wordsworth is right. We must not confuse information about the life of a poet, or his time, or his materials, with the poem itself. For the reader of poetry Lamb is right. What is important is the poem itself and not the psychological process whereby it was created. But in another sense both Wordsworth and Lamb are wrong. What we can learn about the origin of a poem may, if we do not confuse origin and poem, enlarge our understanding and deepen our appreciation.*

In thinking of the origin of a poem we may distinguish two general aspects of the question: first, the *materials* of the poem, and second, the *process* whereby the poem is made.

The materials of a poem are various. We can, for instance, say that language itself is a material of poetry. It is one of the things the poet shapes and uses. We have to know something of the language a poet is using before we can appreciate his poem—before we can see how the poem came to be. This applies not only to poems in foreign languages but also to poems in our own tongue. The English of one time is not like the English of another. Words are born and die and, to make matters more complicated, the meaning of a word may change from one period to another. Furthermore, the poet himself may twist and wrench the language he uses so that words get new meanings.

To take another example, we may regard literary convention as a material for poetry. When Campion came to write "Blame Not My Cheeks" (p. 217), he used as one of the elements in his poem the Petrarchan convention of the lover who is abject and self-pitying before the cruel lady who despises him. Actually, in the course of the poem, this convention is brought into contrast with other attitudes, and the almost whimsical irony of the last line, which yet remains

---

* This gain in understanding and appreciation is not merely, in fact not primarily, of the poem whose development we can trace because early drafts or information about the poet's experience have been preserved to us. It is, rather, a gain in our understanding and appreciation of poetry in general; when we learn about the materials of poetry and about the poetic process, we also learn something about the nature of poetry. The value of this study of biographical and textual material is to be distinguished sharply, however, from the value of certain historical information which is necessary for the understanding of particular literary works from another age or another culture. For example, we can presumably understand *Hamlet* without knowing Shakespeare's private life or the steps in the composition of the play, but we cannot understand the play unless we know something of the heroic tradition in which revenge is held to be honorable.

serious, is anything but Petrarchan. But the convention provides the starting point. The same is true of the convention of the pastoral elegy in Milton's "Lycidas." Milton is simply using this conventional fiction which had persisted from classical times. It is a material which he adapts in his own way.

Or let us consider the ideas that are available at a given time. Those, too, are materials. Tennyson uses a foreshadowing of the theory of evolution in his "In Memoriam," and Whitman expresses certain notions of democracy. But it is nonsense to read "Sir Patrick Spence" (p. 23) as a statement of modern democratic ideas, for that poem came out of a feudal society. A poet may, of course, do something original with the ideas available to him. But his ideas are conditioned by his time.

So far we have been speaking of some of the materials of poetry that are generally available in a period: the language, the literary conventions, the ideas. But the personal experiences of the poet are also materials. This is not to say that a poet simply reports his personal experiences. Because Shakespeare wrote a play about Macbeth, who killed a king and stole a throne, we do not have to assume that Shakespeare ever committed murder or robbery. Sometimes, very often in fact, the events in a poem are fictitious, are products of imagination. But the imagination is not entirely free; it is conditioned, too, by the experience of the poet. It is true, as Robert Frost says, that the poet needs only samples for the imagination to work on, but it does not work in a vacuum.

The relation between the actual work of a poet and his personal experiences may be a very delicate and tenuous one, but sometimes we find a very close correlation between the actual events and the poetry. Dorothy Wordsworth, the sister of the poet, records in her journal for April 15, 1802, the episode that gave the material for Wordsworth's poem on the daffodils entitled "I Wandered Lonely as a Cloud" (p. 492):

It was a threatening, misty morning, but mild. . . The wind was furious, and we thought we must have returned. We first rested in the large boathouse, then under a furze bush opposite Mr. Clarkson's. Saw the plow going in the field. The wind seized our breath. The Lake was rough. There was a boat by itself floating in the middle of the bay below Water Millock. . . . When we were in the woods beyond Gowbarrow Park we saw a few daffodils close to the water-side. We fancied that the lake had floated the seeds ashore, and that the little colony had so sprung up. But as we went along there were more and yet more; and at last, under the boughs of the trees, we saw that there was a long belt of them along the shore, about the breadth of a country turnpike road. I never saw daffodils so beautiful. They grew among the mossy stones about and about them; some rested their heads upon these stones as on a pillow for weariness; and the rest tossed and reeled and danced, and seemed as if they verily laughed with the wind, that blew upon them over the lake; they looked so gay, ever glancing, ever changing. This wind blew directly over the lake to them. There was here and there a little knot, and a few stragglers a few yards higher up; but they were so few as not to disturb the simplicity, unity, and life of that one busy highway.

It is true that in his poem Wordsworth does more than merely report the scene, but the scene is vividly there, a piece of material from his experience.

And we are fairly safe in concluding that when he came to write the poem two years after the event, in 1804, the interpretation he gave the original event—the notion that experience grows in the imagination and the notion of the sympathetic relation between man and nature—was drawn also from personal experience. The real scene *had* flashed upon his inward eye. We see here how a whole poem, event and interpretation, presumably come as a presentation of real experience, *preceding* the act of composition.

To take another instance, we have an account by William Butler Yeats of a visit to a dying friend, the sister of the artist Aubrey Beardsley, who himself had died young and courageously:

> She was propped up on pillows with her cheeks I think a little rouged and looking very beautiful. Beside her an Xmas tree with little toys containing sweets, which she gave us. . . . I will keep the little toy she gave me and I dare say she knew that. On a table near were four dolls dressed like people out of her brother's drawings. . . . Ricketts had made them, modeling the faces and sewing the clothes. They must have taken him days. She had all her great lady airs and asked after my work and health as if they were the most important things in the world to her. "A palmist told me," she said, "that when I was forty-two my life would take a turn for the better and now I shall spend my forty-second year in heaven," and then emphatically pretending we were incredulous, "O yes, I shall go to heaven. Papists do." . . . Then she began telling improper stories and inciting us (there were two men besides myself) to do the like. At moments she shook with laughter. . . . I lay awake most of the night with a poem in my head. I cannot overstate her strange charm—the pathetic gaiety—It was her brother but her brother was not I think lovable. only astonishing and intrepid.*

If we compare this with Yeats's poem on the same dying lady (p. 403), we find that most of the details and attitudes had already been present in the prose account, either explicitly or implicitly.

In the journal of Dorothy Wordsworth and the letter of Yeats, we have accounts of personal experiences that later become the material of poetry. In these instances, the relation between the experience and the poem is close. We have the impression that the poet had the experience and then did his thinking about its significance before he entered upon composition, before he had the impulse to make a poem.

We may, of course, be wrong about this. Wordsworth may have begun to turn around in his mind the idea of a poem on the daffodils even as he looked marveling at them. But what is important is that the first simple experience is interpreted, is turned about and about, until it gets a meaning for the poet and until he finds words that develop the meaning.

It may be objected here that the thinking about the original experience is also *material,* that it is as much material as the sight of the daffodils, and that it is certainly to be regarded as material if the poet did his thinking and interpreting *before* he actually began the process of composition. Then arises the question of what we mean by the process of composition. Does it begin

---

* Quoted by A. Norman Jeffares, *W. B. Yeats: Man and Poet,* Yale University Press, 1949, p. 166.

when the poet first takes pen in hand, or when, without necessarily intending a poem, he begins to think about the material and try to interpret it?

But does it really matter which view we take? The important thing is to see some line of connection between the experience and the poem which in its finished form interprets the experience.

All poems, however, do not start directly from a personal experience of the poet. A poet may actually start from a general idea—a theme—and seek episodes and images to embody it. For example, Coleridge apparently intended to write a poem about guilt and atonement, and actually began a prose-poem on Cain, long before he lit upon the story of the Ancient Mariner to embody his ideas. And Milton, too, was casting about for a story to embody his ideas on guilt and atonement before he settled on *Paradise Lost* (p. 168). In the manuscript of Milton's minor poems, preserved in the library of Trinity College at Cambridge University (to which Lamb alluded in the passage we quoted on p. 465), there are notes toward a drama on the Deluge as well as a drama on the Fall of Man. Or a poem may start from a story, an episode, or a situation heard about or read. It strikes the poet as interesting, and he begins to try to make a poem of that material, even before he is clear about why it interests him or what it means to him. Or it may start with a casual phrase that pops into the poet's head or is picked up somewhere; or an image of some kind or a comparison may fire his imagination.

However the process may start, what is its nature?

At first glance, the accounts we have of the process seem contradictory and confusing. Some poets work very slowly and carefully. Some work by fits and starts, trusting to the suggestion of the moment. Some poems have been dreamed up in an instant. Some have required years of thought. There is Poe's famous account, in "The Philosophy of Composition," of the creation of "The Raven." After arguing that a poem must make its effect immediately, in a limited time, Poe says:

> Holding in view these considerations, as well as that degree of excitement which I deemed not above the popular, while not below the critical, taste, I reached at once what I conceived the proper *length* for my intended poem—a length of about one hundred lines. It is, in fact, a hundred and eight.
>
> My next thought concerned the choice of an impression, or effect, to be conveyed: and here I may as well observe that, throughout the construction, I kept steadily in view the design of rendering the work *universally* appreciable. . . . That pleasure which is at once the most intense, the most elevating, and the most pure, is, I believe, found in the contemplation of the beautiful. When, indeed, men speak of Beauty, they mean, precisely, not a quality, as is supposed, but an effect. . . . Now I designate Beauty as the province of the poem, merely because it is an obvious rule of Art that effects should be made to spring from direct causes. . . .
>
> Regarding, then, Beauty as my province, my next question referred to the *tone* of its highest manifestation—and all experience has shown that this tone is one of *sadness*. . . . Melancholy is thus the most legitimate of all the poetical tones. . . .
>
> The length, the province, and the tone, being thus determined, I betook myself to ordinary induction with the view of obtaining some artistic piquancy

which might serve me as a key-note in the construction of the poem—some pivot upon which the whole structure might turn. In carefully thinking over all the usual artistic effects . . . I did not fail to perceive immediately that no one had been so universally employed as that of the *refrain.*

Poe continues in this fashion, as systematically as though working out a theorem in geometry. The refrain must be a single word, it must close each stanza, it must be sonorous, it must be melancholy, for that is the already determined tone, by which Poe seems to have meant *mood,* rather than tone as used in this book. So he selects the word *nevermore,* as logically as a mechanic picks up the proper monkey-wrench.

Over against this sytematic approach of Poe (which seems almost too systematic to be true) we can put the account given by Coleridge of the composition of "Kubla Khan" (p. 318):

In the summer of the year 1797, the author, then in ill health, had retired to a lonely farmhouse between Porlock and Linton, on the Exmoor confines of Somerset and Devonshire. In consequence of a slight indisposition, an anodyne had been prescribed, from the effects of which he fell asleep in his chair at the moment that he was reading the following sentence, or words of the same substance, in *Purchas's Pilgrimage:* "Here the Khan Kubla commanded a palace to be built, and a stately garden thereunto. And thus ten miles of fertile ground were inclosed with a wall." The author continued for about three hours in a profound sleep, at least of the external senses, during which time he has the most vivid confidence, that he could not have composed less than from two to three hundred lines; if that indeed can be called composition in which all the images rose up before him as *things,* with a parallel production of the correspondent expressions, without any sensation or consciousness of effort. On awaking he appeared to himself to have a distinct recollection of the whole, and taking his pen, ink, and paper, instantly and eagerly wrote down the lines that are here preserved. At this moment he was unfortunately called out by a person on business from Porlock, and detained by him above an hour, and on his return to his room, found, to his no small surprise and mortification, that though he still retained some vague and dim recollection of the general purport of the vision, yet, with the exception of some eight or ten scattered lines and images, all the rest had passed away like the images on the surface of a stream into which a stone has been cast, but, alas! without the after restoration of the latter.

In between these two extremes there are all sorts of ways of composition. Though Shakespeare never, as far as we know, dreamed up a poem, he apparently did compose with great speed and fluency, and did little revision. Dryden, too, came to have more and more readiness so that, as he says, the thoughts outran the pen. The French poet Bonnard* records that when he composed, all the words seemed to crowd in at the same time so that he had the impression of having a thousand voices. But one part of the same poem may be composed in almost a flash and another part may require long and

---

* N. Kostyleff, *Le Mécanisme Cérébral de la Pensée,* Librairie Félix Alcan, 1914, p. 187.

tedious effort. A. E. Housman provides us with such a poem. He tells us, in *The Name and Nature of Poetry,* how he was accustomed to compose on his afternoon walk, when he was a little drowsy from lunch and beer and his mind was relaxed and free for the movement of association. Under these circumstances, sometimes stanzas, or even whole poems, would come almost in a flash, sometimes merely the germs of poems which had to be developd later. He tells us, for example, that of the poem given below two stanzas came immediately while he was walking along, that another stanza came that same afternoon during teatime, but that another took a year and went through thirteen versions. Unfortunately, Housman did not specify the stanzas, but one critic* has argued that the first and second stanzas must have come spontaneously on the walk, for they make a finished thought, and that the last most probably came at teatime, separate from the first two. Then the problem was to get something that would carry over from the second to the fourth stanza to give balance to the repetition and return of the poem.

I hoed and trenched and weeded,
  And took the flowers to fair:
I brought them home unheeded;
  The hue was not the wear.

So up and down I sow them   5
  For lads like me to find,
When I shall lie below them,
  A dead man out of mind.

Some seed the birds devour,
  And some the season mars,   10
But here and there will flower
  The solitary stars,

And fields will yearly bear them
  As light-leaved spring comes on,
And luckless lads will wear them   15
  When I am dead and gone.

Robert Frost says that many of his best poems came spontaneously, without effort:

I won't deny I have worried quite a number of my poems into existence. But my sneaking preference remains for the ones I carried through like the stroke of a racquet, club, or headsman's ax. It is only under pressure from friends that I can consent to come out into the open and expose myself in a weakness so sacred and in the present trend of criticism so damaging. When I look into myself for the agony I am supposed to lay claim to as an artist it has to be over the poems that went wrong and came to grief without coming to an end; and they made me less miserable than I deserved when I discovered that though lost they were not entirely lost: I could and did quite freely quote lines and phrases of them from memory. I never wrote a poem for practice:

* Donald A. Stauffer, *Poets at Work,* Harcourt, Brace, 1948, pp. 42–43.

I am always extended for the best yet. But what I failed with I learned to charge up to practice after the fact. Now if I had only treasured my first drafts along with my baby shoes to bear me out in all this I should be more comfortably off in a world of suspicion. My word will be more or less taken for it that I played certain poems through without fumbling a sentence: such as for example November Days, The Mountain, After Apple-Picking, The Wood-Pile, Desert Places, The Gift Outright, The Lovely Shall Be Choosers, Directive. With what pleasure I remember their tractability. They have been the experience I couldn't help returning for more of—I trust I may say without seeming to put on inspired airs.*

As Housman spontaneously caught little or much of a poem on his walks, so Hart Crane† tried to evoke the creative process by drink and jazz music, which might hypnotically start trains of verbal association; and so Schiller is reported to have kept a rotting apple in his desk because he found the odor stimulating. And many poets have had little tricks and habits, which seem to make the process easier, more automatic, more like Coleridge's dream, ways to reach what Katherine Anne Porter has called "that undistracted center of being where the will does not intrude and the sense of passing time is lost, or has no power over the imagination."‡

What are we to make of all this? Is there one kind of poetry that comes from calculation and another kind that comes from inspiration?

Perhaps the best way to approach the question is to ask how the composition of poetry compares with other kinds of creative activity, for instance, the

---

* From a letter to Charles Madison, February 26, 1950. The letter continues: "Then for a small chaser of the low-down under the head perhaps of curiosa I might confess the trade secret that I wrote the third line of the last stanza of Stopping by Woods in such a way as to call for another stanza when I didn't want another stanza and didn't have another stanza in me, but with great presence of mind and a sense of what a good boy I was I instantly struck the line out and made my exit with a repeat end. I left the Ingenuities of Debt lying round nameless for forty years because I couldn't find a fourth line for it to suit me. A friend, a famous poet, saw it in 1913 and wasn't so much disturbed by my bad fourth line as he was by the word "terrelation" further on. The same famous poet did persuade me to omit a line or two from the Death of the Hired Man and wanted me to omit the lines Home is the place where when you have to go there they have to take you in. The last three lines of Nothing Gold Can Stay were once entirely different. A lady in Rochester, N.Y., has, I think, the earlier version. I haven't. Birches is two fragments soldered together so long ago I have forgotten where the joint is."

† See "The Roaring Boy," in Malcolm Cowley, Exile's Return, Viking Press, 1941.

‡ "Notes on Writing," in New Directions 1940, James Laughlin, ed., New Directions. And here is Charlie Chaplin's account of how he provokes the unconscious: "There's no use just sitting down and waiting for an inspiration, though. You've got to play along. The main thing you've got to do is preserve your vitality. A couple of days of complete rest and solitude helps. Not seeing anybody. I even conserve my emotions. 'I'm not going to get excited about anybody or anything,' I say, 'until I get this gag worked out.' I go along that way, living a quiet and righteous life, and then I stay out late one night, and have a couple of drinks—perhaps all night—and the next morning the reserve pours out. But you've got to have the reserve. Dissipation is no use except as a release. You've been damming it up inside of you, and all of a sudden you say: 'Oh, here it is!' And then you go to work." (From Max Eastman, Heroes I Have Known, Simon and Schuster, 1942, p. 177.)

discovery of a scientific principle. We find parallels here to the poetic activity. Some scientific discoveries have been made as the result of elaborate calculation, but some have been dreamed up as was "Kubla Khan."

The great German chemist Kekulé quite literally dreamed up his two most important discoveries, dealing with the structure of the molecule. He describes his discovery of the structure of benzene, which came to him one night as he sat at his desk trying to write a section of a textbook on chemistry. "But it did not go well; my spirit was with other things. I turned my chair to the fireplace and sank into a half-sleep. Again the atoms flitted before my eyes." The atoms took the pattern of rings:

> Long rows, variously, more closely, united; all in movement, wriggling and turning like snakes. And see, what was that? One of the snakes seized its own tail and the image whirled scornfully before my eyes. As though from a flash of lightning I awoke; this time again I occupied the rest of the night in working out the consequences of the hypothesis.*

There is the account, too, of William Oughtred, the seventeenth-century mathematician who introduced the multiplication and proportion signs, as given in Aubrey's *Brief Lives:*

> He has told Bishop Ward, and Mr. Elias Ashmole . . . that on this spott of ground (or leaning against this Oake, or that ashe) the Solution of such or such a Probleme came into my head, as if infused by a Divine Genius, after I had thought on it without Successe for a yeare, two, or three.†

The German scientist von Helmholtz almost made a method of getting solutions for his problems from the intuitive flash. Kekulé even went so far as to say to his fellow-scientists: "Let us learn to dream, gentlemen; then perhaps we shall find the truth."

Are we prepared to say that there is a difference between scientific discoveries arrived at by calculation and those dreamed up in a flash? No, we judge them in exactly the same way, by the same standards. The fact that in one instance the scientist had the conscious intention of getting the solution and in the other instance did not have it does not affect the solution.

But people ask: "If poets sometimes write poems in such a crazy way, how can we know what the poet intended? Isn't any interpretation we put on it just what we personally happen to make of the poem?"

But what does the word *intend* mean in such a connection?

It is true that sometimes the poet has a pretty clear idea of what he wants his poem to be. He may be able to state a theme and describe the sort of atmosphere or feeling he wants the whole thing to have. But even in such circumstances, is the process of creation analogous to that of building a house by a blueprint? An architect intends a certain kind of house and he can pre-

---

* Quoted by John R. Baker: *The Scientific Life,* Macmillan, 1943, p. 14.

† Henry D. Smyth, an important physicist, says: ". . . the outstanding mathematicians quite frequently are able to guess at the truth of a theorem. Their problem is then to fill in the proof by a series of logical steps. . . . Thus we have a paradox in the method of science. The research man may often think and work like an artist but he has to talk like a bookkeeper, in terms of precise facts, figures, and logical sequences of thought." (Address at Amherst College, March 23, 1950.)

dict it down to the last nail. The carpenter simply follows the blueprint. But at the best the poet cannot envisage the poem as the architect can envisage the house; and insofar as the poet can envisage the poem, he cannot transfer it into words in a mechanical fashion corresponding to the builder's work on the house. As he begins to work with the poem he is never simply following a plan; he is also exploring the possibilities of imagination and language. Until the poem is actually written down to the last word, the poet cannot be sure *exactly* what it will mean—for we know that the meaning of a poem is fuller than the paraphrasable idea, that the rhythms, the verbal texture, the associations of words, the atmosphere, all the elements, enter into the meaning.

Sometimes, as we have said above, the poet may not have a very clear idea, perhaps not any idea, to start with. He may start with a personal experience as yet uninterpreted, a general, vague feeling, an episode, a metaphor, a phrase—anything that comes along to excite the imagination. Then as he composes, he moves toward his idea—toward his general conception of the poem. At the same time that he is trying to envisage the poem as a whole, he is trying to relate the individual items to that whole. He cannot assemble them in a merely arbitrary fashion; they must bear some relation to each other. So he develops his sense of the whole, the anticipation of the finished poem, as he works with the parts and moves from one part to another. Then, as the sense of the whole develops, it modifies the process by which the poet selects and relates the parts, the words, images, rhythms, local ideas, events, etc. As the sense of the poem develops, as the idea becomes clearer, the poet may have to go back and change his beginnings, revise them or drop them entirely. It is a process in which one thing leads to another, then to a whole, and the whole leads back to single things. It is an infinitely complicated process of establishing interrelations.*

We can trace something of this process in certain passages of Shakespeare. When Shakespeare came to compose a particular passage in one of his plays, he had some notion of the relations of the characters and of the over-all business of the scene, but the local composition often seems to move by a fairly free process of association and suggestion.† In the following passage

* One of the best accounts of the creative process, of the way in which the parts become related to each other and to an envisaged whole, occurs in a letter sometimes attributed to Mozart: "My ideas come as they will, I don't know how, all in a stream. If I like them I keep them in my head, and people say that I often hum them over to myself. Well, if I can hold on to them, they begin to join on to one another, as if they were bits that a pastry cook should joint together in his pantry. And now my soul gets heated, and if nothing disturbs me the piece grows larger and brighter until, however long it is, it is all finished at once in my mind, so that I can see it at a glance, as if it were a pretty picture or a pleasing person. Then I don't hear the notes one after another, as they are hereafter to be played, but it is as if in my fancy they were all at once. And that *is* a revel (*das ist nun ein Schmaus*). While I'm inventing, it all seems to me like a fine vivid dream; but that hearing it all at once (when the invention is done), that's the best. What I have once so heard I forget not again, and perhaps this is the best gift that God has granted me." (Quoted by Josiah Royce, *The Spirit of Modern Philosophy*, Houghton Mifflin, 1920, p. 457.) The letter, though generally taken to be a forgery, may have been drawn from various pieces of testimony by the composer. See Jean-Victor Hocquart, *La Pensée de Mozart*, pp. 315–323.

† The examples here are drawn from E. E. Kellett's "Some Notes on a Feature of Shakespeare's Style" in *Suggestions*, Cambridge University Press, 1923, pp. 57–78.

from *Henry V,* the oration of Henry V to his army before the battle of Agincourt, the italicized words indicate the links of thought: how a word used in one connection prompts its use in another connection and suggests a new idea:

> We few, we happy few, we band of *brothers:*
> For he to-day that sheds his blood with me
> Shall be *my brother;* be he ne'er so vile,
> This day shall *gentle* his *condition*
> And *gentlemen* in England now abed
> Shall think themselves accurst they were not here,
> And hold their *manhoods* cheap whiles any speaks
> That fought with us upon St. Crispin's Day.

Again, let us take the speech of Antony, in *Antony and Cleopatra,* when he sees his followers deserting him for Octavius Caesar:

> The hearts
> That *spanieled* me at heels, to whom I gave
> Their wishes, do *discandy, melt* their *sweets,*
> On *blossoming* Caesar; and this *pine* is *barked*
> That overtopped them all.

The word *discandy* combines the notions of melting and of sweetness; *spanieled* leads to *barked,* but in another sense than that of a dog barking; *barked* leads to *pine* (perhaps with some notion of languishing away or losing strength also leading to the word), and to *blossoming* (though this pine is barked and dies, another, i.e., Caesar, is blossoming).

Here, in a limited way, by verbal suggestion, we can see something of the process that sometimes works more generally.

In these instances, however, the drift is established by the dramatic situation. There is a predetermined direction, more or less general, for the development of a passage. But what of poems that, like "Kubla Khan," spring fully formed, or almost fully formed, without any predetermining intention? Can they be said to express a poet's meaning?

They can be said to embody meaning in exactly the same way as any other poem: by the relations among the various elements that constitute the poem. The scientific discoveries of Kekulé or Oughtred are to be judged as any other scientific theories are judged. In the same way, it is the nature of the poem that counts.

But, granting this, it may still be asked how the dreamed-up poem, the poem that comes by a kind of inspiration, is related to the poet himself. Is the poem that is dreamed up irrelevant to the kind of man the poet is? Can it be said to express him? Or are we to regard it, as the ancients sometimes did, as the words of a god coming through the mouth of a man? Or as a kind of accident? Does it just happen, and might it equally well happen to somebody else?

It is the last question that gives us our clue. Only poets dream up poems, and only scientists dream up scientific discoveries. That is, the thing dreamed up is the product of the kind of mind and the kind of training possessed by the dreamer. As Louis Pasteur said: "Chance favors only the prepared spirits." So with inspiration: it only comes to those who are ready for it. Coleridge could dream up "Kubla Khan" because he had thought long and deeply about poetry, because his mind was stocked with certain materials, images and rhythms and ideas. Kekulé could dream up the benzene ring because he had devoted years of conscious and rigorously logical effort to the study of chemistry. The effortlessness was the result of long effort.*

To sum up this last matter, we may turn to Wordsworth's famous Preface to the second edition (1800) of the *Lyrical Ballads,* the volume of poems that he and Coleridge published together. He says that his poems will be distinguished by a "worthy *purpose,*" and *purpose* we can interpret as theme, meaning, or idea. He continues:

> Not that I always began to write with a distinct purpose formally conceived: but habits of meditation have, I trust, so prompted and regulated my feelings, that my descriptions of such objects as strongly excite those feelings, will be found to carry along with them a *purpose.* If this opinion be erroneous, I can have little right to the name of a Poet. For all good poetry is the spontaneous overflow of powerful feelings: and though this be true, Poems to which any value can be attached were never produced on any variety of subjects but by a man who, being possessed of more than usual organic sensibility, had also thought long and deeply.

We find a parallel to Wordsworth's account of how ideas get into poetry, or may get into poetry, in a letter from T. S. Eliot concerning an essay on the themes of one of his poems:

> I think that this kind of analysis is perfectly justified so long as it does not profess to be a reconstruction of the author's method of writing. Reading your essay made me feel, for instance, that I had been a great deal more ingenious than I had been aware of, because the conscious problems with which one is concerned in the actual writing are more those of a quasi musical nature, in the arrangement of metric and pattern, than of a conscious exposition of ideas.†

What is important here for our purpose is that Wordsworth takes the most spontaneous poem, which might have begun in a burst of feeling and with no preconceived notion of its "purpose" or meaning, to be the fruit of his serious thinking at some earlier time. He took the poem to represent him, and accepted the full responsibility for it. The "objects" that excited the feelings carried along with them the "purpose" without the poet's conscious concern with the purpose. And Eliot, also, emphasizes the poet's conscious concern with the immediate problems of the poem, with the problems of the medium, rather than with the ideas as such. But if the unconscious is, as Coleridge says, the genius in the man of genius, it is still far from independent of the conscious; both the conscious and the unconscious are of the same man.

* The relation of "Kubla Khan" to the background of Coleridge's reading and experience is investigated by John Livingston Lowes, *The Road to Xanadu,* Houghton Mifflin, 1927.
† Letter to Cleanth Brooks, March 15, 1937.

For better or for worse, the poet is responsible for his poem. He can always reject any ideas, images, phrases, etc., that come into his head. He cannot guarantee to himself that the right thing for his poem will come along out of his unconscious, but he can certainly refrain from putting the wrong one down on paper. As the poem grows during the process of composition, as he more clearly senses the kind of poem it is to be, he can more consciously criticize and reject elements that are not adequate or coherent, or do not express him. Some years ago a young scholar who greatly admired Housman's work wrote to the poet and asked him how he managed always to select the right word. Housman replied that he didn't bother about trying to get the right word, he simply bothered about getting rid of the wrong one.* That is, the conscious activity was critical, and the unconscious was productive. But the conscious activity is extremely important. It lays down, as it were, the limits for the activity of the unconscious. And in the end, if a poet feels that a poem doesn't represent him, that it does violence to his ideas, etc., he can always burn the poem instead of publishing it. His veto is absolute.

All this is not to say that the process of rejection and revision is carried on at a fully conscious level, that the poet gives himself the reasons for every rejection he makes. He may simply "feel" that the line isn't right, that the image does not fulfill the idea, that the rhythm is awkward. The rejection, that is, may be spontaneous, too. On the other hand, the poet may be fully aware of the issues, and may argue out each step with himself. But it doesn't matter which line he pursues. His act finally represents him. And if the poem is a good poem we can say that the act, whether the poet consciously reasoned about it or not, is a reasonable act.

Here is Randall Jarrell's account of how "The Woman at the Washington Zoo" came to be:

> Late in the summer of 1956 my wife and I moved to Washington. We lived with two daughters, a cat, and a dog, in Chevy Chase; every day I would drive to work through Rock Creek Park, past the zoo. I worked across the street from the Capitol, at the Library of Congress. I knew Washington fairly well, but had never lived there; I had been in the army, but except for that had never worked for the government.
>
> Some of the new and some of the old things there—I was often reminded of the army—had a good deal of effect on me: after a few weeks I began to write a poem. I have most of what I wrote, though the first page is gone; the earliest lines are

            any color
My print, that has clung to its old colors
Through many washings; this dull null
Navy I wear to work, and wear from work, and so
~~And so to bed~~   To bed
With no complaint, no comment—neither from my chief,
               nor
The Deputy Chief Assistant, ~~from~~ his chief.
Nor   nor
~~From~~ Congressmen, ~~from~~ their constituents—
             thin
Only I complain; this ~~poor~~ worn serviceable . . .

* Letter to Arnold Stein, August 22, 1935.

The woman talking is a near relation of women I was seeing there in Washington—some at close range, at the Library—and a distant relation of women I had written about before, in "The End of the Rainbow" and "Cinderella" and "Seele im Raum." She is a kind of aging machine-part. I wrote, as they say in suits, "acting as next friend"; I had for her the sympathy of an aging machine part. (If I was also something else, that was just personal; and she also was something else.) I felt that one of these hundreds of thousands of government clerks might feel all her dresses one dress, a faded navy blue print, and that dress her body. This work- or life-uniform of hers excites neither complaint, nor comment, nor the mechanically protective *No comment* of the civil servant; excites them neither from her "chief," the Deputy Chief Assistant, nor from his, nor from any being on any level of that many-leveled machine: all the system is silent, except for her own cry, which goes unnoticed just as she herself goes unnoticed. (I had met a Deputy Chief Assistant, who saw nothing remarkable in the title.) The woman's days seem to her the going-up-to-work and coming-down-from-work of a worker; each ends in *And so to bed,* the diarist's conclusive unvarying entry in the daybook of his life.

These abruptly opening lines are full of duplications and echoes, like what they describe. And they have about them a familiar wrongness—lie under the curse of all beginnings: either there is too much of something or it is not yet there. The lines break off with *this worn serviceable*—the words can apply either to her dress or to her body, but anything so obviously suitable to the dress must be intended for the body. *Body that no sunlight dyes, no hand suffuses,* the page written the next day goes on; then after a space there is *Dome-shadowed, withering among columns, / Wavy upon the pools of fountains, small beside statues . . .* No sun colors, no hand suffuses with its touch, this used, still-useful body. It is subdued to the element it works in: is shadowed by the domes, grows old and small and dry among the columns of the buildings of the capital; becomes a reflection, its material identity lost, upon the pools of the fountains of the capital; is dwarfed beside the statues of the capital—as, year by year, it passes among the public places of this city of space and trees and light, city sinking beneath the weight of its marble, city of graded voteless workers.

The word *small,* as it joins the reflections in the pools, the trips to the public places, brings the poems to its real place and subject—to its title, even: next there is *small and shining,* then (with the mark beside it that means *use, don't lose*) *small, far-off, shining in the eyes of animals;* the woman ends at the zoo, looking so intently into its cages that she sees her own reflection in *the eyes of animals, these wild ones trapped / As I am trapped but not, themselves, the trap . . .* The lines have written above them, now, *The Woman at the Washington Zoo.*

The next page has the title and twelve lines:

This print, that has kept the memory of color
Alive through many cleanings; this dull null
Navy I wear to work, and wear from work, and so
To bed (with no complaints, no comment: neither from my chief,
The Deputy Chief Assistant, nor her chief,

> Nor his, nor Congressmen, nor their constituents
> ~~wan~~
> —Only I complain); this ~~plain,~~ worn, serviceable
>   sunlight
> Body that no ~~sunset~~ dyes, no hand suffuses
> But, dome-shadowed, withering among columns.
> Wavy beneath fountains—small, far-off, shining
>   ~~wild~~
> In the eyes of animals, these beings trapped
> As I am trapped but not, themselves, the trap . . .

Written underneath this, in the rapid ugly disorganized handwriting of most of the pages, is *bars of my body burst blood breath breathing—lives aging but without knowledge of age / Waiting in their safe prisons for death, knowing not of death;* immediately this is changed into two lines, *Aging, but without knowledge of their age, / Kept safe here, knowing not of death, for death—* and out at the side, scrawled heavily, is: *O bars of my own body, open, open!* She recognizes herself in the animals—and recognizes herself, also, in the cages.

Written across the top of this page is *2nd and 3rd alphabet*. Streets in Washington run through a one-syllable, a two-syllable, and a three-syllable (Albemarle, Brandywine, Chesapeake . . .) alphabet, so that people say to you, "Let's see, that's in the second alphabet, isn't it?" It made me think of Kronecker's, "God made the integers, all else is the work of man"; but I felt that it was right for Washington to have alphabets of its own—made up the title of a detective story, *Murder in the Second Alphabet*. The alphabets were a piece of Washingon that should have fitted into the poem, but didn't; but the zoo was a whole group of pieces, a little Washington, into which the poem itself fitted.

Rock Creek Park, with its miles of heavily wooded hills and valleys, its rocky stream, is like some National Forest dropped into Washington by mistake. Many of the animals of the zoo are in unroofed cages back in its ravines. My wife and I had often visited the zoo, and now that we were living in Washington we went to it a great deal. We had made friends with a lynx that was very like our cat that had died the spring before, at the age of sixteen. We would feed the lynx pieces of liver or scraps of chicken and turkey; we fed liver, sometimes, to two enormous white timber wolves that lived at the end of one ravine. Eager for the meat, they would stand up against the bars on their hind legs, taller than a man, and stare into our eyes; they reminded me of Akela, white with age, in the *Jungle Books,* and of the wolves who fawn at the man Mowgli's brown feet in *In the Rukh.* In one of the buildings of the zoo there was a lioness with two big cubs; when the keeper came she would come over, purring her bass purr, to rub her head against the bars—almost as our lynx would rub his head against the turkey-skin, in rapture, before he finally gulped it down. In the lions' building there were two black leopards; when you got close to them you saw they had not lost the spots of the ordinary leopards—were the ordinary leopards, but spotted black on black, dingy somehow.

On the way to the wolves one went by a big unroofed cage of foxes curled up asleep; on the concrete floor of the enclosure there would be scattered two or three white rats—stiff, quite untouched—that the foxes had left. (The wolves left their meat, too—big slabs of horse-meat, glazing, covered with flies.) Twice when I came to the foxes' cage there was a turkey-buzzard that had come down for the rats; startled at me, he flapped up heavily, with a rat dangling underneath. (There are usually vultures circling over the zoo; nearby, at the tennis courts of the Sheraton-Park, I used to see vultures perched on the tower of WTTG, above the court on which Defense Secretary McElroy was playing doubles—so that I would say to myself, like Peer Gynt: "Nature is witty.") As a child, coming around the bend of a country road, I had often seen a turkey-buzzard, with its black wings and naked red head, flap heavily up from the mashed body of a skunk or possum or rabbit.

A good deal of this writes itself on the next page, almost too rapidly for line-endings or punctuation: *to be and never know I am   when the vulture buzzard comes for the white rat that the foxes left   May he take off his black wings, the flesh of his head, and step to me as man—a man at whose brown feet the white wolves fawn—to whose hand of power / The lioness stalks, leaving her cubs playing / and rubs her head along the bars as he strokes it.* Along the side of the page, between these lines, two or three words to a line, is written *the animals who are trapped but are not themselves the trap   black leopards   spots, light and darkened, hidden except to the close eyes of love, in their life-long darkness, so I in decent black, navy blue.*

As soon as the zoo appeared, all the things of the poem settled into it and were at home there; now it begins to be plain that all the things of the poem come out of, and are divided between, color and colorlessness. Colored women and colored animals and colored cloth—all that the woman sees as her own opposite—come into the poem to begin it. Beside the typed lines are many hurried phrases, most of them crossed out: *red and yellow as October maples   rosy, blood seen through flesh in summer   colors wild and easy natural   leaf-yellow cloud-rose leopard-yellow, cloth from another planet the leopards look back at their wearers, hue for hue   the women look back at the leopard.* And on the back of the vulture's page there is a flight of ideas, almost a daydream, coming out of these last phrases: *we have never mistaken you for the others   among the legations one of a different architecture women, saris of a different color   envoy   impassive   clear bullet-proof glass   lips, through the clear glass of a rose sedan color of blood   you too are represented on this earth . . .*

One often sees on the streets of Washington—fairly often sees at the zoo—what seem beings of a different species: women from the embassies of India and Pakistan, their sallow skin and black hair leopardlike, their yellow or rose or green saris exactly like the robes of Greek statues, before the statues had lost their color. I was used to saying in a serious voice, about the sun red over the horizon, the moon white over the ocean: "It's like another planet"; partly because of this joke, the saris seemed to me cloth from another planet. After I had worked a little longer, the poem began as it begins now:

The saris go by me from the embassies.

Cloth from the moon. Cloth from another planet.
They look back at the leopard like the leopard.

And I . . . This print of mine, that has kept its color
Alive through so many cleanings; this dull null
Navy I wear to work, and wear from work, and so
To my bed, so to my grave, with no
Complaints, no comment: neither from my chief,
The Deputy Chief Assistant, nor his chief—
Only I complain; this serviceable
Body that no sunlight dyes, no hand suffuses
But, dome-shadowed, withering among columns,
Wavy beneath fountains—small, far-off, shining
In the eyes of animals, these beings trapped
As I am trapped but not, themselves, the trap,
Aging, but without knowledge of their age,
Kept safe here, knowing not of death, for death
—Oh, bars of my own body, open, open!

It is almost as if, once all the materials of the poem were there, the middle
and end of the poem made themselves, as the beginning had just made itself.
After the imperative *open, open!* there is a space, and the middle of the poem
begins evenly—since her despair is beyond expression—in a statement of accomplished fact: *The world goes by my cage and never sees me.* Inside the
mechanical official cage of her life, her body, she lives invisibly; no one feeds
this animal, reads out its name, pokes a stick through the bars at it—the cage
is empty. She feels that she is even worse off than the other animals of the
zoo: they are still wild animals—since they do not know how to change into
domesticated animals, beings that are their own cages—and they are surrounded
by a world that does not know how to surrender them, still thinks them part
of itself. This natural world comes through or over the bars of the cages, on
its continual visits to those within: to those who are not machine-parts, con-
victs behind the bars of their penitentiary, but wild animals—the free beasts
come to their imprisoned brothers and never know that they are not also free.
Written on the back of one page, crossed out, is *Come still, you free;* on the
next page this becomes

The world goes by my cage and never sees me.
And there come not to me, as come to these,
The wild ~~ones~~ beasts, sparrows pecking the llamas' grain,
Pigeons ~~fluttering to~~ settling on the bears' bread, turkey-buzzards
~~Coming with grace first, then with horror~~   ~~Vulture seizing~~
Tearing the meat the flies have clouded . . .

In saying mournfully that the wild animals do not come to her as they come
to the animals of the zoo, she is wishing for their human equivalent to come
to her. But she is right in believing that she has become her own cage—she has
changed so much, in her manless, childless, fleshless existence, that her longing wish has inside it an increasing repugnance and horror: the innocent
sparrows *pecking* the llamas' grain become larger in the pigeons *settling on* (not
fluttering to) the bears' bread; and these grow larger and larger, come (with
grace first, far off in the sky, but at last with horror) as turkey-buzzards seiz-
ing, no, *tearing* the meat the flies have clouded. She herself is that stale left-
over flesh, nauseating just as what comes to it is horrible and nauseating. The
series *peck, settling on,* and *tearing* has inside it a sexual metaphor: the stale
flesh that no one would have is taken at last by the turkey-buzzard with his
naked red head and dangling wattles.

Her own life is so terrible to her that, to change, she is willing to accept even this, changing it as best she can. She says: *Vulture* (it is a euphemism that gives him distance and solemnity), *when you come for the white rat that the foxes left* (to her the rat is so plainly herself that she does not need to say so; the small, white, untouched thing is more accurately what she is than was the clouded meat—but, also, it is euphemistic, more nearly bearable), *take off the red helmet of your head* (the bestiality, the obscene sexuality of the flesh-eating death-bird is really—she hopes or pretends or desperately is sure—merely external, *clothes,* an intentionally-frightening war-garment like a Greek or Roman helmet), *the black wings that have shadowed me* (she feels that their inhuman colorless darkness has always, like the domes of the inhuman city, shadowed her; the wings are like a black parody of the wings the Swan Brothers wear in the fairy tale, just as the whole costume is like that of the Frog Prince or the other beast-princes of the stories) *and step* (as a human being, not fly as an animal) *to me as* (what you really are under the disguising clothing of red flesh and black feathers) *man*—not the machine-part, the domesticated animal that is its own cage, but man as he was first, still must be, is: the animals' natural lord,

> The wild brother at whose feet the white wolves fawn,
> To whose hand of power the great lioness
> Stalks, purring . . .

And she ends the poem when she says to him:

> You know what I was,
> You see what I am: change me, change me!

Here is the whole poem:

The Woman at the Washington Zoo

The saris go by me from the embassies.

Cloth from the moon. Cloth from another planet.
They look back at the leopard like the leopard.

And I . . .
          This print of mine, that has kept its color   5
Alive through so many cleanings; this dull null
Navy I wear to work, and wear from work, and so
To my bed, so to my grave, with no
Complaints, no comment: neither from my chief,
The Deputy Chief Assistant, nor his chief—   10
Only I complain; this serviceable
Body that no sunlight dyes, no hand suffuses
But, dome-shadowed, withering among columns,
Wavy beneath fountains—small, far-off, shining
In the eyes of animals, these beings trapped   15
As I am trapped but not, themselves, the trap,

Aging, but without knowledge of their age,
Kept safe here, knowing not of death, for death
—Oh, bars of my own body, open, open!

The world goes by my cage and never sees me.   20
And there come not to me, as come to these,
The wild beasts, sparrows pecking the llamas' grain,
Pigeons settling on the bears' bread, buzzards
Tearing the meat the flies have clouded . . .
        Vulture,   25
When you come for the white rat that the foxes left,
Take off the red helmet of your head, the black
Wings that have shadowed me, and step to me as man,
The wild brother at whose feet the white wolves fawn,
To whose hand of power the great lioness   30
Stalks, purring . . .
      You know what I was,
You see what I am: change me, change me!

Let us take an example from A. E. Housman (see pages 484–485). Here the poet has left no record of his reasoning. We must, then, try to reconstruct the stages by which the poet moved from his original idea to the finished poem. Our poem is "The Immortal Part." In its finished form on the right, the poem has forty-four lines, but the version on the left is much shorter and very early. This early version is an exact reproduction in type of an actual manuscript page (with line numbers added); therefore, we will refer to it as "the manuscript." It is clearly not the first version; on the manuscript we can see erasures beneath the first visible text. Let us try to reconstruct the stages of the poem.

First we notice that the manuscript has a title, "The Immortal Part." Very rarely does Housman give a title to a poem, and so we can hazard that the title was the start of the poem, that the germ is the ironical idea that the bones are the immortal part of man.

The first line has been erased, but as far as we can now tell it ran

   Every——night and day.

And was followed by

   (2) I hear my bones within me say
   (3) "Another eve another morn

The next line, 4, intended to rhyme with 3, had two versions, both of which are erased, but we can make out that the second version ended with *born*. But the stanza was unsatisfactory. For one thing, "Every——night and day" is a rather flat line. And for another thing, it doesn't seem to be enough preparation for line 2. Furthermore, the sharp, succinct effect of what the bones say would be weakened by the addition of another line, and the line ending in *born* was, in all likelihood, but a descriptive elaboration. So Housman began again on the right margin, lines 2a and 3a. The erasure here leaves little legible, but line 2a seems to end with *betray*. We may guess that Housman was with his new rhyme trying to get a new preparation for line 2.

In any case, this couplet did not work out. So Housman came back to lines 2 and 3, and by changing *eve* and *morn* in line 3 to *night* and *day*, got the sharp, epigrammatic couplet to embody his key idea, where before the idea had been split between the last line of one couplet and the first of another. So we have what, except for punctuation, is the final version:

I hear my bones within me say
"Another night another day,

The next line, 5, came fairly well:

When shall this slough of flesh be cast,

But line 6 caused more trouble. Under the erasure we see something that looks like:

This flame——be past.

And above the erasure the word *life*, which seems to have been a revision of the rejected line, perhaps something like, "flame of life." Another try gives us:

This dust of thought be laid at last.

But the word *thought* is not satisfactory to Housman, probably because it does not somehow associate with *flesh*, the key word of the above line. So he cancels *thought* and substitutes *life* (suggested perhaps by the revision of the earlier version of the same line), a word that pairs more readily with *flesh*. Neither line is now in its final form, but the poet, as we shall see, probably did not touch them again until he had worked out his last stanza.

Now we face a question. We see that the next two lines on the manuscript, 7 and 8, though in their final form, are not in their final place. Did Housman jot them down here as they came into his mind, realizing that they were to be placed later, or did he first think of them as coming after line 6 and leading up to line 11? Under any circumstances, lines 7 and 8 could not lead up to lines 9 and 10.

So far in the poem, Housman is thinking in couplets, not in stanzas, and he is not establishing a very clear progression from one couplet to the next. It is true that we do get a progression from lines 2–3 to lines 5–6, but otherwise what we seem to find are germinal bits, points of focus, pegs on which the poem is to be hung as it develops.

In the next four lines, however, Housman composes a rounded stanza, one that is clearly intended to end the speech of the bones. In line 11 he repeats the night-day motif, which starts the speech of the bones, but after he has struck on the phrase "endless night" in the next line, he comes back and changes *nights* to *morn* and *days* to *eve,* to avoid repetition. But this stanza is not to survive.

After the speech of the bones, the turn of the poem comes, the consequence of the speech:

(15) Therefore I shall have my will
(16) Today while I am master still,
(17) And flesh and soul, now both are strong,
(18) Shall lug the sullen slaves along,

The immortal part

(1)   ~~Every~~   ~~night and day~~

(2)   I hear my bones within me say   (2a) ~~This~~   ~~betray~~
     night   day,

(3)   "Another ~~eve~~, another ~~morn~~   (3a) ——— ~~xxxx~~ ———

(4)   ~~It's long~~   (4a) ~~It's~~   ~~born~~

(5)   When shall this slough of flesh be cast
      life

(6)   This dust of ~~thought~~ ∧ be laid at last
      life
This flame   past

(7)   The immortal bones obey control

(8)   Of dying flesh and dying soul

(9)   This tongue that talks, these lungs that shout,

(10)   These thews that hustle us about

      morn   eve

(11)   When will ~~nights~~ and ~~days~~ be gone

(12)   And the endless night come on?

(13)   Another night, another day,

(14)   So my bones within me say
      they shall do

(15)   Therefore ~~I shall have~~ my will

(16)   Today while I am master still,

(17)   And flesh and soul, now both are strong,
      haul

(18)   Shall ~~lug~~ the sullen slaves along,
      this   sense

(19)   Before ~~these~~ fires of ~~flesh~~ decay,
      thoughts

(20)   This smoke of ~~soul~~ blow clean away,

(21)   And leave with ancient night alone

(22)   The ~~immortal~~ and enduring bone.
      ~~senseless~~
      stedfast

The Immortal Part

When I meet the morning beam
Or lay me down at night to dream,
I hear my bones within me say,
"Another night, another day.

"When shall this slough of sense be cast,
This dust of thoughts be laid at last,
The man of flesh and soul be slain
And the man of bone remain?

"This tongue that talks, these lungs that shout,
These thews that hustle us about,
This brain that fills the skull with schemes,
And its humming hive of dreams,—

"These to-day are proud in power
And lord it in their little hour:
The immortal bones obey control
Of dying flesh and dying soul.

" 'Tis long till eve and morn are gone:
Slow the endless night comes on,
And late to fulness grows the birth
That shall last as long as earth.

"Wanderers eastward, wanderers west,
Know you why you cannot rest?
'Tis that every mother's son
Travails with a skeleton.

"Lie down in the bed of dust;
Bear the fruit that bear you must;
Bring the eternal seed to light,
And morn is all the same as night.

"Rest you so from trouble sore,
Fear the heat o' the sun no more,
Nor the snowing winter wild,
Now you labor not with child.

"Empty vessel, garment cast,
We that wore you long shall last.
—Another night, another day."
So my bones within me say.

Therefore they shall do my will
To-day while I am master still,
And flesh and soul, now both are strong,
Shall hale the sullen slaves along,

Before this fire of sense decay,
This smoke of thought blow clean away,
And leave with ancient night alone
The steadfast and enduring bone.

5

10

15

20

25

30

35

40

The form of statement in line 15 throws the emphasis off the bones, the key word; and so "I shall have my will" is altered to "they shall do my will." And in the last line of the stanza *lug* becomes *haul,* which, in the final version, becomes *hale.*

The first change in line 18 may be argued like this: the word *lug* sets up too positive an alliteration on *l* in the line, and a nonfunctional forced pause between *shall* and *lug.* Housman uses alliteration very freely but rather discreetly. As for the forced pause, the general notion of the line is that flesh and soul get their will done effortlessly, masterfully, and freely, and the impediment of the pause destroys this impression. Furthermore, the word *lug* means carrying an absolutely dead weight—and that is not what a man does to his bones, which are active, or what a master does to his slaves. So Housman tries *haul.* This does avoid the forced pause and the obvious alliteration; the *l* sound is not initial and is lightly absorbed into the texture of the line. Also the word doesn't imply as much dead weight as *lug,* it is not quite as chunky a word, as it were. But it still fails on this general score: the bones are still passive. But sometime between this version and the last, Housman strikes on *hale,* an easy sound association derived from *haul.* The new word fulfills all the requirements indicated above, and brings, besides, a new element. The a-sound in *hale* provides an assonantal binder with the a-sound in *slaves,* and emphasizes the flow and unity of the line, but discreetly.

This brings us to the last stanza. In line 19 the first version "these fires of flesh" becomes "this fire of sense," and in line 20 "smoke of soul" becomes "smoke of thoughts." But it seems unlikely that these changes were made until Housman had written the last two lines. We might argue in this way: Line 21 with "ancient night" is really an echo of line 12. Then in line 22 Housman first put down "immortal and enduring," the word *immortal* coming almost automatically from the title, which, as we have said, probably contained the germ of the poem. But the word didn't suit. Perhaps it is too closely associated with *soul,* used above, carrying some notion of lightness, of delicacy, of an aspiring quality, of a continuity in life. So *senseless* comes next. This try indicates something of Housman's objection to *immortal.* The new word covers part of the objection, but it does not retain the idea of permanence in *immortal.* Then he finds what he in the manuscript spells as "stedfast." This word avoids the objections to *immortal* and yet carries the idea of permanence, but permanence by solidity, by weight, by massive indestructibility, with the faint hint of some sort of moral victory in its permanence. We may notice, too, that *enduring* carries a sort of double meaning, mere durability as its primary sense and a capacity for surviving suffering as its secondary sense. But to return to *steadfast,* the word introduces a new rhythm, a *spondaic effect* (see Appendix B, p. 497) that adds appropriately to the solidity and heaviness of the line, and to the final stoical temper of the poem.

It is the revision of this last line, further, that may react on the poem to instigate other revision. Perhaps the try at *senseless* for *immortal* suggested *sense* for *flesh* in line 19: if the bones are "senseless," then the flesh is "senseful," and the contrast between flesh and bone becomes more precise. But once having struck on *sense* in 19, Housman cannot let *soul* stand in the next line. In traditional psychology, the aspects of consciousness to be associated are sensation and thought, and thought was supposed to derive from sensation; so the "fire of sense," which, by the way, is a good image for man's appetite for the immediate experience of the world, leads to the "smoke of thought," the evanescent, useless thing that comes from man's experience.

Of course, Housman may have arrived at the sense-thought notion before he wrote the last line. He may have simply objected to *soul* because it did carry the idea of immortality, and he wished to imply that the only immortality was in the bones. Thus, having rejected *soul* he would have to start on a new train of thinking; and then he may have picked up the rejected *thought* of line 6. But in any case, having set up the last stanza, he went back at some point, as we know from the final version, and changed the *flesh* in line 5 to *sense*, and the *life* in line 6 back to *thoughts*. It is even possible that the version of line 6 as we have it in the manuscript was not written at all until after the last stanza, that Housman came back and erased his earlier line 6 which may very well have had *soul* in it to pair with *flesh* above, and then got his "dust of thought" idea and changed *thought* to *life* on a bad hunch that he later had to revoke. The precise order of events here is not what is important. What is important is a kind of relation among them.

To sum up, we may say that Housman probably struck on the idea of man's bones as being his immortal part. That gave the germ of the poem, and the title. Next he struck on the idea that the bones would speak in pitying protest against their enslavement to flesh. After jotting down several almost unrelated couplets, which served as notes, as it were for the speech of the bones, Housman worked seriously at what was to be the climax of his poem, the response to the bones. Even in this first manuscript these last two stanzas, with the exception of one word in line 18, come out in final form. This much may have come on a walk and at the hour of teatime, but the actual time involved here is not very significant. It *is* significant that we have here the germ of a poem, the development of its plan (introduction, speech of bones, reply), the establishing of its theme and tonality. What the poet had to do later was to get a satisfactory introduction to the speech of the bones, and then fill in the speech. This meant finding a principle of continuity for the speech, and, in fact, the splitting of the one stanza, lines 11–14, already set up in this section. The process may have required a long time, but the control by which it would take place already existed.

Let us take another example, from another poet, the second stanza of Keats's ode "To Autumn" (p. 87). In the original draft it began:

> Who hath not seen thee? for thy haunts are many
> Sometimes whoever seeks for thee may find

Keats, according to one critic,* sees that *many* is going to be a difficult rhyme, and so starts over again, "feeling also no doubt a kind of thin abruptness in the half-line question, and a certain feebleness both of sound and sense in *for thee*." Almost immediately, for the manuscript shows signs of haste, Keats composes the first four lines of the stanza:

> Who hath not seen thee oft amid thy stores?
> Sometimes whoever seeks abroad may find

---

* M. R. Ridley, *Keats' Craftsmanship*, Clarendon Press, 1933, pp. 285–287.

> Thee sitting careless on a granary floor
> Thy hair soft lifted by the winnowing wing

Then Keats strikes off the final *s* of *stores* to make his rhyme with floor, and changes *wing* to *wind*.

Ridley continues the analysis:

> However, whatever small problems there may have been in the first four lines, they were soon and easily solved. Now the real troubles begin.

husky

> While bright the Sun slants through the / barn,
>   Or sound asleep in a half reaped field
> Dosed with read poppies, while thy reeping hook
>   Spares form Some slumbrous

At this point the lines, which have clearly been going from bad to worse, have petered out altogether, and no rhyme for *field* is in sight anyway. The next stage is some minor tinkering. The line about the sun, and the next line, are deleted altogether, and the second rewritten as

> on on a half reap'd furrow sound asleep

(i.e., intending not to delete the *Or* and to write *on* once only), then *Some slumbrous* is deleted, and under it written

> minutes while wam slumpers creep

So that now he has in front of him

~~husky~~

> ~~While bright the Sun slants through the~~   barn
>   on on a half reap'd furrow sound asleep
> ~~Or sound asleep in a half reaped field~~
> Dosed with read poppies; while thy reeping hook
>   Spares form ~~Some slumbrous~~
>   minutes while wam slumpers creep

That has at least achieved a rhyme; but if the line about the sun is to disappear altogether the rhyme is in the wrong place; none of it is very satisfactory; and the *eep* sound has got out of hand. So Keats cancels the whole passage with some vigorous cross-hatching, and begins all over again, using the rewritten sixth line as the fifth, and improving the old seventh for use as the new sixth.

> Or on a half reap'd furrow sound asleep
>   Dos'd with the fume of poppies, while thy hook
> Spares for ~~one~~some slumbrous minutes the next swath;

So far, so good; and as any troubles about a rhyme for the unpromising *swath* are still four lines off he goes on his way rejoicing:

> And sometimes like a gleans thost dost keep
>   Steady thy laden head across the brook
>   Or by a Cyder-press with patent look
> Thou . . .

Well, and now what about the swath, waiting four lines above for its rhyme? But the Cyder-press is going as well as can be, so for the moment confound the swath, and finish

> watchest the last oozing hours by hours

and now go back and get the rhyme, even if we have to sacrifice in the process the idea of the tenacious *slumpers* which has hung onto existence through two corrections.

> Spares the next swath and all its twined flowers;

The copy in the Woodhouse letter omits to notice the cancellation of the *s* of *stores;* corrects some spellings, but writes *Stready* for *Steady;* does some punctuating; reads *a brook* for *the brook,* and *Dased* for *Dos'd,* either an easy misreading of a word so written that it might be either, or a deliberate alteration; and greatly accentuates the opiate *z* sound of the last line by reading *oozings* for *oozing.**

Questions

1. Below are three versions of Housman's "To an Athlete Dying Young." Version A is very early, but Version B is approaching the finished form, which appears below. Study both versions in comparison with the finished poem. On the basis of this evidence write an account of the development of the poem. Try to define the reasons for the changes in text.

(To an Athlete Dying Young: no title on manuscript)

VERSION A

```
                    your
(1)    The day you won the town the race
                      through
(2)        We chaired you in the market place,
       ———— folk
(3)    ————————stood cheering by,                    xxxxxxxxxxxxxxx
       And home                                      xxxxxxxxxxxxxxx
(4)    Home we brought you shoulder-high.            xxxxxxxxxxxxxxx
(5)        So——————————fade   (5a)——————————————betrayed (?)
             feet (?)                  So set, before its echoes fade,
(6)        ————race, sill of shade,  (6a)  Set foot upon the sill of shade
                 low                        The fleet foot on
(7)    And hold to the dark lintel up
(8)    The still defended challenge cup.
(9)                                    Wise lad, to steal betimes away
(10)                                   From fields where victory will not
                                                                      stay
                                                     xxxxxxxxxxxxx
(11)   A garland briefer than a girl's    A garland briefer than a————
(12)   xxxxxxxxxxxxxx                      ——————————that night has shut
(13)   ————————see your record cut
                 that young
(14)   And round your early laurelled head
(15)   Will throng to gaze the strengthless dead
                 find unwithered on
```

---

*For instructive accounts of methods of creation, in science as well as the arts, see Brewster Ghiselin, *The Creative Process,* University of California Press, 1952.

(16)   And ~~yet unfaded round~~ its curls
(17)   ~~The xx~~ The garland briefer than a girl's.
(18)   Of runners whom renown outran
         ~~Or~~
(19)   And the name died before the man

VERSION B

                        time
(1)   The ~~day~~ you won your town the race
(2)   We chaired you through the market place;
(3)   Man and boy stood cheering by,
(4)   And home we brought you shoulder-high.
(5)   Today, the road all runners come,
(6)   Shoulder-high we bring you home,
(7)   And set you at your threshold down,
(8)   Townsman of a stiller town.
         Well done,
(9)   Wise lad, to slip betimes away   Smart lad,
                     glory
(10)   From fields where ~~victory~~ will not stay.
(11)   ~~And glory for the runner braids~~   And early though the laurel grows
                                               lasts no ~~longer~~ better a
(12)   ~~A chaplet briefer than a maid's~~   It withers sooner than ~~the~~ rose.
                                                    cloudy
(13)   ~~He~~ whose eye the night has   Eyes the shady night has shut
              shut   ~~Will never~~
(14)   ~~Never sees his record cut~~   never see the record ~~cut~~
                             sounds no worse than
(15)   And silence ~~is the same~~ as cheers
                             ~~his~~
(16)   After earth has stopped the ears.
                        have   swelled,
(17)   ~~And~~ Now you will not ~~join~~ the
              throng   swell   No fear you now should join
                                                           the throng
                        stayed spell
(18)   Of lads that lived a ~~day~~ too long,
(19)   Runners whom renown outran
(20)   And the name died before the man.
(21)   So set before its echoes fade,
(22)   The fleet foot on the sill of shade,
(23)   And hold to the low lintel up
(24)   The still defended challenge-cup
                        that your
(25)   And round ~~that~~ early-laurelled head
(26)   Will flock to gaze the strengthless dead
(27)   And find unwithered on its curls
(28)   The garland briefer than a girl's
                        Eyes the cloudy
(29)   ~~Now the eye that~~ night has shut
(30)   Will never see the record cut,
(31)   And silence sounds no worse than cheers
                        After

(32) ~~Now that~~ earth has stopped the ears.
(33) Cannot see the record cut
Now you'll never
(34) ~~xxxxxxxxx~~ swell the rout
(35) Of lads that wore their honours out.

To an Athlete Dying Young

The time you won your town the race
We chaired you through the market-place;
Man and boy stood cheering by,
And home we brought you shoulder-high.

Today, the road all runners come,   5
Shoulder-high we bring you home,
And set you at your threshold down,
Townsman of a stiller town.

Smart lad, to slip betimes away
From fields where glory does not stay   10
And early though the laurel grows
It withers quicker than the rose.

Eyes the shady night has shut
Cannot see the record cut,
And silence sounds no worse than cheers   15
After earth has stopped the ears:

Now you will not swell the rout
Of lads that wore their honors out,
Runners whom renown outran
And the name died before the man.   20

So set, before its echoes fade,
The fleet foot on the sill of shade,
And hold to the low lintel up
The still-defended challenge-cup.

And round that early-laureled head   25
Will flock to gaze the strengthless dead,
And find unwithered on its curls
The garland briefer than a girl's.

2. Below is a section rejected by Yeats for his "Upon a Dying Lady." Study it carefully and compare it with the sections which he published (p. 403). What grounds can you give for his rejection of these lines? Are there elements here better developed in the poem as we finally have it?

Although she has turned away
The pretty waxen faces
And hid their silk and laces

For mass was said today
She has not begun denying   5
Now that she is dying
The pleasures she loved well
The strong milk of her mother
The valor of her brother
Are in her body still   10
She will not die weeping
May God be with her sleeping.*

3. On page 466 we have quoted a passage from Dorothy Wordsworth's
journal in which she describes the incident on which the following poem is
presumably based. Note that in the poem Wordsworth makes the speaker of
the poem say that he had been wandering alone. What, do you think, led him
to do this? What other changes do you observe in Wordsworth's treatment of
the material of the journal?

I Wandered Lonely as a Cloud

William Wordsworth [*1770–1850*]

I wandered lonely as a cloud
That floats on high o'er vales and hills,
When all at once I saw a crowd,
A host of golden daffodils;
Beside the lake, beneath the trees,   5
Fluttering and dancing in the breeze.

Continuous as the stars that shine
And twinkle on the milky way,
They stretched in never-ending line
Along the margin of a bay: 10
Ten thousand saw I at a glance,
Tossing their heads in sprightly dance.

The waves beside them danced, but they
Outdid the sparkling waves in glee:—
A poet could not but be gay   15
In such a jocund company:
I gazed—and gazed—but little thought
What wealth the show to me had brought.

For oft when on my couch I lie
In vacant or in pensive mood,   20
They flash upon that inward eye
Which is the bliss of solitude,
And then my heart with pleasure fills,
And dances with the daffodils.

* Quoted in A. Norman Jeffares, *W. B. Yeats: Man and Poet,* Yale University Press,
1949, pp. 166–167.

METRICS

Appendix B

Foreword

We are all aware of, and, in varying degrees, respond to, the rhythms of sound and movement all about us: the clickety-clack of the rails as a train passes over them, the throb of an idling automobile engine, the murmur of a rapidly flowing stream, the tick-tock of the clock on the table. Rhythm may be defined as a regularly patterned flow of sounds or of movements. We add, "of movements," because we can speak of the rhythm of the tides as they rise and fall, or the alternation of daylight and dark, or the succession of the seasons of the year; but in this book we shall use the term *rhythm* primarily with regard to sounds, and more especially to those pertaining to human speech.

Different languages have their characteristic rhythms, and even the different varieties of English have their special rhythmic patterns. The voice of an Englishman seems to be following a different "speech tune" from that followed in most of the American varieties of English. The rhythms of an utterance may also have an important expressive function. A moving sermon, an impassioned political speech, or even the tirade of an enraged motorist berating someone who has bumped his car tend to take on pronounced and characteristic rhythmic patternings as opposed to, let us say, the speech of ordinary conversation. Written English, also, even when read silently, to a great extent depends for its effect on its rhythmic qualities. A dull piece of prose, to the inner ear, "reads" dull. Good prose, on the contrary, has a

493

perceptible rhythm: it reads as if it were going somewhere, with its sense of direction implicit in its rhythmic makeup.

Here, for example, is the conclusion of Winston Churchill's speech to the British Parliament on June 4, 1940, after the British army had just been successfully evacuated from Dunkirk:

> Even though large tracts of Europe and many old and famous States have fallen or may fall into the grip of the Gestapo and all the odious apparatus of Nazi rule, we shall not flag or fail. We shall go on to the end, we shall fight in France, we shall fight in the seas and oceans, we shall fight with growing confidence and growing strength in the air, we shall defend our island, whatever the cost may be, we shall fight on the beaches, we shall fight on the landing-grounds, we shall fight in the fields and in the streets, we shall fight in the hills; we shall never surrender, and even if, which I do not for a moment believe, this island or a large part of it were subjugated and starving, then our Empire beyond the seas, armed and guarded by the British Fleet, would carry on the struggle, until, in God's good time, the New World, with all its power and might, steps forth to the rescue and the liberation of the Old.*

Here is another passage (from James Joyce's *Ulysses*†) which embodies a different rhythm and reflects a very different mood. It represents a portion of the somber meditation of a bitter young intellectual, Stephen Dedalus, as he walks along Sandymount beach near Dublin:

> The grainy sand had gone from under his feet. His boots trod again a damp crackling mast, razorshells, squeaking pebbles, that on the unnumbered pebbles beats, wood sieved by the shipworm, lost Armada. Unwholesome sandflats waited to suck his treading soles breathing upward sewage breath. He coasted them, walking warily. A porter-bottle stood up, stogged to its waist, in the cakey sand dough. A sentinel: isle of dreadful thirst. Broken hoops on the shore; at the land a maze of dark cunning nets; farther away chalkscrawled backdoors and on the higher beach a dryingline with two crucified shirts. Ringsend: wigwams of brown steersmen and master mariners. Human shells.

If rhythm is an important aspect of all discourse and if it has, even in prose, an important expressive function, one would expect it to be even more important in poetry. As we have often observed, for the man in the street, rhythm is of the very essence of poetry. And in rhythm, as in other things, poetry does tend to be more elaborately patterned than prose. Where, as is usual in poetry, the rhythm has been regularized and systematized, we say that a work is written in *verse;* that is, in *meter.*

Before turning to a detailed discussion of verse and meter, however, we may comment on the general effect of such highly organized rhythm. In "Poetry as a Way of Saying," we have already discussed the natural sources of

---

* Winston Churchill, *Their Finest Hour,* Houghton Mifflin, 1949, p. 118.
† Modern Library Edition of 1961, pp. 40–41.

rhythm and have referred to aspects of rhythm in poetry (pp. 1–3). Though
not the only factor involved, it is, as we have said, important in establishing
the "form" of a poem, in bringing its materials into a sharp focus of attention. Furthermore, rhythm is fundamentally associated with emotion, and, as
we have remarked, utterances springing from pain, grief, joy, and so forth,
tend toward a marked rhythm; and conversely, rhythm, in music and poetry,
tends to evoke emotion in the hearer, or at least to predispose him toward it.

To introduce a new matter in connection with rhythm, in what seems to
be a paradoxical fashion, the strongly marked rhythm of verse also tends to
create a hypnotic effect. Often we assume that the general condition of
hypnosis is sleepiness, dullness, and sluggishness, but actually, the characteristic
quality of the hypnoidal state is a sharpened focus of attention and heightened
suggestibility. As the subject is drawn to focus attention on the hypnotist and
to accept his suggestions, so we, as the readers, are influenced by meter to
free our imaginations from the bonds of the ordinary world and to accept
what Coleridge calls the "willing suspension of disbelief." As Coleridge,
like Wordsworth a Romantic poet, goes on to say, meter tends "to increase
the vivacity and susceptibility both of the general feelings and of attention. . . .
As a medicated atmosphere, or as wine during animated conversation, they
[the dispositions created by meter] act powerfully, though themselves unnoticed." *

Accentual-Syllabic Verse

To turn to poems themselves, the importance of rhythm comes out most
obviously, of course, in those that have a pronounced and characteristic
rhythm. Of the poems so far read, "Danny Deever" (p. 35) and "Inversnaid"

---

* *Biographia Literaria,* ch. xviii. The French poet Paul Valéry has also remarked,
though more generally with reference to music, on this hypnotic effect: music "unites
the liberties of sleep with the development and consistency of extreme attention."
"Introduction to the Method of Leonardo da Vinci," translated by Thomas McGreevy,
Selected Writings of Valéry, 1959, pp. 89–101. The ideas of Coleridge and Valéry
imply that the body itself, as we have pointed out in "Poetry as a Way of Saying"
(p. 2), is a locus of rhythms in a universe of rhythms. When we attend to the
rhythm of poetry or music (or to any other kind of rhythm), we undergo, even
though often unconsciously, a complex physical reaction, most obviously in our
organs of speech but also in the body generally; and the *fusion* of this physical response with other elements in a poem—for instance, imagery, drama, and idea—is a
basic factor in the power that poetry exercises and the pleasure it gives. This notion
takes us again to the fact that to read poetry we must as fully as possible surrender
ourselves to its quality as language, to the rhythm of the movement and the texture
of the words. And the best way for a person more or less inexperienced in poetry to
approach a poem is by reading it aloud, over and over, until he really feels the
rhythm and the verbal quality. This does not mean that the reader should be striving
for elocutionary effects: merely that he should try to surrender himself to both what
is being said and the way of the saying. Such an organic base of poetry has, of course,
long been observed. For instance, the French poet Charles Baudelaire, in the Preface
to his famous book of poems *The Flowers of Evil,* asserts that "rhythm and rhyme
answer in man to the immortal needs of monotony, symmetry, and surprise." A
student interested in this idea may well consult *The Seamless Webb,* by Stanley
Burnshaw.

(p. 83) probably furnish the clearest instances. It would be hard to imagine either poem's retaining its special flavor and force if the poet had given it a different rhythm—had written it, for instance, in a quieter, less assertive verse, or in something moving toward the flattened rhythms of prose. Compare the first stanza of "Inversnaid" with the following version, which preserves most of the diction but makes use of a smoother verse:

> The darksome burn is horseback brown,
> Its rollrock stream runs headlong down.
> In comb and coop its fleece of foam
> Flows down into the lake, its home.

Having been deprived of its special rhythmic character, it has lost much of its force as poetry.

The significance of the rhythmic element in T. S. Eliot's "Preludes" (p. 91) may not appear quite so obvious. Its beat is not so emphatic. Yet it will not be difficult to show what expressive force its particular rhythm lends to its words. Consider, for example, lines 39–42:

> His soul stretched tight across the skies
> That fade behind a city block,
> And trampled by insistent feet
> At four and five and six o'clock. . . .

Various factors are here involved, but the most obvious is the pronounced stress on the hours, *four, five,* and *six,* which reinforces the trampling of the "insistent feet."

In the pages that follow, we shall investigate much more specifically the function of verse in a number of poems, but for the present let us return to a general discussion of the nature of verse and—since verse is merely metrical discourse—of meter.* There are several kinds of verse in English, and we come to them later; but we begin with what is called *accentual-syllabic verse*—that is, with what is generally taken as the standard verse of poetry in English.

What does "accentual-syllabic" mean? The pattern of such verse is based not only on the number of syllables in a line, but also on the relation to each other of the accented and unaccented syllables. Consider, for example, the third stanza of Housman's "Farewell to Barn and Stack and Tree" (p. 36):

> My mother thinks us long away;
> 'Tis time the field were mown.
> She had two sons at rising day,
> To-night she'll be alone.

Inspection will reveal that the first and third lines have eight syllables apiece, whereas the second and fourth lines have six. But we notice, too, that in this poem every other syllable is accented; and this pattern of one unaccented

---

* We here use the word *verse* in a general sense. When we use the word particularly, however, as when we refer to the "second verse of a poem," we mean a line, verse in this sense meaning simply a metrical line. The use of the word to mean a stanza is non-technical; it is not so used in this book.

syllable followed by an accented syllable is what determines the "measure" of the verse in this poem. We call such a basic unit of the verse a "foot."*

The foot in this poem consists of one unaccented syllable followed by an accented: to give it its technical name, an *iamb* or an *iambic foot* (e.g., ∪ ⁄ away). The first and third lines in this stanza have four such feet (i.e., they are *tetrameter* lines), whereas the second and the fourth lines have three (i.e., *trimeter* lines).

Feet and Line Lengths: Terms Defined This is a good place to list the five kinds of accentual-syllabic feet that concern us in this book:

IAMB   one unaccented followed by an accented syllable (a∪wa⁄y)

ANAPEST   two unaccented syllables followed by an accented syllable
              (inter∪ve∪ne⁄)

TROCHEE   an accented followed by an unaccented syllable (on⁄ly∪)

DACTYL   one accented syllable followed by two unaccented syllables
              (ha⁄ppi∪ly∪)

SPONDEE   two accented syllables (This is best understood in an actual line
              of verse, as in this one from Shakespeare's *Antony and Cleopatra*:
              "Unarm, Eros, the long da⁄y's ta⁄sk is done." Here *day's task* may
              be taken as a spondee. But in the system of scansion used in this
              book such a foot would be treated as iambic with a secondary
              accent on the first syllable: *da⁄⁄y's ta⁄sk*. See the discussion of
              secondary accent, p. 500. Such a situation might be referred to,
              however, as a "spondaic effect.")

It may also be convenient to list here the various lines to be found in accentual-syllabic verse:

MONOMETER   one foot
DIMETER   two feet
TRIMETER   three feet
TETRAMETER   four feet
PENTAMETER   five feet
HEXAMETER   six feet (also called an ALEXANDRINE)
HEPTAMETER   seven feet (Yet it should be observed that since a line serves
              as a unit of attention, lines composed of more than six feet
              tend to break up into smaller units. Thus, a heptameter line
              tends to break up into a tetrameter line and a trimeter line.)

---

* In *syllabic verse* (which is, for example, the verse of most poems written in French) we don't need the concept of "feet," for our only concern is with the number of syllables to the line. But since accentual-syllabic verse counts stresses as well as syllables, its basic unit has to be a combination of an unaccented syllable (or syllables) and an accented syllable. Hence, the line in accentual-syllabic verse consists of so many units of this sort—that is, so many metrical "feet." See *Versification: Major Language Types*, ed. W. K. Wimsatt, New York University Press, 1972, pp. 177 ff. and pp. 191–203.

To return to the Housman stanza, a convenient way to mark off the feet and to indicate the accents is illustrated in the following scheme:

> ˘ / ˘ / ˘ / ˘ /
> My mo | ther thinks | us long | away
> ˘ / ˘ / ˘ /
> 'Tis time | the field | were mown.
> ˘ / ˘ / ˘ / ˘ /
> She had | two sons | at ris | ing day,
> ˘ / ˘ / ˘ /
> To-night | she'll be | alone.

In marking off the foot divisions and indicating the syllables that are stressed and unstressed, we have *scanned* the stanza. (If you have a sensitive ear, you may have wondered, as you scanned line 3, whether the word *two* should not get as heavy an accent as *sons*. We will take up this matter on p. 500.)

In looking at the scansion above, you have, no doubt, accepted it as natural. Even so, we must comment on three aspects.

First, the structure of an individual word has no necessary relation to a foot. In line 4, for instance, there are two disyllabic words, *to-night* and *alone*, and each happens to coincide with a foot (*To-night*; *alone*); but in line 1 the word *mother* is divided between two feet, with the first syllable (*mo-*) providing the accent for the first foot, and the second syllable (*-ther*) being the unaccented syllable of the second foot (My mo | ther thinks). Observe, however, that the scansion must follow the natural accent of an individual word of more than one syllable. Suppose the line had been:

> Mother now thinks us long away.

Even in a poem prevailingly iambic, as this is, we could not scan as follows:

> ˘ / ˘ /
> Mother | now thinks . . .

Meter cannot violate the natural accentuation of a word. *

---

* Though meter cannot violate the natural accentuation of a word, it may metrically recognize minor, or secondary, accents in a word. For instance, the word *immortality* has five syllables, accented as follows (see a dictionary):

> // / //
> im mor tal i ty
> 1 2 3 4 5

The major, or primary, accent is on the third syllable, and in ordinary speech the other accents would seem almost lost. But notice this stanza in a poem by Emily Dickinson (p. 256) in which the word occurs:

> Because I could not stop for Death—
> He kindly stopped for me—
> The Carriage held but just Ourselves—
> And Immortality.

If we scan the last line we see that all three accents must be recognized in the meter:

> ˘ / ˘ / ˘/
> And Im | mortal | ity.

When a word of more than one accent appears in meter, it tends to get "stretched" or "lifted up"—to get a special emphasis not naturally in the word in ordinary usage. Take the first line of Milton's *Paradise Lost*:

> Of man's first disobedience, and the fruit

Our second comment on looking back over the scansion of the Housman stanza is that the monosyllabic words that would be unimportant in a normal prose reading of a phrase or clause are unaccented in the meter and that key words are accented. What we have just said is not, however, always applicable; it is merely a good working guideline, not an absolute principle.

Our third comment is that naive readers may believe that the more neatly the stresses of normal conversation are made to conform to those of the metrical pattern, the better a poem is. They may even admire the tidy workmanship of such verse. How steadily it ticks along! But there is such a thing as monotonous regularity, like that of the metronome, with no sense of the vitality of human speech. Good verse does not subside into numbing regularity. For instance, Housman would not have improved his poem if, in the interest of making the metrical accents conform more exactly to speech, he had begun the poem as follows:

> Goodbye to barn and stack and tree,
> > Goodbye to Severn shore,
> Elaine, you've looked your last at me,
> > You'll never see me more.
>
> The sun is hot upon the hill
> > And so the blood has dried,
> The blood of him who lies so still;
> > The knife sticks in his side.

Poets most certainly must not allow themselves to be "used" by their verse; but on the other hand, they must not depart too much from the accents dictated by their verse pattern. If they do that, we won't hear their utterance as verse at all. Suppose Housman had written:

> Mother wants us back right away;
> > That field's certainly mown.

We note that the first line still has the required eight syllables, and the second the required six, but the accents no longer fall into the iambic pattern—or

---

If we scan it we find the word *disobedience* (five syllables, with the word accented:
/ᴗ /ᴗ ᴗ
dis o be di ence) receives two metrical accents, and thus receives special emphasis: the word *disobedience* is the very key of the poem—the Fall of Man in the Garden of Eden—and affirms the theme of the epic.

In scanning you might, of course, try the following:
ᴗ / ᴗ / ᴗ/ ᴗ/ ᴗ ᴗ /
Of man's | first dis | obe | -dience | and the fruit
This, however, seems very unnatural, in that it violates our feeling of the word *disobedience*. So we must get:
ᴗ / ᴗ / ᴗ/ ᴗᴗ / ᴗ /
Of man's | first dis | obe | dience and | the fruit
At first thought, you may feel it wrong to put the accent on the ordinarily unemphatic word *and*. On a moment's reflection we realize, however, that this is exactly what the sense sometimes dictates in common speech. The excited child telling about a party may well say, "We had cookies and nuts and bananas *and*—ice cream!" This emphatic *and* announces some important item, some climactic idea. And the fruit of the tree in Eden, as the next line of Milton's poem tells us, "Brought death into the world, and all our woe"—an event important and climactic enough. We may call such *and* the "annunciatory *and*," for not too infrequently we have use of such a phrase.

into any pattern that we can make out. *What good verse embodies is both a pattern and a vital variety.*

RHETORICAL VARIATION

We are now ready to look at an exception that we have earlier warned might have to be made in stanza 3 of Housman's poem. On page 498 we scanned the third line as follows:

$$\smile \;/ \quad \smile\;/ \quad \smile\;/ \quad \smile \quad /$$
She had | two sons | at ris | ing day

Yet if we look more closely at the actual sense of the line we realize that the word *two* requires a good deal of stress—perhaps as much as *sons* (which claims the metrical accent). This alteration of the regular metrical pattern is an example of what is called "rhetorical variation"—that is, a variation of meter forced by considerations of expressive emphasis. The murder of Maurice (see line 7, p. 36) robs the mother of *both* sons, not merely of one; for she will have lost one by death and the other by flight. But the reader scarcely needs the logical and emotional situation spelled out for him. Grasping the dramatic situation, he will, in reading the line, automatically put a heavier stress on *two*.

In our first scansion of the stresses in this stanza we clearly misled the reader when we blindly followed what the metrical pattern called for and marked the accents as we did. How, then, ought we to scan it?

$$\smile \;/ \quad /\quad/ \quad \smile\;/ \quad \smile \quad /$$
She had | two sons | at ris | ing day   (?)

But if we scan it this way, we make it appear that the line has, not the normal four accents, but five, and so misrepresent the true situation as established in the body of the poem.

Suppose we mark *two* with a secondary accent, thus: *two sons.** This has the virtue of letting us recognize the established metrical pattern but of indicating that the word *two* gets far more stress than, say, *at* or *of*. It has the added virtue of reminding us that a variation occurs here—something that alters the smooth run of the succession of normal iambs.

How strong is a secondary accent? Half as strong as a full stress? A quarter as strong? The truth is that the stress on *two* will seem to most readers fully as strong as that on *sons.*† Realistically speaking, there are many degrees of

---

* A secondary accent in the metrical sense is not to be confused with a secondary accent used in marking the accent in a word in the dictionary.

† Some authorities would argue that we really *divide* the accent between the two syllables, hesitating between them rather than giving a more emphatic stress to one or the other. The accent thus is said to "hover" between the two. A hovering accent may be indicated thus: *two sons.* How shall the student handle such problems? We would suggest: under no hard-and-fast rule. You will not be wrong if you always mark such a foot *two sons.* The important matter is that you should notice—whatever marks you choose to set down—the effect of heavy secondary accents on the rhythm of the line. They tend to slow the movement of the line and often give what is called a *spondaic movement,* especially when several such feet are clustered in a line. See p. 497.

stress in the syllables of human utterance—ranging from the slightest we can think of—as in an unaccented *a* or *the* ("It was *a* wisp of smoke from *the* roof")—on up to the cry of "Fire! Fire!" But if we tried to take account of all such gradations in our scansion, we would need at least a dozen symbols. Our scansion of a single poem at that rate would come to look more like the notes and directions of a teacher of elocution. But we are not concerned with elocution—with reading as performance. Our scansion is not intended to compete with a tape-recording. It is necessarily arbitrary in the same sense as an abstract scheme like a map, which does not pretend to be a photograph of the area to which it applies, but which can be very useful—for certain purposes, more useful than a photograph.

Let us be frankly arbitrary then. We shall agree to let the secondary accent (marked //) stand for every degree of accent between the lightest and the heaviest. To mark a syllable as taking a secondary accent will be a way of pointing to the fact of *variation*. It will say, in effect: this syllable, which, according to the metrical scheme, ought to be unaccented, does in fact carry a degree of accent, and whether it is quite strong or only moderately so, it is an accent *not accounted for* in the metrical pattern.

Substitution of Feet   The secondary accent is not, of course, the only variation from the norm of a meter. There are various types of substitutions of feet for those called for in a metrical pattern. One example occurs in the fifth stanza of Housman's poem:

> I wish you strength to bring you pride,
>   And a love to keep you clean,
> And I wish you luck, come Lammastide,
>   At racing on the green.

This stanza reveals two metrical substitutions. Line 2 has not the expected six syllables, but seven, and the only scansion that makes sense is the following:

$$\cup \ \cup \ / \quad \cup \ / \quad \cup \ \ /$$
And a love | to keep | you clean

What the poet has done here is to substitute an anapest (two unaccented syllables followed by an accented syllable) for the iamb. Inspection will show that another anapestic substitution has been made in the first foot of the third line. The scansion of the stanza is otherwise regular except that it is arguable that *come* in the third line ought to be marked with a secondary accent. Most thoughtful readers will put a fairly strong stress on this word and con-

$$// \quad /$$
sider the foot *come Lam-* as an instance of rhetorical variation.

Or let us take a more extreme example, this from "The Wood-Pile" by Robert Frost:

> Out walking in the frozen swamp one gray day,
> I paused and said, " I will turn back from here.
> No, I will go on farther—and we shall see."

From the first line, one would never guess that the poem is to be basically iambic pentameter, and only on going into the poem a few lines does one discover that the basic meter is indeed iambic pentameter, though often distorted to such a degree by ordinary speech rhythms that the pattern is almost lost.

Defective Feet One form of substitution is the defective foot, a foot from which one (or more) weak syllable is missing. There is an example also in Housman's poem:

    /   ᵕ /   ᵕ /   ᵕ   /
Long | for me | the rick | will wait
  ᵕ   /   ᵕ   /   ᵕ /
And long | will wait | the fold,
  ᵕ /   ᵕ /   ᵕ /   ᵕ /
And long | will stand | the emp | ty plate
  ᵕ   /   ᵕ   /   ᵕ /
And din | ner will | be cold.

What are we to do with the first foot in the first line? Clearly *Long* takes a primary accent, and clearly the three feet that follow in the line are normal iambs. But there aren't enough unaccented syllables in the line to complete the first foot as an iamb. So in scanning the line, we call *Long* a defective foot and show that fact by using a caret to point up the missing syllable, thus:

      / ᵕ /   ᵕ /   ᵕ /
    ᴧ Long | for me | the rick | will wait.

Omitting the normal unaccented syllable is the reversed counterpart of what we found in the preceding stanza, viz., the adding of an extra syllable by anapestic substitution. The one tends to make us linger on and draw out the accented syllable (*Long*) of the defective foot. The other is a device of syncopation: we speed up the line a bit to "get in" the extra syllable. But neither variation drastically disturbs the normal iambic pattern. These variations not only give added expressiveness to the lines; they make the rhythm richer and more complex and bring it closer to a rhetorically expressive rhythm as opposed to a strict metrical reading.

In this connection, we may look back to "The Fall of Rome" by Auden (p. 44) and "Hell Gate" by Housman (p. 59) to find poems in which the defective first foot of a line becomes a normal metrical practice, giving a crisp, driving effect. We may frequently notice elsewhere that a defective foot may occur within a line, as in "After Long Silence" by Yeats (p. 515):

    /   ᵕ ᵕ /   /   ᵕ / ᵕ /
Speech af | ter long | ᴧ si | -lence; it | is right

We may notice here how effective is the pause we automatically assume for the lost weak syllable of the third foot.

A more complicated example is to be found in Tennyson's "Break, Break, Break," the first stanza of which follows:

     /   /   /
  ᴧ Break, ᴧ break, ᴧ break,
    ᵕ ᵕ /   /   // /   // /
On thy cold | gray stones, | O Sea!
  ᵕ ᵕ /   ᵕ ᵕ /   ᵕ / ᵕ
And I would | that my tongue | could utter
    ᵕ   /   ᵕ ᵕ / ᵕ /
    The thoughts | that arise | in me.

The stanza is trimeter, but we notice the heavy, retarded effect of the three imperfect iambs constituting the first line. This effect is, we notice, continued in the second line, with the secondary accents on the two iambs that conclude it; and we may notice the sense of release in the third line, with its anapests. Our point here, however, is simply to illustrate the high degree of complication, with imperfect iambs, secondary accents in iambs, and normal iambs and anapests in a metrically controlled passage.

SIGNIFICANCE OF RHETORICAL VARIATION

Such rhetorical variations are most important. They serve to give expression and vitality to the verse. They relieve it of a mere monotonously mechanical beat. The sense of vitality that we find in good verse arises from a tension between the tug of the metrical pattern toward a flat uniformity on the one hand and, on the other, the special stress on certain words that is demanded by the rhetorical pattern. The abstract pattern of the meter sets up certain expectancies as to where the stress is to fall, but the expressive importance of this or that particular word forces us to modify or even to violate the pattern.

What is wanted is neither a dead mechanical beat nor a jumble of patternless incoherence, but the rich expressiveness of a verse that is alive with the tension of living speech.

If you, as the reader, perform a number of scanning exercises, you will soon find that you have to become sensitive to the occurrence of rhetorical variation.

Can you find and mark the secondary accents in the fourth stanza of Housman's "Farewell to Barn and Stack and Tree"?

> And here's a bloody hand to shake,
>   And oh, man, here's good-bye;
> We'll sweat no more on scythe and rake,
>   My bloody hands and I.

Since we have admitted that scansion is an arbitrary notation—an *abstract* simplification of a poem as *experienced*—and that not all secondary accents have the same stress, perhaps we ought to go further and admit that, in actual rhythm, neither do all primary stresses have quite the same value, nor, for that matter, do all "unaccented" syllables. One can perhaps make this point best by representing it in graphic form. Suppose we choose a line of iambic pentameter that seems to scan with absolute regularity, this from Shakespeare's Sonnet 55:

$$\breve{\text{Not}} \text{ mar} \mid \acute{\text{ble}} \text{ nor} \mid \text{the gild} \mid \text{ed mon} \mid \text{uments.}$$

Our graph would be something like this:

Not marble nor the gilded monuments

The peaks occur over the accented syllables; the valleys over the unaccented. But this graph clearly misrepresents a normally expressive reading, for the conjunction *nor* (even if it is taken as annunciatory, see p. 499 fn.) would not receive as much emphasis as is demanded by the syllable *mar-*, the accented syllable of the important word *marble;* nor could *-ments* (in *monuments*) receive as much emphasis as that which falls on *mon-*. If we graph the line

so as to take into account what we have called rhetorical variation, we get
something like this:

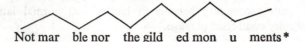

Not mar   ble nor   the gild   ed mon   u   ments*

To summarize what has been said: In this line from Shakespeare's sonnet,
as in all verse, two principles are at work: (1) a principle of metrical regularity, which conditions our reading toward a fixed recurrence of stress and
tends to level out divergencies from the norm; and (2) a principle of dramatic
and rhetorical emphasis, which demands stresses that sometimes coincide with
those of the metrical pattern and sometimes diverge from them. The characteristic rhythm of a piece of verse comes from the *interplay of these two
principles*. There is not only an interplay—there is a positive tension, which
is necessary if verse is to have vitality and its unique expressiveness. The fact
of meter does indeed modify our awareness of a line, and therefore our reading of it, but *only because of this tension*.

When the meter as such dominates meaning, we approach doggerel. As
Robert Frost said, "You save it [a poem] from doggerel" by "having enough
dramatic meaning in it for the other thing to break the doggerel. But it
mustn't break *with* it. I said years ago that it [verse in which the meter and
the meaning have a proper relation] reminds me of a donkey and a donkey
cart; for some of the time the cart is on the tugs and some of the time on
the hold-back."

SOME PRACTICAL NOTES ON SCANSION

Many students become confused when they are asked to scan a poem—
and needlessly so. It will do no harm, therefore, to set down a few ground
rules to make the task simpler, all th⋅ more so in view of the fact that scansion
is, as we have seen, at some point⋅ an arbitrary scheme, and in all arbitrary
schemes we have to agree to observe certain rules—not because they represent some absolute truth, but because it is useful for us to adopt them as
conventions. Here, then, are the guidelines that we suggest should be used:

1. Every foot we mark off should have one primary syllable and only one.
Let's agree not to scan line 11 of Housman's poem as *two sóns*, but to mark
it instead *twó sóns*.

2. Every foot has one or more unaccented syllables. If it lacks any, the
missing syllable should be indicated by a caret in order to show that the foot
is defective.

3. Let us always try to keep the treatment of variations, substitutions, and

---

* Though the graph is useful as a way of pointing out the different degrees of stress
among metrically accented syllables, *we are not suggesting that degrees of emphasis
such as these and other nuances ought to be—or even can be—indicated in the scansion*. In fact, we are not referring to scansion at all; the purpose of scansion is to
indicate succinctly the *basic pattern* and the *principal variations* from it, and what we
are here trying to indicate is *the rhythms resulting from the interplay of meter and
rhetorical factors*.

other literary devices as close as possible to the established metrical pattern. Thus, we could conceivably scan line 3 of Housman's poem in this way:

$$\text{/ ᴗ ~~~~~ / ~~ ᴗ ~~~ / ~ ᴗ ~~ /}$$

Terence, | look your | last at | me, ʌ

In this scansion we have correctly indicated all the primary accents and we have marked off the line into the expected four feet; but we have shown three trochaic substitutions and a defective foot for the expected iamb (a trochee consists of an accented syllable *followed* by an unaccented). Such a scansion, however, violates the established metrical pattern, which we have previously determined is iambic, with a *rising rhythm.** But the scansion we have set down above gives a falling rhythm. Accordingly, the following scansion more accurately describes the line:

$$\text{/ ᴗ ~~~~ / ~~ ᴗ ~ / ~ ᴗ ~ /}$$

ʌ Ter | ence, look | your last | at me,

If you object that this scansion divides the name *Terence* rather than keeping it all within one foot, you should remember that, as we have said earlier, any normal scansion constantly divides words this way. To repeat, *metrical feet do not necessarily correspond to words.*

So much for the ground rules under which we shall operate. Now for several cautions:

1. Remember that *sound,* not *spelling,* counts in scansion. Diphthongs such as those in *howl, oil,* and others normally (but with some exceptions) count as *one* vowel sound. In general, remember that spellings that employ two vowels must not be allowed to mislead us: for example, we spell *sweat* with an *e* and an *a,* but we pronounce it as though it was spelled *swet.* (A word like *naive,* of course, is another matter.) Again, *polished* has two syllables, not three. The final *-ed* is not sounded.† Remember too, that muffled and muted sounds, if they are audible at all, count as vowels: thus a word like *principle* has to be taken as a trisyllable: *prin- ci- ple.* (Note here that under certain metrical situations the syllable *-ple* might even receive a metrical accent: The prin | ciple | of all | delight | that blooms.)

2. In determining the meter (kind of foot and number of feet to a line) in order to scan a poem, one should take the poem as a whole and not merely a line at a time, for the lines may not be metrically identical. One should try, thus, to get a sense of the basic pattern. Always one should read a poem aloud, at least several times, to establish the initial acquaintance. Any line of a poem, it must be remembered, may be irregular—even the first line.

---

* Iambic and anapestic feet give us a rising rhythm; that is, the movement from weak stress to strong. The trochee and the dactyl, since they move from strong stress to weak, yield a falling rhythm.

† In the *-ed* forms of verbs ending in a *-t* or a *-d* sound, it usually is sounded, e.g., *executed, shaded,* etc. Moreover, the poet may specifically mark the *-ed* as sounded, e.g., "And there she lullèd me asleep." See Keats's "La Belle Dame sans Merci," p. 63.

Questions

1. Scan the first four stanzas of "The Workbox" (p. 42). To start you off, here is a scansion of the first stanza:

<pre>
     ̷̷ ́   ∪ ́   ∪ ́ ∪ ́
"See, here's | the work | box, lit | tle wife
   ∪ ∪ ́   ∪ ́ ∪ ́
That I made | of pol | ished oak."
  ́ ∪ ∪ ́   ∪ ∪ ́   ∪ ́
He was | a join | er, of vil | lage life;
    ̷̷ ́   ∪ ́   ∪ ́
She came | of bor | ough folk.
</pre>

Note that the poem records a conversation, and so one would naturally expect a good deal of rhetorical variation. But there are also instances in this poem of the substitution of feet (an anapest and a trochee). Note, too, that "He" and "She," because rhetorically important, get strong secondary stress. Take note also of how we have handled them in our scansion: we have treated *He was* as a trochee, but *She came* as an iamb with a secondary accent on *She*.

2. Scan the stanzas excerpted from "The Palace of Art" (p. 98). We offer a scansion of the first stanza:

<pre>
    ̷̷ ́   ̷̷ ́   ∪ ́   ∪ ́   ∪ ́
One seem'd | all dark | and red— | a tract | of sand,
   ∪ ́   ∪ ́   ∪ ́   ∪ ́
And some | one pac | ing there | alone,
   ̷̷ ́   ∪ ́   ∪ ́ ∪ ́   ∪ ∪ ́
Who paced | for ev | er in | a glim | mering land,
  ́ ∪ ∪ ́   ̷̷ ́
Lit with | a low | large moon.
</pre>

Do you agree with the scansion that we suggest? With, for example, the secondary accents on *One* and *all* in the first line? With the trochaic substitution that we note in the first foot of the last line? Would you agree also that the poet has so managed matters as to make it difficult to read the last line rapidly? If you think so, does the scansion of the line help to explain why?

Note that we have marked the fifth foot in line 3 as an anapestic substitution. Tennyson might have avoided the substitution by writing *glimm'ring*. Why do you suppose he wanted to keep the extra syllable?

Tennyson is famous for his fine ear and his virtuosity in handling rhythms. See whether instances of this virtuosity are revealed in your scansion of the next five stanzas.

3. On pp. 47–48 we indicated that "Channel Firing," with the mention in its last stanza of place names charged with venerable associations in English history, moves into a different dimension of feeling. The poet's handling of the metrical situation powerfully reinforces this shift.

When we discussed "Channel Firing" on pp. 46–47 and 95–96, you presumably did not have the technical equipment to allow you to understand how Hardy had achieved this effect through his disposition of the accents—though you may very well have become aware, even at your first reading, of an increased gravity and even majesty in the movement of the last lines. The poet has rendered this last line almost proof against an inappropriately glib utterance. Scan the last stanza in order to see more clearly how he has done it.

(a) Scan stanza 1. How many secondary accents do you find? Attempt to describe the effect of these in setting the mood of the poem.

(b) Scan stanzas 5 and 6.

Anapestic and Dactylic Meter Edgar Allan Poe's "Ulalume" comes very close to being a fully "anapestic" poem. Here, for example, is the first stanza scanned. Note that lines 1, 4, 6, and 8 have a *feminine ending,* that is, an added unaccented syllable. Note also how this ending is indicated in our scansion; it is not regarded as a separate foot in its own right.

```
      ˘   /     ˘    ˘ /    ˘  ˘  /   ˘
The skies | they were ash | en and so | ber;
      ˘   /     ˘    ˘  /   ˘  ˘  /
The leaves | they were cris | ped and sere—
      ˘   /     ˘    ˘   /    ˘  ˘  /
The leaves | they were with | ering and sere,
   ˘  ˘  /     ˘  ˘   /    ˘  // /  ˘
It was night, | in the lone | some Octo | ber
   ˘   ˘   /    ˘  ˘  / ˘˘ /
Of my most | immemo | rial year:
  ˘  ˘  /    ˘  ˘  /   ˘  ˘  /   ˘
It was hard | by the dim | lake of Au | ber
    ˘  ˘   /    ˘  ˘ /   ˘  ˘   /
In the mis | ty mid re | gion of Weir;
   ˘  ˘  /     ˘  ˘  /   ˘  ˘  /  ˘
It was down | by the dank | tarn of Auber
  ˘  ˘   /    ˘  ˘   /    ˘  ˘   /
In the ghoul- | haunted wood | land of Weir.
```

The strongly assertive rhythms of almost pure anapestic (or dactylic) verse are often associated with the emphasis, *in isolation,* of musicality (see p. 544). But such meters, as we have already remarked, easily come to seem mannered and artificial, and readily lend themselves to parody. Aldous Huxley did, in fact, write a famous parody of "Ulalume" (see p. 546).

As we have noted earlier (p. 505 fn.), both the iamb and anapest are feet of rising rhythm; that is, we move from unaccented to accented syllable. Now we consider feet of falling rhythm, the trochee and the dactyl.*

Poems in which the staple foot is trochaic are not very numerous in English poetry, and in many of them the line terminates in an accented syllable —that is, ends technically with a defective foot. We can scan the opening stanza of Longfellow's "Psalm of Life" as follows:

```
 /   ˘   /  ˘    /   ˘   /  ˘
Tell me | not, in | mournful | numbers
 /  ˘   /  ˘   /   ˘  /
Life is | but an | empty | dream! †
 /   ˘   /  ˘   /   ˘   /  ˘
For the | soul is | dead that | slumbers
  /   ˘   /  //    /  ˘  /
And things | are not | what they | seem.
```

Here follows a poem that is basically trochaic, but one that offers some instructional variation:

* We might note in passing that the iamb and the trochee are instances of duple rhythm; the anapest and dactyl of triple rhythm—triple, because they have *three* syllables rather than two.

† Often in the scansion of trochaic verse the caret marking the missing syllable in a final defective foot is omitted, as here and also in line 4.

Why So Pale and Wan?

Sir John Suckling [1609–1642]

Why so pale and wan, fond lover?
　　Prithee,[1] why so pale?
Will, when looking well can't move her,
　　Looking ill prevail?
　　Prithee, why so pale?

Why so dull and mute, young sinner?
　　Prithee, why so mute?
Will, when speaking well can't win her,
　　Saying nothing do't?
　　Prithee, why so mute?

Quit, quit for shame! This will not move;
　　This cannot take her.
If of herself she will not love,
　　Nothing can make her:
　　The devil take her!

Questions

1. Is the speaker's attitude one of matter-of-fact rationality? Indignation? Light-hearted gaiety? Is there any change of attitude in the course of the poem? Try to define the attitude as clearly as you can and indicate any devices used to suggest any changes in the tone of voice of the speaker.

2. Let us now scan the first stanza:

$$/ \;// \quad / \quad \cup \quad / \quad // \quad / \; \cup$$
Why so | pale and | wan, fond | lover?
$$/ \quad \cup \quad / \quad // \quad /$$
　　Prithee, | why so | pale? ∧
$$/ \quad \cup \quad / \quad \cup \quad / \quad \cup \quad / \quad \cup$$
Will, when | looking | well can't | move her,
$$/ \quad \cup \quad / \quad /$$
　　Looking | ill pre | vail? ∧
$$/ \quad \cup \quad / \; // \quad /$$
　　Prithee, | why so | pale? ∧

Would you agree that the prevailing trochaic meter, with its falling rhythm, has some appropriateness here—that it may be taken as related to the dejection of the lover? Even though in a spirit of parody—parody, because the speaker does not fully sympathize with the lover's attitude?

3. Scan the remaining two stanzas. Undoubtedly, you will find that the third stanza will not accept the pattern of the first two. In fact, all sorts of wrenchings occur here, and the falling movement disappears. The speaker of the poem has, in the first two stanzas, given himself (even if in the mood of parody) to the mood of the lover, but in the third he is saying, "Stop this

---

[1] clipped form, now archaic of "I pray thee," i.e., "I ask you"

nonsense and self-pity. Buck up, be a man! If she won't have you, to hell with her!" How does the metrical change relate to this tone? *

Of the four standard accentual-syllabic feet, the dactyl is the least common in English, but it does occasionally occur.† Henry Wadsworth Longfellow used dactylic hexameter in his *Evangeline,* which begins:

> / ∪ ∪ / ∪ ∪ / ∪ ∪ / ∪∪ / ∪ ∪ ∪ / ∪
> This is the | forest pri | meval, the | murmuring | pines and the | hemlocks ∧

Longfellow's experiment has never been regarded as very successful, and the artificiality is generally apparent. The verse, necessarily, is based on stress, not quantity, and most readers feel it as accentual-syllabic verse, a basic anapestic line with *feminine* ending (p. 507):

> / ∪ ∪ / ∪ ∪ / ∪ ∪ / ∪∪ / ∪ ∪
> ∧∧This | is the for | est prime | val, the mur | muring pines | and the
> / ∪
> hem | locks

The emergence of this rhythm instead of the dactylic suggests how powerful in English is the rising rhythm. As Paul Fussell, Jr., puts it in a recent study, "When it is poetically organized, the English language appears to tend toward rising rhythms; that is, the main instinct in English prosody is for iambic or occasionally anapaestic movements rather than for trochaic or dactylic."‡ And Robert Frost insists that the iambic is the basic English verse.

For one more illustration of dactylic verse, let us turn to "Hesperia" by Algernon Charles Swinburne, a poet famous for complex metrical effects. Here are the first eight lines:

---

* A famous example of trochaic verse appears in Tennyson's "Boadicea." Boadicea was a queen of the Britons, technically an ally of Rome, but actually under Roman control. On some pretext she was seized, flogged, and her daughters raped, on which provocation the queen raised a bloody revolt. Tennyson's poem is, fictionally, her speech of incitement to the Britons. Here is a section:

> Burst the gates and burn the palaces, break the works of statuary,
> Take the hoary Roman head and shatter it, hold it abominable,
> Cut the Roman boy to pieces in his lust and voluptuousness,
> Lash the maiden into swooning, me they lashed and humiliated,
> Chop the breast from off the mother, dash the brains of the little one out,
> Up my Britons, on my chariot, on my chargers, trample them under us.

The critic Gilbert Highet has described the poem as composed of "long racing trochaic lines, one two, one two, one two, kill them, kill them, kill them—which, instead of pausing at the end of each measure, dash off into a frenzy of excitement" (*The Powers of Poetry,* Oxford University Press). Scan the passage above, remembering Highet's remarks on the end of each measure.

† The dactyl was one of the most important verse forms in classical poetry; for example, it is used in the *Iliad* and the *Odyssey* and in the *Aeneid,* all written in dactylic hexameter. But neither Greek nor Latin used accentual verse, and the classical dactyl was composed of one *long* plus two *short* syllables—not, as in English, of one accented syllable followed by two unaccented. *Quantity* (involving the relative length and brevity of syllables) is only a subsidiary in English verse (see p. 520), and all attempts to base verse on it have failed.

‡ *Versification: Major Language Types,* ed. W. K. Wimsatt, New York University Press, 1972, p. 196.

/ ᴗ ᴗ | / ᴗ ᴗ | / | // | / | ᴗ ᴗ | / ᴗ ᴗ | / ᴗ
Out of the | golden re | mote wild | west where the | sea without | shore is ʌ

/ ᴗ ᴗ | / / // | ᴗ / ᴗ ᴗ | / | ᴗ ᴗ | / ᴗ ᴗ | /
Full of the | sunset, and | sad, if at | all, with the | fulness of | joy ʌ ʌ   2

ᴗᴗ / | ᴗ / | ᴗ ᴗ | / ᴗ ᴗ | / ᴗ ᴗ | / | ᴗ ᴗ | / ᴗ ᴗ
As a | wind sets ʌ| in with the | autumn that | blows from the | region of |

/ ᴗ
    stories ʌ   3

/ ᴗ ᴗ | / ᴗ ᴗ | / ᴗ ᴗ | / ᴗ ᴗ | / | ᴗ ᴗ
Blows with a | perfume of | songs and of | memories be | loved from a |

/
    boy ʌ ʌ   4

/ ᴗ ᴗ | / ᴗ ᴗ | / / ᴗ | / ᴗ ᴗ | / ᴗ ᴗ | / ᴗ
Blows from the | capes of the | past over | sea to the | bays of the | present ʌ

/ ᴗ ᴗ | / ᴗ ᴗ | / ᴗ ᴗ | / ᴗ ᴗ | / ᴗᴗ | /
Filled as with | shadow of | sound with the | pulse of in | visible | feet ʌ ʌ

// | / ᴗ ᴗ | / ᴗ ᴗ | / ᴗ ᴗ | / ᴗ ᴗ | / | //
Far | out to the | shallows and | straits of the | future, by | rough ways

ᴗ | / ᴗ
    or | pleasant ʌ   7

ᴗ ᴗ | / ᴗ ᴗ | / | // | / ᴗᴗ | , ᴗ ᴗ | / // | ᴗ
Is it | thither the | wind's wings | beat? Is it | hither to | me, O my |

/
    sweet? ʌ ʌ   8

In view of our preceding remarks, it is not surprising that in the last foot of each line one or both of the expected unaccented syllables have been omitted (*catalexis* or *double catalexis,* to speak technically), thus inviting the rising movement. An even more difficult problem is raised by the first feet of lines 3, 7, and 8. What are we to do with these extra syllables? One solution is to regard them as compensating, in each case, for the omitted syllables in the last foot of the preceding line. In theory, this would seem to work for line 3, but in line 7 we have only *one* extra syllable to compensate for *two* omitted syllables at the end of line 6, and in line 8, two extra syllables for one at the end of line 7. Even when one can work out a scansion for such verse as that of "Hesperia," it is fair to ask what we actually hear, and some authorities say that even when a dactylic scansion can be worked out, it is more reasonable to regard the work as a form of *accentual verse.**

End-Line and Internal Pauses We do not always pause at the end of a line of verse, for the sense unit does not necessarily coincide with the metrical unit—that is, with the verse line. When it does, we say the lines are *end-stopped;* when it does not, we have *run-on lines,* or an instance of *enjambment.* The following lines by Alexander Pope (1688–1744) are definitely end-stopped:

> Know then thyself, presume not God to scan;
> The proper study of Mankind is *Man.*
> Plac'd on this Isthmus of a middle state,
> A Being darkly wise, and rudely great. . . .

But the following lines by John Keats (1795–1821), though written in the same meter and rhyme scheme, show considerable enjambment:

---

* See Joseph Malof, *A Manual of English Meters,* Indiana University Press, 1970, p. 34. Our discussion of *accentual verse,* in contrast to accentual-syllabic verse, appears later, pp. 553–560. There four lines of "Hesperia" are scanned as accentual verse.

> A thing of beauty is a joy forever;
> Its loveliness increases; it will never
> Pass into nothingness; but still will keep
> A bower quiet for us, and a sleep
> Full of sweet dreams, and health and quiet breathing. . . .

There are internal pauses as well as those that come at the ends of lines, and these, too, exert a considerable influence on the rhythm of the verse. In English poetry, lines that have four, five, or six stresses, almost invariably exhibit a strong internal pause, which is called the *caesura*. It marks the end of a sense unit—not a metrical unit—and in scansion is indicated thus:

> Know then | thyself, || presume | not God | to scan. . . .

or

> Its love | liness | increas | es: || it | will never. . . .*

In addition to the main pause or caesura, there may be secondary pauses that mark off less important sense divisions (though we do not usually indicate them in scansion). The location of the caesura and of the secondary pauses is extremely important in influencing the rhythmical quality of a line. More is at stake here than mere variety. In good verse there is usually a significant interplay between the handling of pauses and such factors as rhetorical variation and quantitative variation. Pauses and variation relieve the monotony of mechanical adherence to the abstract metrical pattern, and indeed *use* the abstract pattern to point up the expressiveness of the poetry. By postponing, or emphatically confirming, or even occasionally violating, the expectations set up by the metrical pattern, they make the most of the expressive potential.

What has just been said about the poet's handling of the pauses internal to the line applies, of course, in full measure to the handling of pauses at the ends of lines. As in the five lines quoted from Keats above, we may have the extreme of a full pause at the completion of a statement (here marked by a semicolon), scaling down to the extreme of no pause at all except that suggested by the metrical conclusion of the line, such "run-on" lines being technically referred to as *enjambment*); and in between, of course, we may find all sorts of pauses, from very strong to minimal, punctuated or not, as the case may be. To illustrate the importance of the poet's handling of pauses let us return once more to a poem with which we are familiar, Hardy's "Channel Firing":

> That night | your great | guns, || un | awares,   **1**
> Shook all | our cof | fins || as | we lay,   **2**

---

* Notice that since the caesura marks off a unit of sense, not of meter, it may come *within* a metrical foot; that is, strictly speaking, it is a rhetorical factor. The caesura usually—though not necessarily—occurs somewhere toward the middle of the line.

⌣ ╱   ⌣ ╱   ⌣   ╱   ⌣ ╱
And broke | the chan | cel || win | dow-squares,   3

╱╱ ╱   ⌣ ╱   ⌣ ╱   ⌣ ╱
We thought | it was || the Judg | ment-day   4

⌣   ╱ ⌣ ╱   ⌣ ╱   ⌣╱
And sat | upright. || While drea | risome   5

⌣ ╱   ⌣ ╱   ⌣ ╱   ⌣   ╱
Arose | the howl || of wak | ened hounds: 6

⌣   ╱   ⌣ ╱   ⌣╱ ⌣   ╱
The mouse | let fall || the al | tar-crumb,   7

⌣   ╱   ╱╱   ╱   ⌣╱   ⌣ ╱
The worms | drew back || into | the mounds,   8

⌣   ╱   ╱╱   ╱   ⌣   ╱   ╱╱   ╱
The glebe | cow drooled. || Till God | called || "No;   9

⌣   ╱   ⌣⌣   ╱   ⌣   ╱   ⌣ ╱
It's gun || nery prac | tice || out | at sea . . .   10

Note that in line 1 the caesura comes late in the line. Some readers would argue for two caesuras, the first coming after *night*. At any rate, a considerable pause is clearly demanded after *night,* and these two strong pauses, situated as they are, tend to lighten the normal end-of-line pause and give something approaching the effect of enjambment with line 2, for the sense hurries us on to *Shook.* The carrying-over of the sense from line 4 to line 5 gives us an obvious instance of enjambment, emphasized by the fact that line 4 has ended a stanza. But line 5 stops in midcourse with a very heavy caesura pointed up by a full stop after *upright.* There is another run-on from line 5 to line 6, and then the more normal patterning of caesuras resumes in lines 6, 7, and 8.

Line 9, however, repeats the situation in line 1—in fact, pushes it to a further extreme: we have a heavy caesura after *drooled;* but then the sense insists on a heavy pause after *called*—one quite as strong as that after *drooled.* Since the syllable that ends the line—the word to which "Till God called" leads up—is a powerful *No,* uttered with thunderous force, the movement of this whole quatrain is rendered exciting and dramatic.

The metrical situation throughout the ten lines we have quoted above is complex, and its power is not to be accounted for by any simple explanation. Rhetorical variation in these lines, for example, is obviously important; but Hardy's disposition of his pauses, primary and secondary, internal and at the ends of lines, plays an important part too.

In scansion, how does one determine where the caesura falls? By inspection; by reading the line, preferably aloud, and noting where the principal internal pause comes. But even where no punctuation occurs, one's sense of the principal "joints" in the pattern of meaning will usually suffice. Sometimes the caesura is only faintly marked; at other times a secondary pause may be nearly—or quite—as strong as the primary. (See our discussion, above, of lines 1 and 9 of "Channel Firing.")

In the following excerpt from Robert Frost's "The Code" (p. 51), the caesuras fairly shout their presence by punctuation or line breaks. In the last two lines they are, however, less emphatic.

> The town-bred farmer failed to understand.
> "What is there wrong?"
>   "Something you just now said."

"What did I say?"
                  "About our taking pains."
"To cock the hay?—because it's going to shower?
I said that more than half an hour ago.
I said it to myself as much as you."

Like as the Waves

William Shakespeare [*1564–1616*]

Like as the waves || make towards the pebbled shore,
So do our minutes || hasten to their end;
Each changing place || with that which goes before,
In sequent toil || all forwards do contend.
Nativity, once in the main of light,   5
Crawls to maturity, wherewith being crown'd,
Crooked eclipses 'gainst his glory fight,
And Time, that gave, doth now his gift confound.
Time doth transfix the flourish set on youth,
And delves the parallels in beauty's brow;   10
Feeds on the rarities of nature's truth,
And nothing stands but for his scythe to mow:
    And yet, to times in hope my verse shall stand,
    Praising thy worth, despite his cruel hand.

Questions

1. Scan the poem.
2. Mark the caesuras in lines 5 through 14.
3. Are there any lines that seem to lack a caesura? Are there any that seem to have more than one principal pause?
4. Can it be said in the first four lines that the placement of the caesura (in contrast to its placement in the rest of the sonnet) is actually, in this context, expressive, and therefore justified?
5. Do the caesuras in lines 5 through 14 grow out of the "rhetorical situation" in the lines? Do they accord with the rhetorical emphasis?

To Heaven

Ben Jonson [*1573–1637*]

Good and great God! can I not think of thee,
But it must straight my melancholy be?
Is it interpreted in me disease,
That, laden with my sins, I seek for ease?
O be thou witness, that the reins[1] dost know   5

[1] loins

And hearts of all, if I be sad for show;
And judge me after, if I dare pretend
To aught but grace, or aim at other end.
As thou art all, so be thou all to me,
First, midst, and last, converted One and Three!   10
My faith, my hope, my love; and, in this state,
My judge, my witness, and my advocate!
Where have I been this while exiled from thee,
And whither rapt, now thou but stoop'st to me?
Dwell, dwell here still! O, being everywhere,   15
How can I doubt to find thee ever here?
I know my state, both full of shame and scorn,
Conceived in sin, and unto labor born,
Standing with fear, and must with horror fall,
And destined unto judgment, after all.   20
I feel my griefs too, and there scarce is ground
Upon my flesh t' inflict another wound;
Yet dare I not complain or wish for death
With holy Paul, lest it be thought the breath
Of discontent; or that these prayers be   25
For weariness of life, not love of thee.

Questions

1. Scan this poem.
2. Can you justify, on rhetorical grounds, the frequent trochaic substitutions and the frequent use of secondary accents? Consider in particular the first ten lines.
3. Where do the caesuras fall in lines 1, 2, 10, 11, and 12?
4. Discuss the whole system of pauses in line 15. How are they forced by metrical and rhetorical considerations?

Ah, Sunflower

William Blake [*1757–1827*]

Ah, Sunflower, weary of time,
    Who countest the steps of the sun;
Seeking after that sweet golden clime
    Where the traveller's journey is done;

Where the Youth pined away with desire,   5
    And the pale virgin shrouded in snow,
Arise from their graves, and aspire
    Where my Sunflower wishes to go!

This poem is prevailingly anapestic in meter. This meter often tends to give a mechanical effect (see pp. 506–507). But this poem does not give such an effect, and, as a matter of fact, is characterized by its delicate and lingering rhythm. We can notice that the first feet in lines 1, 2, and 7 constitute iambic substitutions. Relate these substitutions to the context. But the most important item in securing the characteristic rhythm of this poem is the use of what might be called the secondary accent on the first syllable of the anapest. For example, the following line might be scanned:

$$\overset{//}{Seek}\overset{\cup}{ing}\overset{/}{aft} \mid \overset{\cup}{er}\overset{\cup}{that}\overset{/}{sweet} \mid \overset{//}{gol}\overset{\cup}{den}\overset{/}{clime}$$

The first and the third feet are obviously different in effect from the second foot, which is a normal anapest. This retardation of the anapest is what one poet has said we can't "afford to miss" in this poem.

> For example, "Seeking after that sweet golden clime." You can't afford to hurry over "golden." It's just as important as "sweet." . . . Yes, and this one: "And the pale virgin shrouded in snow." There you can't possibly subordinate your "virgin" to "pale" and "shrouded." And so that's very bold. . . . I think it may be that "virgin". . . . comes out stronger in its unaccented position than it would otherwise. . . . We have to overcome our initial impulse to subordinate it and drive on to "shroud—" then, don't we? So we set it up and it emerges more significant to us.*

Questions

1. Scan the entire poem, being careful to mark all secondary accents.
2. State the theme of the poem. Do you see any relation between what you take to be the theme and the tension between the secondary and primary accents in the poem?

After Long Silence

William Butler Yeats   [*1865–1939*]

> Speech after long silence; it is right,
> All other lovers being estranged or dead,
> Unfriendly lamplight hid under its shade,
> The curtains drawn upon unfriendly night,
> That we descant and yet again descant   5
> Upon the supreme theme of Art and Song:
> Bodily decrepitude is wisdom; young
> We loved each other and were ignorant.

The dramatic situation implied by the poem is easily defined. The two lovers are in a shadowed room alone, the lamplight being almost hidden by the shade. One of the lovers is speaking to the other, and before we comment on what he says, several points may be rehearsed. The lovers are evidently old. The relationship has not been a constant one, for we are told that all other

---

* John Crowe Ransom, in Cleanth Brooks and Robert Penn Warren, eds., *Conversations on the Craft of Verse,* pamphlet and tape recording.

lovers are "estranged or dead." The first line suggests that there has been a long silence after they have "descanted" upon the "supreme theme of Art and Song." (The nature of this theme will be discussed later.) This silence has been broken by more talk on the same subject, apparently now the only subject left to them, and one of the lovers makes the comment which constitutes the poem itself.

The speaker says, in effect, this: one lover can no longer take pleasure in the physical beauty of the other (for the lamplight, which would reveal the decay of age, is described as "unfriendly"). Furthermore, the outside world has no more use for them (for the world outside their drawn curtains is likewise "unfriendly"). It is right that, having passed through the other phases of their lives, they should now talk of the "theme of Art and Song," which is "supreme" because it involves the interpretation of their own previous experience. Wisdom, the power to reach an interpretation, comes only as the body decays. The poet sees the wisdom as a positive gain, but at the same time he can regret the time of beauty and youth when the lovers could dispense with wisdom. The basic point of the poem is the recognition, with its attendant pathos, of the fact that man cannot ever be complete—cannot, that is, possess beauty and wisdom together.

Why is the poem so much richer and more moving than the bare statement of our summary? In part, one would say, because the poet has dramatized the general statement—that is, he has made us feel that the idea as embodied in the poem has behind it the weight of experience involving real people; in part, one would say, because of the suggestiveness of the images used in the first four lines. And other reasons for the dramatic power of the poem will occur to the reader. But surely one of the most important reasons for the power of the poem is the beautiful adaptation of the verse to the rest of the poem so that we are made to read it with full expressiveness.

This poem is written in iambic pentameter, but the first line is highly irregular, and there are several substitutions made in the course of the poem. There are also some very interesting and expressive secondary accents forced by rhetorical considerations.

Questions

1. Scan the poem. (If there seem to be alternative ways of handling certain lines, after consideration, choose the one that seems to be the simplest. What is important is that one should take into account—whatever the particular scansion adopted—the accents and secondary stresses that actually occur in the line.)

2. In line 3, how does the metrical situation throw emphasis upon the idea of light hidden?

3. Line 6 is metrically very interesting. Note the instance of internal rhyme. How does it work with the other factors—what are these other factors?—to throw emphasis upon the word *theme?* What is the rhetorical justification for special emphasis upon this word?

4. In line 7, the last word, *young,* is obviously an important word, a pivotal word in the poem. How does the metrical situation in the line work to throw special stress upon this word? Where does the caesura fall in this line?

Rose Aylmer

Walter Savage Landor [*1775–1864*]

Ah, what | avails | the scep | tred race,
Ah, what | the form | divine!
What ev | ery vir | tue, ev | ery grace!
Rose Ayl | mer, all | were thine.

Rose Ayl | mer, whom | these wake | ful eyes
May weep, but nev | er see,
A night | of mem | ories and | of sighs
I con | secrate | to thee.

This poem seems perfectly straightforward in its statement. But the statement alone does not give us the poem—that is, other factors are required to make the statement come alive for us. One thing that serves very obviously to convert the bare statement into poetry is the use made of the various elements we have already discussed in this appendix.

In the first stanza, in the first foot of every line, we may note the heavy secondary accent, and the length of the first syllable of the foot. These factors tend to give an unusual emphasis to those feet, especially since the remainder of each line is characterized by a very positive difference between accented and unaccented syllables; and those feet, by the repetitions, set the basic attitude of questioning. The marked regularity of the metrical pattern of each line, the definite stop at the end of each line, and the repetition involved in the first three lines—all of these factors contribute to a formal and elevated tone. (We can notice the formal tone supported, further, by the repetitive balance of the first and second lines, which is repeated by the balance within the third line. "What every virtue" is balanced against "[what] every grace." And we can notice how the distinction between the first and second parts of the line is marked by the pause, which tends to cause greater emphasis to fall on the first syllable of *every*.)

The first line of the second stanza, with the repetition of the name *Rose Aylmer*, picks up the metrical pattern characteristic of the first stanza, providing a kind of transition between the rhythm characteristic of the first stanza and that characteristic of the second. The difference in the rhythm of the second stanza is caused chiefly by the run-on lines, the absence of the secondary accents on the initial syllables of the last three lines, and the metrical accenting of syllables not usually accented. We may try to relate some of these special details to the meaning of the poem.

The first run-on line serves to emphasize the word *weep:* since the sense unit is so radically divided by the line end, when we do pick up the rest of the clause at the beginning of the second line, it comes with a feeling of emphatic fulfillment, which is further supported by the marked pause after the word *weep*. The emphasis on the word *weep* is, of course, rhetorically right because it is set over in contrast with the word *see* at the end of the second line. And we may also observe how the alliteration of the word *weep* with the word *wakeful* in the preceding line helps to mark the association of the two ideas: it is not merely weeping which is to be contrasted with seeing, but the lonely weeping at night when the sense of loss becomes most acute.

The third line is also a run-on line, giving a kind of balance to the structure of the stanza, which functions as do the various balances of structure in the first stanza. Although neither the first line nor the third line of the second stanza is punctuated at the end, we can see that the tendency to run on into the next line is not so strong in the third line as in the first; we can see that the phrase "whom these wakeful eyes" strikes us with a more marked sense of incompleteness than does the phrase "A night of memories and of sighs." This is especially true because the first of the two phrases, coming early in the stanza, is less supported by a context, by the sense of things preceding it. But, even though the tendency to run on is not so strong in the third line as in the first, the tendency is still marked; and such a tendency to *enjambment* (see p. 510) fixes our attention on the clause, "I consecrate," which begins the last line, and forces a pause after that clause.

The word *consecrate*, which is thereby emphasized, is very important. We can see how important it is, and how effective it is in avoiding a sentimental or stereotyped effect, by substituting other words which convey approximately the same meaning. For instance, the lines might be rewritten

> A night of memories and of sighs
> I now will give to thee.

We immediately see a great difference. The rewritten passage tends toward sentimentality. The word *consecrate* means "to set apart perpetually for sacred uses"; it implies the formality and impersonality of a ceremony. This implication in conjunction with the formality of tone, which has already been discussed in connection with the technique of the first stanza, helps to prevent any suggeston of self-pity.

Another technical feature appears in the use of the word *consecrate*, which does not appear in the rewritten line

> I now will give to thee.

The word *consecrate* is accented in ordinary usage on the first syllable. But when the word is used in this poem, meter dictates an additional accent on the last syllable, for the line is to be scanned as follows:

> ˘ / ˘ / ˘ /
> I con | secrate | to thee.

Thus the metrical situation tends to give the word an emphasis which it would not possess in ordinary prose usage; and this is appropriate because of the importance of the word in the poem.

Questions

1. What would have been the difference in effect if the poet had written, in the next to the last line, "an age" instead of "a night"?

2. Discuss the effect of the accent on the ordinary unimportant word *and* in the same line.

A Deep-Sworn Vow

William Butler Yeats [*1865–1939*]

> Others because you did not keep
> That deep-sworn vow have been friends of mine;
> Yet always when I look death in the face,
> When I clamber to the heights of sleep,
> Or when I grow excited with wine,
> Suddenly I meet your face.

The theme of this poem is the lasting impression made by a love affair which has been broken off, apparently long ago, and which has been superseded by other relationships. On the conscious level of the mind, the loved one has been forgotten, but the image is still carried indelibly imprinted on the deeper, unconscious mind. When we come to consider how this theme is made concrete and forceful in its statement in the poem, we must consider, of course, matters like diction, imagery, structure of incidents, and so on. For example, there is the contrast of the informality of the opening lines of the poem and the note of excitement with which the poem ends. One notices also the arrangement of the three instances which the lover gives of the moments when the face suddenly appears to him: at moments of great danger, in sleep when the subconscious is released, and in moments of intoxication. The last item balances the first: the poet does not intend to falsify the experience by saying, "Only when I look death in the face, I remember you." The memory comes also when the occasion is one of no seriousness at all—merely one of conviviality. And yet the three classes of occasions, though they contrast with each other in their associations, all reinforce one particular idea: the face appears when concern for the immediate, self-conscious everyday existence has been let down—for whatever reason. Yet important as are all the details of this sort, we shall have to examine the metrical arrangement and rhyme scheme of this poem before we can account for its effectiveness.

The poem is highly irregular. There is a considerable variation in the kinds of lines, trimeter, tetrameter, and pentameter; though the basic foot is of two syllables, some feet have three. Moreover, there are, we notice, many feet having secondary accents. But the irregularities in this poem are far from haphazard.

Questions

1. Do you agree with our statement that "the irregularities in this poem are far from haphazard"? Scan the poem carefully before you frame your answer.

2. How many metrical substitutions do you find? How many instances of secondary accent? Do you believe these variations from the normal metrical pattern add to the expressive force of the poem?

QUANTITATIVE VARIATION AND FORCED PAUSES

There is another factor that influences rhythm and yet finds no specific place in the scansion of English verse. Some syllables—those containing long vowels or clusters of consonants—take longer to pronounce than others. The meter of Greek and Latin poetry is indeed based upon the count (and the distribution) of "long" and "short" syllables.* Though this is not true of English meter, and though in general the length of the syllable in English verse tends to ride along with the incidence of stress, nevertheless, what may be called the *quantitative aspect* of language does exist and has its influence on the felt rhythm.

One iambic foot, for example, may be longer than another iambic foot, or one iambic pentameter line longer than another. Both of the following lines are iambic pentameter:

'Mid hushed, cool-rooted flowers fragrant-eyed
from John Keats, "Ode to Psyche"

How soon they find fit instruments of ill
from Alexander Pope, *Rape of the Lock*

But a normal reading of the Keats line will take longer than a normal reading of the Pope line. In the Keats line, the foot *cool-root-*, though it can be treated as an iamb, has two long syllables. This length, coupled with the fact that *cool* takes a rather heavy secondary accent—rhetorical considerations demand this—slows the reading of the foot and helps to give a grave and deliberate emphasis to the middle portion of the line. The quantitative aspect of verse is constantly interplaying with the strictly metrical aspect. The mere fact of this interplay gives a certain vitality to verse. But the good poet is able to control the quantitative factor in language, as in the line quoted from Keats, in order to produce (or assist in producing) special effects.

Associated with the retardation that may be caused by quantity, there is that which comes from what we may call a *forced pause*. Let us examine instances that occur in the last stanza of a poem by Thomas Hardy:

Since then, keen lessons that love deceives,
And wrings with wrong, have shaped to me
Your face, and the God-curst sun, and a tree,
And a pond edged with grayish leaves.

First, in the phrase "God-curst sun" the transition from the "d" sound of *God* to the "hard" (guttural) sound of "c" in *curst* is not easy. Nor is that

* The vowels in *hit, met, hot,* and *pull* are short, or are perceived as such though they also differ qualitatively from the vowels which we think of as their long equivalents, the vowels of *heat, mate, father,* and *pool*. To the long vowels just listed should be added those of *bowl* and *bawl*. The vowels of *at, but,* and the blurred vowel of unemphatic *the* are also short. A syllable is long if it contains a long vowel; but even if it contains a short vowel it may become long if followed by more than one consonant or by a lengthening consonant: for instance, the syllable is long in *man, path, pass, laugh, dash,* and *buzz*. The reader ought to be warned, however, that this list does not pretend to be exhaustive and it admits of many exceptions. Nothing short of a course in phonetics will give an exact exposition of what makes syllables sound long or short in various linguistic situations, but for present purposes the more or less attentive reader's impression will suffice.

from the final "st" sound of *curst* to the "s" of *sun.* A pause is "forced" on us, as becomes immediately clear if we consider the contrast with the transitions in the opening lines of "The Choric Ode" from Tennyson's "The Lotus-Eaters":

> There is sweet music here that softer falls
> Than petals from blown roses on the grass. . . .

But to return to Hardy's lines, the problem of transition is different, and even more difficult, between *pond* and *edged,* and between *grayish* and *leaves:* here the pause is forced in order to avoid a nonsensical jumble, such as *pon-dedged,* or a nonsensical elision, such as *gray-shleaves.*

To take another instance:

> When Ajax strives some rock's vast weight to throw,
> The line too labors, and the verse moves slow.

In moving from *Ajax* to *strives,* the reader must negotiate the consonants *k-s-s-t-r;* from *strives* to *some, v-z-s;* * and from *rock's* to *vast, ksv.* One aspect of the general difficulty of such transitions is the pronunciation in succession (as with *pond* and *edged* above) of the same or related consonants; for example, *s* and *s,* or *s* and *z.* The difficulty of such transitions makes the line "labor," as Alexander Pope puts it, in writing "The line too labors, and the words move slow" (p. 522).

Effects such as these are, in general, unpleasant when considered in isolation. They are examples of what is called *cacophony,* to use the technical term, which means literally "bad sounding" (as contrasted with *euphony,* "good sounding"; see pp. 542–545). Sometimes, however, a transition may be slow and complicated without being intrinsically unpleasant. For instance, such a combination may be one of the factors in lengthening the foot *cool-rooted,* to which we have referred on p. 520. The consonants *l* and *r* are both *liquids,* and it is impossible to move from one to the other without taking a slight pause.

Pleasantness or unpleasantness is not, however, what is at stake in the examples we have given. In both examples, the poet has been aiming at dramatic expressiveness, not at versification agreeable in itself.† For example, let us consider the entire poem from which the first illustration is drawn:

Neutral Tones

Thomas Hardy [*1840–1928*]

> We stood by a pond that wintry day,
> And the sun was white, as though chidden of God,

---

* With regard to "strives some": though we spell *strives* with a final *s,* the actual sound is that of a "voiced" *s;* that is, a *z.* Because *z* and *s* are such closely related consonants, a too rapid or careless utterance will give us *strive zum* or even *stry some.* In an effort to pronounce both words without slurring, we have to pause at least briefly to avoid a distorting glide from one word into the other.

† See "The Music of Verse," p. 542.

And a few leaves lay on the starving sod;
    —They had fallen from an ash, and were gray.

Your eyes on me were as eyes that rove   5
Over tedious riddles solved years ago;
And some words played between us to and fro
    On which lost the more by our love.

The smile on your mouth was the deadest thing
Alive enough to have strength to die;   10
And a grin of bitterness swept thereby
    Like an ominous bird a-wing . . .[1]

Since then, keen lessons that love deceives,
And wrings with wrong, have shaped to me
Your face, and the God-curst sun, and a tree,   15
    And a pond edged with grayish leaves.

Questions

We have said that the forced pauses in the last stanza are dramatically effective. After meditating on the poem, would you accept this judgment? To answer the question, you would, of course, have to interpret the poem. For one thing, what is the significance of the fact that the poem is a recollection, in which the words spoken represent the very act of reaching back into the past in an attempt to establish its meaning?

To turn to the passage from which our second illustration is drawn:

Sound and Sense

Alexander Pope   [1688–1744]

True ease in writing comes from art, not chance,
As those move easiest who have learned to dance.
'T is not enough no harshness gives offense,
The sound must seem an echo to the sense:
Soft is the strain when Zephyr gently blows,   5
And the smooth stream in smoother numbers flows:
But when loud surges lash the sounding shore,
The hoarse, rough verse should like the torrent roar:
When Ajax strives some rock's vast weight to throw,
The line too labors, and the words move slow;   10
Not so, when swift Camilla scours the plain,
Flies o'er th' unbending corn, and skims along the main.
Hear how Timotheus' varied lays surprise,
And bid alternate passions fall and rise!

                          from "An Essay on Criticism"

[1] no omission; dots are part of the poem

Though this passage is in iambic pentameter couplets, there is actually a great deal of variety in the verse. Moreover, Pope is here practicing what he preaches: he is making the sound "seem an echo to the sense."

Questions

1. We have just indicated the relation of the forced pauses in lines 9 to 10 to the "sense." What other factors in these lines support the dramatic effect?
2. What do you observe of dramatic aptness in lines 11 and 12? Or elsewhere?

Rhyme

All of our previous discussion in this section of the book has been concerned with aspects of rhythm. We have pointed out that rhythm is a constant factor in all uses of language, and that its use in verse is a special adaptation. But there are other factors that tend to shape and bind poetry, factors that are not ever-present in the use of language.

For centuries the most obvious among these factors and the one most commonly and systematically appearing as a structural device has been rhyme, a correspondence in sound between the accented syllable of two or more words (*grow–know, rebound–astound*). When the rhyming words end in one or more unaccented syllables, these, too, must correspond in sound (*potato–Plato*). Rhyme is a phenomenon of *sound,* never of mere spelling (*buy–why–sigh–eye*). Observe, too, that the introductory consonants in rhyme (when one exists; see *eye* above) are *not* identical.*

Rhyme serves usually, as we have already said, to bind lines together into larger units of composition. We have already seen that the metrical scheme of a single line does its work by setting up in the mind of the hearer or reader an anticipation of regular recurrence. In the same way a fixed pattern of rhyming, a *rhyme scheme,* will, in conjunction with a fixed pattern of line lengths, a *stanza,* define a group of lines as a unit. In stanzas where rhyme is employed, the rhyme emphasizes the stanza pattern by marking the end of each line unit. But rhyme, it should be said, is sometimes used irregularly; in such cases, it still exerts a binding and unifying effect, though much less forcefully. In addition, irregular rhyme may appear as a device of emphasis, insofar as it has not been used consistently in the poem or passage. The basic function of rhyme, however, has already been described: the unifying and "forming" function, which is most positively exhibited, as we shall see, in the reinforcing of the line pattern of stanzas.†

* For further distinctions in rhyme: *masculine* when the rhymed, accented syllables conclude the word (rebound–astound); *feminine* (or *double*) when the rhymed accented syllables are followed by identical unaccented syllables (*forever–never*); *triple* when the rhymed accented syllables are followed by two syllables that are identical (*slenderly–tenderly*). *Internal rhyme* occurs when, instead of rhymes appearing only at the end of lines, a word within a line rhymes with a word at the end: ("The splendor *falls* on castle *walls*" or "So Lord Howard past *away* with five ships of war that *day.*")

† Though here we emphasize the structural function of rhyme, we should refer to "Poetry as a Way of Saying," in which the intrinsic pleasure in rhyme is emphasized. See also p. 543 for a discussion of the function of rhyme in establishing the musicality of verse.

Related to rhyme as we have here described it are other elements of repetition of identical or related sounds: *alliteration, assonance,* and *consonance.*

In poetry of the Old English period the device of alliteration was regularly used for the purpose of establishing a verse scheme. (Alliteration is, in fact, sometimes called "front rhyme.") The following lines illustrate, in modern English, the way alliteration was used to give lines unity, just as meter tends to unify a line:

> Now *B*eowulf *b*ode in the *b*urg of the Scyldings,
> Leader be*l*oved, and *l*ong he ru*l*ed
> in *f*ame with all *f*olk, since his *f*ather had gone
> a*w*ay from the *w*orld, till a*w*oke an heir. . . .*

from *Beowulf*, trans. by Francis B. Gummere

But now alliteration is rarely used in verse according to any regular scheme. Where it occurs frequently, as in the work of Swinburne, it often impresses the reader as a mechanical and monotonous mannerism or a too gaudy decoration (see p. 547). Most poets use it with discretion to give a line or a group of lines a greater unity, to support musical effects, or to emphasize the words alliterated. In the following lines we can see how alliteration is used to emphasize and support the contrast in the second line and to relate the contrast to the word, *forgot:*

> Hast thou *f*orgot me then, and do I seem
> Now in thine eye so *f*oul, once deemed so *f*air

from *Paradise Lost,* Book II

Assonance, which may be called *interior rhyme,* depends on the identity of vowel sounds in accented syllables, without the identity of following consonants. It, too, may serve the purposes of binding or of emphasizing musicality. In the following line from Keats we see a good example of assonance used for emphasizing an effect:

> 'Mid hushed, *cool-rooted* flowers fragrant-eyed. . . .

To take another example of assonance used to emphasize an entirely different effect, we may turn to these lines of Pope's:

> Or Alum styptics with contracting pow'r
> Shrink his thin essence like a riveled flow'r;
> Or, as Ixion fixed, the wretch shall feel
> The giddy motion of the whirling Mill . . .

from *Rape of the Lock,* II

Here it is obvious that the sustained assonance, involving both accented and unaccented syllables, gives a high degree of unification. We can also see that emphasis is secured by the repetition in new combinations of the vowel sounds of the more important syllables. But the quality of the par-

---

* For the survivals of this meter in modern English poetry, see "Accentual or Stress Meter," pp. 553–560.

ticular "run" here is of some significance, for the tight frontal sound is appropriate to, and supports, the general idea of the passage.

Consonance involves a similarity between patternings of consonants.* In the following lines we see consonance serving to link lines in the same way as rhyme:

> You are the one whose part it is to *lean,*
> For whom it is not good to be *alone.*
> Laugh warmly turning shyly in the *hall*
> Or climb with bare knees the volcanic *hill.* . . .

from W. H. Auden, Poems, "III"

Consonance serves here as a "slant rhyme" to establish a pattern, but it may occur internally in a single line as a sort of binder or device of emphasizing musicality, as with assonance. But for such purposes it occurs more rarely than alliteration and assonance.

Stanza Forms

There are many different stanzas in use in English poetry. Some acquaintance with the more common forms is certainly desirable,† *but any given type of stanza must be regarded as an instrument at the poet's disposal and not as a thing important in itself.* The same instrument may be used for widely different purposes. Any given type of stanza is used in conjunction with so many other poetic factors that a reader must be very wary of attributing special effects to special stanza forms. Only the most general principles may be arrived at concerning stanza forms considered in isolation from other poetic factors. For instance, though it is fair to say that, in general, complicated stanza forms such as the *Spenserian stanza* have certain disadvantages for use in long narrative poems because the involved form may become monotonous and may impede the movement of the action, we should remember that Edmund Spenser, who invented the stanza, did use it in his *Faerie Queene,* an epic poem—and that it did suit his special purposes and poetic temperament. To take another instance, the folly of asserting, as many critics have done, that the sonnet is especially adapted for love poetry will be demonstrated by the following pair of poems, both sonnets.

---

* The vowel varies, but the consonantal pattern is identical: viz., *own–inn* or *leave–love.*

† The reader has already encountered a number of rhyme schemes and stanza forms in the earlier pages of this book: blank verse, for example, in " 'Out, Out—' " (p. 18) and "The Code" (p. 51); pentameter (or heroic) couplets in "To Heaven" (p. 513) and "Sound and Sense" (p. 522); various kinds of quatrains in "Sir Patrick Spence" (p. 23), "The Demon Lover" (p. 27), "The Workbox" (p. 42), "The Fall of Rome" (p. 44), and "Channel Firing" (p. 45); and such elaborate patterns as the sonnet—for example, "Like as the Waves" (p. 513). Other well-known stanzas are: rhyme royal: iambic pentameter, ababbcc (used by Shakespeare in *Venus and Adonis*); ottava rima: iambic pentameter, abababcc (used by Keats in *Isabella*); and the Spenserian stanza: iambic pentameter except for the last line which is iambic hexameter, ababbcbcc (used by Spenser in *The Faerie Queene*).

How Do I Love Thee?

Elizabeth Barrett Browning [*1809–1861*]

How do I love thee? Let me count the ways.
I love thee to the depth and breadth and height
My soul can reach, when feeling out of sight
For the ends of Being and ideal Grace.
I love thee to the level of everyday's   5
Most quiet need, by sun and candle-light.
I love thee freely, as men strive for Right;
I love thee purely, as they turn from Praise.
I love thee with the passion put to use
In my old griefs, and with my childhood's faith.   10
I love thee with a love I seemed to lose
With my lost saints,—I love thee with the breath,
Smiles, tears, of all my life!—and, if God choose,
I shall but love thee better after death.

from *Sonnets from the Portuguese*

On the Late Massacre in Piedmont

John Milton [*1608–1674*]

Avenge, O Lord, thy slaughtered saints, whose bones
Lie scattered on the Alpine mountains cold;
Ev'n them who kept thy truth so pure of old,
When all our fathers worshipped stocks and stones,
Forget not: in thy book record their groans   5
Who were thy sheep, and in their ancient fold
Slain by the bloody Piedmontese, that rolled
Mother with infant down the rocks. Their moans
The vales redoubled to the hills, and they
To heav'n. Their martyred blood and ashes sow   10
O'er all the' Italian fields, where still doth sway
The triple Tyrant that from these may grow
A hundredfold, who, having learnt thy way,
Early may fly the Babylonian woe.

These sonnets, both being of the type called the *Italian sonnet,* are in iambic pentameter and are rhymed abbaabbacdcdcd. But the difference in subject and treatment is obvious, and this simple example should indicate why one should be extremely cautious in assuming that any effect or subject matter is absolutely associated with a particular stanza form. The proper approach to the study of the significance of stanza form may be through this question:

How does the poet use a particular stanza form in any given poem to pro-duce the special effect of that poem?

Let us look more closely at Milton's sonnet, one of the most famous in our language. As for the subject: in 1655, in North Italy, a number of the Waldensian sect of Protestants, in spite of the fact that they had been en-joying freedom of worship, were massacred by Catholic troops quartered among them. Milton, who, as secretary to Cromwell, wrote an official letter of protest to the Duke of Savoy, composed the sonnet as a personal and direct expression of his sense of outrage. But we must not assume that the heinousness of the event and the sincerity of the author's sense of outrage are what give the poem its power. It is the realization—the imaginative projection—of those things into language that counts: the relation of idea, image, and rhythm.

Let us scan the first two lines:

$$\overset{\cup\ \prime}{\text{Avenge,}} \mid \overset{\prime\prime\ \prime}{\text{O Lord,}} \mid \overset{\cup\ \prime}{\text{thy slaught}} \mid \overset{\cup\quad\prime}{\text{ered saints,}} \mid \overset{\prime\prime\quad\prime}{\text{whose bones}}$$

$$\overset{\prime\prime\ \prime}{\text{Lie scat}} \mid \overset{\cup\ \prime}{\text{tered on}} \mid \overset{\cup\quad\prime}{\text{the Al}} \mid \overset{\cup\qquad\prime}{\text{pine mount}} \mid \overset{\cup\quad\prime}{\text{ains cold.}}$$

In general, we may say that the massing of accents, primary and secondary, gives weightiness and force. More particularly, the massing of four accents in the fifth foot of line 1 and the first foot of line 2 focuses the symbolic force of the passage on the image of the bones, and the metrical accent on the word *on* (which in ordinary reading would be rhetorically insignificant) makes the image of the scattered bones in the desolate scene come with vivid immediacy, an effect supported by the falling away into regular accentuation in the subsequent feet. But notice, too, how the isolation of the single word and syllable *cold,* after the previous run of polysyllables, reinforces our sense of the desolation of the scene. This is simply a limited analysis of how the power of Milton's poem is developed—and developed in a sonnet that has not the slightest connection with the subject of love.

Questions

1. Scan the entire poem, and comment on any details that seem significant.
2. Do you observe any significant instances of alliteration?
3. Consider the distribution of pauses, both within and at the end of lines. What effect do you get from the large number of run-on lines? Do you see any relation between this fact and the temper, the emotion, of the poem?

In our last question above, we have been leading to a fundamental con-sideration about the use of a stanza. We have said earlier that the stanza is, like meter, a device for giving form to a poem, and so it is. But, like meter, it is, abstractly regarded, a rigid form; and just as meter exists in a fluctuating tension with rhetorical and other factors in the language of a poem, so does the stanza. To return to "On the Late Massacre in Piedmont," we notice that in the first quatrain the basic pentameter line is firmly estab-lished; in line 1, with the last three feet, the firm iambic beat is clear, and even though there is enjambment, we sense the line. So with lines 2 and 4: we have the final full stop for each, and with line 3, a definite pause at the end. With line 5 and on through line 12, there is not a single pause at a line end, much less a full stop. The passage begins with the exhortation, "Forget not"—and the sudden rush of movement outside the line pattern represents the passionate piling up of things that must not be forgotten, and then, with line 10, what amounts to another exhortation to vengeance. Here the stanza form is burst, as it were, by the violence of the feeling, the disintegration (or near disintegration) of the stanza being emphasized, indeed, by the presence of strong pauses, even full stops, within lines. Finally, with lines 13 and 14, the poem looks forward to a "happy ending"—the fact that the blood of martyrs will bear the fruit of salvation; and with these lines the pattern is reestablished, by pause and end-stop, and, we may add, with the full rhythmical effect of the precise meter of the last four feet of line 14.

To take another example of tension between the stanza form and the rhetorical factors, we may return to Hardy's "Channel Firing (p. 45). In discussing the question of line pauses and enjambment, we have been also demonstrating how violent are the tensions in that poem between the rhetoric and the stanza form, especially in stanzas 1 and 2, with the last line of each spilling over to a full pause in the first line of the following stanza, and in the long speech by God in stanzas 3, 4, 5, and 6, with the run of enjambments.

Let us turn to a poem with a rather complicated stanza form to observe how the poet has played off a great deal of rhetorical (and metrical) variety within the pattern.

To Daffodils

Robert Herrick [1591–1674]

Fair daffodils, we weep to see
  You haste away so soon:
As yet the early-rising sun
  Has not attained his noon.
    Stay, stay,   5
  Until the hasting day
    Has run
  But to the Even-song;
And, having prayed together, we
  Will go with you along.   10

We have short time to stay, as you,
  We have as short a spring,
As quick a growth to meet decay,
  As you, or anything.
    We die,   15
  As your hours do, and dry
    Away,
  Like to the summer's rain;
Or as the pearls of morning dew
  Ne'er to be found again.   20

First, note that, even with caesura in line 1, the first four lines are close to a jingle; but then note how the line variations in the stanza, and the rhymes (along, of course, with pauses within the lines) create a much more complex rhythm—a rhythm growing more complex in stanza 1, we observe, as the gravity in the metaphor emerges. (The life of man and that of the flower metaphorically coincide, and man and flower having prayed together, both being God's creatures, are ready, after evening service, for the night.) If we reduce the first stanza to the iambic 4,3,4,3 of the first four lines (with a few revisions to make things fit), we readily see what has been gained by the variations in the lengths of the last six lines of the stanza:

> Fair daffodils, we weep to see
>> You haste away so soon:
> As yet the early-rising sun
>> Has not attained his noon.
> Stay yet until the hasting day
>> Has run to the Even-song,
> And, having prayed together, we
>> Will go with you along.

This is not to imply that an accomplished poet might not take the near-doggerel of our imabic 4,3,4,3,4,3,4,3 arrangement and yet produce authentic poetry. But our regularized stanza may, nevertheless, serve to point up what Herrick has gained by his special patterning of lines. For example, his use of short lines serves as a kind of punctuation, as it were—a punctuation not based on the conventional rhetorical considerations. In this connection, observe how lines 6 and 7, which rhetorically have no pause, are given, by the way in which Herrick has set them off in his stanzaic pattern, a slight end-of-line pause, one that importantly alters the rhythm of the whole passage. Compare our altered version in which this pause is totally lost by the running together of lines 6 and 7: viz., "Has run to the Even-song."

A more specific effect is observable in the handling of the stanza in the following poem:

The Blossom

John Donne [*1573–1631*]

> Little think'st thou, poor flower,
>> Whom I have watched six or seven days,
> And seen thy birth, and seen what every hour
> Gave to thy growth, thee to this height to raise,
> And now dost laugh and triumph on this bough, 5
>> Little think'st thou
> That it will freeze anon, and that I shall
> Tomorrow find thee fallen, or not at all.
>
> Little think'st thou poor heart
>> That labor'st yet to nestle thee, 10

And think'st by hovering here to get a part
In a forbidden or forbidding tree,
And hop'st her stiffness by long siege to bow:
  Little think'st thou,
That thou tomorrow, ere that sun doth wake,   15
Must with this sun, and me a journey take.

  But thou which lov'st to be
  Subtle to plague thy self, wilt say,
Alas, if you must go, what's that to me?
Here lies my business, and here I will stay: 20
You go to friends, whose love and means present
  Various content
To your eyes, ears, and tongue, and every part.
If then your body go, what need you a heart?

  Well then, stay here; but know,   25
  When thou hast stayed and done thy most;
A naked thinking heart, that makes no show,
Is to a woman, but a kind of Ghost;
How shall she know my heart; or having none,
  Know thee for one?   30
Practice may make her know some other part,
But take my word, she doth not know a Heart.

  Meet me at London, then,
  Twenty days hence, and thou shalt see
Me fresher, and more fat, by being with men,   35
Than if I had stayed still with her and thee.
For God's sake, if you can, be you so too:
  I would give you
There to another friend, whom we shall find
As glad to have my body as my mind.   40

The stanza presented here is very complicated: iambic 3,4,5,5,5,2,5,5. The basic tension of the poem is between the complexity and formality of the stanza and the dramatic variety of utterance that constitutes the poem. In stanzas 1 and 2, for instance, we observe that a single sentence, with very complicated subordinate constructions, is threaded into the stanza pattern, maintaining the fluency of speech, and with a number of run-on lines, but not violating too drastically the sense of the stanza. In this last matter, we must notice that the sentences themselves, in the first five lines of each stanza, give a sort of complicated preliminary to the statement of the last two lines of each stanza, this statement being introduced in each case by echoing the first line of the stanza: "Little think'st thou . . ."; and this repetition sets up a secondary pattern that reinforces the formal structure of the stanza itself.

With stanzas 3, 4, and 5, the whole effect is more agitated and dramatic, more broken in movement, by rhetorical and secondary accents, and by more positive pauses within the lines. But notice that the poet ends with a rather pat, ironic, even witty turn with a close, tidy metrical effect, a summing up of the complex and sometimes rather violent shifts and turns of movement and feeling.

Questions

1. Scan stanzas 1 and 5. What differences do you observe?
2. Comment on differences in sentence structure as related to stanza pattern.

There are a number of very complicated stanza forms dating back to the Middle Ages, such as the *rondeau,* the *ballade,* the *sestina,* and the *villanelle.** Generally speaking, nineteenth-century poems that make use of such forms have seemed academic or overly "poetical" or "romantic." But the very associations that for a time seemed to disqualify such complicated forms from use by a serious poet have actually been exploited by some modern writers; that is, the irony of the contrast between the literary association of the form and a modern content and realistic language became part of the effect of the poem.

Let us first take a villanelle in the traditional romantic manner:

Villanelle of the Poet's Road

Ernest Dowson   [*1867–1900*]

> Wine and woman and song,
>> Three things garnish our way:
> Yet is day over long.
>
> Lest we do our youth wrong,
>> Gather them while we may:
> Wine and woman and song.
>
> Three things render us strong,
>> Vine leaves, kisses and bay:
> Yet is day over long.

5

---

* The *rondeau* is an Old French form: 15 lines (of usually 8 syllables each) in 3 stanzas; the opening words of the poem become the refrain: rhymed aabba, aabc, aabbac. The French *ballade* was adopted for a poem with the strophe form ababbcbc. In the fourteenth century the ballade had 3 strophes, often octosyllabic lines, with an envoi (final summary stanza). The chant royal was similar, but of 5 strophes. The French *sestina* has a fixed poetic form: 6 stanzas, 6 lines each, envoi of 3 lines; usually unrhymed, but repeating as final words those of the first stanza, in the following order (each letter represents the final word of a line):

stanza						
1	A	B	C	D	E	F
2	F	A	E	B	D	C
3	C	F	D	A	B	E
4	E	C	B	F	A	D
5	D	E	A	C	F	B
6	B	D	F	E	C	A
envoi	B D F *or* A C E					

Often the envoi uses all the final words, 2 to a line: B E; D C; F A. The French *villanelle* consists of five 3-line stanzas aba, and a final quatrain; all on two rhymes. The first and third lines are alternately the last lines of the remaining tercets, and together are the last lines of the quatrain.

Unto us they belong,   10
   Us the bitter and gay,
Wine and woman and song.

We, as we pass along,
   Are sad that they will not stay;
Yet is day over long.   15

Fruits and flowers among,
   What is better than they:
Wine and woman and song?
   Yet is day over long.

In contrast to Dowson's use, let us set a villanelle by a poet with the modern spirit:

Missing Dates

William Empson [*1906–*]

Slowly the poison the whole blood stream fills.
It is not the effort nor the failure tires.
The waste remains, the waste remains and kills.

It is not your system or clear sight that mills
Down small to the consequence a life requires;   5
Slowly the poison the whole blood stream fills.

They bled an old dog dry yet the exchange rills
Of young dog blood gave but a month's desires;
The waste remains, the waste remains and kills.

It is the Chinese tombs and the slag hills   10
Usurp the soil, and not the soil retires.
Slowly the poison the whole blood stream fills.

Not to have fire is to be a skin that shrills.
The complete fire is death. From partial fires
The waste remains, the waste remains and kills.   15

It is the poems you have lost, the ills
From missing dates, at which the heart expires.
Slowly the poison the whole blood stream fills.
The waste remains, the waste remains and kills.

Such ironical contrast, however, is not the effect of a villanelle by another modern poet, which, instead, is vividly emotional:

Do Not Go Gentle into That Good Night

Dylan Thomas [*1914–1953*]

Do not go gentle into that good night,
Old age should burn and rave at close of day;
Rage, rage against the dying of the light.

Though wise men at their end know dark is right,
Because their words had forked no lightning they
Do not go gentle into that good night.

Good men, the last wave by, crying how bright
Their frail deeds might have danced in a green bay,
Rage, rage against the dying of the light.

Wild men who caught and sang the sun in flight,
And learn, too late, they grieved it on its way,
Do not go gentle into that good night.

Grave men, near death, who see with blinding sight
Blind eyes could blaze like meteors and be gay,
Rage, rage against the dying of the light.

And you, my father, there on the sad height,
Curse, bless, me now with your fierce tears, I pray.
Do not go gentle into that good night.
Rage, rage against the dying of the light.

Here is an example of a modern use of the sestina:

Paysage Moralisé

W. H. Auden [*1907–1973*]

Hearing of harvests rotting in the valleys,
Seeing at end of street the barren mountains,
Round corners coming suddenly on water,
Knowing them shipwrecked who were launched for islands,
We honor founders of these starving cities
Whose honor is the image of our sorrow,

Which cannot see its likeness in their sorrow
That brought them desperate to the brink of valleys,
Dreaming of evening walks through learned cities
They reined their violent horses on the mountains,
Those fields like ships to castaways on islands,
Visions of green to them who craved for water.

They built by rivers and at night the water
Running past windows comforted their sorrow;
Each in his little bed conceived of islands   15
Where every day was dancing in the valleys
And all the green trees blossomed on the mountains,
Where love was innocent, being far from cities.

But dawn came back and they were still in cities;
No marvellous creature rose up from the water;   20
There was still gold and silver in the mountains
But hunger was a more immediate sorrow,
Although to moping villagers in valleys
Some waving pilgrims were describing islands . . .

"The gods," they promised, "visit us from islands,   25
Are stalking, head-up, lovely, through our cities;
Now is the time to leave your wretched valleys
And sail with them across the lime-green water,
Sitting at their white sides, forget your sorrow,
The shadow cast across your lives by mountains."   30

So many, doubtful, perished in the mountains,
Climbing up crags to get a view of islands,
So many, fearful, took with them their sorrow
Which stayed them when they reached unhappy cities,
So many, careless, dived and drowned in water,   35
So many, wretched, would not leave their valleys.

It is our sorrow. Shall it melt? Ah, water
Would gush, flush, green these mountains and these valleys,
And we rebuild our cities, not dream of islands.

Onomatopoeia and Related Effects

The word *onomatopoeia* means name-making. Specifically, in this context, it means name-making by using a sound that suggests the object named. Words imitative of their own literal meanings are onomatopoeic—for example, *bang, fizz, hiss, crackle, murmur, moan, whisper, roar.* We may observe that all of the words listed here denote special sounds. *The sound of a word can be imitative only of a sound, and only to such words can the term* onomatopoeia *be strictly applied.*

In dealing with poetry it is important to insist upon at least a relatively strict interpretation of the term onomatopoeia and of onomatopoeic effects, for it is very easy for an unwary critic to attribute to onomatopoeia effects that arise from other causes. Such critics attribute a particular imitative meaning to the sound of a word, when at best only a general suitability can actually be observed. For example, here is what one critic has written of a certain line of Edna St. Vincent Millay's poetry:

But she gets many different effects with clusters of unaccented syllables. With the many *f*'s and *r*'s and *th*'s a fine feeling of fluffiness is given to one line by the many unaccented syllables:

Comfort, softer than the feathers of its breast,

sounds as soft as the bird's downy breast feels.

But another critic challenges this interpretation, as follows:

> ... The effect [is said to be] a fine feeling of fluffiness and a softness as of the bird's downy breast, while the cause is said to be the many unaccented syllables, assisted by the many *f*'s, *r*'s and *th*'s. But I will substitute a line which preserves all these factors and departs from the given line mainly by rearrangement:
>
> Crumpets for the foster-fathers of the brats.
>
> Here I miss the fluffiness and the downiness.*

In the same way, one might imagine a critic stating that the following line by Keats is onomatopoeic, and identifying the suggestion of coolness and repose with the presence of certain vowel and consonant sounds:

> 'Mid hushed, cool-rooted flowers fragrant-eyed.

The line gives a suggestion of coolness and repose, *but the effect is not to be identified with specific vowels or consonants, nor are specific vowels and consonants to be defined as the cause of the impression.* What one can say of the sound effect of the line is this. The scarcely resolved accentuation of the foot *cool-root-* and the length and sonority of the vowels repeated in the foot emphasizes these words, which with the accented word *hushed* just preceding, set the whole impression of coolness and repose; but the words set this impression primarily by their literal meanings. The function of the verse as such is highly important, but important in supporting and stressing literal meaning.

With this caution in mind, we may look at what is a famous example of extended onomatopoeia—that is, onomatopoeic effect in a passage and not in a single word. The passage is from Tennyson's "Come Down, O Maid":

> The moan of doves in immemorial elms,
> And murmuring of innumerable bees.

We notice that only two words here, *moan* and *murmuring,* are in themselves onomatopoeic (three words, if *bees,* with its hint of literal buzzing, may be taken in this way); but the onomatopoeic effect is extended and, more importantly, intensified by repetition of sound in normally non-onomatopoeic words, most obviously in *immemorial, elms,* and *innumerable.* We may note, too, how the sibilance at the end of *doves* and *elms* also reinforces the onomatopoeic force of *bees.*

What we have above is, of course, a few key words that are, strictly speaking, onomatopoeic and give the base for further association and reinforcement.

* John Crowe Ransom, *The World's Body,* Charles Scribner's Sons, 1938, pp. 96–97.

Sometimes a further extension may occur by association with sounds. Look, for instance, at this group of words: *gleam, glow, glint, gloss, glimmer, glister, glitter,* and *glare.* These all suggest light (as, in one sense, does *glory,* a word without that literal denotation, though Latin *gloria,* from which our *glory* derives, does mean a light). What we find in common here is the initial consonantal *gl.* And we may even observe that the words *gloaming* and *gloom* are also associated with the idea of light, though light by diminution. These last words, in fact, lead us to another associational group: *groan, gloom, doom, woe, forlorn.* These words, which have a common association of sadness, contain rounded "back" vowels, and have, with one exception, a nasal consonant at the end.* The word *gloaming,* with the same structure, literally means twilight, but twilight has a sort of secondary association with dimness, sadness, diminution. Let us sort out some of the other "light" words listed above. Take *glint, glitter, glimmer,* and *glister.* These are words in which the characteristic vowel is the short *i,* a sound strongly associated with smallness, quickness, and sharpness, as found in *little, tittle, wink, thin, bit, slit, chink, sliver, twit, twitter, snip, twinkle, flicker, kitten.* So with this particular cluster of *gl* words the idea of light is connected with smallness, quickness, and sharpness.

Many other such groups exist. For example, the terminal *-er* (not as indicative of an agent, as in *kill-er*) and terminal *le* suggest a continuous and repetitive process: *twitter, twinkle, ripple, flicker, clatter, whisper, mutter, bubble* (verb), *shimmer, glitter, flutter, jangle.* And notice that with *glitter,* we have the combination of three associational groups: *gl* (light), *i* (small, etc.) and *-er* (continuing process).

We must caution ourselves that we are not dealing here with a strictly fixed code of certain sounds meaning certain ideas or feelings. The word *gloomy* may sound sad and "gloomy," but the word *broom* doesn't and the word *groom* doesn't—certainly not when it is a *bridegroom.* Though in certain verbal groups there may well be a broad, general correlation between feeling and the muscular experience of uttering the sound, we are primarily dealing with associations of meaning, as we are (in poetry in general) with imagery, for instance, or rhythm.

Questions

1. Select the words here that are *strictly* onomatopoeic.

gabble	bingo	slime	flamboyant	lissom
rabble	bang	slather	flame	linger
scrabble	yammer	mucus	chatter	bolder
skitter	murmur	bulge	chitter	boulder
skillet	mutter	slump	clatter	prattle
scramble	slick	slap	clutter	slop
slobber	flash	whisper	mellow	mist
kiss	hiss	bum	bumptious	bountiful
bound	blunt	flare	chop	crack
creak	bosom	cringe	crisp	rattle
flash	fling	flicker	whisk	whimper

* The examples we have just quoted represent all three: *oh, oo, and aw.* All three vowels are made with the tongue in back position together with a good deal of lip-rounding.

2. What associational groupings may be selected from the list above? Describe each group.

3. What words in the list below do not, in your view, belong in the associational group involved here? Describe the group that is here.

flare	glare
pair	mare
stare	blare
dare	fare

What we are concerned with here is the fusion of sound with other elements into a dramatic meaning. Let us take a very simple instance, one in which the very lack of metrical or phonetic variety and resonance is dramatically effective, a line from Pope's *Rape of the Lock*.

And wretches hang that jurymen may dine.

The prevailing feel of the line is "tight" and "thin";* the syllables *And, wret--ches, hang, that, -y-, men,* and *may* are all in the same verbal bracket, and the line does lack variety and resonance. But, perhaps, this particular line *should* lack variety and resonance. The line is satirical, a sharp, caustic, biting observation on human nature and the administration of justice. Contempt, sardonic humor, and a controlled anger are the basic emotions here, and it is easy to sense a correlation between these emotions and the physical experience of the line. Try reading the line without uttering the sounds but making all the muscular movements of pronunciation. How does it feel? What emotions would seem to be associated with these muscular movements? Resonance, depth, variety, musicality—all would be out of place here.

For another, more complex, example, read the following sonnet; then read it aloud a number of times.

God's Grandeur

Gerard Manley Hopkins [*1844–1889*]

The world is charged with the grandeur of God.
It will flame out, like shining from shook foil;
It gathers to a greatness, like the ooze of oil
Crushed. Why do men then now not reck his rod?
Generations have trod, have trod, have trod;   5
And all is seared with trade; bleared, smeared with toil;
And wears man's smudge and shares man's smell: the soil
Is bare now, nor can foot feel, being shod.

---

* "Tight" and "thin" are rather subjective and impressionistic terms used in an attempt to suggest the general "feel" of this line. The phonetician would be compelled to use more technical terms in his description. He might begin by saying that in this line nearly all the vowels are "front" vowels, and, like all front vowels in English, without lip-rounding. Here, then, there are almost no rounded back vowels with their resonance and orotundity.

> And for all this, nature is never spent,
>   There lives the dearest freshness deep down things;   10
> And though the last lights off the black West went
>   Oh, morning, at the brown brink eastward, springs—
> Because the Holy Ghost over the bent
>   World broods with warm breast and with ah! bright wings.

In the first quatrain, the grandeur of God is proclaimed, in a passage full of verbal resonance and a rhythm straining the bounds of meter. The second quatrain describes what man has done to the world that should shine with God's grandeur. In line 5, the onomatopoeic effect of the repetition of *have trod* is obvious, but something less obvious, and very important, is the effect associated with the word *generations*. The content—the indeterminate millions over the ages—is, of course, clear, but the rhythm deserves comment. In the four syllables of the word, two of the metrical accents fall, with a consequent lengthening of the word, a lengthening that opens up into the emphatic mounting repetition of *have trod*. With lines 6 and 7 we have a very powerful expressive effect. The most obvious device is the vowel run (emphasized by the rhyme) in *seared*, *bleared*, *smeared* (with the word *trod* very close), which piles up the suggestion of ruin and dirtiness. It is not merely that the words have such denotations; if that were true, we should get an equivalent effect by substituting another series, say, *seared*, *blotched*, *fouled*.* But we get nothing. In the original version, the verbal quality itself is significantly intensifying. We may attribute much or little force to the muscular stances and phonetic quality of the words in the original run, but the mere repetition and interweaving of the sounds intensify meaning. This process is, of course, continued by *smudge* and *smell*, which pick up the initial consonant sound of *smear*, and set up a new verbal run of intensification, an intensification that makes man's smell indeed foul. Notice, too, in line 7, the intensifying effect in the rhyme of *wears* and *shares* and the repetition of *man's* with each: the earth is doubly infected (*wears*, *shares*) with man's filth, as it were. We may also remark on the intensifying alliteration in *foot* and *feel*, and how the word *shod*, by rhyme, echoes the strong effect of the repetitions of *have trod* in line 5. It is also important to observe how this second quatrain, in contrast to the vigorous, bursting-out rhythm of the first, has a movement that continues, though somewhat less mechanically, the monotonous effect of line 5. To sum up, the passage, in its very lack of musicality, is especially expressive.

The following passage from "The Passing of Arthur" by Tennyson is famous for the extended onomatopoeic effect. At this point in the poem Sir Bedivere, one of the Knights of the Round Table, after the disastrous last battle, is carrying the wounded Arthur across a rugged and wintry landscape, down to a lake where the mystic barge waits to bear him away ("He" refers to Sir Bedivere):

> He heard the deep behind him, and a cry
> Before. His own thought drove him like a goad.
> Dry clashed his harness in the icy caves
> And barren chasms, and all to left and right

---

* We may now reverse the process and set up a new series to see what effect we get. For instance with the line: "And all is bleared with trade; blotched and smutched with toil."

The bare black cliffs clanged round him, as he based
His feet on juts of slippery crag that rang
Sharp-smitten with the dint of armèd heels—
And on a sudden, lo! the level lake,
And the long glories of the winter moon.

Some of the effects here come from onomatopoeia and extended onomatopoeia and other verbal details, and some from the rhythm. To begin with, let us observe how the strictly onomatopoeic words (*clashed, clanged, rang,* for example) serve, as we may put it, as "governors" for the extended effects. Notice how the vowels of these words are seeded into the long run of related sounds in *clashed, barren, chasms, bare, black, clanged, crag, rang.* There is a short subsidiary run (*dry, icy, right*); and a long one (founded on short *i*) which includes *him* (three times), *his* (three times), *cliffs, slippery, smitten, with, dint.* Notice, too, how the nasals enter into the effect with prolongation and resonance and, too, the frequent alliteration of the hard * sound combinations containing a hard *c* (or *k* sound), e.g., *clashed, chasm,* and so on.

As for the rhythm, the basic iambic pentameter is obviously modified by several factors. First, there is the great number of monosyllabic words. Second, there are a great number of secondary accents, with heavy spondaic effects. Third, many of the transitions in sound are difficult, and *forced pauses* between words are common. Fourth, the proportion of hard sound combinations is high. In other words, we have here *cacophony* as opposed to euphony (p. 543). To illustrate, let us scan a few lines, and also indicate forced pauses with an inverted caret (˅), and hard sound combinations by italics:

$$\overset{\cup\quad/\quad//\; ˅\;/\quad//\quad ˅\;/\quad/\;//\cup\;/}{\text{The bare }\textit{black cliffs clanged}\text{ round him as he based}}$$

$$\overset{\cup\;/\;\cup\cup\;/\;\cup\cup\;/\;\cup\cup\;/˅\;\cup\;/}{\text{His feet on juts of slippery }\textit{crag that rang}}$$

$$\overset{//˅\;/\cup\;/\;'\;\cup\;/\;\cup\;/\;\cup\;/}{\textit{Sharp-smitten}\text{ with the dint of armed heels—}}$$

But another significant factor in the passage emerges in the last two lines: when Sir Bedivere has reached his goal, there is a "sudden" contrast in the verbal quality of the verse, with the fluent run of "lo! the level lake," marked by easy accentuation and the alliteration of the liquid *l* sound. The last line is particularly interesting. To scan it:

$$\overset{/\qquad\cup\;//\quad/\quad\cup\;/\quad\cup\;/\quad\cup\quad/}{\text{˄ And }|\text{ the long glor }|\text{ ies of }|\text{ the win }|\text{ ter moon}}$$

It would be possible, of course, to take *And the long* as an anapest, but the scansion above seems more natural and effective with the "annunciatory *and*" taken as an imperfect iamb introducing the summarizing and, it may be said, redemptive image of the glorious moon. To return to the rhythm itself: As scanned above, there is only one anapest in the line, which is followed by three iambs: $\overset{/\qquad/\qquad/}{-ies\;of\;the\;winter\;moon.}$ But in this line the rhetorical thrust is so strong that the weak accent on *of* is, for all practical purposes, annulled in this rhythm:

* By "hard," we mean syllables that are clogged with consonants. *Cliffs* and *clanged* furnish good examples.

∧And | the long glor | ies of the win | ter moon

Here the rhythm would be based on three strong rhetorical accents (*And, glories, and win–*), with *long* and *moon* as secondary. Thus the rhythm amounts to two wide swings (one "swing" actually four syllables: *–ies of the win–*), a powerful release from the gnarled and tortuous movement of the preceding lines stabilized in the more muted iambs at the end. And note here how the word *long* functions. It offers the distance and openness suggested by *level* in the line before, again the sense of release; and this is supported by the resonant, orotund vowel sounds of *long, glories,* and *moon,* and the three nasals, contrasted, again, with the difficult verbal qualities preceding.

No More Be Grieved

William Shakespeare [*1564–1616*]

No more be grieved at that which thou hast done;
Roses have thorns, and silver fountains mud;
Clouds and eclipses stain both Moon and Sun,
And loathsome canker lives in sweetest bud
All men make faults, and even I in this,   5
Authorizing thy trespass with compare,
Myself corrupting, salving thy amiss,
Excusing thy sins more than thy sins are:
For to thy sensual fault I bring in sense,
(Thy adverse party is thy Advocate)   10
And 'gainst myself a lawful plea commence:
Such civil war is in my love and hate,
   That I an accessory needs must be
   To that sweet thief, which sourly robs from me.

The following analysis of this poem has been made by a modern critic:

The first four lines we may say, both in movement and imagery, are . . . straightforward. The fifth line begins by continuing the excuses, 'All men make faults,' but with an abrupt change of rhythm Shakespeare turns the generalization against himself: 'All men make faults, and even I in this,' i.e. in wasting my time finding romantic parallels for your sins, as though intellectual analogies ('sense') were relevant to your sensual fault. The painful complexity of feeling (Shakespeare is at the same time tender towards the sinner and infuriated by his own tenderness) is evident in the seventh line, which means both, 'I corrupt myself when I find excuses for you' (or 'when I comfort myself in this way') and 'I'm afraid I myself make you worse by excusing your faults'; and although there is a fresh change of tone towards the end (the twelfth line is virtually a sigh as he gives up hope of resolving the conflict), the equivocal 'needs must' and the sweet-sour opposition show the continued civil war of the emotions.

Some such comment as this was unavoidable, but it is upon the simplest and most obvious of technical devices that I wish to direct attention. In the first quatrain the play upon the letters *s* and *l* is mainly musical and decorative, but with the change of tone and direction the alliterative *s* becomes a hiss of half-impotent venom:

All men make faults, and even I in thi*s*,
Authorizing thy tre*s*pa*ss* with compare,
My*s*elf corrupting *s*alving thy ami*ss*,
Excusing thy *s*in*s* more than thy *s*in*s* are:
For to thy *s*en*s*ual fault I bring in *s*en*s*e . . .

The scorn is moderated here, but it is still heard in the slightly rasping note of the last line,

To that sweet thief, which sourly robs from me.

From the fifth line, then, the alliteration is functional: by playing off against the comparative regularity of the rhythm it expresses an important part of the meaning, and helps to carry the experience alive into the mind of the reader.*

The Expense of Spirit

William Shakespeare [*1564–1616*]

The expense of spirit in a waste of shame
Is lust in action; and till action, lust
Is perjured, murderous, bloody, full of blame,
Savage, extreme, rude, cruel, not to trust;
Enjoyed no sooner but despisèd straight;   5
Past reason hunted; and no sooner had,
Past reason hated, as a swallowed bait,
On purpose laid to make the taker mad:
Mad in pursuit, and in possession so;
Had, having, and in quest to have, extreme;   10
A bliss in proof, and proved, a very woe;
Before, a joy proposed; behind, a dream.
    All this the world well knows; yet none knows well
    To shun the heaven that leads men to this hell.

Questions

1. Taking suggestions from Knights's discussion of "No More Be Grieved," write an interpretation of this sonnet.

2. Turn to Keats's "To Autumn" (p. 87). This poem, too, is a famous example of an extended onomatopoeic effect, though, of course, of one very different from that in "Arthur." Read the first stanza aloud a number of times, giving yourself to it as fully as possible; then write a technical account of it.

3. Write an account of the onomatopoeic effects, strict and extended, in Whitman's "Battle of the *Bonhomme Richard* and the *Serapis*" (p. 31).

* L. C. Knights, "Shakespeare's Sonnets," from *Explorations*, George W. Stewart, 1947, p. 65.

The Music of Verse

The phrase "the music of verse" is common. Exactly what is meant by it? And what, we may add, is the relation of such music to the expressiveness of verse?

In the course of this book we have often suggested that you read some selection aloud to get a feel for its rhythms. But the physical dimension of speech involves more than rhythm, heard or felt. The most obvious effect of the physical dimension of speech comes from the fact that it *is* physical: the flux of muscular and nervous activity is inevitably involved with the emotional and intellectual aspects of speech, and is continually modifying our basic stance, our general feeling, toward what is happening at the level of content. Even when we read to ourselves, in some part of our being the shadowy muscular play and flow of sensation continue. Poetry, in this as in other ways, insists on the unity of experience: mind and body, idea and emotion.*

This physical factor in speech is not regularized in verse (as is the stress on meter); it is, rather, one of the factors that modify the regularity of meter and make a special contribution to the actual rhythm. The most obvious contribution is, as we have suggested, the sense of vital involvement, and in general (with exceptions to be noted) it is the constant and lively flux that is important. Take, for instance, these lines from Keats's "Ode to a Nightingale" (p. 355):

> O for a draught of vintage! that hath been
> Cooled a long age in the deep-delvèd earth,

If one reads this aloud, preferably several times, and perhaps even exaggerates a little the muscular flux in the syllabification, the variety and range will be obvious. This is even more obvious if we set these lines in contrast to another line (from "If Poisonous Minerals," by John Donne, p. 330):

> I think it mercy if Thou wilt forget.

Here, clearly, the vowel range is very slight,† and the basic tone "thin," and in comparison with the lines from Keats, we think of this as "unmusical."

The variety and range of syllabic relations is, obviously, involved in what we ordinarily think of as the musicality of verse. Certainly, meter, too, has some connection with musicality, but taken by itself—and meter is, strictly speaking, "abstract," as we have insisted—it is not the determining fact here. Perhaps the best way to approach this question is to submit ourselves as fully as possible to a passage that would generally be regarded as "musical"; "Choric Song" from Tennyson's "The Lotus-Eaters."

> There is sweet music here that softer falls
> Than petals from blown roses on the grass,

---

* When you read to yourself you should try to be aware subvocally of the muscular experience—should get the feel of what you are reading. "Rapid reading," whatever its merits for informational reading, is the death of literature, certainly of poetry. Language is the *medium* of literature.

† Most of the vowels are formed high and toward the front of the voice chamber: short *i* and short *e* are examples.

Or night-dews on still waters between walls
Of shadowy granite, in a gleaming pass;
Music that gentlier on the spirit lies,
Than tired eyelids upon tired eyes;
Music that brings sweet sleep down from the blissful skies.
Here are cool mosses deep,
And through the moss the ivies creep,
And in the stream the long-leaved flowers weep,
And from the craggy ledge the poppy hangs in sleep.

At this point, go back and read again the passage from "The Passing of Arthur," also by Tennyson (pp. 538–539). We have seen how crabbed and clang-y that verse is, how the poet has, in fact, made an expressive virtue out of the lack of musicality. By contrast, in the present selection, Tennyson, who was a great technician of verse (as well as a poet), has used all his resources to achieve musicality.

In reading this passage, one of the first features that we notice will be the prominence of vowel sounds—and such prominence is characteristic of musical verse. The vowels, that is, are musical tones. Furthermore, if we notice the muscular motions involved, we are immediately aware not only of the range and variety of vowel sounds, but also of the ease—and the fluidity—of the transition of one sound—and one word, one syllable—to the next. In musical verse, the consonants—which are, we may say, mere "noise" in comparison to the vowels—are set in fluent relation so that we make an unforced transition when we move from one word to another. In other words, in musical verse the forced pause, arising from whatever situation, is avoided; in musical verse we would never find, for instance, such a line as the last of Hardy's "Neutral Tones" (see pp. 521–522 and discussion):

And a pond edged with grayish leaves.

In the passage from Tennyson above, notice how different are the transitions: for instance, from *sweet* to *music* and *softer* to *falls* in line 1, and *than* to *petals* and *blown* to *roses* in line 2. As the forced pause and the difficult transition make, as we have said, for cacophony (p. 521), so the transitions in "Choric Song" make for euphony—for "well sounding," not ill-sounding, verse.

But other factors enter into the creating of euphonious verse. As we have seen (pp. 538–539), the repetition of sounds—in rhyme, alliteration, assonance and consonance—may give a pattern beyond a metrical pattern, and such repetitions may also work to emphasize sounds basic to the "music" of a passage. We observe that, in the first two lines, with the long vowel sounds in *sweet, music, softer, blown,* and *roses,* and the droning nasal consonants of *m* and *n* in *music, than,* and *blown,* the effects are established that are basic for the stanza and are more fully developed as it proceeds.

We may inspect, too, the following lines from Keats's "Ode to a Nightingale" ("the same" refers to the song of the bird):

The same that oft-times hath
Charmed magic casements, opening on the foam
Of perilous seas, in faery lands forlorn.

Here we notice the assonance of the closely related vowels in *hath, magic,* and *lands,* and that of the closely related vowels in *oft, o-, on, foam,* and *forlorn,* and, again, the run of nasals from the syllable *same* to the last one, *-lorn.* But we must notice, also, the two runs of alliteration: of *f* in *foam, faery, forlorn,* and of *l* in *-lous, lands,* and *-lorn.* These runs give a sense of unifying structure to the passage, not only by the mechanical fact of repetition, but by establishing the basic musical tone and temper.

Musicality of verse does, in itself, give a pleasure, but it is a fundamental error to hold that this particular kind of pleasure (which, in itself, is minimal) is the end of poetry. Poetry is not music. It involves a special use of language, and insofar as musicality is one of the potentials of language it *may* be involved in poetry. The basic fact is, however, that language has a primary function quite distinct from musicality, and musicality in poetry becomes important only insofar as, directly or indirectly, it is related to, or, better still, fused with, the primary function of language. By language we create symbols embodying events, ideas, and emotions, and in poetry, by means of a special refinement of language, we may fuse the musicality with the other dimensions of meaning. As Alexander Pope puts it in "An Essay on Criticism":

'Tis not enough no harshness gives offense,
The sound must seem an echo to the sense.

It is not enough, in fact, to say that musicality is not the end of poetry. Some very powerful poetry, we know, is quite unmusical, and may even seem quite difficult or, to some readers, ugly. We may cite a passage from *Paradise Lost* on page 168 and that from one of Donne's "Holy Sonnets" on page 330. These passages are, however, powerfully expressive, and expressiveness, not musicality, is the end of poetry. Some poetry is, of course, highly lyrical, but even in such cases, the verbal content remains important and the relation— the *expressive* relation—between the content and the musicality is crucial. Speech (p. 144, Question 7) is the root of poetry, and the expressive heightening of language—of speech, if you will—is of the essence. Musicality is, then, simply one of the ways of heightening language.

The heightening of language by musicality, however, is not always expressive. Sometimes musicality may, even, be the enemy of poetry. Let us look at a stanza from Poe's most famous poem, "The Raven":

Ah, distinctly I remember it was in the bleak December,
And each separate dying ember wrought its ghost upon the floor.
Eagerly I wished the morrow;—vainly I had sought to borrow
From my books surcease of sorrow—sorrow for the lost Lenore,
For the rare and radiant maiden whom the angels name Lenore:
Nameless here for evermore.

The question is: Do the very obvious verbal effects, including the assertive meter and emphatic rhyming, overwhelm the other aspects? The image presented is of a man, bereaved of his beloved, sitting late into the night and trying to forget his grief in study, but does the "feel" of such a situation survive the demanding musicality? Does the effect seem, in the end, just a little ludicrous? Poe was enormously skillful in a certain kind of technique, and could, on occasion, create very haunting effects, but it may be instructive to turn to a poem which Poe is supposed to have plagiarized in "The Raven." Here is one stanza:

As an egg, when broken, never
Can be mended, but must ever
Be the same crushed egg forever—
So shall this dark heart of mine!
Which though broken is still breaking,
And shall never more cease aching
For the sleep which has no waking—
For the sleep which now is thine!

This poem, "To Allegra Florence in Heaven," also about grief, is, though lined differently, in the same metrical and rhyme scheme and aims at the same kind of verbal richness, but because the author, Thomas Holly Chivers, had no shred of Poe's talent and because of the absurdity of the image of the egg, we can see more readily the split between the verbal assertiveness—the mistaken musicality—and the content.

Let us take the first stanza of "Ulalume" (already scanned, p. 507), in which Poe also exhibits his technical virtuosity:

The skies they were ashen and sober;
　　The leaves they were crispèd and sere—
　　The leaves they were withering and sere.
It was night, in the lonesome October
　　Of my most immemorial year: 5
It was hard by the dim lake of Auber,
　　In the misty mid region of Weir:
It was down by the dank tarn of Auber,
　　In the ghoul-haunted woodland of Weir.

The English novelist and critic, Aldous Huxley, has written a destructive comment on "Ulalume":

These lines protest too much (and with what a variety of voices!) that they are poetical, and, protesting, are therefore vulgar. To start with, the walloping dactylic meter is all too musical. Poetry ought to be musical, but musical with tact, subtly and variously. Meters whose rhythms, as in this case, are strong, insistent and practically invariable offer the poet a kind of short cut to musicality. They provide him (my subject calls for a mixture of metaphors) with a ready-made, reach-me-down music. He does not have to create a music appropriately modulated to his meaning; all he has to do is to shovel the meaning into the moving stream of the meter and allow the current to carry it along on waves that, like those of the best hairdressers, are guaranteed permanent. . . . A quotation and a parody will illustrate the difference between ready-made music and music made to measure. I remember (I trust correctly) a simile of Milton's:—

　　　　Like that fair field
Of Enna, where Proserpine gathering flowers,
Herself a fairer flower, by gloomy Dis
Was gathered, which cost Ceres all that pain
To seek her through the world.

Rearranged according to their musical phrasing, these lines would have to be written thus:—

> Like that fair field of Enna,
>   where Proserpine gathering flowers,
> Herself a fairer flower,
>   by gloomy Dis was gathered,
> Which cost Ceres all that pain
> To seek her through the world.

The contrast between the lyrical swiftness of the first four phrases, with that row of limping spondees which tells of Ceres' pain, is thrillingly appropriate. Bespoke, the music fits the sense like a glove.

How would Poe have written on the same theme? I have ventured to invent his opening stanza:—

> It was noon in the fair field of Enna,
>   When Proserpina gathering flowers—
>   Herself the most fragrant of flowers,
> Was gathered away to Gehenna
>   By the Prince of Plutonian powers;
> Was borne down the windings of Brenner
>   To the gloom of his amorous bowers—
> Down the tortuous highway of Brenner
>   To the god's agapemonous bowers.

The parody is not too outrageous to be critically beside the point; and anyhow the music is genuine Poe. That permanent wave is unquestionably an *ondulation de chez Edgar*. The much too musical meter is (to change the metaphor once more) like a rich chasuble, so stiff with gold and gems that it stands unsupported, a carapace of jewelled sound, into which the sense, like some snotty little seminarist, irrelevantly creeps and is lost. This music of Poe's— how much less really musical it is than that which, out of his nearly neutral decasyllables, Milton fashioned on purpose to fit the slender beauty of Proserpine, the strength and swiftness of the ravisher and her mother's heavy, despairing sorrow!

What Huxley has been emphasizing is the fact that the insistence of the "musicality" smothers the meaning, and that into the stream of verbal effects Poe is willing to shovel almost anything that comes to mind that may help to establish his notion of a mysterious and morbid atmosphere. Huxley, in his parody, simply carries this process to an absurd extreme. What has Gehenna (the valley of Hinnom, near Jerusalem, where sacrifices were sometimes made to the pagan god Moloch) to do with the Greek legend of the rape of Proserpina by Pluto? Or what has Brenner (the Brenner Pass between Italy and Austria?) to do with Pluto's descent into the Greek Hades? With the adjective *agapemonous* Huxley has out-Poe-d Poe. The adjective (meaning "beloved"?) is not in the *Oxford English Dictionary* and seems to be Huxley's coinage from a Greek root. This, of course, is the whole point of the jest: Poe, so Huxley implies, was more impressed with the grandiose or musical sound of a word and its metrical possibilities than with its meaning.

Like Poe, the English poet Algernon Charles Swinburne aimed at extremes of euphony, and was indeed the author of some of the most melodious and metrically intricate verse ever written in the language. Here follow the concluding stanzas of his "The Garden of Proserpine" (here he is thinking of Proserpine as the Greek goddess of Death):

> We are not sure of sorrow,
>   And joy was never sure;
> Today will die tomorrow;
>   Time stoops to no man's lure;
> And love, grown faint and fretful
> With lips but half regretful
> Sighs, and with eyes forgetful
>   Weeps that no loves endure.
>
> From too much love of living,
>   From hope and fear set free,
> We thank with brief thanksgiving
>   Whatever gods may be
> That no life lives for ever;
> That dead men rise up never;
> That even the weariest river
>   Winds somewhere safe to sea.
>
> Then star nor sun shall waken,
>   Nor any change of light:
> Nor sound of waters shaken
>   Nor any sound or sight:
> Nor wintry leaves nor vernal,
> Nor days nor things diurnal;
> Only the sleep eternal
>   In an eternal night.

Like Poe, Swinburne, with his strain of morbidity and insistence on musicality, could be led into such excesses as the following stanza from his "Dolores":

> O lips full of lust and of laughter,
>   Curled snakes that are fed from my breast,
> Bite hard lest remembrance come after
>   And press with new lips where you press.
> For my heart, too, springs up at the pressure,
>   Mine eyelids, too, moisten and burn;
> Ah, feed me and fill me with pleasure,
>   Ere pain come in turn.

Here follows a not ill-natured parody of the Swinburne manner. The author, A. C. Hilton, entitled his poem "Octopus," indicating in the subtitle that the parody was "Written at the Crystal Palace Aquarium." We print the first and the last two stanzas.

> Strange beauty, eight-limbed and eight-handed,
>   Whence camest to dazzle our eyes?
> With thy bosom bespangled and banded
>   With the hues of the seas and the skies;

Is thy home European or Asian,
　　O mystical monster marine?
Part molluscous and partly crustacean,
　　Betwixt and between. . . .

O breast, that 'twere rapture to writhe on!
　　O arms 'twere delicious to feel
Clinging close with the crush of the Python,
　　When she maketh her murderous meal!
In thy eight-fold embraces enfolden,
　　Let our empty existence escape;
Give us death, that is glorious and golden,
　　Crushed all out of shape!

Ah! thy red lips, lascivious and luscious,
　　With death in their amorous kiss!
Cling round us, and clasp us, and crush us,
　　With bitings of agonized bliss;
We are sick with the poison of pleasure,
　　Dispense us the potion of pain;
Ope thy mouth to its uttermost measure
　　And bite us again!

How absurd the musicality (such as exists in the verse) turns out to be when the verse has this content! As we have remarked earlier, the poet's true medium is not sheer sound; it is words, and though he is concerned with their phonetic qualities, he is also (and primarily) concerned with their meanings. The tonal and rhythmic properties are only one—and not even the most important—aspect of language. Thus, when an adult reader calls a particular poem "musical," he is using the adjective in a very special sense. He cannot mean simply the rippling of syllables devoid of meaning or the chime of nonsense rhymes. The "music" that he hears in poetry is inseparable from the meanings and emotional associations of words.

Let us take an example. When Milton refers to the beauty of the nightingale's song by writing,

Sweet Bird that shunn'st the noise of folly,
Most musicall, most melancholy,

someone may be inclined to say: Milton's own musical lines catch the very quality of the nightingale's song. We know what that person is trying to say, but Milton's lines can't be said to sound *literally* like the bird's song. More important still, if these lines were read to a Japanese or to a Hungarian who had no idea of the *meaning* of the words and had no familiarity with the sound patterns employed in English verse, the lines wouldn't sound "musical" to him—and certainly not like a bird's song. They might sound like some strange and perhaps faintly pleasant gibberish. They could conceivably strike his ear as definitely unpleasant.

To sum up: the poet's skill in handling the element of sound in his poetry is indeed important, but not as sheer sound. In poetry the purely phonetic element is rarely—if, indeed, ever—divorced from other aspects of language.

Though it may play an important part in developing the total effect of the poem, it does not do so as *pure music*—as an isolated thing that can be enjoyed for its own sake even though people have long talked as if it did, saying that "just the pure music of certain great poems" was delightful in itself, quite without reference to the meanings of the words.

The British critic I. A. Richards, in order to undeceive such believers in the *absolute beauty* of melodious verse, constructed a nonsense poem which was an almost exact phonetic mock-up of one of the stanzas of a poem noted for its musical quality. Here is the phonetic dummy that he concocted:

> J. Drootan-Sussting Benn
> Mill-down Leduren N.
>   Telamba-tras oderwainto weiring
> Awersey zet bidreen
> Ownd istellester sween
>   Lithabian tweet ablissood owdswown stiering
> Apleven aswetsen sestinal
> Yintomen I adaits afurf I gallas Ball.*

There is, certainly, such a thing as melodious verse and it can be a subtle and powerful factor in poetic effect. Take the poem below:

Voices

Walter de la Mare [*1873–1956*]

> Who is it calling by the darkened river
>   Where the moss lies smooth and deep,
> And the dark trees lean unmoving arms,
>   Silent and vague in sleep,
> And the bright-heeled constellations pass   5
>   In splendor through the gloom;
> Who is it calling o'er the darkened river
>   In music, "Come"?
>
> Who is it wandering in the summer meadows
>   Where the children stoop and play   10
> In the green faint-scented flowers, spinning
>   The guileless hours away?
> Who touches their bright hair? who puts
>   A wind-shell to each cheek,
> Whispering betwixt its breathing silences,   15
>   "Seek! seek!"?
>
> Who is it watching in the gathering twilight
>   When the curfew bird hath flown

---

* *Practical Criticism*, p. 220. The dummy is arranged from a particular stanza of Milton's "Ode on the Nativity." It is interesting to compare the effect of the dummy with the original. Can you find the stanza for which Richards constructed his phonetic parody?

On eager wings, from song to silence,
   To its darkened nest alone?   20
Who takes for brightening eyes the stars,
   For locks the still moonbeams,
Sighs through the dews of evening peacefully
      Falling, "Dream!"?

Questions

Suppose lines 9 to 12 were revised as follows:

Now who goes walking in the summer meadows
   Where the children skip and play
Among the pretty, fragrant flowers, spinning
   The happy hours away?

What, in various ways, has been lost?

Turn to "Tears, Idle Tears," discussed in Section 4 (p. 242). This poem is one of the "songs" sung in *The Princess,* a long narrative poem. There, it is sung at the request of the Princess, who, however, doesn't like it, referring to it as a voice out of "the moulder'd lodges of the Past," "sweet," indeed, but "vague" and "fatal to men," specifically a glorification of the Middle Ages and romantic heroism. Tennyson himself reports that it was written at Tintern Abbey (on which Wordsworth had written a famous poem), "when the woods were yellowing with autumn, seen through the ruined windows," adding that it was "distance" that charmed him "in the landscape, the picture and the past, and not the immediate to-day in which I move." * The poem is generally taken to be a poem about the personal past (sometimes as Tennyson's personal past). But whether the poem be taken as referring to history or to an individual's experience, the general temper is the same.

Questions

1. Describe that temper, with relation to the "musicality" of the material in the poem. Be as precise as possible.
2. Do you find any thematic or emotional development in the poem?

The Dream

Theodore Roethke [*1908–1963*]

1

I met her as a blossom on a stem
Before she ever breathed, and in that dream
The mind remembers from a deeper sleep:
Eye learned from eye, cold lip from sensual lip.
My dream divided on a point of fire;   5

* See F. W. Bateson, *English Poetry,* p. 227.

Light hardened on the water where we were;
A bird sang low; the moonlight sifted in;
The water rippled, and she rippled on.

2

She came toward me in the flowing air,
A shape of change, encircled by its fire.   10
I watched her there, between me and the moon;
The bushes and the stones danced on and on;
I touched her shadow when the light delayed;
I turned my face away, and yet she stayed.
A bird sang from the center of a tree;   15
She loved the wind because the wind loved me.

3

Love is not love until love's vulnerable.
She slowed to sigh, in that long interval.
A small bird flew in circles where we stood,
The deer came down, out of the dappled wood.   20
All who remember, doubt. Who calls that strange?
I tossed a stone, and listened to its plunge.
She knew the grammar of least motion, she
Lent me one virtue and I live thereby.

4

She held her body steady in the wind;   25
Our shadows met, and slowly swung around;
She turned the field into a glittering sea;
I played in flame and water like a boy
And I swayed out beyond the white seafoam;
Like a wet log, I sang within a flame.   30
In that last while, eternity's confine,
I came to love, I came into my own.

Questions

1. What differences do you note between the last stanza of the poem and the following revision of it?

'Twas motionless she held herself in the wind;
Our shadows came together, then around;
She turned the field into a shining sea;
I played with fire and water like a boy
And I went out beyond the sea's white foam;
Like a log that's wet, I simmered in the flame.
During that time, as long as eternity,
I fell in love, and that's enough for me.

2. Here are two versions of the same passage (the original by Keats). Which do you prefer? Why?

a) The tunes you hear are sweet, but the ones unheard
   Are sweeter, therefore, you gentle pipes, play on;
Not to the physical ear, but more endeared
   To the deep heart, make a music of no tone.

b) Heard melodies are sweet, but those unheard
   Are sweeter; therefore, ye soft pipes, play on;
Not to the sensual ear, but more endeared,
   Pipe to the spirit ditties of no tone.

3. Turn back to page 41 and reread "Meeting at Night." Analyze the poem for onomatopoeic and other verbal effects.

All Day I Hear

James Joyce [*1882–1941*]

All day I hear the noise of waters
    Making moan,
Sad as the sea-bird is, when going
    Forth alone
He hears the winds cry to the waters'   5
    Monotone.

The gray winds, the cold winds are blowing
    Where I go.
I hear the noise of many waters
    Far below.   10
All day, all night, I hear them flowing
    To and fro.

Questions

1. Comment on any verbal elements that heighten meaning in this poem. Use all of your resources, including your knowledge of metrics. What, by the way, does the poem "mean"?

2. Return to "The Goat Paths" by James Stephens (p. 209), and after a careful reading, write a study, interpretive and technical.

We do not intend to imply that there is some easily established norm for the relationship of musicality to other elements in poetry. There is more than one kind of poetry, and the virtues of Tennyson's "Choric Ode," de la Mare's "Voices," and Joyce's "All Day I Hear," with their incantatory dependence on language to create a mood, are not the virtues, to go to another extreme, of Donne's "If Poisonous Minerals" (p. 330) or Shakespeare's "The Expense of Spirit" (p. 541), with their tight logicality of structure and dramatic density of language. In between such extremes are many other kinds of poems, some such as Roethke's "The Dream" (p. 550), Auden's "Lullaby" (p. 143), and Thomas Campion's "Blame Not My Cheeks" (p. 217), each with a high degree of musicality coupled with intellectual density and dramatic force.

It is impossible to set out to establish a norm here beyond the requirement that there be some vital relation between the euphony (or the cacophony) of the verse and the other elements of a poem.

Accentual or Stress Meter

Thus far we have discussed *accentual-syllabic verse*. We have mentioned *syllabic verse* and given a brief description of it on p. 497 fn. Our brevity is justified on two counts: (1) Syllabic verse occurs but rarely in English poetry and there is only one example of it in the poems included in this text.* (2) Since the lines in syllabic verse are determined by a simple count of syllables, it is the easiest kind of pattern to describe and need detain us no further here. *Accentual meter,*† however, is a very different matter. It is important enough to warrant a discussion in some detail.

In accentual verse, the matter of consequence is the number of stressed syllables; the number of unstressed syllables may vary greatly and their number plays no part in a definition of the meter. In Old English poetry, the stresses were four in number, and this four-stress line was divided in half by a strongly marked caesura. Furthermore, the stressed syllables were marked by alliteration, usually three of these syllables being so linked. Here is a brief sample from the Old English epic *Beowulf:*

> Waes sē grimma gæst   Grendel hāten
> mære mearcstape   sē þe mōras hēold[1]

This basic four-stress pattern has survived into modern English. For example, we find the measure in many nursery rhymes:

> Sing a song of sixpence,
> Pocketful of rye;
> Four-and-twenty blackbirds
> Baked in a pie.

If asked to scan this, many people would produce something of this sort:

> Sing a | song of | sixpence,
> Pocket | ful of | rye;
> Four and | twenty | blackbirds
> Baked in a | pie.

But if we arrange the verse as follows, in two long lines, we more readily sense the Old English stress meter as natural:

> Sing a song of | sixpence, || pocketful of | rye
> Four and twenty | blackbirds || baked in a | pie

* "No Swan So Fine" by Marianne Moore, p. 367.
† It is sometimes also called *stress meter* or *strong-stress meter* or referred to as the *old native meter.*
[1] translation by D. H. Crawford: "Grendel his name was—a savage spirit. / great stalker of marches, he that held the moors."

In this scansion we have noted the secondary accents, but the fact of secondary accents does not destroy the basic four-beat pattern: it does no more than enrich and complicate it.

The four primary beats and the strong caesura dividing them two and two suggest the Old English ancestry of this nursery rhyme and related kinds of folk poetry. But accentual or stress verse as it has survived in folk poetry is not necessarily confined to a line composed of four primary accents. Thus the following nursery rhyme has a pattern of three accents to the line:

$$
\begin{array}{llll}
/ & / & \cup & / \\
\end{array}
$$
Peas | porridge | hot,
$$
\begin{array}{llll}
/ & / & \cup & / \\
\end{array}
$$
Peas | porridge | cold,
$$
\begin{array}{lllll}
/ & / & \cup & // & \cup & / \\
\end{array}
$$
Peas | porridge in the | pot
$$
\begin{array}{lll}
/ & / & / \\
\end{array}
$$
Nine | days | old.

The common ballad meter employs a stanza composed of alternating lines of four and three accents.

$$
\begin{array}{llllll}
\cup & / & / & \cup & // & / & \cup & / \\
\end{array}
$$
The king | sits in | Dumferling | toune,
$$
\begin{array}{llll}
/ & \cup & \cup & / & // & / \\
\end{array}
$$
Drinking the | blude-reid | wine:
$$
\begin{array}{lllll}
// & / & \cup & // & / & / & / \cup \\
\end{array}
$$
"Oh whar | will I get | guid | sailor,
$$
\begin{array}{llllll}
\cup & / & \cup & / & \cup & / \\
\end{array}
$$
To sail | this schip | of mine?"

There are still other stanzaic patterns of accentual verse. What all have in common is the primacy of the main accents. The count of other syllables is relatively unimportant. Consider the first line of "Sing a song." We find such groupings as a primary accent followed by one unaccented syllable, one secondary accent, and a second unaccented syllable (*Sing a song of*) [/ ∪ // ∪]; a primary accent followed by a secondary (*six pence*) [/ //]; a repeat of the first grouping; and a primary accent standing alone (*rye*) [/]. (You might observe what other variations are to be found in the lines from "Peas porridge hot" and the first quatrain of "Sir Patrick Spence.")

It is interesting and may be illuminating to regard the preceding fragments of poems under what is called the Dipodic Principle. We may best begin by saying that in a great many of the folk meters the accented syllables and their accompanying secondary and unaccented syllables are treated as having the same *duration of time* in utterance; that is, they constitute "isochronous" (equal-time) units. Thus, "Peas," "porridge," and "hot" are allowed the same duration, or, to take a more extreme case, "pie" is allowed as much time as "Four-and-twenty." (Read these nursery rhymes aloud and see if you are not reciting them in just this way.)

But how does one make one syllable "isochronous" with three or four? By keeping the beat on the primary accents: by hurrying the unaccented syllables, stretching out the primaries where necessary, and making use of pauses. Thus, in "Sing a song," you get two beats to the line and two more-or-less equal units of duration in each line, in spite of the fact that there are six syllables in each of the first three lines but only *four* in the fourth.

Let us consider the next stanza of "Sing a song":

> When the pie was opened
> The birds began to sing;
> Wasn't that a dainty dish
> To set before the king?

How do we read these lines? With accents on *pie* and *op-* (line 1); on *birds, began,* and *sing* (line 2); on *was-, that, dain-,* and *dish* (line 3); and *set, -fore,* and *king* (line 4)? Is there any metrical consistency? Does line 1 have two accents; lines 2 and 4, three; and line 3, four? Line 3 presents special problems. Do we, as rhetorical considerations seem to demand, accent *that?* Rhetorical considerations also call for stress on *Was-* (After all, the word signals a question.) What about *dain-* and *dish?* Both seem to have substantial claims to accent. But if we honor all of these claims we have a line of four accents, ill sorting with the others.

Joseph Malof answers our questions as follows: ". . . it doesn't matter. The true structure does not depend on whether [line 3] has three or four stresses, but rather on whether it has exactly two *primary stresses.*" * "It doesn't matter" because here we are not dealing with accentual-syllabic verse, in which the count of the total number of syllables is important. In accentual meter the count of the primary stresses is all-important, and as for unaccented syllables and secondary accents, a varying number of these may be accommodated into this rather loose but quite coherent verse.

The stanza can be scanned as follows:

> When the pie was | opened
> The birds began | to sing;
> Wasn't that a | dainty dish
> To set before | the king?

One might add a further instance from the other nursery rhyme we have cited: in

> Peas | porridge | hot,
> Peas | porridge | cold,
> Peas | porridge in the | pot
> Nine | days | old.

what do we do with the third line? Do we read it as scanned above? Or do we accent the word *in* and thus get four accents rather than the expected three? We can say as Malof has said: it doesn't matter. Even if we put an extra empha-

* Op. cit., p. 128.

sis on *in* as the rhetorical pressure rather forces us to do, we nevertheless tend to crowd all of the phrase "porridge in the" into one time unit. The isochronous (equal durational) quality is kept even if we do place a fairly heavy stress on *in*.

What, then, is a dipod? In Greek, it means a two-syllable foot. Malof defines it as follows: "The basic measure or 'foot' of the regularly isochronous folk line consists of one primary stress plus one secondary stress or its equivalent (in a pause or hold). This two-stress foot is a dipod." In this foot the primary stress can either follow or be preceded by a secondary stress. It is important to note further that these two stresses (primary and secondary) may be separated by one, two, or even three unaccented syllables, or by none at all. Though there always has to be a primary stress, *the secondary stress may be replaced by a pause*. For example, the line "Nine days old" is composed of three dipodic feet, but in every one of them the syllable with secondary accent is missing and is replaced by a pause. (If you don't believe that the pauses are there and are a necessary part of the structure of the line, then read the jingle through, and listen to the way you are forced to read that last line.)

If we use accentual verse norms, the scansion of the first stanza of "Danny Deever" (p. 35) might come out—give or take a little—something like this:

"What are | the bu | gles blow | in' for," || said Files | -on- | Parade.
"To turn | you out, | to turn | you out," || the Co | lor-Ser | geant said.
"What makes | you look | so white, | so white?" | said Files | -on- | Parade.
"I'm dread | in' what | I've got | to watch," || the Co | lor-Ser | geant said.
For they're hang | in' Danny Deever, || You can hear | the Dead March play,
The Regiment's | in 'ollow square || —they're hang | in' him today;
They've taken | of his buttons off || and cut | his stripes away,
An' they're hang | in' Danny Deever || in the mornin'.

Note that in this scansion several matters become clear: (1) the caesura in these lines is very heavily marked and resembles the heavy caesura that divides every line in Old English poetry; (2) the disposition of accents in the ends of lines (such as "said Files-on-Parade") is best accounted for by the accentual system: the heavy beat *Files, on,* and *Parade,* and the general slowing down of the line is accounted for more naturally than if measured by an accentual-syllabic norm; (3) the rhythm of this poem is thus close to that of the old folk ballad.

One can show this last point by calling attention to the fact (see p. 497) that lines of seven accents tend to break down into two lines, one of four and one of three syllables, and that the caesura in "Danny Deever" is heavy and comes regularly at the same place in the lines.

Indeed, one is tempted to rearrange the lines in this fashion:

What are | the bu | gles blow | in' for,
  Said Files- | on- | Parade. . .

If we do arrange the first four lines in such fashion and keep the other lines as they are, noting that they call for far fewer primary accents than those that precede them, we get this pattern:

4
3
4
3 } *the standard ballad measure*
3
4
3

4
4 } *a variation of the standard ballad measure*
4
3

The fact that each of these last four lines contains approximately the same number of syllables as each of the first four lines but only *four* (or *three*) primary accents rather than the seven we've been accustomed to may help to account for the sense of quickened movement that we feel as we read the second half of the stanza. We have suddenly to get in more syllables between our four main beats—and this sense of acceleration suggests why some readers now "hear the drums" of the marching regiment after having been forced to listen to the laconic and long-drawn-out responses of the Color-Sergeant.

This important point shows up more sharply if we attempt to use the accentual-syllabic scheme. The first four lines, it is true, are readily amenable to the accentual-syllabic system. But look what happens when we try to use this norm to scan the last four lines of the stanza.

For they're hang | in' Danny Deev | er You can hear | the Dead March play

or | er You can hear | the Dead March play

If we follow the normal rhetorical accents, we can scan the first foot as an anapestic substitution, but the next three call for complicated feet that may occur in the quantitative meters of ancient Greece and Rome, but which are clearly unnatural in English and, if used, would complicate our account of the metrical situation to no good purpose. Still, this attempt to scan the line as accentual-syllabic verse has told us something: it has reinforced the point we made in an earlier paragraph. That is, the poet has crowded his four-beat line with syllables that have to be negotiated rapidly: indeed, he has crammed it to the point at which the conventional verse system splits at the seams. But the *poem* does not split. Drawing on the old folk meter, a traditional resource available to verse in the English language, the poet has developed a rhythmic shift that is strikingly effective for the material in hand.

If, however, a poem like "Sir Patrick Spence" (p. 23) is really best regarded as written in accentual verse (and according to the dipodic principle), how is it that we can scan so many of its lines as accentual-syllabic verse? We can do so because there is a large overlap between the two systems. Thus, the fifth stanza falls rather easily into an accentual-syllabic pattern.

"Mak hast, | mak hast, | my mir | ry men all
Our guid | schip sails | the morne:"

> ˵ /   ˵ /   ∪ /   ∪ /
> "O say | na sae, | my mas | ter deir,
>   ∪ ˵ /   ∪ /   ∪ /
> For I feir | a dead | lie storme.

Many poems, though clearly influenced by the older accentual verse, can be scanned readily enough in iambs and anapests. For example, though the following lines from William Morris's poem "Love Is Enough" reflect the old native meter, they can easily be described in normal English meter:

> ∪ /   ∪ ∪   /   ∪ ∪ /   ∪ ∪ /   ∪
> If thus | the king's glo | ry, our gain | and salva | tion
> ∪ /   ˵   ∪ /   ∪ ∪   /   ∪ ∪ /   ∪
> Must go | down the wind | amid gloom | and despair | ing.

On page 510 above we suggested that Swinburne's "Hesperia" might best be scanned in accentual verse. Here is a possible scansion of the first four lines:

> /   /   /   /   /
> Out of the golden remote wild west where the sea without shore is
> /   /   /   /   /   /
> Full of the sunset, and sad, if at all, with the fulness of joy
> /   /   /   /   /   /
> As a wind sets in with the autumn that blows from the region of stories
> /   /   /   /   /   /
> Blows with a perfume of songs and of memories beloved from a boy . . .

Note that we have marked only the primary accents. Readers will differ on the foot divisions. But as we have seen, in stress verse only the placing of the primary accents—not the determination of the secondary accents, unaccented syllables, or the division into feet—is really important.

A great deal of poetry, however—and not merely folk poetry—stoutly resists an accentual-syllabic scansion. The American folk ballad "Jesse James" (p. 20) will illustrate. If we try to treat it as accentual-syllabic verse, we get something like this:

> ∪ ∪ /   ∪ /   ∪   /   ∪   /   ∪ /   ∪   /
> It was on | a Wed | nesday night, | the moon | was shin | ing bright,
>   ˵ /   ∪ /   ∪ /
> They robbed | the Dan | ville train.
> ∪   ∪ /   ∪ /   ∪ /   ∪   /   ∪ /   ∪ /
> And the peo | ple they | did say, | for man | y miles | away,
>   ∪ ∪ /   ˵ /   ∪ /   ∪ /
> 'Twas the out | laws Frank | and Jes | se James.

Yet to most of us this scansion will seem arbitrary and forced. (Note, among other things, that it is impossible to find more than three feet in line 2, though line 4 must have four.) Moreover, in the refrain there is a direct invitation to the reader to place a heavy accent on the first syllable of the first word, "Jesse." If we do so, we will be forced, if we attempt to use accentual-syllabic feet, into the following arbitrary scansion:

> / ∪ ∪   ∪ /   ∪ /   ∪ /   ∪ /
> Jesse had | a wife | to mourn | him all | her life.

In view of such complications, it is surely more natural to describe the meter as accentual. When we do so we find that, not unexpectedly, we are dealing with the old ballad meter.

stresses

ŭ ŭ / ŭ / ŭ // ŭ / ŭ // ŭ /
It was on | a Wednesday night, the moon | was shining bright   4

// / ŭ / ŭ /
They robbed | the Dan | ville train.   3

ŭ ŭ / ŭ // ŭ / ŭ / ŭ // ŭ /
And the people | they did say, | for many | miles away   4

ŭ / // / ŭ // ŭ /
'Twas the out | laws Frank | and Jesse James.   3

/ ŭ ŭ ŭ / ŭ / ŭ // ŭ /
Jesse had | a wife | to mourn him | all her life,   4

ŭ / ŭ / ŭ /
The chil | dren they | are brave.   3

ŭ ŭ / ŭ // ŭ / ŭ / // ŭ / ŭ
'Twas a dir | ty little coward | shot Mister | Howard   4

ŭ / // ŭ / ŭ ŭ /
And laid | Jesse James | in his grave.   3

In modern poetry accentual meter is by no means confined to folk poetry. For example, W. H. Auden used it (with the alliteration that accompanies it in Old English poetry) as the meter for his long poem *The Age of Anxiety*. But one of the most interesting ways in which the accentual meters appear in present-day verse is as a kind of counterpoint to accentual-syllabic verse. Modern poets play the accentual meter off against the more conventional meter so as to develop a rich and complicated rhythm. Monroe Beardsley and W. K. Wimsatt have described the strategy as follows:

A wise and shifty modern poet [T. S. Eliot], always in search of rhythmical invention, writes a stanza containing in the middle such a line as:

Her hair over her arms and her arms full of flowers,

and at the end:

Sometimes these cogitations still amaze
The troubled midnight and the noon's repose.

This is playing in and out of the metrical inheritance. Part V of *The Waste Land* begins:

After the torchlight red on sweaty faces
After the frosty silence in the gardens
After the agony in stony places . . .

Coming after four parts of a poem written largely in strong-stress meter, these lines, with their marked swinging parallel of construction, will most likely be read at a fast walk as strong-stress meter, four stresses to the first, three each to the second and the third. But each is also a perfectly accurate pentameter line, each complicated in the same two traditional ways, the inverted beginning and the hypermetric ending. ("Whether 'tis nobler in the mind to suffer . . .")

It is probably not until about the time of Mr. Eliot and his friends that the free and subtle moving in and out and coalescing of strong-stress and syllable-stress [equivalent to "accentual-syllabic" in our terminology] meters in the same poem, the same stanza, begin to appear with any frequency. This is something remarkable in the history of metrics. But the understanding of it depends precisely upon the recognition of the few homely and sound, traditional and objective, principles of prosody. . . . Without recognition of the two distinct principles of strong-stress and of syllabic-stress meter, it seems doubtful if anything at all precise or technical can be said about Mr. Eliot's peculiar rhythms and tensions.*

In this same general connection, one might also note the following observation by Paul Fussell:

> Some modern metrical critics and theorists (among them C. S. Lewis and Northrop Frye) have suggested that even beneath the iambic pentameter line of blank verse or the heroic couplet of Modern English we still catch a faint echo of the four-stress Old English line. And some have suggested that what we are talking about when we speak of "metrical variations" is really the modern line's apparent indecision about whether to adopt a four- or a five-stress structure. . . .†

Another theorist, Joseph Malof, says that

> there is a significant tendency in the [iambic pentameter] line to lead a double life, to qualify for strict iambic pentameter through such devices as "promotion" of a medial stress to the rank of a full one, and yet to assert beneath the surface the four strong beats of our native meter.‡

But Fussell goes on to argue that such theories are overstatements of the case, for "although Old English verse can be recalled and imitated (as in Auden's *Age of Anxiety*), nothing really like it can be recovered: the language has changed. . . ." §

Questions

Turn to Auden's "As I Walked Out One Evening (p. 245). Discuss the role of accentual meter.

Free Verse

What is "free verse" free from? The Imagists, as we have observed (see p. 73), often wrote in free verse and sometimes made an association between their special kind of verse, on the one hand, and their emphasis on the image (with freedom from commentary, generalizing, and moralizing), on the other. Strictly speaking, however, the freedom of free verse refers only to the versification—or, rather, to the freedom from versification in any traditional sense. Certainly the phrase *free verse* does not mean "freedom from form," more generally conceived. No form, no poem: and the poet writing in free verse must

---

* Monroe Beardsley and W. K. Wimsatt, "The Concept of Meter: An Exercise in Abstraction," *PMLA*, 74 (1959), p. 598.
  † Essay on English versification in *Versification: Major Language Types*, ed. W. K. Wimsatt, New York University Press, 1972, p. 197.
  ‡ Op. cit., p. 197.
  § Fussell, op. cit., p. 197.

accept the necessity of creating a form without the systematic metrical structure of verse. What such forms may be is a topic we shall come to later in this appendix, but the general principle should be constantly held in mind from the beginning—no form, no poem.

Another idea that is essential, certainly in the beginning of this discussion, is that there is no black-and-white distinction between verse and free verse; there is, rather, a sort of scale with a grayish section in the middle. As we have emphasized at various times, especially in connection with the tension between rhetorical considerations and with questions concerning metrical substitutions and quantitative factors, there is always a vital pull against the abstract conception of meter. We see this very clearly in the contrast between Shakespeare's early blank verse and his practice in his later plays. In the early work, the metrical form is rather precise, as in this passage from *The Comedy of Errors:*

> Upon my life, by some device or other,
> The villain is o'er-raught[1] of all my money.
> They say this town is full of cozenage,[2]
> As nimble jugglers that deceive the eye,
> Dark-working sorcerers that change the mind,
> Soul-killing witches that deform the body,
> Disguisèd cheaters, prating mountebanks,
> And many such-like liberties of sin.
>
> I, ii, 95–102

We can readily see that such verse would be monotonous on the stage, and that it could not accommodate the great variety of feelings and ideas that are central to the dramatic effect of the stronger plays. The dramatic flexibility and depth that Shakespeare aimed at meant, in the end, a loosening of his meters, and in a late play such as *Cymbeline* we find metrical disintegration like this:

> A father cruel, and a step-dame false;
> A foolish suitor to a wedded lady,
> That hath her husband banish'd;—O, that husband!
> My supreme crown of grief! and those repeated
> Vexations of it! Had I been thief-stolen,   5
> As my two brothers, happy! but most miserable
> Is the desire that's glorious: bless'd be those, . . .
>
> I, vii, 1–7

In line 1 we do have ten syllables, and the line can be scanned as iambic pentameter; but the dominant rhythm is that of the four-beat stress meter:

A fáther crúel, and a stép-dame fálse.

Line 2 shows the same arrangement—ten syllables but best read as a four-stress line. Lines 3 and 4 do submit to accentual-syllabic scansion, but lines 5 and 6 are impossible to scan in accentual-syllabic terms. Even worse, if we read the passage aloud, we are aware of irregular rhythmic thrusts that swamp any metrical sense.

We can see something of the same process, a generation later than Shake-

---

[1] swindled   [2] cheating

speare, in Milton's *Samson Agonistes,* in which the prevailing measure is blank verse but which exhibits such violations as in these lines (spoken by the Chorus as it discovers the prisoner Samson brooding alone):

> This, this is he; softly a while;
> Let us not break in upon him.
> O change beyond report, thought, or belief!
> See how he lies at random, carelessly diffused,
> With languished head unpropt,   5
> As one past hope, abandoned,
> And by himself given over,
> In slavish habit, ill-fitted weeds
> O'er worn and soiled.
> Or do my eyes misrepresent? Can this be he,   10
> That heroic, that renowned,
> Irresistible Samson? whom, unarmed,
> No strength of man, or fiercest wild beast, could withstand;
> Who tore the lion as the lion tears the kid;
> Ran on embattled armies clad in iron,   15
> And, weaponless himself,
> Made arms ridiculous, useless the forgery
> Of brazen shield and spear, the hammered cuirass,
> Chalybean-tempered steel, and frock of mail
> Adamantean proof: . . .   20

Certain lines in this passage are readily perceived—granted the presence of some reasonable variation—as iambic pentameter, the meter of blank verse—lines 1,* 3, 15, 17, 18, and 19. Others can, with wrenching, by absorbing a number of accents as merely secondary in a telescoped foot, be put into the pattern. Still others here, though not pentameter, can be treated as iambic. But other lines burst entirely out of the pattern, even if Milton's metrical practice in blank verse is in itself somewhat violent and idiosyncratic. In fact, we may say that here, when the standard of the blank verse line is withdrawn, certain feet that, in Milton's practice of blank verse, could be absorbed, tend to take on another shape. In any case, all the freedom of this passage is clearly set against the declared background of formal verse.

It is interesting to observe the same transition from iambic pentameter to free verse (or something approaching it) in a modern poet, T. S. Eliot. Notice how the ghost of blank verse lurks behind this passage from one of his *Four Quartets:*

> The inner freedom from the practical desire,
> The release from action and suffering, release from the inner
> And the outer compulsion, yet surrounded
> By a grace of sense, a white light still and moving,
> *Erhebung* without motion, concentration   5
> Without elimination, both a new world

---

* In line 1, the first two feet are defective, a strongly marked pause compensating for the missing unaccented syllables: This, | ʌ this | is he; | softly | a while

And the old made explicit, understood
In the completion of its partial ecstasy,
The resolution of its partial horror.

If we summon forth the ghost of the blank verse here we get something like
this:

This inner freedom from all sharp desire
Release from action; the release from inner
Compulsion and from outer, yet surrounded
By grace of sense, a white light still and moving,
Ehrebung without motion, concentration   5
Without elimination, a new world
The old now made explicit, understood—
Completion of its partial ecstasy
The resolution of its partial horror.

The point is not that our more neatly metrified version is better. Far from it.
The original is not only richer and more complex in sense; it is richer and more
satisfyingly complex in sound. But our smoothed-out version should serve to
make plain how "real" is the ghost of blank verse that lurks just behind Eliot's
version and actually emerges in lines 5 and 9 (normal blank verse except for the
feminine ending).

If Eliot has pushed too far (as we are inclined to believe) the theory that
some meter must always lurk behind even the most free "free verse," and if
there are some kinds of free verse that abandon any reference, however
ghostly, to meter, there are nevertheless a great variety of instances to which
the principle will apply. For instance, though Walt Whitman is generally taken
to be the father of modern free verse (or at least of one kind of it) and often
practices great swinging rhythms that are totally unscannable, in the following
passage from the poem later entitled "Song of Myself" (from the first version,
1855, of *Leaves of Grass*) we find pentameter in several lines—in some, even
iambic pentameter (lines 3 and 12–15):

Have you reckoned a thousand acres much? Have you reckoned the
    earth much?
Have you practiced so long to learn to read?
Have you felt so proud to get at the meaning of poems?

Stop this day and night with me and you shall possess the origin of
    all poems,
You shall possess the good of the earth and sun . . . . there are millions
    of suns left,   5
You shall no longer take things at second or third hand . . . . nor
    look through the eyes of the dead . . . . nor feed on the
    spectres in books,
You shall not look through my eyes either, nor take things from me
You shall listen to all sides and filter them from yourself.

I have heard what the talkers were talking . . . . the talk of the
    beginning and the end,
But I do not talk of the beginning or the end.   10

There was never any more inception than there is now,
Nor any more youth or age than there is now;
And will never be any more perfection than there is now,
Nor any more heaven or hell than there is now.

Urge and urge and urge,   15
Always the procreant urge of the world.*

In the following passage by Ezra Pound, one of the masters of free verse in this century (from *The Cantos,* number XVII), we observe another way in which pentameter may be the ghost behind free verse:

    ... cliff green-gray in the far,
   / / // /
In the near, the gate-cliffs of amber,
And the wave
    / // / //
    green clear, and blue clear,
   / / // / //
And the cave salt-white and glare-purple,   5
    / / /
    cool, porphyry smooth,
    / / //
    the rock sea-worn.
 / // / /
No gull cry, no sound of porpoise,
 / // // / //
Sand as of malachite, and no cold there,
    / / /
    the light not of the sun   10

Recognizing some margin for debate in this scansion, and employing secondary accents, lines 3 and 4 taken together would constitute a pentameter line, and so also lines 5, 6, and 9. Occasionally, in fact, Pound actually writes straight iambic pentameter lines—and sometimes, going to the other extreme, prose rhythms dominate a passage.

The ghost of meter behind a free verse poem may, however, be other than iambic pentameter. For instance, we scan the first eleven lines of H.D.'s "Pear Tree" as follows (see p. 100 for the poem in full):

  / /
Silver dust
 /   /
lifted from the earth,
 /   / //
higher than my arms reach,
 // /
you have mounted.
// /
O silver,   5
 /   / //
higher than my arms reach
 / // / //
you front us with great mass;
  / /
no flower ever opened

* See also pp. 31, 81, 126, 567, 588 for other examples of Whitman's verse.

/   / //
so staunch a white leaf,

/   /   /
no flower ever parted silver   **10**

/ // /
from such rare silver. . .

There may well be some disagreement about the scansion as marked here.* For instance, in line 4, some readers might wish to give a primary accent to *you*, or a primary accent to *O* in line 5. Or, again, in line 10, the first syllable of *silver* might be given a secondary accent. Even with such debatable lines, however, most people would probably sense a dimeter line from which develop the variations.

With the same concerns in mind, we may turn to a section of a poem by Yvor Winters with the poet's own scansion indicated:

/   /
Earth darkens and is beaded

/ // / //
with a sweat of bushes and

/ //
the bear comes forth:

/ //
the mind stored with

/ // / //
magnificence proceeds into

/ // / //
the mystery of Time, now

/ // /
certain of its choice of

/   // / //
passion but uncertain of the

// /
passion's end.

/
             When . . . †

Again, there may be some debate about the scansion, although the poet himself has marked it thus. But even if we depart substantially from the scansion as given, we shall still find that there is a prevailing pattern under the variations —again a dimeter.

For another type of metrical base we scan the first six lines of a poem by William Carlos Williams:

/   /   /
By the road to the contagious hospital,

/   /   /
under the surge of the blue

//   /   /   /
mottled clouds driven from the

/ // /
northeast—a cold wind. Beyond, the

/   / // /
waste of broad, muddy fields,

/   // / /   //
brown with dried weeds, standing and fallen. . . .

---

* In formal poetry the presence of the metrical pattern tends to prevent disagreement. In free verse there is, inevitably, more uncertainty.

† Yvor Winters, *Primitivism and Decadence,* Arrows Editions, 1937, p. 103.

Again there is room for some debate about the scansion. Some readers might, for instance, want to give the first syllable of *fallen,* in line 6, a primary accent, and call the line a four-beat variation from the three-beat norm. But most readers, going through the entire poem, would probably accept the three-beat norm, despite such possible variations, and feel trimeter as the ghost meter of the whole poem.

Question

The whole of the poem by Williams is on p. 570. Scan the whole poem. Would you agree with the statement above?

If we look back at the passages from H.D., Yvor Winters, and W. C. Williams quoted above, we notice that the line unit seems to bear little relation to syntactical units such as phrase or clause; that in fact there are a number of examples of run-on lines of a violent kind, ending with articles, conjunctions, or prepositions. In these poems some conception of rhythm (though not meter in any ordinary sense) determines the line. But let us look at another kind of free verse:

There Was a Crimson Clash of War

Stephen Crane [*1871–1900*]

> There was a crimson clash of war.
> Lands turned black and bare;
> Women wept;
> Babes ran, wondering.
> There came one who understood not these things.
> He said, "Why is this?"
> Whereupon a million strove to answer him.
> There was such intricate clamor of tongues,
> That still the reason was not.

Clearly, the lines here *are* based on syntactical units, all of the lines, in fact, except one (line 8) being sentences or at least independent clauses. But in the following poem, though some of the lines (for example, lines 1–5) are based on syntactical units, a number are based on units of content, such as the image of the prostitute or the demand that begins "Come and show me another city. . . ." Notice, too, that in some of the long lines no rhythmical unity whatever can be detected.

Chicago

Carl Sandburg [*1878–1967*]

> Hog Butcher for the World,
> Tool Maker, Stacker of Wheat,
> Player with Railroads and the Nation's Freight Handler;

Stormy, husky, brawling,
City of the Big Shoulders. 5

They tell me you are wicked and I believe them, for I have seen your
    painted women under the gas lights luring the farm boys.
And they tell me you are crooked and I answer: Yes, it is true I have
    seen the gunman kill and go free to kill again.
And they tell me you are brutal and my reply is: On the faces of women
    and children I have seen the marks of wanton hunger.
And having answered so I turn once more to those who sneer at this my
    city, and I give them back the sneer and say to them:
Come and show me another city with lifted head singing so proud to be
    alive and coarse and strong and cunning. 10
Flinging magnetic curses amid the toil of piling job on job, here is a tall
    bold slugger set vivid against the little soft cities;
Fierce as a dog with tongue lapping for action, cunning as a savage
    pitted against the wilderness,
    Bareheaded,
    Shoveling,
    Wrecking, 15
    Planning,
    Building, breaking, rebuilding,
Under the smoke, dust all over his mouth laughing with white teeth,
Under the terrible burden of destiny laughing as a young man laughs
Laughing even as an ignorant fighter laughs who has never lost a battle, 20
Bragging and laughing that under his wrist is the pulse, and under his
    ribs the heart of the people, laughing!
Laughing the stormy, husky, brawling laughter of Youth, half-naked,
    sweating, proud to be Hog Butcher, Tool Maker, Stacker of Wheat,
    Player with Railroads and Freight Handler to the Nation.

We have said that a number of lines of "Chicago" are based on content; that
is, on rhetorical considerations. The following passage from Whitman's "Song of
Myself," even more specifically than "Chicago," illustrates how rhetorical considerations may provide the basic form, and be the basic determinant of line.

I speak the pass-word primeval, I give the sign of democracy,
By God! I will accept nothing which all cannot have their counterpart
    of on the same terms.
Through me many long dumb voices,
Voices of the interminable generations of prisoners and slaves,
Voices of the diseas'd and despairing and of thieves and dwarfs, 5
Voices of cycles of preparation and accretion,
And of the threads that connect the stars, and of wombs and of the
    father-stuff,
And of the rights of them the others are down upon,
Of the deform'd, trivial, flat, foolish, despised,
Fog in the air, beetles rolling balls of dung. 10
To behold the daybreak.

Concerning traditional verse, we may say, speaking metaphorically, that the metrical form (and stanzaic form, if any) "contains" the material of the form, which develops within that form. In that same fashion, we may say that here the development of the material "contains" the development of the rhythms. To be specific: in this poem the most obvious form is the rhetorical one. In the first two lines, Whitman makes a statement about democracy and his general attitude in relation to it. In the next seven lines he develops his role as a "voice"—this by a series of parallel constructions, each of which determines a line unit (but notice how the original series of "Voices" in lines 4, 5, and 6 slips into another set of parallels based on "And of"). In lines 10 and 11, in a very strange and poetically exciting justaposition of items, Whitman sums up his feeling. As we have said, within this rhetorical structure the rhythms are developed, most obviously in the long swinging series of parallels. But observe how in the last two lines, the rhythm draws in toward an effect approaching metrical control. We might scan it as follows:

Fog in the air, beetles rolling balls of dung.

To behold the daybreak.

We should remind ourselves here that there are certain types of free verse more radical and unpredictable than any we have thus far illustrated. For instance, the following example in which not only meter and rhetorical structures are rejected, but even words are found inadequate as units:

Impressions, Number III

E. E. Cummings [1894–1962]

> 1 was considering how
> within night's loose
> sack a star's
> nibbling in-
>
> fin   5
> -i-
> tes-
> i
> -mal-
> ly devours   10
>
> darkness the
> hungry star
> which
> will e
>
> -ven   15
> tu-
> al

-ly jiggle
the bait of
dawn and be jerked   20

into

eternity.   when over my head a
shooting
star
Bur   s   25
        (t into a stale shriek
like an alarm-clock)

We must not assume that the fracturing process here is intended to be merely amusing or whimsical (though Cummings is often amusing or whimsical). The process is intended to set up a rhythm of its own, one that will dramatize the "impression" and emotion that is the poem.

We have made a distinction between free verse that is based primarily on the line as a rhythmical unit and free verse in which the line is primarily a syntactic or rhetorical unit. This distinction seems clear if we compare the poem by Yvor Winters, from which we have quoted, with that by Stephen Crane, but we must remember that the distinction is a matter of emphasis, and it must be assumed that in all poems both principles are, in some fashion and allowing for differences, recognized.

With this in mind, we take two poems by William Carlos Williams that we have previously referred to. The first is "Red Wheelbarrow," which we have discussed as an example of Imagism (p. 73), but which we now scan:

So much depends
upon

a red wheel
barrow

glazed with rain
water

beside the white
chickens

What we have here is a poem of alternating dimeter and monometer lines, but the lining is so arbitrary that the metrical scheme is reduced to "ghostliness," and what we feel primarily is the tension between the words isolated in an arbitrary line and the logic of the sentence to which they belong.

To develop this notion, we turn to the second poem by Williams, the first six lines of which we scanned on page 565.

Poem

William Carlos Williams [*1883–1963*]

By the road to the contagious hospital,
under the surge of the blue
mottled clouds driven from the
northeast—a cold wind. Beyond, the
waste of broad, muddy fields,   5
brown with dried weeds, standing and fallen,

patches of standing water,
the scattering of tall trees.

All along the road the reddish,
purplish, forked, upstanding, twiggy   10
stuff of bushes and small trees
with dead, brown leaves under them
leafless vines—

Lifeless in appearance, sluggish,
dazed spring approaches—   15

They enter the new world naked,
cold, uncertain of all
save that they enter. All about them
the cold, familiar wind—

Now the grass, tomorrow   20
the stiff curl of wildcarrot leaf.

One by one objects are defined—
It quickens: clarity, outline of leaf,

But now the stark dignity of
entrance—Still, the profound change   25
has come upon them; rooted, they
grip down and begin to awaken.

The most striking feature of this poem, at first glance, anyway, is the apparent arbitrariness of the lining. The first line does have a phrasal unity, but each of the next three lines ends with a violent slashing across the sense structure—*blue* without its noun, and *the,* twice without its noun. Such runovers can, of course, occur in formal verse (though in any kind of verse the ending of a line with an article is rare), but when there is a formal meter, the presence of the meter makes the effect seem less arbitrary: the metrical order compensates in part for the disordered grammar, syntax, and rhetoric. Here, as we have earlier pointed out in scanning this poem (p. 565), there is a ghost of meter, a submerged meter, which gives some sense, however minimal, of a line structure. Even so, in this case the apparent arbitrariness makes us take a special look.

At one level, the arbitrariness of the lining, the apparent disintegration of the line, fuses with the content to give an effect of openness, blankness, bareness, a sense of the late winter scene. But on a level more pertinent to our immediate concern, the insistence on a line—however arbitrarily determined—is a way of declaring that the composition is poetry; at least, there is the negative claim that this is *not* prose, and the lining insists that the content somehow be regarded differently, in itself and for itself, in a way other than the way we regard individual elements in prose.

But here we must reflect on the fact that if every line were arbitrarily determined, if every line, that is, slashed across syntax, grammar, and sense, then the arbitrariness of itself would cease to be significant; the arbitrariness, to be significant, must be played off against some other principle. One such principle is, of course, the ghost of meter; but another, and sometimes in free verse an even more important one, is the logic of the sentence to which it belongs. What we have, then, is a shifting between the line as conforming to some sentence element (or, more rarely, as in the extreme case of "There Was a Crimson Clash of War," p. 566, to a whole sentence) and the line as a violation of sentence structure, or even phrasal or clausal structure. With the withdrawal of formal meter, such shifting relation between lines based on sentence logic and those purely arbitrary, and the relation among line units of varying weight based on sentence structure, may provide a device capable of great subtlety of effect.

We may now try to summarize the ideas that have emerged from our discussion of free verse·

1. In free verse (as in accentual verse) the syllable count is scarcely relevant to the line; a number of syllables may cluster around, and be carried by, the accent. The accents that are to be counted are, by and large, the main rhetorical ones (though sometimes juxtaposition may determine an accent, as in metrical verse).

2. The count of the main accents may be variable, variation being determined by rhetorical and rhythmical considerations taken in conjunction.

3. Around the accents, a number of secondary accents may appear—and usually do appear. These secondary accents are the great determinants of the weight, speed, and flexibility of the verse.

4. The relation of the verse line to the sentence line—the degree of arbitrariness in relation to the rhetorical, syntactical, and grammatical order—is more important in free verse than in formal verse. In formal verse the most important interplay is between the meter and the rhetorical consideration *within the line;* in free verse the most important interplay—the basis of the vital tension—is primarily between the verse line and the sentence line. This, of course, is subject to modification and enrichment by the interplay between the accents of the line and the secondary accents, plus the time of the varying number of unaccented syllables.

This is not to be taken as a final account of free verse. It is intended merely to be suggestive, and to lead the student to make his own study, thereby sharpening his awareness of the factors that enter into free verse.

Overland to the Islands
Denise Levertov   [1923–   ]

Let's go—much as the dog goes,
intently haphazard. The
Mexican light on a day that
"smells like autumn in Connecticut"
makes iris ripples on his   5
black gleaming fur—and that too
is as one would desire—a radiance
consorting with the dance.

        Under his feet
rocks and mud, his imagination, sniffing,   10
engaged in perceptions—dancing
edgeways, there's nothing
the dog disdains on his way,
nevertheless he
keeps moving, changing   15
pace and approach but
not direction—"every step an arrival."

Questions
1. Scan the poem.
2. Discuss what you consider the primary principle of the line here.

Poetry*
Marianne Moore   [1887–1972]

I, too, dislike it: there are things that are important beyond all this fiddle.
  Reading it, however, with a perfect contempt for it, one discovers in
    it after all, a place for the genuine.
      Hands that can grasp, eyes
        that can dilate, hair that can rise   5
          if it must, these things are important not because a
high-sounding interpretation can be put upon them but because they are
  useful. When they become so derivative as to become unintelligible,
    the same thing may be said for all of us, that we
      do not admire what   10
        we cannot understand: the bat
          holding on upside down or in quest of something to

---

* The text printed here is the 1927 version. In the *Complete Poems* (1967), the poem reads, in its entirety: "I, too, dislike it. Reading it, however, with a perfect contempt for it, one discovers in it after all, a place for the genuine."

eat, elephants pushing, a wild horse taking a roll, a tireless wolf under
    a tree, the immovable critic twitching his skin like a horse that
        feels a flea, the base-
ball fan, the statistician—   15
    nor is it valid
        to discriminate against 'business documents and

school-books'; all these phenomena are important. One must make
    a distinction
however: when dragged into prominence by half poets, the result
    is not poetry,
nor till the poets among us can be   20
    'literalists of
    the imagination'—above
        insolence and triviality and can present

for inspection, 'imaginary gardens with real toads in them,' shall we have
    it. In the meantime, if you demand on the one hand,   25
    the raw material of poetry in
        all its rawness and
    that which is on the other hand
        genuine, you are interested in poetry.

Questions

1. Would you say that there is a "ghost" of meter here? If not, on what does the rhythm depend?

2. Suppose that the poem were continuous, without stanzas. What would be lost? What would be the effect if each stanza were self-enclosed—that is, ending with a full stop?

3. State in your own words—as elaborately as you feel necessary to make yourself clear—what definition or description Marianne Moore here offers.

Nine Birds

E. E. Cummings [1894–1962]

    nine birds(rising

    through a gold moment)climb:
    ing i

    -nto
    wintry   5
    twi-

    light
    (all together a

    manying
    one   10

-ness)nine
souls
only alive with a single mys-

tery(liftingly
caught upon falling)silent!   **15**

ly living the dying of glory

Questions

1. If you find this poem satisfying, how would you describe the rhythmical effect, and how would you relate that to the overall sense of the poem?

2. Comment on the principle of the rhythmical composition of "For the Union Dead" by Robert Lowell (p. 155).

3. Choose some poem (perhaps an elaborate stanza from some long poem such as Keats's "Ode to a Nightingale," p. 355) and recast it into free verse.

We began our discussion of free verse with a question, "What is free verse free from?" We have said that it is not free from the necessity of creating a form. It is free, however, to create a form outside of certain fixed structures accepted as a base for formal verse. In referring to the rhetorical principle of organization in Whitman's verse (p. 568), we have said that in traditionally formal poetry, the meter (and stanza, when one is used) may be said to "contain" the material of the poem, and that in Whitman's work, the material "contains" the rhythmic form—determines it. This is one way of describing what we may call the *fixed* form of traditional verse as contrasted to what we may call the *emergent* form of free verse.*

In the preface to a collection of his poems in 1919, D. H. Lawrence emphasized, in other terms, the sense of the emergence of form, by insisting that traditional poetry had been oriented toward the past or the future:

> The poetry of the beginning and the poetry of the end must have that exquisite finality, perfection which belongs to all that is far off. It is in the realm of all that is perfect. It is of the nature of all that is complete and consummate. This completeness, this consummateness, the finality and the perfection are conveyed in exquisite form: the perfect symmetry, the rhythm which returns upon itself like a dance where the hands link and loosen and link for the supreme moment of the end. Perfected bygone moments, perfected moments in the glimmering futurity, these are the treasured gem-like lyrics of Shelley and Keats.

---

* In this sentence we have been tempted to make a drastic and even misleading oversimplification, and one that violates the basic assumptions of this book. In the final sense, the form of a poem, even of the most traditional type, is always emergent: the poem itself does not exist until the concrete, nonpredictable elements have fulfilled themselves in the context of the abstract and predictable (i.e., meter, stanza, etc.). When that occurs, the abstract predictable elements have, insofar as the poem is successful, entered into an expressive fusion with the concrete and nonpredictable to create an expressive form. But with this warning, the oversimplification above may be useful.

But free verse, he declared, is concerned with the immediate present, with "no goal in either eternity." For such poetry of "the instant; the quick; the very jetting source of all will-be and has-been," there can be no "externally-applied law." The law of its being—its form—"must come new each time from within."

What Lawrence says of the immediacy of free verse is, at the same time, both profoundly true and profoundly false. What he says of free verse—of certain kinds of free verse, anyway—has to do with the *impression,* the *illusion,* that it creates. Whitman, whom Lawrence takes as the great archetypal poet of free verse, does give the impression of a bursting out into immediate eloquence —and this impression is dramatically effective and dramatically appropriate for his doctrine of immediacy, of naturalness, of the untrammeled interplay of instinctual life. But this dramatically effective illusion did not imply effortless immediacy in the composing of the poetry. And we do not have to assume this to be true, or to guess about it: for Whitman kept rewriting his basic work for years. The impression of spontaneity is often very hard-earned.

Furthermore, not all free verse aims at an illusion of immediacy and spontaneity. The poem we have quoted just above by Marianne Moore does not, nor does much of Ezra Pound. Some free verse is very elaborately wrought, and, in fact, to compensate for the absence of the more obviously formal elements, a writer of free verse may make profound demands on all other verbal resources. Pound, for instance, suggested as early as 1917 that at least part of the impulse to free verse arose from the resurgence of "the sense of quantity . . . after years of starvation." But his recognition of the complication and density possible in free verse is implicit in his statement:

> I think one should write *vers libre* only when one "must," that is to say, only when the "thing" builds up a rhythm more beautiful than that of set metres, or more real, more a part of the emotion of the "thing," more germane, intimate, interpretative than the measure of regular accentual verse [here meaning accentual-syllabic]. . . .

Then Pound quotes Eliot on this point: "No *vers* is *libre* for the man who wants to do a good job."

Afterword

Considering some of the arid complexities that may appear in the study of metrics and other such technical matters, we may well ask why bother with it at all. Poets write by ear anyway, not by eye, and so why should the reader not simply submit himself to what he hears and let the effects come effortlessly?

This question is justified, certainly, insofar as it suggests that what we want in the end is the *experience of the poem,* including the experience of its rhythms as part of the total effect. But our bothering with metrical patterns and such problems does justify itself in that it gives some notion of how verse "works" and how the "good ear" of a poet may make rhythm serve his genera poetic needs and feelings. Such a study justifies itself in that it is a way o learning to "hear." The study stimulates a kind of attention that may not come naturally, or if it does come naturally, will come much more slowly and painfully. Let us ask, by way of a parallel, who is likely really to "hear" music—the person who has done some studying or the one who happens to like it naturally and listens now and then?

But with this we are back at the principle discussed at the end of "Poetry as a Way of Saying" (p. 16). We try to "understand" in order to return more fully and devotedly to the experience of the poem.

Metaphor and Symbol Compared and Contrasted

Appendix C

It may be useful to draw up a kind of balance sheet—not of virtues and defects, of course, but of contrasts and differences of emphasis.

METAPHOR

Metaphor tends to be (or at least to seem) more *consciously* analogical than symbol. Though it need not be intellectual and witty, such tends to be its character in *vers de société,* and witty effects *can* occur in deeply serious poems of romantic love or religious devotion. Donne and Marvell are two of the great users of such metaphors, but one can also find such metaphors in abundance in the plays of Shakespeare.

SYMBOL

Symbols seem to be more "natural" and spontaneous than metaphors. They almost never seem shocking or startling, as metaphors sometimes do. Unless the symbol has a conventional and arbitrary meaning, such as the Cross (signifying Christianity) or the Stars and Stripes (signifying the U.S.A.), the symbol may impress one as simply having its meaning from the beginning. But closer inspection will show that successful symbols depend very much on the supporting context, and the poet whose symbolism seems to grow quite effortlessly out of the poem has usually found—whether by conscious intellection or mere instinct or inspiration—a context properly developed to bring out the symbolism in the object (or action or process) that becomes the vehicle for that meaning. Just as the metaphysical poets (Donne, Marvell) were the great masters of the daring and complex metaphor, so the Romantic poets (Wordsworth, Coleridge, Keats) were typically the poets who developed a symbolism such as we find in "She Dwelt Among the Untrodden Ways" (p. 220), or "Yew-Trees" (p. 109), or "Ode to a Nightingale" (p. 355).

If a symbol is nourished by some sense of general likeness, so that Wordsworth's yew trees become a symbol of eternal nature itself, something outside the realm of human history, yet nurturing and enduring history, the metaphor derives its strength from contrast—very often from the very unlikeness of the things compared. The unity of a pair of romantic lovers is not ordinarily thought of as in any sense like that of the legs of a compass. The effectiveness of the comparison derives in good part from its incongruity. Dr. Samuel Johnson made this point in observing that the imagery of the metaphysical poets involved "heterogeneous ideas yoked by violence" together. Most of us would say that the best of such imagery achieves a real unity and is not simply "yoked by violence." But metaphor does always work to some degree *through* incongruity and by the shockingly unlike proving to be really "like" after all.

The late Cecil Day Lewis, a modern poet, put this matter of unlikeness and shock very happily when he observed that with metaphor "We find poetic truth struck out by the collision rather than the collusion of images." I. A. Richards has got at the same point in defining a metaphor as a "transaction between contexts" (*The Philosophy of Rhetoric*, Oxford University Press, 1936, p. 94). If the contexts are too nearly similar, not much force is generated. For a powerful metaphor, we must have a sense of very different contexts having been linked together. Thus, for example, Donne's comparison of the souls of the lovers to the legs of an instrument used in geometry links two vastly different contexts (p. 240).

W. K. Wimsatt—though without reference to Richards's definition of a metaphor as the linchpin tying together two sharply different contexts—points the difference between such metaphor and the sort of symbol we associate with the method of the Romantic poets by saying that, in their characteristic method, the tenor (the thrust of the comparison) and the vehicle (the concrete objects or processes used in the comparison) are usually "wrought out of the same material," i.e., the poet does not draw on two sharply different contexts, but makes use of essentially the same context: e.g., Lucy is sweet, wholesome, and "natural" like a violet or like a star. One consequence, as Wimsatt puts it, is that with Romantic imagery "the element of tension in disparity is not so important as for metaphysical wit," and he goes on to say that Romantic nature imagery "favors implication rather than overt statement," and thus is "far closer than the metaphysical to symbolist poetry . . ." (*The Verbal Icon*, University of Kentucky Press, 1954, pp. 110, 116).

One must not, however, oversimplify the situation by suggesting that metaphor is more artificial and less natural than symbol. Symbol too can be rather exactly and formally structured (e.g., as in allegory).

In allegory we have symbols arranged in a rather rigid and sometimes complicated pattern. To take a fairly simple case, in Bunyan's *The Pilgrim's Progress,* the hero, who is named Christian, decides to flee from the City of Destruction (i.e., the worldly city) and sets out on his pilgrimage (i.e., his

Yet metaphor is in fact a perfectly "natural" process. It is not necessarily cold-blooded or intellectual. Language itself probably began as metaphor. Certainly our present language is filled with evidence of this, for many of our present expressions are now "dead" metaphors. Thus, we speak of the "eye of a needle," the "bed of a river," the "foot of a bed," the "head of a nation," and use other such phrases. What causes metaphors to die? Their ceasing to be transactions between sharply different contexts and becoming, through habitual use, frozen in one context; e.g., the "eye of a needle."

The sense of freshness (a sense of real "transfer") is indeed 'absolutely necessary if we are to feel that a metaphor is really "alive." In fact one definition of metaphor calls it a "new naming." (To call the hole in the end of a needle an eye was presumably once "new" and a felt metaphor.) Defining metaphor as a "new naming" provides an easy bridge to Christine Brooke-Rose's statement that a metaphor "replaces" a more ordinary way of naming an object, an action, or a process (p. 206).

life's journey) to the Celestial City. In the course of his journey he encounters various difficulties. He nearly drowns in the Slough of Despond. He is for a time imprisoned by the Giant Despair, and so on. Allegories can be naive or sophisticated, mechanical or rich and subtle. This method will neither guarantee a good poem nor condemn it to failure. But it does represent a special and not necessarily a typical handling of symbol. The point is that it can be just as self-conscious as the most complicated use of metaphor.

You may receive a sense of freshness and discovery when you first grasp the symbolism developed by an author. Thus, the letter *A*, which Hester Prynne (in *The Scarlet Letter*) was required to wear because she had been condemned as an adulteress, in time, because of the later actions of Hester's life, came to mean to the community something else, *Able*, the person who was able to help the sick or afflicted. But though symbols can be manipulated—even created —by the author or changed from their "fixed" meaning to new meanings, much symbolism has certain basic connections with the world in which we live. Many symbols are so deeply rooted in human experience that they can be regarded as archetypes. For example, the sun is the great life-giving power in our solar system. It provides the heat and light that make our life pos-

sible. Small wonder that from time immemorial we have talked of the "sun
of righteousness" or "the light of truth
dispelling the powers of darkness," or
the nurturing sun of spring putting to
rout the forces of death. Yet the sunlight can have more sinister aspect· it
can be the fierce glare of the desert
sun that withers and parches everything—a force of death.

In short, though there is a relation
between the symbol as used in literature and the universal archetypes, the
individual author's imagination nevertheless determines the fitness of the
symbol and its import. A poet cannot
simply go through the files to find an appropriate archetype, in the confidence
that this archetype will then automatically do his work for him.

To sum up: metaphor and symbol represent ways in which the literary artist
can make a concrete particular of some sort—an object, an action, a process
—convey a further meaning. Each mode can be used (and each can be misused)
Both are parts of the universal analogical process by which we discover patterns
in the jostling and often heterogeneous elements of our experience. As ways
of unifying our experience and making sense of it, we use metaphors and symbols constantly in our daily living—not merely in our literature. Symbol and
metaphor have their own special, individual characters, but, as we have said
earlier, they sometimes overlap. Occasionally, it may be difficult to determine
whether the device in question, though strictly speaking a metaphor, more
closely resembles a symbol or whether it ought to be called a symbol with
strong metaphoric overtones. How, for example, should we describe the violet
in "She Dwelt" (p. 220) or the rose in "Go, Lovely Rose" (p. 213)?

Parodies

Appendix D

A good parody is amusing, but it can also be revealing. If the parodist has been able to catch the tone and manner of the poem being "taken off," the parody may reveal defects and limitations—and even, paradoxically, powers—in the original poem. If, for example, the original is pretentious or oversolemn or sentimental, a good parody, by altering the angle of vision or widening the context or inviting us to take an ironic squint at the original poem, may expose its defects; but the parody of a good poem may make us more keenly aware of the virtues that survive parody.

Yet a good parody is not necessarily merely destructive. It can make the skill of the poet parodied obvious by showing that the diction and imagery were appropriate to the special purpose. An altered subject matter or an altered context as effected by the parodist may reveal through contrast the original author's good taste and good judgment in using particular methods to produce a special effect and in not straining beyond what could properly be done. In general, a good parody may bring into sharp delineation the special characteristics that are the hallmark of a genuine poet.

The parodies in this appendix are amusing—at least we have found them so—but your sense of their wit and point will obviously depend on knowing the original. Your appreciation of the wit and humor will also depend very much on seeing how clearly the parodist has caught the special manner of the original. A mere gross caricature will not seem very funny and will not claim our attention very long.

Dwight Macdonald, in his *Anthology of Parodies,* includes a very interesting appendix entitled "Some Notes on Parody." In it, he makes distinctions among travesty, burlesque, and parody proper. Travesty, he observes, "raises laughs, from the belly rather than the head, by putting high, classic characters into prosaic situations, with a corresponding stepping-down of the language. Achilles becomes a football hero, Penelope a suburban housewife, Helen a beauty queen." In short, a dignified or exalted character is degraded through a series of pratfalls.

Burlesque "is a more advanced form since it at least imitates the style of the original. It differs [, however,] from parody in that the writer is concerned with the original not in itself but merely as a device for topical humor. Thus the writer of burlesque recreates a recognizable edition of the form of the original but he fills it with a very different kind of content."

Macdonald considers parody the highest of these three related modes because the parodist gives the reader "a recognition of both the style and the content." Macdonald goes on to say that therefore, "at its best, [parody] is a form of literary criticism."

In the parodies that follow,* you may find it interesting to see into which category each take-off falls. Thus "Chard Whitlow" (p. 589) is an excellent parody and amounts to a shrewd examination of the limitations and the specialized qualities of Eliot's later poetry.

The foregoing comments, however, are not meant to muffle the humor. Although parody may occasionally become a kind of literary criticism, furthering the reader's recognition of significant aspects of the original work, a prime index of its effectiveness is its humor. If the reader does not find a parody genuinely funny, then the parodist has indeed failed—or else the reader has missed the point.

One of the best examples of parody comes from *Alice's Adventures in Wonderland,* the classic tale by Lewis Carroll (Charles Lutwidge Dodgson) that was first published in 1865. Alice, newly arrived in Wonderland, is conversing with the Caterpillar, who is sitting on a mushroom, smoking a hookah. Alice remarks sadly to the Caterpillar that she can't remember things as she used to be able to.

"Can't remember *what* things?" said the Caterpillar.

"Well, I've tried to say '*How doth the little busy bee,*' but it all came different!" Alice replied in a very melancholy voice.

"Repeat '*You are old, Father William,*' " said the Caterpillar.

Alice folded her hands, and began:

* See also the following parodies: Aldous Huxley's on Poe's "Ulalume," p. 546; A. C. Hilton's on Swinburne's "Dolores," p. 547, I. A. Richards's (a phonetic one) on Milton's "Ode on the Nativity," p. 549.

You Are Old, Father William

Lewis Carroll [*1832–1898*]

"You are old, Father William," the young man said,
"And your hair has become very white;
And yet you incessantly stand on your head—
Do you think, at your age, it is right?"

"In my youth," Father William replied to his son, 5
"I feared it might injure the brain;
But now that I'm perfectly sure I have none,
Why, I do it again and again."

"You are old," said the youth, "as I mentioned before,
And have grown most uncommonly fat; 10
Yet you turned a back-somersault in at the door—
Pray, what is the reason of that?"

"In my youth," said the sage, as he shook his grey locks,
"I kept all my limbs very supple
By the use of this ointment—one shilling the box— 5
Allow me to sell you a couple."

"You are old," said the youth, "and your jaws are too weak
For anything tougher than suet;
Yet you finished the goose, with the bones and the beak—
Pray how did you manage to do it?" 20

"In my youth," said his father, "I took to the law,
And argued each case with my wife;
And the muscular strength, which it gave to my jaw,
Has lasted the rest of my life."

"You are old," said the youth, "one would hardly suppose 25
That your eye was as steady as ever;
Yet you balanced an eel on the end of your nose—
What made you so awfully clever?"

"I have answered three questions, and that is enough,"
Said his father; "don't give yourself airs! 30
Do you think I can listen all day to such stuff?
Be off, or I'll kick you downstairs!"

"That is not said right," said the Caterpillar.

"Not *quite* right, I'm afraid," said Alice, timidly; "some of the words have got altered."

"It is wrong from beginning to end," said the Caterpillar decidedly, and there was silence for some minutes.

What the Caterpillar had in mind when he asked Alice to test her memory by reciting was the poem by Robert Southey that follows.

The Old Man's Comforts and How He Gained Them

Robert Southey [*1774–1843*]

"You are old, Father William," the young man cried;
  "The few locks which are left you are gray;
You are hale, Father William—a hearty old man:
  Now tell me the reason, I pray."

"In the days of my youth," Father William replied,   5
  "I remembered that youth would fly fast,
And abused not my health and my vigor at first,
  That I never might need them at last."

'You are old, Father William," the young man cried,
  "And pleasures with youth pass away;   10
And yet you lament not the days that are gone:
  Now tell me the reason, I pray."

"In the days of my youth," Father William replied,
  "I remembered that youth could not last;
I thought of the future, whatever I did,   15
  That I never might grieve for the past."

"You are old, Father William," the young man cried,
  "And life must be hastening away;
You are cheerful and love to converse upon death:
  Now tell me the reason, I pray."   20

'I am cheerful, young man," Father William replied;
  "Let the cause thy attention engage;
In the days of my youth, I remembered my God,
  And He hath not forgotten my age."

The Last Ride Together
(From Her Point of View)

J K. Stephen [*1859–1892*]

When I had firmly answered "No,"
And he allowed that that was so,
I really thought I should be free
For good and all from Mr. B.,
  And that he would soberly acquiesce.   5
I said that it would be discreet
That for awhile we should not meet;
I promised that I would always feel
A kindly interest in his weal;

I thanked him for his amorous zeal;
   In short, I said all I could but "yes."   10

I said what I'm accustomed to;
I acted as I always do.
I promised he should find in me
A friend,—a sister, if that might be;   15
   But he was still dissatisfied.
He certainly was most polite;
He said exactly what was right,
He acted very properly,
Except indeed for this, that he   20
Insisted on inviting me
   To come with him for "one more last ride."

A little while in doubt I stood:
A ride, no doubt, would do me good;
I had a habit and a hat   25
Extremely well worth looking at;
   The weather was distinctly fine.
My horse, too, wanted exercise,
And time, when one is riding, flies;
Besides, it really seemed, you see,   30
The only way of ridding me
Of pertinacious Mr. B.;
   So my head I graciously incline.

I won't say much of what happened next;
I own I was extremely vexed.   35
Indeed I should have been aghast
If any one had seen what passed;
   But nobody need ever know
That, as I leaned forward to stir the fire,
He advanced before I could well retire;   40
And I suddenly felt, to my great alarm,
The grasp of a warm, unlicensed arm,
An embrace in which I found no charm;
   I was awfully glad when he let me go.

Then we began to ride; my steed   45
Was rather fresh, too fresh indeed,
And at first I thought of little, save
The way to escape an early grave,
   As the dust rose up on either side.
My stern companion jogged along   50
On a brown old cob both broad and strong.
He looked as he does when he's writing verse,
Or endeavoring not to swear and curse,
Or wondering where he has left his purse;
   Indeed it was a sombre ride.   55

I spoke of the weather to Mr. B.,
But he neither listened nor spoke to me.
I praised his horse, and I smiled the smile
Which was wont to move him once in a while.
    I said I was wearing his favorite flowers,   60
But I wasted my words on the desert air,
For he rode with a fixed and gloomy stare.
I wonder what he was thinking about.
As I don't read verse, I shan't find out.
It was something subtle and deep, no doubt,   65
    A theme to detain a man for hours.

Ah! there was the corner where Mr. S.
So nearly induced me to whisper "yes";
And here it was that the next but one
Proposed on horseback, or would have done,   70
    Had his horse not most opportunely shied;
Which perhaps was due to the unseen flick
He received from my whip; 't was a scurvy trick,
But I never could do with that young man,—
I hope his present young woman can.   75
Well, I must say, never, since time began,
    Did I go for a duller or longer ride.

He never smiles and he never speaks;
He might go on like this for weeks;
He rolls a slightly frenzied eye   80
Towards the blue and burning sky,
    And the cob bounds on with tireless stride.
If we aren't home for lunch at two
I don't know what papa will do;
But I know full well he will say to me,   85
"I never approved of Mr. B.;
It's the very devil that you and he
    Ride, ride together, forever ride."

See Robert Browning, "The Last Ride Together," page 397.

Camerados

Bayard Taylor *[1825–1878]*

    Everywhere, everywhere, following me;
    Take me by the buttonhole, pulling off my boots, hustling me with the
            elbows;
    Sitting down with me to clams and the chowder-kettle;
    Plunging naked at my side into the sleek, irascible surges;
    Soothing me with the strain that I neither permit nor prohibit;   5

Flocking this way and that, reverent, eager, orotund, irrepressible;
Denser than sycamore leaves when the north-winds are scouring Paumanok;
What can I do to restrain them? Nothing, verily nothing.
Everywhere, everywhere, crying aloud for me;
Crying, I hear; and I satisfy them out of my nature;   10
And he that comes at the end of the feast shall find something over.
Whatever they want I give; though it be something else, they shall have it.
Drunkard, leper, Tammanyite, small-pox and cholera patient, shoddy and
      codfish millionaire,
And the beautiful young men, and the beautiful young women, all the same.
Crowding, hundreds of thousands, cosmical multitudes,   15
Buss me and hang on my hips and lean up to my shoulders,
Everywhere listening to my yawp and glad whenever they hear it;
Everywhere saying, say it, Walt, we believe it:
Everywhere, everywhere.

The reader familiar with Walt Whitman's "Song of Myself" will recall
passages such as

2

Houses and rooms are full of perfumes, the shelves are crowded with
    perfumes,
I breathe the fragrance myself and know it and like it,
The distillation would intoxicate me also, but I shall not let it.
The atmosphere is not a perfume, it has no taste of the distillation,
    it is odorless,
It is for my mouth forever, I am in love with it,   5
I will go to the bank by the wood and become undisguised and naked,
I am mad for it to be in contact with me.
The smoke of my own breath,
Echoes, ripples, buzz'd whispers, love-root, silk-thread, crotch and vine,
My respiration and inspiration, the beating of my heart, the passing
    of blood and air through my lungs,   10
The sniff of green leaves and dry leaves, and of the shore and dark-
    color'd sea-rocks, and of hay in the barn,
The sound of the belch'd words of my voice loos'd to the eddies of
    the wind,
A few light kisses, a few embraces, a reaching around of arms,

and

4

Trippers and askers surround me,
People I meet, the effect upon me of my early life or the ward and
    city I live in, or the nation,
The latest dates, discoveries, inventions, societies, authors old and new,
The real or fancied indifference of some man or woman I love,
My dinner, dress, associates, looks, compliments, dues,   5

The real or fancied indifference of some man or woman I love,
The sickness of one of my folks or of myself, or ill-doing or loss
        or lack of money, or depressions or exaltations,
Battles, the horrors of fratricidal war, the fever of doubtful news, the
        fitful events;
These come to me days and nights and go from me again,
But they are not the Me myself.   10
Apart from the pulling and hauling stands what I am,
Stands amused, complacent, compassionating, idle, unitary,
Looks down, is erect, or bends an arm on an impalpable certain rest,
Looking with side-curved head curious what will come next,
Both in and out of the game and watching and wondering at it.

With Rue My Heart Is Laden

Samuel Hoffenstein [1890–1947]

With rue my heart is laden
For many a lass I had.
For many a rouge-lipped maiden,
That's got a richer lad.

In rooms too small for leaping   5
Such lads as I are laid,
While richer boys are keeping
The girls that do not fade.

With Rue My Heart Is Laden

A. E. Housman [1859–1936]

With rue my heart is laden
   For golden friends I had,
For many a rose-lipt maiden
   And many a lightfoot lad.

By brooks too broad for leaping   5
   The lightfoot boys are laid;
The rose-lipt girls are sleeping
   In fields where roses fade.

Chard Whitlow
(Mr. Eliot's Sunday Evening Postscript)

Henry Reed [1914–]

As we get older we do not get any younger.
Seasons return, and today I am fifty-five,
And this time last year I was fifty-four,

And this time next year I shall be sixty-two.
And I cannot say I should like (to speak for myself)   5
To see my time over again—if you can call it time:
Fidgeting uneasily under a draughty stair,
Or counting sleepless nights in the crowded tube.

There are certain precautions—though none of them very reliable—
Against the blast from bombs and the flying splinter,   10
But not against the blast from heaven, *vento dei venti*,
The wind within a wind unable to speak for wind;
And the frigid burnings of purgatory will not be touched
By any emollient.
                    I think you will find this put,
Better than I could ever hope to express it,   15
In the words of Kharma: "It is, we believe,
Idle to hope that the simple stirrup-pump
Will extinguish hell."
                    Oh, listeners,
And you especially who have turned off the wireless,
And sit in Stoke or Basingstoke listening appreciatively to the silence,   20
(Which is also the silence of hell) pray, not for your skins, but your souls.

And pray for me also under the draughty stair.
As we get older we do not get any younger.

And pray for Kharma under the holy mountain.

See T. S. Eliot's "Four Quartets." Eliot himself enjoyed this parody. He wrote: "Most parodies of one's own work strike one as very poor. In fact one is apt to think one could parody oneself much better. (As a matter of fact some critics have said that I have done so.) But there is one which deserves the success it has had, Henry Reed's 'Chard Whitlow.' "

Just a Smack at Auden

William Empson [*1906–*   ]

Waiting for the end, boys, waiting for the end.
What is there to be or do?
What's become of me or you?
Are we kind or are we true?
Sitting two and two, boys, waiting for the end.   5

Shall I build a tower, boys, knowing it will rend
Crack upon the hour, boys, waiting for the end?
Shall I pluck a flower, boys, shall I save or spend?
All turns sour, boys, waiting for the end.

Shall I send a wire, boys? Where is there to send?   10
All are under fire, boys, waiting for the end.
Shall I turn a sire, boys? Shall I choose a friend?
The fat is in the pyre, boys, waiting for the end.

Shall I make it clear, boys, for all to apprehend,
Those that will not hear, boys, waiting for the end,   15
Knowing it is near, boys, trying to pretend,
Sitting in cold fear, boys, waiting for the end?

Shall we send a cable boys, accurately penned,
Knowing we are able, boys, waiting for the end,
Via the Tower of Babel, boys? Christ will not ascend,   20
He's hiding in his stable, boys, waiting for the end.

Shall we blow a bubble, boys, glittering to distend,
Hiding from our trouble, boys, waiting for the end?
When you build on rubble, boys, Nature will append
Double and re-double, boys, waiting for the end.   25

Shall we make a tale, boys, that things are sure to mend,
Playing bluff and hale, boys, waiting for the end?
It will be born stale, boys, stinking to offend,
Dying ere it fail, boys, waiting for the end.

Shall we go all wild, boys, waste and make them lend,   30
Playing at the child, boys, waiting for the end?
It has all been filed, boys, history has a trend,
Each of us enisled, boys, waiting for the end.

What was said by Marx, boys, what did he perpend?
No good being sparks, boys, waiting for the end.   35
Treason of the clerks, boys, curtains that descend,
Lights becoming darks, boys, waiting for the end.

Waiting for the end, boys, waiting for the end.
Not a chance of blend, boys, things have got to tend.
Think of those who vend, boys, think of how we wend,   40
Waiting for the end, boys, waiting for the end.

Empson's parody makes its smack not only at Auden's manner but at what Empson at least takes to be the matter—the content—of Auden's early work. Auden began to be known as a poet with the beginning of the Great Depression and the growing sense of the end of the world as men had known it —a time of impending violence and revolution. The early poems are full of passages such as these:

The tall unwounded leader
Of doomed companions
"Missing"

Control of the passes was, he saw, the key
To this new district, but who would get it?
"The Secret Agent"

> *All this time was anxiety at night,*
> *Shooting and barricades in the street.*
> *Walking home late I listened to a friend*
> *Talking excited of final war*
> *Of Proletariat against police.*
>
> > "1929"

The world pictured is that of the dying of old comfort and privilege:

> *It is time for the destruction of error.*
> *The chairs are being brought in from the garden,*
> *The summer talk stopped on that savage coast*
> *Before the storms, after the guests and birds.*
>
> > "1929"

At the same time in Auden's work there appeared poems with the following tone:

> *Stop all the clocks, cut off the telephone,*
> *Prevent the dog from barking with a juicy bone,*
> *Silence the pianos and with muffled drum*
> *Bring out the coffin, let the mourners come.*
>
> > "Twelve Songs, IX"

Squeal

Louis Simpson [1923–]

> I saw the best minds of my generation
> Destroyed—Marvin
> Who spat out poems; Potrzebie
> Who coagulated a new bop literature in fifteen
> Novels; Alvin   5
> Who in his as yet unwritten autobiography
> Gave Brooklyn an original *lex loci.*
> They came from all over, from the pool room,
>
> The bargain basement, the rod,
> From Whitman, from Parkersburg, from Rimbaud   10
> New Mexico, but mostly
> They came from colleges, ejected
> For drawing obscene diagrams of the Future.
>
> They came here to L.A.,
> Flexing their members, growing hair,   15
> Planning immense unlimited poems,
> More novels, more poems, more autobiographies.
>
> It's love I'm talking about, you dirty bastards!
> Love in the bushes, love in the freight car!
> I saw them fornicating and being fornicated,   20
> Saying to Hell with you!

America.
America is full of Babbitts.
America is run by money.

What was it Walt said? Go West!   25
But the important thing is the return ticket.
The road to publicity runs by Monterey.
I saw the best minds of my generation
Reading their poems to Vassar girls,
Being interviewed by *Mademoiselle*.   30
Having their publicity handled by professionals.
When can I go into an editorial office
And have my stuff published because I'm weird?
I could go on writing like this forever . . .

The title is a takeoff on Allen Ginsberg's "Howl" (1955), the first nine
lines of which appear on page 162.

The Dover Bitch
A Criticism of Life
Anthony Hecht [*1923–*]

for Andrews Wanning

So there stood Matthew Arnold and this girl
With the cliffs of England crumbling away behind them,
And he said to her, "Try to be true to me,
And I'll do the same for you, for things are bad
All over, etc., etc."   5
Well now, I knew this girl. It's true she had read
Sophocles in a fairly good translation
And caught that bitter allusion to the sea,
But all the time he was talking she had in mind
The notion of what his whiskers would feel like
On the back of her neck. She told me later on
That after a while she got to looking out
At the lights across the channel, and really felt sad,
Thinking of all the wine and enormous beds
And blandishments in French and the perfumes.
And then she got really angry. To have been brought
All the way down from London, and then be addressed
As sort of a mournful cosmic last resort
Is really tough on a girl, and she was pretty.
Anyway, she watched him pace the room
And finger his watch-chain and seem to sweat a bit,
And then she said one or two unprintable things.

But you mustn't judge her by that. What I mean to say is,
She's really all right. I still see her once in a while
And she always treats me right. We have a drink
And I give her a good time, and perhaps it's a year
Before I see her again, but there she is,
Running to fat, but dependable as they come,
And sometimes I bring her a bottle of *Nuit d'Amour.*

Questions

1. A good parody can often point up not only the weaknesses but the strengths of the poem parodied. What light, if any, does Hecht's parody throw on Arnold's "Dover Beach" (p. 333)? Note that Hecht has taken as his subtitle a phrase that Matthew Arnold made famous in calling poetry a criticism of life. Is the girl addressed by the man who speaks "Dover Beach" a "mournful cosmic last resort"? If "Dover Beach" is a criticism of life, of what is "The Dover Bitch" a criticism?

2. What is the real object of Hecht's spoof? Arnold's view of the state of the culture, now deprived of its faith? Or Arnold's lugubrious solemnity? Or Arnold's feeling that the love relationship between a man and a woman could make up for Darwin's revelation that man had not been created by God from the dust, but was the descendant of a hominoid mammal? Or what?

3. Is it conceivable that the woman addressed in Arnold's poem would be a girl like the amiable "bitch" who figures in "The Dover Bitch"? If not, does this fact rob the parody of any real point? Or is it the very point of the joke?

Index
of Authors, Titles, and Terms